THE ENGLISH SECULAR CATHEDRALS
IN THE MIDDLE AGES

PLATE I
A CANON OF WELLS CATHEDRAL

THE
ENGLISH SECULAR
CATHEDRALS
IN THE MIDDLE AGES

A CONSTITUTIONAL STUDY WITH SPECIAL REFERENCE
TO THE FOURTEENTH CENTURY

BY

KATHLEEN EDWARDS
M.A., Ph.D.
Reader in Medieval History in the University of Aberdeen

MANCHESTER UNIVERSITY PRESS
BARNES & NOBLE INC., NEW YORK

Published by the University of Manchester at
THE UNIVERSITY PRESS
316–324 Oxford Road, Manchester 13

First published 1949
2nd edition, revised throughout and reset, 1967

U.S.A.
BARNES & NOBLE, INC.
105, Fifth Avenue, New York, N.Y. 10003

Printed in Great Britain by Butler & Tanner Ltd., Frome and London

CONTENTS

LIST OF ILLUSTRATIONS

vii

PREFACE TO THE FIRST EDITION

THE object of this book is to describe the organization of the secular cathedral chapters in England in the middle ages, and especially during the fourteenth century, when the number of clergy attached to the cathedrals was greater than at any other period. The subject has an obvious interest both for the history of the later medieval church and for medieval constitutional and administrative history in general. The cathedral churches were among the leading churches in Europe. It is often said that neglect of duty and a lack of efficiency and enthusiasm on the part of the higher clergy were largely responsible for the widespread discontent which culminated in the Reformation and the break with Rome; it is important to test this statement by finding out as much as possible about the character of ecclesiastical government and administration in the later middle ages. The constitutional development of the secular cathedrals is no isolated subject. It runs parallel with, influenced by and perhaps occasionally influencing similar developments in other ecclesiastical bodies or in the royal administration. The cathedral canons themselves, who helped to frame the cathedral statutes, were often important men in church and state: royal clerks holding high office in government departments; administrators and lawyers prominent in the service of king, pope, archbishops, or bishops; distinguished scholars, cardinals, foreigners, with a wide knowledge of affairs. Many of them were provided to their prebends by the popes, since the popes largely depended on cathedral prebends for their disposal of benefices in the medieval church. Investigation of the appointments of such non-resident canons may incidentally throw light on the working of papal provisions, which became vital to the machinery of ecclesiastical government.

Study of the cathedral constitutions in the later middle ages is made both more interesting and more fruitful by the wealth of available evidence. As in other departments of church and state, the fourteenth century was the great legislative and codifying age, when cathedral customs were defined and elaborated, and when the keeping of administrative records, such as detailed financial accounts and minutes of chapter meetings, was greatly extended. A good proportion of these records have been preserved at English cathedrals, yet compared with contemporary monastic records they have so far been surprisingly little explored. There is no modern work giving in adequate detail a view of the duties and functions of the various officers and ministers of the secular cathedrals.[1]

The subject of capitular organization in the later middle ages naturally cannot be discussed without constant reference to origins and early development. Yet generally developments during the twelfth, thirteenth, and fourteenth centuries seem to have been more important in moulding the form of the secular constitutions than any formal plan adopted at their foundations. The plans which William the Conqueror's bishops, St. Osmund, Remigius, and Thomas of Bayeux, made in 1090-1 for their cathedrals of Salisbury, Lincoln and York seem to have been vaguer and slighter than has sometimes been supposed. Certain of the great dignitaries as well as many lesser officials and *ministri inferiores* are known to have been instituted at a much later date; and there were important differences in the early customs adopted at different cathedrals. In the late twelfth century Peter de Blois wrote of the great variety in the customs of English secular cathedrals.[2] This variety persisted and in some ways increased, especially in matters

[1] The most useful general account is contained in Professor Hamilton Thompson's *Cathedral Churches of England* (S.P.C.K.), 1925. In this, the space devoted to secular cathedral constitutions is necessarily limited, for the book deals with the architectural as well as the constitutional history of the cathedrals, and includes the cathedral monasteries and the secular cathedrals of the New Foundation in addition to the medieval secular cathedrals. Also, Professor Hamilton Thompson has sometimes modified the conclusions reached in this book in a long series of books and articles on special aspects of the subject published since 1926. To all his work I am greatly indebted. Other books are not sufficiently general in character. M. E. C. Walcott's *Cathedralia: A Constitutional History of Cathedrals of the Western Church*, 1865, is little more than a mass of useful facts; in any case much further information has become available since he wrote. The work of Henry Bradshaw, published in the massive introduction to three volumes of *Statutes of Lincoln Cathedral*, 1892–7, is indispensable for any serious study of the subject; but the form is rather too diffuse and the subject-matter too specialized for the general reader. Several useful accounts are available for particular cathedrals. Details of these will be found in the bibliography at the end of this book.

[2] '*Petri Blesensis Opera*', in *Patrologia Latina*, ccvii, 497.

of detail, throughout the middle ages, as the chapters adapted their organization to correspond with local needs. But at the same time, in spite of the growing complexity of cathedral organization and the multiplication of offices, there is by the thirteenth and fourteenth centuries a growing unity or at least similarity in general outline. The way in which this similarity was developing is made clear in the extant correspondence of the chapters, in their minutes of chapter meetings, and in their collections of written customs. The chapters consulted one another on the best way to deal with particular problems of organization created by changing conditions, or with episcopal claims to exercise jurisdiction over them. Often they wrote to ask neighbouring chapters to lend them copies of their customs; long passages from the statute books or customaries, especially of Salisbury, Lincoln and St. Paul's, are quoted *verbatim* in the statutes of other secular chapters. As a result of this 'cross-fertilization' of customs, the nine English chapters had come, by the fourteenth century, to form constitutionally a remarkably homogeneous group. The number, titles, and order of precedence of their dignitaries varied less than those of the six secular cathedral chapters of the French province of Rouen.

As in the history of all constitutions, development has also been largely the result of conflict. It was the clash of interests between the different dignitaries, officers, and groups of cathedral clergy which caused each side to define and expound its claims, and which finally led to important legal decisions and a more elaborate organization. Naturally, these conflicts assumed greater proportions, and the legal issues became more involved, as the chapters came to possess greater wealth, property, jurisdiction, and privileges. Thus the growth of the chapter as a privileged body within the diocese caused its interests to clash with those of its early head, the bishop. Some of the bitterest constitutional conflicts of the later middle ages were fought over the chapter's efforts to win exemption from his jurisdiction, and over the bishop's determination to retain some rights of supervision over his chapter. Within the chapter, too, there were conflicts between the dean and canons, when the dean tried to extend his authority over the chapter or to act independently; while the jurisdiction and functions of different dignitaries and officers often overlapped and had to be defined. In the later middle ages, when the *ministri inferiores* at the cathedrals,

such as the vicars choral or chantry chaplains, began to receive
separate endowments of money, lands, and jurisdiction, they in
their turn asserted their claims to have an independent organization and privileges, and the chapters were forced into the position
of conservative bodies trying to retain their powers of correction
and discipline over the lesser cathedral clergy. The *acta* of the
secular chapters in the later middle ages contain long accounts of
these conflicts; it was necessary that careful records should be kept
of all legal precedents and claims, while other interests and activities of the canons, for example in learning, might not be recorded in the official registers. A modern reader might form the
impression that medieval cathedral clergy spent most of their
time in bickering. The very detail with which the disputes are
recorded increases the difficulties of the historian in giving a clear
picture of what was happening. Yet the settlement and definition
of points of detail often led to important results. Their importance
is plainly seen when the impressive structure of the constitutions
of the highly organized secular cathedral bodies of the later middle
ages is compared with the life of the early episcopal *familiae*.

In approaching the subject it will first be necessary to give some
account of the origin and early development of the secular chapters; the materials on which the investigation is based, particularly the cathedral statutes and chapter acts, will also be
described, since they are not generally very well known. The
work will then be divided into four parts. First, the secular canons
themselves and their residence in the later middle ages will be
discussed. One of the chief problems connected with the history of
the secular cathedrals was that of non-residence, and the need for
finding a satisfactory solution for it was a main factor in stimulat-
ing constitutional development. An attempt will be made to see
what kind of men the canons were; how they were appointed;
what were their numbers, emoluments, and interests; how many
of them actually lived in the cathedral city and performed the
offices which their founders had intended them to perform; how
many were non-resident, and what kind of work these did. Next,
the bishop's position in his cathedral church in the later middle
ages is interesting: it is in striking contrast to his position there
both before the Conquest and after the Reformation, and illustrates well the remarkable independence and powers of the medieval chapters. The similarity in general outline of the English

secular cathedral constitutions in the later middle ages makes it possible to discuss and compare the duties, functions, and authority of the various officers, from the dignitaries down to the beadle or janitor of the close, grouped according to the different departments of cathedral life in which they served. In discussing the chancery, special attention will be paid to the development and organization of the cathedral schools. Little is known of the work of these schools in England, either in the early or later middle ages; it is important to see how the English secular cathedrals provided for education, which, in the twelfth century, was recognized as one of their chief duties. Finally, the various groups of *ministri inferiores*, the vicars choral, chantry chaplains, the clerks of the second form, and the choristers, have a special interest and importance. They formed the most numerous element in the fourteenth-century cathedral close, and were, in effect, the working staff of the cathedral. The development of self-governing corporations among the vicars and chaplains, within the larger body of cathedral clergy controlled by the chapter, was one of the most interesting constitutional experiments at the secular cathedrals in the later middle ages.

I should like to express my gratitude to Dr. E. F. Jacob for his unfailing help and encouragement at every stage of this work, which was begun at Manchester under his supervision in preparation for a Ph.D. degree. Special thanks are also due to Professor C. R. Cheney, who has given me most generous advice and constructive criticism in the work of revision; and to the late Mr. Lewis C. Loyd for generously lending me his unpublished memorandum, and for placing at my disposal his wide knowledge of Norman secular cathedrals in the eleventh and twelfth centuries. Professor Margaret Deanesly, Mr. W. A. Pantin, Dr. Kathleen Wood-Legh, and Chancellor F. Harrison have kindly given me the benefit of their special knowledge on different sections of the book. I am further deeply indebted to Dr. Beryl Smalley, who has read and criticized each chapter as it was written; and to Dr. Joan Hussey, Dr. Decima Douie, Mr. John Dickinson, and many other friends who have contributed of their knowledge and time to the work. I should also like to take this opportunity of thanking Professor Sir Maurice Powicke, who has done much to make it possible for me to continue my researches. The use of manuscripts at Lincoln and Salisbury was made possible by the kind permission of the Deans and Chapters, and the help at Lincoln of Miss Kathleen Major, Archivist to the Bishop of Lincoln, and at Salisbury of the late Canon J. M. J. Fletcher, Librarian to the Dean and Chapter. I have received much expert advice from Mr. H. M. McKechnie, Secretary of the University Press, and am indebted to Miss Mabel Mills for help in preparing the index. Finally, I must express my gratitude to the Delegacy of Ashburne Hall, Manchester, for the Ashburne Hall Research Studentship, and to the British Federation of University Women for the Junior British Scholarship, which enabled me to begin this work in the form of a thesis in 1937–9; to the Council of St. Hugh's College, Oxford, which elected me to the Mary Gray Allen Senior Scholarship for a further two years in order that I might write the book; and to the Committee of the Tout Memorial Publication Fund for a generous grant towards the cost of publication.

KATHLEEN EDWARDS

KING'S COLLEGE,
ABERDEEN
December, 1947

PREFACE TO THE SECOND EDITION

THIS book has been out of print for over eleven years, and I am grateful to the Manchester University Press for this second edition. It has generously allowed me to make a more thorough revision of the text than would have been possible in a less costly photographic edition. Over a hundred alterations have been made. Some represent only minor changes or additions; others have involved the rewriting of several paragraphs or pages. The bibliography has been brought up to date, and I have been able to substitute different illustrations for some of the rather disappointing reproductions of photographs in the first edition.

The main purpose of the book was to provide a comparative study of the constitutions of the English secular cathedral chapters in the later middle ages. At the time this was something new, which, as some continental reviewers commented, had not and probably could not yet be attempted for their countries.[1] It was possible for England because of the small number of nine secular out of a total of nineteen cathedral churches in the middle ages, the large amount of surviving original material for their history, and the existence of a number of local and some general studies. Since the publication of the first edition there has been increasing interest in the history of these secular cathedrals and much more material has become available. More records of the chapters have been printed and more studies of individual chapters have appeared, including the important work of Professor C. N. L. Brooke on the medieval chapter of St. Paul's and of Sir Charles Clay on that of York; Miss Major's studies of the financial administration of Lincoln chapter from the twelfth to the fourteenth century and of the office of chapter clerk there; and my account of the history of Salisbury chapter from 1075–1950. A number of theses, not yet published, have also dealt with the medieval history of particular chapters. I am indebted to Mrs. Hester Jenkins, Miss

---

[1] E.g. M.-L. Ménier in *Bibliothèque de l'Ecole des Chartes*, cviii, 1950. Cf. W. Holtzmann in *Zeitschrift der Savigny Stiftung für Rechtsgeschte: Kanonistische Abteilung*, xxvi, 1950, who remarked that for Germany there were many modern monographs on medieval cathedral chapters but no detailed and adequate general survey of their constitutions.

Marjorie Jones, Mr. D. J. B. Hindley and Mr. A. R. B. Fuller for their kindness in allowing me to read their theses on the chapters and bishops of Lichfield, Hereford and Exeter, and on the minor canons of St. Paul's. Outside England Mr. Geoffrey Hand and Mr. Greenway have studied the influence of the English secular cathedral constitutions on those of St. Patrick's, Dublin, and St. Mary's, Limerick, in Ireland, and of St. David's in Wales; while Professor David Douglas's work on the Norman secular cathedral chapters before the Norman Conquest of England and two unpublished or partly published papers of Professor Brooke on the English cathedral chapters and the Norman conquest, which he has generously allowed me to read, have thrown more light on the continental origins of the English chapters. There have been many articles on special subjects. All these works have suggested some corrections and modifications and many additions. None, however, have seemed to make necessary major changes in the general conclusions or structure of the book. I am told that as a constitutional study it stands firm and is still useful to students.

Much further material is of course also available on other aspects of the history of the English secular cathedrals in the middle ages, such as the liturgy, music and architecture of the cathedral churches, the contents of cathedral libraries, the economic history of the chapters' estates, the composition or personnel of the chapters and minor corporations. A few reviewers suggested that I should have tried to incorporate more about some or all these subjects in a second edition. It is perhaps worth while to explain here why I have not done this.

All these subjects are closely connected with the constitutional history of the cathedrals and with each other, as I tried to show. No rigid line can be drawn between the liturgical and constitutional customs of a cathedral church. The constitution was largely designed for the liturgy, the perpetual celebration of which is the main purpose of a cathedral church; therefore the cathedral statutes set out the duties of the dignitaries, canons and lesser clergy in the daily services. The architecture of the cathedral church and of other buildings in the close was designed both for the liturgy and for the constitution or way of life of the clergy celebrating it. The long nave, aisles and ambulatory of the church were necessary for the processions and ceremonies; the chapter house for chapter business. The separate houses of the residentiary canons and the houses, common halls or colleges of the lesser clergy reflected the constitutions of the secular chapter and minor corporations. The cathedral library and its contents, sometimes a grammar school or theological lecture room, suggested some other of the clergy's activities or interests. The rapid increase in the chapters' property especially in the twelfth century was a chief reason for the increase in numbers of the cathedral clergy, for their growing independence of their bishop and for the development of their various systems of home government, while the management of their estates throws light on the working of their constitutions. Knowledge of the kind of men who formed the chapters helps to explain both the reasons for framing many of their statutes and the ways in which they were observed or interpreted.

It would obviously be impossible to study the constitutional history of the cathedrals in isolation from these other subjects, but to give detailed information about all of them would mean writing several books the size of this one. A comprehensive history of the English secular cathedrals in the middle ages, giving a full picture of their life in all its different aspects, is much needed, but before it can be written a vast amount of original material on subjects other than the constitutional, much of it highly specialized and technical, and full of pitfalls for the general historian, will have to be examined and interpreted. The recent work of Mr. Neil Ker has shown the difficulties for the non-specialist of research on the contents of medieval cathedral libraries. Investigation of liturgical development, of the influence of the different English secular uses, and of changes in the chant and music calls for an understanding of liturgical and musical manuscripts and for special knowledge of these subjects. The history of cathedral architecture requires understanding of building techniques and of art history. The economic history of the chapters' estates is a part of general economic history and cannot be interpreted without frequent reference to the history of other estates. The personnel of the chapters is a subject which can be more easily tackled by the general or constitutional historian, and study of it has been made easier in recent years. Dr. A. B. Emden's important biographical registers of the universities of Oxford and Cambridge to 1500 have provided a mine of information for the careers of graduate members of the chapters; a new edition of Le Neve's *Fasti Ecclesiae Anglicanae* is in progress, and a number of the local

B

studies already mentioned have investigated in detail the personnel of particular chapters over limited periods. The time seems to
be approaching when a further synthesis or comparative study
might be attempted on the composition and methods of recruit-
ment of the various English secular chapters in different periods of
the middle ages. Such a study would be highly desirable, but the
materials which would have to be examined for the personnel of
all the nine secular chapters are immense, and the subject is too
large and important to be dealt with adequately in additions to the
present book. The revised bibliography includes recent publica-
tions which are helpful for the study of all these aspects of the
chapters' history except the art and architecture, but no attempt is
made in the text to give much further information about them.

A section of the book which I should in some ways have
liked to rewrite in a longer form is the introductory chapter on
the origins and early development of the chapters. Here is much
that could be added. I have not done this because a fuller chronological account might have obscured the general plan for a
comparative study of the nine medieval constitutions with special
reference to the fourteenth century. In any case there are now
available several fuller accounts of the early development of individual chapters, particularly that of Professor Brooke on St.
Paul's and my own on Salisbury, which can be used to supplement the present introductory sketch.

I am very grateful to Dr. Beryl Smalley and Dr. A. B. Emden
for the help, encouragement and advice they have so kindly and
freely given me both in discussions on the nature of this second
edition, and at every stage of the work. Special thanks are also due
to Professor C. N. L. Brooke, who has not only generously lent
me his unpublished work, but who has read and criticized the
typescript of the revision with great care and made many valuable
suggestions. I am further indebted to Professor C. R. Cheney, Mr.
W. A. Pantin and Mrs. Dorothy Owen for information on particular aspects of the subject and for advice on additions to the
bibliography. I should like to thank Mr. T. L. Jones, Secretary of
the Manchester University Press, for his interest and care in seeing
the work through the press.

KATHLEEN EDWARDS

KING'S COLLEGE,
ABERDEEN. *January*, 1966

ABBREVIATIONS

B.J.R.L.	*Bulletin of the John Rylands Library.*
C.C.R.	*Calendar of Close Rolls.*
C.C.W.	*Calendar of Chancery Warrants.*
C.Ch.R.	*Calendar of Charter Rolls.*
C.F.R.	*Calendar of Fine Rolls.*
C.M.H.	*Cambridge Medieval History*
C.P.L.	*Calendar of Papal Letters.*
C.P.R.	*Calendar of Patent Rolls.*
C.Q.R.	*Church Quarterly Review.*
C.S.	*Statutes and Constitutions of the Cathedral Church of Chichester,* ed. Bennett, Codrington, and Deedes.
Cathedral Commission Rept.	*Report of the Royal Commission on the State and Condition of the Cathedral and Collegiate Churches in England and Wales.*
Concilia	*Concilia Magnae Britanniae et Hiberniae,* ed. D. Wilkins.
E.H.R.	*English Historical Review.*
Hemingby's Reg.	*Hemingby's Register,* ed. Helena M. Chew.
H.M.C.	*Reports of the Royal Commission on Historical Manuscripts.*
Hereford Charters	*Charters and Records of Hereford Cathedral,* ed. W. W. Capes.
Hinschius	P. Hinschius, *Das Kirchenrecht der Katholiken und Protestanten in Deutschland. System des Katholischen Kirchenrechts.*
Hist. Church York.	*Historians of the Church of York and its Archbishops,* ed. J. Raine (Rolls Series).
J.E.H.	*Journal of Ecclesiastical History.*
J.T.S.	*Journal of Theological Studies.*
Jones, *Fasti Sar.*	W. H. R. Jones, *Fasti Ecclesiae Sarisberiensis.*
L.S.	*Statutes of Lincoln Cathedral,* ed. H. Bradshaw and C. Wordsworth.
Le Neve–Hardy	J. le Neve, *Fasti Ecclesiae Anglicanae,* ed. T. Duffus Hardy.
Le Neve–I.H.R.	J. le Neve, *Fasti Ecclesiae Anglicanae,* 3rd edn., Institute of Historical Research, London, 1962–65 (in progress)
Lit. Cant.	*Literae Cantuarienses,* ed. J. B. Sheppard.
Livre Noir	*Antiquus Cartularius Ecclesiae Baiocensis,* ed. V. Bourrienne.
M.R.A.	*Great Register of Lichfield Cathedral known as Magnum Registrum Album,* ed. H. E. Savage.
Mansi	*Sacrorum Conciliorum Nova et Amplissima Collectio,* ed. J. D. Mansi.
Monasticon	*Monasticon Anglicanum,* ed. W. Dugdale.
P.L.	*Patrologia Latina,* ed. J. P. Migne.
P.M.L.A.	*Publications of the Modern Language Association of America.*
Proc. Y.A.A.S.	*Proceedings of the Yorkshire Architectural and Archaeological Society.*
R.S.S.P.	*Registrum Statutorum et Consuetudinum Ecclesiae Cathedralis Sancti Pauli Londinensis,* ed. W. Sparrow Simpson.

Reg. Antiquissimum .	*Registrum Antiquissimum of the Cathedral Church of Lincoln*, ed. C. W. Foster and Kathleen Major.
Reg. Corffe, Reg. Coman, etc. .	Corffe Register, Coman Register, etc. Act Books of the Dean and Chapter of Salisbury.
Reg. Orleton, Reg. Winchelsey, etc. .	*Registrum Adae de Orleton, Episcopi Herefordensis, 1327–27*, ed. A. T. Bannister (Canterbury and York Soc.); *Registrum Roberti Winchelsey, Archiepiscopi Cantuariensis, 1294–1313*, ed. Rose Graham (Canterbury and York Soc.), etc.
Reg. S. Osmund .	*Vetus Registrum Sarisberiense alias dictum Registrum S. Osmundi Episcopi*, ed. W. H. R. Jones (Rolls Series).
Rev. d'hist. eccl. .	*Revue d'histoire ecclésiastique.*
S.C. . . .	F. Madan and H. H. E. Craster, *Summary Catalogue of Western Manuscripts in the Bodleian Library*. Oxford, 1922. In progress.
S.S. . . .	*Statuta et Consuetudines Ecclesiae Cathedralis Beatae Mariae Virginis Sarisberiensis*, ed. C. Wordsworth and D. Macleane.
Salisbury Ceremonies	*Ceremonies and Processions of the Cathedral Church of Salisbury*, ed. C. Wordsworth.
Sarum Charters .	*Charters and Documents Illustrating the History of the Cathedral, City, and Diocese of Salisbury in the Twelfth and Thirteenth Centuries*, ed. W. H. R. Jones and W. D. Macray (Rolls Series).
St. Nicholas' Cartulary	*Fifteenth Century Cartulary of St. Nicholas' Hospital Salisbury*, ed. C. Wordsworth.
Swainson . .	*History and Constitution of a Cathedral of the Old Foundation Illustrated from Documents in the Registry and Muniment Room of the Cathedral of Chichester*, ed. C. A. Swainson.
T.R.H.S. . .	*Transactions of the Royal Historical Society.*
Use Exeter . .	*Use of Exeter Cathedral according to Bishop Grandisson. Abstract of Chapter Acts, etc.*, ed. H. E. Reynolds.
Use Sarum . .	*Use of Sarum*, ed. W. H. Frere.
V.C.H. . . .	*Victoria History of the Counties of England*, ed. W. Page.
Valor Eccl. . .	*Valor Ecclesiasticus* (Record Commission).
W.A.M. . . .	*Wiltshire Archaeological and Natural History Magazine.*
W.S. . . .	*Wells Cathedral: Its Foundation, Constitutional History and Statutes*, ed. H. E. Reynolds.
Y.A.J. . . .	*Yorkshire Archaeological Journal.*
Y.S. . . .	*Statutes of the Cathedral Church of York*, ed. J. Raine.
York Chantry Certificates .	*Certificates of the Commissioners Appointed to Survey the Chantries, Guilds, Hospitals etc. in the County of York*, ed. W. Page (Surtees Soc.).
York Fabric Rolls .	*Fabric Rolls of York Minster*, ed. J. Raine (Surtees Soc.).

INTRODUCTORY

1. THE ORIGINS AND EARLY DEVELOPMENT OF THE SECULAR CHAPTERS

'IT is by an abuse of terms that we have come to be called *seculars*,' wrote a canon and prebendary of Utrecht cathedral in the mid-fourteenth century: 'not that we should live a secular life, but because as seculars, we can have possessions and dispose of them.' [1] A long tradition of regular, common life forms the historical background of the secular cathedrals of medieval Europe, and is evidently at the root of this protest. In the fourth or fifth centuries the city was the bishop's parish (diocese), and its clergy were the bishop and the clerks of his *familia* or household. These served the city churches, which were, so to speak, chapels of ease to the principal basilica or cathedral church, of which the diocesan clergy formed the chapter. All were then called simply 'clerks' or 'canonical clerks'. The earliest meaning of the term *clericus canonicus* was any clerk living under ecclesiastical law, or according to the canons or rules of the church.[2] As Christianity spread to the more remote districts, the same name was at first used also for the priests and clergy living in the country or in towns distant from the cathedral city. Then, gradually, those clerks living with the bishop and acting as his council were given certain titles of honour, such as 'clerks of the first rank', 'the bishop's councillors', 'the crown and senate of the church', 'cardinal clerks',[3] to

[1] 'Per abusum transiverimus in nomen denominativum *seculares*, ut non seculari vita vivamus, sed quia ut seculares propria habere et de ipsis disponere possumus' (*Het Rechtsboek van den Dom van Utrecht*, ed. S. Muller, p. 153). The writer was Master Hugh Wstinc, compiler of the fourteenth-century statute book of Utrecht cathedral.

[2] C. de Clercq, *La législation réligieuse franque de Clovis à Charlemagne*, pp. 18-19. The word canon is derived from the Greek word κανών meaning law or rule. Abbot Chapman, *St. Benedict and the Sixth Century*, pp. 43-4, 65, 68, in tracing the connexion between Justinian's code, St. Benedict's rule, and the collections of canon law of Dionysius Exiguus, shows that 'canon' and *regula* were used interchangeably by St. Benedict and Dionysius in the same sense as κανών in Justinian's code.

[3] *Clerici primi gradus, consiliarii Episcopi, corona et senatus Ecclesiae, clerici cardinales.*

distinguish them from the rural or country clerks (*clerici forastici* or *corregionales*). But in councils of the Merovingian period the description 'canon' was still used for both these groups of city and town or country clerks, apparently because both lived in more or less close dependence on their bishop, doing the work which he assigned to them; while it was not given to the third group of clerks, who served oratories on private domains, and were dependent on the proprietors of the domains.[1]

No specific rules of common life were enjoined universally on bishops and their cathedral clerks at this time. From the first there had always been a party in the church that, following *The Acts of the Apostles* and interpreting the early christians as the clergy, thought that all clerks ought to lead the apostolic, that is, the communal life: 'No man said that he had anything of his own, but they had all things in common.' [2] St. Augustine's success in making his clergy lead a communal life at Hippo at the end of the fourth century was widely known through the lessons on his feast day, but there were two reasons why the rule supposed to have been followed by his community was unsuitable for medieval Europe. The first part of this rule, much the most important from the legislative point of view, enumerated in detail the hours of a very ancient office, which did not at all correspond to the liturgy of the western church in the early middle ages. It also laid down a very austere time-table of prayer, manual labour, and reading, with a single meal a day at three in the afternoon.[3] Though

[1] C. de Clerq, *op. cit.*, pp. 18–19, 23, 93.

[2] Acts iv. 32. The influence of the apostolic life on ecclesiastical thought throughout the early middle ages has been amply illustrated by P. Mandonnet in his study of the Augustinian rule in *Saint Dominique: l'Idée, l'Homme, et l'Œuvre* (1937), ii, 149 *et seq.*

[3] Cf. *ibid.*, pp. 131–5. Mandonnet, following the brilliant work of Amort in the eighteenth century on the surviving texts of the Augustinian Rule, maintained that this part of the Rule was written by St. Augustine as early as 388 for his first monastery at Thagaste. He also believed that the second part, which is four or five times as long, and consists chiefly of general spiritual precepts, was added to this by St. Augustine as a kind of commentary about three years later. This second part, however, is almost identical with the *Regula Sororum* appended to St. Augustine's letter 211, which he sent to an erring nunnery towards the end of his life about 423. More recent work suggests that there is still much to be said for the traditional view which recognizes St. Augustine's authorship of Letter 211 alone, and regards the second part of the Augustinian Rule as an adaptation of it made a little later, to which was added at the same

possible for clerks living in Africa, such a time-table was very difficult to follow under the climatic and economic conditions of western and northern Europe. It left those bishops of Merovingian and Carolingian Gaul, who desired their clergy to live a common life, with the task of making a rule for themselves.

There was a communal element in the life of most episcopal *familiae* in Merovingian Gaul, but this seems to have been chiefly due to economic motives of convenience. Though most of the inferior clergy lived in common buildings, all received stipends, both in money and in kind, while certain of the higher clergy might have private houses and were men of some patrimony.[1] Then, in the eighth and early ninth centuries, a much stricter form of common life was advocated by Boniface and the later Carolingian reformers. They saw in the revival of a strict common life a chief means of reforming and disciplining the clergy, particularly of enforcing celibacy. They maintained that a common life ought to be lived by clergy of all churches with an endowment large enough to support more than a single clerk or priest, and especially by cathedral clerks. Now that the missionary stage in the expansion of the church in Gaul was past, and the diocese more adequately supplied with clergy, the cathedral clerks had mostly ceased to travel about the diocese to different churches. Their duties were becoming much more limited to the daily public celebration of the office in the cathedral church. To the reformers it seemed that these duties could best be performed by clergy living a kind of semi-monastic life in common buildings grouped round the cathedral.

Several bishops drew up rules of common life for their cathedral clergy at this time. The most famous and successful was that of Bishop Chrodegang of Metz, written about 755. Chrodegang did not actually call his production a rule. He described it in his preface as a '*decretulum*', assuming that the sacred canons meant his clergy to live this way; but, as in fact they did not, he drew up this *parvum decretulum* for them. He borrowed largely from the

---

or a slightly later date in the fifth century the first part (J. C. Dickinson, *Origins of the Austin Canons and their Introduction into England*, 1950, pp. 255–72).

[1] For the life of the episcopal *familiae* in Gaul in the seventh century, see M. Deanesly, 'The *Familia* at Christ Church, Canterbury', in *Essays to Tout*, pp. 2–4.

Benedictine rule.[1] Chastity and obedience to the bishop were enforced; the clerks lived in common, with a common dormitory,
refectory, and cloister; their enclosure was as strict as that of
Benedictine monks, and their duties in the divine office practically
the same. The chief way in which Chrodegang's *decretulum* differed both from the Benedictine and Augustinian rules was in its
requirements for individual poverty. Though his clerks were supposed to give up all their property to the church, they were
allowed distributions not only of food and clothing, but of alms.[2]
This left the way open for later abuses, when the *pars eleemosyna-
rum* was interpreted as meaning that they might have regular
distributions of money, and, in some cases, private houses. Yet at
the time Chrodegang's *decretulum* appeared to contemporaries as a
convenient *norma* for leading a perfect canonical life. It was em-
bodied almost word for word, though not by name, in the canons
of the Council of Aix-la-Chapelle of 816–17 and in those of subsequent councils. Under the name *Institutio Canonica* it became the
basis for the widespread adoption of a common life for clerks at
cathedral and collegiate churches throughout the Empire.

It was now that the word *canonicus* began to acquire a stricter,
more specialized meaning in addition to its older significance.
Chrodegang seems to have been the first to use the term *ordo
canonicus* as meaning a group of clerks bound to an observance
stricter than that of the ancient canons. In the councils and capitularies of the last half of the eighth and of the ninth centuries, the
clerici canonici were usually those clerks who observed a definite
rule or canon, and the canonical or regular life (*canonica* or *regularis
vita*) came to be practically synonymous terms for the common
life either of clerks under the Chrodegangian or some similar rule,
or of Benedictine monks.[3] This meaning of 'canon' was well
known to writers of the ninth to twelfth centuries. Godwin,
precentor of the secular cathedral of Salisbury, writing about 1140,
declared that canon meant rule, and that therefore a canon was
one who lived according to a rule.[4] As late as the mid-fourteenth

[1] See the analysis of Chrodegang's rule by C. de Clercq, *op. cit.*, pp. 146–55.
[2] *Old English Version of Enlarged Rule of Chrodegang, with Latin Original*, ed.
A. S. Napier, pp. 48–9.
[3] Cf. C. de Clercq, *op. cit.*, pp. 135, 148–55, 164, 166, 175, 195–7, 211, 218,
224–5, 232, 234, 238–9, 245, 296–7.
[4] *Meditaciones Godwini Cantoris Salesberie, ad Rainilvam Reclusam*, Digby MS.
96, ff. 20b–21a.

century, Hugh, secular canon of Utrecht, could still write, 'For
we are canons, that is, we are living under a canon, that is, under a
rule.'[1]

From the ninth century onwards, however, two increasingly
divergent influences can be traced in the history of the organization of communities of canons. On the one hand, reformers were
trying to enforce the observance of a strict form of common life
based on the *Institutio Canonica*. At some cathedral and collegiate
churches this seems to have worked well for a time, and had a
strong influence on the constitutions of certain chapters throughout
the middle ages.[2] Yet capitularies issued from 824 onwards show
that in many parts it was meeting with resistance, and that local
bishops were finding it difficult to put the reforms into execution.[3]
The other tendency was towards the break-up of the common
life. Cathedral canons acquired private property, lived in separate
houses, and, in the course of the tenth and eleventh centuries,
divided up a large part of the common estates and goods of their
churches into separate portions or prebends for themselves. Because of these separate possessions they came to be called 'secular'
canons, which, as contemporary chroniclers were fond of pointing
out, was, strictly speaking, a contradiction in terms, equivalent to
saying *irregulares regulares*.[4]

The acceptance of this division of common goods was recognized as permissible on the continent about the middle of the
eleventh century. This led, in the religious revival of the same
period, to a renewed demand for clergy to live the 'apostolic' life.[5]
The name of St. Augustine is often met with in writings of this
period, but at first this does not necessarily mean that the rule of
the bishop of Hippo had been precisely adopted, or even that it

---

[1] 'Quia canonici sumus, hoc est sub canone, hoc est sub regula viventes' (*Het
Rechtsboek*, p. 153).

[2] E.g. Utrecht cathedral, throughout the middle ages, kept many traces of
its early organization for a common life. Though the canons received separate
incomes as prebends, these were administered in common, and further distributions from the common fund continued to be made in kind as well as in
money. This may have been why Hugh, in the fourteenth century, insisted that
their life was still, in truth, regular.

[3] Cf. E. Amann, *L'Époque carolingienne* (1937), pp. 265–6.

[4] E.g. Hospinian, quoted by Smith and Cheetham, *Dict. Christian Antiquities*,
s.v. Canonici.

[5] Mandonnet, *op. cit.*, pp. 167–82. *La vita commune del clero nei secoli xi e xii*,
Milan, 1962.

was known. The Augustinian institution seems to have been invoked simply because it was a synonym of a common clerical life and of the absolute abandonment of individual property. Occasionally attempts were made to follow the complete rule of St. Augustine. At the same time a movement began to 'decapitate' the rule by papal permission, cutting out the impossible antique time-table and austerities, and 'modernizing' the offices.[1] In the early twelfth century this solution became increasingly popular. The second part of the rule consisted largely of spiritual precepts which could form an excellent basis for the life of any religious house. To this, particular houses or orders could add their own legislation, while keeping the prestige of the Augustinian rule as a kind of banner for their organization. The communities of canons, which followed a strict common life under the second part of the Augustinian rule were called 'Augustinian' or 'regular' canons, an expression which, in earlier times, would have been redundant.

The general break-up of the old canonical life in the ninth, tenth, and eleventh centuries was due partly to the invasions and unrest, which led to a relaxation of ecclesiastical discipline everywhere. At the same time the influence of feudalism and their growing riches, granted in the form of lands and privileges by kings and magnates, transformed the chapters into powerful feudatories, which might rival the bishops in their social and economic importance, and they strongly resented close episcopal control, such as had been prescribed by Chrodegang and other eighth-century reformers. The development of the new secular organization was also in many ways an answer to the needs of a new age. Changes in the structure of society and in the centres of civilization, the growth of towns and of education, were creating demands which Benedictine monks or clerks living a semi-monastic life in their cloisters could not meet. The Benedictine institution had been admirably suited to serve the spiritual needs and to adapt itself to the economic life of a feudal society. But, in the eleventh and twelfth centuries, preoccupied with the spiritual perfection of its members, weighed down by its institutions, its house situated generally at a distance from the towns, it could not exercise the same influence on the new world which was coming

[1] Fr. Dereine (*Scriptorium* II, i, 1948, pp. 28 ff.) shows that this movement began earlier and was a more gradual and less uniform process than Mandonnet thought.

into existence. The new work in the towns had to be done by clerks or canons; naturally there grew up fresh conceptions of the kind of life they should lead. At first they were chiefly needed to serve in the city churches, to teach, and to help their bishop in administrative work. Then, in the late eleventh and twelfth centuries, the demand for trained clerks in the rapidly expanding administrations of the royal and papal courts became more insistent. Without some arrangement for separate prebendal incomes for canons and some relaxation of the rule binding them to continual residence in the cloister, it would have been impossible for them to do this work; and, in the absence of banks and ready money, kings, popes, and bishops would have been hard put to find any means other than prebends with which to provide for the busy clerks in their service. Godwin, precentor of Salisbury in the early twelfth century, himself a secular canon, pointed out that secular canons and clerks should not be called 'irregular' merely because they had possessions. They did not use their property in feasting and vanity, in buying fine clothes or piling up wealth, but for the necessities of their work for the faithful, and for ecclesiastical needs.[1] He emphasized that monks, regular canons, secular canons, and clerks were all members of one body, the church universal. Naturally, different members of a body had different functions; their way of life had to vary in a number of unimportant details simply in order that they might more easily perform their different duties.[2]

The later history of the secular and regular canons shows that in time they came to fill very different places in the church and society. During the first fifty years of the existence of the canons regular, a number of their communities, inspired by the clerical ideals of St. Peter Damiani and the eleventh-century reformers, managed to combine the practice of individual poverty and pastoral preaching in the towns. But in the course of the twelfth century they came under the very strong influence of the reformed Benedictines, especially the Cistercians.[3] New Augustinian houses were founded either in the country or outside the gates of the towns; the monastic ideal of personal salvation became more important to them; they insisted more on the communal life than on

[1] Digby MS. 96, f. 21a.   [2] *Ibid.*, ff. 22a–24a.
[3] For this later phase in the history of the regular canons, see Mandonnet, *op. cit.*, p. 182.

pastoral work. While earlier houses had often been formed from members of episcopal chapters or the ordinary clerks of the church, the new foundations consisted chiefly of men who had not previously been clerks. These came together to live a religious life which had more similarities with that of Benedictine monks than with that of secular canons. In the meantime the secular canons had been finding their interests increasingly in the outside world, at the royal and papal courts, in the service of archbishops and bishops, and in the schools. It was the secular cathedral schools of the eleventh and twelfth centuries which prepared the way for and sometimes developed into the universities of the thirteenth century.

In England there is little evidence for the early life of the cathedral clergy, particularly before the Norman Conquest. The conversion took place later than in France, and the Danish invasions of the ninth century destroyed much of the ecclesiastical organization set up in the seventh and eighth centuries, especially in the north and east midlands. The available evidence does, however, show that the idea that a bishop's cathedral clerks ought to live the apostolic, communal life was prevalent in England as in France. A communal life for clerks, not the Benedictine life, was followed by St. Augustine and his companions at Christ Church, Canterbury.[1] When bishops' sees were founded at London and Rochester in 601 and 604, the arrangements at the cathedrals were, it is thought, modelled on those of Canterbury; the clergy had a common refectory and dormitory; many of them were men who had previously made a monk's profession, yet the cathedrals at this time were not Benedictine monasteries.[2] By the eighth and early ninth centuries, private property and separate houses for the higher clergy seem to have been accepted at many English minsters. But, following on the revival of a strict common life in cathedrals of the Empire, Archbishop Wulfred about 813 introduced a rule of common life at Canterbury, similar to that of Chrodegang.[3] In

---

[1] Different views are held about the early practice of the common life at Christ Church (see e.g. M. Deanesly, *loc. cit.*, pp. 1–13; J. A. Robinson in *J.T.S.* (1926), pp. 225–40; M. D. Knowles, *ibid.* (1938), pp. 126–31; *The Monastic Order*, pp. 619–20, 696–7). However, it seems clear that, even if Christ Church became a Benedictine monastery for a short time after Augustine's death, the common life practised there during his lifetime was not Benedictine.

[2] F. M. Stenton, *Anglo-Saxon England*, p. 109.

[3] M. Deanesly, *loc. cit.*, pp. 10–13.

the eleventh century, before the Conquest, there is further evidence for attempts to enforce the canonical life at English cathedral and collegiate churches. About 1050, Bishop Leofric moved his see from Crediton to Exeter, where he built a refectory and dormitory for his canons, and gave them the rule of Chrodegang.[1] About ten years later Bishop Giso introduced a regular common life at Wells with great success:[2] while at Hereford the same may have been done shortly before the Conquest by Bishop Walter (1061–79).[3] All these bishops had been either born or educated in Lorraine; their introduction of the canonical life at English cathedrals is generally attributed to their Lotheringian training, and it is sometimes assumed that this kind of organization was foreign to Englishmen. Yet as early as about 1009, at the Council of Ænham, English canons had been admonished to live according to their rule.[4] The fifth and sixth codes of King Ethelred laid down that wherever canons had sufficient revenues for a refectory and dormitory, they should maintain regularity and celibacy, as their rule prescribed.[5] Furthermore, the policy of Leofric seems to have been anticipated in northern England. Between 1060 and 1069 Archbishop Ealdred enriched the three great minsters of York, Southwell, and Beverley. At York and Southwell he established refectories for the canons, but at Beverley he is said to have completed the refectory and dormitory which Archbishops Ælfric and Cynesige had begun during the period from 1023 to 1051.[6] Other English cathedrals may also have been influenced by this movement. The canons of St. Paul's, shortly before the Conquest, had their own *Regula Sancti Pauli*, adapted from the *Institutio Canonica*.[7]

[1] The copy of Chrodegang's rule which Leofric gave to Exeter is at Corpus Christi College, Cambridge, MS. 191. It was edited by A. S. Napier for the Early English Text Society, 1916. Cf. R. W. Chambers, *Exeter Book of Old English Poetry*, p. 7.

[2] '*Historiola de primordiis Episcopatus Somersetensis*', in *Eccl. Documents*, ed. J. Hunter (Camden Soc.), pp. 16–20.

[3] For the evidence and arguments, see A. T. Bannister, *Cathedral Church of Hereford*, pp. 25–6.　　　　　　　　　　　[4] *Concilia*, i, 292–3.

[5] *Laws of the Kings of England from Edmund to Henry I*, ed. A. J. Robertson, pp. 80–1, 92–3.

[6] R. R. Darlington, 'Ecclesiastical Reform in the Late Old English Period', in *E.H.R.* (1936), li, 404.

[7] C. N. L. Brooke in *Hist. St. Paul's Cathedral*, ed. R. Matthews (1957), pp. 12, 263; *Early Charters of St. Paul*, ed. M. Gibbs, p. xviii; cf. Bannister, *loc. cit.*, p. 26.

But in pre-conquest England Chrodegang's rule from the mid-tenth century had a rival in the Benedictine rule as a basis for regular cathedral organization. The monastic revival of the tenth century had led to the introduction of Benedictine monks in the place of clerks at certain cathedrals, to serve the church and to form the chapter. This practice, during the later middle ages, was almost peculiar to England.[1] St. Ethelwold in 964 was the first bishop in the south of England violently to eject the clerks from his cathedral church of Winchester and to put Benedictine monks in their place. St. Oswald followed his example more gradually at Worcester, by a process of slow transformation of the body of clerks into a fully organized monastic community. A little later the plan was adopted also at Sherborne and probably at Canterbury.[2] There the movement ceased for the time being. But, during the ecclesiastical reorganization after the Norman Conquest, Lanfranc decided to have Benedictine monks in at least some English cathedrals. He dissuaded those of the Conqueror's bishops who had at first wanted to turn out the monks. Through his influence the monastic cathedrals were increased to as many as nine,[3] that is, to about half the full number of English medieval cathedrals. This

---

[1] Among the rare medieval examples of monastic cathedrals outside England were Monreale in Sicily, where the abbey was made a bishop's see in 1176, perhaps with English precedent in mind; and Downpatrick in Ireland, where monks from Chester were imported to form a cathedral monastery about 1185 (M. D. Knowles, *The Monastic Order*, p. 619). The tradition of the early monastic bishops of Lindisfarne and the Northumbrian church, living as monks in their monasteries, probably had little direct influence on the arrangements of Dunstan, Ethelwold, and Oswald, though, through the writings of Bede, it influenced later generations (*ibid.*, pp. 620–1).

[2] It seems likely that St. Dunstan began gradually to introduce monks at Canterbury, and that the process was completed by one of the archbishop's immediate successors about the year 1000. On the other hand, the community never became, or certainly did not remain fully and purely monastic in spirit, and, more than any other house, it became secular in outlook under the Confessor (*ibid.*, p. 697).

[3] These were Canterbury, Winchester, Worcester, Rochester, and Durham, which had all been bishops' sees before the Conquest. The new see of Ely was carved out of the large diocese of Lincoln *c.* 1109, and the bishop was given Ely Abbey as his cathedral and its monks as his chapter. The sees of Elmham (removed to Thetford *c.* 1071), Lichfield (removed to Chester *c.* 1075) and Wells acquired Benedictine chapters on their later removals to Norwich, Coventry, and Bath. One Saxon cathedral monastery, Sherborne, became secular when it was removed to Salisbury.

result may have been due to pressure from the monks as well as to Lanfranc's own *esprit de corps* as a monk, and to his desire to preserve existing institutions in England. It was also probably bound up with his policy of using monasticism as an instrument of reform. A chief demand of the reformers was still for a celibate clergy, especially at the cathedrals.[1] Various attempts to enforce the communal life through adopting Chrodegang's rule or the 817 version of it had not, in fact, proved adequate to keep the cathedral clergy celibate. Lanfranc may well have introduced the Benedictine rule at English cathedrals because he thought it would secure this.

Many other far-reaching changes took place at English cathedrals after the Norman Conquest. The sites of many cathedrals were moved from small villages to the most important town in the diocese.[2] The number of cathedrals was increased from fifteen to nineteen, two bishops eventually having double chapters (one monastic and one secular) with two cathedral churches at Bath and Wells and at Coventry and Lichfield. Many chapters were founded afresh or reorganized under the influence of Norman ideas. As a result there came to be nine secular cathedrals, Salisbury, Lincoln, York, London, Exeter, Hereford, Lichfield, Chichester, Wells, now called the cathedrals of the Old Foundation, and ten served by regular clergy: nine by Benedictine monks, and one, Carlisle, founded in 1133, by Augustinian canons. This arrangement remained unchanged until the Reformation. Then, after the dissolution of the monasteries, most of the cathedral monasteries were refounded as chapters of secular canons, and became known as cathedrals of the New Foundation.

Before the Conquest there is little evidence for the adoption at English cathedrals of the new secular system, which allowed separate prebendal incomes to the individual canons. Clerks or canons holding estates, later known to be cathedral prebends, sometimes appear among a bishop's tenants in Domesday Book.[3]

---

[1] See Mandonnet's account of the reform movement of the mid-eleventh century, especially of the writings and teachings of St. Peter Damiani (*op. cit.*, pp. 167–82).

[2] In addition to the changes noticed above, p. 10, n. 3, the sees of Dorchester and Selsey were moved to Lincoln and Chichester.

[3] See e.g. W. Page, 'Some Remarks on the Churches of the Domesday Survey', in *Archaeologia*, 2nd ser., xvi (1915), 94.

At St. Paul's there was apparently an embryo prebendal system.[1]
But normally those chapters which followed neither a specific rule
of canonical life nor the Benedictine rule seem still to have been
supported from common revenues. It was the Conquest which
opened the way to the adoption of the new type of secular organization then coming into use on the continent.

The first English secular cathedral chapters to emerge from the
Norman refoundation after the Conquest were Salisbury, Lincoln, York, and London. London was exceptional among the four
in having an unbroken history from before the Conquest. Its
bishop, Maurice, gradually completed the prebendal system of
30 prebends and established a hierarchy of the dean and archdeacons probably about 1090.[1] The other three chapters were all
founded or reconstituted by their bishops, Osmund of Salisbury,
Remigius of Lincoln, and Thomas of York, on a secular basis
between about 1089–91. There is little precise contemporary information about the constitutions which they set up. Those of
York and Lincoln are described very briefly and generally by the
chroniclers, Hugh the Chanter at York, and Henry, Archdeacon
of Huntingdon, who had been brought up in the household of
Robert Bloet, the successor of Remigius.[2] St. Osmund is the only
bishop known to have given a written constitution to his cathedral. The earliest surviving copies of his Institution were written
in the early fourteenth and early fifteenth centuries, and the texts
used may have been brought up to date towards the middle of the
twelfth century.[3] They seem however to be substantially accurate
copies of genuine lost originals. It is moreover interesting to
notice that, according to the available copies, both Osmund's
foundation charter and his Institution at Salisbury are witnessed by
Archbishop Thomas of York, Bishop Remigius of Lincoln, and

[1] See C. N. L. Brooke in *Camb. Hist. Jour.*, x, 111–19 and *Hist. St. Paul's Cathedral*, pp. 18–22.

[2] Hugh the Chanter, *Hist. Church York* (R.S.), ii, 108; Henry of Huntingdon, 'Epistola de contemptu mundi' in *Hist. Anglorum* (R.S.), pp. 301–2.

[3] They have been printed several times: in *L.S.*, ii, 7–10; *Use Sarum*, i, 259–261; *Canonization S. Osmund*, pp. 50–2; *S.S.*, pp. 26–35. For discussion of their accuracy see A. F. Leach, *Medieval Schools*, pp. 106–13; Frere, *Use Sarum*, i, xvii–xx, xxxvii; K. Edwards in *V. C. H. Wilts*, iii (1956), 156–8 and below, pp. 19–21, 181–3, 218, 263, 319–20. Professor Brooke in his papers read at Oxford, 1952, and Stockholm, 1960 (below, p. 371) supports the authenticity of the surviving texts of the Institution.

Bishop Maurice of London, while the foundation charter of Lincoln cathedral of 1090, extant in a later copy of the confirmation granted by William Rufus to Remigius, is witnessed by Osmund of Salisbury, Thomas of York and Bishop Maurice of London.[1] Thus the bishops may quite possibly have discussed together their plans for their cathedral constitutions. Bishop Maurice does not seem at any time to have been an ardent reformer, and his plans (or absence of plans) were more individual and apparently less disinterested than those of the other bishops.[2] But so far as we know the arrangements of Osmund, Remigius, and Thomas were on similar lines. Furthermore, one at least of these bishops, and probably all three, had had experience in Normandy of arrangements in Norman secular cathedrals. Archbishop Thomas had been treasurer of Bayeux cathedral, while Remigius, although a monk of the exempt abbey of Fécamp, would presumably be familiar with the organization of the cathedral of Rouen. There is no evidence for St. Osmund's origin,[3] though his name and position as king's chancellor point to Normandy. These facts have led many historians to suppose that the constitutions which the three bishops gave to their English cathedrals were precisely modelled on the constitution of a particular Norman cathedral. Bradshaw described the characteristic, fully-developed, medieval constitutions of the English secular cathedrals as 'four-square', because they were founded on four great dignitaries, the dean, precentor, chancellor, and treasurer, with their stalls at the four corners of the choir. Assuming that such constitutions were instituted in a more or less complete form by Osmund, Thomas, and Remigius at their cathedrals in 1090-1, he made a determined effort to discover in northern France a cathedral with the same four dignitaries. In 1873 he wrote that he had found just such a constitution at Bayeux. He

[1] *S.S.*, pp. 22-3, 32-3; *Reg. Antiquissimum Lincoln*, i, 8.
[2] C. N. L. Brooke, *Hist. St. Paul's Cathedral*, pp. 18-22.
[3] A fifteenth-century document preserved at Salisbury (*Sarum Charters*, p. 373) says that St. Osmund was the son of Henry, Count of Séez, by Isabella, daughter of Robert, Duke of Normandy, and sister of William the Conqueror. This document is almost certainly a fairy story. The writer shows an entire ignorance of Norman history. He starts with a duke of Normandy named Robert, whom he makes father of Rollo; no such person existed. There never was a count of Séez, whether named Henry or anything else. Nor is there any evidence that Duke Robert, father of King William, had a daughter named Isabella.

c

declared that Bayeux cathedral was the 'real mother' of the English secular cathedral constitutions.[1]

Unfortunately, the only evidence which Bradshaw seems to have used for the constitutions of the Norman and French cathedrals was a list of forty-four of them which he had compiled from the *Gallia Christiana*.[2] The information given by the *Gallia Christiana* is confined to the titles of the dignitaries and the number of canons; furthermore, these scanty details represent the state of affairs at a date much later than the eleventh century. Therefore the possibility of change and development during the intervening centuries has to be taken into account. Since Bradshaw wrote, other historians have sometimes questioned his assumption that the constitutions of all the English secular cathedrals were derived ultimately from Bayeux, through the arrangements adopted by Osmund, Remigius, and Thomas. Canon Bannister at Hereford and Dean Savage at Lichfield have pointed out that the medieval constitutions of their cathedrals and of Lincoln cathedral had more similarities with that of Rouen than with that of Bayeux.[3] More recently, however, the researches of the late Mr. Lewis C. Loyd have suggested that neither Bayeux nor Rouen, nor any other Norman secular cathedral, could in the late eleventh century have formed a precise model for the particular 'four-square' constitution, which, by the late twelfth or early thirteenth century, later than Bradshaw supposed, had become characteristic of English secular cathedral government. Mr. Loyd, working chiefly from charters and other Norman cathedral records, published since Bradshaw wrote, compiled further lists of dignitaries actually known to have been present in the six Norman secular cathedrals[4] in the eleventh and twelfth centuries. He very kindly lent me his notes and allowed me to quote them here.[5]

[1] G. W. Prothero, *Memoir of Henry Bradshaw*, p. 345, cf. p. 283; *L.S.*, i, 33–6,101–3.

[2] *Memoir of Henry Bradshaw*, p. 283. The list is now lost (*L.S.*, i, 35 n.).

[3] A. T. Bannister, 'Origin and Growth of the Cathedral System', in *C.Q.R.*, civ (1927), 95–6 and n.; H. E. Savage, Introduction to *Magnum Registrum Album of Lichfield Cathedral* (1928), pp. xxvi–vii; cf. E. Bishop, *Liturgica Historica*, pp. 276–300.

[4] The seventh Norman cathedral, Séez, was served by regular canons after 1129. Little is known of its earlier constitution.

[5] Fuller information from Mr. Loyd's memorandum and elsewhere is now also available in D. Douglas, 'The Norman Episcopate before the Conquest', in *Camb. Hist. Jour.* (1957).

Although there were a dean and cantor at Bayeux from about 1077 and a treasurer from before 1070 there is no evidence in the eleventh century for a cathedral chancellor. In 1147 a bishop's chaplain appears, who, about 1153, took the title of *archicapellanus*.[1] In 1156 he is first known to be described as chancellor.[2] But his functions were quite different from those of chancellors in English secular cathedrals. Raoul Langevin, canon of Bayeux, described them about 1270 in his treatise on the statutes and customs of Bayeux cathedral: they were to keep the bishop's seal, and to attend constantly on the bishop, both when the bishop was ministering in his cathedral, and when he was travelling about his diocese.[3] Clearly this was the bishop's chancellor, not the cathedral chancellor. He was not bound to residence in the cathedral, and his position as a cathedral dignitary, like that of the archdeacons, was merely an honour accorded to an episcopal official. The dignitary who, at Bayeux, throughout the middle ages, performed the functions corresponding to those of an English cathedral chancellor, was the *scholasticus* or *magister scholarum*. He probably existed from the time of Bishop Odo,[4] but his precedence was low. Langevin, writing about 1270, puts him at the foot of the list of seven dignitaries, below the subdean and succentor.[5] This looks as if he may have counted as the holder of an officium or *personatus* rather than, as in English cathedrals, as a principal dignitary.

Thus the chapter of Bayeux cannot be said to have formed a precise model for the particular 'four-square' constitution adopted at English secular cathedrals. Nor does evidence for dignitaries at the other five Norman secular cathedrals suggest that any of them provided such a model. Rouen was the only Norman cathedral which ever came to have a cathedral chancellor. But from 1091 to

[1] *Antiquus Cartularius Eccl. Baiocensis (Livre Noir)*, ed. V. Bourrienne, nos. 52, 73, 102, 128, 133, 148; V. Bourrienne, *Philippe de Harcourt*, Pièces justificatives, nos. 3, 5, 6, 15, 18, 20, 22.

[2] The title of chancellor at Bayeux only gradually superseded that of *archicapellanus* in the last half of the twelfth century; see e.g. *Livre Noir*, nos. 45, 96, 125, 150.

[3] *Ordinaire et Coutumier . . . de Bayeux*, ed. U. Chevalier, pp. 299, 307–8, 317.

[4] A certain Richard, *grammaticus et scholasticus*, attested two unpublished charters of Bishop Odo (S. L. Gleason, *An Ecclesiastical Barony of the Middle Ages*, p. 14 n.). This is probably the earliest occurrence of the *magister scholarum*, who appears in printed records in 1151 (*Livre Noir*, no. 106).

[5] *Ordinaire*, pp. 300, 319.

1092, when a dignitary with the functions of the later chancellor first appears in the records, until 1140 he was called either *scholasticus* or *magister scholarum*; the first undoubted instance of his being described as chancellor is in 1151.¹ At other Norman cathedrals, the dignitary in charge of the schools and of the chapter seals continued, throughout the middle ages and later, to be called *scholasticus* or *magister scholarum* and usually ranked fairly low among the dignitaries.

As for the other dignitaries, it is clear that Norman practice with regard to their titles, precedence, and numbers, was by no means settled in 1090, that it remained uncertain for the greater part of the twelfth century, and varied considerably at the different cathedrals. Rouen, for instance, had a *secretarius* in 1091–2, who in 1146 was described as *sacrista*, but who did not apparently come to have the title of treasurer until 1151.² The order of witnesses to twelfth-century charters is no reliable guide to their actual precedence; the order in which dignitaries of the same cathedral witnessed charters of about the same date might vary considerably. But by the mid-thirteenth century, the precedence of the dignitaries in both Norman and English cathedrals was more or less settled. Then, it is significant of different development in the two countries that, while in English cathedrals the treasurer usually had the fourth place, in Norman cathedrals he generally ranked as third dignitary, above the *magister scholarum*, *scholasticus*, or chancellor. In addition, there are certain minor differences in the number of dignitaries finally instituted in the Norman and English cathedrals. None came to have so many as certain cathedrals in northern France, such as Chartres, where in the fourteenth century there were seventeen.³ But whereas, in English cathedrals only the dean,

---

¹ The gradual change of title at Rouen during the last half of the twelfth century from *magister scholarum* or *scholasticus* to chancellor has been traced in detail by Mr. Loyd from a number of attestations to contemporary charters. A charter of Malger, archbishop of Rouen, for St. Père-de-Chartres (*Cartulaire*, ed. Guérard, p. 176), which cannot be later than 1055, is witnessed by Fulbert 'cancellarius'; the occurrence of a chancellor at so early a date is startling, but the charter does not seem to be otherwise open to suspicion.

² This change, also, has been carefully traced by Mr. Loyd in his unpublished memorandum. The title *thesaurarius* did not finally supersede that of sacrist until about 1190.

³ See L. Amiet, *Essai sur l'Organization du Chapitre Cathédrale de Chartres*, pp. 2 *et passim*.

precentor, chancellor, and treasurer, with the archdeacons, were normally described as dignitaries, Norman cathedrals sometimes gave the title of dignitary to other officers, such as the subdean and succentor at Bayeux, and the *capicerius* or treasurer's deputy at Lisieux; these dignitaries came in several cases to take precedence of the *magister scholarum* or *scholasticus*.[1] Furthermore, the constitutions of the Norman churches were by no means uniform among themselves. Coutances was exceptional in having no dean;[2] Evreux had no *scholasticus*.

Thus, although marked similarities in general outline may be observed between the functions of dignitaries in Norman and English cathedrals in the twelfth century, it is clear that the Norman cathedrals do not exhibit anything like the uniformity or parallelism of design shown by the 'four-square' constitutions of English secular cathedrals of the late twelfth or thirteenth century. The knowledge of cathedral constitutions of Osmund, Thomas, and Remigius is unlikely to have been limited to those of Normandy. They had before them in northern France a large number of solutions of the problems of secular cathedral government roughly similar to those which they introduced into England. Attention may be drawn in particular to two cathedrals just south of Normandy, Angers, and Le Mans, for which there is a larger amount of eleventh-century evidence available than for the Norman cathedrals. At Angers there is express evidence for a dean, treasurer, and chanter as early as 1076, and for a *magister scholarum* in 1104.[3] At Le Mans there is evidence for all four in the eleventh century.[4] It is interesting to notice that Salisbury and perhaps Lincoln had connexions with one or other of these churches in the

[1] See e.g. E. Deslandes, *Étude sur l'Église de Bayeux*, pp. 95–6; *Ordinaire de Bayeux*, pp. 300, 319; H. de Formeville, *Hist. de l'Ancien Évéché-Comté de Lisieux*, i, clxxxiii–ccix. At the English cathedrals of Lincoln, York, and Wells, the subdean was a dignitary, but generally ranked after the four great dignitaries, having precedence only of the simple canons.

[2] Bishop Geoffrey de Montbray is said to have appointed a dean temporarily at Coutances shortly after he founded the chapter in the mid-eleventh century (J. le Patourel, 'Geoffrey de Montbray, Bishop of Coutances', in *E.H.R.*, lix (1944), 141). But the office did not survive, and the cantor acted as head of the chapter.

[3] *Cartulary of St. Aubin*, ed. Bertrand de Broussillon, i, 35, 131.

[4] *Cartulaire de St. Vincent du Mans*, nos. 15, 114, 175, 187, 242, 302, 472; *Cartulaire de St. Pierre de la Couture du Mans*, nos. 7, 15, 16, 25.

late eleventh or twelfth centuries. An Albinus of Anjou was one of the first generation of canons instituted by Remigius at Lincoln, and may possibly have held the office of *magister scholarum* there.[1] Soon after 1107, Guy of Etampes, who had formerly been *magister scholarum* and precentor of Le Mans, was made *magister scholarum* or *scholiarcha* of Salisbury and a canon of Salisbury cathedral. The appointment was the result of direct correspondence between Roger, bishop of Salisbury, St. Osmund's successor, and Hildebert, bishop of Le Mans. Apparently Roger wrote to Hildebert, asking him to recommend a *magister scholarum* for the cathedral school at Salisbury. Hildebert, in reply, sent Master Guy, whom he had trained in his own household, and who was later to succeed him as bishop of Le Mans.[2]

On the whole, it seems unlikely that Osmund, Remigius, and Thomas chose any definite model for their cathedral constitutions. They were probably somewhat eclectic, and, like sensible men, preferred to establish simply the kind of chapter which they thought would work best at their particular cathedrals, and which they could afford. In so far as each English chapter in the twelfth century consisted of a body of canons with separate prebends and with dignitaries at its head, it certainly followed what had become the ordinary practice on the continent. In general outline the division of administrative duties among the dignitaries was roughly similar to that of many cathedrals of northern France. But in matters of detail, particularly the number, titles, and precedence of the different dignitaries, English historians seem to have read developments of the twelfth and thirteenth centuries, both in England and Normandy, too freely backwards in their desire to find for English cathedral constitutions a precisely Norman origin. In any case the English bishops, in naming their cathedral officials may not have been influenced solely by existing cathedral constitutions. Professor Brooke has recently drawn attention to a possible written source, a list of nine or ten officials of 'mother-churches' with descriptions of their functions in Bishop John of Avranches's *De Officiis Ecclesiasticis* of *c.* 1060, a book which, as he shows, may have influenced the early liturgical customs of English

---

[1] Henry of Huntingdon, p. 301, and below, pp. 180-81.
[2] *'Hildeberti Epistolae'* in *P.L.*, clxxi, c. 219; cf. *'Actus Pontificum Cenomannis'*, in *Vetera Analecta*, ed. Mabillon, p. 320.

secular cathedrals.[1] The most important factor, however, was doubtless the resources available for English cathedrals in the late eleventh and early twelfth centuries. It is unlikely that English bishops of this time had sufficient resources to appoint the full number of dignitaries, officers and *ministri inferiores* associated with the highly developed cathedral constitutions of the later middle ages. St. Osmund's Institution itself may well have been a statement of principles, forecasting the lines on which he hoped his chapter would develop, rather than a statement of a constitution in being. Much more than is generally realized was due to the way in which the bishops' plans were developed at the different English cathedrals in the course of the twelfth, thirteenth, and fourteenth centuries.

This development will be discussed in later chapters. For the present it can be said that the arrangements introduced at Salisbury, Lincoln, and York in 1090–1 appear to have filled a definite need, and soon became widely popular at other English cathedrals. The years following the Conquest saw the end of the eleventh-century revival of the canonical life at English cathedrals. At York when Archbishop Thomas took possession of his cathedral in 1070, he found almost everything destroyed by the recent 'harrying of the north'; at first he attempted to restore Ealdred's system of the communal life,[2] but by 1090 had decided to abandon it in favour of the kind of organization familiar to him in Normandy. At Exeter, decay seems to have set in after Leofric's death in 1072; while at Wells Giso's reforms were abrogated by his successor, John of Tours, who destroyed the refectory, dormitory, cloister, and other offices built by Giso, and turned the canons out to live 'with the people'.[3] At Wells, a new stage in the history of the chapter began with the appointment of Bishop Robert of Lewes. From 1136 onwards he gradually introduced a secular constitution very similar to that of the neighbouring cathedral of Salisbury.[4] Other chapters whose organization in the twelfth century came to

---

[1] In his two papers read at Oxford 1952 and Stockholm, 1960 (see below, p. 371). The list was derived in part from an interpolated letter of St. Isidore of Seville. The book was recognized as the official use of Rouen.

[2] Hugh the Chanter, *Hist. Church York*, ii, 108.

[3] *Historiola de primordiis Episcopatus Somersetensis*, p. 22.

[4] See C. M. Church, *Chapters in the Early History of the Church of Wells*, pp. 11–21; J. A. Robinson, *Somerset Hist. Essays*, pp. 55–61; *Dean Cosyn and Wells Cathedral Miscellanea*, ed. A. Watkin (Somerset Record Soc., 1941), pp. xxv–vi.

be modelled fairly closely on that of Salisbury were Chichester and Lichfield.[1] The three at which the change from a communal to a secular organization seems to have been most individual and gradual were London, Exeter, and Hereford. Throughout the middle ages their customs and statutes kept traces of their pre-conquest organization for a common life. This is seen particularly in their distributions of commons in kind, their arrangements for feeding the choir, and at Exeter, in the common administration of the canon's prebends.[2] But, in the late eleventh, twelfth, and early thirteenth centuries, most other features of their constitutions were gradually assimilated to the more usual Anglo-Norman model, the institution of prebends and dignitaries coming later at Exeter and Hereford than at St. Paul's.

The ideal of St. Osmund and Remigius was probably that the great majority of their canons should be resident fairly continuously, serving the *opus dei* in the cathedral church. It is difficult to know how far the three bishops allowed for non-residence of the canons. The fourteenth and fifteenth century copies of St. Osmund's Institution required only two archdeacons to be present at the cathedral, while the others fulfilled their duties in their archdeaconries; they further permitted the archbishop, bishop, and king to keep one or three canons in their service; and the canons were allowed leave of absence for a third part of the year if this were obviously necessary for the common good of the church or their prebends. Dispensations might also be granted to canons to be absent at the schools.[3] These concessions were doubtless all necessary from the beginning. Prominent royal and episcopal clerks are known to have held prebends at the secular chapters in the late eleventh and early twelfth centuries and it must also have been common for bishops of newly founded chapters to send some of their canons away to study. But whatever the legal position at the cathedrals may have been, non-residence clearly

---

[1] See *C.S.*, pp. 1 *et seq.*, and the statutes for Lichfield of the time of Bishop Nonant in *L.S.*, ii, 11–28.

[2] At Wells also, traces of the earlier communal administration survived in the equal division of the revenues of the large manor of Combe among fifteen prebendaries. The chapter of Wells also continued to pay part of its commons in kind until about the middle of the thirteenth century. In churches such as Salisbury, which had been secular from its foundation, this system was apparently never practised.

[3] *S.S.*, pp. 26–9.

increased at an alarming rate throughout the twelfth century, creating a major problem at the cathedrals and for the church generally.

Working solutions were found in time. It was recognized that, under changed conditions, a certain number of cathedral prebends, which were without cure of souls, must provide the salaries of busy clerks in the service of king, pope, archbishop, and bishop, and be used as scholarships for university students. Therefore the position of such non-resident canons was legalized; their emoluments and duties were strictly defined and regulated in the cathedral statutes; while at the same time the situation at the cathedrals was met by increasing the number of subordinate officers and ministers. All this has generally been regarded as a decline from the ideal and purpose of a cathedral church, and it is as a story of steady decline that the history of the secular cathedrals during the later middle ages has usually been written. The cathedral schools of the twelfth century are sometimes thought to have rendered important services to learning. But after the rise of the universities, most historians have supposed that they ceased to provide much teaching. At the same time the growing wealth and privileges of the chapters seem to have caused the residentiary canons, who, in the later middle ages, became fewer and fewer, to centre their interests increasingly on the assertion of their rights and privileges. In describing the quarrels to which their claims so often led, Dom Leclercq has written that it is impossible not to wonder how the life of the chapters was able to endure for so many centuries without either a sudden decay or some spiritual revival.[1] Yet all this time the religious work of the cathedrals was not left undone, and the chapters became in many ways far more important and powerful bodies, economically, socially, and politically, with much wider interests and contacts than the early Saxon chapters, drawn chiefly from the local clergy of the diocese. For the greater part of the middle ages, at any rate until the fourteenth century, the development of their constitutions was towards greater elaboration and specialization of functions. This was in conformity with the tendency of the age, in both secular and ecclesiastical administration. In the fourteenth century the number of clergy attached to the cathedrals was usually greatest. In 1390 there were over a

---

[1] *Dict. d'Archéologie Chrétienne et de Liturgie, s.v.* Chapitre, c. 505.

hundred and thirty clergy at Salisbury;[1] in 1337 there were eighty-nine, excluding the annuellars, at the small cathedral of Exeter;[2] St. Paul's, with its seventy-three chantries, must have had many more than Salisbury. Towards the end of the fourteenth and in the fifteenth centuries there was a tendency at some cathedrals to reduce the number of *ministri inferiores*. This gradual process of simplification was accelerated at the Reformation. But no general reform of the chapters took place until the great revision of their endowments and customs in the nineteenth century.

2. THE MATERIALS

The various collections of statutes and customs of the chapters must form the basis of any attempt to reconstruct the cathedral constitutions; it is only from such material that a connected picture of the different aspects of cathedral life can be drawn, and the more scattered information from the administrative records linked together. A good proportion of the cathedral statute books and customaries have been published. The three most important editions are those of the Lincoln statutes by Bradshaw and Wordsworth,[3] of the Salisbury statutes by Wordsworth and Macleane,[4] and of the St. Paul's statutes by Sparrow Simpson.[5] But, with the exception of Exeter, a fairly adequate selection of their medieval statutes is available in print for all the English secular cathedrals.[6] For Exeter I have used the valuable manuscript collections of statutes at the British Museum and the Bodleian Library.[7]

The making of new statutes was a fairly late development at most secular cathedrals. Custom, which, throughout the middle ages, was regarded by the chapters as in no way inferior to their

[1] Jones, *Fasti Eccl. Sar.*, p. 203.

[2] *Ordinale Exon.*, i, 6.

[3] *Statutes of Lincoln Cathedral*, 1892–7, 3 vols. This includes the medieval customs of Hereford and York, with the earliest known statutes of Lichfield cathedral.

[4] Salisbury, 1915.

[5] *Registrum Statutorum et Consuetudinum Eccl. Cathedralis S. Pauli*. London, 1873.

[6] A list of printed statutes is given below in Section A of the bibliography to this book.

[7] Harl. MS. 1027; MS. Rawlinson Statutes 38 (*S.C.* 15892); MS. Wood Empt. 9 (*S.C.* 8597); MS. Top. Devon, c. 16 (*S.C.* 22769).

written statutes,[1] was at first by nature unwritten. Usually the chapter would only agree to have its customs reduced to writing either when they were in danger of being forgotten through their growing detail and complexity;[2] when there was urgent need to produce written evidence of the chapter's rights; or when neighbouring chapters made requests to know what its customs were.[3] For a long time statutes were regarded simply as a declaration of ancient custom, and the idea of new legislation, introducing changes in the cathedral constitution, was rarely considered. Indeed, at Lincoln, where Bradshaw wrote that, 'more perhaps than at most places, custom, unwritten or imperfectly registered, seems to have been the law',[4] new statutes framed before the fifteenth century, were relatively few. As late as 1442, the dean and chapter found in the supremacy of custom over statute law a powerful weapon to block the fresh legislation which Bishop Alnwick attempted to introduce in his *Novum Registrum* of Lincoln statutes. The canons of Lincoln looked on the statutes in their Black Book as a declaration of the ancient law of their church which there was no gainsaying, and maintained that the *Novum Registrum* did not declare their peculiar law.[5]

Yet custom could become a stimulus rather than a check to legislation when existing customs were found no longer to correspond with, and sometimes to be directly contrary to ancient customs declared in writing.[6] At first, statutes, designed to remedy

---

[1] E.g. see the motto from Isidore appended to the Lincoln Black Book: 'Consuetudo est jus quoddam moribus institutum quod pro lege suscipitur cum deficit lex, nec differt an racione an scriptis consistat' (*L.S.*, i, xxi). In discussing the canons' oaths of admission to Lincoln cathedral, in which they swore to obey the 'reasonable and approved customs of the church', Bradshaw argued that, while the *statuta et consuetudines approbatae* referred to customs which had been reduced to writing, the *consuetudines rationabiles* were unwritten (*ibid.*, p. 157).

[2] E.g. *ibid.*, iii, 163; *S.S.*, pp. 82–3.

[3] At Lincoln the first known written statement of customs of 1214 was due to a request from the newly founded chapter of Moray to be informed of what the Lincoln customs were (*L.S.*, i, 40–1).

[4] *Ibid.*, p. 30.

[5] Cf. *ibid.*, p. 158.

[6] This had evidently become fairly common at cathedrals by the mid-thirteenth century. Hostiensis, the contemporary canonist, discusses the problem of canons bound by oath to obey ancient customs, which were contrary to the present utility and honour of their church (*Summa Aurea*, c. 909). See also *R.S.S.P.*, p. 99.

this state of affairs, were still regarded as declarations of existing as opposed to ancient custom, but gradually the framers of legislation became bolder, and introduced definite changes. At Salisbury this transition took place unusually early, possibly because the up-heaval in cathedral life caused by the removal from Old to New Salisbury in the early thirteenth century made changes desirable. The new residence statute of 1214,[1] agreed upon when the removal was under consideration, showed a remarkably early willingness on the part of the dean and chapter to experiment.

At Lincoln, Bradshaw has defined the years from 1214, but more especially from the making of the Black Book of cathedral customs about 1300, until 1442, as 'the legislative period, a period of constitutional struggle, which led to the constant moulding and re-moulding of the cathedral statutes', and added that, in 1442, 'we take leave of the period of original books, and enter upon that of the transcripts'.[2] This is generally true of the position at other English secular chapters. Some statutes, defining ancient or existing customs, survive at most cathedrals from the last half of the twelfth century.[3] The more important early statements of customs at Salisbury were probably written in the last quarter of the twelfth century; at Chichester and Hereford in the first half and about the middle of the thirteenth century; at Exeter in the third quarter of the thirteenth century; and at York between 1221 and 1325.[4] But none of these has the fullness of detail of the great codes or registers of customs, such as those of Salisbury, compiled in 1319 on the initiative of Bishop Roger Martival; of St. Paul's, made by Ralph Baldock, dean of St. Paul's from 1294 to 1305; of the Lincoln Black Book, begun about 1300, or of Bishop Aln-wick's *Novum Registrum*, rejected by the chapter of Lincoln in 1442.[5] Usually the late thirteenth- and early fourteenth-century

---

[1] *S.S.*, pp. 42–3.　　　　　　　　　　　　　　[2] *L.S.*, i, 158–9.

[3] E.g. *R.S.S.P.*, pp. 63, 109–10, 124–34; *C.S.*, pp. 1–3; Harl. MS. 1027, ff. 4a–6b; MS. Top. Devon, c. 16, ff. 3–4; MS. Wood Empt. 9, f. 1; *L.S.*, ii, 11–28.

[4] Frere, *Use Sarum*, i, xx, xxxiv–v; *C.S.*, pp. 3–17; *L.S.*, ii, 44–85; Harl. MS. 1027, ff. 6b–20b; MS. Rawl. Statutes 38, ff. 1–8; MS. Wood Empt. 9, ff. 2–8; MS. Top. Devon, c. 16, ff. 6–30. The earliest surviving text of ancient customs at York is the codification made as the result of an order of 1307 (cf. C. T. Clay in *Y.A.J.*, xxxv, 128 n.), and printed in *L.S.*, ii, 90 *et seq.* This edition includes statutes dating at any rate from 1221.

[5] *S.S.*, pp. 134–275; *R.S.S.P.*, pp. 9–79; *L.S.*, 1, 269–427; iii, 268–363.

material is the most bulky and the most valuable for historical purposes. By the fifteenth century the main outlines of the constitutions had been defined, and legislation declined in quantity.

The actual making of statutes by the bishop, dean, and chapter will be discussed later.[1] For the present it may be of interest to notice some of the forms in which customs and statutes were written down and collected. These varied very widely. Certain of the codes were elaborate pieces of work. Dean Baldock at London divided his subject-matter into five books, beginning with the number and order of the dignities, canonries, and prebends, and their value. Then came the entry of the canons to the cathedral body; their progress through residence, and their duties in the church; their exit by death, resignation, or translation. Lastly there was a statement of the duties of the *ministri inferiores*. The only English medieval cathedral code which can compare with this in comprehensiveness and logical arrangement is Bishop Alnwick's draft of his rejected *Novum Registrum* for Lincoln. He adopted the complete skeleton of Baldock's five books, transferring word for word whole passages, sections, chapters, and even prefaces, and attempting, upon this groundwork, to incorporate whatever was characteristic of Lincoln.[2] Elsewhere, the codes were generally slighter and more selective. That of Salisbury of 1319 gave a fairly full account of the life and government of the canons, but, after the twenty-first chapter, consisted mainly of decisions on particular points needing definition at the time. Hereford produced one of the most original and practical codes. Its mid-thirteenth-century collection of customs began with the new canon's collation, admission, and oath to the church. Certain rules were then set down in the order in which they were to be expounded to him. First in importance was that he should not reveal the secrets of the chapter. There followed a list of customs, first of the church, secondly of the choir, which it was essential for him to know. Finally the scribe concluded: 'This is enough of the chapter's customs to remember at present.'[3] The canon was to learn the rest from experience.

In fact, the codes were never exhaustive, and the statute books

[1] See below, pp. 115–19, 145, 278.
[2] See Bradshaw's and Wordsworth's analysis of these two codes, *L.S.*, i, 155–6; ii, clxxxii–iii, cxcii.
[3] *Ibid.* ,ii, 78.

contain a wealth of additional material. In the Lincoln Black Book, a short digest of 'customs and offices' is followed by a long series of privileges, awards, and compositions. There are also extracts from the chapter acts, together with statutes on particular points, formally made and confirmed by the dean and chapter. Then comes the *Consuetudinarium de divinis officiis*, giving directions for the celebration of the *opus dei*. Lastly is a series of miscellaneous later entries, recorded at intervals from the fifteenth to the nineteenth centuries, which includes some further chapter acts, and the oaths of admission to the cathedral body. This miscellaneous character of the medieval statute and custom books illustrates their essentially practical nature. They were in constant use, both for providing evidence of the chapter's rights to jurisdiction and property, and as the authority by which difficulties and disputes at the cathedral might be solved. It was those statutes and customs most likely to be needed for these purposes which were copied into the registers. Later decisions and interpretations of custom were added as they were made; and so the statute book seldom kept the precise character of a legal code, but frequently developed more or less in the way of a contemporary register of episcopal or chapter acts.

Most chapters had more than one register containing statutes and customs. The Black Book enjoyed exceptional prestige and authority at Lincoln as the main source of chapter law; yet Bradshaw and Wordsworth have compiled two large volumes of further Lincoln documents, illustrating and supplementing its contents.[1] The modern editors of the statutes of Salisbury and Chichester have had to collect their materials from a variety of books and registers in the possession of the dean and chapter or bishop. Most cathedral customaries, whether they have been compiled by medieval or modern editors or scribes, are incomplete. Statutes and customs may be found not only in those registers officially described as statute or custom books, but also in chapter act books and cartularies; in chapter registers of a more miscellaneous kind, such as the Wells *Liber Albus*, the Lichfield *Magnum Registrum Album*, or the Salisbury Register of St. Osmund; in bishops' registers, among visitation injunctions or judicial awards; in the papal registers, where papal confirmations and exemplifications of cathedral statutes are entered; in the patent and

---

[1] There are in the Lincoln muniment room nine manuscript volumes containing capitular statutes and customs (*L.S.*, i, v, 30–96).

close rolls of the royal chancery, in cases of royal confirmations of statutes.

Elaborate precautions were sometimes taken to try to ensure the observance of certain of the more formal later medieval statutes. They might be witnessed by one or more notaries. The confirmation of the bishop, archbishop, king, or pope might be obtained. Some statutes were specially ordered to be registered, and read aloud in chapter at fixed intervals, once a year, once a month, or once a week.[1] Others were included in the canons' oath to observe the statutes.[2] Copies were made available to canons at their own expense,[3] while copies of statutes concerning the vicars choral might be hung in the vicars' common hall.[4] Yet clearly the same amount of trouble was not taken with all statutes. Throughout the middle ages many cathedral customs and statutes remained scattered, imperfectly registered, or without formal ratification. Some customs were never even reduced to writing. Even the codes might be left without the confirmation or acceptance of bishop or chapter. The Lincoln Black Book itself was never formally sealed or approved, and the Hereford collection of customs has no note of its date or authority. Later, all this was the cause of much uncertainty about the chapters' customs. After the Reformation the statutes of the cathedrals of the Old Foundation were described as *pretensas ordinaciones*, difficult and obscure, having no legitimate or sufficient authority.[5] Orders were sometimes issued for their reform, and the chapters had to accept royal injunctions on particular points. But generally little was done. In the nineteenth century, when reform was at last undertaken, nobody knew what the statutes really were, and many blunders were made. Contemporary ignorance of the statutes acted as a stimulus to research. This was the immediate reason for Bradshaw's monumental work on the statutes of Lincoln cathedral.

In addition to the statutes, a great wealth of administrative and

[1] E.g. *Reg. Bronescombe*, p. 77; *Reg. Grandisson*, ii, 863; Harl. MS. 1027, ff. 48b, 58a; MS. Rawl. Statutes 38, f. 206.

[2] E.g. *Reg. Rede*, i, 137. The 'ancient' form of the canons' oath at Salisbury was said in 1388 to include special mention of statutes concerning the non-residents, their obligations for repairs on their prebends, and for contributions to defend the rights and liberties of the cathedral church (Reg. Dunham, f. 40).

[3] *L.S.*, ii, 448; *Reg. Grandisson*, ii, 863.

[4] *Salisbury Ceremonies*, p. 153.

[5] E.g. *W.S.*, p. cliii.

other records is extant at the cathedrals, very little of which has been printed. The most valuable for the present investigation are the registers of chapter acts and the financial accounts of the common fund. Both these types of records were kept fairly regularly at most English cathedrals from about the late thirteenth or early fourteenth century.

The chapter act books or minutes of chapter meetings are a characteristic record of the secular chapters. At the monastic chapters there is nothing really comparable to them. The monastic registers or letter books, which begin to appear about the same time as the act books of the secular chapters, consist chiefly of various letters issued by the abbot and convent, or by the abbot alone.[1] The abbot had more power than the dean of a secular chapter to make decisions without always obtaining the chapter's consent. At a secular chapter it became necessary to record the *acta* because the consent of a majority of the residentiary canons was legally required for all business. Therefore the act books illustrate in detail the actual working of cathedral government. From them it is possible to fill in gaps left in the picture of cathedral life given by the statute books and customaries; to find out how the statutes were interpreted in practice; to gain much additional information about the functions of the cathedral officers and ministers. Much more than the statutes, the *acta* were contemporary documents, written in the chapter house probably soon after chapter meetings,[2] and so the actual practice at a particular time can be discovered from them. In this way they provide a valuable check to the statutes. It can be seen how far the statutes were declaring ancient custom which no longer corresponded with contemporary practice; how far they were laying down new rules which, like the Salisbury plan requiring every canon to reside at

[1] Cf. W. A. Pantin, 'English Monastic Letter Books', in *Essays to Tait*, pp. 201–22; *Chapters of the English Black Monks*, i, xv.

[2] At Salisbury in 1394 it was ordered that chapter acts must be written in the chapter house, and never elsewhere, except by chance in the house of the dean or his *locum tenens*, or the canon who had charge of the registers. Every chapter clerk had to swear on admission to observe this (Reg. Dunham, f. 258). Sometimes chapter meetings at Salisbury were held, not in the chapter house, but in the treasury or in one of the canons' private houses; this may explain why the clerk was occasionally allowed to write the minutes in such places. The *acta* were probably copied into the registers at leisure after the meetings. The care with which the Salisbury registers were written suggests this.

the cathedral for a quarter of the year in turn, might never be fully adopted in practice.

Some of the best examples of capitular registers of *acta* are at Salisbury, Lichfield, and Lincoln. At Salisbury a long series is extant, dating with a few gaps from 1329 to the present day. Those relating to the fourteenth century consist of five large volumes of from ninety-five to three hundred folios each, named after the chapter clerk who wrote them. Together they cover forty-five years of the century, 1329–58 and 1385–1400. Admissions of canons, vicars, and cantarists, the granting of the chapter's farms and canonical houses, entries of canons into residence, judgements on neglect of duty or moral offences of the *ministri inferiores*, are among the earliest and most frequent entries. In addition there are records of decanal visitations of the cathedral chantries; appointments of commissaries to visit the chapter's lands and houses; discussions of the chapter's lawsuits or requirements of the cathedral fabric; taxation of the prebends for these or other purposes; decisions on various aspects of cathedral government, such as the administration of the cathedral schools during the illness or absence of the chancellor; the settlement of disputes on jurisdiction between officers of the chapter; definitions of the obligations of canonical residence. Yet none of these different groups of entries, not even that recording admissions of the canons, seems to be complete. In the earliest register of John Hemingby, some classification of the material was at first attempted, while at the same time there were a larger number of miscellaneous entries than in later registers. Later in the century a straightforward chronological method was adopted, of which the advantages are at once apparent. The writing of the chapter clerks became larger, clearer, and well spaced out, and regular forms were adopted.

The earliest known register of Lichfield chapter acts is MS. Ashmole 794 at the Bodleian Library, a large volume of two hundred and two leaves, written in different hands, and dating from 1321 to 1384.[1] Its form and contents are generally similar to those of the Salisbury act books. The act books at Lincoln begin in 1305, and consist, for the fourteenth century, of eight volumes of about sixty to a hundred and forty folios each, known as *Liber Primus*, *Liber Secundus*, *Liber Tertius* and so on. Between them they

---

[1] There are gaps for the years 1342–52 and 1366–9. The later registers of Lichfield chapter acts are at Lichfield cathedral and at the British Museum.

D

cover about fifty-four years of the century.[1] Again, admissions of canons and vicars, and entries of canons into residence are among the most important early entries. But generally the Lincoln books seem to be neither so well written nor so carefully kept as those of Salisbury. The folios are not always numbered consecutively; *memoranda* of different years are mixed up together with no apparent object of arranging them according to subject-matter; there are crossings out and interlinear additions; the writing is usually small and heavily abbreviated. More than the Salisbury *acta*, they have the appearance of notes hastily jotted down at chapter meetings; though documents, such as papal privileges for non-residence, produced before the chapter, are sometimes copied out at length, and were presumably added after the meeting. Printed examples of medieval chapter acts for English cathedrals are few. Recently the first act books of Salisbury and Chichester have been printed; acts contained in the various registers at Wells are calendared in the reports of the Historical Manuscripts Commission; some for Exeter, beginning in 1380, are included by H. E. Reynolds in his *Use of Exeter*. For the three large collegiate churches of Beverley, Ripon, and Southwell, we have valuable printed editions of medieval chapter act books.[2]

Many different kinds of registers, in addition to statute books and registers of *acta*, were kept by medieval secular chapters. Cartularies or collections of documents concerning capitular property and privileges were naturally among the earliest to be made. A number of these, dating from the twelfth and thirteenth centuries, such as the *Registrum Antiquissimum* at Lincoln or the *Liber Pilosus* at St. Paul's, have been printed,[3] and provide interesting information for the existence and rights of cathedral dignitaries and officers before the time when statute material becomes available. Then, in the thirteenth and early fourteenth centuries some chapters produced registers of a much more miscellaneous character. Both the Wells *Liber Albus* and the Lichfield *Magnum Registrum Album*, which contain a number of charters and privileges, include also chapter acts and statutes. The Wells *Liber Albus* I [4] can,

---

[1] The biggest gap in the fourteenth-century act books comes almost at the same time as the gap in the Salisbury registers, from 1356 to 1384.

[2] See below, Bibliography, pp. 356-8, 362.

[3] See below, Bibliography, pp. 356-8.

[4] This is calendared in *H.M.C. Wells*, i, 1-304.

perhaps, be best described as a combination of a cartulary and a letter book or register of documents. Admissions of canons and vicars of Wells do not seem to have been recorded regularly until a separate register of chapter acts was begun in *Liber Ruber* II,[1] but *agenda* for general chapter meetings and decisions on current business are entered from about 1243 in *Liber Albus* I. It is interesting to find at Salisbury also, that the first known records of chapter acts, for the years 1320–6, are written on blank pages of the chapter's cartulary, *Liber Evidentiarum C*.[2] Later in the middle ages separate registers of judicial proceedings might be kept at certain chapters. At Salisbury, capitular judgements on moral offences and causes of the *ministri inferiores* continued to be entered in the chapter act books. But at York such cases were heard, not at chapter meetings, but in the court of the dean and chapter's peculiar jurisdiction, presided over by their auditor of causes; here a separate register was kept of this court's proceedings.[3]

In the case of the chapter's financial records, much less is available in print. A few examples of medieval accounts kept at York, Wells, Hereford, and Exeter have been published; at Lincoln and Salisbury I have used unpublished material. Accounts of the common fund have naturally been of greater interest for the present investigation than those of the fabric. Commons, from the end of the twelfth century, were normally paid only for residence; thus, in addition to the light which accounts of the common throw on the business administration of the chapter, they are often extremely valuable in giving details of the canons' residence. Both the method of recording these accounts and their present state of preservation vary considerably at different churches. At Salisbury, where, from the fourteenth century, the communar or keeper of the common drew up brief quarterly statements of accounts on parchment rolls, there are now many gaps, while a number of those rolls which survive are faded and torn.[4] But at Lincoln the accounts were kept in much greater detail, and were copied out at

---

[1] Calendared *ibid.*, ii, 101–237.   [2] ff. 452–9.

[3] Cf. J. S. Purvis, *A Medieval Act Book at York*, York, 1943. The court book which Canon Purvis describes dates from 1396 to 1485. At Ripon judicial proceedings form a separate section in the volume of chapters act for 1452–81 (*Ripon Chapter Acts*, Surtees Soc., 1875, pp. 1–189).

[4] Only nineteen quarterly rolls are now extant at Salisbury for the period before 1400; of these the earliest is dated 1343. For the fifteenth century a larger number has survived, but they are by no means complete.

length into bulky volumes known as Audit Accounts of the Dean and Chapter. These volumes, extant for fifty-eight complete years of the fourteenth century,[1] are often two or three times as thick as the Lincoln act books for the same period, and are among the most valuable material there.

Much further material has been found in a variety of sources. The duties in choir of the dignitaries, canons, and *ministri inferiores* are best illustrated in the liturgical books of the chapters, such as the *Use of Sarum*, and the various ordinals, processionals, and con- suetudinaries, many of which have been printed by the Henry Bradshaw Society and elsewhere.[2] Fewer chroniclers are con- cerned with secular than with monastic chapters, though several are useful, particularly for the twelfth-century chapters. Bishops' registers, papal registers, the calendars of enrolments of the royal chancery, the great collections of ecclesiastical documents, such as Mansi's collection of the councils or Wilkins' *Concilia*, often throw light on the canons' organization and activities.

---

[1] They cover the years 1304–19, 1320–30, 1332–3, 1334–40, 1357–8, 1360–9, 1378–87, 1389–91, 1392–7, 1399–1400. Each book is called after the clerk of the common fund who wrote it.

[2] See below, Bibliography, Section A.

CHAPTER I

THE CANONS AND THEIR RESIDENCE

THE canons were the most important and necessary group of cathedral clergy, and so their numbers naturally became fixed before those of other groups of inferior *ministri*, such as vicars choral, secondaries, or choristers. In England the foundation and endowment of the canons' prebends (their separate 'provender', income or estates) was generally the work of the late eleventh, twelfth, and early thirteenth centuries. St. Osmund is said to have established thirty-two or thirty-six canons and prebendaries at Salisbury in the late eleventh century.[1] Remigius at Lincoln constituted twenty-one; his successor, Robert Bloet, added another twenty-one.[2] For the most part the founding of additional prebends from grants of land and churches made by bishops, kings, and magnates was a gradual process which can sometimes be only partially traced in the extant cathedral cartularies. The result by the thirteenth century was to make Lincoln, Salisbury, and Wells the three largest English secular chapters. Lincoln had fifty-eight, Wells fifty-five, and Salisbury fifty-two prebendaries. York came next with thirty-six, Lichfield had thirty-two, and Chichester thirty. St. Paul's had thirty major and twelve minor canons.[3] Hereford and Exeter were the smallest English secular cathedral chapters with twenty-eight and twenty-four prebendaries respectively. Thus, while the number of the canons at the English secular cathedrals could not rival those in the greatest medieval French chapters, such as Chartres, which had seventy-seven prebendaries at the beginning of the fourteenth century,[4] they were about equal to and sometimes greater than those in the Norman secular cathedrals, which had between twenty-five and fifty.[5] Generally

[1] *S.S.*, pp. 24–5; *Canonization S. Osmund*, p. 50; *Scottish Chronicle of Holyrood*, p. 110.

[2] John de Schalby in *Giraldi Cambrensis Opera*, vii, App. E., p. 195.

[3] For the minor canons, see below, pp. 253 et seq.   [4] Amiet, *op. cit.*, p. 2.

[5] Rouen had forty-nine prebends; Bayeux forty-nine or fifty; Evreux thirty-one; Avranches twenty-five; Coutances twenty-six; Lisieux thirty-one full prebends, two half-prebends, and six *praebendae volantes* which did not carry with them the right to share in the daily distributions from the common fund.

the number of prebendaries in the English chapters remained practically unchanged throughout the middle ages. In the thirteenth, fourteenth, and fifteenth centuries, when canons in excess of the statutory number were provided to the cathedrals by king or pope, these had to remain as 'expectant' canons until prebends fell vacant for them. Although an expectant canon might be assigned a stall in choir, he received no prebendal income and was excluded from chapter meetings.

In the later middle ages the English secular cathedral canons formed a very miscellaneous group of men, drawn from different social ranks and having a variety of outside interests and employments. Unlike some continental chapters, such as Lyons, which laid down that all its canons must have at least four strains of nobility in their blood,[1] or Cologne and other Rhineland chapters which consisted almost exclusively of ecclesiastics belonging to local noble families,[2] men of all social ranks except freedmen and serfs could be admitted to English chapters. Indeed English chapters normally included many new men, particularly clerks who had risen in the royal service or at the universities, appointed chiefly through the influence of king or pope. All were supposed to be in holy orders and therefore at least twenty-two years of age, that is, the earliest age at which by canon law a clerk could be ordained a subdeacon. Yet in practice boys in minor orders were sometimes admitted by special dispensation of the pope; the statutes of Salisbury and Wells made provision for them to sit on the lowest form in choir among the boy choristers.[3] Originally there had been all orders of clerks in the early episcopal *familiae*; throughout the middle ages the canons' statutory choir duties required that they should be fairly equally divided among the three orders of priest, deacon, and subdeacon, for purposes of ministering at the high altar. At most cathedrals the prebends had been constituted in the eleventh or twelfth centuries as priest, deacon, or subdeacon prebends, the priest prebends being usually the most valuable. But by the later middle ages the distinction between the orders of the canons who held them had generally disappeared. A priest canon could always minister at the altar

---

[1] Amiet, *op. cit.*, p. 4.

[2] F. R. Lewis, 'Prelates and Nobles in the Rhineland', in *History*, xxii (1937), 195–6.

[3] *S.S.*, p. 64; *W.S.*, p. 1.

when necessary in the offices of deacon or subdeacon; at Exeter it was laid down by statute that all canons should be in priests' orders.[1]

By this time many duties in the cathedral choir were performed by the body of vicars choral, supervised and directed by a constant though slowly diminishing group of residentiary canons, who, both in choir and chapter, bore the 'heat and burden of the day' in place of the full body of canons. Residence, at any rate from the early thirteenth century, was optional; if a canon wished to become a residentiary he now made a formal entry into residence and swore a special oath on the gospels, distinct from the oath which he took on his first admission to the church. In the late twelfth or thirteenth centuries there was rapidly growing up a division of the canons into two more or less distinct groups of residentiaries and non-residents, each with their carefully defined duties and privileges.

This, very roughly, was the solution worked out at the cathedrals to deal with the frequent and often unregulated non-residence of the canons, which had reached alarming proportions in the twelfth century. It was both practical and highly important. The chief object of cathedral statutes was no longer to force or even to encourage all canons to reside, but simply to try to ensure that a sufficient proportion of the whole body of canons would be present at the cathedral to maintain its services and work. In this way they provided a working answer to contemporary conditions and laid down the lines of future development. Successive modifications of these statutes in the fourteenth, fifteenth, and sixteenth centuries drew much more clearly the distinction between the two bodies of resident and non-resident canons, who in time naturally developed different and sometimes opposing interests. Gradually the residentiaries came to form a close corporation which gained almost complete control over the cathedral government and business. They are said to have tried deliberately to restrict the entry of new residentiaries to their body so that they might keep a larger share of the common goods of the church for themselves. In the sixteenth and seventeenth centuries the number of residentiaries was limited and fixed by statute.

Throughout the history of the secular cathedrals, from their

[1] *Ordinale Exon.*, i, 6.

foundation almost until the present day, canonical non-residence has been a main cause of controversy and one of their most pressing problems. Probably more cathedral statutes are concerned with it than with any other subject; both contemporaries and later historians, in comparing the situation at the medieval cathedrals served by constantly resident monks or regular canons with that at the secular cathedrals, have argued that the justification of the secular cathedrals depended on their capacity to deal with the non-resident canon. Investigation of canonical residence at the English secular cathedrals would therefore be important at any period, but in the thirteenth and fourteenth centuries it has a special interest. First, because the decision recently taken to accept and make legal the position of the non-resident canons marked a turning-point in its history. Secondly, because English secular cathedrals at this time have received rather more than their fair share of condemnation, particularly from historians of the nineteenth century. Capes, for instance, drew what he described as a 'sorry picture' of fourteenth-century cathedral life, writing that

'the dignitaries, on whom residence was specially incumbent, were seldom there to set a higher standard of decorum . . .; the canons . . . neglected their duties; . . . curtailed their residence; gave each other dispensations, and let their prebendal houses go to ruin. . . . Neglect of duty spread downwards on its natural course. The vicars came straggling into choir after the service had begun and left before it was quite over.' [1]

Freeman considered that the cathedral system, in origin 'most wisely and beautifully ordered', was ruined by 'the vice' of non-residence, which was given a legal status in the later middle ages.[2]

It is true that the cathedral statutes which made legal the position of the non-resident were drafted and passed by the canons themselves. But contemporaries generally recognized that the ideal of continuous residence by all the canons was unattainable and in some ways undesirable in the changed conditions of the later middle ages. Popes and bishops confirmed and approved capitular statutes defining the status of the non-residents; directions about them were included in the official body

[1] W. W. Capes, *The English Church in the Fourteenth and Fifteenth Centuries*, pp. 251–2.

[2] E. A. Freeman, *Wells Cathedral*, pp. 55, 58; 'Cathedral Churches of the Old Foundation', in *Essays on Cathedrals*, pp. 145–57.

of canon law. Non-resident canons of the fourteenth century were no longer denounced for neglecting their duties with such moral indignation as Richard of Devizes had denounced secular canons of the twelfth century who left the cathedral services to be conducted by their ill-paid vicars.[1] Censure in the later middle ages was more often reserved, not for the non-residents, but for the canons who had sworn to reside and failed to keep the conditions of their residence.[2]

Circumstances had probably made necessary a certain amount of non-residence from the time when the canons were granted their separate prebends. The prebends often included a church or manor at a distance from the cathedral, and the prebendaries were responsible for their administration. Probably from as early as 1091 canons of Salisbury were allowed to spend a third part of the year attending to the needs of their prebends, while there were apparently also exemptions from residence for canons in the service of king, archbishop, or bishop, and for some scholars.[3] In the course of the twelfth century, the increase in the number of canons and the growth of bodies of vicars choral probably made the constant attendance of all canons seem unnecessary for the conduct of the cathedral services. But from the late twelfth and thirteenth centuries onwards the factor of over-riding importance was that pluralism, or the holding of more than one benefice by a clerk, and the resulting non-residence of the clerk in some or all of his benefices had, in spite of many efforts to check them, become established and necessary parts of both secular and ecclesiastical administration.[4] In the absence of ready money the only way for king, pope, and bishops to pay the salaries of the many clerks employed in their services was to obtain ecclesiastical benefices for them. Cathedral prebends were the most convenient benefices for the purpose, for they were usually remunerative, and had been declared by canon law to be without cure of souls; therefore legally one other benefice with cure and others without cure

---

[1] *Cronicon Richardi Divisensis*, ed. J. T. Appleby, 1963, pp. 70–1.
[2] This was a usual reason given for condemnation of the canons in fourteenth-century visitation injunctions and cathedral statutes.
[3] See above, p. 20.
[4] For the history of pluralism and its results in the fourteenth century, see A. H. Thompson, 'Pluralism in the Medieval Church', in *Associated Archit. Socs. Repts.*, xxxiii, 35–73.

could be held with them. Tout and Professor Hamilton Thompson have stressed the importance of the endowment of the civil service and learning which this system made possible.[1] They point out that non-residence at a fourteenth-century cathedral did not necessarily imply laziness in other spheres of life. Often the non-resident civil servants, or the scholars who used the incomes from their prebends to support them at the universities, represented the ablest professional and academic ability of the day. Throughout the middle ages the royal and papal administrations were constantly expanding and opening up a greater number and variety of clerical careers to talent; naturally an increasing proportion of the higher cathedral clergy were attracted to them. The situation made it necessary for the chapters to recognize that some canons would be absent for practically the whole year, perhaps attending only a few specially important general chapter meetings; and that statutes which required every canon to reside even for as short a period as three or six months a year were unworkable.

Yet in spite of much interesting work done recently on the problem of canonical residence, there is still little precise information of the numbers of canons actually resident at the different cathedrals in the later middle ages; nor is it known how far the residentiaries were able adequately to carry out the duties and functions of the full body of canons. This may be partly because historians in recent years have more often approached the subject from the point of view of the history of the royal administration and of the universities than from that of the secular cathedrals. At the cathedrals the chapters usually found that they could regulate residence most effectively through the canons' emoluments, particularly their shares in the common fund. It is here proposed to examine the way in which they did this: to compare the different sources of income payable to the two groups of resident and non-resident canons, and to discuss the many statutes in which the chapters defined the obligations and the privileges of residence. Finally an attempt will be made to discover some of the practical results of these statutes.

[1] E.g. Tout, *Chapters in Medieval Administrative History*; A. H. Thompson, *loc. cit.*; *The Medieval Chapter* (York Minster Hist. Tracts), pp. 11–15; Introduction to *Rot. Gravesend*, pp. xxvii–viii; cf. G. Barraclough, *Papal Provisions*, pp. 159–62.

1. THE CANONS' EMOLUMENTS

Three main sources of income were open to the canons: their prebends; their share in distributions from the chapter's common fund; and a further share in distributions made at obits or services held on the anniversary of the death of some pious benefactor who had left an endowment to the cathedral. By the thirteenth century only the separate prebends were granted to them unconditionally whether they resided or not; and at least three English chapters, Salisbury, Lichfield, and Lincoln, imposed a heavy tax of a fifth or a seventh on the prebendal incomes of the non-resident canons. The various distributions of commons, which earlier had been claimed by all the canons, were now almost everywhere reserved for the residentiary canons and for those absent on special business approved by the chapter.

The prebends at most English cathedrals were very unequal in value. Possibly, when the first prebendal estates had been carved out of the common estates of the chapter in the late eleventh or early twelfth century, there may have been an attempt at some cathedrals to see that certain of them were roughly equal in value. But after the estates had passed under the separate administration of individual prebendaries some would naturally increase in value with time, while others would become poorer. Moreover, the value of additional prebends founded by individual benefactors varied in proportion with the wealth and generosity of the founders. According to the taxation of about 1291, Masham Vetus at York was the wealthiest English prebend, assessed at 250 marks a year; its actual value would of course be far more, for the assessments were very low. Some other York prebends were then taxed at over 100 marks a year and many at more than 50 marks.[1] At Hereford, on the other hand, the most valuable prebends were not usually taxed at more than 19 li. a year, while one, *Pratum Minus* was assessed at the end of the thirteenth century at only a truss of hay worth twopence.[2] Apart from York, the richest

---

[1] *Taxation of Pope Nicholas*, p. 297; cf. *L.S.*, ii, 133–4.
[2] A. T. Bannister, *Cathedral Church of Hereford*, p. 160. By 1532 the annual value of this prebend had risen to four shillings and fourpence-halfpenny (*ibid.*, p. 61 n.). The holder of the only Hereford prebend of much value, that of Moreton and Whaddon, was forbidden to receive any commons except the daily canonical bread (*L.S.*, ii, 58).

prebends in England were mostly at Salisbury and Lincoln, where a fair number were assessed at about fifty or sixty marks a year.[1] Wells, too, had at least nineteen prebends taxed at twenty marks a year or more.[2] But all three cathedrals also had prebends assessed at only four or five marks a year; while between five and ten marks was about the average taxable value of the small manorial prebends of St. Paul's.[3]

This system of individual prebendaries administering separate prebendal estates which yielded very unequal incomes was usual at Norman secular cathedrals.[4] But at some other continental chapters, where the common life lived in the eighth or ninth centuries had left a deeper impression, there were attempts to keep the prebendal incomes as equal as possible. The thirty 'full' prebends at Utrecht cathedral, for example, were all supposed to be equal in value. As late as 1341 the chapter decided to return to the old method of administering them in common, because, through the bad administration of certain prebendaries, some goods of the church had been alienated or lost, and the portions had become unequal, causing hatred and strife among the canons. In future all the fruits of the prebends were to be divided into equal portions.[5] At Chartres the individual prebendaries were found to be better administrators of the estates than the four provosts who had administered them in common until 1171. But in order to prevent any serious inequalities from developing, a fresh division or share-out of the prebends among the canons was made every five, nine, or twelve years.[6] In England, Exeter was the only secular cathedral where the principle of equal prebends for all the canons was maintained, probably as a survival of the rule of common life introduced there by Bishop Leofric in the eleventh century. The stewards of the cathedral exchequer continued throughout the middle ages to administer all the chapter lands in common, merely distributing an annual sum of six

[1] See *ibid.*, iii, 171–2 (1330), 307–11 (1440); *S.S.*, pp. 339–43; *Sarum Charters*, pp. 206–8 (*c.* 1226); Jones, *Fasti Sar.*, pp. 350 *et seq.*, *s.v.* the particular prebends.

[2] *W.S.*, pp. 97–9.

[3] *R.S.S.P.*, pp. 24–5 (1300); *Taxation of Pope Nicholas*, pp. 19–20.

[4] E.g. Pommeraye, *Histoire de l'Église Cathédrale de Rouen* (1686), pp. 183–5; Deslandes, *op. cit.*, pp. 183–9.

[5] *Het Rechtsboek Utrecht*, pp. 108–9.

[6] The very complicated procedure of the periodical 'partages' is described in detail by Amiet, *op. cit.*, pp. 185–214.

marks for his prebend to each of the twenty-four canons.[1] At Wells there were traces of a similar arrangement in the equal division of the revenues of several large manors among fifteen of the canons, known as the prebendaries of Combe I to Combe XV.[2]

The different incomes which canons received from their prebends clearly had some influence on their residence. In the twelfth century Peter de Blois, who held a five-mark prebend at Salisbury, refused to reside for it, saying that his income would not pay for the journey to Salisbury, and arguing that the constitutions of Osmund and Jocelin were designed for those wealthy prebendaries who could afford to build houses and easily procure what they needed for residence.[3] On the other hand, vacancies in the richer prebends were carefully watched by king and pope, who tried to secure them for high officials in their service. Therefore it often happened, especially in the later middle ages, that the richest prebends were held by the non-residents.

But by this time the chapters had found means to redress the balance and to make it economically possible, and in many cases profitable, for a canon with a small prebend to perform his residence in the close, keeping a house and *familia* there, and dispensing the required hospitality. This result was achieved by appropriating large increases in the common fund almost exclusively to the use of the residentiaries. When separate prebends had first been formed out of the common estates of the chapters, part of these estates had always been kept back in order to provide both a reserve fund for common expenses of the chapter, and daily or weekly distributions of food or money for the cathedral clergy. Gradually in the course of the twelfth century it was made clear that such distributions could only be paid to those actually present at the church. Then, as the number of prebends became fixed, and the growth of non-residence began to alarm contemporaries, benefactions to the cathedrals more frequently took the form of grants to the common fund, given with the express purpose of encouraging the canons to reside.

Distributions of commons to the canons were everywhere

[1] Harl. MS., 1027, f. 8a; cf. *Use Exeter*, p. 84; MS. Top. Devon, *c.* 16, ff. 1–3; MS. Rawl. Statutes 38, f. 1.
[2] *W.S.*, p. 93; *Reg. Shrewsbury* (Somerset Record Soc.), pp. lxiv–viii.
[3] *P.L.*, ccvii, *c.* 395, Ep. 133.

divided into two kinds. First there were the daily commons, sometimes paid weekly, for attendances at the daily canonical hours. Secondly, termly (that is, yearly, half-yearly, or quarterly) distributions from the surplus revenues in the fund were made only to those canons who had resided for the statutory number of days in each term. This system forced those canons who wished to receive their full share of commons to be regular both in their daily attendances at the cathedral services, and in making up their full number of days' residence in each term. At the same time it enabled the chapter to keep enough money in hand during each term to meet any extraordinary cathedral expenses.

The daily commons were the most stable item in the residentiary's income, for the amounts payable were fixed by statute, and every simple canon had the opportunity to earn an equal sum. Greater allowances, however, were due on feast days, and, at some churches, such as Salisbury, dignitaries were granted double commons because of their special responsibilities.

At Salisbury precise evidence is available of the annual value of these commons: in the first quarter of the year the maximum amount payable to a simple canon was fifty-three shillings and fourpence; in the second quarter, forty-nine shillings and sixpence; in the third, fifty-two shillings and ninepence; and in the fourth, fifty-one shillings.[1] Thus a canon who completed his full residence in every quarter of the year could add ten pounds six shillings and sevenpence to his annual income from this source alone. Yet daily commons at Salisbury in the later middle ages were meagre compared with those of Lincoln, York, and Lichfield, the three other chapters which apparently from the first paid all their commons in money, not in kind. About the last half of the thirteenth century these chapters all raised their distributions from sixpence or eightpence a day to at least twelve pence a day, with extra allowances of from two shillings to ten shillings on double or principal feast days.[2] In 1360–1 greater residentiaries at Lincoln (that is, those who resided for two-thirds of the year or more)

---

[1] These were the sums laid down in Bishop Poore's time (*c.* 1214) as payable to the canons for daily commons (*Sarum Charters*, pp. 206–7 n.). The unpublished communar account rolls at Salisbury show that the same sums were being paid in the fourteenth and fifteenth centuries.

[2] *L.S.*, i, 347; ii, 106; iii, 165, 338; *Monasticon*, VI, iii, 1260; cf. *Fabric Rolls of York Minster*, p. 123.

were receiving about seventeen or twenty pounds a year for daily commons, with an extra four or five pounds for wine on feast days.[1] A York account of 1371 shows that twelve pounds five shillings was then a possible sum for commons for half a year's residence:[2] and the canon could probably double this during the remaining six months of the year. In 1242 the chapter of Wells decided to abolish its practice of paying part of the commons in white or black loaves, and adopted money payments similar to those of Salisbury: twelve pence a day was payable to the four principal *personae* and the archdeacon of Wells, and sixpence to the simple canons.[3]

Elsewhere it is more difficult to assess the value of commons to residentiaries because they continued to be paid partly in kind. Moreover, at St. Paul's and Hereford the non-residents succeeded in maintaining their claims to share in some of the distributions. At St. Paul's residentiaries about 1300 received only a shilling a week from the chamber, but every canon, resident or non-resident, was entitled to 21 loaves and 30 gallons of ale a week from the bakehouse and brewery.[4] Hereford also distributed bread, grain instead of ale, and pence to its canons, the non-residents being allowed a share of the 'little' as distinct from the 'great' commons;[5] while from 1269 additional payments of 'mass pence' were made to all canons attending the daily high mass in the cathedral.[6] In the late thirteenth and early fourteenth centuries canons of Hereford could earn as much as four or five pounds a year from mass pence alone, but in the last half of the fourteenth century these distributions, which were derived from Diddlebury church, fell to only about a quarter of that sum.[7] Probably the most valuable daily commons paid to residentiaries of any English secular cathedral were at Exeter. There they received twelve pence a day in money with three daily canonical loaves, fifteen pence on days when the choir was ruled, and eighteen pence with the usual loaves on doubles and greater feasts.[8] The exceptional value of the Exeter commons was doubtless meant to

---

[1] Audit Accounts D. and C. Lincoln, Bj/2/6, ff. 63a–64b.
[2] *Fabric Rolls of York Minster*, p. 123. [3] *H.M.C. Wells*, i, 60.
[4] *R.S.S.P.*, pp. 35, 75 n., 173 n. [5] *L.S.*, ii, 47–8, 51–2.
[6] *Hereford Charters*, p. 124. [7] Cf. *ibid.*, pp. x, 168–9.
[8] Harl. MS. 1027, ff. 10a, cf. 26a–27b; MS. Rawl. Statutes 38, f. iia; *Reg. Grandisson*, ii, 858.

counter-balance the meagre bursal prebends and probably did much to encourage residence. An Exeter prebend would be worth little to its canon unless he resided.

The terminal distributions of surplus commons were everywhere a much more variable and unreliable source of income for the residentiary. In years when the chapter lands yielded a good harvest, when rents and farms were paid promptly, and when there were few extraordinary cathedral expenses, it was often very valuable; in the lean years it might be almost negligible. It used to be thought by Dean Milman at St. Paul's and by some other historians of the chapters that at most English secular cathedrals there was a large increase in the residentiaries' shares of the surplus in the last half of the fourteenth century. They supposed that this led to a rush of canons to enter residence and that the rush led in its turn to restrictions being imposed by the close chapters of resident canons, who were alarmed at the prospect of their share being reduced in value as the distributions had to be divided among an increasing number of canons. They declared that this situation was a chief cause of a sharp fall in the number of residentiaries at the end of the fourteenth and in the fifteenth centuries.[1] Yet none of them was able to quote figures to prove this remarkable and somewhat unlikely increase in surplus commons in the last half of the fourteenth century. An attempt will therefore be made to see whether evidence can be found of the actual sums received at terminal distributions in the fourteenth century.

The most important evidence comes from Lincoln, where records are extant of the distributions paid to all greater residentiaries for fifty-eight years of the fourteenth century.[2] Unfortunately the shares named did not represent the full amount due and subsequently paid to each canon for his residence in any given year. At the time when the annual surplus was distributed arrears always remained to be levied from the chapter lands; these often amounted to as much as a half or two-thirds of the

---

[1] H. H. Milman, *Annals of St. Paul's*, pp. 83, 139–40, 143; W. R. W. Stephens, *Memorials Chichester*, pp. 329–30, 337; E. A. Freeman, *Hist. Wells*, pp. 91–2; 'Cathedral Churches of the Old Foundation' in *Essays on Cathedrals*, pp. 151–2; W. W. Capes, *Hist. English Church in Fourteenth and Fifteenth Centuries*, p. 249.

[2] In Audit Accounts of the Common Fund, Muniments D. and C. Lincoln, Bj/2/4–10. See the lists printed below, Appendix I.

first sum, and were paid to the canons in small additional shares as they came into the cathedral chamber, sometimes as long as four or five years after they were due. It must therefore be remembered that for most years the canons would ultimately receive a considerably larger sum from the surplus than that quoted in the first account. Even so, the figures available show clearly that there was no steady, consistent rise in the surplus revenues distributed in the last half of the fourteenth century. In the first half of the century, between 1304 and 1340, the shares varied from eight pounds seventeen shillings and twopence in 1314 to forty-eight pounds seven shillings and threepence in 1330. In only one year, 1314, were they less than ten pounds; in ten years they were between ten and twenty pounds; in fourteen years between twenty and thirty pounds, and in three years between forty and forty-eight pounds. During the last half of the century fluctuation in the value of the shares was greater. The extremes were reached with the distribution of fifty-eight pounds five shillings and eightpence three-farthings to each residentiary in 1381, and of only two shillings and sevenpence-halfpenny in 1397. But the average share in this half-century seems to have remained at between twenty and thirty pounds. The records are complete for twenty-six years: in six of these years the shares were under ten pounds; in five years they were between ten and twenty pounds; in six years between twenty and thirty pounds; in five between thirty and forty pounds; in two between forty and fifty pounds, and in two between fifty and sixty pounds. Thus the state of the Lincoln common fund in the last half of the fourteenth century suggests no adequate reason for an especially large number of canons pressing to be allowed to enter residence.

No evidence comparable to that of the detailed Lincoln accounts has been found at the other English secular cathedrals. Shares in the division of surplus commons at York were probably exceptionally valuable: in 1371 each residentiary received thirty-one pounds two shillings and eightpence at a half-yearly distribution,[1] but it is not known whether this represents an increase on distributions made in the first half of the century. Summaries of five Wells communar accounts for the fourteenth century available in print, suggest that the average yearly shares there were

---

[1] *Fabric Rolls of York Minster*, p. 125.

about equal to, or slightly less than, those at Lincoln.[1] Further, it is interesting to notice that the shares in the earliest printed account, for 1327–8, and in that for 1400–1 were almost identical: both amounted to about twenty-four pounds. At Salisbury a separate division of the surplus was made at the end of every quarter, and nineteen quarterly accounts have survived for the century. Again there was considerable variation in the amounts paid. A full share for one quarter of the year might vary from about three pounds to about nine pounds;[2] probably the average was about five pounds; and so a canon who resided in all four quarters of the year might receive as much as twenty pounds a year from this source. Here again there is no suggestion that the value of the shares rose sharply towards the end of the fourteenth century. At Hereford Canon Capes' researches have shown definitely that the termly distributions of surplus grain and money to the residentiaries decreased in value from about the middle of the fourteenth century. He writes that any restrictions imposed by the chapter at this time on the number of canons entering residence were due to poverty, not to increased wealth of the common fund.[3] At St. Paul's too Professor Brooke's recent work suggests that production on the manors was falling in the late fourteenth century and that a reason for the fall in the number of stagiaries at this time was that the expenses of a new residentiary could no longer be balanced by the perquisites of residence.[4]

The third chief means by which the residentiary could supplement his income was by attending obit or anniversary services in the cathedral. The distributions payable at these services naturally did not amount to as much as the daily commons. But by the later middle ages, when many wealthy benefactors had left legacies to the cathedrals for the celebration of services on their obit days, a canon who attended fairly regularly might easily earn an extra four or five pounds a year. One hundred and eleven obits were

---

[1] *H.M.C. Wells*, ii, 1–11, 22–30, 34–7. The shares are given for the years 1327–8, 1343–4, 1392–3, 1394–5, and 1400–1, and vary in value from about fourteen to twenty-four pounds. These sums exclude payments of arrears from previous years, which might nearly double the distributions.

[2] Full shares of two pounds nineteen shillings and elevenpence were paid in the second quarter of 1347, and of eight pounds fifteen shillings and fivepence in the first quarter of 1361 (Muniments D. and C. Salisbury, Press II, Communar Rolls).

[3] *Hereford Charters*, pp. x–xii.   [4] *Hist. St. Paul's Cathedral*, pp. 88–9.

celebrated annually at St. Paul's in the early fourteenth century,[1] while at Hereford, one of the poorest cathedrals, there were at least fifty.[2] The normal payment to a canon for his attendance at an obit service was between sixpence and two shillings: when the founder was rich and generous it might be considerably more. Certain other sources of revenue were open for most of the residentiaries. They might be elected to chapter offices, such as those of the keeper of the common fund, keeper of the fabric, or *custos munimentorum*, to which small salaries were attached. In addition, estates belonging to the common fund were often farmed out to the residentiaries, who paid a fixed rent or farm to the chapter, and kept any further profits from the lands for themselves. These farms were evidently profitable, for there was keen competition in some chapters for the richest farms, and it had to be emphasized by statute that senior residentiaries were always to have first choice.[3]

Is it possible to reach any general conclusions as to the relative proportions of the cathedral's revenue drawn by the two groups of resident and non-resident canons? These proportions naturally varied greatly at different cathedrals and at different periods; the question is complicated by the different values of prebends, by the many kinds of distributions allotted to the residentiaries, and, often, by the absence of precise information in the accounts. At Exeter, where non-resident canons could only receive four pounds a year each as prebends,[4] the proportion of the cathedral's revenues which went to them was obviously very small. Elsewhere, it amounted to much more. Yet, so far as can be judged from available records, the non-resident canons of most English

[1] W. S. Simpson, 'Statutes of Chantry Priests', in *Archaeologia*, lii, 146.

[2] A. T. Bannister, *op. cit.*, p. 156.

[3] E.g. *S.S.*, pp. 188–9; *H.M.C. Wells*, i, 230; *L.S.*, i, 298–9; ii, 117, 120–1; iii, 339–40; Harl. MS. 1027, ff. 11a–b, 22b–23a; *R.S.S.P.*, pp. 35–6, 128. Rents payable by the canons for their leases varied at Wells in 1332 from thirty-three pounds six shillings and eightpence to ninety pounds, and at York *c.* 1290 from ten pounds to eighty marks (*H.M.C. Wells*, i, 230; *Reg. Shrewsbury*, pp. 97–8; *Y.S.*, pp. 29–32). For the Salisbury farms see *V.C.H. Wilts*, iii, 174, 182–3; *Hemingby's Reg.*, pp. 49–54, 57.

[4] If dignitaries were non-resident they naturally received more. According to the *Taxation of Pope Nicholas, 1291*, p. 145, the annual value of the deanery at Exeter was fifty-six pounds; of the precentorship, ten pounds; of the chancellorship, ten pounds; of the treasury, twenty pounds.

cathedrals in the fourteenth century seem, as a group, to have received less from their cathedral than the much smaller group of residentiaries. This is apparently true even at a cathedral such as Lincoln, where many valuable prebends were held by non-residents. A list of non-resident canons at Lincoln and their prebends, made in 1304–5 by the clerk of the common fund, is printed below.[1] Together, the value of their thirty-seven prebends, as estimated by the clerk for purposes of levying the tax of a seventh, amounts to six hundred and eighty-seven pounds nineteen shillings and sevenpence.[2] Sixty-six pounds must be deducted from this sum for payments of forty shillings by thirty-four of the canons to their vicars choral,[3] and a further sixty or seventy pounds for their contributions to the seventh.[4] In addition to thirty-seven prebends, the deanery and the two archdeaconries of Oxford and Northampton were held by non-resident prebendaries. These dignities must have brought the total revenues received by non-residents during this year up to about eight hundred and fifty-nine pounds.[5] In the same year eleven greater residentiaries and three minor residentiaries received from their prebends, according to the same taxation, three hundred and thirty-eight pounds three shillings and fourpence;[6] from the

[1] Appendix I, pp. 327–9.

[2] This sum has been reached by adding up the sevenths given by the clerk, and multiplying by seven. The prebends of St. Botolph, omitted by the clerk, and of Nassington and Banbury, described by him as *in sequestro*, are not included in the calculation.

[3] Four non-residents held prebends on which vicars' stipends were not charged (cf. *L.S.*, iii, 165).

[4] Many non-residents apparently claimed exemption from this tax, either because they were in the bishop's service; because they held papal privileges or dispensations, or for other reasons. By the end of the financial year 1304–5, the clerk had succeeded in raising from them sixty-one pounds eighteen shillings and twopence (Audit Accounts D. and C. Lincoln, Bj/2/4, f. 6a).

[5] The seventh was not levied from dignities, and so the clerk gives no estimate of their value. This has been taken from the estimates made in 1440 and *c.* 1445–55 (*L.S.*, iii, 307–11, 538), which probably differed from their value in 1304–5. The precentorship was vacant in 1304–5, and the archdeacons of Lincoln, Buckingham, and Huntingdon apparently did not hold prebends.

[6] This taxation, on which the seventh was levied, is not given for the residentiaries' prebends in the 1304–5 account, but is printed in *L.S.*, iii, 171–2, from a list made *c.* 1330 by John de Schalby. Estimates of the value of two prebends, Aylesbury and North Kelsey, which John omits, have been supplied from the *Taxation of Pope Nicholas, 1291*, pp. 33, 56, and from that of 1440

dignities of chancellor, treasurer, and subdean, and from the archdeaconries of Stow, Bedford, and Leicester, about one hundred and sixty-three pounds seventeen shillings and eight-pence.[1] Their distributions for daily commons, wines, and obits are not listed in this account, and can be only roughly estimated from accounts of later years, where such information is given in detail.[2] Possibly they shared about two hundred and eighteen pounds as commons, about sixty pounds for wine on feast days, and about forty-eight pounds for attending the celebration of obits. The distribution of surplus commons in 1304-5 was said to be one hundred and fifty-nine pounds eleven shillings and a farthing, but this was considerably less than an average annual distribution at Lincoln in the fourteenth century; about two hundred and fifty pounds was more normal,[3] and a further one hundred and twenty-five to one hundred and seventy-five pounds might also be paid in the form of arrears for previous years. No information is available for the residentiaries' profits from their administration of chapter farms, or from their tenure of salaried offices at the cathedral. Yet, excluding these profits, the total annual revenues drawn from the cathedral by an average group of residentiary canons of Lincoln in the early fourteenth century, might be said very roughly to amount to about one thousand two hundred and fifty to one thousand three hundred pounds. This would seem to be sufficient for a body of twelve or thirteen canons supporting the expenses of residence in the close.

Thus by the later middle ages a working solution had been found for the financial aspects of the problem of residence. The chapters generally had to acquiesce in many of their richest prebends being held by non-resident papal or royal nominees. But, if the residentiaries performed their duties regularly and conscientiously, they could earn additional distributions, which, with their prebends, normally amounted to sums much greater than those drawn by non-resident canons.

(*L.S.*, iii, 307–11). In the case of these prebends, the two taxations are practically identical.

[1] Again, the value of the dignities has had to be estimated from the taxations of 1440 and *c.* 1445–55 (*ibid.*, pp. 307–11, 538).

[2] E.g. the accounts for 1360–7 (Bj/2/6).

[3] See the distributions listed below in Appendix I.

2. THE OBLIGATIONS OF RESIDENCE

(a) THE MINIMUM ANNUAL PERIOD OF RESIDENCE

One of the most pressing needs of the twelfth-century chapters in dealing with canonical non-residence had been to fix and enforce a minimum annual period during which every canon who wished to count as a full-residentiary canon (*plenus et integer canonicus et residentiarius*) must be present in the cathedral city. At all English secular cathedrals the rules for a minimum annual residence were apparently defined and reduced to writing within a period of about sixty years, dating from the late twelfth to the mid-thirteenth centuries. Yet, in spite of legislating within a fairly short time of each other, the chapters varied considerably in their judgement of what was a reasonable length of time for a residentiary canon to spend annually in the cathedral close.

The residence of the four principal dignitaries or parsons (*personae*), the dean, precentor, chancellor, and treasurer, and of the archdeacons was everywhere different from that of the simple canons (*canonici simplices*). The *personae* had cure of souls and special duties in the cathedral which made residence obligatory on them for the greater part of the year. Their residence was described as 'continuous' or 'assiduous'; in point of fact, it usually amounted to two-thirds or three-quarters of the year.[1] Archdeacons, on the other hand, because of their diocesan duties, could often enjoy the privileges of residentiaries in return for much shorter periods of residence than those imposed on the simple canons. At York an archdeacon's minimum annual residence was only three months,[2] that is, half the period required from a simple canon; while at Lincoln it was forty days a year, made either continuously or at intervals.[3]

---

[1] *L.S.*, ii, 100, 144; iii, 164, 280, 305; *W.S.*, pp. 44, 55, 57; *H.M.C. Wells*, i, 60, 141, 154; *S.S.*, pp. 26–7, 42–3, 72–3, 154–5; cf. pp. 444–7; *M.R.A.*, p. 280; Swainson, p. 30; Harl. MS. 1027, ff. 31a–b, 48a, 55a–b; *Ordinale Exon.*, i, 5. At Lichfield the position was exceptional: only the dean was said to make 'continuous' residence, and so he was the only dignitary given double commons for his residence (*Monasticon*, VI, iii, 1260, 1265; *M.R.A.*, p. 280). Elsewhere, when the subdean and succentor ranked as dignitaries, they also had to take the oath to reside assiduously.   [2] *L.S.*, ii, 105; cf. 118.

[3] This was sufficient to exempt an archdeacon at Lincoln from paying the tax of a seventh on the income of his prebend, which was exacted from non-resident canons (*ibid.*, p. 144). For the practice at Salisbury, see *S.S.*, pp. 26–7, 70–3; *Reg. S. Osmund*, i, 338–9.

In discussing the residence of the simple canons, a broad distinction may be drawn between the rules in force at Salisbury, Lichfield, Wells, and Exeter, which enforced the same obligations on all their residentiary canons, and those of St. Paul's, Lincoln, York, Chichester, and Hereford, which required a new residentiary to perform a probationary period of especially strict residence, varying from six months to three years, before proceeding to the 'lesser' or 'minor' residence, in which he could continue for the rest of his life. The rules for the greater residence have sometimes been regarded as one of the expedients worked out in the later middle ages by the close chapters of residentiaries, who wished to discourage the entry of new residentiaries to their body. But actually they were formulated at all five churches by 1251, and were also in force at an early date at a number of continental cathedrals. Rouen had a greater and lesser residence similar to that of Lincoln.[1] The idea of the probationary greater residence seems to have been that a canon ought to give some proof of his ability and purpose to reside before being permanently admitted to the residentiary body. In this sense it has similarities with the monk's novitiate.

The chapter of St. Paul's under Dean Ralph de Diceto in the late twelfth century was one of the first English chapters to draw up written rules for a greater residence. This was to last for one year from the time of the canon's decision to enter residence. He had to be present at the cathedral for at least three-quarters of this year, attending services, dispensing hospitality, and being allowed no more than six days' absence in the first quarter and twenty-seven in each of the last three quarters.[2] Later, new and stringent rules, probably of the early fourteenth century, greatly increased the burdens and expenses of this greater residence at St. Paul's.[3] Afterwards, when the canon had been admitted as a 'stagiary' (that is, the name used at St. Paul's for a full residentiary), he only had to be present for twenty-four weeks in the year.[4]

At Lincoln and Hereford the greater residence lasted for three

[1] Pommeraye *op. cit.*, pp. 195–8.

[2] *R. de Diceto Opera* (Rolls. Ser.) ii, lxix–lxxii.

[3] *R.S.S.P.*, pp. 125–30, where they are described as statutes of the time of Dean Ralph de Diceto. For the reasons for and probable date of their publication see C. N. L. Brooke in *Hist. St. Paul's Cathedral*, pp. 41, 86–7, 363, and below, pp. 57, 61–3.

[4] *R.S.S.P.*, pp. 35, 83–4, 167.

years. But while, at Hereford, new residentiaries were given no commons at all during this period, greater residentiaries at Lincoln received far more than minor residentiaries. As a result, canons of Lincoln who had completed their greater residence might well prefer to continue as greater residentiaries, instead of entering upon the less onerous but much less remunerative duties of the lesser residence. Greater residentiaries at Lincoln had to reside for thirty-four weeks and four days a year.[1] In return they were exempt from providing and paying a vicar choral,[2] and the entire yearly surplus of commons was divided among them alone. Minor residentiaries need only be present for one-third of the year; but the only commons which they received were the daily or weekly distributions made when they were actually present at the cathedral. The ordinary residence at Hereford, made after completion of three years' greater residence of heavy duties without commons,[3] bears no comparison to the short minor residence at Lincoln. Thirty-six weeks' residence a year was the minimum at Hereford, and the remaining sixteen weeks' absence could normally only be taken in periods not exceeding seven weeks at a time.[4]

Chichester was peculiar in having three forms of residence. First came a period of greater residence lasting for one year; this was apparently continuous, and involved heavy choir and hospitality duties. Afterwards the canon might proceed to 'full residence', which allowed him three weeks' absence a quarter. The 'half residence', amounting to six months a year, was granted only by special grace of the dean and chapter; a 'half residentiary' received only half a share in the quarterly distributions of surplus commons.[5] The fifth chapter which enforced a preliminary

---

[1] *L.S.*, iii, 163–4, 324. [2] *Ibid.*, ii, 144.
[3] Cf. *C.P.L.*, *1198–1304*, p. 223.
[4] *L.S.*, ii, 48–50. There was a complicated system in force at Hereford in the mid-thirteenth century, by which a residentiary might go away for a period longer than seven weeks, provided that he resigned his residence and commons, and was readmitted to them in less than twelve weeks. Such resignations and readmissions could be accepted twice a year. But if the canon stayed away for more than twelve weeks, he was 'abjudicated' on his return; that is, he was condemned to make continuous residence for a period equal to his absence, attending every daily and nightly office, and receiving no terminal distributions of surplus commons.
[5] *C.S.*, pp. 9, 17.

greater residence was York. Here it lasted for only six months. During this time the new residentiary had to be present continuously without commons. Afterwards he was only bound to reside for twenty-four weeks a year.[1]

Thus all these five chapters required most of their residentiary canons, even after completing their greater residence, to be present at the cathedral for between three-quarters and half the year. Three-quarters of the year was equal to the residence normally demanded from the four principal *personae*; it left little time for regular work in other parts of the country. Under such conditions, residentiaries might easily come to form a small and exclusive permanent body, with their interests centring at the cathedral, and having little in common with the larger body of non-resident canons. But at the remaining four English cathedrals, which imposed no probationary greater residence, the obligations of 'full residence' were often much less onerous, allowing the canons more opportunities for maintaining other interests and work outside the close.

Salisbury and Lichfield, in particular, seem to have approached the problem of residence with a rather different attitude from that of other English secular chapters. Instead of requiring a long annual residence from those canons who chose to profess residence, they continued, throughout the thirteenth and fourteenth centuries, to regard a short period of residence as obligatory on all canons, subject only to those exemptions for clerks in the service of king, archbishop, and bishop, and for university students said to have been granted by St. Osmund. The minimum period of annual residence decided upon by both chapters was three months, or a quarter of the year, and their aim was that a quarter of their canons should always be in residence together. Any canon who did not keep his quarterly residence at the statutory time, and who could show no dispensation or reasonable excuse for not doing so, was bound, as a punishment, to pay a fifth of his prebendal income to the common fund for the use of the residentiaries.

The first known evidence of rules for this quarterly residence is in statutes made at Archbishop Hubert Walter's legatine visitation of Lichfield cathedral in 1195.[2] The arrangement of the residentiary quarters was then laid down in accordance with the order of the canons' choir stalls. Each quarter of the year was

[1] *L.S.*, ii, 100-2.   [2] *Concilia*, i, 500.

allotted respectively to one of the four principal *personae*, and the canons were divided into four corresponding groups: six canons were to reside during the same three months as the dean; five with the precentor; four with the treasurer, and three with the chancellor. Probably these rules were modelled on an earlier version of the order for the quarterly residence of canons contained in Dean Richard le Poore's New Constitution made at Salisbury in 1214.[1] The original Salisbury table of residence, like that of Lichfield, is thought to have assigned the four quarters of the year respectively to the four dignitaries, and to have arranged that the canons called upon to reside in any one quarter of the year should be those whose choir stalls were in the same *quarterium* of the choir as that of the *Persona* responsible for the three months' residence.[2] But in 1319, when Bishop Martival published his code of Salisbury statutes, the table or rota of residence there, 'as collected from other documents', was different. In every quarter of the year a different quarter of the canons was still to come into residence; but now they were to be drawn not from one-quarter of the choir only, but roughly half from the *decani* and half from the *cantoris* side of the choir; each quarter was to include members of all three groups of priest, deacon, and subdeacon prebendaries.[3]

Clearly these tables represent an artificial arrangement which was not observed in practice in the fourteenth century. The various attempts made at Salisbury during the century between the *Nova Constitutio* of 1214 and Bishop Martival's code of 1319 to enforce the quarterly residence on all the canons, or to compel them to pay the statutory fine,[4] suggest that at no time did the scheme work satisfactorily. In 1319 it was decided to recognize and provide by statute for the difficulties and inconveniences caused by a rota which arbitrarily imposed residence on each canon during the particular three months of the year required by his prebend. 'Owing to the many hindrances which have increased in modern times, it often happens that a canon cannot conveniently begin his residence at the right time, nor complete

---

[1] S.S., pp. 42–3. Lichfield chapter had already reproduced the greater part of the constitutional section of Richard le Poore's *Tractatus de Officiis* in its statutes of 1190–8, and it is assumed that an earlier manuscript of this part of the *Tractatus* was lent to Lichfield in the late twelfth century. (Cf. Frere, *Use Sarum*, i, xxxiv–v.)

[2] Cf. *S.S.*, p. 157 n.   [3] *Ibid.*, pp. 156–9.

[4] E.g. *ibid.*, pp. 88–91, 160–1.

it.'[1] Therefore the old rota of residence was followed in the code of statutes by a decree which practically abolished some of its most important provisions. In future a canon might choose any one quarter or parts of all four quarters of the year in which to complete his three months' residence; and so long as he earned forty shillings in daily commons during the year, he was to be legally exempt from the fine imposed on the non-residents.[2] Forty shillings of daily commons could be earned in twelve days less than the full three months' residence. Thus the concession allowed to residentiary canons an additional twelve days' leave of absence during their quarter. In the same way Lichfield chapter also cut down its quarterly residence to two months by statutes which allowed all Lichfield residentiaries to take thirty days' absence in their quarters.[3]

In practice, however, as will be seen later,[4] residence at Salisbury and Lichfield in the fourteenth century seems usually to have approximated far more closely to the longer residence required by such chapters as St. Paul's, York, or Hereford, than appears likely on a first reading of the statutes. At the same time it is interesting to notice the later influence of Salisbury's plan for a three-monthly residence. Between the sixteenth and eighteenth centuries it was gradually adopted as the rule for the small fixed number of residentiary canons at most English secular cathedrals of the Old Foundation,[5] and in the nineteenth century was taken as the model by the Ecclesiastical Commissioners. The Cathedrals Act of 1840 resulted in the establishment of practically uniform rules for a quarterly residence at all English secular cathedrals.[6]

The remaining two cathedrals, Wells and Exeter, both imposed a minimum residence of six months on their residentiary canons; but, unlike Salisbury and Lichfield, did not allow any residentiary to be absent for six months continuously. In 1259 the chapter of Wells laid down that every full residentiary must be present at the cathedral for six weeks and four days in each of the four terms of the year.[7] In 1354 a mandate of Bishop Grandisson to resi-

---

[1] Cf. *S.S.*, pp. 160–1.   [2] *Ibid.*

[3] *Monasticon*, VI, iii, 1260.   [4] Below, pp. 76–81.

[5] E.g. *C.S.*, p. 26; *Hereford Charters*, p. xii; *Y.S.*, pp. 54–7; *Cathedral Commission, First Rept.*, 1854, p. 15.

[6] See the summary of the residence rules in force at different cathedrals after this act (*ibid.*, pp. 2–31).

[7] *H.M.C. Wells*, i, 141, cf. 60; *W.S.*, p. 57.

dentiaries at Exeter cathedral implied that a similar rule was in force there.[1]

(b) THE DAILY LIFE AND DUTIES OF THE RESIDENTIARY CANONS

(i) *Attendance at the Cathedral Services*

There was little difference in the later middle ages between the daily round of services in an English secular cathedral and in an English cathedral monastery. The object of both was the perpetual celebration of divine worship by a body of men set apart for the purpose. Thus the recitation of the seven canonical hours and the celebration of the daily high mass were everywhere the chief duties of the community of residentiary canons and vicars choral.

The day began with matins. Often this is described in the cathedral statutes and customaries as being in the middle of the night (*in media nocte*). At Lincoln the custom of midnight matins between Michaelmas and Easter survived until 1548, when it was abolished by royal injunction;[2] but between Easter and Michaelmas it was always postponed until about five a.m. Elsewhere the term 'night matins' apparently continued to be used for the service long after it had been transferred to the early morning. Statutes of 1319 at Salisbury suggest that matins there followed immediately after the morrow mass at dawn.[3] During the rest of the day the services followed the same general pattern at all the cathedrals, though there was much diversity of detail and variations of local customs in the directions of their different uses. In the later middle ages these tended to become more uniform as the Use of Salisbury was gradually adopted as the norm for liturgical observance in England. Everywhere Lauds was immediately after matins. Then there was an interval filled by the successive chantry masses until the mass of the Virgin in the Lady Chapel at about nine a.m. The bell for prime was rung as soon as the Lady Mass was over: afterwards the canons met in chapter.

---

[1] Harl. MS. 1027, ff. 52b–53a. This mandate warned the residentiaries that they were bound to serve in person in any parish churches they might hold in the diocese, except during the forty-six days of each quarter when they were resident at the cathedral.

[2] *L.S.*, iii, 588.　　　　　　　　　　　　　[3] *S.S.*, pp. 258–9.

Tierce was said while the celebrant was preparing for high mass at ten a.m. Feast days of different degrees of solemnity, greater doubles, doubles, semi-doubles, and simples, introduced variety into the order. On the greater festivals the hours of tierce, sext, and nones might be said together in the interval between the procession and high mass; and on these days high mass began rather later than usual and lasted longer. But on ordinary days sext and nones were said after mass, and concluded the morning offices at about eleven a.m. The midday breakfast was followed by a break in the early afternoon. Evensong was said at three p.m.; on obit days it included vespers for the dead in choir. Then came vespers of the Blessed Virgin Mary, and compline was soon afterwards. The canons and vicars had supper at six p.m. or earlier. Curfew was rung at sundown in summer: in winter, when sundown was very early, it was rung at a convenient time after dark.

During the canon's probationary greater residence strict attendance at most of these services was required. The St. Paul's statutes probably of the early fourteenth century warned new residentiaries that they must be healthy and well when they came to the church in order to stand the strain of their labour.[1] 'Residencia debet esse laboriosa, non desidiosa.' St. Paul's and Chichester laid down that new residentiaries must be present at all the seven canonical hours and at the daily high mass during their first year of residence;[2] while York did not allow them to spend a single night outside the close during the twenty-six weeks of their greater residence.[3] But for the ordinary full residence the rules were much laxer; and by the thirteenth century it was generally recognized that the main burden of the *opus dei* should fall on the vicars choral.

'We exact but a moderate assiduity, not that he (the residentiary)

[1] *R.S.S.P.*, p. 127.

[2] *Ibid.*, p. 127; *C.S.*, p. 17. According to the earlier statutes of Dean Diceto and Dean Baldock at St. Paul's, however, this attendance was to be 'ad humanum modum assiduus' and assiduity was defined as 'not that the canon should be present at every hour of the day and night, but at those at which he is bound to be present unless hindered by illness'. This interpretation of the rules was restored by Bishop Braybrooke in 1399 (*R. de Diceto Opera*, ii, lxxii; *R.S.S.P.*, pp. 33, 152).

[3] *L.S.*, ii, 101. At Hereford strict attendance at all the hours was enforced only during the first forty days of the three years' greater residence (*ibid.*, p. 51).

should be forced to be present at all the ecclesiastical hours, but at one principal hour every day, or high mass, unless he is being bled or is ill, or is otherwise occupied in the business of the church.'[1]

Most churches allowed their residentiaries to take one night's leave a week or one or two days' leave a fortnight for recreation or blood-letting, so long as they arranged to be present at the cathedral for the greater feasts.[2] Attendance at matins was usually held to be the canons' most important duty. At some churches the daily commons were paid only to those canons present at matins.[3] At Chichester, however, from 1247, commons were paid for attendance at one service, which might be matins, high mass, or vespers.[4] Exeter required its canons to be present at two services a day: either matins and high mass, or prime, or vespers.[5] The strictest rules seem to have been those of York, which ordered daily attendance at all three services of matins, high mass, and vespers.[6]

In addition every residentiary had to take his turn both as 'hebdomadary canon' or canon of the week, and as ruler of the choir for a fortnight at a time. During this week or fortnight, which usually came round about once a quarter, his duties in the cathedral were naturally much heavier, and he had to be constantly present at the services. The hebdomadary's duty was to minister as priest at the high altar: vicars choral usually acted as deacon and subdeacon hebdomadaries, but it was irregular for anyone but a canon to officiate at the high altar either at mass, matins or evensong. On greater feasts the dean or greatest dignitary present usually celebrated in place of the hebdomadary canon. Two canons were appointed by the precentor to rule the choir for a fortnight at a time. During the first week the principal rector pre-intoned the antiphons, psalms, and hymns, and worked alone on ordinary days at all the hours. His *socius* did the same the next week. But on double feasts and feasts of nine lessons they ruled

---

[1] *Ibid.*, iii, 325; cf. *R.S.S.P.*, p. 37.

[2] E.g. *ibid.*, pp. 37–8, 83, 89; *L.S.*, ii, 106; iii, 164; Harl. MS. 1027, f. 9b.

[3] E.g. *L.S.*, ii, 52.

[4] *C.S.*, p. 9; cf. pp. 2, 8. The canonical bread, distributed daily in addition to the money commons, continued to be given only for attendance at matins (*ibid.*, pp. 6–7; *Reg. Rede*, i, 114).

[5] Harl. MS. 1027, ff. 9b, 67b; cf. *Ordinale Exon.*, i, 6.

[6] *L.S.*, ii, 102.

PLATE II
THE CHOIR OF OLD ST. PAUL'S CATHEDRAL, INTERIOR

PLATE III

AERIAL VIEW OF SALISBURY CATHEDRAL CLOSE FROM THE SOUTH-EAST

the singing together in silk copes at the principal services and in processions; while on greater and medium doubles there were usually four rectors ruling from specially draped forms in the middle of the choir.[1]

(ii) *Hospitality, Feasting, and Entrance Fees*

The idea of liberal hospitality by all the residentiary canons, particularly to the inferior ministers of the church, 'in order to make life more pleasant for them', was a tradition firmly rooted in medieval cathedral life. An oath to practise hospitality regularly was sworn by all Salisbury canons on their admission to residence;[2] in 1328 the chapter of Exeter pronounced that a form of *ficta residencia* to be deplored equally with the canons' absence from the cathedral services was their neglect of hospitality to the poor, to the inferior ministers and to the boys of the church.[3] Often the hospitality duties of the residentiaries were expensive and burdensome. But everywhere they were carefully defined by custom, and the additional commons granted to the residentiaries were intended to help to pay for them.

For the ordinary residentiary, who had proved his good residence, hospitality was heaviest during his week as hebdomadary canon. Then, at Lincoln, he had to feed the deacon and subdeacon hebdomadaries, and one vicar choral, and to provide breakfast daily for two bell-ringers. On Sunday he entertained from nineteen to twenty-six members of the choir to the substantial midday meal at his house.[4] But on the greater feasts the dean or other dignitaries gave the *honorifice pastus* or feasts to the whole choir. At other times residentiaries were expected to issue invitations at matins to breakfast or supper through their vicars to other vicars or choir ministers.[5] There were special feasts for the choir at Christmas and on Holy Innocents' Day. At St. Paul's every stagiary had to feed the whole choir at least once a year.[6] Important strangers passing through the cathedral city, or royal visitors, had to be entertained at the canons' houses.

---

[1] See *Use Sarum*, i, 27-8, 30-3, 35-40; *R.S.S.P.*, p. 50; *W.S.*, pp. 6-7; *Ordinale Exon.*, i, 15-18, 20-2; *Monasticon*, VI, iii, 1259.
[2] *Salisbury Ceremonies*, p. 113.   [3] Harl. MS. 1027, f. 42a.
[4] *L.S.*, i, 294, 389; iii, 178-80, 322, 325-7.
[5] E.g., *S.S.*, pp. 236-7, 336; *Use Exeter*, p. 9; *L.S.*, ii, 103.
[6] *R.S.S.P.*, p. 131.

For these reasons the maintenance of a canonical house and *familia* in the close or at least near the cathedral was a necessary condition of residence at all the secular cathedrals. The four-teenth-century chapters declared that no canon wishing to count as resident might lodge in another canon's house, lest, by so doing, he might avoid providing his fair share of hospitality;[1] and certain distributions could be denied to a new residentiary until he had actually set up house.[2] In the early thirteenth century, when Salisbury cathedral was moved from the hill on Old Sarum to the sheltered valley of New Salisbury, the canons were all expected to build their own houses on spacious sites allotted to them in the new close: the expenses of building proved so great that for three years in succession the chapter decided to reduce temporarily the minimum annual residence to only forty days.[3] Afterwards these houses might be sold by their canons' executors to succeeding residentiaries. But by the fourteenth century most houses had been acquired by the dean and chapter: the chapter assigned them to new residentiaries in return for a yearly rent of about thirteen shillings and fourpence to forty shillings, which usually went to maintain the annual obit service in the cathedral of a former owner of the house.[4] Elsewhere some houses might be attached to particular prebends or dignities; others were in the gift of the bishop or dean and chapter.[5]

The canons were responsible for the upkeep and repair of their houses. In the case of the larger and more desirable houses this might entail considerable outlay. Some of the canons are known to have added new and costly buildings to their houses in the fourteenth century.[6] In 1402 a survey of the house called South Canonry in the south-west corner of Salisbury close described a very large house, with a hall, many chambers, a private bake-house, brewhouse, kitchen, buttery, stables, and dove-cote.[7] The household or *familia* required in such a house would also be large. Some residentiaries, as late as the fourteenth century, still had

---

[1] *H.M.C. Wells*, ii, 5; *W.S.*, p. 75.　　　　[2] E.g. Reg. Holme, f. 87.

[3] *S.S.*, pp. 70–1.

[4] For the building of the houses in Salisbury close, and the gradual changes in their ownership and in the method of their assignment to canons, see K. Edwards, 'The Houses of Salisbury Close in the Fourteenth Century', in *British Archaeological Journal*, 3rd ser., iv (1939), 63–73.

[5] See *ibid.*, pp. 71–3.　　　　[6] E.g., below, p. 79.

[7] Reg. Draper, ff. 3–4.

their vicars choral living with them;[1] various references have been found in cathedral records to the canons' chaplains, cooks, chamberlains, esquires, yeomen, and other *servitores, commensales,* and *domicelli*.[2] Provided the canons could maintain discipline among the members of their *familiae* they were allowed entire control of them; they might bring their clerical *familiares* to follow the choir in the cathedral church, wearing the cathedral habit.[3]

From early times it was customary for a new residentiary, on being assigned his house of residence, to invite his brother canons to a feast in it, as a house-warming and to celebrate his admission into residence. At Lincoln, as soon as he had sworn in chapter to reside, he was taken by the dean and residentiaries to a vacant canonical house by the church, and assigned it. There he immediately gave bread and drink to all present, and, within his first year of residence, would invite the whole choir to a formal *honorifice pastus,* which was commonly called his Entry.[4] In time these entrance feasts became a heavy burden on the new residentiaries everywhere. Bishop Martival at Salisbury condemned them, saying that they 'swallowed up in one short hour provisions which had been calculated to serve for many days'.[5] But it was at those churches which imposed a probationary greater residence that the initial obligations of hospitality fell most heavily on the new residentiaries.[6]

The most detailed and exacting hospitality rules were those drawn up probably towards the end of the chapter's peak period of economic prosperity about 1320–30 for the greater residence at St. Paul's.[7] There the new residentiary had to feed daily for a year two minor canons, two chantry chaplains, four vicars, two almonry boys or choristers, the vergers, and bell-ringers. In addition, the bell-ringers had to be given bread, ale, and cakes every night when they came to wake him for matins. He was to

---

[1] See below, pp. 270–1.

[2] E.g. *S.S.,* pp. 256–7; *L.S.,* ii, 72, 79–80, 113; iii, 327–8; *M.R.A.,* p. 339; *C.S.,* p. 1; *R.S.S.P.,* pp. 125–6; *Use Exeter,* p. 8.

[3] *W.S.,* p. 61; *L.S.,* ii, 113; *Monasticon,* VI, iii, 1261; *S.S.,* pp. 256–7.

[4] *L.S.,* iii, 323, 325.

[5] *S.S.,* pp. 144–5.

[6] For hospitality rules during the greater residence at York, Hereford, and Chichester, see *L.S.,* ii, 101; Bannister, *Cathedral Church of Hereford,* p. 157; *C.S.,* p. 17.

[7] *R.S.S.P.,* pp. 125–9.

F

have bread and ale taken with him nightly to the church for the juniors in the choir, and once or twice a quarter was to invite them back to a breakfast (*gentaculum*) at his house after matins. On his first day he had to feed all who came to his house, including the squires of the stagiaries' households. The canons stagiary themselves were to be invited to special banquets every quarter, 'not at the same time, but successively, so that he might prove to them his good residence'. The two greatest feasts of his entry were to be, one within the first month of his greater residence, the other in his last quarter. All the canons stagiary and the whole choir were to be invited, as well as the bishop, if he were in the city, and the mayor, sheriffs, aldermen, justices, and greater people of the court 'so that the liberties and honour of the church might be maintained, and friendship continued between the church and city, and so that the royal court look more favourably at us'. Less important feasts were to be prepared for the choir, without the stagiaries, on the morrow of these great feasts; and for all the canons and ministers at Christmas and at the beginning of Lent, when there was to be 'a good fire in the middle of the house', and a 'plentiful supply of ale, spices, and red and white wine for all'.

The reasons for these rules are not easy to judge. They were apparently a forgery, purporting to be a copy of statutes of Dean Diceto of about 1192.[1] They may have been thought a justifiable expansion of his directions for the greater residence, sanctioned by recent customs of rich financier canons of the early fourteenth century, who were anxious to ensure that their future colleagues would continue to be wealthy clerical gentlemen able to maintain the dignity of the cathedral. Possibly they were also in part a ruse to keep down the number of stagiaries so that those in residence could enjoy a larger share of the profits. But by the late fourteenth century, which was apparently a time of falling production on the St. Paul's manors, they were found to be impracticable. A steady fall in the number of residentiaries led in 1399, on the initiative of the reforming Bishop Braybrooke, to a drastic reduction in the cost of hospitality in the first year of residence from the startling sum of seven hundred or a thousand marks to three hundred marks.[2] In 1403 the hospitality of the greater residence was

[1] Cf. C. N. L. Brooke in *Hist. St. Paul's Cathedral*, pp. 86–7, 363.
[2] *R.S.S.P.*, pp. 151–4, 198; *C.P.L. 1396–1404*, p. 529.

abolished altogether and replaced by an entrance fee of three hundred marks to be divided between the cathedral fabric and those choir members who had formerly been fed at the new residentiary's table.[1] Finally, in 1417, the entrance fee was reduced to one hundred marks.[2] Thus the qualifications of private wealth required from a new residentiary were very much less in the early fifteenth century than they had been during the fourteenth century.

In many ways the position at St. Paul's chapter, with its close connexion with the city and Westminster, and the large proportion of wealthy king's clerks among its canons, was exceptional. The rich chapter of York is the only other English secular chapter at which the expenses of hospitality during the greater residence are ever known to have reached as much as a thousand marks.[3] This prohibitive sum may well have been a reason for the very small proportion of canons who resided at York in the later middle ages. Elsewhere, the expenses of becoming a residentiary were much less, although, between the mid-thirteenth and the sixteenth centuries most of the English secular cathedral chapters, whether or not they imposed a greater residence, were coming to demand an entrance fee from new residentiaries.

It is interesting to notice the variety of causes which led to the imposition of entrance fees at different chapters. At Wells and Exeter it was substituted for extravagant feasting, though these chapters' judgement of extravagance in hospitality differed widely from that of the canons of St. Paul's. The canons of Wells were said in 1401 to have been spending a hundred and fifty or two hundred marks on useless entertainments at their entries, and were ordered instead to pay a hundred marks to the cathedral fabric fund.[4] In 1507 the much poorer chapter of Exeter introduced the very moderate entrance fee of forty pounds, to be paid for the support of the common burdens of the church in place of

[1] *Ibid.*, pp. 530–1.

[2] *R.S.S.P.*, pp. 200–2.

[3] They were said in 1541 to cost a thousand marks. From this year the expenditure was forbidden (*Y.S.*, pp. 43–4).

[4] *C.P.L. 1396–1404*, p. 400. In 1433 the chapter was apparently allotting ten marks of this sum to the fabric, ten marks to the vicars, and the remainder to general purposes of the chapter. After the Reformation it again became usual for a new residentiary to provide a feast in addition to the entrance fee (E. A. Freeman, *Hist. Wells*, p. 175).

the customary entertainments.[1] Chichester, on the other hand, had imposed an entrance fee of fifty marks in addition to the usual feasting and house-warming as early as 1251.[2] Possibly at this time the chief purpose of the fee had been to draw more clearly the distinction between the two groups of resident and non-resident canons: it represented a pledge that the canon definitely intended to make residence according to the statutes, and it proved that he had means to support the expenses of residence.

One of the clearest cases of a secular chapter imposing a money pledge with the object of restricting the number of its residentiary canons, or at any rate of ensuring that they should all be wealthy men, was at Lichfield. Here the evidence comes from the late thirteenth or early fourteenth century. In statutes of about 1300 the chapter ordered that, on account of the burdens of residence, no canon of whatever birth or scholarship should be admitted to residence, unless he were able to spend forty pounds a year beyond his commons,

'of his own money, or of his patrimony of the church of Lichfield, or outside it, lest, like a drone among bees, or like a thief entering upon the labours of others, he should seem to eat the honey from which those labouring day and night in the vineyard of the Lord ought to be sustained, and should so destroy the apiary'.[3]

A growing number of Lichfield canons were wishing to reside, and it was feared that, unless these new residentiaries had an adequate private income, they would be unable to meet the expenses of hospitality without making demands on the common fund which would reduce all the canons to poverty. Therefore the chapter reserved to itself the right of refusing entry to those canons whose residence seemed to it inexpedient for the church.[4] The act books show that the forty-pound pledge became an entrance fee and was usually spent on a feast. About 1385 it was diverted to the

[1] *H.M.C. Var. Coll.*, iv, 20.
[2] *C.S.*, p. 17. This fee does not seem to have been increased in the later middle ages. In 1574 the chapter reaffirmed that no residentiary ought to be admitted without paying half a hundred marks, saying that an old statute requiring this had been discontinued through negligence (*ibid.*, p. 25).
[3] *Monasticon*, VI, iii, 1262.
[4] *Monasticon*, VI, iii, 1262. All canons wishing to enter residence were required to give at least forty days' notice to the dean and chapter. Then the chapter was to debate whether their residence would be expedient or not.

cathedral fabric,[1] and in 1420 was raised to a hundred marks for the benefit of the cathedral.[2]

It is impossible to form conclusions on the meaning of the statute of 1300 without knowledge of the accounts of the Lichfield common fund at this time. The chapter of residentiaries may have developed into a selfish and exclusive body, whose object was to keep valuable profits of surplus commons for itself. On the other hand, the common fund at Lichfield was always small, and the rise in prices in the later middle ages may well have caused the money distributions of commons to be inadequate for a large number of residentiaries to provide the lavish hospitality customary at secular cathedrals. Certainly the cost of hospitality must have risen everywhere about this time. There are a number of suggestions in cathedral records that residentiary canons were finding it difficult to meet their obligations.

At Salisbury, for instance, Bishop Martival pronounced in 1319 that, 'even though all [the residentiaries'] property were held in peaceful possession, they were compelled by reason of their residence to spend much more than they could acquire for themselves from their titles in the church or from common property'.[3] But the chapter of Salisbury reacted in a different way from Lichfield to this situation. It invited the non-resident canons to make trial of residence at their cathedral, and, in order to encourage them, reduced drastically the burden of the entrance feast, forbidding any new residentiary to spend more than the annual value of his prebend on the feast.[4] At the same time some pledge of the canon's purpose to reside was necessary, and so he was required to pay forty shillings as a kind of security that within a definite time he would either provide an entrance feast in his house or pay a fine of forty pounds to the cathedral fabric.[5] The chapter act books show that during the following years most new residentiaries at

[1] H. Jenkins, Lichfield Cathedral in the Fourteenth Century (Oxford B.Litt. thesis, 1956), pp. 19–20, 71.
[2] *Monasticon*, VI, iii, 1262.   [3] *S.S.*, pp. 152–3.
[4] *Ibid.*, pp. 144–7.
[5] Records of the payment of such pledges are entered in the chapter act books, e.g. *Hemingby's Reg.*, pp. 63, 123, 162; Reg. Corffe, f. 19. Possibly the forty-shilling payment had some connexion with the order in Bishop Poore's *Tractatus* that every canon obtaining a prebend at Salisbury was to pay one ounce of gold to the dean, and forty shillings or a day's provision to the canons for love's sake (*S.S.*, p. 61).

Salisbury preferred to pay the fine rather than to provide the entrance feast. Moreover, the chapter of residentiaries did not show a grasping attitude towards the exaction of the fine. Several times it reduced the amount from forty to twenty pounds, or agreed that payment should be postponed for as long as two years if the new residentiary had difficulty in paying at once.[1] Salisbury seems to have been one of the first English chapters at which an entrance fee for residence thus came to be substituted for feasting, and the amount of the fee was very moderate throughout the greater part of the fourteenth century.

Then, towards the end of the fourteenth and in the fifteenth centuries, a change took place in the practice at Salisbury. In 1386 a chapter act laid down that the custom of either a formal entrance feast or payment of a fine must be strictly observed.[2] From this time onwards increasingly heavy fines were paid by the new residentiaries: in 1404 Master Henry of Harborough paid a hundred marks for his entrance;[3] in 1406 and 1413 the chapter declared that no entrance fee should be less than forty pounds and that it had the right to demand a greater sum.[4] Finally, in 1428, all entrance feasts were forbidden, and in their place every simple canon entering residence was ordered to pay a hundred and seven marks, six shillings and eightpence, and every dignitary a hundred and fifty-seven marks, six shillings and eightpence.[5] The immediate reason for this change of policy is probably to be found in the pressing need of the chapter to raise money at this time. In the late fourteenth and early fifteenth centuries, particularly after 1412, it was spending large sums at the Roman curia in pressing forward the business of the canonization of its founder, St. Osmund.[6] The canonization was finally achieved in 1457. In the meantime there is definite evidence that entrance fees from the new residentiaries were devoted to the expenses of the canonization.[7] Thus at Salisbury the increased fee was evidently imposed as a tax for a definite purpose, not simply as a means of increasing the profits of a close chapter of residentiaries. Yet it also seems

[1] E.g. *Hemingby's Reg.*, p. 112.   [2] Reg. Coman, ff. 32–3.
[3] Reg. Draper, f. 29.   [4] *Ibid.*, f. 53; Reg. Vyring, f. 111.
[5] *S.S.*, pp. 308–11. This statute was confirmed by Pope Eugenius IV in 1442.
[6] *Canonization S. Osmund*, ed. A. R. Malden, p. v.
[7] E. F. Jacob, 'Some English Documents of the Conciliar Movement', in *B.J.R.L.*, xv, 384 n. Cf. *Canonization S. Osmund*, pp. v–vi.

significant that the order for the increased fee followed very soon after the chapters of St. Paul's, Lichfield, and Wells had all decided to fix their entrance fees at a hundred marks.[1] By the fifteenth century there was clearly a growing uniformity in the expenses of becoming a residentiary at the different cathedrals.

(iii) *Chapter Business*

In addition to their duties at the cathedral services and in dispensing hospitality, residentiary canons of the later middle ages were also responsible for the conduct of the greater part of the business affairs of the cathedral and chapter. They were bound by oath to serve in any office belonging to the common of the residentiaries to which they were elected,[2] and are frequently found acting as financial officers of the chapter, keepers of the common fund and of the fabric, masters of the choristers, keepers of the muniments. They were appointed as chapter commissaries to visit or administer the common estates; to hold inquisitions about repairs needed in the prebends, on chapter farms, or in the canonical houses of residence. They collected taxes from the prebends; they might be sent to conduct chapter lawsuits or other business at the Roman curia, in the king's courts, or at the court of Canterbury, or to undertake negotiations with the bishop or monastic houses.

Most of these appointments and other current business were settled at the ordinary daily or weekly chapter meetings, from which non-resident canons, and, at some churches, new residentiaries in their first year were normally absent.[3] General chapters of all the canons, resident and non-resident, were held occasionally for specially important matters affecting the whole body of canons;[4] for these, written summonses were sent out. But for the short daily chapters after prime, the ringing of a bell was the only summons. On a Saturday this chapter was often concerned with the discipline of the choir: the vicars choral and other *ministri*

---

[1] At Hereford, also, an entrance fee of a hundred marks was customary in 1593 (Bannister, *op. cit.*, p. 157). It is not known when this was first imposed.

[2] *Salisbury Ceremonies*, p. 113.

[3] E.g. At St. Paul's and Lincoln no new residentiary was allowed to be present at the chapter's counsels and business meetings unless specially invited by the dean and chapter (*R.S.S.P.*, p. 129; *L.S.*, iii, 324).

[4] For discussion of the general chapters, see below, pp. 91-3.

inferiores were then ordered to attend, and received correction from the dean and chapter for any faults or negligence observed in their conduct in the preceding week; the weekly commons were distributed; and the *tabula* or list of ministers assigned for duties at the cathedral services during the following week were read out. But especially on feast days, there was little time to deal with lengthy business after prime, and the dean had the right to summon meetings of the residentiaries at other times. Sometimes, as at Lincoln under the rule of Dean Macworth in the first half of the fifteenth century, such chapters might be after the midday breakfast: the canons are said to have objected strongly to their dean's habit of calling them to frequent chapters on frivolous excuses at inconvenient times, especially *post prandium*.[1] The chapter of Lichfield in the second half of the fourteenth century preferred to transact most of its business on Fridays;[2] at Salisbury meetings recorded in the chapter act books were apparently held on any convenient day of the week. All residentiary canons present in the city were supposed to attend, and were bound by oath not to reveal the secrets they heard there.

The fourteenth-century registers of chapter acts at Salisbury and Lichfield illustrate well the variety and importance of the business dealt with at these chapters by the residentiary canons. The temporal administration of the chapter's estates, the assignment of farms and canonical houses, business concerning the cathedral fabric naturally took up a considerable amount of time. Reports and accounts of the financial officers of the common fund and of the fabric fund were heard and discussed. There were admissions of new canons and of their vicars choral to the cathedral body. A number of collations to benefices, especially cathedral chantries and vicarages on the chapter's estates, were made jointly by the dean and chapter. Appointments of other choir ministers and cathedral officers had to be discussed. The chapter of residentiaries had some control over all departments of cathedral life. Together with the dean or his *locum-tenens*, it exercised discipline and juris-

[1] 'Potissime post horam prandendi, quando nonnulli non adeo bene disponuntur sicut ieiunii' (*L.S.*, iii, 375, cf. 377–8, 390).

[2] Most of the *acta* in the chapter register MS. Ashmole 794 are dated on Fridays; cf. also *Monasticon*, VI, iii, 1261. At Bayeux, also, the day for ordinary chapter business was Friday (Deslandes, *op. cit.*, p. 180); at Chartres in 1740, following ancient usage, ordinary chapters were said to be on Mondays, Wednesdays, and Saturdays, unless these were feast days (Amiet, *op. cit.*, p. 167).

diction over the various groups and corporations of lesser cathedral clergy; over all the cathedral servants, and over the tenants living on its estates. It might sometimes intervene in the work of the principal dignitaries; if the cathedral grammar school were not being efficiently run, or the theology lectures not given regularly and adequately, it could require the chancellor to make correction. Often it made statutes, or enforced the observance of earlier statutes. Always it was much concerned in the conduct of the chapter's lawsuits. The secular chapters usually included eminent canon and civil lawyers among their canons. They might pay subordinate proctors or agents to act for them at Rome or in the courts of the king or archbishop, but the direction of the lawsuits remained in their own hands. They took a lively interest in solving legal problems; members of the residentiary chapter might be sent to Rome or London to conduct the case in person, or to secure the help of some influential non-resident canon, or lay or clerical *confrater* of the church.[1]

Thus residentiary canons who fulfilled all their duties conscientiously led a busy life, particularly in the later middle ages, as their numbers became fewer, and as the conduct of the cathedral services and chapter business was left more completely to them. Life in the close may have seemed limited and monotonous to some non-residents, who had been attracted by prospects of power and wealth at court, or adventure and excitement in diplomatic work. Yet it had variety. The cathedral services formed the main pattern of residentiary life, but this pattern was never uniform. The liturgy and chant varied daily. The numerous feast days, the different liturgical colours used at their appropriate seasons, the processions and psalmody, all needed careful study and organization. There

---

[1] An interesting case of a distinguished *confrater* of Salisbury chapter, William Gray, the future bishop of Ely, proctor of Henry VI at Rome, and a close friend of Pope Nicholas V, giving help to canons of Salisbury at Rome occurred in the mid-fifteenth century. In 1452 Nicholas Upton and Simon Huchyns, canons of Salisbury, who had been sent to promote the canonization of St. Osmund, wrote to their bishop that, on entering the city of Rome, 'we . . . straightway . . . went to Master William Gray, delivering your letters to him. Having read them, he declared himself a son and brother (*confrater*) of your church of Salisbury; wherefore he promised to do everything possible in the matter' (*Canonization S. Osmund*, pp. 94–6). Subsequent letters of the two Salisbury proctors (*ibid.*, pp. 99–144 *passim*) show that William Gray fulfilled his promises. For the fraternities of the chapters, see below, pp. 318–19.

was scope at the cathedrals for the able administrator, the lawyer, the scholar, the preacher, the theologian, the man interested in finance or estate management, and the man with a flair for entertaining and dispensing hospitality.

3. THE PRACTICE OF RESIDENCE IN THE FOURTEENTH CENTURY

(*a*) THE SIZE OF THE RESIDENTIARY BODY

An attempt will now be made to discover roughly the proportion of canons who chose to profess residence at English secular cathedrals in the fourteenth century. Generally, estimates of the size of the residentiary bodies at this time have been low. Financial records of the chapters, particularly accounts of the common fund, and the registers of *acta capitularia* are usually the only sources in which more or less definite evidence can be found of the numbers of residentiary canons; and these, even when extant, have rarely been printed, or used much for this purpose. Moreover, York, where much work has been done on the composition of the medieval chapter, was in many ways exceptional: it seems to have had fewer residentiary canons than any other English secular cathedral in the later middle ages. But some writers have merely accepted the evidence of visitation records and chronicles, which stressed the fewness of the residentiaries.[1] They have been prepared to believe that in the fourteenth century the number of residentiaries was not much more than that fixed by statute after the Reformation. At St. Paul's and Lincoln this number was four; at Lichfield and Chichester, four with the dean; at Hereford and Salisbury six; at Wells eight, and at Exeter nine.

Yet, as long ago as 1897, the late Canon Wordsworth pointed out that an early surviving fragment of a Lincoln *Re* and *Ve* roll (*recedendi et veniendi*, or a roll recording the 'comings and goings' of the canons, so that the clerk of the common fund should know how much to pay them for their commons), showed that far more canons were present at Lincoln during fifteen weeks of the year 1278–9 than had previously been thought possible.[2] Twenty-nine out of fifty-two canons of Lincoln were entered as appearing

[1] E.g. W. W. Capes, *Hist. English Church in Fourteenth and Fifteenth Centuries*; W. R. W. Stephens, *Memorials Chichester*.
[2] *L.S.*, ii, ccvi–viii.

at Lincoln during these fifteen weeks: twenty of them kept more than a couple of weeks residence. There were usually about sixteen in residence at a time, never less than thirteen, and occasionally as many as twenty or twenty-one. Unfortunately no more *Re* and *Ve* rolls are extant at Lincoln until 1437, and the next printed by Wordsworth, for 1471–2, shows that the total number of canons receiving distributions in a whole year had by then fallen to nine.[1] Clearly, therefore, a big change had taken place in the size of the residentiary body in the two intervening centuries.

The unpublished fourteenth-century 'Audit Accounts' of the common fund at Lincoln[2] provide a means of seeing how this change came about, and of how far the size of the residentiary body in the fourteenth century was intermediate between its size in the late thirteenth and in the late fifteenth centuries. The distributions of commons recorded in these accounts are based on information supplied by the *Re* and *Ve* rolls, and therefore indicate the time which each canon had resided. No mention is made of canons in residence for less than four months in the year, but the information about the different kinds of distributions paid to all the full residentiaries is more detailed than that of other contemporary cathedral accounts which I have seen. Moreover, the accounts at Lincoln are exceptionally well preserved and are available for fifty-eight complete years of the century.

Two interesting points emerge from a study of these accounts. First, Canon Wordsworth was completely justified in suggesting that the size of the residentiary body at Lincoln had been underestimated. In the fourteenth century twelve or thirteen was the average number of canons resident at various times throughout the year: in only one year did it drop as low as seven, and in five years it was as many as fifteen. No special preponderance of the higher numbers in the earlier years, or of the lower numbers towards the end of the century can be traced.[3] Secondly, the vast majority of Lincoln residentiaries in the fourteenth century chose to make the greater residence of eight months in the year, rather than the minor residence of four months: the names of the same canons occur year after year, until their death, in the lists of the

[1] *Ibid.*, iii, 800–23.
[2] Muniments D. and C. Lincoln, Bj/2/4–10.
[3] For extracts from these accounts, see below, Appendix I.

greater residentiaries. In the early years of the century, from 1305 to 1315, there were usually one or two minor residentiaries. But there were never more than three at a time, and after 1315 they are very rarely found at all. The evidence of the 1278 *Re* and *Ve* roll suggested that at the end of the thirteenth century a number of Lincoln canons were coming into residence for short periods at a time; while the 1471 roll showed that all the nine residentiaries then stayed at Lincoln for the greater part of the year. Possibly, therefore, the early fourteenth century was the period at Lincoln when the distinction between the two bodies of resident and non-resident canons became definite and more or less rigid. Gradually those canons who went to the expense of acquiring a house of residence and making their formal entry, came to make their permanent and comfortable homes in the close. They did not usually attempt to carry on with work outside the cathedral city, but preferred a long residence which entitled them to the distributions of surplus commons. Most of the non-resident canons were busy in active careers in other parts. Thus the residentiaries were left with almost entire control of the cathedral close and its government. Yet even at the end of the fourteenth century they did not form a close oligarchy, comparable to that of the late fifteenth or sixteenth centuries. Their numbers were still considerably more than the six or nine which became usual in the course of the fifteenth century: there were no restrictions, other than the outlay of hospitality, on entry to their body; even in the 1380's there were still a very few minor residentiaries; and non-resident canons are still occasionally found taking part in chapter business.

A few fourteenth-century accounts of the common fund or chapter acts of five other English secular cathedrals have been either printed in full or calendared. Though the evidence from these is not nearly so detailed or complete as that for Lincoln, it gives valuable indications of the size of other residentiary bodies.

In 1881 H. E. Reynolds published a definite contemporary statement at Wells that fifteen canons were in residence there in 1331.[1] It has sometimes been supposed that this must have represented the maximum number present at Wells in any one year during the century; Professor Hamilton Thompson has written that nine or ten was apparently the normal number of residen-

[1] *W.S.*, p. 130.

tiaries at Wells at this time.[1] Yet the five calendared communar's accounts of the fourteenth century, printed in the Reports of the Historical Manuscripts Commission,[2] suggest that fifteen was nearer the minimum than the maximum number of Wells residentiaries at this time. In 1326–7 there were sixteen residentiaries at Wells; in 1327–8, fifteen; in 1342–3, seventeen; in 1343–4, nineteen; in 1391–2, nineteen again; in 1392–3, twenty. This number was maintained in 1393–4 and 1394–5, though it dropped to seventeen in 1400. For the fifteenth century a larger proportion of communar's rolls have survived; it is clear that there was no marked falling off in numbers until 1417–18, when only eleven canons resided.[3] From 1418 to 1445 there were still about fifteen canons in residence in most years,[4] and it was not until the last half of the fifteenth century that ten, eleven, or twelve became normal.[5] In 1575, when the number of canons allowed to reside at Wells was limited by statute to eight, there were still eleven residentiaries there, and provision had to be made that the statute should not take effect until three of them had died, so that all might continue in residence for the rest of their lives.[6] Judged by previous estimates, Wells seems to have had an unusually large residentiary body throughout the later middle ages.

Wells, however, like Lincoln and Salisbury, had a large chapter of over fifty canons. Even more remarkable evidence has been found for two of the smallest English secular cathedral chapters, Exeter and Hereford, both, like Wells, in the south-west or west of England.

At Exeter, where the full number of prebends was twenty-four, fourteen canons were described as residentiaries in 1302.[7] There were sixteen residentiaries in 1384,[8] and fourteen in 1386;[9] while in the lists of the chapter's 'Expenses Extraordinary' of 1388–1402, between sixteen and twenty-three canons are normally said to have been resident in a year.[10] This is a much higher proportion of resident to non-resident canons than has been found at any other English secular cathedral at the same period; and it is interesting to notice that in the sixteenth century, when the number of

[1] *Cathedral Churches*, p. 174.   [2] *H.M.C. Wells*, i, 1–11, 22–30, 34–7.
[3] *Ibid.*, p. 58.   [4] *Ibid.*, pp. 58–73.
[5] *Ibid.*, pp. 77 et seq.   [6] *W.S.*, p. 247.
[7] *Reg. Bytton*, p. 409.   [8] *Reg. Brantyngham*, i, 516.
[9] *Use Exeter*, p. 2.   [10] *Ibid.*, pp. 56–9.

residentiaries was everywhere fixed by statute, Exeter allowed a higher number of its canons, nine, to enter residence, than any other cathedral of the Old Foundation. The explanation of the very general practice of residence at Exeter in the later middle ages lies probably in the economic system of the chapter. All the prebends were equal in value and very meagre, while the bulk of the chapter revenues payable to the canons was distributed as commons to the residentiaries. Canonries at Exeter were therefore worth little to non-residents, and would rarely attract royal clerks or papal nominees. Many canons in the Exeter chapter acts and *fasti* have Cornish names. A large proportion of the chapter was apparently made up of local men, whose chief interests were in the diocese, and who preferred residence with an adequate income from the common fund to careers in other parts.

At Hereford, also, meagre prebends resulted in the provision of comparatively few royal and papal clerks. Here the researches of Canon Capes and Canon Bannister among the unpublished compotus rolls of the chapter have proved that the mid-fourteenth century was the turning-point in the development by which a small body of residentiary canons came gradually to replace the much larger number of canons present at the cathedral in the late thirteenth century. In 1294–5 the names of twenty-one out of the full number of twenty-eight Hereford canons are entered on the roll of mass pence as having attended masses at the cathedral:[1] fifteen of them attended over ninety masses in the year, and so must have resided for at least three months, and some attended as many as two hundred and eighty-eight. During the first half of the fourteenth century these numbers were maintained: the rolls of mass pence show that a good proportion of from twelve to fifteen canons made large attendances.[2] But in the mid-fourteenth century the entire income of the chapter from lands and tithes in Hereford, including the rents which provided the mass pence, was reduced almost by half.[3] As a result the number of residentiaries fell rapidly. For the rest of the century there were seldom more than eight or nine canons in residence during any one year; while in the early fifteenth century there were only six or seven. The number rose slightly to eight or nine again in the reigns of

---

[1] This roll has been printed by Canon Capes in *Hereford Charters*, pp. 168–9.
[2] *Ibid.*, p. x.
[3] Bannister, *op. cit.*, p. 156; *Hereford Charters*, p. x.

Henry VII and Henry VIII, but under Elizabeth it was limited to
six.[1]

St. Paul's and York, on the other hand, always attracted large
numbers of royal and papal nominees; York because of its rich
prebends, and St. Paul's largely because of its nearness to Westminster and the government offices. In consequence they seem
never to have had as many residentiary canons as the other English
secular cathedrals, though at St. Paul's, where royal clerks were
sometimes able to keep residence at the same time as working in
government departments, there were a fair number in the early
and middle years of the fourteenth century. At least twelve out of
thirty major canons were stagiaries in 1319 and 1320;[2] in 1364 there
were nine stagiaries.[3] But from about 1389 the number fell steadily
until in 1400 there was only one. By 1403 there was a recovery to
five and by 1447 to eight.[4] Thus the sharpest drop in the number
of residentiaries at St. Paul's came in the last years of the fourteenth
century. At York very few canons were in residence even at the
beginning of the century. Professor Hamilton Thompson's detailed study of the chapter under Archbishop Greenfield, from
1306 to 1315, shows that not more than six or seven out of the
thirty-six canons were normally resident.[5] Moreover, the residentiaries of York like those of St. Paul's were apparently more
occupied in affairs of state, and less often present in the cathedral
close, than the residentiaries of other English secular cathedrals.
Early in 1305 John Nassington, residentiary of York, wrote to
John Risinden, the auditor of Beverley chapter, about some business concerning Beverley which was to have been dealt with at the
next chapter meeting at York. He warned Risinden that little
business was being done at York these days, because Robert
Pickering, one of the chapter's most energetic members, was
absent at parliament with certain of the brethren, and only two
canons remained in the close. He (John Nassington) did not wish,
without Pickering, 'inopportunely to wake the sleeping dog', and
therefore advised Risinden to send details of his business and the
proposed date of the meeting to Pickering and the other absent

---

[1] *Ibid.*   [2] *R.S.S.P.*, pp. 107, 109.
[3] *H.M.C. Ninth Rept.*, App. i, 53b.
[4] C. N. L. Brooke in *Hist. St. Paul's Cathedral*, pp. 89–91; *C.P.L. 1396–1404*,
p. 530.
[5] Introduction to *Reg. Greenfield*, i, xviii.

canons at Westminster.[1] A chamberlain's account of York's common fund for half of the year 1371 suggests that the residence situation had not substantially altered by then: seven canons were present at York for periods varying from six to twenty-one weeks.[2]

It has sometimes been suggested that a reason for canonical non-residence at the secular cathedrals in the later middle ages was the limited number of residentiary houses in the close and their bad state of repair. Investigation of the houses in Salisbury close has been possible from various charters and indentures giving the position of the houses; from records of the assignment of houses in chapter; and from payments of obit rents charged on them. From these it is clear that there was ample housing accommodation for a very large body of residentiary canons in the fourteenth-century close.[3] Besides the deanery and two houses appropriated to the cathedral prebends held by the abbots of Sherborne and St. Mary Montebourg, there were at least fifteen and probably seventeen canonical houses of residence: only one of these was said to have been in an exceptionally bad state of repair, and that only in the last years of the century; others were frequently repaired and enlarged at the canons' expense. In addition, thirteen smaller houses, usually inhabited by vicars choral, were allowed by their title deeds to be assigned to canons, and canons are occasionally known to have lived in them. At different times in the fourteenth century canons have been found living in about twenty-seven different houses in the close.

Yet, in spite of having detailed information of this kind, it is in some ways more difficult at Salisbury than at other cathedrals to reach definite conclusions about the size of the residentiary body. This is chiefly due to the state of the extant accounts of the common fund, which elsewhere usually provide the most reliable evidence. At Salisbury they are few, in a bad state of repair, and difficult to use, because they were drawn up to fit in with the complicated system of the quarterly residence. Only nineteen rolls survive from the fourteenth century,[4] and each covers only a quarter of a year. In order to count as a full residentiary a canon

---

[1] *Beverley Chapter Acts*, i, 61–2.
[2] *Fabric Rolls of York Minster*, pp. 123, 125.
[3] For the evidence, see K. Edwards, *loc. cit.*, pp. 55–115.
[4] Muniments D. and C. Salisbury, Press II.

had to earn forty shillings in daily commons. Therefore those who earned between thirty and forty shillings a quarter were set down by the communar in his roll as three-quarter residentiaries; those with twenty to thirty shillings were half residentiaries; those with ten to twenty shillings quarter residentiaries; and those with less than ten shillings were omitted altogether from the total. The four chief dignitaries received double commons; so, if one of them earned forty shillings, he counted as two residentiaries. By these methods, the communar, at the end of a quarter, judged that thirteen and a half, eleven and three-quarters, or twelve and a quarter canons had completed their full residence, and were entitled to share in the quarterly distribution of surplus commons; while, towards the end of the century, when more dignitaries resided, the total might rise to fifteen, sixteen, or seventeen and three-quarter full residentiaries. But the payments of daily commons to individual canons show that a completely different number of canons, ranging from about sixteen to as many as twenty-three, were present at Salisbury for some period during the quarter. Not all these would be residentiaries: some, receiving only two or three shillings for commons, were clearly non-residents visiting the cathedral for a few days, possibly to attend a general chapter meeting. Others, with more than ten shillings, might be intending to earn the rest of their forty shillings in the remaining three-quarters of the year, and so may have been full residentiaries for the year. The difficulties experienced in trying to discover how many of them did this are chiefly due to no complete set of four communar rolls being extant for any one year in the century. Two quarterly rolls are available for each of the years 1343, 1369, 1371, and 1380; but the remaining eleven rolls are all for different years.

It is therefore necessary to supplement the evidence of the accounts by drawing largely on lists of the canons' chapter attendances recorded in the chapter acts. These *acta* are available for forty-two years of the fourteenth century; but their information is much less precise and satisfactory than that of the accounts, from the point of view of finding out how many canons were actually in residence. At the beginning of his minutes of each chapter meeting, the chapter clerk wrote down the names of the canons present. But clearly all the canons in residence were not present at all chapter meetings. As many as twelve or thirteen

G

might attend for important business; other matters might be transacted in the presence of only four or five; while sometimes, when several matters were dealt with on the same day, the names of canons said to be present at the different meetings varied. Moreover, the *acta*, at any rate for some years, are incomplete. The number of ordinary chapter meetings of residentiaries recorded in a year varies from five to forty-six. There must obviously have been more meetings in some years; the subject-matter of the entries frequently shows that certain business, such as the assignment of a farm or house, or even the admission of a canon or vicar, has been left unrecorded.

In order to form some idea of the proportion of the full body of fifty-two canons performing their statutory residence at Salisbury in the course of a year, the evidence of the *acta* and of the accounts must be collated. This has been done for six years of the fourteenth century, 1343, 1347, 1350, 1394, 1398, 1399, for which material is available from both sources.[1] The result shows that in these years the majority of residentiaries were present in the cathedral city for longer or shorter periods in all four quarters of the year, not only in a single quarter. The eight to twelve canons who earned their full forty shillings commons in a single quarter generally continued to reside for the rest of the year: it is their names which appear most frequently in the lists of witnesses to chapter acts during the remaining quarters. The three-quarter, half and quarter residentiaries of the accounts were also often present at chapter meetings in other quarters of the year, though not so regularly as those in the first group. Therefore few additions can be made from the lists of chapter witnesses to the residentiaries named in the quarterly accounts.

This conclusion is supported by study of the canons' chapter attendances over a longer time. For two periods of the fourteenth century, 1334–58 and 1385–1400, when the chapter acts are most complete, a group of about eight to eleven canons is seen to be in residence almost continuously throughout the year. They did not attend every chapter meeting, but were present at a sufficient number to suggest that they were making up a full quarter's residence or more in each quarter of the year. During those quarters for which communar rolls are extant they generally earned more than their forty shillings commons a quarter. In the

---

[1] Tables of the evidence for these years are given below, Appendix II.

earlier period from 1334 to 1358 this constant, stable element in the residentiary chapter was formed by men like Ralph de Querendon, formerly a clerk of Bishop Ghent's consistory court and his sequestrator general,[1] who professed his residence, and settled down in a house in the close on being made subdean; Walter de Wyville, the treasurer; the two archdeacons, Robert of Luffenham, archdeacon of Salisbury, notary public, who was also a canon of Wells,[2] and John Kirkby, archdeacon of Dorset; Elias of St. Albans, the long-lived and irascible chancellor, who caused many difficulties in chapter in his old age;[3] John de Camera, the precentor; John of Salisbury; James of Havant; and Thomas Buckton. All these men apparently made their permanent homes in the close. Then, towards the end of the century and in the early fifteenth century, a group of rather more distinguished ecclesiastics came into residence. Thomas of Montacute, kinsman of the Earl of Salisbury, was the first resident dean of Salisbury in the fourteenth century,[4] and was succeeded as dean by another residentiary, John Chaundler, the Wykehamist, formerly a king's clerk, and future bishop of Salisbury.[5] Adam Mottram, after long experience of provincial and diocesan administration as chancellor of the archbishop of Canterbury, commissary of the archbishop's prerogative and archdeacon of Canterbury, became a residentiary on being made precentor of Salisbury in 1397.[6] William Loring, residentiary, was both a theologian and a lawyer, owning a large collection of books; he left his Roman law books to the University Library at Cambridge, some of his theological books to Merton College, Oxford, and directed that others should be sold by his executors to provide funds for Merton scholars.[7] At Salisbury he went to great expense in repairing and adding new buildings to his house called 'Hemingsby' in the close.[8] Other

---

[1] *Reg. S. de Gandavo*, pp. 794, 912.

[2] Cf. E. H. Pearce, *Thomas de Cobham*, p. 49.

[3] See below, pp. 195, 201.

[4] Thomas was appointed dean in 1382, but did not begin to reside until 1394 (Reg. Dunham, f. 257). A number of reforms of the cathedral statutes and administration took place under his leadership (*ibid.*, ff. 257–62; *S.S.*, pp. 306–7).

[5] Notes on his career have been collected by Dr. Jacob in *Reg. Chichele*, ii, App. 645.

[6] For Adam's career, see *ibid.*, p. 666.   [7] *Ibid.*, ii, 79–82.

[8] Reg. Dunham, f. 154; Reg. Vyring, f. 109.

residentiaries of the time were John Norton, LL.D., the chancellor, Robert of Ragnall, archdeacon of Dorset; George Louthorpe, John Maidenhead, John Turk, Richard Postell, Robert Croucheston, and Richard Pitts. Together they undertook large schemes: the reform of the cathedral statutes; the settlement of a long series of disputes with their bishop; the repair of the cathedral fabric; and the canonization of their founder, St. Osmund.[1] One of their main objects in this last plan is thought to have been to popularize the Use of Salisbury, which was gradually being adopted as the normal liturgy in most English churches. The interests of these canons were not confined to their cathedral church. Dr. Jacob has pointed out that some were keenly interested in the political thought of the time and the problems of the conciliar movement: he has described them as representing the most progressive minds of the day.[2] In many ways the residentiary chapter at Salisbury at the end of the fourteenth century seems to have been a more vital, distinguished, and interesting body of men than that of the middle years of the century. It may be compared with the thirteenth-century chapter, when canons of Salisbury had given leadership to the English church, and when the cathedral school had nearly developed into a *studium generale*.[3]

In addition to this main group of residentiaries, who made a long annual residence lasting for the greater part of the year, it is interesting to find at Salisbury, throughout the fourteenth century, a smaller group of canons, who apparently still came up to the cathedral for little more than their statutory three months' residence a year. In the period from 1334 to 1358 the chapter acts show that at least four men, Robert Baldock, William Salton, Peter Inkpen, and Richard Chaddesley, though admitted as residentiaries, were attending far fewer chapter meetings than the other residentiaries. In the communar's quarterly accounts they were counted as half or quarter residentiaries; but their scattered chapter attendances throughout the year suggest that they managed to

---

[1] For their plans and activities, see Reg. Coman, ff. 70–7; *Canonization S. Osmund, passim*; Reg. Dunham, ff. 257–62; *S.S.*, pp. 306–7.

[2] 'Some English Documents of the Conciliar Movement', in *B.J.R.L.*, xv, 387.

[3] Cf. M. Gibbs, *Bishops and Reform*, pp. 32 n., 51, and below, pp. 191–2. Salisbury still had a learned chapter in the early fourteenth century (*ibid.*, pp. 88, 201).

make up at least three or six months' residence in most years. For the year 1343 there is proof that two of them did so. Two account rolls for the quarters January to April and July to October are available. Robert Baldock earned a three-quarter share of the surplus commons in the January to April quarter, and another quarter share in July to October; William Salton made half his residence in each of the quarters. Possibly both of them may have earned another full or part share in the two remaining quarters, for they are known to have attended a few more chapter meetings then. In the later years of the century Thomas Spert, Peter Barton, John Cheney, John Chitterne, and William Spaldwick made similar short periods of residence.

What did these 'lesser residentiaries' do when they were not living in the cathedral city? Some may have preferred to spend part of the year on their prebends[1] or chapter farms or other benefices. Some, such as William Salton, Robert Baldock, and John Cheney, undertook diocesan work in the service of the bishop of Salisbury or of bishops of other dioceses.[2] University students and masters, as, for example, St. Edmund of Abingdon in the thirteenth century,[3] might make up their three months' residence at the cathedral during the university vacations. Perhaps some of the most interesting evidence for the outside activities of certain Salisbury residentiaries comes from the Wells chapter records. Four canons, Robert Baldock, William Salton, Thomas Spert, and Peter Barton, known to have made a quarterly or half-yearly

[1] St. Edmund Rich, treasurer and prebendary of Calne at Salisbury, is a well-known example of a famous canon who conscientiously fulfilled his duties on his prebend. In 1233-4 the messengers sent to announce to him his election as archbishop of Canterbury, found him living on his prebend at Calne, 'attending to the spiritual and temporal needs of those of whom he had oversight' (*Use Sarum*, i, xvi n.; *Fasti Sar.*, p. 258).

[2] William Salton and Robert Baldock received commissions from the bishop of Wells while residentiaries at Salisbury and Wells, and John Cheney was vicar general of the bishop of Hereford (*Reg. Shrewsbury*, pp. 44, 65, 86, 147, 727; *Reg. Gilbert*, p. 1). The printed registers of Simon of Ghent, bishop of Salisbury, and of William Greenfield, archbishop of York, include many commissions to residentiary canons of their cathedrals.

[3] Father Daniel Callus has shown that St. Edmund was actually lecturing at Paris while treasurer and residentiary at Salisbury. He points out that the dates when Edmund is known to have been at Salisbury were usually in the university long vacations (*Introduction of Aristotelian Learning to Oxford* (Proc. British Academy, xxix), pp. 13–14 and n.).

residence at Salisbury, were at the same time residentiaries of Wells cathedral: they maintained houses of residence at Wells, and attended Wells chapter meetings.[1] The nearness of Wells to Salisbury would make it fairly easy for them to do this, although the Wells statutes, by ordering that part of the six months' residence at Wells should be made in each quarter of the year, must have caused them frequent travelling: these statutes probably explain why Robert and William resided for a few weeks in every quarter at Salisbury instead of making three months' continuous residence. The holding of residentiaryships at two cathedrals in the same year would naturally be impracticable at two churches which both demanded more than six months' residence a year.

Throughout the fourteenth century, with the exception of the abnormal plague years about 1350,[2] there seems rarely to have been much less than a quarter of the fifty-two canons making full residence at Salisbury cathedral in any quarter of the year; sometimes there were considerably more. The communar's accounts show that these numbers were maintained well into the fifteenth century, at any rate until 1461. They were achieved largely through the majority of residentiaries making a much longer residence than their statutory three months, in place of the absent canons. But at the same time the rules requiring only one quarter's residence a year from each canon remained in force, and, together with the absence of any onerous greater residence, evidently helped to make the residentiary chapter both larger and more varied in personnel than it might otherwise have been. Moreover, it gave the residentiaries opportunities to maintain their interests and work outside the close and diocese. Conditions of residence at Salisbury may well have attracted canons with a certain amount of spare time, particularly scholars and those interested in diocesan work, who at other cathedrals might have decided to be non-resident. On the other hand, the many rich prebends at Salisbury resulted in the provision of many royal and papal clerks, who could not manage even the three-monthly residence. There-

---

[1] *W.S.*, pp. 78, 130, 149, 153; *Reg. Shrewsbury*, pp. 66–7, 631, 670, 708, 735, 779; *H.M.C. Wells*, i, 222, 236, 240–3, 274–5, 281–3, 293, 295, 299–300, 303–4, 378, 415, 535, 538, 541–3; ii, 11, 22, 25–6.

[2] The one quarterly communar's roll extant for 1350 shows that only four canons, instead of the usual eight to twelve, made up the full three-monthly residence in this quarter.

fore the Salisbury residentiary body was never so large as that of Exeter, though it had a much less local character.

At Lincoln, Wells, and Salisbury, the investigation has shown that a good proportion of between a quarter and a third of the canons normally professed residence in the fourteenth century;[1] while at Exeter residentiaries formed about three-quarters of the whole body. This is in striking contrast to the practice in the late fifteenth and sixteenth centuries: by then a sharp fall in the number of residentiaries had taken place everywhere. At Hereford and St. Paul's this fall apparently took place in the middle or later years of the fourteenth century; at York there were rarely more than six or seven residentiaries from the beginning of the century.

(b) The Non-Resident Canons

The non-resident canons formed a very large and miscellaneous body of men. It is impossible, in the limited space available, to attempt any detailed analysis of the composition of this body, which in any case varied considerably at different chapters. But it may be interesting to notice a few examples, at certain of the richer cathedrals, of the proportion of non-residents who were royal clerks, *sublimes* or magnates, foreigners, scholars, clerks assisting their bishops in diocesan work, or resident in other ecclesiastical benefices. Generally the non-residents fall fairly naturally into groups of this kind.

The number of foreigners, especially cardinals, is in striking contrast at the beginning and end of the fourteenth century. Up to 1378, many of the richest dignities and prebends, particularly at Salisbury, Lincoln, and York, were held by non-resident cardinals provided by the Avignon papacy.[2] Professor Hamilton Thompson, in his detailed studies of the personnel of York chapter, has shown that, under Archbishop Corbridge (1300-4), eleven appointments of foreigners to York prebends as against three

---

[1] The recent researches of Mrs. H. Jenkins have shown that the same was true at Lichfield cathedral in the fourteenth century (Oxford B.Litt. thesis, 1956, pp. 60, 69, 71-87).

[2] See *L.S.*, ii, cxliv-vii, where Canon Wordsworth has collected evidence of the provision of cardinals to the three churches; C. Moor, 'Cardinals beneficed in Sarum Cathedral', in *W.A.M.*, l (1943), 136-48; R. E. G. Cole, 'Some Papal Provisions in the Cathedral Church of Lincoln, 1300-20', in *Associated Archit. Socs.' Repts.*, xxxiv (1918), 219-58.

Englishmen were recorded.[1] As a result the proportion of foreigners to Englishmen in the chapter on Archbishop Greenfield's accession in 1306 was one in three. It remained at about this figure throughout his pontificate.[2] But in the mid-fourteenth century, under Archbishop Melton, the provision of foreigners rose to as many as twenty-six out of fifty-one appointments entered in the archbishop's register.[3] A similar situation appears at Salisbury and Lincoln in the unpublished lists of non-resident canons drawn up by the clerks of the common fund, who were trying to levy the fines imposed by these chapters on canons non-resident without a papal dispensation. Only one such list, for 1320–1, has been discovered at Salisbury.[4] It shows that fourteen out of twenty-nine non-resident canons, that is, over a quarter of the whole chapter, were then foreigners. At Lincoln lists of canons *Nullo Modo Residentes* were entered annually in the accounts of the common fund:[5] beside each canon's name was written the amount of the seventh of the income of his prebend, payable by him as a fine for his non-residence, together with some abbreviated sign, evidently meant to guide the clerk engaged in levying the tax. Generally, in the early and middle years of the fourteenth century, about a quarter of the forty or so non-residents were foreigners, described in the lists as *Romanus* or *Cardinalis*: these nearly all had the sign 'pr' (*privilegia*) written by their names, indicating that they held a papal privilege exempting them from the seventh.

Then at the time of the Schism, the English government officially took the side of Urban VI, and the parliament at Gloucester in 1378 adhered with enthusiasm to the decision to confiscate all the English benefices of the French cardinals supporting Clement VII. Details collected by M. Perroy of the nature and value of the benefices surrendered by these cardinals in the following years illustrate the extent to which some of the most important English secular cathedral dignities, the deaneries of York and Salisbury, the treasurership of Salisbury, the chancellor-

---

[1] *V.C.H. Yorks.*, iii, 378.

[2] Introduction to *Reg. Greenfield*, i, xvii–xviii.

[3] *V.C.H. Yorks.*, iii, 378. Not all these aliens succeeded in obtaining installation, so the actual proportion of them in the chapter may not have been much greater than in the early fourteenth century.

[4] Liber Evidentiarum C., ff. 452a–454b.

[5] Muniments D. and C. Lincoln, Bj/2/4–10. Two of these lists, for 1304–5 and 1305–6, are transcribed below, Appendix I.

ship of Hereford, the archdeaconries of Exeter, Taunton, Berkshire, Dorset, Wells, and Leicester, together with rich prebends of Salisbury, Lincoln, York, and Wells had been in their hands.[1] Naturally Urban VI tried to substitute his Italian cardinals in place of the Frenchmen in these benefices. At first it looked as if the English government would acquiesce.[2] But its resistance gradually stiffened. In 1384 statistics furnished by an inquest into the number of benefices held by foreigners in English dioceses, show that foreign provisors, especially cardinals, were much fewer than they had been earlier in the century.[3] The results at the cathedrals can be plainly traced in records of the residence made by the principal dignitaries. At Lincoln in the early and middle-years of the fourteenth century there were rarely more than one or two of the four principal *personae* in residence. But in the 1390's, after the confiscation, all four *personae* were present together with the sub-dean and, usually, one or more of the archdeacons.[4] In 1432, at Bishop Gray's visitation, the chapter was still almost without a foreign element.[5] The Salisbury chapter acts, communar's accounts, and *fasti* reveal a similar situation. From 1297 to 1379 all six deans and four out of eight treasurers were non-resident aliens, mostly cardinals:[6] the only period in the century when all four principal dignitaries have been found in residence together was in the late 1390's. Then they all had English names.

A large proportion of non-residents holding the richest prebends at the cathedrals was made up of government officials. At York, especially, their preponderance in the chapter throughout the fourteenth century was overwhelming. It has been worked out in detail by Professor Hamilton Thompson.[7] He points out that the position of the royal clerks at York at this time was exceptional, because, from the late thirteenth century, nearly all of them were Yorkshiremen, who continued to take a strong interest in the business of the chapter and diocese while working in the king's service. This connexion between York and the government apparently arose mainly through the influence of Robert

[1] E. Perroy, *L'Angleterre et le grand schisme d'Occident*, pp. 59–62.
[2] *Ibid.*, pp. 272–3, 282–3.   [3] *Ibid.*, pp. 284–5.
[4] See below, Appendix I.   [5] *Lincoln Visitations*, i, 174.
[6] See Jones, *Fasti Sar.*, pp. 313–15, 344–5.
[7] In *The Medieval Chapter* (York Minster Tracts), pp. 12–15; *V.C.H. Yorks.*, iii, 378; Introduction to *Reg. Greenfield*, i, xviii.

Burnell, Edward I's chancellor, who, during his tenure of the archdeaconry of York, discovered the most prominent recruits for the chancery in young Yorkshiremen. As time went on, these held their chief preferments in the church of York. Men like William Greenfield and William Hambleton, who succeeded Burnell as chancellors, began their careers as Yorkshire clerks, and rose to be canons, and later deans or archbishops of York; and they continued Burnell's practice of introducing their fellow-countrymen and kinsmen to high offices in the king's service and in the church of York. The tradition seems to have been unbroken until Archbishop Scrope's rebellion in the early fifteenth century. After this, the importance of Yorkshiremen in the affairs of state diminished, and the royal clerks appointed to York prebends were supplied from outside.[1] Elsewhere many of the richer prebends were held by royal clerks, who may or may not have had local connexions. At Salisbury the fourteenth-century prebendaries of Shipton, Charminster and Bere, Bedwyn, Bedminster and Redcliffe, Blewbury, Horton, Lyme and Halstock, and Preston, were frequently said to have been appointed *per literas regias*;[2] many were civil servants well-known in the pages of Tout's *Chapters in Medieval Administrative History* and in the printed calendars of patent and close rolls. The Lincoln lists of *Nullo Modo Residentes* always included a good proportion of this sort of men.[3]

Perhaps some of the most interesting evidence for civil servants holding cathedral prebends is to be found in the bishop's returns of pluralists staying in their dioceses, compiled in 1366 as a result of Urban V's decree *Consueta*, and entered for Canterbury province in the register of Archbishop Langham. These have now been printed.[4] They show that by far the largest class of pluralists, at

[1] *The Medieval Chapter*, p. 15.

[2] See the lists in Jones, *Fasti Sar.*, pp. 350 *et seq.*

[3] E.g. see below, Appendix I. In the 1305–6 list there were John Droxford, the able wardrobe clerk, who later became bishop of Bath and Wells; the queen's treasurer; John Langton, chancellor of England, and bishop of Chichester from 1306; and James of Spain, Queen Eleanor's nephew, chamberlain of the exchequer. In 1320, James of Spain was also called upon to pay his fifth for non-residence at Salisbury, where he held the prebend of Lyme and Halstock (Liber Evidentiarum C., f. 453b).

[4] *Reg. Langham* (Canterbury and York Soc.), pp. 5–109; *Reg. Sudbury* (Canterbury and York Soc.), ii, 148–82; cf. A. H. Thompson, 'Pluralism in the Medieval Church; with notes on Pluralists in the diocese of Lincoln, 1366', in *Associated Archit. Socs.' Repts.*, xxxiv, 1–26; xxxv, 87–108, 199–242; xxxvi, 1–41.

least a fifth of the whole in two dioceses of London and Lincoln, were officials of the chancery, exchequer, privy seal, wardrobe, almonry, and clerks in personal attendance on the king, or attached to other members of the royal house. Together these men enjoyed nearly half the ecclesiastical revenues listed in the returns from the two dioceses;[1] and a good proportion came from cathedral dignities and prebends. William de Wykeham, keeper of the privy seal, was by far the mightiest pluralist in both lists. His benefices amounted to eight hundred and seventy-three pounds six shillings and eightpence a year; they included the archdeaconry of Lincoln, valued at three hundred and fifty pounds a year; the prebend of Sutton in Lincoln cathedral of two hundred and sixty marks; the prebend of Laughton at York of one hundred and ten marks; the prebend of Tottenhall at London of sixteen marks; the prebend of Fordington at Salisbury of twenty-five marks; and the provostry of Wells with a prebend of sixty-eight marks.[2] No other clerk in the lists had an income at all comparable with this. David de Wollore, who had served in the chancery for over forty years, and who was now the king's principal clerk, came next, with ecclesiastical revenues of two hundred and seventy pounds four shillings a year.[3] Other civil servants rarely received more than a hundred pounds a year from their benefices, while many had under thirty pounds in spite of their pluralism. Furthermore, it is interesting to find that the type of magnate pluralist, living in ease on the fruits of his many benefices, who had been common enough in the thirteenth and early fourteenth centuries,[4] was now almost unknown. There were doubtless some idlers, but pluralism, as practised on the grand scale in the thirteenth century, had been effectively checked. Most pluralists of 1366 were busy men, actively employed in government work or in the service of pope or bishop. They usually kept within the law, holding only one incompatible benefice (that is, a benefice with cure of souls), with other compatible cathedral or collegiate prebends.[5]

---

[1] See the analysis of the London returns by Professor C. Jenkins, *Reg. Sudbury*, ii, xxxvi–xli.

[2] *Reg. Sudbury*, pp. 164–5; *Associated Archit. Socs'. Repts.*, xxxvi, 31–4.

[3] *Ibid.*, pp. 26–30; *Reg. Sudbury*, ii, 166–7. Of this sum one hundred and sixteen marks were contributed by three prebends of York, London, and Lincoln.

[4] Cf. A. H. Thompson, *loc. cit.*, xxxiii, 49–59. Bogo de Clare was a striking example of this kind of pluralist in the last half of the thirteenth century.

[5] *Ibid.*, p. 59 *et seq.*

Scholars, apart from lawyers in official positions, seem to have been comparatively rare among non-resident pluralists of the mid-fourteenth century. In the 1366 returns for London diocese twenty-six clerks were described by academic titles, and between them received one thousand two hundred pounds eight shillings and elevenpence annually from ecclesiastical preferments; but the great majority of these were either qualified in law or engaged in its study.[1] There is not a single master of theology in the lists, and only one bachelor of theology, William Durant, canon of Hereford, with expectation of a dignity and prebend, whose benefices produced only twenty-three pounds six shillings and eightpence a year. The complaints of the University of Oxford in the last half of the fourteenth century that men of learning were unduly neglected in the distribution of ecclesiastical benefices, appears from the evidence of these returns to have had plenty of foundation. Moreover, at Salisbury in 1320, only one canon, Master John de Grave, prebendary of Major Pars Altaris, was definitely described in the list of non-residents as licensed to be absent for study without paying the fine for non-residence;[2] the Lincoln lists of *Nullo Modo Residentes* throughout the century rarely included more than one or two canons said to be exempt from payment of the seventh because they were 'in scholis'. On the other hand, certain chapters, particularly in the early years of the century, are known to have had a fair proportion of University masters and students among their canons. Simon of Ghent, bishop of Salisbury, 1297–1315, collated a group of distinguished theologians to Salisbury chapter: Walter Burdon, Roger Martival, and William de Bosco, all former chancellors of Oxford University; Henry de la Wyle, Richard of Winchester, John of Winchelsea, and James Berkeley.[3] Probably most became residentiary rather than non-resident canons. They might receive licences of absence for study for certain periods; but sometimes they would be able to make up their residence in the university vacations, and on the completion of their studies might set up house permanently in the cathedral close.

Other pluralists might prefer residence at another cathedral or on one of their other benefices. Two non-resident canons of

---

[1] *Reg. Sudbury*, ii, xli–iii.   [2] Liber Evidentiarum C., f. 454a.
[3] K. Edwards, 'Bishops and Learning during the Reign of Edward II', in C.Q.R., cxxxviii (1944), 72.

Wells, Nicholas de la Wyle and Robert de Luffenham, chose to
enter residence at Salisbury, where Nicholas held the precentorship and Robert the archdeaconry of Salisbury.[1] The career of
Nicholas Tingwick, canon of Salisbury, provides examples of
various reasons for non-residence. He was a student of theology or
canon law, and, in his youth received licences of absence for
study.[2] Then he became a doctor of medicine and was appointed
physician to Edward I.[3] He held two prebends in succession at
Salisbury,[4] and at one time acquired a house of residence in the
close there.[5] But in 1320 he was summoned before the chapter to
pay his fine for non-residence and in 1328 granted a lease of his
house.[6] The explanation seems to be that, after Edward I's death,
Nicholas preferred living at his rich rectory of Reculver in Canterbury diocese, to which Edward had presented him in 1306.[7] In
1324 he was physician to Henry of Eastry, prior of Christ Church,
Canterbury,[8] within easy riding distance of Reculver.

Naturally some non-resident canons were engaged in ecclesiastical work in the service of their bishop or archbishop, or of bishops
of other dioceses. By canon law, two canons of any cathedral
church, absent with the bishop or in his service, might receive the
fruits of their prebends as if resident, notwithstanding any contrary
custom of their chapter.[9] Similar provisions were included in the
statutes of most English secular cathedrals;[10] and it is clear from the

[1] In 1338 they sent proxies as non-residents to a general chapter at Wells
(*W.S.*, pp. 78–9).

[2] *Reg. S. de Gandavo*, pp. 848, 858, 871. He was then rector of Coleshill in
Salisbury diocese. For his benefaction to Oxford University, see A. G. Little,
'Grammar Schools of Oxford', in *E.H.R.*, vi, 152–3.

[3] *Ibid.*

[4] These were the prebends of Major Pars Altaris in 1309 and Bedwyn in
1312, to which he was appointed *per literas regias* (*Reg. S. de Gandavo*, pp. 708,
749, 792).

[5] K. Edwards, 'Houses of Salisbury Close', *loc. cit.*, p. 104.

[6] *Ibid.*; Liber Evidentiarum C., ff. 453a–454a.

[7] *C.P.R. 1301–7*, p. 461. This was during Winchelsea's suspension and exile.
The rectory was assessed at one hundred and thirteen pounds six shillings and
eightpence a year and there was already a perpetual vicar. I have to thank Dr.
Rose Graham for kindly sending me these references to Nicholas's career; cf.
'Sidelights on the Rectors and Parishioners of Reculver from the Register of
Archbishop Winchelsey', in *Archaeologia Cantiana*, lvii, 9–12.

[8] *Lit. Cant.*, i, 120. He died before 1354. (*Ibid.*, ii, 319.)

[9] *Corpus Iuris Canonici*, Decretal. Greg. IX, Lib. III, tit, iv, cc. vii, xv.

[10] E.g. *S.S.*, pp. 26–7; *Use Sarum*, i, 11, 259; *L.S.*, iii, 164; *C.S.*, p. 13.

fourteenth-century episcopal and capitular registers that the English bishops used their right of collating to cathedral prebends as a means of introducing members of their household to the chapter. In spite of the influence of king and pope, who usually secured the richest prebends for their nominees, the bishop was generally able to provide some economic support from the cathedral chapter for his more important diocesan assistants, and at the same time to gain through them some influence in the chapter body. At Wells, Bishop Droxford's treasurer, Thomas of Retford, became chancellor of the cathedral; and the bishop's chancellor, John Martel, obtained a prebend there.[1] John of Kempsey, chaplain and household steward of Richard de Swinfield, bishop of Hereford, was treasurer of Hereford cathedral;[2] John de Schalby, registrar of John Dalderby, bishop of Lincoln, was a canon and prebendary of Lincoln;[3] and Ralph de Querendon, Bishop Ghent's sequestrator-general and a clerk of his consistory court, obtained a prebend and the subdeanery at Salisbury.[4] These men might continue in their bishop's service for some years after their collation to cathedral prebends; then, in their old age or after their bishop's death, they often retired to canonical houses of residence in the cathedral close. Thus Ralph de Querendon entered residence at Salisbury after Bishop Ghent's death; and John de Schalby, after many years of active life as bishop's registrar, became a residentiary at Lincoln in 1308, where he made good use of his knowledge of ecclesiastical archives in compiling a valuable collection of Lincoln cathedral customs.[5] Evidently fourteenth-century bishops were able to claim exemption from non-residence fines for considerably more canons in their service than the two or three allowed to them by statute. The Lincoln lists of *Nullo Modo Residentes* show that in most years from five to eight non-resident canons were exempted from paying their seventh on grounds that they were in attendance on the bishop (*cum episcopo*).[6]

What connexions, if any, did these different groups of non-resident canon have with their cathedrals and with the residentiary

---

[1] *Reg. Drokensford*, pp. 42, 59, 109, 115–16.

[2] *Reg. Swinfield*, pp. 475–6; *Roll of Household Expenses of Richard de Swinfield*, p. lxxxii.

[3] *Reg. Antiquissimum Lincoln*, i, xxx.

[4] *Reg. S. de Gandavo*, pp. 794, 912.

[5] *Reg. Antiquissimum Lincoln*, i, xxx–xxxiii.   [6] See below, Appendix I.

body there, apart from drawing the revenues of their prebends, and paying or resisting payment of their fines for non-residence? At some French cathedrals, such as Chartres and Bayeux, the medieval statutes contained directions for holding two or three general chapters at fixed dates every year.[1] These chapters would last for two or three days: some were devoted to temporal business; others to ecclesiastical discipline; and all non-resident canons living in the kingdom had to attend them in person or send a proxy. But for the English secular chapters in the middle ages, few precise regulations of this kind survive. It was not until 1560, in obedience to injunctions of Queen Elizabeth, that Salisbury chapter adopted the custom of holding Pentecostal Chapters for the discussion of matters of general interest, such as the taxation of the prebends for repairs of the fabric, the granting of leases or modifications of the cathedral statutes. The canonical house called 'Leadenhall' was then set aside for the non-resident canons, who were expected to stay in the close for eight days over Whitsun.[2]

In the middle ages the custom at most English secular cathedrals was to summon extraordinary general chapters of all canons living in the kingdom, whenever business arose in which it seemed likely that they could help.[3] It is clear from the printed bishops' registers that such chapters were summoned as a matter of course for elections of bishops and deans, and for episcopal and archiepiscopal visitations:[4] a few non-residents, including certain of the busiest of the king's clerks,[5] would attend in person; others sent proctors; the remainder, usually a minority, who took no notice of the summons, were pronounced contumacious, and ordered to

---

[1] At Chartres, in addition to extraordinary general chapters which could be summoned for special business at any time, there were always two ordinary general chapters a year: the first on the feast of the Purification, when matters of ecclesiastical discipline, revision of ceremonies and liturgy, and other spiritual business were debated; the second on the feast of St. John the Baptist, which was reserved chiefly for temporal interests and the appointment of officials (Amiet, *op. cit.*, pp. 172–7). Similar general chapters were held regularly at Bayeux on the morrow of the Purification, and on the feast of St. Raven and St. Rasiphe (24 February) (Deslandes, *op. cit.*, p. 179).

[2] See *V.C.H. Wilts.*, iii, 187–8; Jones, *Fasti Sar.*, ii, 256–7.

[3] Cf. *L.S.*, iii, 285, 321.

[4] E.g. *Reg. Greenfield*, i, 44–50; *Lincoln Visitations*, i, 131; *Reg. Rede*, ii, 366–7.

[5] E.g. John Sandall, chancellor of England, placed the great seal in commission when he went as a canon to Lincoln in 1315 to take part in the election of a dean (*C.C.R.*, 1313–18, p. 314).

be punished for neglect of duty. But records of the more interesting sort of general chapters, to which non-residents were summoned to take part in deliberations, not merely to record a vote or to show their titles to the bishop, are usually contained only in the chapter acts, which have been comparatively little used by historians. It has usually been supposed that in the later middle ages, as the distinction between the two bodies of residentiary and non-resident canons became clearer, the residentiaries took over more and more completely the conduct of chapter business, and gradually almost ceased to summon the non-residents to share in their deliberations; while the non-residents, even when summoned, rarely took the trouble to attend in person.

Yet Canon Wordsworth, in compiling a list of general chapters held at Lincoln cathedral between 1258 and 1890, found that these were much more frequent, particularly in the thirteenth and fourteenth centuries, than had previously been thought, and that a good proportion of non-resident canons attended them.[1] Similar evidence is available in the unpublished chapter act books at Salisbury, and in the *acta* of Wells chapter calendared in the Reports of the Historical Manuscript Commission. It is not possible to draw up a full list of general chapters held at Wells and Salisbury, for the records are very incomplete; but it is interesting to see the kind of business discussed and the proportion of non-residents attending.

On 29th July 1387, for instance, there were present in chapter at Salisbury as many as twenty-two canons in person, five more by sufficient proxies, and three by insufficient proxies.[2] This was an especially important general chapter lasting for over a week: the agenda included discussion of the plan to promote the canonization of the chapter's founder, St. Osmund; of the dangerous state of discord between bishop and chapter, which had continued for eight years; and of the threatened collapse of the tower and spire. As a result the canons unanimously agreed to a tax of a seventh on the incomes of their prebends to meet the situation.[3]

At Wells also a number of general or 'special' chapters in the thirteenth and fourteenth centuries ended in grants from all prebendal incomes to the common expenses.[4] But the chapter of Wells apparently valued not only the consent to taxation of its

[1] *L.S.*, ii, cciv–xiv.   [2] Reg. Coman, f. 69.   [3] *Ibid.*, ff. 76–7.
[4] E.g. *H.M.C. Wells*, i, 180–1; *W.S.*, pp. 78–9, 129–30.

non-resident members, but also their counsel and assent in difficult business. In 1319, when a speedy decision had to be reached about the chapter's attitude to a threatened visitation by Bishop Drox-ford, a *quorum* of residentiaries immediately decreed that all residentiaries of that and the previous year should be summoned to take counsel for the defence of the church; and that canons at a distance should be asked to give their opinion in writing.[1] This order has sometimes been quoted as illustrating the cleavage at Wells between the two bodies of resident and non-resident canons.[2] But it also suggests co-operation between them: the small inner chapter was evidently anxious to have the considered opinions of the non-residents, though shortness of time made it impossible for them to be present at the discussions. In 1322–3 the residentiaries at Wells prepared a long *agenda* of thirteen articles to be discussed in a special chapter with the non-residents. These articles ranged from the administration of the cathedral manors and the state of the fabric fund to problems of the lights in choir; the church's sanitation; the proposed building of vicars' houses, and the claim of a non-resident cardinal's chaplain to share in distributions of the common fund. All but nine of the canons summoned were said to be present at the debates which followed.[3]

General chapters, then, were apparently a useful way of keeping the large body of non-resident canons informed of the state of affairs at the cathedral, of obtaining their consent to taxation, and their support and advice in difficult decisions. Unfortunately the records are not full enough to judge whether the non-residents took much part in the actual deliberations. Probably the residentiaries, who were on the spot and familiar with the details of the business and procedure, would lead the discussions, and have fairly complete control of the execution of the decisions.

At the same time some residentiary bodies seem to have been ready to welcome non-resident canons at their small ordinary chapters, whenever non-residents happened to be passing through the cathedral city. At Salisbury the names of one or two non-resident canons were sometimes entered as witnesses to chapter acts, while occasional payments of commons were made to these same canons for attending cathedral services.

Canons assisting the bishop in his diocese, with some of the

[1] *H.M.C. Wells*, i, 190.   [2] A. H. Thompson, *Cathedral Churches*, p. 173.
[3] *H.M.C. Wells*, i, 180–2.

H

university masters and students, were usually among those non-residents who found it easiest to keep in touch with their cathedral. There was in any case frequent interchange of personnel between these two groups of non-residents and the residentiary body. At St. Paul's canons working in government offices at Westminster were also in a very convenient position to give help and advice; and most chapters seem to have recognized that those of their canons who held official positions in the government or who were lawyers in the royal or archiepiscopal courts might be very useful members of their societies. In 1392 John de Bere, dean of the royal chapel, and a non-resident canon of Salisbury, was using his influence, evidently at the request of the residentiaries, to obtain a royal licence, which they had been refused, for their proctor to go to Rome.[1] The chapter of Wells in the early fourteenth century appealed to one of their canons, who was dean of the archbishop's court of the Arches, for help against the demands of a papal nuncio, and at the same time thanked the canon for past services.[2] Non-resident French and Italian cardinals, who could rarely visit their English cathedrals, received long letters from the chapters asking them to promote their cathedral's business at the Roman court.

Thus, although the non-resident canons contributed little to the main purpose of the cathedral church, the conduct of its services, they could often give practical help in legal or other temporal business. Moreover, many of the non-residents were distinguished men in church and state. At a time when residentiary bodies were growing smaller, and when their interests were becoming more closely centred at the cathedral close and diocese, contacts with such men in London, at the Roman curia, at universities, or at other cathedral churches, might well help to counteract tendencies to exclusiveness and narrowness of outlook at the local chapters.

There was inevitably some friction between the two bodies of resident and non-resident canons at the English chapters in the fourteenth century. Non-residents of Lichfield and Salisbury resisted the levying of fifths from their prebends[3] and at a number of churches, particularly St. Paul's, protested against the increasing

---

[1] Reg. Dunham, f. 203.   [2] *H.M.C. Wells*, i, 237.
[3] H. Jenkins, *op. cit.*, p. 85; S. Overton, Ralph Erghum, Bishop of Salisbury (B.Litt., thesis, Oxford, 1960), p. 141.

expense of becoming a residentiary. The most serious trouble was apparently at St. Paul's, where Professor Brooke has traced in the records indications of hostility between stagiaries and non-residents during the greater part of the century.[1] He thinks the reason for the disputes between them was that the second main problem of canonical residence, that of residentiaries who refused to reside, was becoming acute. He writes that by the end of the fourteenth century conditions similar to those at many cathedral churches in the sixteenth and seventeenth centuries may already have developed, with some non-resident canons attending regularly in the cathedral in their retirement without being able to afford the extravagance of a stagiaryship, while rich stagiaries, having performed their probationary greater residence, were absent on government service or other affairs.[2]

At London, however, conditions were probably exceptional. There were both more opportunities for contact between the two bodies of canons and a more rigid distinction between them. Elsewhere, except perhaps at York, the solution found for the non-residence problem of the twelfth century, of increasing the emoluments of canons who were willing to profess residence while recognizing the right of others to be non-resident, still seems to have been working fairly well. At Salisbury, Lichfield, and Lincoln the records suggest that in the fourteenth century the residentiaries normally lived in the cathedral close for the greater part of the year, attending services and dealing with chapter business, while the non-residents were occasional but not unwelcome visitors. The residentiary body was smaller at most English chapters than it had been in the thirteenth century and more clearly divided from the non-residents. Yet a larger proportion of canons was apparently present, particularly at cathedrals in the south and west of England, than has generally been supposed. With the help of a large staff of *ministri inferiores*, greater in numbers than at any other period, they can have had little difficulty in maintaining the work of the cathedral.

The fourteenth century is an interesting transition period in the history of canonical residence, which has sometimes been regarded too much in the light of later developments. It contained the germs of the much attacked system of residence which

[1] C. N. L. Brooke in *Hist. St. Paul's Cathedral*, pp. 86–90.
[2] *Ibid.*, p. 41.

developed in the sixteenth and seventeenth centuries, when the residentiaries formed a small privileged oligarchy, whose numbers were strictly limited by statutes. There were considerable differences at different cathedrals. But the most usual reason for non-residence in the fourteenth century was still that many canons had work to do outside the cathedral and had been given cathedral prebends to support them while doing it. They were prepared to give up their share of the common fund in order to do it. The idea that a small exclusive body of residentiaries was trying to prevent other canons from joining it and sharing its revenues apparently had little foundation at most English churches at this time. Even at St. Paul's and York, where the excessive expense of entering residence has given some colour to this charge, the financial conditions of the entry were made very much easier at the end of the century.

CHAPTER II

THE BISHOP IN HIS CATHEDRAL CHURCH

'There are by right in one cathedral church only the bishop and the chapter who make one body, of which body the bishop is the head and the chapter are the members. Therefore to argue that the dean is another head is to argue two heads in one body, which is like a monster, and prejudicial to the bishop.' [1]

This reasoning was used by Lincoln canons of the early fourteenth century who were trying to prevent their dean, Roger Martival, from exercising jurisdiction independently of the chapter. It represents a curious mixture of tradition and of extreme medieval pretensions of the chapters. In early days when the bishop had lived a common life with his cathedral clergy he had been their only head. The metaphor of bishop and chapter as head and members of one body was appropriate then and continued to be common throughout the middle ages and later, long after the rise of the dean or some other official had given the chapters a second head concerned with the home government of the cathedral in the bishop's absence. Originally the rise of the dean had been a sign of the chapter's growing independence of their bishop. But the canons of Lincoln of 1313 were not weary of this independence as their argument might at first sight suggest. In attacking their dean they had no idea of reverting to the old state of subordination to their bishop, but were really asserting their independence of both. They seem to have wanted not one head but no head at all, for they maintained in the same plea that the chapter was the fount of episcopal jurisdiction: in a vacancy of the see such jurisdiction returned to the chapter as to its source, and after enthronement no bishop could exercise it without the chapter's consent and counsel. This view had no historical foundation, either in the bishop's election, which originally was *a clero et populo*, or in the holding of property by bishop and chapter.[2] Possibly the Lincoln canons never ex-

---

[1] *L.S.*, ii, lxxvii.
[2] Cf. the views of Bracton on the separate holding of property by bishop and chapter (*De Legibus et Consuetudinibus Angliae*, ed. G. E. Woodbine, iv, 373;

pected their arguments to be taken seriously. Yet these arguments well illustrate the difficulties of the relations of bishop and chapter in the thirteenth and fourteenth centuries. In all parts of Europe cathedral chapters were challenging the claims of their bishops to exercise authority over them, claiming exemption from their visitations, and refusing them the right to sit in chapter; in 1269 the registrar of the archbishop of Rheims informed his lord that, 'whoever is archbishop of Rheims has two principal adversaries: the chapter of Rheims and the citizens'.[1] The legal position was still largely undefined.

Originally the cathedral church was the bishop's church, taking its name from his *cathedra* or throne. In early times he celebrated in it regularly, assisted by his cathedral clergy, who also formed a kind of council for the bishop, advising and helping him in the administration of his diocese, and carrying on the work of the diocese with the help of neighbouring bishops during a vacancy of the see.[2] But gradually the bishop was more and more drawn away from his cathedral city, both on affairs of state and through the increasing duties of looking after a large diocese. During his long absences there began to develop some sort of home government among the cathedral clergy. The archdeacon or provost, and later in northern France the dean, came to be recognized as their immediate head; various other officers were instituted. By the ninth or tenth centuries a division of the common goods of the church had been made between bishop and chapter in many parts of Europe.[3] The chapter could thus control its own affairs and

---

Makower, *Const. Hist. of the Church of England*, p. 301, n. 16). The canons of Lincoln quote Hostiensis as their authority. But Maitland, who admits that there are in Hostiensis' *Summa* several sentences favourable to the canons' contention, doubts very much that the great lawyer would have committed himself to the statement making the chapter the fount of the bishop's jurisdiction (letter quoted in *L.S.*, ii, lxxvi–vii n.).

[1] 'Sciat dominus quod quicumque est remensis archiepiscopus duos habet principales adversarios, viz. capitulum remense et cives' (*Archives legislatives de la ville de Reims*, ed. P. Varin, i, 30; cf. 18 n.).

[2] For the work of the chapters during this early period, see H. Leclercq in *Dict. d'Archéologie Chrétienne et de Liturgie*, s.v. Chapitre; P. Fournier, *Les Officialités*, pp. xvii–xviii, xxv.

[3] Cf. P. Viollet, *Hist. des Institutions de la France*, i, 379. In England the separation seems sometimes to have been made rather later. But the *familia* at Christ Church, Canterbury, had a small separate endowment as early as 799,

property without regard to the bishop's absence, or to the complications of royal claims to administer the temporalities on the bishop's death. Increasingly it began to assume the position of an independent corporation. It became wealthy and privileged, receiving many fresh endowments and grants of liberties from king, pope, and magnates. The reforming papacy of the eleventh century saw in the growing powers of the chapters a means of establishing what it called 'free canonical elections' to bishoprics: in the twelfth century cathedral chapters frequently took the place of the whole clergy and people as the electoral body; the decree of the fourth Lateran Council of 1215, which recognized them as having the sole right to elect the bishop, marked in some ways the peak of the chapters' powers in relation to the bishop.[1]

Yet in point of fact the popes of the late twelfth and thirteenth centuries were already using these so-called 'free' elections to influence the chapter in favour of their own nominees. Their intervention in disputed elections sometimes appears as an anticipation of the later practice of provision,[2] even though, as Professor Barraclough points out, the initiative in bringing these cases before the pope was usually taken by the parties concerned.[3] The great development of the practice of papal provision in the thirteenth and early fourteenth centuries arose largely from different causes; it was bound up with the increasing centralization of the church, and with the financial policy of the papacy.[4] In England by the mid-fourteenth century it had become the normal method of appointing to bishoprics and here usually represented a compromise between the claims of royal and papal candidates. Though the theory of episcopal election by the chapters continued to be quoted and formally observed, this had ceased to have any practical value. But although the English chapters were not powerful enough to enforce their rights against king and pope, they con-

---

and the canons of St. Paul's from about 867 (M. Deanesly in *Essays to Tout*, pp. 10–13; J. A. Robinson in *J.T.S.*, xxvii, 235–8; E. John in *J.E.H.*, vi, 144–5).

[1] For the growth of the chapters' electoral powers in France from the ninth to the early thirteenth century, see Imbart de la Tour, *Les Elections Episcopales de France du ixe au xiie siècle*.

[2] Cf. the large number of papal interventions in episcopal elections listed in N. Valois, *Guillaume d'Auvergne*, pp. 12–13; M. Gibbs and J. Lang, *Bishops and Reform, 1215–1272*, pp. 72–83.

[3] G. Barraclough, 'The Making of a Bishop in the Middle Ages', in *Catholic Hist. Rev.*, xix, 296 *et seq.*   [4] Cf. *ibid.*, p. 314.

tinued to claim increasing independence of their bishops. The residentiary canons, who now had few diocesan duties, found some of their chief interests in legal and constitutional questions concerning their own rights and privileges. They were so sensitive of these rights and privileges that bishops usually found it advisable to stay away from their cathedral cities as much as possible. The dean and chapter came to be regarded as the rulers of a kind of autonomous ecclesiastical republic within the diocese.

Yet in spite of the growing detachment, both moral and material, of the chapter from the bishop and diocese, certain of the old links remained. During a vacancy of the see the chapter still had definite functions and responsibilities. In England in the southern province the archbishop of Canterbury in the course of the thirteenth century had assumed rights of episcopal jurisdiction in the vacant sees which may formerly have been exercised by the chapters.[1] But as late as the reign of Edward II the four chapters of Salisbury, Lincoln, London, and Exeter took over fresh responsibility for episcopal property when they made fine with the king to have custody of the temporalities of the vacant bishoprics, giving as their reason the many losses suffered by their churches in time past through the waste and destruction of the royal escheators and keepers.[2] Once the see had again been filled the consent of the chapter remained necessary throughout the later middle ages for certain episcopal acts, such as the alienation of ecclesiastical property, changes in the state of benefices, or the grant of important privileges.[3] The cathedral church was still the mother church of all the churches in the diocese: at special times in the year the clergy and laity of the diocese were supposed to visit it.[4] In some ways it was a centre of diocesan government, for

[1] Cf. I. J. Churchill, *Canterbury Administration*, i, 161 *et seq*. These rights of the archbishop were apparently essentially English rights not exercised by metropolitans on the continent. They were gained for the metropolitan see of York by Archbishop Wickwane later in the thirteenth century (R. Brentano, *York Metropolitan Jurisdiction 1279–96*, Camb., 1959, pp. 19–22, 175).

[2] *C.F.R.*, *1307–19*, pp. 272, 348–9; *ibid.*, *1319–27*, pp. 38–9; cf. 425–6. The compositions at the first three churches were intended to be permanent, but that at Exeter was only for the vacancy following the death of Bishop Walter of Stapleton.

[3] Cf. Hostiensis *Summa Aurea*, cc. 902–7; Hinschius, *Kirchenrecht*, ii, 153–61; Fournier, *Les Officialités*, pp. xxiii–iv.

[4] The great occasion of the year was Whitsun when they came in processions to lay their pentecostal offerings on the high altar (see e.g. *S.S.*, p. 207 n.). For

a part of it was usually reserved for the holding of the bishop's consistory court.[1] A special grievance of York chapter against Archbishop Neville was that, from 1384 to 1388, during his long dispute with Beverley chapter, he caused his official's court to be removed from York to Beverley, which thus became the capital of the diocese for the time being.[2] In addition the bishop usually summoned his diocesan synod to meet in the cathedral church; he might hold ordinations there; and the chapter was frequently the guardian of important diocesan records and treasures.

Clearly, therefore, the relations of bishop and chapter in the later middle ages were complicated, and there were many reasons for uncertainty and friction about their respective rights and jurisdiction. For present purposes the enquiry will be limited to discussion of two main aspects of the problem: the bishop's place in the choir and chapter of his cathedral church; and the extent of his jurisdiction over the cathedral clergy and their estates.

1. THE BISHOP IN CHOIR AND CHAPTER

At the secular cathedrals in the later middle ages a broad distinction can generally be drawn between the position of the bishop in the choir of his cathedral church and in its chapter house. This was natural, for it was obviously much easier for a privileged chapter to put restrictions on its bishop's activities in the stronghold of its separate organization than in his own church. The cathedral church was the bishop's spouse, to which he was united by a marriage which only death or a special dispensation from the pope could dissolve. No English chapter, therefore, attempted to deny the bishop's headship and pre-eminent dignity in choir, although the strictly defined customs of the church and a number of practical limitations prevented his power there from being absolute.

The most elaborate ceremonial was reserved for the three special occasions when the bishop came to his cathedral church in

other similar customs, see *H.M.C. Ninth Rept.*, App. i, 53; Harl. MS., 1027, f. 29b.

[1] At Salisbury this was to the south-west of the porch, with the plumbery or paradise on its east and the cloister on its south (*Salisbury Ceremonies*, facing p. 72).

[2] See the account of this dispute by A. H. Thompson, *The Medieval Chapter* (York Minster Hist. Tracts), p. 11.

state: for his enthronement, on his first arrival at visitation, and on his return from parts beyond the sea.[1] At such times the cathedral bells were tolled, and the bishop was met by the whole choir in silk copes at the west door of the church, where he was censed and sprinkled with holy water by the principal dignitary, and then led in procession to the high altar. At an enthronement the procession might go further to meet him, to the close gates or the road. Much store was laid by medieval bishops on the custom of the *reverencialia* or tolling of the bells on their arrival at the cathedral. At St. Paul's, where there was comparatively little friction between bishop and chapter, it was agreed that this should be done whenever the bishop attended the church.[2] But Lincoln chapter allowed it only when the bishop had been absent for more than a quarter of a year.[3] At Salisbury there was a long struggle on the subject. In 1392 Bishop John Waltham obtained the right of having the cathedral bells tolled at his coming and going whenever he pleased, provided he gave due notice to the dean or his *locum tenens*; but his successors might only have it at stated times.[4]

Special honour was shown to the bishop whenever he was present in choir. If another were officiating, the bishop was always to be asked to give the blessing at matins, to say *Confiteor* at prime, compline, and mass, and the collect at evensong, and to give absolution.[5] When the bishop officiated the precentor intoned all chants begun by him; the chancellor ministered the legend to him, and the treasurer the collect.[6] The bishop was always censed first when the choir was censed, and sprinkled with holy water first. He kissed the gospels first, and received the kiss of peace first at mass.[7] The cathedral clergy bowed to him whenever entering,

[1] *L.S.*, ii, 273; iii, 273–4; *R.S.S.P.*, p. 11. Detailed accounts of a bishop's enthronement are given in *Salisbury Ceremonies*, pp. 104–9; Reg. Dunham, ff. 80–5; Reg. Holme, ff. 44–5; *W.S.*, pp. 91–2; *L.S.*, iii, 273–4, 553–5; *Reg. Courtenay* (Hereford), pp. 4–5. Cf. *Reg. Grandisson*, i, 95.
[2] *R.S.S.P.*, p. 11.
[3] *L.S.*, i, 273. The *Novum Registrum* added that the tolling of the bells was also usual at Lincoln on the bishop's arrival at the church to celebrate orders or to consecrate chrism (*ibid.*, iii, 274).   [4] *S.S.*, pp. 300–1.
[5] E.g. *Use Sarum*, i, 46–7, 50, 65, 117; *W.S.*, p. 18; *R.S.S.P.*, pp. 12, 80; *L.S.*, iii, 276; *Monasticon*, VI, iii, 1260; *Ordinale Exon.*, i, 28.
[6] *Use Sarum*, i, 113; *W.S.*, pp. 45, 55; *L.S.*, i, 274, 284; ii, 17, 95; iii, 275, 298, 300. At St. Paul's it was the chancellor who ministered the collect or chapter to the bishop (*R.S.S.P.*, p. 13).
[7] *Ibid.*, p. 12; *W.S.*, p. 10; *L.S.*, i, 370; ii, 26–7.

leaving or crossing the choir. In some churches they apparently did not always bow to the dean in the bishop's presence;[1] while at St. Paul's and Lincoln the bishop might, if he so wished, sit in the dean's stall in choir instead of in his throne, thus forcing the dean to perform his duties from the *cantoris* side of the choir.[2] But at Salisbury the bishop was content to sit in his prebendal stall of Potterne when he did not use his throne;[3] and at both Salisbury and Wells the clergy were ordered to bow to the bishop only if they entered from the east end of the choir, and to the dean if they entered from the west.[4]

Every cathedral had its special feast days when the bishop was expected to take the principal part, celebrating at the high altar and walking in procession in mitre and with pastoral staff, with the two principal dignitaries on his right and left.[5] The making of the chrism and blessing of the holy oils, supplied by the cathedral to all the churches of the diocese, were, if possible, to be performed by him in person.[6] He sprinkled the ashes on Ash Wednesday and ejected the penitents from the church, assisted by the archdeacon of the city. Then on Maundy Thursday he received them back, and the whole choir was invited to share his Maundy loving cup.[7] In the bishop's absence the dean or senior person present would normally take his place.[8] At other times the bishop, in spite of his dignity, had no legal right to celebrate out of his turn or to preach without permission from the precentor or chancellor, to whom the ordering of the services belonged. If he expressed a wish to officiate the turns of the others might give way to him; but such requests, if frequent, might lead to conflict.[9]

[1] E.g. at Lichfield and Lincoln (*Monasticon*, VI, iii, 1259; *L.S.*, ii, 150).

[2] *R.S.S.P.*, pp. 12–13, 80; *L.S.*, i, 274, 368; iii, 276.

[3] Jones, *Fasti Sar.*, p. 206 n.   [4] *Use Sarum*, i, 14; *W.S.*, p. 2.

[5] See *L.S.*, i, 273, 281; ii, 17, 62, 92–3; iii, 283; *Use Sarum*, i, 3; *Ordinale Exon.*, i, 3; *R.S.S.P.*, pp. 11, 182.

[6] E.g. *Use Sarum*, i, 201–5; *W.S.*, pp. 43–4, 105–8.

[7] *Salisbury Ceremonies*, pp. 60–4, 68–72, 80–1; *Use Sarum*, i, 138, 143–4; *W.S.*, p. 104; *L.S.*, ii, 92.

[8] At Salisbury, however, the bishop's vicar choral apparently had certain rights. In 1381 the chapter decided that the benediction and sprinkling of the holy water on Sundays belonged in the bishop's absence to his vicar choral (Reg. Dunham, f. 59).

[9] E.g. The St. Paul's chapter thought it necessary to declare that when the bishop celebrated out of his turn, the hebdomadary canon should still receive the oblations (*R.S.S.P.*, pp. 12, 185–6).

Certain chapters might pay daily commons to their bishop, as to any other member of the cathedral body, when he attended the cathedral services. Sometimes his share was that of a simple canon; sometimes he had the double commons of the dignitaries; and sometimes more than the dignitaries.[1] Salisbury chapter, always suspicious of its bishop, declared in 1355 that Bishop Wyville was trying to take an unfair share of its common goods by his practice of residing and attending the services.[2] Yet the communar account rolls extant at Salisbury for the fourteenth and fifteenth centuries show that normally the canons had little cause to worry on this account. In most years the bishop received no commons at all: when he did, the sums paid to him amounted to little more than sixpence or twelve pence a quarter, representing a stay of only one or two days at the cathedral.[3]

English medieval bishops, indeed, seem rarely to have been present at their cathedrals, even for the ceremonies and feasts in which they had the right and duty to take the leading part. Simon of Ghent, bishop of Salisbury from 1297–1315, is only known to have been in Salisbury for one Christmas and five Easters during the eighteen years of his episcopate.[4] Richard of Gravesend, bishop of Lincoln, 1258–79, who always maintained excellent relations with his chapter, spent Easter at Lincoln in 1265 and 1270; possibly also in 1264 and 1269, and was probably there for the Christmas of 1272.[5] Of the two fourteenth-century bishops of Exeter who spent vast sums on their cathedral fabric, Bishop Stapleton, in an episcopate of twenty years, spent only six Easters in Exeter; Bishop Grandisson in more than forty years apparently never stayed there for one of the great feasts, although he may have occasionally come in for the cathedral services from one of the

[1] See e.g. *H.M.C. Wells*, i, 60; ii, 6, 23, 27, 34, 40, 44, 49, 60, 66 *et seq.*; Bannister, *Cathedral Church of Hereford*, p. 159 n.; *Hereford Charters*, p. ix; *Monasticon*, VI, iii, 1260.

[2] Reg. Corffe, f. 111. Salisbury was one of the chapters which allowed only the single commons of a simple canon to its bishop, presumably because he drew his commons, not as bishop, but as prebendary of Potterne.

[3] Commons paid to the bishop are recorded in seven out of the nineteen extant communar rolls for the fourteenth century, and in others for the fifteenth century. The highest sum he is ever said to receive in these rolls is five shillings and fourpence for the quarter January to March, 1410.

[4] A. H. Thompson, Review of *Reg. S. de Gandavo* in *E.H.R.*, li (1936), 320. A full itinerary of Bishop Simon is available in his register.

[5] *Rot. Gravesend*, p. xv.

country houses where he usually resided.[1] The very full itinerary of Simon of Sudbury, bishop of London, gives a long list of dates when he was in London, but although these include eight Easters he is never known to have been there at Christmas. He may have attended two or three feasts of St. Erkenwald and three or perhaps six feasts of St. Paul, the importance of which was stressed by St. Paul's customs.[2]

The need for constant travelling in order to supervise a large diocese, together with political work, naturally made it impossible for the bishops to attend often at their cathedral churches, but motives of prudence also dictated that they should prefer to stay at their manor houses in the country districts rather than risk conflict with the dean and chapter in their cathedral cities. When they did not observe this customary precaution, cathedral dignitaries might easily forget the honour due to their bishop in choir. In the twelfth century, when their reactions were possibly more violent than they would have been in similar circumstances in the later middle ages, Roger de Howden told how the canons of York locked the archbishop's stall in choir and the door which led into the nave from his palace, and stopped the cathedral services, when they disagreed with him on the appointment of a dean.[3] On another occasion in 1189 the treasurer of York cathedral ordered the tapers in the church to be extinguished and so put an end to vespers, because Archbishop Geoffrey had come late to the service and had insisted on beginning it again.[4]

Some of the most interesting constitutional differences at the cathedrals are to be found in the varying positions accorded to the bishop in chapter. Canonists are generally agreed that the bishop had the right to summon the chapter and to preside over it, if he wished to ask its advice on affairs of the bishopric; for in such a case the chapter would assemble in its ancient capacity as the bishop's council or senate, not as a separate corporation.[5] Similarly the bishop would naturally preside in chapter during his visitations, provided he could establish his claim to visit. But he had no legal claim to be consulted about the holding of chapter meetings at which the dean and chapter proposed to order their own

[1] *E.H.R.*, li, 320.   [2] *Reg. Sudbury*, ii, 144–7.
[3] *Chronica R. de Houedene*, iii, 223.
[4] *Ibid.*, pp. 31–2.
[5] Hinschius, *Kirchenrecht*, ii, 128.

affairs.[1] The only way in which he could gain admission to these meetings was through the particular custom of different churches. Moreover, even if he were allowed to attend some meetings, it was often very uncertain whether he should then assume the presidency of the chapter, or take a subordinate seat below the dean or provost.[2]

In England the bishop's right to sit in chapter seems to have been less restricted than in some of the great continental churches. At Chartres the bishop was not allowed to enter the chapter house on any pretext: when business touching his prerogatives was debated there, even canons of Chartres holding office under him, such as his vicar general or official, were ordered to withdraw.[3] At Utrecht he had no voice in chapter, even if he were a canon with a prebend, though he was bound to come to chapter, when summoned by the dean or president.[4] The practice at English cathedrals seems to have approximated more or less to that in Norman cathedrals, where, at Rouen and Bayeux, the bishop apparently kept the right to preside in chapter in the middle ages.[5] But even among the different English chapters custom varied considerably. York was apparently the only English secular cathedral which denied to its bishop all statutory right to sit in chapter. Its earliest known customs declared, 'They say that in the church he [the dean] is greater than anyone after the archbishop, and in chapter he is greater than all.'[6] At Exeter, on the other hand, it was ordained that the bishop was head in chapter;[7] and both the Lincoln Black Book and the St. Paul's code of statutes laid down, 'It belongs to the bishop's dignity to have pre-eminence in honour shown to him in choir, in chapter, and in all places, above the dean and above all the parsons and canons of the church.'[8] The

---

[1] Hinschius, *Kirchenrecht*, p. 127; Bouix, *Tractatus de Capitulis*, p. 70; Fournier *Les Officialités*, p. xxiv.

[2] Cf. Thomassin, *Dictionnaire de Discipline ecclésiastique*, c. 404; Hinschius, ii, 127–8; Fournier, pp. xxiv–v.

[3] Amiet, *op. cit.*, p. 168.

[4] *Het Rechtsboek Utrecht*, p. 6. For the custom in some other continental churches, see Hinschius, ii, 127.

[5] Cf. Pommeraye, *op. cit.*, p. 189; Deslandes, *op. cit.*, p. 114.

[6] *L.S.*, ii, 93.   [7] Harl. MS. 1027, f. 3b.

[8] *L.S.*, i, 273; cf. *ibid.*, iii, 273. The St. Paul's form is slightly different: 'Dignitas Episcopi est in Choro, Capitulo et in omnibus locis supra omnes Canonicos et Ecclesie ministros in exhibitione honoris habere preminenciam' (*R.S.S.P.*, pp. 11, 217).

St. Paul's statutes added specifically that the bishop, as head of the chapter, discussed with the chapter the business and secrets of the church;[1] while the draft *Novum Registrum* of 1440 at Lincoln forbade the dean and chapter to discuss matters concerning episcopal rights in the bishop's absence; declared that the dean was 'first both in place and voice' only 'after the bishop'; and maintained that the power of summoning a general convocation of resident and non-resident canons belonged to the dean and chapter either on their own authority, or by the bishop's mandate.[2]

Although these statements of the *Novum Registrum* may appear suspect on grounds that they were prepared by a bishop and never formally accepted by the chapter, they apparently represented contemporary practice. Bradshaw and Wordsworth have collected twelve examples from the Lincoln chapter act books and statutes of bishops presiding in chapter in the late thirteenth and in the fourteenth and fifteenth centuries.[3] Certain of these meetings were evidently general chapters including some non-resident canons: at others only a few residentiaries attended. In addition the bishop presided at Lincoln at two other meetings in 1293 and 1355, when statutes were made;[4] and about 1195 Bishop Hugh of Avalon was present in chapter and confirmed there an ordinance which concerned him.[5] At Exeter, St. Paul's and Lichfield also, the bishop might sometimes preside in chapter when statutes were made;[6] and occasional examples of his doing so have been found at Wells and Chichester.[7] Yet English bishops who presumed too

---

[1] *Ibid.*, p. 23. [2] *L.S.*, iii, 279, 321, 334. [3] *Ibid.*, ii, cciv.
[4] *Ibid.*, i, 347–50, 362. These are not noticed in the list, *ibid.*, ii, cciv.
[5] This was when the dean and chapter ordained a fresh division of the psalter among the canons, assigning certain psalms to the bishop for daily recitation (*ibid.*, i, 300–1, and below, p. 112). Few other chapter acts or statutes are extant for this early period, but it would seem from the *Magna Vita S. Hugonis* (ed. Decima L. Douie and H. Farmer, 1961) i, 124, that Bishop Hugh was frequently present in chapter and normally presided when he was there. According to his biographer Hugh used to say that the unruffled harmony between him and his canons was not because they found him mild and gentle. 'On the contrary I am more astringent and biting than pepper, and when I am presiding in chapter the least thing often rouses me to anger.'
[6] E.g. Harl. MS. 1027, ff. 30b–31b, 49a–51b, 61b–62a; MS. Top. Devon, c. 16, ff. 4, 39–41, 74–78, 96–7; *R.S.S.P.*, pp. 87, 95–6, 98, 151–4; *L.S.*, ii, 15–16, 28, 31–4; *Monasticon*, VI, iii, 1255–65. For cases of statutes being made at episcopal visitations of cathedrals, see below, pp. 115–16.
[7] E.g. *W.S.*, pp. 57–8; *C.S.*, p. 3.

far on their right of entry to the chapter house might be severely rebuffed. In 1393 Bishop Trefnant forced Hereford chapter to submit to his presidency at the election of a dean.[1] At most secular cathedrals the right of free election of their dean was one of the canons' most closely guarded privileges. Bishop Trefnant secured a signal triumph when he induced the canons to elect his own candidate. But the next day, when he presumed still further on their good will by collating the archdeacon of Hereford to the prebend customarily annexed to the deanery, he was not admitted to the chapter house. He complained bitterly of having to wait about in the church and cloisters until eleven in the morning, while the canons deliberated in the chapter house, and their messengers planned conspiracies in corners of the church.[2]

Salisbury is the only other English secular cathedral at which medieval bishops are known to have exercised their claim to share in the election of the dean.[3] This is the more remarkable because the Salisbury customs and statutes gave far less prominence to the bishop's office and dignity than those of Lincoln and St. Paul's; while in the fourteenth century at any rate there were constant disputes between bishop and chapter at Salisbury. But the position of the bishop of Salisbury in his chapter differed fundamentally from that of his fellow English bishops, because, from the foundation of the cathedral at Old Sarum, he had a prebend permanently annexed to his office. Therefore he was able to attend chapter meetings in his capacity as prebendary when he might have been excluded as bishop. In 1219 Bishop Richard Poore stated in his letters patent that

'since Blessed Osmund and his chapter by unanimous and deliberate counsel constituted that the bishop of Salisbury should be admitted to the secrets of the chapter like a canon and should have a prebend with his bishopric, and since this prebend [i.e. the prebend of *Major Pars Altaris*] consisted in uncertain profits, namely the pentecostal oblations at the high altar, we and the chapter have now provided that for the future the prebend of Horton shall be annexed to the bishopric, . . . lest at any time the bishop should lack a prebend and so be excluded from the secrets of the chapter.'[4]

[1] *Reg. Trefnant*, pp. 51–8.   [2] *Ibid.*, pp. 58–60.
[3] Cf. *Reg. S. Osmund*, ii, 15–16; *H.M.C.*, *Var. Coll.*, i, 355; Jones, *Fasti Sar.*, p. 208.
[4] *Sarum Charters*, p. 95.

In 1254 Alexander IV sanctioned the exchange of the prebend of Horton, then held by the bishops, for that of Potterne,[1] which the bishop of Salisbury still holds. After his enthronement he was solemnly admitted as canon and prebendary to his stall in choir and place in chapter. He wore the canonical habit and swore the usual canonical oath to observe the ancient and approved customs of the church, to keep the secrets of the chapter, and to pay his vicar choral's stipend regularly. Only the canon's promise to obey the dean was omitted.[2]

This holding of prebends at their cathedrals was a recognized expedient both in England and on the continent by which bishops tried to gain access to the chapter meetings, but it raised a number of difficult constitutional problems. The chief of these was whether the bishop, when he attended chapter as a canon or prebendary, had the right to the first seat and the presidency there. Hinschius declares that he had, although the custom of the bishop attending chapter as a canon was little known in Germany.[3] Yet Fournier says that in medieval France it was a disputed question;[4] and Thomassin has pointed out that the decretal *Postulastis*,[5] which mentions the double capacity in which bishops might be present in chapter either as bishops or canons, leaves undecided the question of where they should sit.[6] He also quotes earlier canonists as saying that, while it was desirable for a bishop attending chapter as a canon to take a seat below the president, it was nevertheless necessary to observe the custom of the particular church.[7]

Custom at Salisbury seems definitely to have been that the bishop, in his capacity as prebendary, should not attempt to assume the presidency of the chapter. Possibly this was why he was able, throughout the middle ages and afterwards, to maintain

---

[1] *Reg. S. Osmund*, i, 196–7. The reason given for the exchange was that Horton was in the diocese of Worcester, and it was unseemly for the bishop of Salisbury to be subject to the bishop of Worcester in his capacity as prebendary. In 1393 there was a further proposal, which evidently did not take effect, to annex the prebend of Charminster and Bere to the episcopal *mensa* of Salisbury (*C.P.L. 1362–1404*, p. 463).

[2] *Salisbury Ceremonies*, pp. 107–9. Accounts of the admission as canon and prebendary of Potterne of Bishop Waltham and Bishop Mitford are given in Reg. Dunham, ff. 84–5 and Reg. Holme, f. 45.

[3] *Kirchenrecht*, ii, 127.   [4] *Les Officialités*, pp. xxiv–v.

[5] Decretal. Greg. IX, Lib. III, Tit. viii, c. xv.

[6] Thomassin, *Dictionnaire*, c. 404.   [7] *Ibid.*

I

his position in a chapter so sensitive of its independent rights. In 1319 Bishop Martival gave his consent in chapter to the code of statutes which he himself had prepared, not as bishop and president, but as prebendary of Potterne.[1] In the mid-fourteenth century, when Bishop Wyville attended chapter meetings to discuss the appointment of a coadjutor to the cathedral chancellor and to make arrangements for the granting of chapter farms, he is not said to have presided.[2] Later, at the Pentecostal Chapters held at Salisbury for resident and non-resident canons, c. 1560–1740, the dean always took the chair, though the bishop might be present.[3] There were naturally other occasions at Salisbury when the bishop sat in chapter *in loco suo principali*, as at visitations,[4] and possibly when the chapter, as his council, gave its consent to appropriations of churches, to manumissions of his serfs, or to grants of land from the episcopal estates.[5] Moreover, he might at one and the same meeting be called upon to act in his two different capacities. The 1392 composition between Bishop Waltham and his chapter declared that 'on any day the bishop can enter the chapter as a canon, and, if any things be referred to his correction he as bishop can enjoin that they be corrected'.[6]

At other English secular cathedral and collegiate churches in the middle ages several bishops attempted, without any permanent success, to secure a place in chapter similar to that of the bishop of Salisbury. At Beverley the claim of Alexander Neville, archbishop of York, to be a prebendary of the college in virtue of his corrody there caused one of the bitterest ecclesiastical disputes of the fourteenth century. But he went further than the bishop of Salisbury by trying to exercise the chapter's jurisdiction as its head.[7] The result was a clerical strike at Beverley which lasted over five years. Most of the canons and all the vicars choral refused to perform the services and left the church in a body. The archbishop had to summon vicars from York to take their places; and the

---

[1] *S.S.*, pp. 138–9.　　　　　　　　　　[2] Reg. Corffe, ff. 83, 88, 112.
[3] Jones, *Fasti Sar.*, p. 219.　　　　　　[4] E.g. Reg. Dunham, f. 272.
[5] E.g. Reg. Corffe, ff. 71, 109; Reg. Dunham, ff. 221, 223. On these occasions his name was written first in the list of canons present at the meeting, though the place in which he sat is not specified.
[6] *S.S.*, pp. 290–1.
[7] See the account by A. F. Leach, 'A Clerical Strike at Beverley Minster in the Fourteenth Century', in *Archaeologia*, lv (1896), 1–20, and the documents in *Beverley Chapter Acts*, ii, 202–65.

quarrel only came to an end with Neville's exile from the king-dom.[1] Elsewhere there does not seem to have been such fierce opposition on the part of the cathedral clergy to the bishops' efforts to obtain prebends. Yet when Bishop Henry of Wingham of London obtained an indult from Alexander IV in 1260 to have, with the consent of his chapter, 'a place as canon, and the right to hold any prebend that does not of right belong to another',[2] his privilege was revoked after only two years by a bull of Urban IV;[3] while at Lincoln and Lichfield prebends were not per-manently annexed to the office of bishop until the eighteenth century.[4] Bishops might hold prebends for short periods. In the mid-fifteenth century Bishop John Chedworth apparently held a succession of prebends at Lincoln.[5]

Yet apart from such occasional tenure of a prebend, the bishop of Lincoln was apparently recognized, throughout the middle ages, as a canon of the church without holding a prebend. Brad-shaw wrote that, from the foundation of the church the bishop was a canon in the brotherhood of canons in which all were on a level.[6] He could find no documents at Lincoln to prove this, but showed that, when chapters were formed on the model of Lincoln at Elgin and Aberdeen in Scotland, the bishop was represented as

[1] Mr. Leach maintains (*loc. cit.*, p. 16) that the archbishop's claim was hope-lessly wrong as regards historical usage and constitutional law: 'If we go to the historical root of things, probably the Archbishop among his canons, was merely *primus inter pares*, a president among his ministers, who probably had all things in common. But . . . after the chapter estates were divided from those of the Archbishop and the Archbishop had the lion's share, it was absurd for him to claim to come in and take a new share as a simple canon. . . . It was idle for an archbishop in the fourteenth century to pretend to go back to a state of things which had ceased by the eleventh century.' Yet from the evidence at other churches, it seems that Archbishop Neville was not such a 'historical pedant, mistaking history for law', as Leach supposed. Apparently he was only trying to realize, by rather tactless methods, the actual legal position as a prebendary held by certain of his brother bishops both in England and abroad.

[2] *C.P.L. 1198–1304*, p. 373.

[3] Quoted from Lambeth MSS. 644, 57, in *V.C.H. London*, i, 420.

[4] Le Neve-Hardy, i, 600; ii, 121.

[5] *L.S.*, ii, ccv n. Bradshaw and Wordsworth here identify him with the John Chedworth who held the prebend of Castor in 1454. He quitted this in 1457 on being made archdeacon of Northampton. In 1458 he held the prebend of Thame; in 1464 the archdeaconry of Lincoln, and from 1465 until his death in 1471 the prebend of Sutton cum Buckingham.

[6] *Ibid.*, i, 107–8.

one of the simple canons, although his canonry was relieved from the duties of residence.[1] Furthermore, the bishop of Lincoln shared with the canons in the daily recitation of the psalter,[2] and was thus included by implication in the whole body of canons. The order of about 1145 assigned the first four psalms to the bishop.[3] About 1195 an ordinance of bishop, dean, and chapter, made a fresh division of the psalter and reduced the bishop's psalms to three;[4] while in the *Novum Registrum* proposed by Bishop Alnwick in 1440 the first psalm *Beatus Vir* was still allotted to the bishop.[5] This part of the *Novum Registrum* definitely represented Lincoln custom uninfluenced by the St. Paul's code of statutes from which Bishop Alnwick took so much of his material: at St. Paul's the bishop, though recognized as head of the chapter, had no share in the daily recitation of the psalter.[6] But there were parallels to the Lincoln custom elsewhere. At Wells and Salisbury, the bishop was allotted psalms for daily recitation,[7] although at Salisbury these were assigned to him, not as bishop, but as prebendary of Potterne.

One further piece of evidence survives for the bishop's canonical status at Lincoln. An order of 1527 for the bishop's enthronement provided that, after enthronement, he should exchange his pontificals for a canon's dress and enter the chapter house as a canon, led by the two chief dignitaries. There he was to be admitted as a canon, assigned a place (unspecified) in chapter, and given twelve pence as commons for the day.[8] No mention is made of this custom either in the *Liber Niger* or in the *Novum Registrum*. Generally in the middle ages possession of a prebend was the only means, even for cathedral canons and dignitaries, by which entry could be had to the chapter house.[9] The 1527 order may therefore represent a new development, disregarding medieval custom, adopted after the order of enthronement proposed by Bishop Alnwick in 1440 had been put aside. But, on the other hand, it does seem to have had some foundation in the Lincoln tradition of the bishop as a member of the canonical body; it may help to

---

[1] *L.S.*, i, 108.

[2] This custom of allotting certain psalms to each prebendary for daily recitation, in order that the entire psalter should be said each day by the chapter, was practised at most English secular cathedrals in the middle ages and later.

[3] *Ibid.*, iii, 789.   [4] *Ibid.*, i, 300–1.

[5] *Ibid.*, iii, 308.   [6] Cf. *R.S.S.P.*, p. 31.

[7] *W.S.*, p. 69; Jones, *Fasti Sar.*, p. 200.   [8] *L.S.*, iii, 555.

[9] Cf. *ibid.*, p. 706; above, p. 34; and below, pp. 135, 143–4, 247–8.

explain why bishops of Lincoln throughout the middle ages were able, apparently without much friction, to preside in chapter when it suited them.

2. THE BISHOP'S JURISDICTION OVER HIS CATHEDRAL CLERGY

The great disputes on jurisdiction between bishop and chapter in the later middle ages, described by Professor Hamilton Thompson as among 'the epics of cathedral history',[1] are much too long and complicated to be examined in detail here. All that can be done is to indicate in general terms the extent to which English bishops in the later middle ages could still exercise supervision over their cathedral clergy and over the chapter's estates in the diocese.

The fourteenth century is a particularly interesting time at which to investigate the outcome of the clash of episcopal and capitular jurisdiction. Many of the chapters' most extreme claims to independence had been made earlier, in the late twelfth and thirteenth centuries. By the mid-thirteenth century there were signs that English bishops, led by Grosseteste, were preparing for more vigorous assertion of their rights.[2] Yet at the same time bishops in the later middle ages were naturally more ready than their predecessors to recognize that 'a cathedral church and college could not exist unless it had privileges and customs.'[3] They often preferred to adopt a policy of negotiation and legal definition rather than of open warfare with their chapters. The chapters too, with their many lawyer canons, were often willing and almost eager to continue the long negotiations and lawsuits for indefinite periods, and to enjoy to the full the legal and constitutional interest of the situation. As a result, many outstanding disputes were settled. The age was one of definition and compromise.

[1] *Cathedral Churches*, p. 192.
[2] See below, pp. 128–9.
[3] These were the words of John Waltham, bishop of Salisbury in 1388: faced by a defiant chapter, he declared that he wished to avoid an open quarrel, and was ready to negotiate about the canons' demands (Reg. Dunham, f. 72).

THE BISHOP'S OATH

In England there seems to have been no precise parallel to the custom by which medieval German chapters, such as Passau, exacted 'capitulations' from their bishops before election.[1] But the English secular chapters in the fourteenth century, like many French chapters,[2] usually succeeded in forcing their bishops to swear an oath on the gospels at the west door of the cathedral, before their admission for enthronement.[3] This oath bound the bishop to observe and defend the customs and liberties of the cathedral church. It was no vague formula, for it meant that the bishop had to observe the very definite statements of chapter law and privileges in the cathedral's statute books. The importance attached to the oath is well illustrated at Salisbury, where it formed the subject of one of the bitterest disputes between Bishop John Waltham and his chapter in 1388. Both sides were so determined that the canons eventually threatened to refuse to attend Bishop Waltham's enthronement, even though the king himself should come to it, unless the bishop would agree to swear the oath in the form which they maintained was customary.[4] John finally gave way. But at his enthronement when the cathedral chancellor had read the words of the oath aloud to him, Bishop John, repeating them, added on his own account, 'saving the rights and customs of our church of Salisbury and our pontifical dignity'.[5]

[1] These capitulations laid down a series of conditions which had to be accepted by any candidate for the bishopric. Those at Passau form the basis of a detailed study by J. Oswald, *Das alte Passauer Domkapitel bis zum dreizehnten Jahrhundert und sein Wahlkapitulationswesen*, Munich, 1933, which is reviewed by C. de Clerq in *Rev. d'hist eccl.*, xxix, 1002–4. Capitulations were common at monasteries (e.g. U. Berlière, *Les Elections abbatiales au Moyen Âge*, pp. 50 et seq.; E. H. Pearce, *Walter de Wenlock, Abbot of Westminster*, pp. 142, 144, 225).
[2] Cf. Luchaire, *Manuel des Institutions Françaises*, p. 62.
[3] E.g. *Reg. Charlton* (Hereford), p. 1; *L.S.*, i, 400; ii, 34; *Anglia Sacra*, i, 450; *W.S.*, p. 91.
[4] Reg. Dunham, f. 57.
[5] *Ibid.*, ff. 81–2. His successor, Bishop Mitford, added a similar saving clause to his oath in 1396 (Reg. Holme, f. 44); but the clause is not given in the fifteenth-century copy of the oath in *Salisbury Ceremonies*, p. 105.

THE MAKING OF THE CATHEDRAL STATUTES

What power had bishops in the later middle ages to share in the making of the cathedral statutes which they swore to observe? The constitutions of the secular cathedrals were less rigid than those of the English cathedral monasteries. This arose in the first place because the monastic constitutions were founded on the rule of St. Benedict; secondly, because from 1215 the priors and convents had to observe the orders made in the general and provincial chapters of the English black monks. Thus there might appear to be less opportunity for bishops having monastic cathedral chapters to introduce new legislation at their cathedrals. Yet the flexibility of the secular constitutions did not always give the bishop greater power to legislate, because the deans and chapters were usually bent on asserting their own control over the development of their statutes.

One of the chief ways in which bishops in the later middle ages might initiate legislation at their cathedrals was through their visitation injunctions. Statutes sent by them in this form to their cathedral monasteries seem generally to have been regarded as judicial mandates, and accepted on the bishop's authority alone.[1] But at the secular cathedrals it was more usual for them to be formally accepted and confirmed by the dean and chapter before being included among the approved constitutions of the church. The chapter seal was affixed, and the preamble to the statutes usually stated that they had been made 'with the express consent and assent', 'the unanimous counsel and consent,' or 'the common and unanimous consent and will of the dean and chapter'.[2] The dean and chapter's consent was apparently considered necessary if the injunctions were concerned with any fresh definition or interpretation of custom. It might be omitted if they were merely cor-

---

[1] Cf. C. R. Cheney, *Episcopal Visitation of Monasteries in the Thirteenth Century*, pp. 96–9; E. H. Carter, *Studies in Norwich Cathedral History* (1935), pp. 3–30. No evidence has been noticed to suggest that the abbot or prior and convent normally confirmed their bishop's visitation injunctions, though they sometimes appealed against them, e.g. C. R. Cheney, 'Norwich Cathedral Priory in the Fourteenth Century', in *B.J.R.L.*, xx, 104; *Lit. Cant.*, ii, 394–8.

[2] E.g. *R.S.S.P.*, pp. 99–100, 145–51, 163–73, 204–13; *C.S.*, pp. 18, 137; *S.S.*, p. 312; Harl. MS. 1027, ff. 35a–40b; MS. Rawl. Statutes 38, ff. xxvib–xxviia; MS. Top. Devon, c. 16, ff. 51–60, 117.

recting abuses or enforcing existing rules;[1] but in such cases injunctions might not be registered in the statute books, and have often disappeared.[2] When Bishop Gray of Lincoln sent visitation injunctions in 1432 to the dean and chapter in the form of a mandate without mention of their consent or confirmation, the chapter is thought to have refused to accept them.[3]

A further way in which bishops might take a leading part in cathedral legislation may be seen in the long series of awards on matters of jurisdiction made by the bishops of Lincoln in the fourteenth and fifteenth centuries.[4] These were in effect additional statutes framed by the bishop. Yet here again the unanimous consent of the dean and chapter had to be given beforehand in their *compromissio* and *submissio* to his judgement. If there were any irregularities in their submission, or if the dean and chapter were not present at the judgement, the award might be declared null and void.[5] In 1257/8 Giles of Bridport, bishop of Salisbury, promulgated statutes for his cathedral chapter in his diocesan synod;[6] while in the early thirteenth century Bishop Jocelin of Wells made an ordinance for the provostry of Wells cathedral while beyond the sea, with the assent of Ralph, the dean of Wells, and other canons then with him.[7] But these were probably only early and isolated examples of bishops adopting a rather high-handed attitude towards their chapters, which does not seem to have been repeated. In each case it is significant that the chapter's assent is recorded.

Secular cathedral statutes in the later middle ages were normally framed in the chapter house. The consent of the dean and chapter was essential. Generally this meant the consent of a majority of the residentiary canons.[8] The knowledge and consent of the non-residents was required only for statutes affecting their interests, or the common interests of all the canons.[9] If the bishop were con-

---

[1] E.g. Harl. MS. 1027, ff. 12a–25b, 28a–30b, 44b–49a, 54a–58b; MS. Top. Devon, c. 16, ff. 18–39, 67–74, 82–9.

[2] Cf. Frere, *Visitation Articles*, i, 115–16. Some survive in bishops' registers.

[3] *Lincoln Visitations*, i, 137–45. These injunctions were not copied into the Lincoln Black Book.

[4] E.g. *L.S.*, i, 319–22, 340–4; iii, 182–231, 249–67.

[5] *Ibid.*, ii, 220.   [6] *Concilia*, i, 715.   [7] *H.M.C. Wells*, i, 58.

[8] For possible difficulties when the dean was absent, see below, p. 145.

[9] In such cases those present in England would be summoned by the dean and chapter to a general meeting, which they might attend either in person or, if legitimately prevented, by proxy.

cerned in legislation, he might, at most English cathedrals, sit in chapter either as president or, at those cathedrals where a prebend was annexed to his office, as a canon and prebendary. But usually, by the fourteenth century, his only apparent share was that of assent, as constitutional head of the cathedral, to statutes discussed and agreed upon by the dean and chapter. In such cases his formal ratification of statutes, strengthened by the affixing of his official seal, was often dated at a different place, and some days later than that of the dean and chapter.

Yet for some statutes the bishop's consent was neither required nor formally given. Already in the thirteenth century the problem was causing difficulties and being discussed. In 1221 a ruling of Honorius III, sent to the chapter of Paris, laid down that the chapter could not change the approved constitutions or customs of their church or introduce new ones, without the advice and consent of their bishop.[1] Later, several English bishops and chapters made further definitions of their own. At Lincoln, Bishop Alnwick's award of 1439 decreed that the chapter might legislate *super levibus et minoribus*, never *in gravibus vel arduis*, without their bishop's authority or consent;[2] in 1440 the same bishop declared in his *Novum Registrum*, never officially received by the chapter, that the dean and chapter might make ordinances on matters touching the utility and honour of the church, provided that neither his rights nor those of his successors or absent persons were involved.[3] At Exeter an early statement of custom, probably of the twelfth century, declared that the canons without their bishop could not make statutes touching the general state of the church or the bishop or his rights, though they might do so on matters concerning *sua singularia negocia*.[4] But in 1277 Bishop Walter Bronescombe ordained that all Exeter cathedral customs not strengthened by the written witness of himself or his successors should be quashed and null until they had been so confirmed.[5]

The dean and chapter of Exeter apparently took Bishop Bronescombe's warning to heart; all statutes from the twelfth to

[1] *Corpus Iuris Canonici*, Decretal. Greg. IX, Lib. I, tit. iv, c. ix. For further discussion of the problem, see Hinschius, ii, 131 *et seq.*

[2] *L.S.*, iii, 208. [3] *Ibid.*, p. 334.

[4] Harl. MS. 1027, f. 3b. This statement is undated, but must have been made before the foundation of the deanery at Exeter in 1225, since it refers to the archdeacon or provost taking the second place in chapter after the bishop.

[5] *Ibid.*, f. 19b.

the fifteenth centuries entered in the Exeter statute books at the British Museum and Bodleian library were promulgated or confirmed by the bishop, regardless of subject-matter.[1] But elsewhere there was no uniformity of practice. Important statutes, such as the *Nova Constitutio* of 1214 at Salisbury[2] which introduced definite changes into the constitution of the chapter, might be made on the authority of the dean and chapter alone. At most English cathedrals the personality of the bishop and the attitude to him of the dean and chapter seem to have been the chief factors in determining whether or not the statutes should be confirmed by the bishop. A strong bishop would try to insist on his consent being asked to all important legislation. This was especially vital to him if his own rights were involved. In certain cases the chapter would not object. The bishop's official sanction gave greater authority to their statutes, and, if particular statutes were liable to be disputed either from within or without the chapter, it was advisable to obtain his confirmation. On the other hand, if important matters were unlikely to arouse controversy, this precaution might be omitted. If the bishop were staying near his cathedral church, it would be comparatively simple to get his consent; if he were abroad or outside the diocese, only the more urgent or controversial statutes might be sent to him.

Episcopal confirmations of statutes were not the only kind sought. Certain cathedral statutes might receive in addition the confirmation of pope, king, or archbishop, often as a result of considerable trouble and expense undergone by the chapters.[3] Moreover, the share of all these authorities, like that of the bishop, in making the cathedral statutes, might sometimes go further than mere confirmation. The archbishop might take some share in framing statutes of the cathedral chapters of his province when he came into contact with them during his metropolitan visitations.[4]

[1] Harl. MS. 1027; MS. Rawl. Statutes 38; MS. Wood empt. 9; MS. Top. Devon, c. 16.

[2] *S.S.*, pp. 40–53. At this time the dean of Salisbury, Richard Poore, was the brother of the bishop, Herbert Poore; possibly they had some kind of understanding.

[3] Hereford chapter in particular set much store by the value of papal confirmations of its statutes. Its canons' oath to observe the ancient and reasonable customs of the church included the phrase not found in similar oaths at other English cathedrals: 'maxime [consuetudines] que sunt auctoritate apostolica confirmata' (*L.S.*, ii, 45).   [4] E.g. *Concilia*, i, 500; *Reg. Brantyngham*, ii, xxiii.

The pope might send mandates to English chapters, sometimes in the form of judicial awards, sometimes as ordinances correcting abuses in their customs.[1] Particularly towards the end of the fourteenth and in the fifteenth century, there are instances of the Crown intervening in arrangements at cathedrals. Often this happened when the king was asked by one or both parties to a capitular dispute to provide a solution. The practice sometimes led to orders being issued by king and council on matters as closely connected with the internal government of the cathedral as the administration of the chapter's brewery and bakehouse at St. Paul's; the residence rules for the canons; or the order of the chantry masses at Hereford.[2] Possibly the influence gained by the crown over the chapters at this time may foreshadow the royal statutes and injunctions sent to them in the sixteenth century. In the period after the Reformation the chapters lost much of their medieval powers of independent legislation. At the same time the control over their statutes by their bishop, working in co-operation with the crown, increased.

THE BISHOP'S SHARE IN THE APPOINTMENT OF THE CATHEDRAL CLERGY

The method of appointments to the chapter body, though of special importance to the bishop, was a matter on which there were comparatively few disputes between bishops and their secular chapters in medieval England, and very little variation in the customs of different churches. Moreover, the English bishop's legal position, according to these customs, was remarkably strong in comparison with that of some continental bishops. By canon law the appointment of cathedral dignitaries and canons could only be made through the exercise of the *vis simultanea* of bishop and chapter. In French chapters this varied in every conceivable way. Sometimes the bishop and chapter would nominate jointly; sometimes alternately. Their turns might come according to the week or month of the year. The whole chapter might nominate as a body in its turn, or the two sides of the choir might act alternately.[3] At Chartres, where the method was nomination by the

---

[1] E.g. *C.P.L. 1396–1404*, pp. 400, 529–30.

[2] *R.S.S.P.*, pp. 195–7; *C.P.R. 1399–1401*, pp. 121–2; cf. *Reg. Trefnant*, pp. 20–1.

[3] Cf. Benson, 'Relation of Chapter to Bishop', in *Essays on Cathedrals*, pp. 254–6; Fournier, *op. cit.*, p. xix.

bishop, the chapter asserted its right to examine his candidate.[1] But in England, as at Rouen and Bayeux, the bishop normally collated to all canonries and dignities except the deanery 'in his *camera* or wherever he wished, by bread or book or any other way by his own authority',[2] merely sending a mandate to the dean and chapter to admit his nominee. St. Paul's chapter had an early tradition of independence in the appointment of canons, and York chapter in 1106 asserted that the archbishop could not appoint to canonries without its counsel and assent.[3] But by the thirteenth century the powers of the archbishops of York and the bishop of London to nominate canons do not seem to have been any more restricted than those of bishops at the other English secular cathedrals.[4]

Indeed, in legal theory the bishop appears to have had greater influence on the composition of the chapter body at an English secular cathedral than at an English cathedral monastery. In a cathedral monastery the bishop, as titular abbot, might sometimes be able to nominate monks, especially at his accession, but his general claim to receive professions of the novices was often disputed by the prior;[5] while in the appointment of obedientiaries he usually had, by the later middle ages, only limited rights of nomination, choosing from two or three names submitted to him by the prior and convent.[6] But the appointment of a secular

---

[1] Amiet, *op. cit.*, pp. 21–7.

[2] *L.S.*, ii, 137. Cf. Pommeraye, *op. cit.*, p. 430; Deslandes, *op. cit.*, p. 66.

[3] C. N. L. Brooke in *Camb. Hist. Jour.*, x, 119, and *Hist. St. Paul's Cathedral*, pp. 22–4, 42; *Visitations and Memorials of Southwell Minster*, p. 193. The Lincoln customs of 1214 said that the bishop could appoint without asking the consent of his chapter (*L.S.*, ii, 137).

[4] It was, however, agreed in the 1290 composition between Archbishop Romeyn and his chapter, that if the chapter refused to install a canon on receiving the archbishop's mandate, the matter should be postponed for further discussion (*Hist. Church York*, iii, 219). The English bishops sometimes asked their chapters' counsel in extraordinary cases of papal provisions or of royal or archiepiscopal collations to canonries (e.g. *Reg. Shrewsbury*, p. 8; *Reg. Corbridge*, ii, 6–7).

[5] E.g. as at Canterbury (*Lit. Cant.*, i, 18, 294–5, 389–90; ii, 131–3, 160–3, 166, 216, 244–6). Cf. Carter, *op. cit.*, pp. 49–50, 63–4.

[6] See e.g. *Lit. Cant.*, i, 117, 308–9, 422–4, 506–10; ii, 106–8, 128–9, 192–200, 276–7, 287–8, 318–19; *Reg. Chichele*, iv, 114–16, 151–3. Norwich cathedral priory in the early fifteenth century seems to have been exceptionally independent of its bishop in appointments of obedientiaries (E. H. Carter, *op. cit.*,

cathedral canon was a much more important affair for powers in the outside world than the admission of a monk; and so in practice the bishop's actual power in the collation of canonries came to be much restricted, both by the growing practice of papal provision, and by the pressure put on him by king, queen, and magnates to provide for their clerks. Yet he was usually able, even in the later middle ages, to gain some influence in the chapter by introducing into it certain of his nominees, and at the same time to find means of support there for some of the officials who helped him in the administrative or judicial work of his diocese.[1]

The English chapters did not completely abandon their canonical right to share in the appointment of new canons. On occasion they were prepared to assert that admission by the dean or dean and chapter was no mere formality, but a necessary part of the appointment which might be withheld.[2] Moreover, there were certain variations of detail in the customs of the different churches which the bishops had to be careful to observe. At Lincoln the bishop had to address his mandate for the admission of a canon to the dean and chapter jointly, not to the dean alone.[3] But at Salisbury the installation and induction of canons belonged solely to the dean, and a mandate sent to the dean and chapter jointly might be declared invalid.[4]

In the appointment of the dean, on the other hand, the choice belonged in England to the chapters by free election when the pope did not provide. Most of the chapters established their right to elect early,[5] and by the fourteenth century the bishops rarely disputed either the fact or the procedure of the elections.[6] But there were again local variations in procedure and in the degree of the bishop's control. Lincoln and St. Paul's, two of the chapters

---

pp. 50–2, 64–5). For the practice before 1216, see M. D. Knowles, *Monastic Order in England*, pp. 626–7.

[1] Cf. the recent studies of appointments of canons at Lichfield in the fourteenth century and at Salisbury 1329–49 in H. Jenkins *op. cit.*, pp. 171–201; *Hemingby's Reg.*, pp. 6–41.

[2] E.g. cf. *W.S.*, pp. cxxxvi n., 45, 55; *H.M.C. Var. Coll.*, iv, 76–7.

[3] *L.S.*, ii, xci–ii.

[4] E.g. Reg. Dunham, f. 175.

[5] Among the last to obtain it were Wells by 1217, Lichfield by 1222, and Exeter, which had no dean until 1225 (*H.M.C. Wells*, i, 65, 151; *Anglia Sacra*, i, 437, 448, 465; *H.M.C. Var. Coll.*, iv, 66).

[6] But cf. *Reg. Trefnant* (Hereford), pp. 52–8.

usually more willing than others to recognize their bishop's authority, were in this respect the most independent. They merely announced the dean's death to the bishop, and, without waiting for a licence, proceeded immediately to the election. The elect was then presented to the bishop for examination, and the bishop was bound to admit him unless there were reasonable and canonical cause for objection.[1] But at Wells, Salisbury, and Exeter, it was apparently customary to ask the bishop's licence to elect.[2]

The point on which controversy mostly centred in the business of appointments in the later middle ages was the oaths of obedience taken by deans and canons on their admission. Usually the dean swore an oath of canonical obedience to the bishop;[3] while the other dignitaries and canons swore theirs to the dean only.[4] Certain bishops, such as Bishop Grosseteste at Lincoln in 1245 and Bishop Rede at Chichester tried, usually without much success, to force them to take an additional oath to the bishop.[5] At Salisbury Bishop Waltham even went so far as to try to suppress the canons' oath to the dean.[6] But Exeter was apparently the only English cathedral at which the bishops established as an accepted rule that all dignitaries and canons should swear an oath to them.[7]

For the most part the bishop's share in controlling the selection of the clergy of his cathedral church stopped short with members

---

[1] *L.S.*, i, 279-80; ii, 137; iii, 279; *R.S.S.P.*, pp. 14, 219-20. The copy of Lincoln customs sent to Moray in 1214 says, with regard to the dean's election 'episcopo tamen super hiis prius requisito'; while that registered at Lincoln declares 'non quidem prehabito cum Episcopo super hoc sermone, nec ipsius requisito assensu' (*L.S.*, i, 43).

[2] *H.M.C. Wells*, i, 65, 151; Jones, *Fasti Sar.*, p. 208; *Ordinale Exon.*, i, 2.

[3] Cf. *ibid.*; *R.S.S.P.*, pp. 15, 220; *Reg. Greenfield*, i, 50, 81. The matter was disputed at Lincoln (*L.S.*, i, 317; iii, 281; *Lincoln Visitations*, i, 133).

[4] Cf. *RS.S.P.*, pp. 16, 21.

[5] *L.S.*, i, 317; *Reg. Rede*, i, 68-9, 101, 103.

[6] Cf. *Reg. Dunham*, f. 193, where the chapter refused to admit Richard Holme to a prebend because Richard's letters omitted to give his proctor powers to swear obedience to the dean. The chapter said that a struggle was then being carried on at Rome between it and the bishop on the question of the oath to the dean, and Richard was known to be on the bishop's side.

[7] *Ordinale Exon.*, i, 2. At Wells in 1325 three dignitaries, the precentor, chancellor, and subdean swore an oath to Bishop Droxford (*Reg. Drokensford*, p. 248). In 1337 the chancellor of Wells refused to take an oath of obedience to the dean and chapter on the ground that he and other dignitaries were subject immediately to the bishop and were not bound to obey the dean and chapter (*H.M.C. Wells*, i, 546, cf. 545).

of the chapter. At Hereford in 1252 Bishop Peter de Aigueblanche claimed the right to nominate vicars of the choir, but the award of arbiters declared that such presentation belonged to the dean and chapter.[1] Elsewhere the vicars choral were the nominees of the individual canons, their lords, and the bishop could usually only appoint by lapse when both canon and dean had failed to provide for the vacant stall. At Exeter the bishop probably had more control than at most cathedrals, for there he could examine the canons' presentees to vicarages in musical ability.[2] At Wells he had the right to collate to vacant choir vicarages during the vacancy of prebends, though not to the prebendal vicarage, should that fall vacant at the same time as the prebend.[3] The right of presenting chaplains to cathedral chantries was sometimes granted to the bishop in the foundation deeds of the chantries; other chantries might fall to his collation by lapse. He might also confer certain minor offices in his church. At St. Paul's he appointed the penitentiary and keeper of the Old Work, and had in his gift one share of bread and beer for a writer and book-binder.[4]

THE BISHOP'S POWERS OF SUPERVISION AT THE CATHEDRAL CHURCH

After the clergy had been admitted to the cathedral church, the bishop's control over them and his cathedral was by the later middle ages very limited. The supervision of the cathedral fabric and administration of the fabric fund is seen in the records to have been almost entirely the concern of the dean and chapter.[5] At St. Paul's the bishop had some share in the supervision of the old fabric,[6] but this seems to have been exceptional. Usually the bishop's part was confined to providing or appealing for funds to carry out the dean and chapter's plans. There is little reason for

---

[1] *Hereford Charters*, pp. 97, 100.   [2] *Use Exeter*, p. 15.
[3] *H.M.C. Wells*, i, 66.   [4] *R.S.S.P.*, pp. 13, 182.
[5] See below, pp. 230–4.
[6] In the late twelfth century the chapter declared that the supervision of both the old and new fabric belonged to the dean and residentiaries, since they must chiefly bear the burden of repairs (*R.S.S.P.*, p. 131). Yet the bishop continued to appoint the keeper of the old fabric (above, n. 4), and in 1308 Bishop Baldock made an agreement with a mason for its supervision and repairs (*Reg. Baldock*, pp. 91–3).

connecting the names of the chief rulers of a see with the actual design of the buildings which came into being during their pontificates.[1] At certain cathedrals, however, the bishop had more control over the canons' houses of residence than over the fabric of the church itself. At Hereford and Lichfield he supervised the repairs of canonical houses and conferred them; while at Chichester he conferred all the houses except those appropriated to the four dignitaries.[2] In the later middle ages, when the number of residentiary canons began to be restricted by statute, this sometimes gave the bishop some influence in deciding who the residentiaries should be. At Wells, too, the bishop collated to a number of canonical houses and to all the vicars' chambers in their hall.[3] Elsewhere certain houses were annexed to particular dignities or prebends, but the majority were in the gift of the dean and chapter.[4]

Otherwise the bishop could generally only intervene at his cathedral if the statutes which he had sworn to observe and maintain were broken or neglected. The four principal dignitaries could only be dispensed from their oath to reside by licence of the bishop or pope.[5] In cases of constant reports of misdoing by subordinate officials or vicars choral, the bishop might order correction to be made by the dean, who was immediately subject to him by his oath of obedience. But he could only correct the canons in chapter. Among the privileges said to have been granted by St. Osmund to the dean and chapter of Salisbury in 1091, and which was certainly in force by the end of the twelfth century, was that 'of making answer to the bishop in no matter, unless it be in chapter, and of complying with the judgement of the chapter only.'[6] This privilege was copied into the statute and custom books of practically every English secular cathedral;[7] while in

---

[1] Cf. A. H. Thompson, 'Cathedral Builders of the Middle Ages', in *History*, x (1925), 139–50.

[2] *Hereford Charters*, p. xxiii; *M.R.A.*, p. 347; *Reg. Swinfield*, p. 547; *Reg. Stretton*, i, 115–16, 121–2, 137, 151 *et seq.*; *C.S.*, pp. 19–20.

[3] *W.S.*, p. cxli; K. Edwards, *op. cit.*, in *British Archaeological Jour.* (1939), pp. 71–3.

[4] *Ibid.*, pp. 66–73.

[5] E.g. *Reg. Grandisson*, i, 586; ii, 710, 723.

[6] *S.S.*, pp. 28–9, 61; *Use Sarum*, i, 8, 260.

[7] E.g. *C.S.*, p. 13; *R.S.S.P.*, p. 18; *W.S.*, pp. 44, 55; *L.S.*, i, 283; ii, 24, 138–9; iii, 295.

time the monks of certain cathedral monasteries claimed a similar privilege from their bishops.[1]

When there were quarrels among the canons the bishop could usually only intervene after the efforts of dean and chapter had failed, and then, at some cathedrals, only at the request of the chapter. Salisbury chapter did not often invite its bishop's intervention. But at Lincoln the early rule was said to be that a quarrelsome canon, still rebellious after three warnings from the dean and chapter, should be brought before the bishop, who, with the dean and other canons, would correct and if necessary expel him.[2] The bishops of London, Lichfield, and Exeter had a similar right to compose quarrels in the chapter.[3] Hereford chapter, however, ordered all its canons to swear on admission that, if discord arose in the chapter or between them and other canons, they would stand by the judgement of the dean and chapter, and not appeal to a higher authority.[4]

Peculiar Jurisdictions of the Dean and Chapter

In addition to the cathedral and close, fairly large parts of the diocese were also subject immediately to the dean and chapter or prebendaries, and practically exempt from the jurisdiction of the bishop and his officers. By the thirteenth century all the chapters had established their right to the ordinary jurisdiction in the churches appropriated to their common fund; while in those appropriated to prebends, the individual prebendaries usually had their own courts, with proof of wills and powers of correction. The deanery might have annexed to it the archdeaconry of the cathedral city and suburbs,[5] and most dignities had their separate estates. The dean and chapter claimed to administer these estates when the

---

[1] E.g. at Canterbury (*H.M.C. Eighth Rept.*, App. p. 317; C. E. Woodruff and W. Danks, *Memorials of Canterbury Cathedral*, pp. 130–2).

[2] *Reg. Antiquissimum*, i, 7. This rule was included in the charter of doubtful authenticity said to have been granted to Lincoln chapter in 1090. Professor Stenton writes that it is not necessarily a mere fabrication. He suggests that a genuine charter of confirmation by William II was conflated with a set of precepts concerning canonical discipline issued by some ecclesiastical authority (*ibid.*, pp. 10–11).

[3] *R.S.S.P.*, pp. 88, 212; *Monasticon*, VI, iii, 1263; Harl. MS. 1027, ff. 19b–20a.

[4] *L.S.*, ii, 47.

[5] See below, pp. 146–7, 153–4.

K

dignities and prebends were vacant. Some chapters and pre-bendaries obtained greater independence than others. At York the powers of the dean and chapter are well illustrated in their Court Book of 1396–1485, described by Canon J. S. Purvis.[1] This records charges against both clergy and laity in the peculiar jurisdiction. It shows the dean and chapter's court being con-ducted on lines similar to those of the archbishop's consistory court. It was the chapter's court, not the archbishop's, which by this time apparently had undisputed right to judge causes in lands and churches of the vacant prebends and dignities.[2] Salisbury, too, seems to have been exceptionally independent of the bishop and his officials in its peculiars.[3] But at Lincoln and Wells, the bishop kept some powers over prebends or vacant dignities, other than the deanery.[4]

In the matter of the administration of the vacant deanery the bishops were especially reluctant to acknowledge the defeat of their claims. This was probably because they felt they had more direct control over the dean, through his oath to them, than over the simple canons. Moreover, exercise of the decanal jurisdiction in a vacancy would give the bishop not only the profits of the jurisdiction, but also, in many cases, the right to visit the lands and churches of the separate prebends and of the common fund.[5] In reply to such claims the chapter maintained that, by electing the dean, it granted to him the decanal jurisdiction which, at his death, returned to the chapter, until it chose to grant it to another.[6] The problem was of such general importance that, in the early fourteenth century, the dean and chapter of Lichfield collected and had transcribed in their Great White Register the customs observed during a vacancy at six other secular cathedrals of Can-terbury province.[7] In spite of the bishops' efforts, Exeter chapter was then the only English chapter ready to acknowledge that its

---

[1] *A Medieval Act Book at York*, York, 1943.

[2] *Ibid.*, pp. 5–6.

[3] *S.S.*, pp. 302–3. Cf. *L.S.*, i, 309–10.

[4] *L.S.*, iii, 278; *H.M.C. Wells*, i, 66; *Reg. Drokensford*, pp. 22–3, 47, 198–9; *W.S.*, pp. 146–7.

[5] The canons' peculiar jurisdictions did not necessarily involve immunity from episcopal visitation, but in a number of cases they did (cf. Frere, *Visitation Articles*, i, 69–70, and below, p. 129 *et seq*).

[6] *L.S.*, ii, lxxxvii.

[7] *M.R.A.*, p. 353.

bishop had some rights in the vacant deanery. It informed Lichfield that

'the internal jurisdiction over the canons and ministers of the church
belongs to the subdean and chapter during a vacancy, both by custom
and right. But as regards the custody of and jurisdiction over the
manors and churches assigned to the dean's *mensa*, the bishop usually
steps in.' [1]

Elsewhere disputes between the bishop and chapter on the
vacant deanery often continued well into the fourteenth century.
Occasionally the bishop obtained certain rights, especially if the
deanery were vacant by causes other than death, such as suspension or deprivation.[2] But generally the chapters had established
their claims by the end of the century.[3] At Salisbury, where
disputes seem to have been hottest during the vacancy following
the death of the dean, Cardinal Reymund, in 1346,[4] and were
again debated by a general convocation of canons in 1387,[5] victory
in the important composition of 1392 was entirely in the hands of
the chapter. This laid down that

'as regards the fruits, commodities and profits of the deanery when
vacant, and the jurisdiction of the same, and all other things accruing
in the time of vacancy, let them belong to the chapter fully, peacefully
and quietly, and let the chapter have and exercise them all fully in
time to come'.[6]

EPISCOPAL VISITATIONS OF THE CATHEDRALS

During the century and a half from about 1240 to 1392 the
claims of English bishops to visit their cathedral chapters became

[1] *M.R.A.*, p. 353. In 1319 Bishop Stapleton had declared that in a vacancy
the dean's power and jurisdiction devolved, not on the bishop, but on the
chapter, and that the chapter was to appoint an official to administer them
(Harl. MS. 1027, ff. 36b–37a). Yet in 1335, on Dean Colton's death, Bishop
Grandisson appointed an official, the treasurer of the cathedral, to exercise the
decanal jurisdiction (*Reg. Grandisson*, ii. 795).

[2] E.g. *H.M.C. Wells*, i, 66; *Reg. Cantilupe*, p. 112. But cf. *ibid.*, pp. 112–15,
118; *Reg. Trefnant*, pp. 50–1, 59–60.

[3] For the course of the disputes at Wells and Lichfield, see *H.M.C. Wells*, i,
148–9, 151, 231, 233; *W.S.*, p. 77; *Reg. Shrewsbury*, pp. 243–6, 626–7; *C.P.L.
1396–1404*, p. 321; *M.R.A.*, pp. 355–7; *H.M.C. Fourteenth Rept.*, App. viii, p. 233.

[4] In this vacancy both bishop and chapter appointed keepers of the deanery.
But the records show that it was the chapter's official who actually exercised
the jurisdiction (*Hemingby's Reg.*, pp. 99–100, 156–64, 257–8).

[5] Reg. Coman, f. 72.   [6] *S.S.*, pp. 302–3.

and generally remained a major issue at the secular cathedrals, leading to some of the most spectacular and long-drawn-out disputes of the later middle ages. The development of the machinery of visitation and the rulings of canon law on the subject have been fully discussed by Frere and by Professor C. R. Cheney.[1] The Sext of Boniface VIII, issued at the end of the thirteenth century, included a ruling of Innocent IV which ordered archbishops and bishops to begin their visitations of their dioceses with the cathedral chapter.[2] Before this, the position at secular cathedrals had been very uncertain. In early days, before the separation of the estates of bishop and chapter, there was apparently no question of the bishop visiting his chapter, because he was then a person within, not without, the cathedral body.[3] During the one and a half centuries following the Norman Conquest, when the bishop became increasingly alienated from the chapter, the custom that English bishops did not visit their secular cathedrals seems to have been maintained. By the mid-thirteenth century the need for some sort of discipline and correction from without was probably urgent. At this time Eudes Rigaud, archbishop of Rouen, was regularly visiting both his own cathedral chapter of Rouen and other secular cathedral chapters of his province, and seems to have met with little opposition.[4] Yet in 1239, when Bishop Grosseteste set out to visit his cathedral chapter of Lincoln, he raised a storm of opposition out of all proportion to that met by bishops visiting English cathedral monasteries. Here there were many disputes on minor problems connected with the visitation, but the bishop's right to visit was not seriously challenged. When visitation became the order of the day at the Benedictine monasteries of the dioceses, it was generally accepted that the bishop would also visit the monks of his cathedral chapter.[5] The secular chapters, on the other hand, asserted that they were exempt from all episcopal visitation. They banded themselves

---

[1] *Visitation Articles*, i, Introduction; *Episcopal Visitation of Monasteries in the Thirteenth Century.* See also Hinschius, ii, 143 *et seq.*; Barbosa, *De Officio et Potestate Episcopi*, Pt. III, Alleg. lxxiii, cc. 428–32.

[2] *Sext.*, Lib. III, tit, xx, i, 1, 6.

[3] Frere, *loc. cit.*, i, 74.

[4] *Regestrum Visitationum Archiepiscopi Rothomagensis*, pp. 35, 122; P. Andrieu-Guitrancourt, *L'Archevêque Eudes Rigaud et la Vie de l'Église au xiiie siècle*, pp. 251–6, 286.

[5] Cf. Frere, *loc. cit.*, p. 80.

together, sending copies of their privileges to Lincoln to support the canons of Lincoln in their opposition to Bishop Grosseteste, and resisting similar attempts of their own bishops to visit them. The bishops, too, worked together on this supremely important question. Bishop Grosseteste wrote that he was winning back the dropped rights of all the bishops of England.[1]

The first important victory in the struggle went to Bishop Grosseteste at Lincoln in 1245.[2] An award of Innocent IV between the bishop and chapter of Lincoln then declared that the bishop had the right to visit the dean and chapter, the other ministers of the cathedral church, and the clergy and parishioners of churches belonging to the canons; but that the chapter was not bound to pay procurations.[3] Obviously this did little more than state the essentials of the position. It left many problems for future generations: such as how often the bishop might exercise his right of visitation; how many clerks and notaries he might bring with him; whether he must visit in person, or whether he might depute commissaries; what powers of correction he might use. The answers to some of these questions are given in the draft copy of Bishop Alnwick's *Novum Registrum* of 1440: others were still unsettled then.[4] Nevertheless, the 1245 award seems to have marked a turning point in the relations of bishops and secular chapters in England. In the last half of the thirteenth and beginning of the fourteenth century episcopal claims to visit the chapters of Exeter and St. Paul's were apparently easily established without any long struggle or submission to outside arbiters.[5]

At York, too, the Lincoln award may have influenced the course of the struggle between archbishop and chapter. But York claimed greater independence of its archbishop's jurisdiction than most

[1] *Roberti Grosseteste Epistolae* (R.S.), pp. 256, 334.

[2] For the course of the struggle at Lincoln and the bishop's arguments see *ibid.*, pp. 199–203, 235–40, 248–9, 253–61, 290–1, 343–6, 357–431.

[3] *L.S.*, i, 315–19.

[4] *Ibid.*, iii, 277–8. A list of episcopal visitations of Lincoln cathedral after 1245 is given *ibid.*, ii, cl–cli. This omits Bishop Gray's visitation of 1432, the records of which are printed in *Lincoln Visitations*, i, 128–45.

[5] *Reg. Bronescombe*, pp. xiv, 77; Harl. MS. 1027, ff. 12b *et seq.*, 37a; *R.S.S.P.*, p. 11, cf. 87, 99 *et seq.*; Frere, *Visitation Articles*, i, 77; *Documents illustrating the History of St. Paul's*, ed. W. S. Simpson, p. 44; *M.R.A.*, p. 182. Episcopal visitations of Exeter cathedral are recorded regularly in the printed bishops' registers throughout the fourteenth century, sometimes as often as every three years, in person or by commissary.

English chapters. It only submitted to visitation after many disputes; and, even when established, the archbishop's powers during visitation always remained more limited than those of the bishop of Lincoln. The composition of 1290 between Archbishop Romeyn and his chapter,[1] which first allowed very limited powers of visitation to the archbishop, was a source of constant strife for the following thirty-eight years. Professor Hamilton Thompson has said that it deprived the character of the visitation of the ordinary features of a judicial enquiry.[2] Possibly it was put out of date by the Sext of Boniface VIII.[3] Finally in 1328, in the pontificate of Archbishop Melton a compromise was reached, which saved the dignity of both parties, and removed the most obvious causes of friction. For the future the archbishop was allowed to visit his chapter every four years after giving two months' notice to the chapter. He might use the services of three or four clerks and a writer or scribe; corrections were to be made by the dean and chapter within six months.[4]

But in the meantime, between the Lincoln and York agreements, the chapter of Salisbury had won for the other side a notable victory, which seems to have delayed the establishment of episcopal claims to visit there and at some other English chapters for well over a century. In 1262 Bishop Giles of Bridport, who had come to Salisbury from the deanery of Wells, revoked his mandate for a visitation of the chapter, stating that from his examination of the constitutions of Blessed Osmund and the Salisbury customs, he had decided that none of his predecessors had exercised or demanded a visitation. He granted for himself and his successors that all members of the cathedral church and of the canons' prebends should for the future be free and exempt from episcopal visitation.[5] Until as late as 1392 Salisbury chapter seems to have maintained this exemption in face of the ruling of canon law. Then, after a thirteen years' struggle with their bishops they

---

[1] *Hist. Church York*, iii, 216–20. The archbishop might visit the chapter only once in five years, after giving three months' notice. No procurations were payable; the enquiry had to be a personal one; and only canons might help the archbishop in the business. The archbishop could only request information in purely general terms, without enjoying answers or putting a verbal or written series of questions.

[2] *The Medieval Chapter*, p. 9.   [3] See above, p. 128.

[4] *The Medieval Chapter*, p. 10; *Concilia*, ii, 547; *Y.S.*, p. 118.

[5] *S.S.*, pp. 96–7.

were at last forced, under pressure from the king and from Boniface IX, to allow certain rights of visitation to their bishop, John
Waltham, and other rights, more restricted, to his successors.[1]

At three churches, Wells, Chichester, and Lichfield, whose
constitutions were closely connected in origin and early development with that of Salisbury, the chapters claimed exemption for
as long as possible, refusing after set-backs to acknowledge their
defeat. The chapter of Wells had joined with Lincoln in its
protests against Grosseteste's innovations,[2] and in the early fourteenth century maintained that its customs with regard to visitation were the same as those of Salisbury.[3] In practice it had to
submit to episcopal visitation long before Salisbury.[4] But in 1321
it did at least obtain its bishop's recognition that the city and
suburbs of Wells and the prebendal estates were exempt from
visitation; while at the cathedral the bishop was not allowed to
examine the canons and other ministers singly: the dean alone
answered questions in the chapter house.[5] Chichester was also
forced to submit to episcopal visitation before the middle of the
fourteenth century. But here, owing partly perhaps to an un-
fortunate choice of arbiter, partly to the insufficient development
of the dean's authority, the bishop's powers during visitation
became much wider than those of most English bishops. In 1340
the award of John Stratford, archbishop of Canterbury and
brother of Robert, then bishop of Chichester, ordered that the
decanal jurisdiction should be entirely superseded by that of the
bishop at time of visitation. Moreover, the bishop might visit the
estates of the prebends and dignities, and the dean's peculiar in the
city and suburbs of Chichester, as well as the cathedral church in
head and members.[6]

---

[1] The composition, confirmed by Pope Boniface, is printed, *ibid.*, pp. 288–99,
302–5. For the future bishops of Salisbury might visit their cathedral once in
seven years, and could bring one notary and one clerk with them. But the
canons' prebends remained exempt from their visitation. For the later history
of episcopal visitation at Salisbury, see Jones, *Fasti Sar.*, pp. 213–14.

[2] *H.M.C. Wells*, i, 99; *L.S.*, i, 61.   [3] *M.R.A.*, p. 182.

[4] Cf. Frere, *loc. cit.*, p. 78; *W.S.*, pp. 133–45, 148–9; *Reg. Drokensford*, pp. 73,
153–4; *H.M.C. Wells*, i, 189–90, 206–7, 533.

[5] *W.S.*, pp. 125–49. Cf. Church, *Chapters Hist. Wells*, pp. 303–5; *H.M.C.
Wells*, i, 541, 543, 545–7.

[6] Swainson, pp. 58–9. Printed records of Bishop Rede's visitations of
Chichester cathedral and city in 1397, 1403, and 1409 are available in *Reg. Rede*,
i, 69–70, 98–127; ii, 363–73.

The final submission of Lichfield chapter, on the other hand, apparently came later than that of Salisbury, possibly because the dean of Lichfield was in an unusually powerful position. Throughout the fourteenth century the dean and chapter went to much trouble and expense in writing for precedents and advice from other secular chapters, and in appealing to the pope against attempts both of their bishops and of the archbishops of Canterbury to visit them. The peaks of the controversy seem to have been in 1322–4 and in 1357–9.[1] In 1397 the chronicler, William de Whitlocke, wrote that Bishop Scrope visited the cathedral church, making decrees there with the consent of the chapter.[2] But it was apparently not until 1428 under Bishop Heyworth that a formal composition on the subject was sealed.[3] By this the bishop's powers were strictly limited. The prebends, as at Salisbury and Wells, were to be entirely exempt except in cases of scandalous neglect; and visitation of the cathedral might take place only once in seven years. Even then the dean retained his authority over all the cathedral clergy. The bishop could only correct the dean or the dean and chapter.

Hereford cathedral seems to have been the last stronghold in England of capitular resistance to episcopal visitation. Both Pope John XXII in 1320 and Martin V in the early fifteenth century granted faculties to the bishops of Hereford to visit their cathedral, notwithstanding any custom to the contrary.[4] But neither Bishop Orleton nor Bishop Spofford are known to have exercised the powers granted to them.[5] After the Reformation, in 1542, the king commanded the chapter to receive its bishop as visitor according to the laudable custom of other cathedrals.[6] Yet in 1563 the bishop reported that the cathedral was still exempt from his

---

[1] Cf. *M.R.A.*, pp. 182, 323–5, 353–4; 'Abstract of Reg. Norbury', in *Coll. Hist. Staffs.*, i, 245–6, 284, 286–7; 'Catalogue of Muniments D. and C. Lichfield', *ibid.*, vi, 52. 'A Form of Proceeding in an Episcopal Visitation of the Lichfield Chapter', undated, but said to be *c.* 1350, is mentioned, *ibid.*, p. 60.

[2] *Anglia Sacra*, i, 451.

[3] *Concilia*, iii, 508; Frere, *loc. cit.*, pp. 76–7. In 1423 the pope had granted power to the bishop of Lichfield to visit his secular cathedral by his ordinary authority (*C.P.L. 1305–42*, pp. 274–5).

[4] *Ibid.*, *1417–31*, p. 196; *Hereford Charters*, p. xxiv.

[5] Cf. *Hereford Charters*, p. xxiv. It is, of course, possible that records of their visitations have been lost.

[6] Reg. Skipworth, f. 40v, quoted by Frere, *loc. cit.* p. 79.

jurisdiction.[1] No visitation is known to have been held at Hereford until the end of the seventeenth century, when it was finally enforced by the Caroline statutes.[2]

The position at Hereford, however, was exceptional and probably irregular. Throughout the middle ages, in this as in other matters, the chapter's constitution remained less subject to the influence of its neighbours than that of any other cathedral in England. Elsewhere, by the early fifteenth century, English secular cathedral chapters had everywhere come to accept visitation. Even in a vacancy of the see, when the archbishop of Canterbury sent his keepers to visit the chapters, no sort of opposition seems to have been offered.[3] This was in striking contrast to the situation in the last half of the thirteenth century. It forms an interesting example of the gradual introduction and enforcement of the rulings of canon law in the English church.

What was the position of the English bishops in their secular cathedrals in the later middle ages? Undoubtedly it was something very different from that of the early bishops living in intimate relations with their cathedral clergy. Both in choir and chapter the bishops' powers were strictly controlled and limited, and few of them dared to appear there frequently. In matters of jurisdiction the chapters often formed almost autonomous ecclesiastical republics within the diocese. Yet it seems that by the middle of the thirteenth century the chapters had mostly reached the peak of their independence. Afterwards their powers were rarely extended on issues vital to the bishop, while in some respects they declined. The decline may be seen both in the history of appointments to bishoprics, and in episcopal visitation of the cathedrals. On certain matters of home government, such as the administration of the vacant deanery, the chapters were still able to advance their claims in the fourteenth century, winning fresh triumphs largely by means of more precise legal definition. Always, too, some chapters, such as Salisbury, Hereford, York, or Lichfield, remained more independent of their bishops than those of Exeter, Lincoln, or St. Paul's. Yet even in the period of greatest capitular independence the English bishops generally succeeded in keeping a fair measure of control over their chapters. They were not faced with any formal organization of the chapters comparable to that

[1] *Ibid.*, pp. 79, 186.   [2] *Hereford Charters*, p. xxiv.
[3] Cf. *Reg. Chichele*, i, xciv–cxiv.

of the 'congregation' of the twelve secular cathedral chapters of the province of Rheims, who in 1330 decided to hold annual assemblies to discuss measures for the defence of their rights and privileges against the archbishop and his suffragans.[1] These assemblies voted financial and legal help to those of their members who were engaged in disputes with their bishops. Instances of the English chapters helping each other against their bishops have been found, but such help rarely went beyond individual chapters sending copies of their rights and privileges to neighbouring chapters whose claims were opposed by their bishops. By their share in appointments to cathedral prebends, even though this was much limited by king, pope, and magnates, the English bishops were usually able to exercise some influence on the composition of their chapters; while in matters of retaining a seat in chapter or in the making of cathedral statutes, they often achieved more than bishops of some continental dioceses. After the Reformation the royal joined with the episcopal power to bring the English cathedral chapters under much stricter supervision than they had ever been since the beginning of the twelfth century.

[1] For the organization of this institution, see H. Nélis, 'La Congrégation des chapitres cathédraux de la province ecclésiastique de Reims à St Quentin (1331–1428)', in *Rev. d'Hist. Eccl.*, xxv (1929), 447–70.

CHAPTER III

THE OFFICERS OF THE CATHEDRAL CHURCH

THE home government of the English secular cathedrals in the later middle ages was everywhere characterized by a very large number of offices: dignities, parsonages (*personatus*) or merely *officia*,[1] all with necessary and practical functions. The fourteenth-century cathedral statutes reveal an elaborately organized system. Officers were drawn from all ranks of the cathedral clergy: from the dignitaries, canons, vicars choral, chantry chaplains, and from the lay *servientes*. Their duties are often described in minute detail. Certain of them, such as the Salisbury communar or the warden of the choristers, were elected by the chapter annually, for a term of years, or for life. The dignitaries' deputies were sometimes appointed by the particular dignitary, sometimes by the dean and chapter or bishop. All took an oath before the chapter to perform their duties faithfully, and were bound to assiduous residence at the cathedral. But none, not even the dignitaries, had the right to sit in chapter by reason of their office. Only the holding of a cathedral prebend could give this right.

Naturally there was diversity in the duties, titles, number and order of precedence of officers in different cathedrals. Some had been instituted in answer to varying local needs, and no officers with exactly corresponding functions can be found in other cathedrals. Frequently their duties overlapped those of other officers. Yet over and above the apparent complexity and confusion of the minor offices, unity and order were given to the constitutions through the four great dignitaries or principal *personae*: the dean, precentor, chancellor, and treasurer. All four were bound to be priests, and, unlike the simple canons, were

---

[1] Attempts, such as those of Bouix, *Tractatus de Capitulis*, pp. 79–81, to draw clear-cut distinctions between *dignitas*, *personatus*, and *officium* are largely academic and without practical value. *Dignitas* was the highest rank in cathedral offices, and *personatus* generally, though not always, implied cure of souls. But the terms were often used interchangeably; while *officium* might be applied to any responsible position.

generally prohibited from holding other benefices with cure of souls. Other officers, such as the archdeacons, subdean or penitentiary, were sometimes given the title and precedence of dignitaries: in some French cathedrals there were as many as fourteen or seventeen dignitaries.[1] But in English cathedrals only these four were described as 'principal' dignitaries or parsons. Simon of Ghent, bishop of Salisbury in the early fourteenth century, wrote that these four, being assiduously resident, ruled the spiritual fabric constructed in their midst like living corner stones or pillars, controlling the lesser ministers, and that their absence might cause the whole fabric to crash in ruin.[2]

This function of binding together and directing the lesser officers was symbolized in many English cathedrals by the assignment to the four *personae* of the four terminal stalls on the two upper rows of the choir.[3] For this reason Bradshaw described the constitutions as 'four-square'.[4] Each of the four was responsible for the direction of a different branch of administration at the cathedral, and, in contrast to the position at English cathedrals of the New Foundation, the dean and chapter had little power to intervene in their particular spheres, save when a dignity was vacant. The dean was president of the chapter and had cure of souls of all the cathedral clergy. The precentor or cantor was in charge of the music and liturgy, and of the song school. The chancellor kept the chapter's seals; acted as its secretary; supervised the schools of grammar and theology; was frequently cathedral librarian and keeper of the archives; arranged the reading of the lessons in choir, and the sermons. The treasurer guarded the church's treasures, and provided the lights and the material necessaries for the services.

Generally, for purposes of comparing and discussing their duties, it will be possible to group most of the minor officials roughly under one of these four main branches of administration. But there are naturally exceptions, and the groups must not be looked upon as forming water-tight compartments. An officer

[1] Cf. G. F. Browne, 'On the Constitutions of French Cathedral Chapters', in *Trans. St. Paul's Ecclesiological Soc.*, iii, 226–40.

[2] *Reg. S. de Gandavo*, pp. 42–3.

[3] This was the custom at Salisbury, Lincoln, Chichester, Lichfield, and Exeter. Elsewhere there were variations. Details and diagrams of the order of the choir stalls at all the nine secular cathedrals are given in *L.S.*, i, 104–5, 136–8.

[4] *Ibid.*, p. 102.

might be supervised by a dignitary at one cathedral, while another officer with similar duties at a different church might be responsible directly to the dean and chapter. Moreover, the existence of officers with different functions at different churches makes any very definite grouping impossible. The financial and business officers of the chapter were not responsible to any particular dignitary, and so must be discussed separately, while the few cathedral duties of the archdeacons were unconnected with any main branch of the administration. For the most part I shall concentrate on describing the functions of the officers in the later middle ages, when the cathedral constitutions were highly developed. But at the same time it will be interesting to see how certain offices came to be instituted, and how they grew or changed in the course of the centuries, in answer to fresh needs or changing conditions.

1. THE DEAN

Between about 1086 and 1225 a dean emerged as sole head under the bishop at all nine English secular cathedral chapters. This was by no means universally the practice in medieval cathedrals. From about the second quarter of the eleventh century, deans were being appointed as the immediate heads under the bishop at most Norman cathedrals,[1] and are also found from the tenth or eleventh century onwards in a similar position of authority at many other cathedral and collegiate churches in Northern France. But elsewhere, at least until the closing centuries of the middle ages there was usually a division under the bishop between the spiritual authority in a chapter (commonly the dean in Germany and the Low Countries, and the archpriest in Southern France and Italy) and the temporal authority of a provost or archdeacon, analogous to the division of authority between the prior and cellarer under the abbot in a Benedictine community. In many of these chapters the provost or archdeacon held the first place among the dignitaries.[2]

[1] D. Douglas in *Camb. Hist. Jour.*, xiii (1957), 111–13. Coutances was exceptional among Norman cathedrals in having no dean. Here, as in the Breton cathedrals of Dol, Tréguier and Léon, the cantor became head of the chapter.

[2] There is no study of cathedral dignitaries over Europe as a whole. Investigations by Professor Hamilton Thompson for his *Archdeacons and Rural Deans*

The origin of the office of cathedral dean is often obscure and difficult to trace. The title dean would seem by the fifth century to have lost its old association with an officer in charge of ten men. It was used in the Imperial civil service and the later Roman law books for an official messenger or intermediary.[1] St. Benedict in the sixth century preferred that monks under their abbot should be entrusted to several deans rather than to one provost, because the authority of the deans was less likely to clash with that of the abbot.[2] But in this early period there seems to be no trace of deans among the bishop's clerks at the cathedrals. From the fourth or fifth centuries archpriests occur at the head of the priests of the bishops' *familiae*, and archdeacons at the head of the deacons.[3] By the seventh century the archdeacon had usually established his authority over his rival, at any rate in matters of ecclesiastical government and jurisdiction over the clergy; but the 'episcopal' or 'city' archpriest, as distinct from the rural archpriest, kept the right to take the absent bishop's place in the celebration of mass and other solemn acts of public worship at the cathedral.[4] Then in the eighth or ninth centuries, with the adoption of Chrodegang's rule, there was also usually a provost of the canons,[5] who came to concern himself chiefly with the economic administration of the community. About the same time deans might be appointed as officers subordinate to the provost, helping him with the internal discipline of the church. It is thought that Chrodegang may have taken the idea of such deans from the Benedictine

---

(1943), pp. 8–9, 21, and 'Notes on Colleges of Secular Canons in England', in *Arch. Jour.*, lxxiv, 160 n., 177–8, by G. F. Browne, 'On the Constitution of French Chapters', in *Trans. St. Paul's Ecclesiological Soc.*, iii, 225–40, and by Hinschius, *Kirchenrecht*, ii, 88–97, suggest that an archdeacon held the first place among the dignitaries in about half of the Italian Cathedrals, and in a few churches in Languedoc and Gascony. In southern and central France, and in Germany a provost often ranked above or in place of the dean as head of the chapter, and about thirty-five cathedrals in northern Italy had a provost at their head. At Milan and Cremona the archpriest was placed first among the dignitaries. There are occasional examples of a treasurer, *custos*, sacrist or cantor being head of a chapter.

[1] See M. Deanesly, *Sidelights on the Anglo-Saxon Church*, pp. 138–45, 155–6.
[2] *Sancti Benedicti Regula*, c. 21.
[3] See A. Amanieu, 'L'Archidiacre' and 'L'Archiprêtre', in *Dict. de Droit Canonique*.
[4] *Ibid.*, cc. 1005–6.
[5] Cf. Hinschius, ii, 89–92.

rule.[1] The title dean is sometimes used for prior in English monasteries in late Saxon times and in German monasteries under the influence of Gorze.[2]

As the head officer of cathedral and collegiate chapters in northern France the dean dates only from the tenth century. He apparently arose in a variety of ways at different churches. In cathedrals which had an archpriest, he frequently succeeded to the archpriest, inheriting his priestly duties and headship in choir; though in some chapters, such as Orléans, and Tours, an arch-priest continued to have cure of souls, and to rank among the dignitaries and *personae* after a dean had been made head of the chapter.[3] Often the dean's rise was due to the gradual abandon-ment by the provost of the spiritual and internal direction of the cathedral clerks for greater concentration on temporal and external concerns. Sometimes, when the canons were oppressed by the provost's economic administration, the provostry was abolished altogether; elsewhere it might be made subordinate to the dean, with its duties strictly limited to those of an economic and business nature, while the dean exercised both spiritual and temporal authority. Then the archdeacons in many churches were slowly forced to give up much of their power of jurisdiction and correction over the cathedral clergy and chapter lands to the dean.[4] This growing concentration of powers in the dean's hand seems to have been bound up with the feudalization of society in northern France. The dean's position was in some ways assimilated to that of a feudal landholder, exercising lay jurisdiction on the cathedral estates, and the king or duke began to influence his appointment. At the same time the chapters with their many grants of land and privileges from king and magnates came to form wealthy and autonomous bodies with a growing corporate spirit. In time they began to elect their dean, sometimes under royal or ducal influence, from among themselves to be their

---

[1] Cf. Hinschius, ii, p. 92. For the influence of the Benedictine rule on Chrodegang's arrangements at Metz, see C. de Clercq, *op. cit.*, pp. 146 *et seq.* In some Benedictine monasteries the title of dean survived until a late date for monks responsible for discipline (E.g. A. H. Thompson, *Archdeacons and Rural Deans*, p. 22 n.).

[2] M. Deanesly, *Sidelights on the Anglo-Saxon Church*, pp. 157–70; K. Hallinger, *Gorze-Kluny* (*Studia Anselmiana*, 1950–1).

[3] Amanieu, *loc. cit.*, c. 1018; A. H. Thompson, *loc. cit.*, p. 21.

[4] *Ibid.*, cc. 990–91.

separate and immediate head. Thus the dean's office became very different from that of the earlier archpriest, archdeacon, provost or pre-feudal dean, who had all been appointed by the bishop simply as his deputies at the cathedral church and had not challenged his real headship of the chapter. There was now a much clearer separation of interests of bishop and chapter and greater independence of the chapter, which often coincided with the development of a secular organization in place of the common life.

In England deans are found occasionally in late Saxon times as the second in command under the bishop at both colleges of clerks, such as Durham cathedral when it was served by clerks under Walcher, and cathedral monasteries such as Canterbury and Worcester.[1] A list of pre-conquest deans of St. Paul's in a copy of the cathedral statutes is unreliable, but the first known dean there, the Anglo-Saxon Wulman, may already have been in office at Bishop Maurice's accession in 1086.[2] He was on one occasion addressed by Bishop Maurice in a charter before the archdeacons;[3] but for the most part the archdeacons were given precedence. It was only from the time of Wulman's Norman successor, William, the nephew of Bishop Richard de Belmeis, that the deans of St. Paul's ceased to be overshadowed by the archdeacons, and that their position as leaders of the chapter was distinctly recognized by the writers of the chapter documents. At the same time the separation of bishop and chapter at St. Paul's seems to have become clearer.[4]

The first introduction to English cathedrals of deans on the northern French model was made by the three bishops, Osmund, Remigius, and Thomas, in their new secular foundations of Salisbury, Lincoln, and York in 1090–1.[5] Throughout the twelfth century the influence of the constitution of Salisbury cathedral especially was strong on other English chapters. The deaneries of Chichester, Lichfield, and Wells, are thought to have been instituted under the influence of Salisbury about 1108, 1139, and

[1] Cf. Makower, *Const. Hist.*, p. 299, n. 6; Frere, *Visitation Articles*, i, 55; M. Deanesly, *Sidelights on the Anglo-Saxon Church*, pp. 157–70.
[2] C. N. L. Brooke in *Camb. Hist. Jour.*, x, 118; cf. *Bull. Inst. Hist. Research*, xxix (1956), 233.
[3] *Early Charters of St. Paul*, no. 59.   [4] *Ibid.*, pp. xxix–xxx.
[5] *S.S.*, pp. 26–9; *Henry of Huntingdon*, p. 301; *Hist. Ch. York*, ii, 107–8.

1140 respectively.[1] At Wells it is interesting to notice that, as in many continental churches, the dean succeeded to a provost who had abused his power over the canons to exploit their estates in his own interests.[2] The first known dean of Hereford was Erchemar *c.* 1108–15.[3] Indeed, usually the dean was among the first of the four great dignitaries to be instituted in the newly organized secular chapters after the Conquest. But at Exeter, which long remained detached from the main current of constitutional development at English cathedrals, he was the last. This was probably due to the persistence of traditions of the common life established by Leofric in 1050. Throughout the twelfth century and later the chapter seems to have lived in much closer relationship with its bishop than other English secular chapters. Although a more secular organization was gradually introduced from about 1133, when the canons moved out of their old church into the new cathedral built in the episcopate of their Norman bishop, William de Warelwast,[4] no evidence has been found to support Oliver's statement[5] that, in the twelfth century, before the appointment of a dean, the cantor presided over the chapter. So far as can be judged from the available lists of witnesses to chapter documents of the twelfth and early thirteenth centuries, only the four archdeacons seem consistently to have had precedence of the other canons;[6] the offices of cantor and treasurer apparently conferred no higher rank than that of their brethren on the canons

---

[1] Odo, the first known dean of Chichester, occurs in 1108 (*Eadmeri Historia Novorum*, ed. M. Rule (Rolls Ser.), p. 205). A dean was apparently the first dignitary instituted by Bishop Robert when he began to reorganize Wells chapter on a secular basis *c.* 1136–40 (J. A. Robinson, 'The First Deans of Wells' in *Somerset Hist. Essays*, pp. 56–62; Church, *op. cit.*, 11–13, 352–4). At Lichfield a dean is first found attesting charters about 1139–40, i.e. about the time when Bishop Roger de Clinton was reorganizing the chapter there (H. E. Savage, *Lichfield Chapter in the Twelfth Century*, p. 11).

[2] Church, *op. cit.*, pp. 5–12, 352–4. At Lichfield, also, the dean's predecessor had been a provost first instituted in 822 (*Anglia Sacra*, i, 448).

[3] Balliol MS. 271, f. 93ᵛ, no. 412. I owe this reference to Miss Marjorie Jones.

[4] Cf. F. Rose-Troup, *The Consecration of the Norman Minster at Exeter*. The move to new buildings seems to have provided a good opportunity for making changes.

[5] *Lives of the Bishops of Exeter*, p. 34.

[6] See e.g. the lists of witnesses printed in *The Crawford Charters*, no. xiii; *H.M.C. Var. Coll.*, iv, 45–66; Oliver, *op. cit.*, pp. 17–18, 28; F. Rose-Troup, *op. cit.*, pp. 16–17, 23.

L

who held them. The archdeacons' pre-eminence would be natural at a cathedral still partially under the influence of Chrodegang's rule. A dean was finally instituted in 1225 by Bishop Brewer on the advice of Archbishop Stephen Langton, in order that Exeter should conform with the practice of other English cathedral churches. Then it was the archdeacons who apparently lost most. The new dean was to have all the jurisdiction which the archdeacon of Exeter then held in the city, together with a house belonging to the archdeacon of Totnes.[1]

'That which belongs to the dean's office is found to be little decided in law; indeed it consists in different things according to various customs of different places; and so it is rooted in custom,'[2] wrote William Alnwick, bishop of Lincoln, as late as 1440. There are few detailed descriptions of the dean's office in cathedral custom and statute books. He seems at first to have been assigned wide though rather indefinite powers in many spheres of cathedral activity. 'Present by day and night, rule thou everything, O Dean,' are the words inscribed over his stall at Exeter.[3] His functions were apparently not defined in any complete or precise form at Salisbury, York, or Lincoln in 1090–1, but were developed and built up gradually: often they can only be discovered by piecing together scattered evidence from judicial awards, charters, statutes, chapter acts, and passing references to his activities in a variety of cathedral documents. Moreover, his powers varied considerably at different cathedrals. At Salisbury his authority was in most respects greater than at Lincoln. At Chichester, where the bishop's position was unusually strong, the dean's power seems never to have developed so fully as in other churches.[4] At Lichfield, after a slow start in the twelfth and early thirteenth centuries,[5] the dean rapidly built up a strong position as against the bishop.[6] Yet nowhere in the English cathedrals of the Old Foundation was the dean able to attain anything approaching the supremacy over the chapter of the dean of the post-Reformation cathedrals of the

[1] *H.M.C. Var. Coll.*, iv, 66. Cf. F. Rose-Troup, 'The Establishment of the Office of Dean in Exeter Cathedral', in *Devon and Cornwall Notes and Queries* (Jan. 1934), pp. 16–20.

[2] *L.S.*, iii, 281.   [3] *Ordinale Exon.*, i, 3.

[4] Cf. Frere, *Visitation Articles*, i, 79.

[5] Until 1222 the dean of Lichfield was nominated by the bishop (*Anglia Sacra*, i, 437).

[6] See above and below, pp. 132, 147; Frere, *Visitation Articles*, i, 76.

New Foundation, where his pre-eminence was not qualified by the presence of other resident dignitaries.

Everywhere the dean's first duty was that of the priest: 'He is pre-eminent over all in the rule of souls and correction of behaviour.'[1] He judged the moral lapses of all the cathedral clergy; visited the cathedral clergy when they were dying; heard their confessions, and ministered extreme unction to them.[2] In choir, as chief priest, he naturally succeeded to the absent bishop's functions. As medieval bishops were present less and less often at their cathedral churches, the honour and reverence due to the head of the church were paid increasingly to the dean. The more solemn duties of divine worship came to be reserved to him: the saying of the *confiteor* at prime and compline; the giving of the benediction; the performance of the special ceremonies on Ash Wednesday, Maundy Thursday, and Palm Sunday; the celebration of the office on all the principal double feasts.[3] He might also be required to preach public sermons on certain great feasts.[4] When resident, he was expected to take his turn as hebdomadary or canon of the week, like the other residentiaries.[5]

In addition the dean had a variety of other duties, in chapter and in matters of administration and jurisdiction, both within and outside the cathedral close. These present more problems than his priestly functions. They made his work more varied and less specialized than that of the other dignitaries, but offered more opportunities for clashes with the authority of the chapter and other cathedral officers.

In chapter the dean was generally recognized as 'first in session and voice, and the more honourable part of the chapter'.[6] But his headship might be limited by the custom which did not allow him to take part in discussing or deciding chapter business unless he held a cathedral canonry and prebend. In 1389 Bishop Trefnant at

[1] *S.S.*, pp. 28–9; *L.S.*, i, 280; ii, 9, 154; iii, 282; *Ordinale Exon.*, i, 3; *C.S.*, p. 13; *W.S.*, pp. 45, 55; *R.S.S.P.*, p. 16.
[2] E.g. *L.S.*, i, 280–1, 294–5; iii, 342–3; *S.S.*, p. 57; *R.S.S.P.*, p. 61.
[3] See e.g. *Use Sarum*, i, 3, 14; *S.S.*, pp. 57, 61, 262–3; *W.S.*, p. 18; Harl. MS. 1027, f. 10b; *L.S.*, i, 282, 366; ii, 25, 31, 62, 92; iii, 294; *R.S.S.P.*, pp. 16–18.
[4] E.g. *L.S.*, ii, 25, 32, 92.
[5] *Ibid.*, p. 62; *R.S.S.P.*, p. 48. At Lincoln he was exempted from his turn *in cursu* (i.e. in place of a non-resident canon), but was bound to perform his week *in propria* (i.e. his own turn), if he held a prebend and resided.
[6] *L.S.*, iii, 279.

Hereford maintained that this was only a local Hereford custom which was evidently null and void, since it contravened the *ius commune* of the church, requiring all deans of cathedrals and colleges to reside and attend chapter meetings.[1] Yet although they were certainly bound to residence, most canonists recognized that in the later middle ages such deans could not attend chapter meetings unless they held a prebend.[2] Salisbury and Wells got over the difficulty by annexing a cathedral prebend permanently to the office of dean as part of his endowment;[3] while the St. Paul's chapter declared that only canons of their church already holding prebends could be elected to their deanery.[4] But this ruling could not be maintained in face of the later papal provisions of deans from outside the body of canons. There were a number of deans of St. Paul's, Lincoln, and York in the later middle ages who were unable to attend debates of their chapters without a special invitation from the canons, until they could be collated to a cathedral prebend.[5]

Yet none of the chapters could meet unless they were specially summoned by the dean or his deputy; and apparently the dean always had the right and duty, even if he were not a canon, to expound in chapter, in person or by deputy, the business for which the meeting was called.[6] After this, he could withdraw if necessary.[7] At Lincoln there was an unusual amount of friction between the dean and chapter, particularly during the deanship of John Macworth (1412–51) on this subject of summoning chapter meetings. When he was present at Lincoln, the dean was said to make overbearing use of his power to summon the chapter of residentiaries on frivolous excuses and at inconvenient

---

[1] *Reg. Trefnant*, pp. 80–3. This was after Bishop Gilbert, his immediate predecessor, and the chapter of Hereford had appropriated the prebend of Bullinghope to the deanery, in order that the dean might be able to reside and attend chapters and councils. Bishop Trefnant refused to allow the annexation.

[2] See the references quoted by Bouix, *Tractatus de Capitulis*, pp. 70–1. The rule was sometimes enforced at Chartres (Amiet, *op. cit.*, pp. 46–8).

[3] Jones, *Fasti Sar.*, p. 217; J. A. Robinson, *Somerset Hist. Essays*, p. 63.

[4] *R.S.S.P.*, p. 87. Even so, there was still a possibility that a new residentiary might be elected dean, and at St. Paul's new residentiaries in their first year were not allowed to attend chapter meetings. In such a case, the chapter decided that the same rule must apply to the dean as to other new residentiaries (*ibid.*, p. 130).

[5] Cf. *ibid.*, pp. 390–1.   [6] E.g. *L.S.*, iii, 285.   [7] *R.S.S.P.*, p. 130.

PLATE IV
THE CHAPTER HOUSE, SALISBURY CATHEDRAL
INTERIOR VIEW, 1810

Plate V

A Group of Canons

times, so that they could attend neither to the cathedral services nor to their studies;[1] while he would refuse to recognize the right of the president and chapter to deal with current business in his absence.[2] The consent of both dean and chapter was normally required for all cathedral legislation. But at Lincoln in view of the dean's frequent absences, Bishop Alnwick declared in his award of 1439 that the chapter might legislate, in the dean's absence, on such minor and unimportant matters as it could legally decide in the dean's presence without the bishop's consent.[3] On the whole medieval cathedral deans in England were given little opportunity to develop autocratic tendencies: the bishop's position was generally fairly strong, and the chapters jealously defended their own powers. The English dean's vote in chapter always remained equal to that of any other canon, not, as in some continental churches, to those of all the rest of the chapter put together.[4] He could not open letters addressed to the dean and chapter except in the presence of his brethren in chapter;[5] nor could he summon a general convocation of resident and non-resident canons without the previous assent of the chapter of residentiaries.[6]

In matters of administration and jurisdiction, both at the cathedral and on the chapter estates, the main problem by the later middle ages was to decide how far the dean could act independently, and how far the chapter shared his powers with him. Lincoln chapter, which, at any rate after the thirteenth century, seems to have feared and resented its dean's authority even more than that of its bishop, gradually established claims to share in nearly all these powers, as the result of a struggle spread over two centuries. The chapters of York and St. Paul's also asserted their control over the exercise of much of the decanal jurisdiction. But the canons of Salisbury in the later middle ages were mainly concerned in curbing their bishop's powers, and generally allowed their dean much more independence of action. At Salisbury the bishop's mandate for the admission of new canons had to be addressed solely to the dean, not to the dean and chapter.[7] Elsewhere the admission of all cathedral clergy was usually a joint act of dean and chapter. But everywhere the dean's consent was

---

[1] *L.S.*, iii, 375, 377-8, 390.
[2] *Ibid.*, pp. 374-5.
[3] *Ibid.*, iii, 208.
[4] Cf. Benson, *The Cathedral*, p. 42.
[5] *L.S.*, iii, 297.
[6] E.g. *ibid.*, ii, 93; iii, 285.
[7] See above, p. 121.

necessary for their admission, and all swore an oath of personal obedience to the dean as well as one of fidelity to the church, and observance of its statutes and customs.[1]

As immediate ordinary at the cathedral, one of the dean's most important functions was his general supervision over and power to correct all the cathedral clergy. Yet severe limitations were often imposed on him in this capacity. A St. Paul's statute declared that he must proceed *modeste* when correcting the major canons; in no case could he expel a major canon from the choir, or punish him without the judgement of his brethren.[2] At Lichfield he was forbidden to meddle in the treasurer's office, because it was distinct from the deanery.[3] Everywhere any formal judgement of the canons had to be in chapter;[4] while the vicars choral and other *ministri inferiores* were cited either before the dean in chapter or before a common auditor of the dean and chapter to answer for their misdeeds and neglect of duty.[5] Lincoln chapter actually claimed that the dean could exercise no power of correction except in common with it.[6] But at Exeter the dean seems to have had more authority over the canons than elsewhere, although he was as the same time less independent of the bishop. The cathedral statutes made him personally responsible under heavy penalties for seeing that the residentiary canons performed their duties, and for enforcing a just distribution of commons.[7] In 1390 there was a recorded case of a canon of Exeter begging the dean's forgiveness for his bad behaviour.[8]

Outside the cathedral, in the more strictly legal sphere, the position was complicated by the varying number of courts. At some English cathedrals the dean was *ex officio* archdeacon of the cathedral city and suburbs; but at most of these churches his authority in this capacity devolved on the subdean, who usually

---

[1] E.g. *S.S.*, pp. 127–30; *L.S.*, i, 397–9. At Chichester the canons swore obedience to the dean and chapter, instead of to the dean alone (Swainson, pp. 8, 21).

[2] *R.S.S.P.*, p. 19. [3] *Monasticon*, VI, iii, 1261.

[4] E.g. *S.S.*, p. 57; *L.S.*, i, 280; ii, 16, 154; iii, 282; *W.S.*, pp. 44, 55. At Hereford the dean might admonish a canon privately at first, or charge him with his faults before two or three canons; but any more formal charge and punishment, brought after these methods had proved unsuccessful, had to be *in pleno capitulo* (*L.S.*, ii, 59).

[5] See below, pp. 271–2. [6] *L.S.*, i, 319–21; iii, 296–7.

[7] Harl. MS. 1027, ff. 16b–17a. [8] *H.M.C. Var. Coll.*, iv, 39.

exercised the archidiaconal jurisdiction whether the dean was present or not.[1] The dean naturally had his own court, like any other dignitary or prebendary, for the proof of wills and other ecclesiastical causes on the estates belonging to his dignity. But in the court which judged causes arising in the lands and churches of the chapter's common fund and heard appeals from the prebendal courts, his jurisdiction had usually to be exercised jointly with the chapter: its extent will be discussed below in connexion with the officers of the court. Everywhere the dean had a special responsibility for the administration of the common lands. In the later middle ages there were also separate elected officers in charge of the lands and profits; but the dean still swore on his admission 'to gather together or reintegrate possessions of the church which may have been unjustly scattered, and revenues dishonestly alienated'.[2] One of the most impressive results of a medieval dean's activity in supervising the chapter's property were the great surveys of lands and churches belonging to St. Paul's chapter, known as the Domesdays of St. Paul's, compiled in 1181, 1222, and 1279 on the initiative of Deans Ralph de Diceto, Robert de Watford, and Ralph Baldock.[3]

In addition to his ordinary jurisdiction over the cathedral clergy, their lands and churches, the dean also claimed to be their visitor. The deans of Salisbury, Lichfield, and Wells apparently established this claim without much difficulty, both at the cathedral and in the prebends.[4] At St. Paul's the chapter elected a residentiary canon to accompany the dean on his triennial visitations of the chapter churches and manors.[5] At

[1] See below, pp. 153–4.
[2] E.g. *Salisbury Ceremonies*, pp. 109–10; *W.S.*, p. 92; Swainson, p. 30; cf. *R.S.S.P.*, p. 15. At Exeter the cathedral statutes assigned to the dean the duty of examining and admitting all officers and commissaries of the common lands (Harl. MS. 1027, f. 36b).
[3] See Stubbs, Introduction to *Hist. Works of Ralph de Diceto*, i, lvi–lxi; W. H. Hale, *The Domesday of St. Paul's* (Camden Soc.).
[4] *S.S.*, pp. 52–3, 302–3; *Reg. S. de Gandavo*, p. 161; *L.S.*, ii, 26–7; *W.S.*, pp. 125–6, 133 *et seq.*; *H.M.C. Wells*, i, 189–90. Records of a decanal visitation of Salisbury prebendal churches in 1220–24 are available in *Reg. S. Osmund*, i, 275–314; and of the cathedral treasury and chantries in 1387 and 1390 in Reg. Coman, f. 94; Reg. Dunham, f. 131. For similar records at Lichfield, see 'Catalogue of Muniments of D. and C. Lichfield', in *Coll. Hist. Staffs.*, vi, 56–60.
[5] *R.S.S.P.*, p. 96. Records of a decanal visitation of St. Paul's treasury and chantries are printed in Dugdale, *Hist. St. Paul's*, pp. 310–35.

Chichester and Hereford the annual or biennial visitation of the common estates had to be made by the dean and canons jointly, and at the common expense.[1] But at Lincoln the dean's position was more difficult. In 1239 Bishop Grosseteste had denied to him all right to visit, saying that a dean was *visor*, not *visitator* of the cathedral. These two functions were incompatible: no one charged with the immediate care of the cathedral church and bound to continuous residence in it could visit there, for a visitor should come from outside; even more definitely the dean could not visit the prebends, dignities, and common lands 'in distant places far and wide', because this would interfere with his first duty of residence and continuous supervision at the cathedral.[2] Nevertheless, in spite of opposition from both bishop and chapter, the fourteenth-century deans of Lincoln did visit both the cathedral church and the prebends and common lands, although sometimes they were forced to send out their summons in the name of the chapter as well as in their own name.[3] In 1314 the chapter scored a victory when it was agreed that the dean must always have three or four residentiary canons with him on visitation to act as his assessors.[4] But the final award on the subject made by Bishop Fleming in 1421 in the king's presence was more favourable to the dean. In future the dean was to be allowed to visit triennially, and the number of his assessors was reduced to two, of whom the dean himself might choose one. [5]

THE SUBDEAN AND PENITENTIARY; OTHER DEPUTIES OF THE DEAN

'In case the dean is absent from the church, let the subdean supply his place.'[6] The meaning of this general statement, apparently first made in England at Salisbury in the Institution of St. Osmund and repeated in the statutes of most other English secular cathedrals, was rarely defined in detail. In practice the subdean's status and duties seem to have varied in different churches more than those of most cathedral officers.

[1] *C.S.*, p. 19; *L.S.*, ii, 60.
[2] *Roberti Grosseteste Epistolae*, pp. 376–7. The object of Grosseteste's letter was of course to prove that only the bishop could visit the cathedral.
[3] Cf. *L.S.*, ii, clix and n.   [4] *Ibid.*, p. civ.
[5] *C.P.R., 1416–22*, pp. 404–6. Cf. *L.S.*, iii, 286–7.
[6] *S.S.*, pp. 30–1, 61; *L.S.*, ii, 23; iii, 307; *Ordinale Exon.*, i, 5; *W.S.*, pp. 45, 56.

At three churches, Lincoln, York, and Wells, the subdean held an important position as a dignitary or *persona*, usually ranking after the archdeacons, as at Bayeux, but having precedence of the simple canons.[1] At Exeter, too, he took precedence of the canons, though he was not given the title of dignitary.[2] Moreover, at all four churches his office was well endowed, sometimes having a prebend annexed to it;[3] while his appointment, like that of the dignitaries and canons, lay with the bishop. At Hereford and Chichester, on the other hand, the subdean was apparently merely the dean's delegate or official in his peculiar jurisdiction.[4] At St. Paul's, also, he held a subordinate place, being chosen from the minor canons by the dean and chapter. He received higher emoluments than the other minor canons, but his office was simply a ministry during the dean's absence, and he had no certain status or choir stall by reason of it.[5] The Salisbury office of subdean was intermediate in rank between these two types. It was perpetual and might be held either by a canon or a vicar. If the subdean were a vicar, he ranked above the other vicars but below the canons; if a canon, as was more usual in the fourteenth century, he took his place among the canons according to the length of his residence.[6] In 1686 he was described by Dean Pierce as a quasi-dignitary.[7]

The office of subdean seems to have been rarer than others at northern French chapters. Rouen never had a subdean. But there was one at Bayeux as early as 1092.[8] Thus it is quite possible, as the Institution of St. Osmund suggests,[9] that Salisbury chapter had

[1] *L.S.*, ii, 94; *W.S.*, pp. 44, 55; *Valor Ecclesiasticus*, i, 133; Deslandes, *op. cit.*, pp. 94-5. At Lincoln his office was given place after the archdeacons in the Black Book (*L.S.*, i, 279), but in the *Novum Registrum* of 1440 he was placed among the principal *personae* taking rank next after the treasurer (*ibid.*, iii, 272). At Chartres the subdean was the third dignitary, having precedence of the chancellor, *capicerius* and archdeacons (Amiet, *op. cit.*, p. 80). But such high rank was unusual for him, and was never adopted in England.

[2] *Reg. Quivil*, pp. 324-5.

[3] See *H.M.C. Wells*, i, 33, 66; *Reg. Gray (York)*, i, 26-7; Le Neve—I.H.R., 1300-1541, i, 128; *Use Exeter*, p. 84.

[4] *Reg. Cantilupe*, p. 2 and n.; A. T. Bannister, *Cathedral Church of Hereford*, p. 39; Swainson, p. 63.

[5] *R.S.S.P.*, pp. 91, 94-5.

[6] Jones, *Fasti Sar.*, pp. 263-70. The emoluments of the office were slight, but in 1443 a house near St. Anne's Gate in the close was annexed to it.

[7] *Ibid.*, p. 263.   [8] *Livre Noir*, no. 22.   [9] *S.S.*, pp. 30-1.

a subdean from its foundation. The earliest known holder of the office there is William, about 1122,[1] and at Lincoln, Humphrey, about 1135.[2] At three other chapters, Wells, Lichfield, and Hereford, a subdean appears fairly soon after their reorganization as secular chapters, about the middle or second half of the twelfth century.[3] But at the remaining four churches the office was a late development. At York it was only founded in 1228;[4] at Exeter in 1284;[5] and at St. Paul's in 1295;[6] while the first known mention of a subdean at Chichester is not until 1306.[7]

The subdean seldom had the right to perform all or most of the absent dean's functions. It was, however, usual for him to take the absent dean's place in choir. At St. Paul's a main object of the institution of a subdean in 1295 was to provide for someone to fulfil the dean's duties in choir during his legitimate absence.[8] In most English cathedrals the subdean's choir stall was near that of the dean,[9] presumably so that he could more easily take the dean's place when necessary; but naturally the same reverence was not paid to him as to the dean. Sometimes the highest dignitary present celebrated at the high altar on greater feasts, when both bishop and dean were absent.[10] At Hereford it was always the

---

[1] *Reg. S. Osmund*, i, 381; cf. *Regesta Regum Anglo-Norm.* (1956), ii, no. 1372, dated 1121-2.

[2] *Reg. Antiquissimum*, ii, 254; Le Neve-Hardy, ii, 37. There seems no evidence for assuming, as Bradshaw does (*L.S.*, i, 31), that 'Felix, exemplum viri clarissimi,' described by Henry of Huntingdon (p. 301) as among the first canons of the church instituted by Remigius, was subdean.

[3] At Wells there was a subdean in Bishop Robert's time (1136-66), and at Hereford two have been traced in the last half of the twelfth century. The Lichfield subdeanery was founded about 1165-7 (Church, *op. cit.*, p. 15; Bannister, *op. cit.*, p. 39; Z. N. and C. N. L. Brooke, *op. cit.*, in *Camb. Hist. Jour.*, viii, 183; Savage, *Lichfield Chapter in the Twelfth Century*, p. 7).

[4] *Reg. Gray*, i, 26-7.

[5] *Reg. Quivil*, pp. 324-5.

[6] *R.S.S.P.*, pp. 94-5. Miss Gibbs gives some doubtful references to a subdean of St. Paul's in 1205 and 1239-41, before the formal institution of the office (*Early Charters of St. Paul*, pp. xxviii-xxix n.).

[7] Le Neve—I.H..R, vii, 6.

[8] *R.S.S.P.*, p. 94. The chapter said that up till now these burdens had not been incumbent *ex officio* on any certain residentiary, and in consequence had been neglected with peril to souls.

[9] For details of the position of his stall in the different cathedrals, see *L.S.*, i, 105, 136-8.

[10] E.g. *ibid.*, iii, 283. But cf. *L.S.*, i, 274; iii, 280, 307; *S.S.*, p. 30 n.

dean's vicar choral, not the subdean, who relieved the dean, when necessary, on eves of feast days and on feasts of nine lessons.[1]

At those churches where the subdean ranked with the dignitaries and canons, he generally had the right to take the dean's place as president of the chapter. At Lincoln he presided, even when greater dignitaries were present;[2] and both here and at Wells and Exeter he apparently exercised also the absent dean's powers of supervising and correcting the cathedral clergy, and of granting licences for a few days' absence to the lesser clergy.[3] Elsewhere his powers were much more limited. At St. Paul's he was expressly forbidden to interfere with the major canons, though he might correct and coerce the minor canons and inferior clergy, and expedite urgent business of the church in the dean's absence.[4] The subdeans of Salisbury, Chichester, Lichfield, and Hereford had no power either to correct in the cathedral or to preside in chapter; the deans of these churches had other deputies or commissaries for such duties.

Three methods might be adopted. Hereford was exceptional in having as its president during the dean's absence the hebdomadary canon or canon of the week.[5] Elsewhere, the senior residentiary present (whether a dignitary or simple canon) might preside *ex consuetudine*,[6] or the dean might appoint any residentiary he pleased to be his lieutenant or commissary in chapter. In 1365 Lichfield chapter decided that this second method was contrary to its statutes; it forced the dean's lieutenant to resign and chose a president.[7] At Salisbury, however, the dean's authority was

---

[1] *L.S.*, ii, 62. He was the only vicar at Hereford allowed to celebrate at the high altar (*ibid.*, ii, 73).

[2] E.g. *ibid.*, iii, 288–9; cf. 292, 307. Letters of Lincoln chapter sent in the dean's absence were made out in the name of the subdean and chapter (e.g. *Reg. Antiquissimum*, i, 126; cf. iii, 322). The York statutes do not mention the presidency of the chapter in the dean's absence, though the subdean's status at York seems to have been similar in most other respects to that of the Lincoln subdean. The subdean of Exeter had the first voice in chapter after the *personae* (*Reg. Quivil*, p. 325).

[3] *Ibid.*, pp. 324–5; *W.S.*, p. 57; *L.S.*, iii, 287–8, 307. At Lincoln he installed the canons and exercised the *sede vacante* jurisdiction with the chapter during the dean's absence (*ibid.*, iii, 280, 289; i, 274).   [4] *R.S.S.P.*, pp. 94–5.

[5] E.g. *Reg. Cantilupe*, pp. 34–5; *Reg. Swinfield*, pp. 138–9, 141, 255; *Reg. Orleton*, pp. 57.   [6] E.g. *R.S.S.P.*, p. 238.

[7] Bodl. Library, MS. Ashmole 794, f. 145. I owe this reference to Mrs. Hester Jenkins.

stronger. Here the fourteenth-century practice can be traced in the chapter act books, especially during the period 1305–85, when six deans in succession were non-resident foreigners. During the early 1340's, Elias of St. Albans, the chancellor, a senior residentiary, usually presided, and was described sometimes as *presidens*, sometimes as *locum tenens decani*, to which latter title was occasionally added '*de consuetudine quam ex commissione*'.[1] But on 30th May 1345 John Kirkby, archdeacon of Dorset, and Robert Baldock, both residentiary canons, received in the chapter house 'a certain mandate or commission to take the dean's place, the dean being *in remotis*'.[2] A year later, John Kirkby, *pro tribunale sedens*, declared in chapter that he could not and did not wish any longer to hold the office of *locum tenens decani*, which he straightway renounced.[3] Then, in July 1348, John de Vienne, a canon who had not previously resided, arrived in the diocese as 'proctor, vicar general, and special commissary of the absent dean, Reginald de Filiis Ursi, with power to visit the canons' prebends and prebendal churches'.[4] The chapter granted him a canonical house of residence in the close,[5] and he held several chapter meetings during a very short tenure of office.[6]

A dispute in 1393 between Thomas Southam, the dean's *locum tenens*, and John Norton, the chancellor, claiming to be president *ex consuetudine*, established definitely that the senior residentiary had no right to act as president when the dean had formally appointed a *locum tenens*. John, during Thomas's temporary absence from the city, had presumed to summon and celebrate a chapter at which he had admitted a new canon and prebendary to the church, and had accepted the fee due to the dean or his deputy for the installation. By judgement of the chapter he was forced to refund the money to Thomas, and was forbidden to hold such a chapter again.[7] The commission granted in 1385 to Thomas Southam by the absent dean, Thomas of Montacute, has

[1] Examples of these various descriptions are in *Hemingby's Reg.*, pp. 65–76 *passim*, 101.

[2] *Ibid.*, p. 118.   [3] *Ibid.*, p. 122.   [4] *Ibid.*, p. 142.

[5] This was Hemingsby House, marked as no. 20 on the plan of Salisbury close in K. Edwards, *op. cit.* in *British Arch. Jour.* (1939), facing p. 73; cf. p. 104.

[6] Reg. Corffe, ff. 6, 8, 11, 15–18, 23–4. He is not mentioned in the chapter acts after April 1349, and on 29 May his house was granted to another canon (*ibid.*, f. 29).

[7] Reg. Dunham, f. 255.

some interest, for it is the first detailed commission to a Salisbury *locum tenens decani* which has been found. The powers granted include

'correcting, punishing and reforming crimes, excesses and faults, including adultery or incest, among any of our subjects, whether canons, vicars, clerks, ministers or servants within the close . . . and, according to the statutes and customs of the church, by judgement of the chapter, removing or pronouncing the removal of vicars, and appointing other suitable and sufficient vicars in their places. Hearing and discussing all causes and business within the close belonging to our decanal jurisdiction, and ending them in the chapter house by the judgement of the chapter; and doing, exercising, expediting and executing everything known to belong to our decanal jurisdiction within the close, . . . with power of canonical cohercion, until we decide to revoke these powers.' [1]

Naturally a subdean, who was also a canon, might be appointed to this office by an absent dean, but in 1463, when William Nessingwick, subdean and residentiary canon of Salisbury, conducted a visitation of prebendal churches in virtue of a commission from the dean, the record of the visitation stated carefully that William acted *non ut subdecanus*.[2]

At Salisbury, Chichester, Hereford, and Wells, the most important part of the subdean's work seems to have been outside the cathedral and close, in the city and suburbs. At Hereford and Chichester he apparently acted there as the dean's official in his peculiar,[3] but at Salisbury he took the dean's place as archdeacon of the city, whether the dean were absent or present:[4] in 1279 it was the subdean, not the dean of Salisbury, who disputed with the chancellor the right of jurisdiction over scholars living in the

---

[1] Reg. Coman, f. 9. Similar fuller commissions granted by Dean Montacute to his lieutenants in 1388, 1389, and 1392 are available in Reg. Dunham, ff. 23–4, 117–19, 213. In addition to the powers detailed in the 1385 commission, these named the right of admitting and installing canons; of collating to vicarages and chantries in the dean's collation by lapse or special right; of proving the wills of canons, vicars, and other *ministri*, of ordering sequestrations and hearing accounts.

[2] Jones, *Fasti Sar.*, p. 267 n.

[3] *Reg. Cantilupe*, p. 2 and n.; *Reg. Swinfield*, p. 327; Bannister, *op. cit.*, p. 39; Swainson, pp. 63, 89–90; *Reg. Rede*, i, 106, 123–4. The subdean of Chichester was normally rector of St. Peter in the cathedral; his parish was the most populous and important in the deanery.

[4] See S.S., pp. 30–1, 61.

city.[1] Wells seems at first to have modelled its office of subdean deliberately on that of Salisbury,[2] but the deans of Wells were bent on retaining their archidiaconal jurisdiction in the city in their own hands so long as they were in residence. At the same time the subdeans of Wells had in other respects acquired greater dignity than those of Salisbury. The result was some stormy passages in the relations of the deans and subdeans. In 1237 Bishop Jocelin laid down that whenever the dean of Wells was present the cognizance of causes in the city and suburbs should be his; when he was absent, and the subdean present, it belonged to the subdean; when both were absent the power of appointing a judge lay with the dean, but a common roll of proceedings was to be kept, which each should cause the other to have in turn.[3] On several occasions in the fourteenth century the subdean of Wells was charged with exceeding his powers of jurisdiction.[4]

During the thirteenth and early fourteenth centuries the subdeans of some cathedrals attained a position more independent of the dean than had previously been customary in England. This seems to have been largely a result of the decree of the fourth Lateran Council of 1215, which required suitable priests to be appointed in cathedral and other conventual churches to act as coadjutors and co-operators of the bishop in preaching, hearing confessions, and enjoining penance.[5] In the course of the following century the chapters of York, Exeter, and Salisbury agreed to annex the title and functions of bishop's penitentiary to the subdeanery. In all these churches the subdean was appointed by the bishop, not by the dean, and was made immediately responsible to the bishop in his new duties.

York was the first English cathedral at which this experiment was made. Indeed, the subdean of York may have been the archbishop's penitentiary from his first institution in 1225. No mention is made of his duties in the foundation deed of Archbishop Gray; but the earliest York statutes, dating at any rate from before the mid-thirteenth century, describe him as *summus*

[1] *S.S.*, pp. 112–13. The final award gave to the subdean jurisdiction and power of correction over the scholars only in moral, not in civil, personal, pecuniary or educational causes. He could of course judge other city clerks in all causes.
[2] Cf. *W.S.*, pp. 45, 56.   [3] *H.M.C. Wells*, i, 49–50.
[4] E.g. *Reg. Drokensford*, pp. 25, 193; cf. 207, 213–14; *H.M.C. Wells*, i, 196–7.
[5] Mansi, xxii, 998–9.

penitenciarius of the archbishop.[1] Then, in 1284, when Bishop Quivil founded and endowed the subdeanery of Exeter, he ordained that whoever held the office should also be the bishop's penitentiary: for two-thirds of the year he should make personal residence in the cathedral, hearing confessions and absolving penitents, or sending them to a higher authority; and once a year he was to travel round the diocese, so that the sick who could not come to the city should receive remedy for the salvation of their souls. Otherwise he was not to be absent from the cathedral for any length of time, especially in Lent and Advent.[2] At Salisbury the offices of subdean and penitentiary were distinct until 1319. Then, as part of his revision of the cathedral statutes, Bishop Martival decided to unite the two offices: at the same time he decreed that for the future the subdean must take an oath of assiduous residence, similar to that of the four principal dignitaries.[3]

Elsewhere the subdean does not seem regularly to have exercised the charge of penitentiary. In French cathedrals a separate prebend or dignity was often appropriated to the office.[4] In England this sytem was adopted at Hereford and St. Paul's.[5] Here the penitentiary was not generally given the title of dignitary, but he held high rank with a prebend, and at Hereford his duties included those of lecturing in theology and canon law, which at most English secular cathedrals belonged to the chancellor.[6]

THE OFFICIAL OR AUDITOR OF THE DEAN OR DEAN AND CHAPTER

The dean or dean and chapter jointly had many other subordinate legal officers in the various courts of the deanery and chapter peculiars, such as the official, auditor or commissary, advocates, proctors, registrar, summoner, apparitor. Most of these would not be cathedral clergy, and generally little is known of them. But the most important, the official or auditor, is sometimes found holding a cathedral chantry or vicarage, and a few

[1] *L.S.*, ii, 94.   [2] *Reg. Quivil*, 324; *Ordinale Exon.*, i, 5.
[3] *S.S.*, pp. 162–5.
[4] Cf. Fournier, *op. cit.*, p. xxi. In French cathedrals the bishop's penitentiary often became the seventh dignitary.
[5] *Hereford Charters*, pp. xxxviii, 228; *R.S.S.P.*, pp. 13, 66–7, 182, 289. In 1724 the penitentiary of St. Paul's was described as the ninth dignitary of the cathedral (*ibid.*, p. 289).
[6] See below, pp. 197–8.

details have been collected about his office and the ecclesiastical courts over which he presided.

The working of his court is well illustrated in records at York. Here the peculiar jurisdiction both in the cathedral city and in the common lands belonged jointly to the dean and chapter,[1] and the earliest statutes laid down that auditors should be appointed by them jointly.[2] An act book of their court for the years 1396–1485 shows the auditor judging charges, chiefly moral, against cathedral and city clergy and laity living within the area of the chapter peculiar;[3] it also gives interesting information about the relations of this court to the thirty-seven or more other peculiar courts of the York dignities and prebends. All these courts had their separate privileges of visitation and discipline, and some powers of dealing with probates and administration of wills by their own commissaries and officials. But there was right of appeal from them to the dean and chapter's court, while in cases of overlapping or contentious jurisdiction, or during the vacancy of dignities or prebends, their jurisdiction might be merged for some months in that of the dean and chapter.[4] Indeed, both then and later, there were signs of efforts to reduce the complexity by the assertion of a stronger central control over the prebendal courts. A number of offices came to be concentrated in the hands of one official: thus in 1536 the same man is found to be acting both as official or commissary of the dean and chapter, and at the same time to be commissary in the peculiars of both the deanery and treasury.[5] A more important step in this direction was taken in 1547, when all dignitaries and prebendaries were forbidden to proceed with the proof or administration of wills in their separate courts without the 'presence and actuarie note of the common register [Registrar] of youre chapter'.[6]

Elsewhere our most definite information is about the Lincoln auditor. His office was annexed to the keepership of St. Peter's altar, the richest chantry in the cathedral, and in consequence his

[1] A survey, made in 1389, gives a detailed definition of the geographical area of the peculiar in the cathedral city, though it takes no notice of places outside the city which were also within the peculiar (J. S. Purvis, *A Medieval Act Book at York*, pp. 41–4, cf. 44–5).

[2] *L.S.*, ii, 94.

[3] The number, nature, and proportion of the charges, as between clergy and laity, are analysed by Canon Purvis, *op. cit.*, p. 4.

[4] *Ibid.*, pp. 5–6, 41.   [5] *Ibid.*, pp. 16–17.   [6] *Ibid.*, p. 6.

cathedral status was almost equal to that of a canon:[1] a number of priests of this chantry in the thirteenth and fourteenth centuries did in fact become canons.[2] After many disputes it was agreed in 1346 that collation should be by the dean and chapter jointly, not by the dean alone.[3] An exception was made to the rule that all chantry priests should reside and follow the choir on pain of forfeiting their commons: the chapter decided that since the auditor had frequently to go out on chapter business and support other burdens, he might have his commons whether absent or present.[4] His judicial duties were defined as hearing and deciding causes and business of the chapter by written commission of the dean and chapter which they could revoke if and when they wished. The dean and chapter might cite persons to appear before him for judgement, and demand execution of decrees by him.[5]

Wells, Exeter, and Lichfield also had an official responsible to the dean and chapter jointly, to hear and decide causes, to punish offences, and to account to them for profits of their jurisdiction.[6] At Lichfield it was suggested that the office should be combined with that of chapter clerk or notary who wrote the chapter's letters.[7] At Wells, Master Richard Baak, official in 1327, had previously been a vicar choral in the cathedral, subtreasurer, warden of the cathedral fabric, rector of a church belonging to the chapter's common fund, and the chapter's proctor at Rome.[8] The position at Salisbury is more obscure. There are scattered references in the chapter act books to an official who was clearly appointed by and responsible to the dean alone. His jurisdiction, unlike that of the York auditor, did not include the cathedral city or close, for the subdean of Salisbury took the dean's place as archdeacon of the city, and had his own official there;[9] while the moral lapses of the vicars choral and proof of wills of the cathedral clergy were

---

[1] *L.S.*, i, 335, 347–8; iii, 165, 353–4. His commons were usually about equal to those of a residentiary canon.

[2] Cf. *ibid.*, i, 325–9. Some had previously been clerks of the chapter's common fund: e.g. Master Hervey de Luda and Richard de Stretton.

[3] *Ibid.*, i, 353–8; iii, 353–4. For earlier disputes on this subject, see *ibid.*, i, 325–30.

[4] *Ibid.*, i, 347–8.   [5] *Ibid.*, iii, 169.

[6] *H.M.C. Wells*, i, 206, 217; *H.M.C. Var. Coll.*, iv, 81; *Monasticon*, VI, iii, 1261.

[7] *Ibid.*   [8] *H.M.C. Wells*, i, 162, 195, 206, 208, 211, 452.

[9] E.g. *Reg. S. de Gandavo*, p. 134.

M

dealt with in chapter before the dean or president.[1] Possibly the authority of the dean's official extended only to the other lands and churches of the deanery. But no other officer has been found judging the dean and chapter's causes in their common lands; and there are cases of the dean's official exercising or attempting to exercise jurisdiction in prebends and vacant dignities.[2] In the dean's absence he sometimes received mandates from the chapter.[3] Salisbury may have been one of the few chapters which allowed its deans to exercise the decanal supervision over the prebends and common lands without much capitular control, at any rate in the appointment of the official.

OTHER COMMISSARIES OF THE DEAN AND CHAPTER

The list of other commissaries, proctors, agents, envoys, or servants appointed jointly by the dean and chapter is necessarily a long one, and its extent can only be indicated here. Such commissaries might be found in many parts of England and abroad, wherever the chapters had interests or influence, as well as in the lands and churches immediately subject to the chapters. Sometimes they were cathedral clergy, canons, vicars or chaplains, entrusted with temporary commissions, such as the administration of vacant dignities, prebends or chapter farms; the holding of inquisitions on dilapidations; the collection of alms for the cathedral fabric; the conduct of lawsuits in London or at the Roman court.[4] Proctors from among the canons represented the chapter in parliament and convocation. There were also more permanent salaried officials, such as the chapter's regular proctors

[1] See below, pp. 271–2.

[2] E.g. In 1387 Dean Montacute addressed a mandate to his official and two notaries, instructing them to warn the canons to repair buildings on their prebends (Reg. Coman, ff. 89–90). In 1346 Master Ralph de Iwern, official of the absent dean, Reymund de Fargis, was cited before the chapter for attempting to hold an inquisition into defects of buildings in the late treasurer's prebend of Calne, to the prejudice of the treasurer's executors and of the chapter; he was inhibited from doing similar things in future (*Hemingby's Reg.*, p. 141).

[3] E.g. in 1320 the official of the absent dean acknowledged mandates from the dean's *locum-tenens* and chapter ordering him to cite non-resident canons to pay the tax of a fifth of the income of their prebends (*H.M.C. Var. Coll.*, i, 359).

[4] Many commissions of this kind are recorded in the Salisbury chapter acts, e.g. *Hemingby's Reg.*, pp. 98–9; Reg. Dunham, ff. 16, 39, 53, 138–9, 171; Reg. Holme, f. 52.

at the Roman curia or the court of Arches, who might or might not hold cathedral benefices.[1] Among a large number of more humble chapter servants there was usually a *cursor nuncius* or 'runner' carrying writs: his wages at York varied from three-halfpence a day in 1371 to tenpence-halfpenny a week in 1405, with three shillings and fourpence a year for his shoes.[2]

2. THE PRECENTOR OR CANTOR

'I acknowledge the great usefulness of this institution [i.e. song] . . . that, through delighting the hearing, the weaker spirit may be uplifted to a pious frame of mind,'[3] wrote St. Augustine. This was in spite of the many warnings issued both by him and other early Christian fathers against allowing the use in church of the less austere kinds of music, which by charming the senses, distracted the people from worship. From the time of St. Augustine the church increasingly recognized the importance of song and music as an aid to worship. Throughout the middle ages it intervened to regulate their use in the liturgy, organizing the repertoire, ordering its execution and correcting abuses. Few ecclesiastical institutions gave such concrete recognition in their constitutions to the power and influence of song as the medieval secular cathedrals. In France, where the titles of the different secular cathedral dignitaries varied considerably, the least variable was that of the cantor, or chanter, the dignitary in charge of the song, who frequently held the second place in the chapter after the dean, archdeacon or provost.[4] All Norman cathedrals had come

---

[1] E.g. Reg. Dunham, ff. 3, 52.

[2] *York Fabric Rolls*, pp. 124, 133. 'Runners' are mentioned as employed by Salisbury and Wells chapters in the fourteenth century in *H.M.C. Wells*, ii, 4; Reg. Corffe, f. 62.

[3] 'Magnam instituti hujus utilitatem . . . agnosco . . . ut per oblectamenta aurium infirmior animus in affectum pietatis assurgat' ('Confessions', in *P.L.*, xxxii, c. 800).

[4] See the lists of dignitaries in *Gallia Christiana* and in G. F. Browne, *op. cit.* At Paris and Orleans the cantor was the second dignitary, though at Sens he held only the fourth, and at Amiens only the sixth, place. Certain cathedrals in Provence and Languedoc were peculiar in having a *capischolus* as their fourth dignitary, who, in the absence of both chancellor and precentor, was presumably responsible for both the grammar and song schools. Professor Hamilton Thompson writes that although the position of the *capischolus* among the dignitaries was lower than that usually accorded to the precentor, his place was

to have a cantor by the last half of the eleventh or in the early twelfth century. At Coutances, which had no dean, and at the three Breton cathedrals of Dol, Tréguier and Léon, the cantor acted as head of the chapter;[1] at Chartres, as late as the eighteenth century, he frequently claimed precedence of the dean in choir.[2]

The English cantor, chanter or precentor was usually, like the dean, one of the first of the four great secular cathedral dignitaries to be instituted. At Salisbury, Lincoln, and York his office dates from the foundation or reconstitution of the chapters in 1090–1.[3] At Exeter there may have been a cantor or *primicerius* from the adoption of the enlarged rule of Chrodegang in 1050: certainly there was a cantor by 1130.[4] Wells already had a precentor, Reginald, holding by hereditary tenure, before Bishop Robert's reorganization of the chapter on a secular basis.[5] At St. Paul's a cantor appears in 1104, although not as a regular officer.[6] At Chichester, Hereford, and Lichfield he is found soon after the appearance of a dean, at any rate by the middle of the twelfth century.[7] In all English medieval secular cathedrals, with the exception of St. Paul's, of Exeter before 1225, and possibly of York in the twelfth and early thirteenth centuries, the cantor was recognized as the second dignitary after the dean, and normally held the north-west terminal stall in choir facing the dean's stall.[8] Thus the north side of the choir came to be called *cantoris*, while

---

probably more closely akin to that of the generally ubiquitous precentor than to the more elastic office of the *scholasticus* or chancellor (*Song Schools in the Middle Ages*, p. 15).

[1] *Song Schools in the Middle Ages*, p. 14; G. F. Browne, *op. cit.*, pp. 227, 231; *Gallia Christiana*, xi, c. 909; xiv, 973, 1040; *Camb. Hist. Jour.*, xiii, 111 n.

[2] Amiet, *op. cit.*, pp. 60–1, 74.

[3] *S.S.*, pp. 26–31; Jones, *Fasti Sar.*, p. 326; Henry of Huntingdon, p. 301; *Hist. Church York*, ii, 108; C. T. Clay, 'Early Precentors of York', in *Y.A.J.*, xxxv, 116.

[4] F. Rose Troup, *Consecration of the Norman Minster at Exeter*, pp. 4, 27. Robert le Blund appears as cantor c. 1130, 1143, and 1159/60.

[5] Early in Bishop Robert's time (1136–66) Reginald surrendered his hereditary tenure to the bishop, receiving as compensation the manor of Combe St. Nicholas for life (Church, *Chapters Hist. Wells*, pp. 16, 18).

[6] *Early Charters of St. Paul*, p. xxviii; C. N. L. Brooke and A. Morey, *Gilbert Foliot and his Letters*, App. iv.

[7] M. E. C. Walcott, *Fasti Cicestrenses*, p. 11; *Monasticon*, VI, iii, 1244, 1249. The first known cantor at Hereford is Robert, 1132 (Balliol MS., 271, f. 88:, no. 388). I owe this last reference to Miss Marjorie Jones and Professor Brooke.

[8] See the diagrams of medieval cathedral choirs in *L.S.*, i, 105, 136–8.

the south side with the dean's stall was the *decani* side. By the time of the earliest surviving collection of statutes and customs at York the precentor of York had also established his right to the second place, above his rival the treasurer, who seems to have ranked next to the dean in the twelfth century.[1] In the early twelfth century the two offices of cantor and treasurer at Exeter are not known to have conferred any special dignity on their holders;[2] but after the institution of a dean and chancellor in 1225 the chapter adopted the normal English arrangement; it was apparently then that Bishop Brewer raised the precentor and treasurer to the rank of dignitaries.[3] Only at St. Paul's where the precentor was made a dignitary *c.* 1204-5, the young holder of the new office failed to oust the archdeacon of London from his traditional place in choir opposite the dean, and he and his successors had to be content to follow the four archdeacons and the treasurer in dignity.[4] Even so, his dignity was in striking contrast to that of the humble position of the precentor in English cathedrals of the New Foundation. In these chapters, founded after the Reformation, the precentor was not a canon, much less a dignitary, but merely a minor canon, elected for one year only, whose office was later made perpetual. At English cathedral monasteries, the precentor, though an important obedientiary, had not rivalled the prior or cellarer in influence or authority.[5]

The precentor or cantor of the medieval cathedral chapters was the descendant of the *primicerius cantorum* of the early church. In

---

[1] *Ibid.*, ii, 94-5. Cf. *V.C.H. Yorks.*, iii, 376, and below, p. 218. As late as 1472 the north side of York choir was described in visitation *detecta* as *pars thesaurarii*, not *cantoris*.

[2] Cf. F. Rose Troup, *loc. cit.*, p. 5.   [3] Oliver, pp. 34-5.

[4] *Early Charters of St. Paul*, p. xxx; C. N. L. Brooke in *Hist. St. Paul's Cathedral*, p. 71. The archdeacon of London, Peter de Blois, appealed to Rome, and the customary dignity of his position was confirmed by Innocent III in a judgement later incorporated into the decretals.

[5] The office of precentor in English monasteries seems to have developed in a rather different way from that of precentor in the secular cathedrals. Dom David Knowles, *Monastic Order in England*, p. 428, writes that by the end of the eleventh century the literary side of the precentor's office at monasteries seems usually to have gained ground at the expense of the musical. The post became the perquisite of the most gifted man of letters in the community. In 1132 it was still normal for him to direct the choir, but he also had charge of all writing and illuminating in the cloister, and directed the work and studies of the younger monks.

the fourth and fifth centuries the direction of song usually belonged to the deacons or archdeacons. Towards the end of the sixth century, when the future Gregory the Great was deacon of Rome, it had become customary to promote simple cantors[1] to the diaconate, without the usual ecclesiastical preparation, merely on account of their fine voices, because it was necessary for deacons to sing the more elaborate pieces. When Gregory became pope he changed all this, abolishing the privileges of the cantor deacons, and reorganizing the *schola cantorum* at Rome.[2] At this school the children were put under the charge of four subdeacon officers: the *primicerius cantorum* (*magister primus*), the *secundicerius*, *tertius*, and *quartus*.[3] The *primicerius*, under the *archicantor*, who was also abbot of the monastery of St. Peter at Rome, directed the instruction and the song.

Gradually, as the Gregorian plain song became famous and spread to different parts of Europe, the organization of the *schola cantorum* was adopted at other cathedral churches. In England the Roman *ordo* and *cantilena* were received with enthusiasm in the newly converted kingdoms. Bede praised especially the master of song called James, *primicerius* of Canterbury, who was raised to the see of York in 633.[4] By the mid-seventh century the *primicerius cantorum*, as chief of the subdeacons and lesser clergy, seems to have been fairly generally recognized, with the archdeacon, or head of the deacons, and the archpriest, or head of the priests, as one of the three pillars (*tria culmina*) of the bishop's church.[5] In 666 the Council of Merida ordered that every cathedral should have an archpresbyter, an archdeacon, and a *primiclerus*.[6] Isidore of Seville stated that the *primicerius* had charge of the acolytes,

[1] These were clerks holding roughly the same rank as lectors, though in the west they did not form one of the seven orders of the church as they did in the east.

[2] H. Leclercq, 'Chantres', in *Dict. d'Archeologie Chrétienne et de Liturgie*, c. 360.

[3] *Ibid.*, c. 361. Gregory's achievement in reorganizing the *scola cantorum* was based on much valuable work of preparation by earlier popes from Celestine and Leo onwards (cf. P. Bayart, 'Chant', in *Dict. de Droit Camonique*, c. 501; G. Reese, *Music in the Middle Ages*, pp. 119–21).

[4] 'Historia Ecclesiastica' in *Venerabilis Bedae Opera Historica*, ed. C. Plummer, i, 126, 205.

[5] Sometimes, however, the *custos* or sacrist was said to form the third pillar of the church with the archdeacon and the archpriest (cf. Hinschius, ii, 103 n.; Smith and Cheetham, *Dict. Christian Antiquities*, s.v. *Capitulum*).

[6] Mansi, xi, 81.

exorcists, psalmysters, and lectors and directed the song; while in the *Ordo Romanus* he was said to occupy a position like that of the archpriest, under the archdeacon, and to have special charge of the teaching and discipline of the deacons and other inferior clergy.[1] In Chrodegang's rule for a common life of clerks the *primiciarius* or *primarius* was a dignitary joined to the archdeacon with a special responsibility for the direction and discipline of the inferior clerks.[2] Later, when the title *primicerius* disappears from the texts, the cantor continues to fill his functions, both in supervising the boy choristers and in directing the song. In England, as in Normandy, his normal title in early twelfth-century documents seems to have been cantor. Later in the century, precentor became more usual at the English cathedrals, probably as a result of expanding functions and greater dignity.[3]

The department of English cathedral life ruled by the precentor was more distinct and compact than those of the other three great dignitaries. His duties in choir might occasionally overlap with those of the chancellor or treasurer.[4] But there was little profitable jurisdiction attached to his office, and so his powers were rarely disputed by other cathedral officers. Moreover, much of his work required specialized liturgical or musical knowledge. There was considerable uniformity in his functions at the different cathedrals, and generally his duties were clearly stated in the statutes.

His first duty everywhere was to rule the choir in strict accordance with the detailed liturgical rules described in the cathedral ordinals and customaries. He set the pitch of the singing; saw that all the choir sang together in regular time and tune; appointed to each singer what he should sing in his time and place, and was responsible for ordering chants appropriate to the variety of days and feasts.[5] Each week, with the chancellor, he drew up the table

[1] *Dict. de Droit Canonique*, s.v. Chantres, c. 512; *Dict. Christian Antiquities*, s.v. *Primicerius*.

[2] 'S. Chrodegangi Regula Canonicorum' in *P.L.*, lxxxix, cc. 1063–4; *Enlarged Rule of Chrodegang*, c. 8.

[3] E.g. as at St. Paul's, c. 1204–5 (cf. M. Gibbs, *Early Charters of St. Paul*, p. xxxiv).

[4] E.g. as in the preparation of the weekly list of singers, ministers, and readers, the care of the books, the giving out of copes, or the discipline of the choristers in choir (below, pp. 164–6, 211, 215, 224).

[5] *Use Sarum*, i, 3; *L.S.*, i, 283–4; ii, 17; iii, 298; *R.S.S.P.*, p. 22; *Ordinale Exon.*, i, 3; *W.S.*, pp. 45, 55; *C.S.*, p. 13. See also the directions for the style of singing in *R.S.S.P.*, p. 66; *L.S.*, ii, 82–3; iii, 352; *Reg. Grandisson*, i, 436–7.

or list of singers, readers, and ministers of the altar. Normally the precentor was responsible for appointing the singers and ministers of the altar, while the chancellor appointed the readers.[1] But at a few churches the chancellor appointed the ministers in addition to the readers;[2] while at Chichester and Exeter the precentor entered the names of all three groups of clergy on the board.[3] The most important singers appointed each week by the precentor were the rulers of the choir (*rectores chori*), that is, those canons who, on ordinary days, exercised in turn some of the precentor's functions in ruling the choir. On double feasts or feasts of nine lessons two of them would rule together in silk copes at the principal services, but on medium or greater doubles there were usually four rulers.[4] On certain greater doubles the precentor would rule in person as principal of the four rulers.[5] He started the antiphon to the *Magnificat* and *Benedictus*; began the processional chants and sequences, and gave his key to the canon celebrating mass at the altar.[6] Whenever the bishop was present he was bound in person to announce to the bishop every chant to be begun by the bishop. Though discipline in choir was normally reserved to the dean and chapter or to the chancellor, the precentor usually had some control over the choristers' behaviour. Furthermore, he was expected to correct faults in the singing, to rouse the negligent to sing, and to rebuke gently or to calm those who caused disturbances by rushing about the choir.[7] When copes were worn, it was his duty at some churches to allot them to their wearers in order of rank.[8] The treasurer or chancellor might sometimes have charge of the service books, but at Lincoln and Hereford their care belonged to the precentor. He had to see that their notation was accurate and uniform; to pay for corrections;

[1] E.g. *Use Sarum*, i, 3–4; *W.S.*, pp. 45, 56.

[2] *L.S.*, i, 285; cf. iii, 300; *R.S.S.P.*, pp. 22–3, 49–50.

[3] *C.S.*, p. 13; *Ordinale Exon.*, i, 3. The usual provisions, however, were made for the chancellors of these churches to coach the readers before they read.

[4] *Use Sarum*, i, 27–8, 32–3, 35–40; *R.S.S.P.*, p. 50; *W.S.*, pp. 6–9; *Monasticon*, VI, iii, 1259; *Ordinale Exon.*, i, 15–17.

[5] *Use Sarum*, i, 3; *R.S.S.P.*, p. 22; *Ordinale Exon.*, i, 3; *L.S.*, i, 283–4; ii, 17; iii, 298.

[6] *R.S.S.P.*, p. 22; *L.S.*, i, 283–4; ii, 17, 63, 94–5; iii, 298; *Use Sarum*, i, 3; *Ordinale Exon.*, i, 3.

[7] E.g. *L.S.*, i, 284; iii, 298–9; *R.S.S.P.*, p. 22.

[8] At Lincoln, Hereford, and St. Paul's he did this through his succentor (*L.S.*, ii, 76; iii, 298; *R.S.S.P.*, p. 22). See also below, p. 224.

and to get them re-bound and mended when they were broken. If new books were required they were written under his charge, and as he appointed.[1]

The choir stalls belonging to the different dignitaries, prebendaries, and vicars were usually strictly defined by custom, and the English cathedral precentor had no power comparable to those of the cantor of Chartres, who could assign stalls according to his pleasure.[2] At some English churches he was said to install the canons on the dean's instructions.[3] But he played a leading part everywhere in the admission of the lesser cathedral clergy, particularly vicars choral and choristers, who were especially concerned with the singing. While each canon had the right to present his own vicar to the dean and chapter, the vicar's actual admission depended upon a favourable report from the precentor on his singing and musical ability. The vicars were examined twice by the precentor or his deputy: once before their first admission to the choir for a probationary period, and again at the end of a year to see if they had sufficient knowledge of the services to be admitted as perpetual vicars.[4]

Naturally the group of choir clerks with whom the precentor was most closely connected was the choristers, whom he chose and admitted, subject to the dean and chapter's approval. At Exeter he was called the *Dux Puerorum*.[5] The early statutes of most English cathedrals assigned to him the instruction and discipline of the boys, both within and outside the choir.[6] At some churches he remained responsible for this throughout the middle ages and later. But endowments given later in the middle ages for the support of the choristers often relieved him of some of his duties. At St. Paul's the almoner housed the choristers, provided their food and clothing, and had them taught grammar. At Lincoln and Salisbury provision was made in the thirteenth and fourteenth centuries for the boys to live together in a common

[1] *L.S.*, i, 284; ii, 63; iii, 299.
[2] Cf. Amiet, *op. cit.*, pp. 76–7. At Chartres special stalls were annexed to eight of the seventeen dignities, but otherwise, so long as the cantor placed dignitaries among dignitaries, simple canons among simple canons, and non-canons among non-canons, he could assign to them any stalls he pleased.
[3] E.g. *L.S.*, ii, 16, 30, 94.
[4] See below, p. 268.
[5] *Ordinale Exon.*, i, 4.
[6] *Use Sarum*, i, 3; *W.S.*, p. 45; *Ordinale Exon.*, i, 3; *L.S.*, i, 283; ii, 17.

house supervised by an elected residentiary canon, who was not necessarily the precentor.[1] At these two churches the precentor apparently lost much of his former authority over the boys.[2] But at Wells, where similar provisions for a chorister's house were made by Bishop Beckington in the fifteenth century, the precentor kept his powers of supervision over both the boys and their master.[3]

THE SONG SCHOOL

Song formed an important part of medieval education. The singing of the church services was based on a detailed and specialized study of metre and harmony; the Gregorian plain chant was a music subtle and sophisticated in its technical expression.[4] Thus it became customary fairly early in the history of the church, in important centres where there were choirs, to teach song in separate schools distinct from the grammar schools. In 796 Alcuin wrote from France to the archbishop of York, his old pupil Eanbald, recommending the separation of three classes of study under separate masters: first there should be a school of book learning or grammar, secondly a school of song, thirdly a school of writing.[5] This distinction was not uniformly observed after Alcuin's time: in the smaller schools kept by parish or chantry priests or by the smaller collegiate churches all three subjects probably continued to be taught by one master throughout the middle ages, and often the teaching of song was overshadowed by that of grammar.[6] But at secular cathedrals the acceptance of the need for the separate teaching of grammar and song was empha-

[1] See below, pp. 310-14.
[2] E.g. at Lincoln he was deprived of his sole right of admitting them. After 1264 he might only present them for admission to the dean and chapter, who could appoint others if they did not consider the precentor's nominees suitable (*L.S.*, i, 410; iii, 162, 298. Cf. *S.S.*, pp. 266-7).
[3] *Dean Cosyn and Wells Cathedral Misc.*, p. 99 *et seq.*, and below, p. 314.
[4] For medieval singing, see H. Leclercq, 'Chant Romain et Gregorien', in *Dict. d'Archéologie Chrétienne et de Liturgie*; P. Bayart, 'Chant', in *Dict. de Droit Canonique*; G. Reese, *Music in the Middle Ages*; F. L. Harrison, *Music in Medieval Britain*, 1958; M. D. Knowles, *The Monastic Order in England*, pp. 545-59; and the medieval treatises on song quoted by A. H. Thompson, *Song Schools*, pp. 4-6.
[5] *Educational Charters and Documents*, ed. Leach, pp. 18-19.
[6] A. H. Thompson, *Song Schools*, pp. 6-7.

sized by assigning the charge of the grammar and song schools to different dignitaries: the schools of grammar and later of theology or law were normally put under the direction of the chancellor or *scholasticus*, and the song school under the precentor.[1] At first these dignitaries probably taught in person in their schools, but by the time of the earliest English cathedral statutes they had both acquired deputies. Usually either the precentor or his principal deputy, the succentor, appointed a subordinate master of song to rule the song school; but at a few of the smaller churches, such as Exeter and Hereford, there might be only one official, the succentor, who ruled the song school in person as well as deputizing for the precentor in his other duties.[2] In cathedrals where the succentor and song schoolmaster were different persons, the master's position seems to have been roughly similar to that of the chancellor's grammar schoolmaster, though his commons and precedence were probably less.[3] He might sometimes share the succentor's duties in choir, helping to draw up the weekly table of singers, or correcting the boys.[4]

The first duty of the ruler of the cathedral song school in the early middle ages naturally was to teach the cathedral clergy, particularly the boy choristers and the younger vicars. But gradually it becomes clear in the records that the cathedral song school was not meant solely for the instruction of the cathedral clergy. Like the master of the grammar school, the song schoolmaster had a monopoly, which was protected by the precentor and by the dean and chapter, of teaching song in the cathedral city.[5] In 1305 certain parish clerks of Lincoln city were charged

[1] This arrangement was not universally adopted in French cathedrals (see above, p. 159 n.).

[2] Cf. *L.S.*, ii, 76, 83; *Reg. Bronescombe*, pp. 77–8. At York, Lincoln, and St. Paul's the precentor appointed a separate master of song in addition to the succentor (*L.S.*, ii, 95; iii, 299; *R.S.S.P.*, pp. 22, 49–50). At Wells the cantor, and at Salisbury and Lichfield the succentor, was said to rule the song school through his official (*W.S.*, pp. 45, 55; *Use Sarum*, i, 8; *L.S.*, ii, 23).

[3] E.g. at Lincoln, on the feast of St. Hugh's Translation, the song schoolmaster received only twelve pence in commons when present at the service while the master of the grammar school had five shillings (*L.S.*, i, 336).

[4] E.g. *R.S.S.P.*, pp. 49–50; cf. 22; *L.S.*, i, 369.

[5] For the similar situation in the thirteenth century at Bayeux, see *Ordinaire et Coutumier de Bayeux*, p. 319. Here the succentor instituted the master of the city song school, and no one was allowed to set up a rival song school without the succentor's permission.

before the chapter with holding adulterine schools to teach boys singing and music to the prejudice of the liberty of the mother church, and were made to swear on the gospels that they would henceforth keep no such schools without licence from the cathedral song schoolmaster.[1] Again in 1367 'divers chaplains, holy water carriers and others' were said to be keeping song schools in parish churches, houses and other places in York to the prejudice and grievance of the precentor's school; they were ordered to stop their schools within a fortnight on pain of ecclesiastical censure.[2] Furthermore, the precentor might sometimes direct the teaching of song throughout the diocese, in much the same way as the cathedral chancellor might sometimes supervise the diocesan grammar schools. The precentor of Lincoln was said to appoint the master of song for both the city and county of Lincoln; the only schools exempt from his supervision were those on the prebendal estates, or schools held by curates or parish clerks for their parishioners.[3]

In the later middle ages, when the cathedral song school-master was steadily gaining more pupils in the city, and acquiring an important position as ruler of the chief song school of the diocese, he gradually ceased at some cathedral churches to have any close connexion with his earliest pupils, the cathedral choristers. This seems to have been due partly to the growing number of pupils at the city song school, partly to special endowments granted to the choristers. It happened for the most part only at the larger cathedral churches, such as Lincoln and Salisbury, where the choristers were given their own private masters for grammar and song. At St. Paul's the almoner still sent the boys to learn singing from the precentor's master of song teaching in the church of St. Gregory; while at Hereford and Exeter the succentor continued to instruct them at the city song school.[4]

---

[1] *Educational Charters*, pp. 236–7.

[2] *V.C.H. York*, i, 419. The earliest York statutes had declared that any cases relating to the school of song at York were to be heard and determined before the precentor, though the execution of his sentence belonged to the dean and chapter after they had received his report.

[3] *L.S.*, iii, 299.

[4] Leach in *Archaeologia*, lxii, 198; *R.S.S.P.*, p. 22; below, p. 311.

THE SUCCENTOR

Apart from differences in the succentor's connexions with the cathedral song schools, his office usually has less interest than that of the dean's deputy, the subdean. The object of both offices was to provide for the execution of their particular dignitary's duties during his absence, and to help him when present. But while the subdean usually had the right to perform only some of the dean's duties in a rather different way from that in which the dean performed them when present, the succentor's functions are described in the cathedral statutes in words almost identical with those describing the precentor's duties. Therefore the main interest of any further investigation of the succentor's office lies not so much in his duties in choir, which have already been discussed, as in the variations of his position or dignity in different churches, and in his relations with the vicars choral. At two English cathedrals, Lichfield and York, he became the permanent head in the later middle ages of the newly formed corporations of vicars choral, thus acquiring new functions, independent of those delegated to him by the precentor.

The office of succentor seems to have been a fairly late institution in most English secular cathedrals. None of them is known to have had a succentor in the late eleventh century. There was one at Salisbury by the mid-twelfth century; at Wells about 1164, and at Lincoln between 1196 and 1203.[1] In Normandy there were earlier precedents. Bayeux already had a succentor in 1092,[2] and Geoffrey de Montbray, Bishop of Coutances from 1049 to 1093, instituted a succentor when he first reorganized the chapter of Coutances on a secular basis.[3] Here, however, the position was exceptional, because Coutances had no dean or subdean. At Rouen there was a subcantor at any rate from 1142.[4]

In some French cathedrals the succentor came to hold high rank. At Chartres he was the fourth dignitary, above the chamberlain, chancellor, *capicerius*, and archdeacons; while at Bayeux, Paris, and Orleans, though he followed the principal dignitaries and

[1] *H.M.C., Var. Coll.*, i, 370–1; Church, *Chapters Hist. Wells*, pp. 15, 355; *Reg. Antiquissimum*, iv, 280.
[2] *Livre Noir*, no. 22.
[3] *Gallia Christiana*, xi, *Instrumenta*, p. 220.
[4] D. Gurney, *Record of the House of Gournay*, i, 107.

archdeacons in rank, he took precedence of the simple canons as a kind of secondary dignitary.[1] But in England Wells was the only secular cathedral where the succentor was sometimes described as a *persona*. Here the unusual importance of his position was emphasized by the bishop's collation of canons to the office: his endowments, though less than those of the subdean of Wells, were greater than those of other English cathedral succentors, and he normally held a canonical house of residence in the close.[2]

The closest parallel at other English churches to the position of the succentor of Wells was at Salisbury, where the succentor, like the subdean, was described as a quasi-dignitary.[3] He took an oath on admission, similar to that of the succentor of Wells, to reside continuously in the manner of the four principal dignitaries, and was given the corresponding stall on the upper row of the north side of the choir near the precentor.[4] He also might be a canon and apparently often was so in the thirteenth and fourteenth centuries when a succentor, Walter de la Wyle, was elected bishop of Salisbury.[5] But towards the end of the middle ages his importance seems to have declined, and he was more often associated with the vicars than with the canons. If he were a vicar he took precedence of the other vicars, but ranked below the canons, and wore an almuce trimmed with fur inferior to the fur of the canons' almuces.[6] Possibly because canons could still hold the office, the Salisbury succentor never became *ex officio* head of the corporation of Salisbury vicars choral; nor did he live in their common hall. In 1440 a separate house of residence in the close was annexed to his office.[7]

The only other English cathedral at which a succentor might be a canon was York. But here the position was peculiar because there were two succentors: a *succentor canonicorum* or *succentor major*, and a *succentor vicariorum*. The succentor of the canons was collated by the archbishop to the stall on the upper row of the south side of the choir next to the chancellor's stall. He took the place of the absent precentor in installing canons and in ruling

---

[1] Amiet, *op. cit.*, pp. 85-6; Deslandes, *op. cit.*, pp. 96-7.
[2] *Reg. Drokensford*, p. 46; *Reg. Shrewsbury*, p. 610; *Valor Eccl.*, i, 134.
[3] Jones, *Fasti Sar.*, p. 263.
[4] *S.S.*, pp. 162-5; *Use Sarum*, i, 13. Cf. *W.S.*, pp. 1, 44, 55; *L.S.*, i, 137.
[5] Jones, *Fasti Sar.*, pp. 270-1.   [6] *Ibid.*, pp. 265-7, 271-2.
[7] Reg. Hutchins, f. 21.

the choir on double feasts.[1] The succentor of the vicars was also bound to be present at installations, but his chief duties were to draw up the weekly table of singers; to warn the singers and ministers in advance of their duties in choir; to coach the choristers in song, and to see that the vicars learnt their 'histories'[2] by heart. He also ruled the choir in the absence of both the precentor and the *succentor major*.[3] Originally he seems to have been the precentor's vicar choral, but the method of his appointment in the later middle ages is uncertain. From the foundation of the Bedern (the York college of vicars choral) in 1248 he apparently always acted as head of the vicars. Yet the vicars had the right to elect their head. Therefore Chancellor Harrison suggests, on the analogy of present-day custom, that the *succentor vicariorum* may from this time have been elected by his fellow vicars.[4]

In the remaining six English secular cathedrals the succentor was apparently always a vicar appointed by the precentor. He either lived with the precentor and received food and yearly robes from him, or was paid an annual stipend by him.[5] The succentor was always one of the leading vicars: at Hereford he judged all questions and causes arising between the other vicars and choir clerks;[6] at Exeter in 1358 he was granted more generous allowances of canonical loaves and money than the other vicars, on grounds that he laboured more than they did.[7] But usually when the vicars of these churches began to live together in colleges and formed corporations, they elected their own presidents, wardens or principals, and the succentor was not necessarily chosen as their head. Only at Lichfield the succentor became *ex officio* president of the vicars.[8] Here his dignity was emphasized by a statute of 1420–47, laying down that henceforth the succentor with the vicars choral of the three other principal dignitaries (the

---

[1] *L.S.*, i, 136; ii, 95. Cf. *Reg. Greenfield*, i, 88.

[2] For the 'histories', see below, p. 265, n. 7.

[3] *L.S.*, ii, 95, 124–5. He was sometimes called precentor of the vicars.

[4] *The Subchanter and the Vicars Choral* (York Minster Hist. Tracts), pp. 3–4; 'The Bedern College and Chapel', in *Proc. Y.A.A.S.*, p. 22.

[5] For details, see e.g. *L.S.*, ii, 63; iii, 164, 358; *Ordinale Exon.*, i, 3–4; *Hereford Charters*, p. 183 n.; *C.S.*, p. 11; cf. *Reg. Rede*, i, 102; ii, 372.

[6] *L.S.*, ii, 77.

[7] Harl. MS. 1027, f. 57a.

[8] *Coll. Hist. Staffs.*, II, vi, 161. The usual style of the corporation of vicars of Lichfield was 'Succentor et Cetus Vicariorum.'

dean, chancellor, and treasurer), should wear a special almuce trimmed with calabur fur, similar to the almuces worn by the Salisbury subdean and succentor when they were vicars.[1] All four deputies were to receive six shillings and eightpence a year more than their fellow vicars, and might take the canon's place in celebrating mass at the high altar on double feasts, should no canon be present. The Lichfield statutes also assigned a further interesting duty to the succentor, not described in the statutes of other English cathedrals: he was required to prepare performances of pastoral plays for Christmas Eve, and of miracle plays on Easter Eve and Easter Monday.[2]

The Organist

All English cathedrals probably had organs and an organist from at least the mid-twelfth century, if not before. Organs were known in England before the time of Bede; their introduction in larger numbers in the ninth and tenth centuries is attributed to the influence of Dunstan and Ethelwold.[3] There is a famous description of an organ in Winchester cathedral about 971 which required two players and seventy blowers, and gave out a thunderous volume of sound. The chief use of these early organs was apparently to provide joyful music to accompany processions or to open some gathering. Their mechanism was still elementary and permitted little modulation or restraint. But towards the end of the eleventh century considerable mechanical improvements were made to the keyboard; the quality of tone became sweeter, and it was possible to use them to accompany the chant. At the Norman church of Coutances, where officers in charge of the music and song were assigned exceptionally high places in the chapter, Bishop Geoffrey de Montbray is said to have appointed an organist in the second half of the eleventh century at about the same time as he instituted a cantor and succentor.[4] But it is a long time before mention is made of organists in the statutes of other

[1] *Monasticon*, VI, iii, 1263; cf. Jones, *Fasti Sar.*, p. 266.

[2] *L.S.*, ii, 23. At Lincoln in 1316 it was the grammar schoolmaster who wrote the Christmas play (see below, p. 196).

[3] See the account of early organs in England by M. D. Knowles, *The Monastic Order*, pp. 559–60.

[4] Cf. J. le Patourel, *op. cit.*, p. 141.

secular cathedrals. Usually the earliest references are found in charters or in documents recording payments of their salaries or commons. At Salisbury the name of an organist is given in a charter of about 1200.[1] In 1307 the organist of Hereford cathedral acknowledged the receipt of his annual pension of five silver marks from the dean and chapter.[2] In 1322 the clerk carrying (and probably playing) the organ at Lincoln cathedral was said to receive distributions of six shillings and eightpence both on the feast of the translation of St. Hugh and at the obit of Robert Grosseteste.[3] Later it seems that there were two distinct pairs of organs, each with a separate organist, at Lincoln, one of which was normally played at the lectern, the other for the Lady Mass at prime.[4] The casual nature of these entries suggests that organists had long been appointed at cathedrals, but that their status was too humble or their duties too obvious to be set out at length in the statutes. It was not generally thought necessary to do this until the fifteenth, sixteenth, or seventeenth centuries, by which time the organist had gained in dignity and importance. This was due largely to the development of the organ as a musical instrument, and to the greater demands made on the organist by the increasing subtlety of musical technique.[5] Furthermore, from the fifteenth century onwards, as a result of the endowment of private schools and boarding houses for the choristers, the organist at several cathedrals had begun to acquire additional duties of instructing and supervising the choristers. Like his other duties, this new work naturally brought him into close contact with the precentor and succentor.

In 1463 the organist at Salisbury is first found to be teaching the choristers in chant. By agreement with the chapter he received emoluments from a vicar's stall, had three yards of broadcloth a year for his livery of the choristers' suit, and twelve pence a week as commons, which he might take wherever he pleased in the close. At the same time he was bound to play the organ daily at the mass of the Blessed Virgin Mary.[6] After the Reformation he

---

[1] *Sarum Charters*, p. 61.   [2] *Hereford Charters*, p. 178.

[3] *L.S.*, i, 337, 338.

[4] A. F. Leach, 'Schools', in *V.C.H. Lincoln*, ii, 436–7.

[5] F. L. Harrison, *Music in Medieval Britain* (1958), pp. 209–18.

[6] This agreement is printed by C. Wordsworth and D. H. Robertson, 'Salisbury Choristers . . . with the History of the Organ', in *W.A.M.*, xlviii, 216. Cf. D. H. Robertson, *Sarum Close*, pp. 72–3.

N

became a lay vicar. Agreements are extant from the years 1569 and 1580 granting him allowances for boarding and clothing the choristers, whom he continued to instruct in music.[1] Similar developments took place at Lincoln, Wells, York, and Exeter. From 1477 the organist of the Lady Mass at Lincoln became also the choristers' music master: he was required to instruct them in 'playnsonge, faburdon, diskant and cowntour', as also in playing on the organ; and was especially to teach playing the clavicord to two or three of them whom he found fit and teachable for such playing. In return he received a hundred shillings a year from the dean and chapter, and three yards of woollen cloth for a gown, besides the thirteen shillings and fourpence a year due to him as a fellow of the Lady Mass altar, and another thirteen shillings and fourpence for playing the organ there.[2] The appointment of Richard Hygons as master of the choristers at Wells in 1479 contains an exceptionally full statement of the duties of an organist.[3] About 1558 T. Heath was appointed organist, master, and instructor of the choristers at Exeter cathedral for life at a salary of ten pounds a year.[4] At York the Reformation statute of 1552 which prohibited organ-playing in the cathedral, mentioned that before this time it had been customary for the master of the choristers to play the organ.[5] At Chichester little evidence has been found for the organist's status in the middle ages; but in post-reformation statutes he appears to be closely connected with the vicars choral. A statute of 1616 directed that whenever he was not playing the organ during the services he was to return into the choir to take his part in singing.[6] In 1680, after the office of succentor had been abolished, it was agreed that the organist should take his turn with the other vicars in carrying out the succentor's duties, and in sharing the emoluments of the office.[7]

[1] *W.A.M.*, xlviii, 218–20. In 1598 the offices of organist and singing master of the choristers were separated, but were combined again after the Restoration.

[2] A. F. Leach in *V.C.H. Lincoln*, ii, 436. A few years later the same organist was also admitted to play the other organ in choir (*ibid.*, p. 437). Except for the years 1524–38 the practice of combining the offices of organist and music master of the choristers has been continued at Lincoln ever since.

[3] F. L. Harrison, *op. cit.*, pp. 179–81, 425.   [4] *Use Exeter*, p. 47.

[5] *Y.S.*, p. 77. A similar practice prevailed also at some English collegiate churches: see e.g. E. H. Fellowes, *The Organists and Masters of the Choristers at St. George's Chapel in Windsor Castle.*

[6] *C.S.*, p. 32.   [7] *Ibid.*, p. 39.

Tabellarii, Punctuatores or Custodes Chori

Two or three lesser choir clerks were normally appointed to help the precentor, succentor, and chancellor in seeing that the duties of singing, serving, and reading at the services were duly carried out each week by those clergy to whom they were allotted in the weekly table or list. The names, rank, and terms of appointment of these officers varied considerably at different cathedrals, but everywhere their chief duties were the same. They had to note daily the faults, neglect of duty, and absences from choir of the ministers, and to report such faults either to the dean and chapter or to the keeper of the common fund in time for them to be punished at the weekly Saturday chapters. The most usual punishment was a deduction for each offence from the culprit's weekly commons.

At Wells there were three of these officers, who were given the expressive titles of *tabellarii, tabularii* or *exploratores* of faults. They were appointed by collation of the chancellor and assignation of the succentor, and were bound by oath to spare none;[1] in 1298 their zeal was encouraged by an order declaring that they should receive half the value of the fines inflicted through their agency.[2] At Exeter they were called 'punctuators'. Two were appointed each term to punctuate the absences of vicars, annuellars, and secondaries or clerks of the second form. Records of their appointments suggest that punctuators were usually secondaries.[3] But the *custodes chori*, who performed corresponding duties at St. Paul's and York, were of higher rank: the succentor of the vicars was one of the York *custodes* in 1294,[4] while at St. Paul's the two cardinals, or heads of the minor canons, with two other minor canons, guarded the choir by day and night, and kept notes of the ministers' faults.[5] At Lincoln the succentor and vice-chancellor apparently shared the work.[6] About 1240 at Lichfield it was decided that a vicar should be regularly appointed to notify the chapter of any absences of vicars or chaplains from the canonical hours.[7]

---

[1] *W.S.*, pp. 64, 99. [2] *Ibid.*, p. 64.
[3] *Ordinale Exon.*, i, 7; *Use Exeter*, pp. 9, 12. For the status and duties of secondaries, see below, pp. 303–7.
[4] *L.S.*, ii, 124. [5] *R.S.S.P.*, p. 103.
[6] *L.S.*, iii, 359. [7] *Monasticon*, VI, iii, 1257.

3. THE CHANCELLOR

By the middle of the thirteenth century the chancellor was the third dignitary in nearly all the English secular cathedrals.[1] He had the greatest variety and in some ways the most interesting combination of functions. In the course of the twelfth, thirteenth, and fourteenth centuries he acquired many deputies and subordinate officials. The origin and development of his office in the late eleventh and twelfth centuries presents many difficulties. Yet during this obscure period in his history the cathedral schools, of which he came to have charge, made their most outstanding contribution to learning. The early development of the chancellor's office, particularly his connexion with the schools, will therefore be discussed in greater detail than that of the other dignitaries.

It has already been seen that in Normandy Rouen was the only cathedral which ever came to have a chancellor in charge of its schools and correspondence, and that there the title was not assumed until the latter half of the twelfth century. In other Norman cathedrals the dignitary who had the supervision of the schools continued throughout the middle ages and later to be called *magister scholarum* or *scholasticus*. This officer often held a subordinate place among the dignitaries; at Bayeux he was the seventh, not the third, dignitary, and at Lisieux the *capicerius*, the treasurer's deputy, took precedence of him.[2] It thus seems necessary to look elsewhere than in Normandy for an explanation of the existence of a cathedral chancellor in twelfth-century England. Before the end of the twelfth century a number of cathedrals in northern and western France had come to have a cathedral dignitary with the title of chancellor,[3] but a long history lies behind his office.

[1] The exceptions were St. Paul's, where the order of the dignitaries was the dean, the four archdeacons, the treasurer, precentor, chancellor (*R.S.S.P.*, p. 13; *L.S.*, i, 136); Wells, where it was the dean, precentor, archdeacon of Wells, archdeacon of Bath, chancellor, treasurer, archdeacon of Taunton, two abbots (*ibid.*, i, 137; *W.S.*, pp. 1–2); and Hereford, where the treasurer was the third, and the chancellor the fourth dignitary (*L.S.*, i, 137; ii, 63–71). This was also the arrangement at Lichfield according to the earliest statutes of c. 1190, but in later statutes the chancellor was given the third place (*ibid.*, i, 138; ii, 16, 20).

[2] See above, pp. 15–17.

[3] E.g. Paris, Orléans, Meaux, and Chartres in the province of Sens; Amiens and Noyon in the province of Rheims; the metropolitan churches of Rouen,

Originally the bishops themselves taught the young lectors who were adopted into their households. Throughout the middle ages *cathedra* meant equally a bishop's throne or a professor's chair. But gradually, by about the seventh century, pressure of diocesan work forced the bishops to delegate much of the teaching in their episcopal schools to one of the senior priests of their *familia*, who became known as the *magister scholarium, magister scholarum, scholasticus* or *capischola*.[1] This priest seems usually to have acted also as the bishop's secretary, keeping his seal and dealing with his official correspondence. As the cathedral clergy came to live apart from their bishop, their separate head, the provost, archdeacon, archpriest or dean, naturally took precedence among them over the *magister scholarum*; but in the new secular chapters of the eleventh century a *magister scholarum* was often included among the cathedral dignitaries. In such cases, in addition to teaching in the cathedral school, he frequently acted as secretary to both bishop and chapter. But, in time, as the bishop was present less and less often in his cathedral city, he usually appointed a separate officer, known as the bishop's chaplain or chancellor, to be his secretary.[2] It was very exceptional for this officer to gain entry in an official capacity to the cathedral chapter.

Tours, and Bourges. There were also chancellors in two cathedrals in eastern France, Metz and Verdun, where the office may have developed early under the influence of the Carolingian court in the Austrasian kingdom. At the same time, throughout the middle ages, a rather larger proportion of French cathedrals kept the older title of *magister scholarum* or *scholasticus* for the dignitary in charge of their schools. In some cases, as at Bayeux, the *scholasticus* is known to have acted also as the chapter's secretary; but at Amiens and Noyon, both of which had a chancellor in addition to a *scholasticus*, the offices may have been distinct. In the churches of Provence and a few immediately adjoining there was usually a *capischolus* or *capischola*, who seems to have combined the functions of *scholasticus* and precentor. About half the cathedrals of medieval France, so far as can be judged from information available in the *Gallia Christiana* and *Pouillés* of the medieval dioceses, seem never to have had dignitaries with the titles of chancellor, *scholasticus*, or *capischolus*.

[1] For the early episcopal and cathedral schools, see M. Deanesly, 'Medieval Schools', in *C.M.H.*, v, 767–78; 'The *Familia* at Christchurch, Canterbury', in *Essays to Tout*, pp. 1–3; *The Medieval Church*, pp. 32–3, 132–4. Fulbert, bishop of Chartres in the early eleventh century, and Ivo of Chartres, bishop in the early twelfth century, seem to have been among the last bishops to teach in person in their cathedral schools (A. Clerval, *Les Écoles de Chartres*, pp. 30, 145).

[2] See below, pp. 205–6.

During the late eleventh and twelfth centuries the office of *magister scolarum* or *scholasticus* in many cathedrals of northern France steadily increased in dignity and importance. This was due both to the remarkable growth of the cathedral schools and to the expanding legal and secretarial business of the chapters. The assumption of the title of chancellor by the *magister scholarum* at some of these chapters seems to have been connected with both these developments, and to have been a sign essentially of his greater dignity. He was not generally styled chancellor until he had another master or masters under him to teach grammar, while he continued to exercise general supervision over the schools, granting the licence to teach, and merely reserving for himself some lecturing in the higher faculties of theology or law. This did not usually happen until the first half of the twelfth century, although at Chartres, where the cathedral school reached an exceptionally high peak of development at a very early period, it is found in the tenth and eleventh centuries.[1] But the first half of the twelfth century, when the change of title normally took place, was also the period when the growth of the chapter's business and the multiplication of official correspondence was causing the *scholasticus*, at those churches in which he acted as the chapter's secretary, to devote much more of his attention than he had previously done to his secretarial duties. These duties were similar in character to those of contemporary royal and other chancellors, and so it was natural for him to assume a title similar to theirs.

In England it seems unlikely that the three new secular chapters of York, Salisbury, and Lincoln would have had dignitaries with the title of chancellor as early as their foundation in 1090–1, when, except for Chartres and Paris, no cathedral in northern France is known to have had a chancellor. Yet Bradshaw maintained that Lincoln and Salisbury had chancellors from the first.[2] York did not, although, unlike Lincoln and Salisbury, it at least had traditions of a highly organized school in the days of Egbert and

---

[1] As early as 931 the title of chancellor was borne at Chartres by the priest Clement who had a vice-chancellor: 'Regenfredus humilis levita ad vicem Clementis presbiteri et cancellarii scripsit' (*Cartul. St. Père de Chartres*, ed. Guérard, p. 28). In the eleventh century both a chancellor and a *magister scholarum* occur at Chartres (cf. *ibid.*, p. 215; *Cartul. la Trinité de Vendôme*, i, 88; *Cartul. de Notre-Dame de Chartres*, i, 94).

[2] *L.S.*, i, 34.

Alcuin.[1] Thomas of Bayeux, who became archbishop of York in 1070, appointed a *magister scholarum* at his cathedral some time before he reorganized the chapter on a secular basis.[2] It has been assumed that, after his institution of the three other dignities of dean, precentor, and treasurer in 1090, the *magister scholarum* became the third dignitary and that his functions and probably his title came gradually to correspond with those of the chancellors of Lincoln and Salisbury.[3] In fact he continued to be called *magister scholarum* or *scholasticus* until 1189 or 1190, when Master Simon of Apulia, a clerk of Archbishop Geoffrey, was appointed chancellor.[4] The compilers of the earliest surviving collection of York statutes, made as the result of an order of 1307, thought it necessary to explain that the chancellor was formerly called the *magister scholarum*.[5] Sir Charles Clay, who has recently published detailed evidence for the early history of the York chancellors, suggests that the change of title was made deliberately by Archbishop Geoffrey possibly with the position at Lincoln in mind, where he had previously been bishop-elect.[6]

There was certainly a chancellor, Hamo, at Lincoln from about 1148–50.[7] But no evidence has been found of any earlier cathedral dignitary with this title. The division of the psalms among the Lincoln canons, made about 1145, allots psalms for daily recitation to the dean, cantor, and treasurer, but not apparently to a chancellor.[8] Yet Bradshaw was so certain that a chancellor had been instituted at Lincoln by Remigius in 1091, that, when he noticed the name of *Robertus cancellarius ecclesie canonicus* among the lists of bishops, abbots, and earls witnessing the foundation charter of Lincoln cathedral, he identified him as Robert, chancellor of Lincoln cathedral.[9] This, however, was almost certainly

---

[1] There is, however, no evidence for the continuity of this school during the three hundred years between the death of Alcuin and the appointment of a *magister scholarum* by Archbishop Thomas.

[2] Hugh the Chanter, *Hist. Church York*, ii, 108.

[3] Cf. *L.S.*, i, 34.

[4] See the evidence quoted by Sir Charles Clay, 'The Early Precentors and Chancellors of York', in *Y.A.J.*, xxxv (1941), 128–37.

[5] *L.S.*, ii, 95.   [6] *Loc. cit.*, pp. 135–6.

[7] He appears as chancellor before Bishop Alexander's death in February 1148 in *Giraldi Cambrensis Opera*, vii, 165, 168. See also *Reg. Antiquissimum*, i, 264; ii, 14, 20, 38, 310; *L.S.*, i, 310.

[8] *Ibid.*, iii, 789–92, 797–9.   [9] *Ibid.*, ii, 5; iii, 945.

Robert Bloet, the king's chancellor, who, again as *cancellarius*, witnessed the foundation charter of Salisbury cathedral a few months later.[1] Furthermore, Bradshaw apparently did not realize that, by counting Robert as the first chancellor of Lincoln, he was contradicting the conclusion which he and Le Neve and many other historians had drawn from a passage in Henry of Huntingdon's *De Contemptu Mundi*, namely, that Hugh was the first chancellor appointed by Remigius.[2] In point of fact, Henry of Huntingdon did not say this. He said that he knew personally all the clerks first instituted in the church by Remigius; and, writing about 1145, gave a brief description of some of them: of Randulf the dean; of Reinerus the treasurer; Felix, *exemplum viri clarissimi*, *Hugo, sacerdos, vir memoria dignus, principium et quasi fundamentum ecclesiae*; Guerno the cantor; and, finally, Albinus of Anjou, *magister quippe meus*. In addition he named the successors of the dean, treasurer, and cantor, and of Hugh 'cui successit Osbertus, vir omnino comis et desiderabilis, in quorum loco jam Willelmus exstat, juvenis magnae indolis'.[3]

This naming by Henry of the successors of only four canons, three of them known to be dignitaries, seems to have been the reason why Hugh has so often been described as the fourth dignitary.[4] Even so, this gives no reasonable ground for the further assumption that Hugh was chancellor. If a dignitary, he may equally well have had the better-known title of *magister*

[1] *S.S.*, p. 23. When the Lincoln foundation charter was reprinted in *Reg. Antiquissimum*, i, 4–9, the editors identified Robert as Robert Bloet (*ibid.*, pp. 8, 301). For doubts about the genuineness of this charter and its list of witnesses, see *ibid.*, pp. 10–11.

[2] *L.S.*, i, 31, 34; Le Neve-Hardy, ii, 91.

[3] *Hist. Anglorum*, p. 301. No other evidence has been found to suggest that Hugh, Osbert, or William held either the title of *magister* or the dignity of chancellor.

[4] It might perhaps be suggested that Osbert and William succeeded Hugh not in a dignity, but in his prebend. In this connexion it is interesting to notice one other reference to a Hugh, canon of Lincoln, about the beginning of the twelfth century. A writ of Henry I of 1100–15 commanded the sheriff of Lincolnshire to cause *Hugo canonicus* to have the land of Hundon if it belonged to the church of Castor (*Reg. Antiquissimum*, i, 35). Should this be the same man as the Hugh mentioned by Henry of Huntingdon it would suggest that Hugh was the first prebendary of Castor. But there would have been nothing to prevent Hugh, Osbert, and William from holding a dignity in addition to a prebend. Furthermore, Henry might well be more likely to remember and to record the successors to dignities than the successors to prebends.

scholarum in use at contemporary cathedrals at York and in northern France. At the same time it is interesting to notice Henry's description of Albinus of Angers as *magister quippe meus*. Henry had been brought up in the household of Robert Bloet,[1] who succeeded Remigius as bishop of Lincoln. He would presumably have attended the cathedral school as a young clerk; thus the passage may suggest that Albinus rather than Hugh was *magister scholarum* at the cathedral. Angers already had a flourishing cathedral school in the late eleventh century, and Remigius, wishing to institute a *magister scholarum* at Lincoln, may well have chosen a canon trained at Anjou. In either case, whether Lincoln in the late eleventh and early twelfth centuries had no fourth dignitary in charge of its school, or whether Hugh or Albinus were then teaching there, the fact remains that we have no evidence for the adoption of the title of chancellor at Lincoln until about the middle of the twelfth century.

At the third church, Salisbury, the position is complicated by doubts about the accuracy of the earliest surviving copies of St. Osmund's Institution.[2] The chancellor is mentioned in one part as ruler of the schools and corrector of the books.[3] Then, later, the *archischola* is said to keep the chapter seal, to compose letters and documents, to hear the lessons, and to mark the readers' names upon the board. If these were different persons, one would have expected Osmund to assign the ruling of the schools to the *archischola* and the keeping of the seal and composition of letters and documents to the chancellor. Mr. Leach thought the available text might read as if the *archischola* were the chancellor's deputy, because the description of his duties followed on after those of the subdean and succentor, the deputies of the dean and cantor.[4] He went to much trouble to show from contemporary practice that it would have been most unlikely for the chancellor to have had a deputy at such an early date.[5] But actually the functions of the *archischola* are coupled with those, not of the succentor, but of the

---

[1] *Hist. Anglorum*, pp. xxxi–ii. 　　　　[2] See above, p. 12.
[3] *S.S.*, pp. 30–1. This latter phrase may be a later interpolation in the original text. As late as 1220 the bishop granted the virgate of land which belonged *ab antiquo* to the correction of the books to any canon he chose (see below, p. 212).
[4] He adopted this interpretation in his article on 'Schools' in *V.C.H. Lincoln*, ii (1906), 421–2.
[5] In *Medieval Schools* (1915), pp. 107–8.

cantor, who is said to do for the singers what the *archischola* does for the readers.[1] Moreover, in the Salisbury Consuetudinary of the late twelfth century, which is largely an expansion and explanation of the Institution, no *archischola* is mentioned, and the functions assigned in the Institution to the *archischola* are attributed to the chancellor. Therefore the *archischola* and chancellor were most probably one and the same person described by different titles. But were both titles used in the original draft of the Institution? Professor Brooke has recently suggested that they were, and that the Institution is the real source for the later use of the title chancellor at the English cathedrals.[2] He writes that St. Osmund could have taken the title chancellor either from the list in John of Avranches's *De Officiis Ecclesiasticis*[3] or from Chartres cathedral, but that there were probably insufficient resources for an appointment to the office in St. Osmund's lifetime. The first known holder of the office was Guy of Étampes, *magister scolarum* at Le Mans, appointed by Roger, bishop of Salisbury, soon after his consecration in 1107.[4] Professor Brooke thinks that at Salisbury Guy preferred to use the title *magister scholarum* previously familiar to him at Le Mans, and that so the alternative title of chancellor proposed by St. Osmund was not generally used until later.

Precision in the use of titles was doubtless less important in the late eleventh than in the late twelfth century. Even so, I am not fully convinced by this explanation. The Institution is a comparatively short instrument, setting out the main features of a cathedral constitution. In such a document lucidity would be of the first importance. To divide up the functions of one of the principal dignitaries, to deal with them in different parts of the document, and at the same time to give this single dignitary different titles in the two parts seems to be something that an experienced administrator such as St. Osmund, who had been the king's chancellor, would want to avoid. It seems to me more probable that the title *archischola* was used for the third dignitary

[1] *S.S.*, pp. 32–3.

[2] In his two papers read at Oxford, 1952, and Stockholm, 1960. (See below, p. 371).

[3] See above pp. 18–19.

[4] Hildebert, Bishop of Le Mans, sent him in answer to Roger's request for a master, praising his learning and character and writing that in him Roger would find many masters ('*Hildeberti Epistolae*', in *P.L.*, clxxi, c. 219).

throughout the original draft. No evidence has been found for the use of the title chancellor at Salisbury in the first four decades of the twelfth century,[1] while there is definite evidence for that of *scholiarcha* or *magister scholarum*. Accounts of Guy of Étampes' life say he was *scholiarcha* (evidently a variant of *archischola*) or *magister scholarum* of Salisbury.[2] Sometime after 1139 King Stephen gave the churches of Odiham Liss and Bentworth *ad opus magistri scholae Sarum*.[3] These churches formed part of the later chancellor's endowment. I would suggest that soon after this grant, with the growing importance of his office, the *archischola* or *magister scholarum* came to be known as chancellor and that the institution was then brought up to date, by inserting the mention of the chancellor, but clumsily, since the *archischola* was not effectively eliminated. The title chancellor was certainly used at Salisbury from about 1155–64 onwards, quite probably from about 1140. [4]

In the course of the twelfth century three other chapters formed their constitutions very largely on the model of Salisbury. Evidence found for a chancellor at these churches does nothing to invalidate and, in one case, something to support the view that at Salisbury the predecessor of the chancellor was the *archischola*, *scholiarcha*, or *magister scholarum*. At Lichfield and Chichester the earliest mention of a chancellor seems to be in the last half of the twelfth century, when there was already a chancellor at Salisbury.[5]

[1] Of the two chancellors named by Canon Jones in his *Fasti Sar.*, p. 335, for this period, the first, Godwin, about 1108, was cantor not chancellor. Canon Wordsworth writes that the reading of the manuscript is definitely 'Godwino cant', meaning *cantore*, not *cancellario*, as is printed by Hatcher and Jones, *Hist. Old and New Sarum*, p. 725; *Reg. S. Osmund*, i, 381 (*P.M.L.A.*, xliv (1929), 640 n.). For the second, John, about 1121, Jones quotes Le Neve, but says he has been unable to trace Le Neve's authority.

[2] *P.L.*, clxxi, c. 219 n.; '*Actus Pontificum Cenomannis*', in *Vetera Analectae*, ed. J. Mabillon (1723), p. 320. Guy succeeded Hildebert as bishop of Le Mans in 1126.

[3] *Sarum Charters*, pp. 8–9.

[4] Philip witnessed a charter of 1155–64 as chancellor (*Reg. S. Osmund*, i, 217–18), and afterwards the succession of chancellors can be traced. Jones, *Fasti Sar.*, p. 335, also has one reference to a Henry, chancellor, in an unprinted charter at Salisbury of about 1148 which I have not traced, but which may well be correct. The titles of both chancellor and *archischola* appear in the *Wells Statuta Antiqua* which are evidently derived from Salisbury. These Wells Statutes are usually dated about 1140 (below, p. 184, n. 1.)

[5] At Chichester the chancellorship was apparently only instituted by Bishop Hilary and his chapter some time between about 1150–60 (*Chartulary of the*

At Wells development seems to be similar, though rather later than at Salisbury. The Wells *Statuta Antiqua*, of about 1140, speak of a chancellor who is also called *archischola*;[1] while the earliest charter evidence for a dignitary in charge of the schools is about 1185, when Peter of Winchester witnessed a charter as master of the schools of Wells.[2] By about 1200 his style had changed to chancellor.[3]

At the remaining three English secular cathedrals, which continued long after the Conquest to keep traces of their early organization for a common life, the chancellorship was naturally a late institution. At Exeter it was only founded in 1225;[4] while at Hereford the earliest known mention of a chancellor was about 1190.[5] At St. Paul's much more material is available. The chapter had a *magister scholarum* at the beginning of the twelfth century, and his history can be traced almost continuously throughout the twelfth century. Shortly after 1200 his style changed to chancellor.[6]

Thus until about the middle of the twelfth century the English secular cathedrals, like those of Normandy, may all have had a *magister scholarum* or *scholasticus* in place of the later chancellor. The title of chancellor is first known to have been used at Lincoln and Salisbury between 1148 and 1160, and, during the last half of the twelfth and in the early thirteenth centuries seems gradually to have been adopted at the other seven secular chapters. An attempt will now be made to examine available evidence both for the teaching at English secular cathedral schools in the middle ages, and for the expansion of the chapters' secretarial work. It

High Church of Chichester, ed. W. D. Peckham (1946), pp. 15–16, 68). At Lichfield a chancellor is mentioned in the earliest collection of customs taken from Salisbury in the late twelfth century (*L.S.*, ii, 20; cf. *M.R.A.*, no. 387).

[1] *W.S.*, pp. 45, 55–6; *Dean Cosyn and Wells Cathedral Misc.*, pp. xxv–vi.

[2] *H.M.C. Wells*, i, 492; cf. Church, *Chapters Hist. Wells*, pp. 61, 355.

[3] *Wells City Charters*, p. 3.

[4] Oliver, *Lives of the Bishops of Exeter*, pp. 34–5, 280.

[5] This was Master Nicholas, probably appointed by Bishop William de Vere (Z. N. and C. N. L. Brooke, 'Hereford Cathedral Dignitaries', in *Camb. Hist. Jour.*, viii, 183). For other canons of Hereford of the last quarter of the twelfth century, who were described as *divinus* or *theologus*, see below, pp. 190–1.

[6] See A. F. Leach, 'St. Paul's School before Colet', in *Archaeologia*, lxii, 191 *et seq.*; *Medieval Schools*, pp. 109–13; *Educational Charters*, pp. 80, 86, 90; *H.M.C. Ninth Rept.*, App., i, 13a–14a, 17a–b, 21b, 26a, 27b, 29a, 38b, 40b, 42a, 45b, 61b; *Early Charters of St. Paul*, pp. xxviii, xxxi–ii, 215–21.

will then be more possible to decide whether the change of title was due to the growing importance of the chancellor's functions, or whether it was merely a formal change.

THE CATHEDRAL SCHOOLS: THE GRAMMAR SCHOOL MASTER AND THE LECTURER IN THEOLOGY

The history of the secular cathedral schools in England in the twelfth century is at present very imperfectly known. The materials are incidental, casual allusions in chronicles, witnesses in charters, letters of papal judge-delegates, stray remarks in prefaces. Many of these have been collected by Dr. Eleanor Rathbone and Dr. R. W. Hunt.[1] I am much indebted to their work for the account in the following pages.

None of the English secular cathedral schools became a university, though some of them seem to have developed during the twelfth and thirteenth centuries in a way similar to French cathedral schools which did. For the first fifty or sixty years after the Conquest we know little except that there were grammar schools connected with the cathedrals: at Salisbury, Exeter, St. Paul's, and Lincoln.[2] Then, in the course of the twelfth century, masters lecturing in theology and sometimes in law begin to appear. As on the continent there was at first no uniformity and not much continuity in their schools. The school depended on the individual master and on the interest of the bishop who appointed him. But it is interesting to see how the schools of some cathedrals began to specialize in different branches of learning, such as theology, law, and occasionally natural science.

Lincoln probably came nearest to developing into a university. About 1158–60 Thorlak, the ecclesiastical lawyer and first saint of the Icelandic church, spent some time at Lincoln, where he is said to have acquired much knowledge useful to himself and others.[3] It

[1] R. W. Hunt, 'English Learning in the Late Twelfth Century', in *T.R.H.S.* (1936), pp. 19–42; E. Rathbone, 'The Intellectual Influence of Bishops and Cathedral Chapters, 1066–1216' (London Ph.D. thesis, 1935). Miss Rathbone's thesis will be the basis of a forthcoming book.

[2] References to the existence of these grammar schools have been collected by Miss Rathbone, *op. cit.*, pp. 133 *et seq.*

[3] *Biskupa Sögur* gefnar út af *Hinu Islenska Bokmentafèlagi* (1858), i, 92, 267. Later, Thorlak's nephew, Paul Jonssen, and one or two more students from Iceland were in England, and it is thought that they probably went to Lincoln

is interesting to notice that his visit was during the time of the first known chancellor, Hamo, and of Bishop Robert de Chesney, who was especially interested in law. A law school was evidently flourishing at Lincoln shortly before 1176. Peter de Blois in a letter then named Lincoln together with three of the most important centres of legal study. He accused the lawyer, Master Robert Blund, of an unrestrained restlessness, which prompted him at one time to dispute cases at Paris, at another to return to Bologna, then to set out for Lincoln, and again to stay in Oxford.[1] After this we hear little more of the law school at Lincoln. In its place a theological school arose under St. Hugh. About 1192 Giraldus Cambrensis, wishing to continue his theological studies, and being unable to go to France, spent several years at Lincoln, where, he said, theological study was more favoured than anywhere in England.[2] His teacher was William de Monte, appointed chancellor of Lincoln about 1190 by St. Hugh, and called *de Monte* because he had previously taught at Paris on the Monte Ste Geneviève. William's influence in England seems to have been very great, judging from the many surviving copies of his works.[3] Though he was praised by contemporaries as the first theological teacher in England, and as almost the equal of Gregory and Augustine, Miss Rathbone writes that it is disappointing to read his works.[4] His chief merit seems to have been that he simplified the theological learning of his time for clergy who were not highly educated. After William's death in 1213 the school becomes obscure. The only successor whose work has survived was Richard Wetherset, chancellor of Lincoln from 1221-9 and then archbishop of Canterbury. He wrote a manual for priests which apparently had a great success in the thirteenth century; but it was an avowed compilation from the works of William.[5]

Exeter also had schools of both theology and law in the twelfth

with its Scandinavian associations (*Hungurvaka, Pals Biskups Saga, ok Pattr af Thorvalldi Vidförla*, pp. 144–5; *Thomas Saga Erkbyskups*, ed. E. Magnusson (R.S.), ii, x–xii; E. W. Benson, *The Cathedral*, p. 26). For possible Scandinavian influence on book-binding at Lincoln about the middle of the twelfth century, see D. Cockerell, 'The Development of Book Binding', in *Trans. Bibliog. Soc.* (1932–3), p. 5.

[1] *P.L.*, ccvii, c. 185.   [2] *Giraldus Cambrensis Opera*, i, 93.

[3] These are discussed by Dr. Hunt, *op. cit.*, pp. 21–2, and by Dr. Rathbone, *op. cit.*, pp. 156–7, 460–2.

[4] *Ibid.*, p. 460.   [5] R. W. Hunt, *op. cit.*, p. 22.

century. There is even a possibility that Robert Pullen taught theology at Exeter as early as 1133 before he lectured at Oxford.[1] About 1159–60 a document of Bishop Robert was witnessed by ten scholars, among them Nicholas of Flanders and Gilbert of Ireland.[2] These may have been studying only grammar. But Thomas de Marlbergh, who became a monk at Evesham in 1194 or 1200, is definitely said to have taught both civil and canon law in Exeter and Oxford before his profession;[3] while Bartholomew, bishop of Exeter, and his archdeacon Baldwin, later bishop of Worcester and archbishop of Canterbury, were both scholars who surrounded themselves with learned men.[4] Baldwin may at one time have been master of the school at Exeter, and is thought to have had something to do with the early collections of decretals in Worcester cathedral library.[5] About the end of the twelfth century, Alexander, prior of Canons Ashby, wrote in his tract on the art of preaching that, when he was a student, there were few masters in England who would teach theology without a fee; but at the time of writing there was one in almost every city: at Northampton an un-named master, at Oxford Master Philip, at Exeter Master John, and others elsewhere.[6] Some time after 1230 Hugh de Wilton, archdeacon of Taunton, left three glossed books of the New Testament to the church of Exeter, 'for the use of poor scholars'.[7]

At York there are suggestions of a school of civil law. Vacarius, the first teacher of civil law in this country, went to York with Archbishop Roger (1154–81), and may possibly have lectured there, as well as at Canterbury and Oxford.[8] Furthermore, the first

---

[1] Cf. E. Rathbone, *op. cit.*, pp. 165–6; R. L. Poole, 'The Early Lives of Robert Pullen and Nicholas Breakspear', in *Essays to Tout*, pp. 61–3; H. E. Salter in *History*, xiv (1929–30), p. 57.

[2] *H.M.C. Var. Coll.*, iv, 49.   [3] *Chronicon Abbatiae de Evesham*, pp. xxi, 267.

[4] Cf. A. Morey, *Bartholomew of Exeter, Bishop and Canonist*, pp. 103–9.

[5] Cf. A. Morey, *Bartholomew of Exeter, Bishop and Canonist*, p. 105; E. Rathbone, *op. cit.*, p. 319; C. Duggan, *Twelfth Century Decretal Collections* (1963), pp. 110–15.

[6] R. W. Hunt, *op. cit.*, p. 20, quoting MS. Camb. Univ. Library, Ii, 1, 24, ff. 173vb–174ra.

[7] MS. Bodl. Auct. D.I. 7, f. iii; cf. *Summary Catalogue of Western MSS. in the Bodleian Library*, II, i, xv, 216. All three MSS. are now in the Bodleian Library: MS. Bodl. 494; MS. Bodl. Auct. D.I. 7, 12.

[8] Cf. *The Liber Pauperum of Vacarius*, ed. F. de Zulueta (Selden Soc.), pp. xix–xxiii.

chancellor of York, Master Simon of Apulia, appointed in 1189–1190, was described by Giraldus Cambrensis as 'a very learned man and a lawyer'.[1] He may be the author of a *Summa* mentioned in the fourteenth-century catalogue of Lantony priory library.[2]

Elsewhere some of the most flourishing twelfth-century schools were at London. The short pontificate of Gilbert of Auxerre, called the Universal on account of his great learning, seems to have attracted both teachers and scholars there. A writ of *c.* 1138, issued by Henry of Blois, who was acting as bishop during the vacancy of the see after Gilbert's death, ordered the chapter of St. Paul's and the archdeacon of London to pronounce sentence of excommunication against any person who presumed to set up a school in the city without the licence of Henry, master of the cathedral school, except the masters of the schools of St. Mary of the Arches and St. Martin's le Grand.[3] These two privileged schools were probably of fairly long standing, but those depending on the licence to teach of the master of the cathedral school were apparently of recent growth. The best account of the London schools later in the twelfth century is by William FitzStephen in his life of Becket. He wrote that the three leading churches had by ancient privilege and right independent schools, but that other schools might be established by special permission, when some famous master wished to teach in the city.

'On holy days the masters of the schools assemble their scholars at the churches whose feast day it is. The scholars dispute, some in demonstrative rhetoric, others in dialectic. Some "hurtle enthymemes", others with greater skill employ perfect syllogisms. Some are exercised in disputation for the purpose of display, which is but a wrestling bout of wit, but others that they may establish the truth. . . . Sophists who produce fictitious arguments are accounted happy in the profusion and deluge of their words; others seek to trick their opponents by the use of fallacies. Some orators from time to time in rhetorical harangues seek to carry persuasion, taking pains to observe the precepts of their art and to omit nothing that pertains thereto. Boys of different schools strive against one another in verse, or contend concerning the principles

[1] *Opera*, iv, 383; cf. William de Newburgh in *Chronicles of Reigns of Stephen, Henry II, and Richard I* (R.S.), i, 340.

[2] 'Summa magistri Symonis de Apuleya, quaternus ligatus' (T. W. Williams 'Gloucestershire Medieval Libraries', in *Trans. Bristol and Glos. Arch. Soc.*, xxxi, 153.

[3] *H.M.C. Ninth Rept.*, App., i, 45b; *Educational Charters*, p. 90.

of the art of grammar or the rules governing the use of past or future. There are others who employ the old wit of the cross roads in epigrams, rhymes and metre; with "Fescennine license," they lacerate their comrades outspokenly, though mentioning no names; they hurl abuse and jibes, they touch the foibles of their comrades, perchance even of their elders with Socratic wit. . . . Each year on Shrove Tuesday . . . boys from the schools bring fighting cocks to their master, and the whole morning is given up to sport; for they have a holiday from the schools that they may watch their cocks do battle. After dinner all the youth of the city goes out into the fields for a game of ball. The scholars of each school have their own ball, and almost all the workers of each trade have theirs also. Older men and fathers and rich citizens come on horseback to watch the contests of their juniors, and after their fashion are young again with the young.' [1]

These schools were evidently chiefly schools of grammar and arts. But in 1170 a Master Ralph, canon of London and priest, was described as an outstanding teacher of theology,[2] so possibly there was also a theological school. Law may have been taught,[3] and possibly there was some interest in astronomy. There were astronomical tables for London for the year 1149–50; Robert of Chester's treatise on the astrolabe is dated London, 1147, and Roger of Hereford, the scientist, perhaps witnessed some documents of Bishop Gilbert Foliot.[4]

At Hereford natural science seems to have been a favourite study at several periods from the Norman Conquest onwards, and there are suggestions that, towards the end of the twelfth century, it was taught there. In the last half of the eleventh century Arabic science had begun to spread through Spain to Lorraine. Lotharingian influence was at this time strong in English ecclesiastical circles. The Lotharingian Robert Losinga, bishop of Hereford, 1079–95, may have introduced the use of the abacus into the English exchequer.[5]

---

[1] The translation is that of Professor H. E. Butler, printed as an appendix to F. M. Stenton, *Norman London* (Hist. Assocn. Leaflet), pp. 27–8, 30. Professor Butler points out the inaccuracies of other editions of the text.

[2] William FitzStephen, *Materials Hist. Becket*, iii, 143. For other references to Master Ralph, *theologus* or *divinus*, about 1183, see *H.M.C. Ninth Rept.*, App., pp. 12a, 38b; *Early Charters of St. Paul*, pp. 52, 129.

[3] In 1234 there is an unexplained reference on the close roll to a suppressed school of law in the city (*Close Rolls*, 1234–7, p. 26). Miss Rathbone (*op. cit.*, pp. 385–408) has studied in detail the work of a group of leading lawyers in the chapter of St. Paul's at the end of the twelfth century.

[4] Haskins, *Medieval Science*, pp. 122–4.   [5] Cf. *Ibid.*, pp. 333–5.

o

He was described by William of Malmesbury as learned in all the arts, particularly astronomy and the science of calculation. He brought the chronicle of Marianus Scotus with its new system of chronology to this country, and made an abridgement of it with such art that the abridgement was said to be worth more than the whole work.[1] He knew that Bishop Remigius would be unable to consecrate his new cathedral by his reading of the stars.[2] His successor at Hereford, Gerard, was said to be interested in the black art: a copy of Julius Firmicus was found under his pillow after his sudden death.[3] Later, in the second half of the twelfth century, the scientist, Roger of Hereford, made astronomical tables for Hereford, which he dedicated to Bishop Gilbert Foliot.[4] Then, when Giraldus Cambrensis became a canon of Hereford, Master Simon de Fresne, a fellow canon, urged him to come to Hereford, where he would receive due honour from a group of men who shared his tastes, and where the seven liberal arts were more studied and taught than anywhere in England.[5] This is interesting, for there is little trace of the teaching of the seven arts at other English secular cathedrals. Furthermore, Simon added that not only astronomy and astrology, but also geomancy was studied at Hereford.[6] Law was read,[7] while, towards the end of the twelfth century, a school of theology may have been growing up. A Master Nicholas *divinus*, possibly the chancellor of *c.* 1190, attested documents of 1173 and 1189, while two other canons of

[1] *De Gestis Pontificum*, pp. 300–1.

[2] *Ibid.*, p. 313.

[3] *Ibid.*, pp. 259 n., 260 n.

[4] Haskins, *Medieval Science*, p. 124 and n. 35.

[5] *Giraldus Cambrensis Opera*, i, 382–3; R. W. Hunt, *op. cit.*, pp. 23–4, 36–7. The description of the subjects taught is not in Brewer's text, but is given by Dr. Hunt from Cambridge, C.C.C. MS. 400, f. 119.

[6] *Ibid.*, pp. 36–7. This is much the earliest reference to geomancy in England. An interest in natural science seems to have been maintained at Hereford after the twelfth century. About 1285 the largest and most carefully drawn medieval wall map of the world to have survived intact was made by Richard of Haldingham or de Bello, later a canon of Hereford, and probably a member of the *familia* of Richard de Swinfield, bishop of Hereford, 1283–1315. (Cf. W. L. Bevan and H. W. Phillott, *Medieval Geography; an Essay in Illustration of the Hereford Mappa Mundi*, p. 5.) This map is now in Hereford cathedral. It was reproduced by the Royal Geographical Society in its Reproductions of Early MS. Maps III, 1954.

[7] R. W. Hunt, *op. cit.*, p. 37.

the period, Simon of Melun and Peter of Abergavenny, were styled *theologus* in the cathedral obit roll.[1]

Strangely enough, it is not until the thirteenth century that we find evidence for one of the most famous theological schools of the English secular cathedrals, that of Salisbury. Here the development of the school in the thirteenth century was so much more akin to what had happened at other English cathedral schools in the twelfth century than to their state in the thirteenth century that it is convenient to discuss it in connexion with the history of the twelfth-century schools. About 1220–30 we know that there was a group of exceptionally learned men in the chapter at Salisbury;[2] their presence was probably largely due to the influence and learning of Richard le Poore, dean, and later bishop of Salisbury, from 1198 to 1228. Among them Master Henry of Bishopstone, who had previously lectured in canon law at Oxford, ruled the school at New Salisbury. In 1238, Oxford students migrated to Northampton and Salisbury.[3] They are thought to have returned from Northampton to Oxford by 1264, but there is evidence for their continuing at Salisbury until at least 1279. In that year an award was made between the chancellor and subdean of the cathedral, who had both claimed jurisdiction over the scholars.[4] The award shows that all the essentials of a *studium generale* or university then existed at Salisbury: numbers of masters were mentioned; the scholars belonged to more than one faculty; and the causes and contrasts which the chancellor was to judge were evidently more than the disputes of schoolboys. Rashdall wrote: It is 'probable that the schools here were of a character which we have no reason for believing existed permanently at such places after the growth of the universities'.[5]

A further reason for regarding thirteenth-century Salisbury as a university town was the foundation there by Bishop Bridport in 1262 of the first university college in England, De Vaux College or the House of the Valley Scholars.[6] The bishop made provision

---

[1] Z. N. and C. N. L. Brooke, 'Hereford Cathedral Dignitaries', in *Camb. Hist. Jour.*, viii, 13, 183; *Hereford Charters*, pp. 23, 24, 37 f.; R. Rawlinson, *Hist. Hereford Cathedral*, Obituary, p. 6.

[2] M. Gibbs and J. Lang, *op. cit.*, pp. 51–2, 193–5, 197; *Reg. S. Osmund*, ii, 16.

[3] Rashdall, *Universities*, iii, 87–8.

[4] *S.S.*, pp. 112–15.   [5] *Universities*, iii, 88–9.

[6] The foundation charter is printed in *Sarum Charters*, pp. 334–6; *S.S.*, pp. 94–5; *The Cartulary of St. Nicholas' Hospital, Salisbury*, ed. C. Wordsworth,

for two chaplains and twenty poor scholars serving God and St. Nicholas and studying Holy Scripture and the liberal arts to live together in a college adjoining the southern boundary of the cathedral close. Their warden was a residentiary canon elected by the chapter, and at first they apparently attended the lectures provided by the chancellor of the cathedral. In 1269 Bishop Wyville founded a collegiate church at Salisbury, called St. Edmund's College, for priests and theologians.[1] With the prior and brethren of St. Nicholas' Hospital, the scholars and priests of both colleges were expected to follow the cathedral choir in processions.[2]

Elsewhere in England the thirteenth century saw no such spectacular developments at the secular cathedral schools. Towards the end of the twelfth and in the early thirteenth centuries the rise of the universities had begun to draw away their best scholars. This process increased in the later middle ages. The pupils of the cathedral schools seem to have been drawn more and more from local clergy who had not the means or opportunity to proceed to a university, with a growing preponderance of cathedral clergy, younger vicars choral, clerks of the second form, and other *ministri inferiores*, some of whom they may have taken to the threshold of the university. Yet these changes, although they naturally affected the teaching and the intellectual contribution of the schools, did not lead to their disappearance. At the same time the schools were steadily gaining in those qualities which they had so conspicuously lacked in the twelfth century, stability, continuity, and a certain uniformity of organization.

How far was the organization and endowment of the schools in the later middle ages due to rulings of canon law? For centuries the church had urged that masters able to teach liberal arts and theology should be appointed in cathedral churches. In the twelfth century, with the intellectual renaissance and the fight against simony in the church, there came a change of emphasis in the

pp. 38–40. For its date see K. Edwards, 'The College of De Vaux, Salisbury' in *V.C.H.*, *Wilts.*, iii, 369 n. The name of the college was probably suggested by that of the regular order of Augustinian canons *de Valle Scholarium*, which in 1229 had begun to build a college in Paris for the students from its different houses (*ibid.*, p. 371).

[1] *St. Nicholas Cartulary*, pp. 40–4.
[2] *Ibid.*; *S.S.*, pp. 256–7. For their later history see below, pp. 202–3.

legislation. Many cathedrals already had a chancellor or *scholasticus*. The chief demand now was that he should not charge fees for granting the licence to teach. In order that teaching should be free the cathedral chapters were required to provide their *scholasticus* with a sufficient benefice to support him without the necessity of charging fees. In 1179 a decree of the third Lateran Council ordered that every cathedral church should institute a master, and supply him with a sufficient benefice to teach the clerks of that church and poor scholars freely;[1] in 1215 the fourth Lateran Council required every cathedral church to support a master of arts, and every metropolitan church a theologian.[2] It has been supposed that these decrees remained largely unfulfilled, at any rate on the continent, because of the difficulty of getting the chapters to give up prebends to support the masters. Mandonnet declared that the decree for the endowment of a teacher of theology in metropolitan churches remained almost a dead letter, and that all education for the ordinary parish clergy was lamentably insufficient until the coming of the friars preacher.[3] From the second quarter of the thirteenth century onwards their theological schools did for the secular clergy what the secular clergy had been unable to do for themselves. Popes and bishops welcomed the establishment of the friars' schools, and no longer found it necessary to insist that the cathedrals should provide theological teaching. In the rare cases when theology was still taught in metropolitan churches the master was usually a friar preacher from a neighbouring Dominican convent.[4]

Yet at many English secular cathedral chapters in the late twelfth and early thirteenth centuries it must have seemed that the educational decrees of the Lateran councils were really demanding less than already existed at their churches. Some permanent endowments had already been granted in the twelfth century for the support of grammar school masters: at York and Salisbury as early as about 1135 and 1139, and at St. Paul's about 1189–98.[5] More followed in the first half of the thirteenth century;[6] while at the

---

[1] Mansi, xxii, 227–8, c. 18. [2] *Ibid.*, 999.
[3] 'La crise scolaire au début du xiiie siècle', in *Rev. d'hist. eccl.* (1914), **xv**, 34–49.
[4] *Ibid.*, pp. 47–8.
[5] C. T. Clay, *loc. cit.*, pp. 129–30; *Sarum Charters*, pp. 8–9; *Early Charters of St. Paul*, pp. 217–19.
[6] E.g. at Wells in 1236 (Church, *Chapters Hist. Wells*, pp. 141–2).

same time further arrangements were being made for the regular provision of theological lectures.

Certainly every English secular cathedral of the later middle ages maintained a grammar school, which was meant to serve the educational needs of the whole city, not only of the choristers and other young clerks attached to the cathedral.[1] For this reason it was normally in the city, not, like the theology schools, in the cathedral close.[2] Some indications of the number of boys taught at the York school are available: in 1369 an advocate of the court of York bequeathed twopence each to sixty poor clerks of the grammar school, 'not being bad boys' to be named by the school-master on a roll, to say the whole of the psalms for the salvation of his soul.[3] In 1535 St. Mary's Abbey, York, was said, from ancient times, to have maintained a boarding house, called Con-clave or The Clee, for fifty boys attending the Minster's school.[4]

At most cathedrals the chancellor was said to rule the grammar school.[5] He administered any endowments granted to the school; appointed a master of arts to teach there, and paid him a small salary. None of the English chapters adopted the recommendation of the Lateran councils of granting the revenues of a prebend to the master. But instead they contributed to his support by allow-ing him to undertake other paid work in the cathedral. He was expected to follow the choir, where his stall was usually superior to that of the priest vicars.[6] In return he was given commons about equal in value to those of the vicars, and might earn further distributions by attending the celebration of obits.[7] In churches

---

[1] Choristers, altarists, and vicars choral were sometimes ordered to attend this school; but at certain churches the choristers were given a separate master, independent of the chancellor's jurisdiction, to teach them grammar (see below, p. 312 *et seq.*).

[2] E.g. at Salisbury the medieval grammar school was in Exeter Street, nearly opposite the east gate of the close, not in the close, as Canon Jones and Mr. Leach supposed (cf. D. H. Robertson, 'Notes on Buildings in the City and Close of Salisbury,' in *W.A.M.*, xlviii, 12–21).

[3] Quoted by Leach in *V.C.H. Yorks.*, i, 420.

[4] *Valor Ecclesiasticus*, v, 6.

[5] E.g. *S.S.*, pp. 30–3; *C.S.*, p. 13; *R.S.S.P.*, p. 23; *W.S.*, pp. 45, 55; *L.S.*, ii, 95–6.

[6] E.g. Jones, *Fasti Sar.*, p. 438, cf. 263, 290; *W.S.*, p. 1; *Educational Charters*, pp. 392–3.

[7] Cf. D. H. Robertson, *loc. cit.*, p. 16; Jones, *Fasti Sar.*, p. 291; *H.M.C. Wells*, i, 176; *L.S.*, i, 276, 291, 336; iii, 315.

such as St. Paul's and Hereford, which had no vice-chancellor, he acted as deputy for the chancellor in his choir duties.[1]

The grammar master's appointment was not always a permanent one. At Lincoln it apparently had to be renewed every year;[2] while at York it was for three years only, with a possibility of extension for a fourth year by special grace.[3] This rule was broken during the period of the Black Death, when the flow of scholars from the universities was scarce. In 1368 the chapter agreed to the appointment of a master, John of York, until he should obtain an ecclesiastical benefice. John was still master of the York school in 1380, when he was admitted a freeman of the city.[4] But later York returned to its old practice of a three years' appointment.[5]

There is often difficulty in tracing continuity in the appointments of the grammar masters, because, if the chancellor kept records of his appointments, he kept them separately from the chapter records, and few have survived.[6] It is only in abnormal times, during a vacancy of the chancellorship, or when things were not going well, that we have evidence for the affairs of the grammar school in the chapter act books. About 1350-2, when Master Henry Nugge was said not to be teaching regularly in the grammar school at Salisbury, the bishop, dean, and chapter decided that Elias of St. Albans, the chancellor who had appointed Henry, was too old and incapable to execute the business of the church. They brought pressure on him to revoke his collation of the grammar school to Henry, and at the same time forced him to admit two residentiary canons to act for him as coadjutors in the chancery.[7] Again in 1468, when the chancellor of Salisbury was

---

[1] See below, p. 215.

[2] Leach, *Medieval Schools*, p. 192; *Educational Charters*, pp. 280-3.

[3] *L.S.*, ii, 96.   [4] *Educational Charters*, p. xxxiv.   [5] *V.C.H. Yorks.*, i, 421.

[6] An exception is in the short collection of letters of William Wickwane, chancellor of York from 1266 to 1268, now in the Bodleian Library (Rawlinson MS., C. 755). This has been edited by Professor Cheney in *E.H.R.*, xlvii, 626-42. It includes two letters dealing with the appointment of a grammar schoolmaster at York (*ibid.*, p. 634).

[7] Reg. Corffe, ff. 54, 83, 87-8, 92. There was much discussion in chapter as to whether the appointment of a coadjutor belonged to the bishop without the chapter, because the chancellor was immediately subject to the bishop; or to the chapter without the bishop, because the chancellor was a canon and residentiary in the close; or to the bishop and chapter jointly. After the protestation of rights by both sides the chapter first agreed to ask Elias to nominate a curator himself. When he refused, they appointed the two canons jointly.

ill, the dean and chapter dealt with a similar situation at the grammar school. They called in an old master of grammar, John Russell, to take over the school until a new man could be found; and gave him a second junior master or *hostiarius* to help him.[1] In normal times there seems little reason to doubt that grammar masters were appointed regularly. Occasionally we hear something of their doings. In 1316 a young clerk ruling the grammar school of Lincoln, wrote two hymns on the life and sanctity of St. Hugh of Lincoln, for a play on Christmas day.[2] In that year there was great scarcity and mortality among men and animals, and the young master said that he wrote the hymns intending to comfort himself and others in their misery. Very probably his name was William of Wheatley or *de Frumenti lege*, the author of a commentary on Boethius' Consolation of Philosophy, which he dedicated, among others, to Henry of Mansfield, dean of Lincoln. He included the two hymns at the end of his longer work.

The monopoly of the chancellor's master to teach grammar in the city was jealously maintained. Only the chancellor could grant the licence to teach there; and, if unlicensed schools were opened, the master of the chancellor's school would appeal to his lord to suppress them.[3] Sometimes too the importance of the chancellor's educational work was emphasized by the bishop allowing him to supervise schools in the diocese outside the cathedral city.[4] About 1266–8 it was the chancellor of York cathedral, William Wickwane, who gave permission to John de Blaby to place his two sons at Guisborough Priory with the schoolmaster who taught the poor children maintained there by the convent.[5] Later, in

---

[1] D. H. Robertson, *loc. cit.*, p. 17.   [2] New College MS. 264, ff. 262a–265b.

[3] Cf. *V.C.H. Yorks.*, i, 420–1; *V.C.H. Lincoln*, ii, 422. In the most thickly populated city, London, the two other privileged churches, St. Mary of the Arches and St. Martin le Grand, maintained their right to appoint a grammar master for their schools independently of the chancellor of St. Paul's. But it was not until the mid-fifteenth century, under pressure of a petition to parliament by the parsons of four other London churches, that two more schools were legally established to meet the growing demand for education in the city.

[4] This is a subject on which much more work needs to be done. In some cases (Amiens, Noyon, Aschaffenberg), the authority of the cathedral *scholasticus* or chancellor extended to schools of the whole diocese (see the note to Rashdall, *Universities*, i, 282). But the practice in England is difficult to trace, and apparently varied in different dioceses.

[5] 'Letters of William Wickwane', ed. C. R. Cheney, in *E.H.R.*, xlvii, 629, 633.

1280, when Wickwane was archbishop of York, he sent injunctions to the same priory forbidding the teaching of wealthy and important scholars, or even of poor scholars, at this school, unless the chancellor of the cathedral approved.[1] At Lincoln the chancellor of the cathedral had the right to collate to all the schools in the county or archdeaconry of Lincoln according to his judgement, except those in the canons' prebends, or others held by parish priests for their parishioners.[2] In a vacancy of the chancellorship this jurisdiction lapsed to the dean and chapter. In a vacancy in 1329, they appointed to six different schools in the county of Lincoln.[3]

In addition to maintaining a grammar school, practically all the English secular cathedral chapters, not only the metropolitan chapter of York, made arrangements for theological lectures to be delivered in their cathedrals. Usually, as with the grammar school, the supervision of the theological school was given to the chancellor, at any rate by the fourteenth century. But there were two exceptions, Hereford and Chichester. The bishop, dean, and chapter of Chichester made their decision fairly soon after the Lateran decree of 1215. In the pontificate of Ralph Neville, 1224–1244, they annexed the cathedral prebend of Wittering permanently to the office of *theologus*, declaring that the canon appointed must always be a master of theology who should take oath to deliver theological lectures.[4] At Hereford there is little evidence between the appearance in chapter records at the end of the twelfth century of *theologi* or *divini*, perhaps distinct from the chancellor, and 1356, when the lectureship is found to be already annexed to the dignity of penitentiary. The chapter then praised the merits of earlier penitentiaries, and went on to declare that for the future the penitentiary must be

'young and vigorous, of excellent life, and knowledge proved in the schools and elsewhere: at least a doctor or inceptor in Holy Scripture,

[1] *Cartularium Prioratus de Gyseburne* (Surtees Soc.), ii, 360.

[2] *L.S.*, i, 285; iii, 300.

[3] *Educational Charters*, pp. 280–3; *Medieval Schools*, p. 192; *V.C.H. Lincoln*, ii, 449–50.

[4] *C.P.L., 1362–1404*, pp. 189–90; *V.C.H. Sussex*, ii, 404; Swainson, p. 39. The danger of this system, which was in accordance with the Lateran recommendation of giving up a prebend to the office, may be seen in the chapter's protests when later bishops or kings conferred the prebend on a clerk, without the necessary university degrees.

or a doctor or bachelor in decrees . . . so that, as is done and should be observed in cathedral churches, he may lecture and teach continuously in theology or canon law at opportune times.' [1]

In other English cathedrals the chancellor was sometimes expected to lecture in theology in person, sometimes by deputy. Statutes of York and Lincoln required the chancellor to rule the school of theology and actually to lecture in it.[2] Deputies would naturally be appointed to take the place of absentee or busy chancellors, especially in the later middle ages. Yet at York, as late as 1332, Master Robert de Riplingham, chancellor of York and a former fellow of Merton, may have lectured in person. He bequeathed his professorial chair and desk to his successor in the chancellorship;[3] and it has been suggested that a picture in the third window from the east in the south aisle of the nave of York minster is meant to represent him teaching in his school.[4] The chapter of Exeter, like Hereford, was prepared to have lectures delivered in either canon law or theology, as the chancellor decided. In 1283 the churches of St. Newlyn and Stoke Gabriel

[1] *Hereford Charters*, p. 228. The Hereford penitentiary had a prebend annexed to his office.

[2] *L.S.*, ii, 95–6; iii, 300–1; cf. i, 284; ii, 158; *C.P.L., 1417–31*, pp. 17–18.

[3] I owe this reference to Chancellor Harrison, Librarian of the Dean and Chapter Library, York, who has kindly inspected Robert's original will for me.

[4] Cf. Leach in *V.C.H. Yorks.*, i, 419. Chancellor Harrison has very kindly sent me all the available evidence of which he knows for this suggestion. At some time someone with an ingenious turn of mind took the middle light of this window to represent a pedagogue chastizing his pupils. But the window was badly damaged by fire in 1840, and badly restored. Twenty-five years ago, when Chancellor Harrison began to study the York glass, he could make nothing of the panel in question, and repeated attempts to see in it a grammar school or the birching of boys were a failure. He preferred to trust to the judgement of James Torre, the antiquary who worked at York in the second half of the seventeenth century, and who saw the glass when it was much better preserved than it is now. Torre says that Riplingham was shown three times in the window: twice in the middle light, and once in the western light. In the first picture of the middle light (i.e. the relevant panel), 'he was accompanied by two old men (in white garments) kneeling before him with hands elevated (as at prayer)'; in the second, by 'two other men standing by him, the one habited *gu*, the other *ut*'. The tale of the chastisement of schoolboys can probably be rejected altogether. In any case the chancellor's pupils in his theological school would be older men, not needing to be birched like boys of the grammar school. There may be a faint possibility that the two older men were older clergy (perhaps vicars choral or others) learning theology from the chancellor. But there is no definite evidence for this.

were annexed to his office to provide for the expense:[1] he was himself to be a doctor or bachelor in canon law or theology, and might appoint a substitute only if legitimately hindered from lecturing in person. At Salisbury and Wells, on the other hand, the chancellor was free to choose whether he would teach in person or appoint a deputy at his own expense.[2] In 1240 Salisbury chapter agreed to the annexation of the prebend of Brixworth to the chancellorship to provide for the lectures.[3] For the school at Wells some lectures on the Apocalypse, given by Dr. John Orum, survive from the first half of the fifteenth century.[4]

The chapter of St. Paul's, which seems to have had a *theologus* before the Lateran decree in 1179, was the last English secular cathedral chapter to make adequate arrangements for the endowment of the office. Richard Junior, canon of St. Paul's in the late twelfth century, left a house to be conferred by the dean and chapter on a residentiary canon 'particularly a doctor in holy scripture or a preacher'.[5] But no further economic provision has been traced until nearly the end of the thirteenth century. Until then the chancellor apparently had no responsibility for the theological school, or jurisdiction over it. In 1281, when the chapter appointed Richard de Swinfield, archdeacon of London, to rule in theology in their school, it lamented that it had no doctor in the holy scripture, nor a suitable preacher, 'but in these things we have been forced to beg to the loss of our honour and good fame'.[6] The chapter relieved Richard of many of the burdens and expenses of the greater residence in order that he should lecture and preach in the cathedral. He was a doctor of theology whose learning and preaching were praised by contemporary

---

[1] *Ordinale Exon.*, i, 4; Oliver, *Lives of the Bishops of Exeter*, pp. 47, 281.

[2] *Sarum Charters*, pp. 259–60; *Reg. Shrewsbury*, pp. 255, 341. But cf. *C.P.L., 1342–62*, p. 284.

[3] *Sarum Charters*, pp. 259–60.

[4] Bodley MS. 859 (*S.C.* 2722), ff. 261a–289v. Dr. John Orum, who died in 1436, had been vice-chancellor of Oxford University. He held the archdeaconry of Barnstaple in Exeter diocese from 1400–29, and was appointed chancellor of Exeter cathedral in 1429. The MS. volume containing the lectures which he delivered in the church of Wells, is said to have been given by the executors of Edmund Lacy, bishop of Exeter, to Exeter cathedral in 1455. It was probably acquired by the Bodleian Library *c.* 1613–20.

[5] Muniments D. and C. St. Paul's, Liber A, f. 46v, quoted by E. Rathbone, *op. cit.*, pp. 177–8.

[6] *R.S.S.P.*, pp. 188–9.

chroniclers.[1] After his promotion to be bishop of Hereford, his successor was apparently another famous lecturer, Robert of Winchelsea, the future archbishop of Canterbury, formerly rector of the University of Paris and chancellor of Oxford University. Birchington says that while he was archdeacon of Essex, Robert resumed his lectures at London.[2] A collection of eight theological *quaestiones* contained in Magdalen College MS. 217 are described in the contemporary table of contents as disputed by Robert de Wynchelse at London when he was lecturing there. They are in substance the same lectures which he had delivered in Oxford in 1283.[3]

Evidently, therefore, lack of endowments did not always prevent the chapter from securing the services of good teachers. But by Winchelsea's time different arrangements may already have been made. Bishop Gravesend, some time between 1280 and 1303, decided to annex the burden of lecturing or of finding a substitute to the chancellorship. He granted a small annual pension to the chancellor for the purpose,

'seeing that, by reason of his office, he seems most suitable for the work, and because in most other cathedral churches in England there have long been and are doctors of theology *de gremio* lecturing in that faculty. But in the church of London, which is thought more famous than the rest, the dean and chapter have hitherto been forced to procure a lecturer *emendicatis suffragiis*.' [4]

The endowment was increased in 1308 when Bishop Baldock appropriated the church of Ealing to the chancellorship to provide additional revenues for the lectures.[5] About 1464–5 Dr. William Ive, the Oxford theologian and canon of St. Paul's, who played a leading part in the quarrel of the secular masters with the Carmelite friars about the poverty of Christ, is known to have kept the schools of St. Paul for over two years and to have held a long course of lectures and disputations there.[6]

[1] E.g. Trivet, *Annales*, p. 306; Rishanger, *Chronica et Annales*, pp. 102–3.
[2] Birchington in *Anglia Sacra*, i, 12.
[3] Cf. A. G. Little, 'Theological Schools in Medieval England', in *E.H.R.*, lv, 625–6.
[4] *Reg. Baldock*, p. 88; *C.P.R. 1307–13*, pp. 149–50.
[5] *Reg. Baldock*, pp. 88–9.
[6] Gregory's Chronicle in *Hist. Collections*, ed. J. Gairdner (Camden Soc. 1876), pp. 230–1; R. du Boulay in *J.E.H.*, vi (1955), 162–3, 168.

At Salisbury the brilliance of the theological school in the second and third quarters of the thirteenth century was not maintained in the fourteenth century. Towards the end of the thirteenth and in the early fourteenth centuries learned chancellors, such as Simon de Micham, William de Bosco and Henry de la Wyle, were still appointed.[1] Ralph of York in 1300 was said to have been the first chancellor who neglected to provide the lectures, and had to be compelled by the bishop and dean to find a lecturer,[2] and after Henry de la Wyle's death in 1329 there seems to have been a lack of ability or inclination among the chancellors or other members of the chapter to teach in person. In 1349, in the time of the aged and difficult chancellor, Elias of St. Albans, the chapter agreed to a friar preacher's lecturing in their school. This, however, was apparently chiefly due to the influence of the Countess of Lancaster, who wrote personally to Elias, asking for the appointment as theological lecturer of John of Newton, friar preacher of Salisbury.[3] There was much opposition in chapter, especially from John Whitchurch, a residentiary canon, who protested that it was contrary to the statutes and customs of the church for anyone except a doctor or bachelor of theology to lecture in their school; and John of Newton, since he had been trained in a Dominican school, was neither.[4] Finally the chapter arranged a compromise. Roger Kington, S.T.P., and archdeacon of Salisbury, was to begin lecturing on the next law day in the chancellor's place. But when he was busy he might substitute Friar John of Newton, 'both for the church's honour and on account of reverence for the friends of the said friar'. The two were to continue lecturing alternately until Christmas, when their reappointment would be deliberated by the chapter.[5] Eight years later, when business concerning the

[1] Henry de la Wyle left a large number of theological manuscripts to the cathedral library (*H.M.C., Var. Coll.*, i, 375–6; N. R. Ker, *Medieval Libraries of Great Britain*, 1964, p. 303). William de Bosco had formerly been a chancellor of Oxford University; some of his and of Henry de la Wyle's theological *quaestiones* are extant (*Snappe's Formulary* (O.H.S.), p. 325; *Oxford Theology and Theologians* (O.H.S.), pp. 253–5).

[2] *Reg. S. de Gandavo*, pp. 41–2. Bishop Ghent said that he had provided Ralph with a house suitable for lecturing, and so Ralph could not excuse himself on grounds that the school had not been repaired.

[3] Reg. Corffe, f. 38.

[4] *Ibid.*

[5] *Ibid.*, ff. 40, 49. Early in 1350 Elias promised the archdeacon ten marks for lecturing for the whole year (*ibid.*, f. 62).

theological school was again brought up in chapter, the chancellor was still employing deputies to give the lectures. Simon of Sudbury, the non-resident chancellor, was then charged with not having found a doctor of theology to lecture for that year. His proctor said that Simon had found a doctor, who had unfortunately been taken ill, and was unable to come to Salisbury.[1] He promised that a lecturer would be found for the next year. This promise was apparently kept. In 1358 William de Fornesete, S.T.P., was granted a papal indult for two years' non-residence at his vicarage of Mildenhall in Norwich diocese, while lecturing in theology at Salisbury.[2]

Possibly the situation at the Salisbury school improved in the first half of the fifteenth century. The chancellors were again learned and distinguished men.[3] They were given a new lecture room in the cathedral in the north part of the new library, and in 1454 agreed that lectures should be given there at least once a fortnight at their expense.[4] More is heard of the Valley Scholars. The history of their college can be traced until its dissolution in 1542.[5] In 1468 it was urged that they might be given an opportunity of preaching in the cathedral.[6] A tradition that they had the privilege on the chancellor of Salisbury's recommendation of taking their degrees at Oxford without any further examination is untrue; so is the legend that there was a special Salisbury Hall in Oxford where they resided constantly.[7] But during the later middle ages a number used their fellowships to study at Oxford and took degrees there in the normal way, returning to their college at Salisbury for the University vacations or after they had

[1] Reg. Corffe, f. 128.

[2] *C.P.L. 1342–62*, p. 596. The indult said that William had been elected to the office by Simon of Sudbury, chancellor of Salisbury.

[3] E.g. Walter Mitford, Henry Chichele, William Chichele, John Stafford, John Fyton, Richard Praty, Andrew Holles, William Ive.

[4] Reg. Hutchins, f. 94; Reg. Burgh, f. 115; cf. C. Wordsworth, 'The Use of Salisbury and the Library of the Cathedral Church', in *Notes on Salisbury Cathedral*, ed. G. H. Bourne and J. M. J. Fletcher, pp. 109–10.

[5] For the history of the college, see K. Edwards, 'The College of De Vaux, Salisbury', in *V.C.H. Wilts.*, iii, 369–85; 'Some Activities of Fellows of De Vaux at Salisbury and Oxford', in *Oxoniensia*, xix (1954), 61–91.

[6] *S.S.*, p. 94 n.

[7] *V.C.H., Wilts.*, iii, 372–3. Cf. A. Wood, *City of Oxford* (O.H.S.), i, 86; *Hist. and Antiq. Univ. Oxford*, ed. J. Gutch (1792), i, 229–30; *St. Nicholas Cartulary*, p. lix; A. F. Leach, *Hist. Winchester College*, pp. 86–7.

graduated. Here some apparently settled down as chantry priests, or undertook legal work in the service of bishop or chapter.[1] In 1526 the chapter, fearing perhaps that the chantry character of the college might lead to its dissolution, ordered that all the scholars should go to Oxford or some other University and none remain in Salisbury, except the two chaplains, two stewards, cook, and butler.[2] Leyland, however, who visited Salisbury about 1540–2, wrote that 'part of these scholars (de Vaulx) remaine yn the college at Saresbyri, and have two chapelyns to serve the church there. . . . The residew studie at Oxford.'[3]

On the whole the English secular cathedrals seem to have more than fulfilled the Lateran decrees of 1179 and 1215. Not only the metropolitan church of York, but also the other secular cathedrals normally supported both a grammar master and a *theologus*, or occasionally a lecturer on canon law. It is difficult to decide how far their arrangements were the direct result of the decrees. In the case of the grammar schools the movement to provide permanent endowments had begun before 1179; while theological lecturers, have also been found at several cathedrals about the end of the twelfth century. At Chichester and Salisbury the grant of endowments for theological lectures followed soon after 1215, and may have been a direct response to the decree. But sometimes, as at St. Paul's or Exeter, economic provision was made later, apparently on the model of other English chapters, rather than in response to papal orders. Moreover, with the single exception of Chichester, the English chapters did not follow the Lateran recommendation of appropriating prebends to the offices of grammar master and *theologus*. They worked out their own system, which was usually one of granting extra endowments to the chancellor, and putting him in charge of the schools, with the obligation of finding and paying masters, or teaching himself. Evidently this had better results than arrangements on the continent. Mandonnet writes that in the rare cases when continental chapters of the early thirteenth century were persuaded to give up a prebend to a *theologus*, they usually could not find a man qualified to lecture. Therefore Honorius III authorized them to give the prebend to one of their own members, who was willing and apt to learn theology, and to allow him five years' non-residence to study at the schools. After

---

[1] *Oxoniensia*, xix, 62–91; *V.C.H., Wilts.*, iii, 378–84.
[2] *Ibid.*, p. 384.   [3] *Itinerary*, i, 268.

he returned qualified to the cathedral, Mandonnet thinks that he rarely undertook the burden of lecturing, because there was no economic inducement for him to do so: he had the prebend whether he taught or not, and all teaching at the cathedrals had to be free.[1] Thus the prebend was made to serve as a university scholarship for a time, but did not usually result in lectures being delivered at the cathedrals. In England, on the other hand, the chancellors paid the masters for actual teaching, not for study, and apparently continued to find both theologians and grammar masters for the cathedral schools more or less regularly throughout the middle ages.

There had clearly been both expansion and changes in the educational duties of the *magister scholarum* or chancellor at the English secular cathedrals since the early twelfth century. The development of his schools in the twelfth century often ran parallel with similar developments at cathedral schools in northern France. A number of English cathedrals, particularly Lincoln and Exeter, had for short periods famous schools with famous masters, and may occasionally have been on the verge of developing into universities, for which they prepared the way; a similar situation arose at Salisbury in the thirteenth century. Furthermore, at most churches, the period when the title of chancellor came into general use was also the time when a developed organization of the schools, with a separate subordinate grammar master, and some evidence for teaching in the higher faculties of theology and law can first be traced. Thus in England, as in France, increasing educational work may well have been a chief cause of the change of style from *magister scholarum* to *cancellarius*. In England the chancellor continued throughout the middle ages to direct this educational work, adapting it to changing conditions. The cathedral grammar schools seem to have done valuable work in most periods, but the rise of the universities and of the theological schools of the friars preacher naturally had a depressing effect on the teaching provided at the cathedrals in theology and law. Little evidence is available from the fourteenth and fifteenth centuries to show either the numbers or class of pupils who attended these lectures; still less is it known how far such pupils benefited from the teaching. At St. Paul's some lectures may have drawn large audiences, but elsewhere, the theologian's pupils

[1] Mandonnet, *loc. cit.*, pp. 38–9, 41.

probably consisted chiefly of younger *ministri inferiores* of the
cathedral, with, perhaps, a few clergy holding benefices within
easy reach of the cathedral, who were unable to go to a university,
but who had been ordered by their bishop to study.[1]

THE CHANCELLOR'S SECRETARIAL DUTIES: THE KEEPING OF THE SEALS; THE CHAPTER CLERKS AND NOTARIES

The other functions of the chancellor at the cathedral and the
various deputies and assistants he came to have must now be discussed more briefly. First in importance were his secretarial
duties. In early days, when the bishop lived a common life with
his cathedral clergy, the same clerk naturally acted as secretary
both to the bishop and to his cathedral clerks. From the sixth or
seventh centuries he seems generally to have been the *scholasticus*
or *magister scholarum* in the bishop's school,[2] and at this time his
secretarial duties were probably light. At first the cathedral clerks
would have little reason for official correspondence independently
of their bishop. But later, as the chapters came to have separate
endowments, they needed someone to write their charters and
privileges. The tenth-century chancellors at Chartres apparently
acted as secretaries to both bishop and chapter;[3] while under
Bishop Fulbert in the early eleventh century, they are said to have
written the letters and kept and applied the seals of the chapter
and bishop.[4] But afterwards the keeping of the bishop's seal ceases
to be included in descriptions of the cathedral chancellor's duties.
In the thirteenth century most bishops probably had a separate
chaplain or chancellor to keep their seals and documents and to
write their letters.[5] Normally this chancellor had no official

---

[1] Hugh of Wells, bishop of Lincoln, 1209–35, ordered priests and clerks of
his diocese to attend the theological school at Lincoln (e.g. *Rotuli Hugonis de
Welles*, iii, 101–2; cf. 35). It is not known how far this practice continued later
in the middle ages.

[2] See above, p. 177.

[3] Clerval, *op. cit.*, pp. 17–18, 23.

[4] *Ibid.*, p. 30.

[5] It is not until about the mid-thirteenth century that there is definite evidence
in England for the appointment of a separate chancellor by bishops having
secular cathedrals. In dioceses with monastic cathedrals the appearance of a
bishop's chancellor was sometimes earlier, in the twelfth century (C. R. Cheney,
English Bishops' Chanceries, pp. 28–43).

P

connexion with the cathedral chapter or with the cathedral schools. The position at Bayeux, where he was a cathedral dignitary, seems to have been quite exceptional.[1]

Wherever the office of chancellor was instituted or developed in the middle ages, in the royal or papal courts, in the households of archbishops, bishops, or magnates, in cathedral or collegiate churches, in monasteries, or at universities, the chancellors had one duty in common: they kept the seal and wrote the letters of the person or body to which they were responsible.[2] In the twelfth century, when the business of writing and sealing chapter letters and documents was steadily increasing, the growing importance of this duty was probably a chief reason for the change of title at the cathedrals from *magister scholarum* to *cancellarius*. The earliest statutes or collections of customs of the English cathedrals, usually of the late twelfth or thirteenth centuries, all stated that it belonged to the chancellor to keep the seal of the church; to compose or dictate letters and documents, and to read aloud in chapter such letters as had to be read there.[3] But secretarial, administrative, and legal work at the cathedrals continued to expand throughout the twelfth, thirteenth, and fourteenth centuries, as the chapters acquired more lands and privileges; undertook more lawsuits to defend them, and kept more careful and detailed records. In time it became necessary to define the chancellor's duties in more detail, and to give him various assistants and subordinates in the chancery. In the case of absentee chancellors, arrangements had to be made for the custody of the seal. The chancellors of the later middle ages did not usually do the work of the chancery in person. For some time they exercised a general supervision. But gradually even the responsibility for much of the work done ceased to belong to them alone: other dignitaries or canons came to share with them the custody of the seals; while subordinate chapter

---

[1] See above, p. 15.

[2] The title *cancellarius* was derived from the classical Latin word meaning a law court usher. The Roman *cancellarius* received his name from the *cancelli fori* or bar of tribunals. Later he did the work of a notary, writing wills and public acts. He is found in this capacity both in the Eastern Empire and in the West, under the Carolingians (Ducange, *Glossarium, s.v. Cancellarius*). In England the title is first known to have been used for a royal chancellor in the reign of William the Conqueror.

[3] *S.S.*, pp. 32–3, 58; *W.S.*, pp. 44, 56; *L.S.*, i, 285; ii, 20, 25, 71; iii, 300; *C.S.*, p. 13; *R.S.S.P.*, p. 23; *Ordinale Exon.*, i, 4; Harl. MS. 1027, f. 68b.

clerks or notaries were often responsible directly to the chapter, not to the chancellor.

All English medieval chapters had at least two common seals, sometimes more. In the later middle ages the great seal was only used to authenticate the more solemn chapter documents, such as charters or especially important agreements. The 'lesser' or 'daily' seal *ad causas, ad causas et negotia, ad petitiones et ad causas* or *ad citationes*, was in much more frequent use for the chapter's ordinary legal and administrative business: the letting of farms or houses, commissions to officers, and citations. There might also be a third seal to authorize business transacted in the office of the keeper of the common fund, but this would usually be in the charge of the communar or provost.[1] Some fine medieval impressions of these seals have survived, in green, black, red, and light coloured wax.[2] Sometimes, as at Salisbury, the seal *ad causas* might be nearly the same size as the great seal, in the form of a pointed oval, measuring about two by three inches. All had elaborately carved representations, usually of the saint to whom the church was dedicated. In cases where the great seal had no counter seal the chancellor might affix his own seal on the reverse,[3] presumably to indicate his responsibility for its issue. A favourite representation on the chancellor's seal was a picture of a chancellor reading at his desk.

Strict precautions, similar to those of Oxford and Cambridge colleges and of other secular and ecclesiastical chanceries, were taken to guard the use of the great seal. In the course of the thirteenth century elected residentiary canons or other dignitaries came to share with the chancellor responsibility for its safe keeping. In 1214 Salisbury chapter laid down that their larger seal must be delivered to the custody of two trustworthy canons, unless the chancellor could himself be present and keep the seal with another canon. This seal was never to be taken out of its case except to execute some *bona fide* writing in the presence of the dean, chancellor and other canons.[4] By 1353 there were three keys to the Salisbury great seal: one of these was always kept by the chan-

---

[1] E.g. as at Lichfield (*Monasticon*, VI, iii, 1265). Cf. *L.S.*, iii, 168, 354.

[2] Many are preserved at the British Museum, and are described by W. de G. Birch, *Catalogue of Seals in the Department of MSS. in the British Museum*, Vol. I. Others may be found in cathedral libraries and muniment rooms.

[3] E.g. Adam de Esseby, chancellor of Salisbury, did this in 1239 (cf. *ibid.*, p. 346).

[4] *S.S.*, pp. 40-1.

cellor, or, in his absence, by a residentiary deputed by him;[1] and the chest containing the seal could only be opened by the use of all three keys. No charter or muniment might be issued under the seal, unless the three residentiaries keeping the keys were present.[2] In 1397, when one of the keepers left the city without handing over his key to a fellow-residentiary, the chapter had to hold a special meeting to authorize the breaking of the lock of the chest, in order to use the seal for urgent business.[3] Elsewhere similar arrangements were made for keeping the great seal under two, three, or four keys.[4] But at Lincoln the chancellor was still said to keep the seal principally, because he had the smallest key which immediately enclosed the seal: the treasurer, and later the provost, had the second key which enclosed the smallest key; and the third key was kept by an elected residentiary.[5] The chapter of St. Paul's decided early that, since the small seal *ad causas et negotia* was more widely known than the great seal, its custody ought to be similar to that of the great seal: for the future no sealing with it was to be done except in the presence of two or three canons.[6]

The actual sealing seems to have remained the chancellor's responsibility throughout the middle ages, though, as at St. Paul's, he might have a special sealer or *sigillarius* to help him.[7] The chancellor of Salisbury had to seal all the chapter's letters in the chapter house at his own expense.[8] At Hereford and Wells the treasurer provided him with wax for sealing.[9] But many people were willing to pay high fees for the chapter's sealed confirmation of their rights and privileges. Sealing became a profitable source of revenue. At St. Paul's the chancellor and chapter shared the profits.[10]

The secretarial work of writing the chapter's letters, keeping the registers of its muniments and recording its *acta* was rarely performed by the chancellor in person in the later middle ages. But at Chichester, Wells, and Lichfield, there are suggestions that

---

[1] Reg. Corffe, f. 100.   [2] Reg. Dunham, f. 125.

[3] Reg. Holme, f. 77.

[4] See *L.S.*, ii, 69; *Monasticon*, VI, iii, 1260; *C.S.*, p. 13.

[5] *L.S.*, iii, 297, 300. In 1236 there had only been two keys to the seal, of which the chancellor held the first and the treasurer the second (*ibid.*, ii, 159).

[6] *R.S.S.P.*, p. 132.   [7] Cf. *H.M.C. Ninth Rept.*, App., i, 26.

[8] *S.S.*, pp. 210–11.   [9] *L.S.*, ii, 69; *W.S.*, pp. 51–2.

[10] *R.S.S.P.*, p. 23. The Wells communar rolls include receipts for the affixing of the chapter seal to various deeds (e.g. *H.M.C. Wells*, ii, 27).

in the thirteenth and early fourteenth centuries the chancellors still had powers of supervision over the chapter clerks and notaries. A Chichester statute of 1232 declared that the chancellor was bound by ancient custom to maintain a notary or letter writer at his own expense to compose the dean and chapter's letters; he must supply the notary with all necessaries for writing without grudging or waste of time.[1] At Lichfield a proposal was made in chapter in the late thirteenth century for the appointment of a chapter clerk with a salary from the common goods to hear the causes of the dean and chapter, and to write their letters by the chancellor's will.[2] In 1316 a section of the Wells register *Liber Albus I*, was headed 'The Register of Thomas of Retford, Chancellor of Wells, from Christmas, 1316'; though another entry in the same register shows that Thomas had a clerk, Robert of Nottingham, to do the work.[3] In 1331 the chapter laid down that charters were to be copied into their register by the chancellor; while again in 1382 a further section of the register was headed 'Chapter Register compiled by Master Thomas Spert, chancellor of Wells'.[4]

Elsewhere there is little evidence for any special connexion between the chancellor and the chapter notaries in the fourteenth century. Usually from about the time when the chapter act books were kept regularly, a notary was formally appointed and paid by the dean and chapter, and took oath before the chapter to keep the registers faithfully and not to reveal the secrets of the chapter. At Salisbury the terms of their appointments show that the notaries had entire charge, subject to the chapter's instructions, of the writing of the registers.[5] Probably as a result of their appointment the chancellor gradually withdrew from his original position of

---

[1] *C.S.*, p. 4.

[2] *Monasticon*, VI, iii, 1261. Cf. *M.R.A.*, pp. xx–xxi. In 1369 William Knyght, notary and chapter clerk, recorded the terms of his appointment, salary and oath to the chapter at the beginning of his section of the Lichfield Act Book (MS. Ashmole, 794, f. 147a). There is here no mention of his supervision by the chancellor.

[3] *H.M.C. Wells*, i, 37, 171. At York, also, William Wickwane, chancellor from 1266 to 1268, had a clerk, probably Henry of Sandford, who kept a kind of letter book containing copies of his master's correspondence (C. R. Cheney, *loc. cit.*, in *E.H.R.*, xlvii, 626–8).

[4] *H.M.C. Wells*, i, 292.

[5] Reg. Coman, f. 1; Reg. Dunham, f. 1; Reg. Holme, f. 5.

chief legal adviser to the chapter. The notaries were naturally men of high legal standing, whose drafting and testimony were necessary for formal legal instruments. Often there were two or three connected with the larger chapters, in addition to the one acting as chapter clerk.[1] From the thirteenth century onwards the compiling of the many registers and cartularies must have employed a fairly large staff.[2] Moreover, the chapter might require the notaries to undertake other legal business outside the cathedral city. At Salisbury commissions were issued to them to conduct chapter business at Rome, or to visit vacant farms or prebends on the chapter's behalf.[3]

CATHEDRAL LIBRARIES: THE CARE OF THE BOOKS AND MUNIMENTS

Originally the *magister scholarum* or chancellor was the obvious person for the secular chapters to put in charge of all the cathedral books. Alcuin at York in the eighth century, and Master Hugh, the first known master of the London schools at the beginning of the twelfth century, combined the offices of *magister scholarum* and cathedral librarian.[4] But during the twelfth century there was great activity in procuring and transcribing manuscripts.[5] The library, like the school, was an essential part of the cathedral system. Study was a recognized duty of the residentiary canons; and scholastic development was reflected in the books acquired. By the fallacious test of surviving books the most important Eng-

---

[1] E.g. The notaries William Tart and Thomas de Chardesle are often mentioned in the Salisbury act books of the later fourteenth century at times when they were not acting as chapter clerks (e.g. Reg. Coman, ff. 77, 89; Reg. Dunham, ff. 138–9). For Lincoln see Miss Major's study 'The Office of Chapter Clerk' in *Medieval Studies presented to Rose Graham*, 1950, pp. 163–88.

[2] See Dean Savage's account of these activities at Lichfield in *M.R.A.*, pp. xx *et seq.*

[3] E.g. the chapter clerk, William Dunham, was one of the visitors of the vacant prebend of Charminster and Bere (Reg. Dunham, ff. 138–9); in 1388 Walter Coman acted as chapter proctor at Rome (*ibid.*, f. 52). Their oaths to the chapter (see above, p. 209, n. 5) required them to do this sort of work.

[4] Leach, *Medieval Schools*, p. 56; 'St. Paul's School before Colet', in *Archaeologia*, lxii (1910), 211; *Early Charters of St. Paul*, p. 216.

[5] Cf. N. R. Ker, *English Manuscripts in the Century after the Norman Conquest*, pp. 1–14, 23–4, 32; M. R. James in A. T. Bannister, *Catalogue of MSS. in Hereford Cathedral Library*, pp. ii–iii.

lish secular cathedral libraries were those of Salisbury, Exeter, Hereford, and Lincoln, but medieval catalogues show how much of interest and value has been lost, particularly from the important collection of St. Paul's, where many books were destroyed in the Great Fire.[1] By the fifteenth century the secular cathedrals were building libraries to house their books, in place of the aumbrey cupboards by the altar, or chests in the treasury, where they had previously been kept.[2] All this expansion meant that the duties of librarian became more important, and took up more time. Catalogues and inventories had to be made; and when books were borrowed, a written acknowledgement or pledge had to be obtained.[3] Different expedients were adopted by the chapters to ease the chancellor's burden. By the end of the middle ages there was great variety in the arrangements at different churches for the care of the books.

Manuscripts belonging to the cathedrals fell naturally into three or four different groups: the scholastic books, the service and music books, and the muniments. The chapters often decided to allot their custody to different keepers. At Lincoln it was laid down that the chancellor should have charge of the theological and other scholastic books, with the *passionarii* and *libri legendarum*; the precentor was to keep the music books, such as *antiphonarii*, *gradalia* and *troparii*; the treasurer had the other service books, including breviaries, missals, *collectarii*, and *martilogia*; while the provost of the common fund kept the charters and muniments.[4] Each officer was responsible for the rebinding and correction of his particular group of books, though new copies were made at the common expense. The first known catalogue of the scholastic books at Lincoln was made about 1150 by the first known

---

[1] N. R. Ker, *Medieval Libraries of Great Britain* (1964), pp. xi, xv. Lists of surviving books of the medieval cathedral libraries with references to printed editions of their medieval catalogues are given *ibid.*, *s.v.* the particular cathedral.

[2] *The English Library before 1700*, ed., F. Wormald and C. E. Wright, p. 20; B. H. Streeter, *The Chained Library*, pp. 16-23; J. W. Clark, *The Care of Books*, pp. 110 *et seq.*; *Camb. Antiq. Soc. Proc.*, ix, 37-60; C. Wordsworth, 'Salisbury Cathedral Library,' in *Notes on Salisbury Cathedral*, pp. 107-10; C. M. Church in *Archaeologia*, lvii, 201-8; Dugdale, *Hist. St. Paul's*, pp. 324-8; R. M. Woolley, *Catalogue of MSS. of Lincoln Cathedral Library*, p. v.

[3] For the rules for borrowing books, see *C.S.*, pp. 3, 14; *H.M.C. Var. Coll.*, i, 192; *H.M.C. Wells*, i, 152; *Use Exeter*, p. 13; *Hereford Charters*, p. 267.

[4] *L.S.*, i, 80, 284-5; iii, 168, 299-300, 302, 355.

chancellor, Hamo.[1] Catalogues were kept in the treasury, and officers had to appear with them once a year before the chapter to show whether any books had been lost or injured.[2]

Elsewhere arrangements seem to have been less precise, and developed more gradually. The muniments, particularly those in constant use, were often kept in the later middle ages by the chapter clerks or notaries.[3] But repair and correction of the music books sometimes continued to belong to the chancellor;[4] while some chancellors still kept the scholastic books.[5] At the same time other dignitaries, particularly the treasurer or precentor, officers, such as the subtreasurer or sacrist, or elected canons or vicars might have charge of different groups of books.

At Salisbury the position is interesting. A virgate of land belonged by ancient custom to the correction of the cathedral books; as late as 1220 the bishop had the right to confer this land with its annexed duty on any canon he chose.[6] But Richard Poore's *Tractatus*, like the earliest known copies of St. Osmund's Institution, assigned the correction of the books to the chancellor;[7] and the virgate of land came to be appropriated to the chancellor's dignity. For some time the Salisbury chancellor was apparently in charge of all the books and manuscripts; then he gradually ceased to have charge of one group after another. In 1319 it was decided that two resident canons should be appointed each year, who, with the chancellor, should inspect the muniments of all places under the chapter's jurisdiction. They were to see that deeds which touched the bishop and others which belonged to the chapter were stored in separate chests under clearly marked headings. Muniments might be borrowed, provided that a written pledge were left, stating the borrower's obligation to restore them safely within a definite period.[8] Later there are suggestions that the chapter notaries and, at one time, the subtreasurer had charge of certain muniments.[9] The binding and repair of books of

---

[1] It is printed by Woolley, *op. cit.*, pp. v–viii.

[2] *L.S.*, i, 285; iii, 300.

[3] E.g. *C.S.*, p. 24, and above, pp. 208–10, below, n. 9.

[4] *Reg. Rede*, i, 103, 115; *L.S.*, ii, 20, 71; *Ordinale Exon.*, i, 4; cf. *W.S.*, pp. 45, 55.

[5] E.g. *R.S.S.P.*, p. 23. [6] *S.S.*, pp. 54–5; cf. pp. 38–9.

[7] *Ibid.*, p. 58. See above, p. 181. [8] *S.S.*, pp. 170–3.

[9] Oaths sworn by Salisbury chapter clerks later in the fourteenth century show that they had charge of some of the registers (see above, p. 209), though

the high altar and of the choir still belonged to the chancellor in 1297–1309 and in 1319,[1] but were repudiated by him on grounds of inadequate revenues at Bishop Beauchamp's visitation of the cathedral in 1475.[2] Until about the end of the fourteenth century the chancellors of Salisbury apparently accepted full responsibility for the scholastic books. Henry de la Wyle, the chancellor who, in 1329, left a valuable collection of theological, philosophical, and historical books to the cathedral, said in his will that they were partly 'in compensation for books of the church received by me in St. Michael's chapel, if the said books have been less well kept, or if by chance some have been lost in my time, which may appear upon examination of receipts and deliveries'.[3] Again in 1388 the chancellor, John Norton, was said to have had a certain ancient book rebound and partly rewritten at his own expense.[4] But after a chapter survey of the books in 1397 it was decided that their state of repair was sufficiently bad to make necessary the appointment of separate librarians. Two residentiary canons, of whom the chancellor was not one, were appointed to the office jointly.[5]

At the secular cathedrals less is known than at the monasteries of the way in which the chapters acquired their books and had them repaired. St. Osmund at Salisbury is said to have transcribed and bound books with his own hands.[6] A group of some 65 extant Salisbury manuscripts apparently written before or shortly after 1100 may have been mainly the work of St. Osmund's canons.[7] But it seems unlikely that secular canons, with their many other activities, would have continued, at any rate after about the middle of the twelfth century, to do this sort of work themselves. A few, such as Thomas Circeter at Salisbury in the fifteenth century, might copy out sermons or make notes on treatises which

---

William Holme promised in his oath to give up all the registers, *codices*, and *raciones* in his hands to the canon deputed by the chapter, whenever the canon should ask for them (Reg. Holme, f. 5). In 1389 the eight registers of the church were ordered to be kept in the chapter house in a chest firmly sealed, and no longer in the custody of the subtreasurer as before (Reg. Dunham, ff. 87–8).

[1] *S.S.*, pp. 210–11.   [2] *Salisbury Ceremonies*, p. 154.
[3] *H.M.C. Var. Coll.*, i, 375–7.   [4] Reg. Dunham, f. 46.
[5] Reg. Holme, f. 50.
[6] William of Malmesbury, *De Gestis Pontificum*, p. 184.
[7] N. R. Ker in *W.A.M.*, liii, 153–5; *English MSS. after the Norman Conquest*, p. 32.

interested them, and later present them to the cathedral library.[1] But probably the nearest approach at the secular cathedrals to the organized *scriptoria* of the monasteries, would be the writing of charters and other letters and the compilation of the various registers by the chapter clerks and notaries. Some of the more richly decorated service books may have been ordered and bought from neighbouring monasteries; many books of all kinds were left to the cathedrals by bishops, dignitaries, and canons, who often acquired them abroad;[2] while others may have been transcribed or bound locally by private book-traders or stationers. The growth of the cathedral schools possibly helped cities such as Lincoln or London to become centres of the book and book-binding trade.[3] Some secular chapters, like some monasteries, may have had one or two regular scribes attached to the cathedral. St. Paul's had a *scriptor librorum*, who was also the official cathedral book-binder, with a salary of fifteen marks a year, and distributions in bread and beer from the common fund equal in value to those of the subdean.[4] At Salisbury in 1389, when complaint was made in chapter that the cathedral had no chronicle, the chancellor ordered the grammar school master to make one.[5]

THE CHANCELLOR'S CHOIR DUTIES; THE VICE-CHANCELLOR; THE SERMONS

Like the other three dignitaries the chancellor had his essential choir duties. These were chiefly drawing up the weekly table of readers of lessons at the cathedral services; of determining the

[1] Cf. E. M. Thompson, *Catalogue of Salisbury Cathedral Library*, nos. 13, 36, 39, 40, 55, 81, 84, 126, 167, 170, 174; N. R. Ker, *Medieval Libraries of Gt. Britain*, p. 303.

[2] See the lists of donors compiled by Mr. N. R. Ker, from inscriptions in books surviving from the medieval cathedral libraries, *ibid.*, pp. 225–325 *s.v.* the particular cathedral. Further information may be found in medieval catalogues of the libraries quoted, *ibid.*, pp. 1–224, *s.v.* the particular cathedral.

[3] At Lincoln there was a Street of Parchmenters in 1147–8 (*Reg. Antiquissimum*, i, 262), and at London Abel *parmentarius* and Anselm *pictor* had houses in Fleet Street *c.* 1188 (*Sarum Charters*, p. 45. Cf. also G. D. Hobson, *English Binding before 1500*, p. 4, and *Trans. Bibliog. Soc.*, 4th Ser., xv, 161–211; xiii, 5).

[4] *R.S.S.P.*, pp. 73, 75 n., 133, 173 n.

[5] Reg. Dunham, f. 102. Early statutes of York cathedral had laid down that it was the chancellor's duty to make chronicles of notable events touching the church (*L.S.*, ii, 96).

length of the lessons, and of hearing the readers practise them beforehand.[1] Fines were inflicted for slovenly reading,[2] and only readers of learning or long experience were not required to have their lessons heard.[3] Sometimes, too, the chancellor was instructed to appoint the weekly ministers at the altar,[4] though at most churches this duty belonged to the precentor. By the thirteenth century the chancellor usually had a deputy to relieve him in these duties. But such deputies had to be fit persons for the work, 'welltaught, with sufficient experience in the manner of pronouncing Latin'.[5] At Lincoln the chancellor had a vice-chancellor, whom he provided with his board and a yearly robe, or sixty shillings a year.[6] This vice-chancellor co-operated with the precentor's deputy, the succentor, in drawing up the weekly table; in seeing that the readers, ministers and singers were warned of their duties, and in filling up gaps when ministers failed to appear in choir.[7] Like the succentor, he was instructed not to burden one more than another in allotting the weekly duties, through fraud, malice, hatred, or favour;[8] together with the succentor, he was invited to dinner with the hebdomadary canon every Sunday.[9] Similar functions were assigned to the subchancellor of York, who received twenty shillings a year from the chancellor's grammar school;[10] and to the chancellor's vicar choral at Lichfield.[11] But at Hereford and St. Paul's the grammar school master entabled the readers and heard the lessons:[12] at St. Paul's he also had to read the first lesson himself on double feasts, and to help his lord to maintain discipline among the *ministri inferiores* in choir.[13]

A further duty of the chancellor of St. Paul's was to introduce the cathedral clerks of the lower form for ordination, and to present to the bishop for ordination other clerks examined in his schools.[14] If the dean were ordained, the chancellor called him to the title of St. Paul.[15]

---

[1] *S.S.*, pp. 32–3, 58; *W.S.*, pp. 45, 56; *C.S.*, p. 13; *Ordinale Exon.*, i, 4; *L.S.*, ii, 20, 71, 96.

[2] *C.S.*, p. 4.   [3] *L.S.*, ii, 83.

[4] E.g. at Lincoln and St. Paul's (*ibid.*, i, 285; iii, 300; *R.S.S.P.*, p. 23).

[5] *C.S.*, p. 4.   [6] *L.S.*, iii, 164.   [7] *Ibid.*, i, 371–88; iii, 358–9.

[8] *Ibid.*   [9] *Ibid.*, i, 378, 389.   [10] *Ibid.*, ii, 96.

[11] *Ibid.*, ii, 25.   [12] *Ibid.*, ii, 71; *R.S.S.P.*, p. 78.   [13] *Ibid.*

[14] *Ibid.*, p. 23. But cf. p. 16, where the dean is said to nominate and introduce those to be promoted to orders.

[15] *Ibid.*, p. 16.

Preaching was rarely given prominence in medieval cathedral statutes. But at Lincoln, Lichfield, and York it was laid down that certain of the more important sermons of the year were to be preached by the chancellor if possible;[1] while arrangements for other sermons were left in his hands subject to some supervision by the dean. At Lincoln there was a public sermon for the people every Sunday, as well as sermons in chapter for the cathedral clergy on certain great feasts. The chancellor might depute strangers to give these sermons only with the dean's consent.[2] After the Reformation greater emphasis was laid on the importance of preaching in the cathedrals. A regular system of preaching turns was organized, usually under the chancellor's direction: every canon, resident or non-resident, had to be responsible for at least one sermon a year.[3] Sometimes the drastic measure was taken of ordering the chancellor to preach sermons instead of giving his traditional course of theological lectures.[4]

4. THE TREASURER

In 1540, when Henry Lytherland, the last treasurer of Lincoln cathedral, saw the medieval treasures of his church being carried away by Henry VIII's commissaries, he flung away his keys of office, exclaiming, 'Now that the treasure is seized, the duties of treasurer come to an end.'[5] From this time no other treasurer has been appointed in Lincoln cathedral. A few years later the treasurer of York also resigned his dignity into Edward VI's hands.[6] Thus in two English cathedrals a dignity ceased to exist, which, under a variety of titles, had been among the most important offices at cathedral churches from about the seventh or eighth centuries. At other English secular cathedrals of the Old Foundation it continued after the Reformation with lighter duties. In cathedrals of the New Foundation the treasurer was no

---

[1] *L.S.*, i, 284–5; ii, 25, 32, 96; iii, 301.

[2] *Ibid.*, i, 284; iii, 301. At Lichfield he was instructed to prefer canons of the church to outsiders, when appointing preachers (*ibid.*, ii, 25; cf. 32).

[3] See Jones, *Fasti Sar.*, pp. 260–3; *Y.S.*, pp. 50–1.

[4] Jones, *Fasti Sar.*, p. 230.

[5] 'Abrepto omni Ecclesiae Thesauro, desiit Thesaurarii munus' (*L.S.*, i, 103; *Monasticon*, VI, iii, 1286).

[6] *V.C.H. Yorks.*, iii, 380.

longer a canon and dignitary, but only a minor canon of no special importance.

The treasurer of the English medieval secular cathedrals was in no sense a financial or business officer concerned with the income derived from the chapter lands. Money belonging to the church might be kept locked in chests in the treasury, together with other valuables, such as the chapter seal, the muniments, or diocesan taxes collected by the chapter. But the keys to these chests would be in the hands of the officers in charge of them, and the treasurer's responsibility for them would be limited to seeing that the treasury was safely guarded. His first duty, as his name suggests, and as Lytherland recognized, was to keep the treasures of the church, the gold and silver vessels, the ornaments, relics, jewels, embroidered silk copes, and altar cloths, while at the same time he provided the lights, bread, wine, incense and other material necessaries for the services. Thus his functions corresponded roughly to those of the obedientiary known as the sacrist in English cathedral monasteries, not at all to those of the treasurers appointed in many Benedictine monasteries from about the end of the twelfth century, whose duties were to institute some sort of central financial control over the incomes of the other obedientiaries.[1]

Like the monastic sacrist, the secular cathedral treasurer was the descendant of the *custos*, *sacrista*, or *cimeliarcha* of the early church. At certain cathedrals there may have been some distinction between these two officers in early times. Hinschius maintains that, while the *custos* had charge only of those vessels and ornaments in everyday use, the sacrist (*custos sacrorum*) kept the more precious treasures which were only brought out on special feast days.[2] In the middle ages, however, the normal arrangement was for one

[1] For these Benedictine treasurers, see R. A. L. Smith, 'The *Regimen Scaccarii* in English Monasteries,' in *T.R.H.S.* (1942), pp. 73 *et seq.*; 'The Central Financial System of Christ Church, Canterbury', in *E.H.R.* (1940), pp. 353 *et seq*; D. Knowles, *Religious Orders in England*, i, 55–63. At some secular collegiate churches, such as Windsor, the title of treasurer was given to elected financial officers (cf. A. K. B. Roberts, *St. George's Chapel, Windsor Castle, 1348–1416*, pp. 50 *et seq.*).

[2] *Kirchenrecht*, ii, 103. Yet the passages which he quotes to illustrate this distinction suggest that the duties of the two officers were very similar. Both were responsible for providing lights in the cathedral, and both were directly subject to the archdeacon.

dignitary to have charge of all the cathedral furniture, utensils and treasures; and, as the cathedrals steadily acquired more riches and treasures, he came to have a number of deputies and assistants. In some continental cathedrals, as in Benedictine monasteries, he kept the old title of sacrist. Elsewhere he was known as *thesaurarius, custos, capicerius,* or *cimeliarcha.*[1] The precedence of this dignitary varied even more than his titles. In a few French cathedrals he became head of the chapter; at Chartres he was the last of the seventeen dignitaries; and examples have been found of his holding many different positions intermediate between these two extremes.[2] Most often he was in the third or fourth place. In Norman cathedrals the variety and uncertainty of his titles and precedence in the twelfth century have already been noticed.[3] Here, however, he seems generally to have been a more important dignitary than the *magister scholarum* or *scholasticus,* and by the end of the twelfth century had usually established his claim to be the third dignitary.

In twelfth-century England, also, the treasurer's place in the cathedrals varied considerably. It was only after the widespread borrowing from Richard le Poore's Salisbury consuetudinary of the late twelfth or early thirteenth centuries that it became customary to give him the fourth place. Even at Salisbury, the Institution of St. Osmund, although it enumerates the dignitaries at the beginning in the usual order (at any rate in the earliest known copies which have survived), further on, in speaking of the duties of the several officers, puts the treasurer before the chancellor, and that twice over.[4] At York, where the treasurership was founded by Archbishop Thomas about 1090–1, it was combined with the rich archdeaconry of the East Riding throughout the twelfth century, and formed one of the most lucrative appointments in the church.[5] Its holders seem often to have ranked next to the dean in dignity; as late as 1197–9 Hamo was promoted from the precentorship of York to the treasury.[6] Only in statutes written down after the separation of the archdeaconry from the treasurership by Arch-

---

[1] *Ibid.*, p. 104; G. F. Browne, *op. cit., passim.*

[2] Cf. *ibid.*; Amiet, *op. cit.*, pp. 123, 129.

[3] Above, pp. 16–17.   [4] *S.S.*, pp. 26–31.

[5] C. T. Clay, 'The Early Treasurers of York,' in *Y.A.J.*, xxxv (1940), pp. 7–33.

[6] *Ibid.*, p. 28; cf. *V.C.H. Yorks.*, iii, 376; and above, p. 161.

bishop Gray in 1218, is the treasurer seen to be established in the fourth place.[1] At Chichester, the treasurership was founded and endowed about 1147, evidently some time before the chancellorship;[2] during this time the treasurer probably ranked next to the cantor. At Exeter, on the other hand, although there may have been a treasurer, Vivian, before 1130,[3] about a century before the chapter had either a dean or a chancellor, the office does not seem to have conferred any special rank or dignity upon its holders, at any rate in the twelfth century.[4] The dignity of the treasurership of the chapter of St. Paul's cathedral was apparently instituted by Bishop Richard de Belmeis some time between 1152 and 1162;[5] as time went on he came to take precedence of both precentor and chancellor, and maintained this position throughout the middle ages.[6] Hereford customs of the mid-thirteenth century assigned to the treasurer the third place in chapter above the chancellor.[7] So did Lichfield statutes of 1191 and 1198; but at Lichfield the normal Salisbury order was adopted in statutes of about 1240.[8] This order was also accepted at Lincoln in the customs of 1214, and at Wells in the earliest available statutes.[9] At Wells, however, the position always remained slightly different, because

[1] *L.S.*, i, 136; ii, 105.

[2] Swainson, pp. 2–3; *Chartulary of the High Church of Chichester*, pp. 15–16, 68. Roger, treasurer, was a witness of Bishop Hilary's charter instituting the chancellorship.

[3] J. H. Round, 'Bernard, the King's Scribe', in *E.H.R.*, xiv, 421.

[4] Cf. F. Rose Troup, *The Consecration of Exeter Cathedral*, p. 5, and above, p. 161. The Salisbury order of the four dignitaries was adopted after 1225.

[5] *Early Charters of St. Paul*, pp. xxxv–vi, nos. 187, 188, 192, 193, 231. Alexander's confirmation (no. 231), dated 1 March 1163 after Bishop Richard's death, was clearly the final step in a long process. Occasional references to the 'treasury' as a fund, or as a place for the deposit of documents, have been found before the time of Bishop Richard (*ibid.*, p. xxxvi).

[6] Cf. *R.S.S.P.*, p. 13; *L.S.*, i, 136.

[7] *Ibid.*, ii, 63–71, cf. i, 137. The first known treasurer occurs at Hereford in 1132. As at Rouen he was sometimes called *secretarius* or sacrist, (Balliol MS. 271, ff. 88ᵛ, 108; *Liber Vitae Ecclesiae Dunelm.*, Surtees Soc., 1841, p. 18). I owe these references to Miss Marjorie Jones and Professor Brooke.

[8] *L.S.*, ii, 16–20; *Monasticon*, VI, iii, 1256, 1258.

[9] *L.S.*, ii, 138; *W.S.*, pp. 1–2. At Lincoln a treasurer had been instituted by Remigius in 1091 (Henry of Huntingdon, p. 301), but there is no definite evidence for his precedence in the twelfth century. Henry mentions him next after the dean. At Wells the office is found in Bishop Robert's time (1136–66), soon after the institution of a dean (Church, *op. cit.*, p. 15).

the two archdeacons of Bath and Wells were said to rank between the precentor and chancellor in dignity; thus, although the treasurer of Wells was the fourth of the four principal *personae*, he had only the sixth place of honour in choir and chapter.

Every treasurer was bound to make and keep an exact inventory of everything in the treasury, and to account regularly before the chapter for its contents.[1] At most churches 'views' or visitations of the treasury were held annually by the dean and one or two elected canons. Numbers of these inventories and visitation records of the treasuries have survived:[2] some describe the treasures in detail. 'Relicks of St. Catherine, enclosed in a head of silver, standing on a pedestal, brought from Rome by Master Heytham in 1270' were in the Salisbury treasury in 1536,[3] together with many precious gifts and legacies from bishops and cathedral dignitaries from St. Osmund onwards. Lichfield's most precious relic in 1345 was the 'head of Blessed Chad contained in a certain painted wooden case'.[4] Lincoln in 1536 had an immense variety of the richest treasures: chalices of gold, set with pearls and precious stones; a reliquary of silver and gilt, 'with twenty pinnacles, and an image of Our Lady in one end and of St. Hugh in the other end'; another 'with four feet and three red stones and two blew stones above in the top'; tabernacles of ivory and silver; images set with jewels and pearls; chests of ivory and crystal, covered with cloth of gold set with pearls; pyxes; crosses; candelabra; 'two great and fair candlesticks of gold, standing on great feet of one fashion, with twenty buttresses of gold in either of them'; censers, with heads of leopards; basons, silver and gilt, 'chased with nine double roses, and, in the circuit of one great rose, a white rose of silver innamelled'; pastoral staffs; crismatories; texts of the gospels, and other books of great price, such as the 'text after Matthew, covered with a plate, silver and gilt, having an image of the Majesty with the four evangelists and four angels about the said image, having at every corner an image of a man, with divers

[1] E.g., *L.S.*, ii, 69, 123, 302.

[2] For some printed inventories, see *Salisbury Ceremonies*, pp. 160–84; 'Catalogue Muniments D. and C. Lichfield', in *Coll. Hist. Staffs.*, vi, 199–213; *Archaeologia*, l (1887), 439–524; Dugdale, *Hist. St. Paul's*, pp. 310–30; *Monasticon*, VI, iii, 1202–10, 1278–92; Oliver, *op. cit.*, pp. 301–78; Hatcher and Benson, *Old and New Sarum*, pp. 718–720.

[3] *Salisbury Ceremonies*, p. 160.

[4] 'Catalogue Muniments D. and C. Lichfield', pp. 199, 207.

stones, great and small'; maniples; stoles, dalmatics; copes and
chasubles of red, white, purple, blue, green, and black, 'broidered
with harts of gold, with orphreys set with swans, roses and lambs
of pearl, having the image of Our Lord with a cross in his hand,
and St. Bartholomew', or another 'old white cope of cloth of
gold, with ostriges' feathers, and a blew orphrey, containing
divers beasts and flowers'; altar cloths of silk, with birds of gold,
and white lions, 'every one of them containing in breadth one ell,
and in length four yards and a half'.[1]

It was the treasurer's duty not only to see that all these treasures
were safely guarded day and night by his officers, but also to keep
them cleaned and in good repair.[2] Therefore he had to employ a
laundress to wash the vestments and altar cloths which were in
daily use, and a seamstress to mend them.[3] He furnished all the
cathedral altars with vessels and other utensils from his treasury,
and was further bound to provide at his own expense all other
material necessaries for the services; the bread, wine, incense,
water, charcoal, and wood. He gave the wine for washing the
altars on Maundy Thursday, and saw that the reed mats, rushes,
and straw in the church were changed at certain times every year.[4]
The most expensive item required from him was the lights, both
of wax and oil. Three hundred and fifty pounds of wax and more
were used yearly at Wells in the early thirteenth century, all of
which had to be found, shaped, and lighted at the treasurer's expense.[5] In order that there should be no misunderstanding, the

---

[1] *Monasticon*, VI, iii, 1278–86.

[2] *S.S.*, pp. 59–60; *C.S.*, pp. 4, 13; *L.S.*, i, 285–6; ii, 17–18, 68–9; iii, 302;
R.S.S.P., pp. 21, 223; *Ordinale Exon.*, i, 4. In 1390 the treasurer of Exeter
begged the chapter not to lay upon him the burden of repairing more ornaments than was distinctly specified in the ordinance of his office (*Use Exeter*,
pp. 7–8).

[3] *H.M.C. Wells*, i, 36; *L.S.*, i, 288; ii, 97, 99; iii, 303, 305; *York Fabric Rolls*,
p. 191.

[4] *S.S.*, p. 60; *Ordinale Exon.*, i, 4; *H.M.C. Var. Coll.*, iv, 82; *C.S.*, pp. 4–6,
13; *H.M.C. Wells*, i, 36–7; *L.S.*, i, 286; ii, 18, 70, 99–100; iii, 303. Only at
St. Paul's it was laid down in Dean Baldock's code of statutes that the chamber
should contribute to the provision of wine and wafers for the altars, because of
the increasing number of chaplains in the church (*R.S.S.P.*, p. 74).

[5] *H.M.C. Wells*, i, 36–7. At Salisbury in 1254, when Bishop William decided
to double the lighting in the cathedral he arranged to supply the treasurer with
an extra two hundred pounds of wax a year from his wardrobe (*Sarum Charters*,
pp. 322–3).

Q

cathedral statutes specified in minute detail the exact number and position of all the lamps, candles, tapers, and mortar lights, which were to be kept burning before the altars and images, carried in processions, or used for lighting the path of the clergy coming to matins.[1] The candles used on feast days varied in weight from the great paschal candle, weighing seven pounds, to those given to every cathedral clerk according to his dignity on the Feast of the Purification. Even the size of the small candles used by the treasurer's officers in their nightly search for robbers in the church was described. At St. Paul's the chamberlain, not the treasurer, was responsible for providing the lights.[2] As a result the treasurer of St. Paul's received a slightly lower income than the precentor. Usually, although the treasurer was normally the least of the four great *personae* in dignity, his income was greater than that of either the precentor or the chancellor, because the expenses of his office were so much heavier.[3]

The treasurer's responsibility extended to the guarding of the whole church and its furniture, including the bells. His officers stayed in the church all night, and had the duty of keeping the laity silent and orderly during the services. The treasurer had to see that the floors of the church and cloisters were swept; that water was provided for the ministers to wash their hands; that the clock was wound, and the bells rung; that bells, bell-ropes and clock were kept in good repair.[4] His personal residence in the close was held to be very necessary. In 1331 Salisbury chapter wrote to its absentee treasurer, Cardinal Arnold, then living at Avignon, imploring him to return to their church, considering the dangers to which its rich treasures were exposed by his absence:

'the most holy relics, the noble vestments, the gold and silver vessels, and various other ornaments . . . the bells suspended in the belfrey with much art, of great weight and price, and sweet sounding to the ears, by the fault of your officers are suffered to decay, and are rendered totally useless for ringing'.[5]

---

[1] *Use Sarum*, i, 4–6; *S.S.*, pp. 59–60; *C.S.*, pp. 4–5, 13; *W.S.*, pp. 49–52; *L.S.*, i, 288–91; ii, 18–20, 63–8, 97–9; iii, 303–5.   [2] *R.S.S.P.*, p. 74.

[3] See the taxation of the various treasurerships in the *Valor Ecclesiasticus* of 1535, and Jones, *Fasti Sar.*, p. 343 n.

[4] *S.S.*, pp. 60, 262–3; *H.M.C. Var, Coll.*, iv, 82; *Ordinale Exon.*, i, 4; *C.S.*, pp. 4, 13; *W.S.*, pp. 51–2; *L.S.*, i, 285–6, 350; ii, 18, 22, 70, 100; iii, 303; *Monasticon*, VI, iii, 1261; *York Fabric Rolls*, p. 191.

[5] *Hemingby's Reg.*, pp. 83–4.

The Subtreasurer and other Treasury Officials

The treasurer needed a large staff of officers, but since much of the work of guarding and cleaning was not highly skilled, he was often allowed to employ laymen, provided that they were sufficiently supervised by responsible clerks. Usually either he or his principal deputy would nominate and pay the salaries of all the treasury officials, and answer for their honesty to the dean and chapter.[1] The number, titles, and organization of these officials varied considerably in the different English cathedrals. But everywhere there was one principal deputy, known either as the subtreasurer, sacrist, or *custos*, who had power to supervise the whole department and to perform the treasurer's duties in his absence.

The most usual name for this deputy was the subtreasurer. He was given this title at six of the nine English churches. At two of these, Wells and Chichester, he was sometimes called also *custos* or sacrist; while at the remaining three churches, Lichfield, Lincoln, and St. Paul's, he was always the sacrist. The sacrist of Lichfield seems to have had a fairly important and secure position. His office was perpetual with a chantry annexed to it.[2] At Lincoln also the *sacrista literatus* (so described to distinguish him from his helper, the lay sacrist) received the same salary of sixty shillings a year or food and drink from the treasurer, as the succentor and vice-chancellor had from their lords.[3] But at Salisbury the subtreasurer was definitely inferior to the succentor,[4] and a subtreasurer might be promoted to be succentor. Indeed, the subtreasurers seem usually to have held office only during the treasurer's pleasure;[5] afterwards they would return to their former position in the choir, and the treasurer would choose another vicar or choir clerk to fill their place as his deputy. The subtreasurer of York received a high salary of fifty marks a year, but this was meant to provide not only for himself, but for the

[1] S.S., p. 60; *Ordinale Exon.*, i, 4; Harl. MS. 1027, ff. 25a, 28b; C.S., pp. 5–6, 21; *Reg. Rede*, i, 115–16; W.S., p. 52; H.M.C. *Wells*, i, 36–7; L.S., i, 286–8, 291–3, 364–5; ii, 18, 20, 69–70, 97; iii, 302–3, 305; *York Fabric Rolls*, p. 191; R.S.S.P., pp. 21–2, 109–10.

[2] L.S., ii, 18; M.R.A., p. 115.

[3] L.S., i, 288; iii, 303. For his other distributions and perquisites at installations, see *ibid.*, i, 336–8, 352–3; iii, 165–6.

[4] Cf. S.S., p. 165 and n.

[5] Cf. Jones, *Fasti Sar.*, p. 235.

maintenance of five other clerks in his service.[1] At Chichester the subtreasurer had forty shillings a year from the treasurer; at Wells only eleven shillings with his food; while at Exeter the treasurer was merely said to have his subtreasurer at table with him when he was present in the city, and to give him yearly robes.[2] These subtreasurers, however, would at the same time be receiving commons and obit distributions at the cathedral, and possibly holding some other vicarage or chantry there.

Statutory descriptions of the subtreasurer's duties differ little from those of the treasurer's duties, except that they suggest a more immediate daily supervision of the church and treasury and of the lesser treasury officials than was required of the treasurer. Thus the Salisbury subtreasurer swore on his admission to office,

'to keep faithfully the goods of the treasury and church; to be present in person every night at the searching of the church; to see that the clerks lie in the church at night in the usual places, and that they behave well; to follow the choir at the nightly and daily hours; not to lend the goods of the church to anyone without special licence from the dean and chapter, and to sleep in the treasury every night without making any excuse'.[3]

The most necessary qualifications for a subtreasurer were said to be *industria, fidelitas, experientia*.[4] He brought the silk copes to choir to be distributed by the succentor, and folded them up again after the service. He supervised the washing and cleaning of the vestments, the repair of the ornaments, the bell-ringing, the locking and unlocking of the doors of the church and vestibule, the provision of the lights, and of the bread and wine for the altars.[5] He answered to the dean and chapter at visitations of the treasury in the treasurer's absence;[6] at Hereford and Wells he was apparently responsible for keeping the treasury accounts.[7]

In addition there would be from three or four other officers working under the treasurer's orders in the smaller cathedrals to as

[1] *L.S.*, ii, 97; *York Fabric Rolls*, p. 191.

[2] *Reg. Rede*, i, 102; *H.M.C. Wells*, i, 36; *W.S.*, p. 99; *Ordinale Exon.*, i, 4–5.

[3] Reg. Hutchins, f. 36; Reg. Dunham, f. 277.

[4] *L.S.*, iii, 302, cf. 355; *R.S.S.P.*, p. 21.

[5] *R.S.S.P.*, pp. 73–4, 101, 109–10; *L.S.*, i, 366–7; ii, 18–25; iii, 355; *Ordinale Exon.*, i, 4–5.

[6] E.g. 'Catalogue of Muniments D. and C. Lichfield', in *Coll. Hist. Staffs*, vi, 199–213; Reg. Coman, f. 94.

[7] *H.M.C. Wells*, i, 187, 193; *Hereford Charters*, p. 183.

many as eleven or twelve in the larger churches. Frequently the
titles of sacrist or *custos* were used also for certain of these subordinate clerks; indeed, these titles might be given to cathedral
treasury officers of almost any rank, from the chief dignitary
down to the verger, bell-ringer or door-keeper. At Salisbury
there were two sacrists, who became vergers after the Reformation;[1] they were immediately subject to the subtreasurer, and had
two boys under them, sometimes called the two minor clerks of
the sacristy.[2] Here the sacrists' duties consisted chiefly of bell-
ringing; of guarding the processions, at which they carried their
wands, and of keeping order among visitors in the church. They
carried round the wine and ale of the bishop's maundy loving cup
to the canons and other clergy.[3] In 1394, when doves were found
to be nesting in the church, the dean and chapter decided that it
was the duty of the sacrists and their boys, with the help of the
fabric clerk, to destroy them.[4] Three sacrists were also employed
at York cathedral, as bell-ringers and vergers; but these were
apparently subordinate to two clerks of the vestibule, who received higher wages than the sacrists.[5] Chichester had two sacrists,
with a door-keeper, a special clerk responsible for the lighting, and
two other *servientes* to ring the bells and clean the church.[6] At
Wells, when the subtreasurer was referred to as sacrist, his second
in command would be called the subsacrist.[7] Exeter had four
custodes or *custores*; the two principal *custores* were annuellars or
chantry priests chosen by the treasurer, and these supervised the
two lesser *custores*, who were clerks of the second form.[8] The
system at St. Paul's was again different. One common servant or
verger was appointed by the dean, and three more lay vergers,
servants, or *custodes* were appointed by the treasurer and responsible to the sacrist.[9] None had been perpetual since 1282, when a
certain manifest crime had been committed in the church for
which the vergers had been expelled. After this all four vergers had
to hand over their wands to the dean every year at Michaelmas,

---

[1] Jones, *Fasti Sar.*, p. 236.   [2] E.g. *ibid.*, p. 203.
[3] *Salisbury Ceremonies*, pp. 80–1, 117; *Fasti Sar.*, pp. 236–7.
[4] Reg. Dunham, f. 257.
[5] *L.S.*, ii, 97, 99, 102, 104, 113; *York Fabric Rolls*, p. 191.
[6] *C.S.*, pp. 5–6, 17–18, 20; cf. *Reg. Rede*, i, 115–16.
[7] *H.,M.C. Wells*, i, 108.
[8] *Ordinale Exon.*, i, 4, 6; Harl. MS. 1027, f. 15a.
[9] *R.S.S.P.*, pp. 20–2, 110.

and received them back for another year only if they had performed their duties faithfully.[1] In addition to the usual vergers'
and sacrists' duties, their responsibility for superintending the
grave digging in the cemetery was stressed in the statutes; they
employed boys for digging.[2] A separate *orologius* was appointed to
have charge of the clock.[3]

The most elaborate system of treasury officers was at Lincoln,
where the three bell-ringers had an especially important position.
Directions for the bell-ringing formed the framework of the
Lincoln consuetudinary: in this, arrangements for all the services
were preceded by full instructions to the bell-ringers as to the
time, duration, and nature of the peals which were to summon the
clergy to church. The first bell-ringer was the lay sacrist: he did
not perform the office of bell-ringing so continuously as the other
two, out of reverence for his lord the treasurer, whom he attended, 'carrying a wand before him in the manner of a beadle'.
He kept a groom, and his dignity was recognized whenever he
went to dinner with the hebdomadary canon; then he sat at table
with the well-born (*generosi*) and the canons, instead of eating
with the humbler *servientes*.[4] The two other bell-ringers were the
candle-lighter and the watchman.[5] All three were given thirteen
or fourteen candles a week in winter and seven each in summer to
search the cathedral twice during the night. After their search all
but the watchman might sleep, but he watched in the church
all night, telling the hours on his flute. In addition there was a
scoparius or sweeper to sweep the dust and dirt from the church; to
see that there was plenty of water for the canons to wash their
hands, and to keep the phials ready filled for the chaplains celebrating anniversaries.[6] A special wax-maker was appointed by the
treasurer; the *sacrista literatus* had his own clerk; two *custodes* or
wardens of the high altar were deputed, one by the treasurer, the
other by the dean and chapter; and the bishop himself paid four
additional servants or beadles, who normally worked under the

[1] *R.S.S.P.*, p. 91; cf. 72–3.
[2] *Ibid.*, pp. 72, 110, 124. They received not more than threepence for digging
a grave.
[3] *Ibid.*, p. 75 n. He received twenty-three gallons of ale from the cathedral
brewery in 1286.
[4] *L.S.*, i, 364–5; iii, 179–80; *Reg. Antiquissimum*, ii, 304–5.
[5] For their duties, see *L.S.*, i, 364–86.
[6] *Ibid.*, p. 365.

orders of the treasurer and sacrist.[1] These bishops' beadles rarely bore their wands except when the bishop came to the cathedral church; but on such occasions they went to meet him at the cathedral door, preceded him into the church with their wands, and stayed with him all the time he remained there. On certain double and semi-double feasts they might assist the wardens of the high altar, walking before the ministers of the altar with their wands. Three of them were carpenters by profession and one a glazier. They were frequently employed on repairs of the cathedral furniture and glass: they put up the Lenten veil, the hangings and the altar cloths in the church; erected the candelabra; lit the candles; washed the altars, vessels, and relics, and sometimes helped with the bell-ringing. For this they received extra payments for drinks from the treasurer.[2] They might be married men, whose wives were allowed special privileges as brewers by the mayor and bailiffs of the city.[3]

Various other officers are occasionally mentioned in cathedral records as keeping watch over certain special relics or shrines in the church, or as guarding the close gates and cemeteries. Sometimes they were appointed by the dean and chapter, and were responsible directly to them; in other cases the method of their appointment is not known. But since all could be described, like the treasurer and his staff, by the general title of *custodes* or wardens, it is convenient to discuss their duties in connexion with those of the treasury officials.

Thus at Lincoln two canons were appointed by the dean and chapter as principal *custodes* of the shrine of St. Hugh, together with three inferior *custodes*, two of whom guarded the shrine by night and one by day.[4] At York an annual pension of twenty shillings was paid from the common fund to the *custodes* of the high altar, shrine and tomb.[5] At Salisbury the chancellor provided a common beadle for the church, who lived with him as his *domesticus* and *familiaris*, and helped the sacrists and janitor in their

---

[1] *Ibid.*, i, 288, 293, 336–8, 349, 366, 378, 389; iii, 178–9, 298, 306, 355. The beadles received their stipends from the bishop through the archdeacon of Lincoln.

[2] *Ibid.*, i, 291–3, 380, 389; cf. 286–7; iii, 179, 276, 327.

[3] *Reg. Antiquissimum*, iii, 300–4.

[4] *L.S.*, i, 336–7; iii, 179.

[5] *York Fabric Rolls*, pp. 124, 132–3.

work.[1] He and the janitor were sometimes present at chapter meetings in the capacity of witnesses,[2] and may possibly have had the duty of guarding the door of the chapter house in the manner of the Lincoln *hostiarius* or door-keeper, who had to prevent strangers from entering the chapter house during secret meetings. Every cathedral had its janitor or porter of the close gates. At Salisbury kings and earls sometimes used their influence to try to secure this office for their servants.[3] At York, in the mid-fourteenth century, the office of janitor was combined with that of master carpenter. The chapter granted to Philip of Lincoln, the holder of the two offices, a house in the close for life, and allowed him to build shops and to take the profits of his shops.[4]

5. FINANCIAL AND BUSINESS OFFICERS

The management of the secular cathedral finances in the middle ages was not entrusted to any one perpetual dignitary or officer. The dean was the only dignitary with special responsibility for supervising the administration of the chapter estates; but he normally exercised his powers in conjunction with the chapter, and the chapter kept a firm hold over the activities of its other business officers. These were usually canons or vicars choral elected by the chapter to serve for one year at a time. They might be re-elected; some are known to have held office for many years in succession. But all had to present their accounts at regular intervals before auditing committees of the chapter, and could be dismissed by the chapter if their administration were found unsatisfactory. The finances of the secular chapters never became so involved as those of Benedictine monasteries, where in the twelfth century the

[1] *Hemingby's Reg.*, pp. 139–40; Reg. Corffe, f. 38.

[2] E.g. *Hemingby's Reg.*, pp. 68–70, 73, 77, 79.

[3] E.g. in 1339 William Bever was granted the office of janitor by the chapter of Salisbury at the instance of the earls of Warenne and Arundel (*Hemingby's Reg.*, p. 143). For other examples, see D. H. Robertson, *Sarum Close*, p. 107. It was the janitor's duty at Salisbury to summon the residentiary canons personally in their houses to attend chapter meetings. He had the perquisites of a fair.

[4] *York Fabric Rolls*, pp. 165, 185–6. Philip's first appointment was in 1346, when it was decided that he should have twenty pence a week for life as master carpenter, and an extra ten shillings a year from the fabric fund for acting as janitor of the close. In 1374 he was granted permission to take also the profits of his shops.

common revenues might be divided up among ten or twenty obedientiaries, all of whom kept separate accounts.[1] Nevertheless there were at several English secular cathedrals a number of overlapping funds, each managed by a different group of officers; this was especially the case at those chapters which, before the Conquest, had been influenced by rules for a common life and afterwards retained some parts of their common organization for the provision of food for the community. After the Reformation there were occasional attempts to institute a general receiver to co-ordinate and supervise all branches of the cathedral's finances. But generally, throughout the middle ages, the financial systems of the secular cathedrals remained complicated, ingenious, and more distinguished by local differences than other departments of English secular cathedral life.

In one important respect, however, the practice of the chapters was uniform. They all drew a clear-cut line of division between the administration of their common fund, used for common chapter expenses, and the fabric fund, which was devoted to the building and repair of the cathedral fabric. Such a division had been recognized in the western church from early times. By 600 it had already been long established in Italy that the revenue of the see should be divided into four portions, for the bishop, the clergy, church fabrics, and the poor. At English medieval cathedrals, whether secular or monastic, it was normally the dean or prior and chapter, not the bishop, who had charge of the portion belonging to the cathedral fabric. Fresh endowments of the fabric, from the twelfth century onwards, were granted to the dean and chapter; all appointments of fabric officers or master craftsmen were made by them and sealed with the chapter seal; and their consent was necessary for any fresh building or major repairs. Ultimately responsibility for the fabric of the cathedral churches always lay with their chapters, not with the great bishops to whom vague popular tradition ascribed it. Since administration of the fabric department and fabric fund was comparatively simple and uniform in most English churches, it will be convenient to

---

[1] For the financial organization of English Benedictine monasteries, see R. H. Snape, *English Monastic Finances in the Later Middle Ages,* and the references quoted above, p. 217. Towards the end of the twelfth century treasurers were sometimes appointed in these monasteries to try to institute some sort of central financial control over the incomes of the other obedientiaries.

discuss this separately, before approaching the more complicated subject of the common fund.

THE FABRIC DEPARTMENT AND THE FABRIC FUND

Professor Hamilton Thompson has shown the influence of the Vulgate interpretation of numerous architectural passages in the Old Testament on medieval arrangements in the cathedral fabric departments. He writes that the fabric offices and grades of labour described in medieval statutes, chronicles, and building accounts were equally familiar to St. Jerome and his contemporaries:

> 'The monk *qui cementariis praefuit* at Canterbury had his prototypes in *praepositi qui praeerant singulis operibus* of 3 Reg. v. 16, and those *qui praeerant operariis* of 2 Par. xxxiv. 10; while the last, *omnes levitae scientes organis canere*, anticipate the vicars choral who acted as clerks of the works at York in the fourteenth and fifteenth centuries.'[1]

This common background may partly explain why the organization of the cathedral fabric departments varied less than that of the chapters' other business departments.

The system in force at Salisbury in the fourteenth century seems to have been fairly typical. Here the immediate management of the fabric fund was delegated by the chapter to two residentiary canons who were called masters of the fabric. They were allotted a chest in the treasury in which to keep the fabric money and jewels; each had a key to this chest as well as to other boxes in which fabric offerings were kept, so that neither could take out money without the assistance of the other.[2] Under them was the clerk of the fabric, usually a vicar choral or chantry chaplain, who was concerned with the collection and receipt of the revenues of the fund, the payment of the workmen, and the drawing up of quarterly accounts for presentation before a committee of audit of

---

[1] *E.H.R.*, li (1936), 357; cf. 'Cathedral Builders of the Middle Ages', in *History*, x (1925), 143, 150. At monasteries the sacrist was ordinarily responsible for the fabric, but, when new building was undertaken, a special *magister* or *custos operum* might be appointed, with duties similar to those of the masters or wardens of the fabric at secular chapters (*ibid.*, pp. 143–4; D. Knoop and G. P. Jones, *The Medieval Mason*, pp. 29–30).

[2] *S.S.*, pp. 276–7.

the chapter.[1] Many of his account rolls, so far unpublished, survive from the fifteenth century. In 1440 it was found necessary to bring the fabric department under closer control by the chapter, as a result of irregularities committed by masters of the fabric, who had lent goods of the church without sufficient security. In future the dean and treasurer were to be jointly responsible with the masters for the jewels and goods of the fabric. The two masters of the fabric were to be elected annually and were each to receive a fixed salary of forty shillings a year; all their expenditure was to be supervised by the dean and treasurer; at the beginning of each year an inventory of fabric goods was to be made by the new masters under the supervision of the former masters.[2]

Variations of this system are found at most other English secular cathedrals. At Lincoln the two elected *custodes* of the fabric were usually residentiary canons,[3] though sometimes a citizen of Lincoln might hold office jointly with a canon.[4] In addition, Lincoln had a special fabric chantry in the cathedral, served by three priests appointed by the *custodes* of the fabric to pray for the souls of all the faithful who made gifts to the fabric.[5] As at Salisbury, a vicar choral or other inferior choir clerk acted as clerk of the works, helping the *custodes* to deal with the receipts and expenditure, and drawing up annual accounts for presentation to the dean and chapter.[6] In a few cases a particular part of the building might be administered separately from the rest of the fabric. At Hereford a special clerk of the works was appointed to have charge of the funds appropriated to the 'new cloister',[7] while at St. Paul's the fabric was divided into two parts, known as the Old and New Fabric. The administration of the Old Fabric was exceptional.

---

[1] *Ibid.* Appointments of the clerk of the fabric are recorded in the chapter act books. In 1394 mention was also made of a sub-clerk of the fabric, John de Mallewayn, chaplain of Roger Clun's chantry. John was accused of not accounting faithfully for the stipends of the church carpenters, and of removing wood, stones, and a gutter from the common house of the fabric workmen in order to repair his own house (Reg. Dunham, f. 263).

[2] *S.S.*, pp. 310–19.   [3] Cf. *L.S.*, iii, 355–6.

[4] E.g. on one occasion Peter of the Bail, mayor of Lincoln, acted as one of the *custodes* (*Reg. Antiquissimum*, iv, viii).

[5] *L.S.*, iii, 168, 358. The masters of the fabric also sent out *nuncii* every year to publish episcopal indulgences for those making gifts to the cathedral fabric, and to exhort people living in the diocese to contribute to the fabric fund (*ibid.*, p. 357).

[6] *L.S.*, iii, 356–7.   [7] *Hereford Charters*, pp. 267–70.

Throughout the middle ages it remained under the bishop's supervision. He appointed both the master craftsmen employed on its repair, and a keeper to collect and administer its revenues.[1] The New Fabric of the cathedral was managed in the usual way, through an elected residentiary canon, and a *custos* or clerk of the works, who in 1312 was a minor canon.[2] These were said to supervise the repairs of the New Fabric; to see that no rain or snow came through the choir roof on to the stalls; to have the gutters cleared after heavy rains, and to render detailed accounts specifying the exact wages paid to all fabric workmen.

It is especially interesting to notice the important part played by vicars choral and chantry chaplains in administering the cathedral fabric departments. At Exeter, Wells, and York, they acted directly under the chapter as wardens or masters of the fabric, or as clerks of the works, without having a specially elected residentiary canon to supervise them. The fabric rolls of these churches, extant from the late thirteenth or fourteenth century,[3] reveal their work in some detail. At York there were always two vicars or chantry priests, elected annually to be clerks of the works; each kept an account roll, so that, as was usual in medieval accounting, the second clerk, known as the *contrarotulator* or controller, could check his companion's roll from his own roll. These clerks were active in administrative and judicial as well as in financial work: they supervised and paid the masons; heard disputes among the workmen; punished offenders who neglected the rules of conduct of the cathedral workshop; and arrested runaways.[4]

Many master craftsmen and workmen were more or less permanently employed at all cathedrals. Of these, the resident master mason enjoyed a position of special importance and influence.[5] Sometimes he was actually the architect of the cathedral,

---

[1] *R.S.S.P.*, p. 13; *Reg. Baldock*, pp. 74–5, 91–3; and above, p. 123.

[2] *R.S.S.P.*, pp. 77–8, 100–1, 131, 228; *H.M.C. Ninth Rept.*, App., i, 54. In the absence of all the residentiary canons the sacrist might deliver money to the *custos* for his expenses.

[3] See *York Fabric Rolls*; *H.M.C. Wells*, ii, 17–101 *passim*; *H.M.C. Var. Coll.*, iv, 27; Oliver, *op. cit.*, pp. 379–407.

[4] *York Fabric Rolls*, pp. 1–120 *passim*, 171–3.

[5] For his office, see Knoop and Jones, *op. cit.*, pp. 33–4, 61–2; A. H. Thompson in *History*, x, 142 *et seq.*; J. Harvey and A. Oswald, *English Medieval Architects*, 1954.

and might be closely associated with the clerk of the works in the administration of the fabric department. At Exeter in 1300 Master Roger, the master mason, kept the duplicate or counter roll, which was used to check the accounts of Robert of Ashprington, the vicar choral who was then warden of the fabric.[1] At St. Paul's the master mason of the Old Fabric had a house of residence in the cathedral precincts annexed to his office, together with two shops to hold freely for the deposit of stone. His duties included the daily scrutiny of all wood and stone of the Old Fabric. As soon as he noticed defects he was supposed to explain them clearly to the *custos* and to engage workmen to make the necessary repairs. If the *custos* were negligent in authorizing or paying for repairs the master mason had to report them directly to the bishop, or, if the bishop were abroad or the see vacant, to the dean and chapter.[2] Other well-known personages among the workmen were the master carpenter, who owed his importance at some cathedrals to the timber roofs of the churches; the glazier, who at Exeter in 1240 was paid one mark a year and a daily livery of bread for repairing glass in the cathedral, with an extra penny for each foot of new glass which he completed;[3] and the plumber. With the increase of specialization among fourteenth-century craftsmen, famous goldsmiths, painters, tomb-makers, or wood carvers, living at a distance, might be engaged to execute some particular piece of work.[4]

In addition to these special craftsmen were the many *artifices* and *operarii* (workmen) organized under the master craftsmen: the skilled workmen and labourers, free and rough masons, carpenters and glaziers, whose numbers varied according to the magnitude of the work going on,[5] and whose wages, materials, and tools were recorded in the fabric account rolls.[6] About 1352 an

[1] Quoted *History*, x, 145.
[2] See the detailed agreement of 1308 between Bishop Baldock and John Weldon, master mason of the old fabric (*Reg. Baldock*, pp. 91–3). A similar agreement of 1359 between the dean and chapter of Hereford and a master mason is printed in *Hereford Charters*, pp. 230–1.
[3] *H.M.C. Var. Coll.*, i, 193; cf. *Use Exeter*, p. 8.
[4] *H.M.C. Ninth Rept.*, App., i, 30; *Hereford Charters*, p. 195.
[5] E.g. in 1371 only fifteen masons were employed at York, but in 1415, when work was being done on the great tower, as many as forty were paid wages there (*York Fabric Rolls*, pp. 3, 33).
[6] For detailed information, based on a careful study of these rolls, of the

ordinance of the chapter of York laid down the order of their lives, both in winter and summer, from sunrise to sunset. It gave details of their hours of work and of their meals; the length of their afternoon sleep in their lodge or workshop in the close, and the time that they might sit drinking in the lodge in an evening. The two master masons and the master carpenter swore in chapter to see that all these ancient customs were observed by the other workmen, and to report to the *custos* of the fabric or his controller any absences or slackness, for which deductions would be made from the culprits' wages.[1]

THE COMMON FUND

The administration of the common fund of the chapters was closely linked with the daily life and government of the cathedral clergy. Originally it was formed out of that part of the chapter's revenues and estates which continued to be held in common after the bulk of the revenues had been divided up into separate prebends for the individual canons. In churches where parts of the organization for a common life were retained, some of the food of the community was still provided from it; elsewhere daily and termly distributions of money, known as commons, were made from it in place of bread, beer, or wine. By the end of the twelfth century payment of commons was everywhere normally restricted to canons actually resident at the cathedral, with the lesser *ministri* who bore the heat and burden of the day in place of the non-residents. The fund thus helped to maintain the large staff of *ministri inferiores*. It also paid the salaries of cathedral officers and other employees of the chapter, and was the fund from which the cost of lawsuits and other extraordinary chapter expenses could be met. During the twelfth and thirteenth centuries it was greatly increased by endowments granted by kings, bishops, and magnates. Such endowments might be granted for special purposes, and so lead to the creation of separate funds or subdivisions of the main fund, requiring separate administration.

The simplest and most unified administration of the common

organization and conditions of work of the masons and other workmen, see Knoop and Jones, *op. cit.*; A. H. Thompson, *loc. cit.*; L. F. Salzman, *Building in England to 1540*, 1952.
[1] *York Fabric Rolls*, pp. 171–3.

was at Salisbury, where commons were paid in money only, not in kind. Every year at the beginning of October the chapter elected a communar (*communarius*) or keeper of the common to serve for the following year. He superintended the collection of the revenue: the farms or rents of chapter estates and other property; the tithes from appropriated churches; the fines from the non-resident canons; other chapter taxes on the prebends, or fines payable for entries into residence; escheats, reliefs, heriots, profits from the chapter seal, and a variety of other casual receipts. He made the distributions of commons to the cathedral clergy, and all other payments authorized by the chapter. Finally he drew up a roll of his accounts every quarter to be audited by the chapter.[1] A salary of twenty marks was allowed him for his expenses,[2] and he was given a vicar choral or other choir clerk, known as the sub-communar, to help him. Among the sub-communar's duties was that of keeping a record of the absences of the residentiary canons to guide the communar in distributing commons.[3] In the fifteenth century all canons had to take an oath on their admission into residence that they would willingly and faithfully administer the common whenever they should be elected to the office.[4] Although complaints were sometimes made that the system of changing communars each year was liable to cause grave inconveniences,[5] the system seems generally to have worked well. No canon was able to establish any perpetual right to administer the common; the chapter could exercise close control over the management of its income, both through the quarterly audit and the annual election. Yet at the same time some continuity of administration was possible in practice: the quarterly account rolls, extant from the fourteenth and fifteenth centuries, show that the same

---

[1] *S.S.*, pp. 190–3. For these rolls, see above, pp. 76–7, and below, App. II. In 1374 minor changes were made in the system of accounting: the communar was ordered to make a separate reckoning at the end of each quarter for uncertain profits and casual receipts not specified in his great roll (*ibid.*, pp. 278–81).

[2] *Ibid.*, pp. 358–9.

[3] Cf. *S.S.*, p. 419 n.; Jones, *Fasti Sar.*, p. 249.

[4] *Salisbury Ceremonies*, p. 113; cf. Jones, *Fasti Sar.*, p. 249 n. The communar had not always necessarily been a canon: the statute of 1319 which described his office spoke of the need for a special oath to be sworn by any communar who was not a canon (*S.S.*, pp. 192–3). But the extant medieval communars' rolls at Salisbury, dating from 1343, seem all to have been drawn up by canons.

[5] E.g. *Salisbury Ceremonies*, p. 152.

canon was frequently elected to the office of communar for several years in succession.

Only two English chapters, Lichfield and Chichester, seem to have organized their finances in ways markedly similar to that of Salisbury. At Lichfield, from the end of the twelfth century, one or two canons or vicars were elected annually to administer the common, and rendered account at the end of the year in the presence of the chapter of residentiaries.[1] At Chichester an arrangement similar to that of Salisbury, of an annually elected communar rendering a quarterly account in chapter, seems to have been in force between 1271 and 1573.[2] But there were probably substantial differences in detail since throughout the middle ages part of the daily commons at Chichester were distributed in the form of canonical loaves; these were known as 'Hilary loaves', because they were provided from a grant made to the canons by Bishop Hilary in the middle of the twelfth century.[3] Officials must have been needed to staff a capitular bakehouse, an institution of which no trace has been discovered at Salisbury.[4]

There was also a communar at Wells, but the status and duties of his office were different from those of the communar at Salisbury. The communar at Wells was usually a vicar choral, who did not administer the whole common.[5] Another elected official, the escheator, had charge of all receipts and expenditure connected with the revenues from prebends vacant by death, of the endowments left to the cathedral for the celebration of obits, and of the offerings and burial fees.[6] He also was usually either a vicar choral or a chantry chaplain. The annual accounts of these two

[1] *Monasticon*, VI, iii, 1261; H. Jenkins, *op. cit.*, p. 61.

[2] *C.S.*, pp. 17, 24; *Reg. Rede*, ii, 370. In 1197 the treasurer and two other canons had been put in charge of the common (cf. *C.S.*, pp. 1–2). For the arrangements after 1573, see *ibid.*, pp. 24, 32, 48.

[3] *Ibid.*, pp. 2, 6–7, 23; *Reg. Rede*, i, 114. The wine, which had formerly been distributed in kind on certain feast days, was commuted to a money payment in 1232 (*C.S.*, p. 6).

[4] The larger canonical houses at Salisbury apparently had their own private bakehouses (see K. Edwards, *op. cit.*, in *British Arch. Journal*, 1939, p. 65). The statute of 1319 allowing cathedral clergy to buy bread from travelling bakers, provided these were of the male sex (*S.S.*, pp. 268–9), also suggests that bread was not distributed at the cathedral.

[5] See the calendars of his accounts in *H.M.C. Wells*, ii, 1–98 *passim*.

[6] The surviving medieval escheators' accounts are calendared, *ibid.*, pp. 11–96 *passim*.

officers were audited at Michaelmas by a committee of three elected residentiary canons, the senior of whom was called the baron of the exchequer. In 1331, it was decided to increase capitular control over the distribution of commons. A fourth canon was for the future to be elected annually to be seneschal or steward, with the duty of selling all grain accruing to the common from tithes and rents, in order that by Michaelmas nothing should remain over from the past year.[1] Professor Hamilton Thompson has traced the later changes in the administration by which the various offices of communar, escheator, and baron of the exchequer were gradually merged in the course of the seventeenth century, until in 1729 all the financial departments at Wells, including the fabric, were united under the supervision of one residentiary canon.[2]

In addition, Wells had a medieval provost whose duties were unconnected with the administration of either the common or the fabric. Instituted by Bishop Jocelin in the early thirteenth century, his chief functions were to administer the lands and distribute the income of the fifteen-fold prebend of Combe and Winsham. He was not a dignitary, and need not be a priest or residentiary. Though he held one of the Combe prebends for himself with a stall in choir next to the succentor, this gave him no voice in chapter, unless the bishop also collated him to another canonry and prebend.[3] Parallels to his office are found in the medieval provostries of a few northern French cathedrals, where, as at Wells, the early provosts ruling the chapters had disappeared, but where provosts were later appointed to administer the funds of divided prebends.[4]

The medieval provostry at Lincoln was of yet another kind. Like most provostries of English collegiate churches until the later middle ages, it was elective and temporary, being granted annually by the dean and chapter to a residentiary canon after the

---

[1] *W.S.*, pp. 130–1.

[2] *Cathedral Churches*, p. 182.

[3] Bishop Jocelin's ordinance for the provostry is printed in full in *Reg. Shrewsbury*, pp. lxiv–lxviii, and calendared with other documents concerning the provostry in *C.Ch.R. 1341–1417*, pp. 25–6.

[4] E.g. at Autun (A. H. Thompson, 'Notes on Colleges of Secular Canons', in *Arch. Journal*, lxxiv, 177 and n.). For the early provosts at Wells, who had charge over the property and internal management of the community, see Church, *op. cit.*, pp. 5–7, 12. Their office was abolished by Bishop Robert soon after 1136.

R

final audit of accounts in September.[1] The office has been well described as a cross between that of the Salisbury communar and the Wells baron of the exchequer.[2] The provost's duties were to supervise the administration of the common; to see that all revenues were paid into the chamber at the correct times; to authorize all expenditure and distributions; to carry the daily seal of the chapter, and the second key to the chest containing the great seal; to examine and seal the ordinary business letters of the chapter; to keep the charters and other muniments, and to visit once or twice a year all churches appropriated to the common.[3] The annual accounts of the common fund at Lincoln were drawn up by the clerk of the common, sometimes called the clerk of the chamber;[4] he was usually a vicar or chantry priest, who often held office for some years in succession. There were also a *clericus scriptor communae*[5] and a *clericus re et ve*, who kept a roll of *re* and *ve* (*recedendi et veniendi*) recording the weekly comings and goings of the residentiary canons, so that the clerk of the common would know how much to pay each canon for his residence.[6] The vicars choral of Lincoln and the clerks of the office of the Blessed Virgin Mary each had their own provost who distributed commons to them.[7]

Two other English secular cathedrals, York and St. Paul's, called the financial department of their common fund the *camera* or chamber. This description was common in cathedrals in France and Germany where chamberlains had frequently succeeded the provosts or cellarers of St. Chrodegang's rule after the break-up of the common life.[8] In such cases the chamberlain was usually a dignitary; but at York and St. Paul's he was not. The chamberlain of York merely received an annual salary of forty shillings for his work in distributing the commons and drawing up the half-yearly account rolls of receipts and expenditure,[9] while a seneschal or steward with a pension of fifty shillings a year supervised the

---

[1] *L.S.*, ii, 168; *Reg. Antiquissimum*, iv, App., p. 282.

[2] A. H. Thompson, *Cathedral Churches*, p. 183.   [3] *L.S.*, iii, 168, 354.

[4] Cf. *ibid.*, i. 389. For all these officers and their work see K. Major, 'Finances of the Dean and Chapter of Lincoln' in *J.E.H.*, v, 149–67.

[5] *L.S.*, i, 378, 389.   [6] *Ibid.*, iii, 800 *et seq.*

[7] *Ibid.*, p. 802, and below, pp. 274–5; *Reg. Antiquissimum*, ii, 56–7.

[8] Cf. Hinschius, ii, 107.

[9] *York Fabric Rolls*, p. 124. Extracts from his account rolls from the late fourteenth century onwards are printed *ibid.*, pp. 121 *et seq.*

administration of the chapter lands and the collection of the rents and other income.[1]

At St. Paul's the chamber was only one of three separate departments concerned with the administration of the common. Its existence has first been noticed in records of about 1181 in the deanery of Ralph de Diceto, and from this time the greater part of the common business unconnected with the provision of food for the community is known to have accrued to it.[2] The chamberlain was responsible for paying the money stipends and pittances of the clergy, and for providing lights in the church; he rendered quarterly accounts which were enrolled in the treasury roll, and his work was supervised by an elected residentiary canon known as the *Custos Camerae*.[3]

At the same time a large part of the farms of the chapter's manors continued to be paid into the much more ancient department of the *Bracinum* or brewery, over which the chamber had no control. The *Bracinum* was supervised by a *Custos Bracini*, who, like the *Custos Camerae*, was an elected residentiary canon, and worked with the *Custos Camerae* to co-ordinate the administration of the farms and the distribution of the commons.[4] Under the *Custos Bracini* was a large department organized to provide food for the community. The two principal officers were the baker and brewer; these were instructed to be present when the *Custos* examined the grain received from the farmers, to make sure that it was good, dry, clean, and suitable for making bread and ale. There was also the *Cervisiae Tractator* (ale-drawer) and numerous other servants and porters staffing the various buildings known as the bakehouse, brewhouse, cellar, and pantry.[5] Ministers of the cathedral were always supposed to receive their distributions of commons from these departments before outsiders. In the thirteenth and early fourteenth centuries much bread and ale seems either to have been given away or sold to augment the chapter income. The *Custos Bracini* rendered monthly accounts of the outgoings sold by the baker, brewer, and *Cervisiae Tractator*.[6]

---

[1] *Ibid.*, p. 124; *L.S.*, ii, 94. He nominated and answered for the bailiffs on the chapter lands.

[2] M. Gibbs, *Early Charters of St. Paul*, pp. xxxvi–vii.

[3] *R.S.S.P.*, pp. 30, 74–5, 127, 132, 174.

[4] *Ibid.*, pp. 30, 75–6, 96, 132, 164–5, 174.

[5] *R.S.S.P.*, pp. 75–6, 174.   [6] *Ibid.*, p. 76.

Archdeacon Hale has worked out that in the late thirteenth century brewings at the cathedral took place nearly twice a week; nearly ten quarters of grain were used at each brewing and an average of 678 gallons was produced each time. In 1283 there was an average of five bakings a fortnight and about 40,266 loaves were produced in the year.[1] The St. Paul's greater loaf was larger than that of any of the neighbouring religious houses.[2] The *Bracinum* however decayed later in the fourteenth century.[3]

The third financial department at St. Paul's, the almonry, was, like the chamber, a Norman addition to the pre-conquest organization of the common. Yet it had more similarities with the almonries of English Benedictine monasteries than with any organization at the English secular cathedrals. In the late twelfth century, in the deanery of Ralph de Diceto, special tithes and rents were assigned to be administered by an almoner.[4] The conversion of the houses of Canon Henry of Northampton into a hospital for the poor, which was apparently a central feature of Diceto's scheme, did not materialize, but the rents from the houses continued to be paid into the almonry in the fourteenth century.[5] The almoner's duties, as described in Dean Baldock's statutes of about 1300, were to make distributions to the poor on the statutory days, according to the ordinances of benefactors who had endowed the almonry; to arrange for the poor and beggars who died in or near the St. Paul's cemetery to be buried there freely; and to feed, clothe, support and teach eight almonry boys suitable for serving in the church.[6] These, like the almonry boys of the English cathedral monasteries, were the cathedral choristers; in 1315 Bishop Newport bequeathed to the almoner a house near the cathedral for 'the maintenance for two years of one or two boys when they shall change their voice'.[7]

[1] *Domesday of St. Paul's*, pp. xlviii–l; *R.S.S.P.*, pp. 75 n., 173 n.

[2] *Ibid.*, pp. 173 n., 176–7. From three years before King Stephen's death the St. Paul's loaf weighed 6½ marks and the lesser loaf 3 marks 2 oz. The canonical loaf at Exeter was said in 1277 to weigh 73/4 (i.e. 5½ marks) when cooked (Harl. MS. 1027, f. 19a).

[3] Cf. C. N. L. Brooke in *Hist. St. Paul's Cathedral*, pp. 62–3.

[4] *Registrum Eleemosynarie D. Pauli*, pp. 1 *et seq*; *Early Charters of St. Paul*; Index *s.v.* almonry. The almoner might be a minor canon (*R.S.S.P.*, pp. 358–9).

[5] *Early Charters of St. Paul*, pp. xxxvii n., 97–8, 125–6, 246–8.

[6] *R.S.S.P.*, pp. 76–7.

[7] A. F. Leach, 'St. Paul's School before Colet', in *Archaeologia*, lxii, 199; *Calendar of Hustings Wills*, ed. Sharpe, i, 281; cf. ii, 21–2. See also below, p. 310.

The continuing influence in the middle ages of pre-conquest rules for a common life can be seen also in the organization of the financial departments of the two remaining English secular cathedrals, Exeter and Hereford. As in the case of St. Paul's, their financial arrangements were individual, showing few similarities with those of other English churches. In the early twelfth century, in William of Malmesbury's time, the canons of Exeter still had an *yconomus* appointed by the bishop who supplied them with food and clothing.[1] This system is thought to have continued only so long as the common buildings of refectory and dormitory survived. In 1133 the canons moved into the new Norman cathedral.[2] Yet afterwards, even when a secular organization had been largely accepted, only the dignitaries were given separate endowments. The rest of the chapter's income continued to be administered in common by two elected residentiary canons known as seneschals or stewards, whose department was called the exchequer. They supervised the farming of the chapter lands, and, from the revenues, paid equal bursal prebends of four pounds a year each to all the twenty-four canons, and one pound to their vicars choral. The remainder was distributed partly in daily or weekly commons of bread, ale, wine, flour, and salt, partly in weekly and quarterly distributions of money.[3] Under the stewards were a chief or superior clerk of the exchequer, who might be a vicar choral or chantry chaplain; a sub-clerk of the exchequer; a rent-collector; bailiffs and other local officials on the chapter's estates; a clerk of the bread chest, who supervised the baker in his buying of wheat 'in foro et alibi', and a baker, who received five shillings a term and one penny for each obit service, which he attended in the cathedral.[4] On certain feast days the city corporation enjoyed the privilege of having bread baked in the canons' oven.[5] A variety of unpublished medieval accounts of the stewards and their subordinate officers survive at Exeter; the *Rotuli*

[1] Malmesbury, *De Gestis Pontificum*, p. 201.

[2] F. Rose Troup, *The Consecration of the Norman Minster at Exeter*, pp. 3–5.

[3] MS. Top. Devon, c. 16, ff. 1–3; MS. Rawl. Statutes 38, ff. 63–6; Harl. MS. 1027, ff. 9b–10a, 14a, 16b–17a, 19a, 24a, 46a; *Use Exeter*, p. 80; *Reg. Grandisson*, ii, 858, 860–1; J. Jones, 'On the Constitution, Discipline and Usages of Exeter Cathedral', in *Archaeologia*, xviii, 396. The chapter lands were supposed to be visited annually by one or two canons elected by the chapter.

[4] *Use Exeter*, pp. 3, 80–2.

[5] E. Lega-Weekes, *Studies in the Topography of Exeter Cathedral Close*, p. 41.

Compotorum Seneschallorum Scaccarii from 1296 to 1525 with some gaps; the *Rotuli Debitorum* or bailiff's accounts from 1331-3 and again with gaps from 1385-1519; some 'Refection Books', the earliest dating from 1305-13, which give the weekly payments to each residentiary for his commons.[1]

The system of accounting at the Hereford exchequer was among the most complicated in use at any English secular cathedral in the middle ages. As at Exeter, two residentiary canons, known as bailiffs, *yconomi*, provosts of the exchequer or keepers of the manors, were elected to supervise the chapter's estates.[2] Under them were two officials, a steward (sometimes a layman), and a receiver (usually a clerk closely connected with the chapter), who prepared general half-yearly accounts of receipts and expenditure. Subordinate to these accounts were the accounts of the local bailiffs and reeves of the chapter's estates, which sometimes give information about other local officials, such as beadles, foresters, and serjeants.[3] A full view of the chapter's income and expenditure cannot, however, be obtained from the receiver's accounts or any other single account roll, because a number of endowments were administered separately from the main part of the common. Separate annual accounts were presented for the canons' bakehouse, by the clerk for mass pence, and by the collectors of the city rents and of heriots and oblations, while the *custos* or provost of the Lady Chapel, a residentiary canon, also accounted separately for distributions made from the tithes of the church of Lugwardine to vicars choral serving the Lady Chapel. Further difficulties were caused through the division of commons into an unusually large number of different payments, such as 'great commons', 'little commons', quotidians, mass pence and obit distributions, made both in money and in kind, on different

---

[1] These accounts are described by Mrs. A. M. Erskine in *Jour. Soc. Archivists*, ii, no. 6, 254-66. Some were used by Mr. D. J. B. Hindley for his M.A. thesis on the Dean and Chapter's Estates in the Fifteenth Century, London, 1958.

[2] *L.S.*, ii, 50-3.

[3] A typescript list of all the surviving Hereford Cathedral Account Rolls, Court Rolls, Rentals and Surveys, ed. B. G. Charles and H. D. Emanuel, 1955, with an index by Penelope E. Morgan, 2 vols., 1957-9, is available at the National library of Wales and at H.M.C., National Register of Archives. The accounts are discussed by Miss Marjorie Jones in her B.Litt. thesis on The Estates of Hereford Cathedral, 1066-1317, Oxford, 1958. Printed examples are in *Hereford Charters*, pp. 130-2, 135-40, 165-6, 168-9, 211-12, 229-30.

occasions and for different reasons.[1] The chapter found it necessary to employ a permanent professional auditor, who might be called upon to give evidence when any canon questioned the amount of commons paid to him. In 1409 John Honte, summoned before the chapter in such a case, declared that for thirty-four years he had held the office of auditor to the dean and chapter, and in his time had ordained distributions to individual canons according to their estate and the revenue of the place, without any favour to one more than another. But he explained that the profits of one year only casually corresponded to those of the next, and that no canon could know the amount of the portion due to him until after the final reckoning.[2]

In the administration of their common revenues the English secular chapters seem generally to have been less sensitive to outside influences than they were in other branches of cathedral government. Similarities can naturally be found in the financial methods of all secular chapters. Yet the comparatively simple and unified financial organization of Salisbury chapter was apparently adopted with modifications at only one or two other cathedrals. Most chapters seem to have preferred to work out their own systems to fit in with their local economic needs, with the conditions of special endowments, and with the particular requirements of their common life. It is especially interesting to see how three or four English chapters retained throughout the middle ages some parts of their pre-conquest organization for the provision of food for the community.

6. THE ARCHDEACONS

The place of archdeacons in secular cathedrals in the middle ages was peculiar. They might hold almost every gradation of rank among the dignitaries and *personae*, yet their chief work was in their archdeaconries outside the cathedral precincts, 'in the care of parishes and in the cure of souls'.[3] No attempt can be made

---

[1] See *L.S.*, ii, 47–61; above, pp. 43, 46–7, and M. Jones, *op. cit.*, pp. 188 *et seq.*

[2] *Hereford Charters*, p. 264.

[3] This was the usual description of the archdeacon's office in English cathedral statutes, e.g. *S.S.*, pp. 30–1, 61; *R.S.S.P.*, p. 20; *C.S.*, p. 13; *W.S.*, pp. 45, 55; *L.S.*, ii, 23; iii, 305.

here to describe the archdeacon's position and duties in his archdeaconry or the diocese as a whole.[1] Discussion must be limited to his connexion with the cathedral church, where, in medieval England, although superior to the simple canons in dignity, he had no jurisdiction and few duties.

This position was in striking contrast to the authority and preeminence which archdeacons had enjoyed at many continental cathedrals before the twelfth century, and which they kept throughout the middle ages and later at many Italian and at a few French cathedrals.[2] Originally the archdeacon had been head of the deacons in the bishop's *familia*, as the archpriest had been head of the priests. At first, in the fourth and fifth centuries in France, there is little evidence to show which of the two was the more important. But by the seventh century, from acting as the bishop's right-hand man and chief administrative officer in the town, the archdeacon had established his authority over all his rivals, both in town and country.[3] St. Chrodegang's rule, both in its original and enlarged forms, placed the archdeacon or other superior (*vel primarius*) at the head of the cathedral clerks. At many cathedrals of the Empire where this rule was adopted, the archdeacon ranked next to the bishop, and had authority over the other cathedral clergy.

In northern France it seems to have been the rise in the eleventh century of the new secular chapters with their separate endowments and greater independence of the bishop, which led ultimately to the decline of the archdeacon's authority at the cathedrals. From the first, the archdeacons sought to be members of these chapters. The *archidiaconus magnus* of the city was nearly always a dignitary, with a prebend permanently annexed to his office; while, from the first half of the twelfth century, many

---

[1] For this see Fournier, *Les Officialités*, pp. xxviii–xxxi; A. H. Thompson, *Archdeacons and Rural Deans*; R. L. Storey, *Diocesan Administration in the Fifteenth Century*, pp. 16–17; C. Morris, 'The Bishop's Commissary' in *J.E.H.*, x, 51–2. By the thirteenth century the archdeacon was no longer the bishop's principal agent in the diocese as a whole, but had jurisdiction in his own right in a defined territorial division of the diocese.

[2] Cf. A. H. Thompson, *loc. cit.*, pp. 8–9. Professor Hamilton Thompson has worked out that, of 285 Italian cathedrals listed by Ughelli, *Italia Sacra*, 141 had archdeacons at their head.

[3] For the early history of the archdeacon, see A. Amanieu, 'L'Archidiacre', in *Dict. de Droit Canonique*, cc. 948 *et seq.*; Frere, *Visitation Articles*, i, 13 *et seq.*

rural archdeacons also obtained prebends.[1] Apparently they thought that the backing of the chapter's wealth and influence would strengthen their position in relation to the bishop. For a time it frequently did so. But the bishops were naturally not anxious for their archdeacons, who were already very powerful subordinates, to gain further power; while the chapters, jealous of their corporate independence, preferred to have as their head an officer elected by themselves rather than an archdeacon appointed by the bishop. Thus bishop and chapter were often ready to co-operate in limiting the archdeacon's authority at the cathedral. In a few cathedrals in southern and eastern France, the *archidiaconus magnus* kept his position as head of the chapter; but usually a dean or provost was instituted in his place.[2] Gradually, as a result of holding prebends and claiming the title of canons, the archdeacons came to be treated as equals rather than as superiors by the other canons.[3] They lost their control over the chapter's lands, jurisdiction, and government. In many dioceses the bishop granted exemption from the archdeacon's jurisdiction to the canons' prebends and common lands, and often allowed it also for the whole district of the cathedral city and suburbs. Naturally, there were disputes in chapter on all these matters, and in the competition and rulings the archdeacons lost prestige. Like the bishop, whose officials they originally were, their authority and activities came to be limited chiefly to spheres outside the cathedral close.

In England before the Conquest there is little evidence for archdeacons.[4] There was an archdeacon at Canterbury in 803; a group of four appeared together in the same diocese between 863 and 870. But elsewhere little trace of them has been found before the eleventh century, when the office is mentioned in the Northumbrian Priests' Law (probably 1002–23). Its appearance here was evidently connected with the expanding work of the large diocese of York. Later in the century when rules of common life were

---

[1] This development is traced by Imbart de la Tour, *Les élections épiscopales*, p. 528. Cf. also Amanieu, *loc. cit.*, cc. 990–1.

[2] See above, pp. 138–40; A. H. Thompson, *loc. cit.*, pp. 8–9.

[3] Amanieu, *loc. cit.*, cc. 990 *et seq.*

[4] For the known evidence, see Frere, *loc. cit.*, pp. 41–52; M. Deanesly, 'The Archdeacons of Archbishop Ceolnoth', in *E.H.R.*, xlii, 1–11; *Sidelights on the Anglo-Saxon Church*, pp. 148–54; W. Levison, *England and the Continent in the Eighth Century*, p. 107; R. R. Darlington, in *E.H.R.*, li, 413 n; F. Barlow, *The English Church 1000–1066*, pp. 151–2, 220, 229, 246 n., 247–9.

adopted at a number of English cathedrals, it seems possible that some may have had an archdeacon at their head.[1] The rule which Leofric gave to Exeter provided for a single archdeacon, and before the end of the eleventh century we meet with three holders of the office.[2] At St. Paul's and Hereford archdeacons are found in the late eleventh century before the appearance of a dean.[3] Furthermore, the unusual precedence enjoyed by archdeacons at both St. Paul's and Exeter in the twelfth century and later suggests that there was some tradition of their authority there. At St. Paul's the deans of the early twelfth century seem only gradually to have established their right to the headship of the chapter in place of the archdeacon of London, while as late as 1205 the archdeacon defeated the precentor's claim to the second place in choir after the dean.[4] At Exeter, where there was no dean until 1225, the four archdeacons normally head the lists of chapter witnesses to documents throughout the twelfth century.[5]

In most English dioceses the institution of territorial archdeaconries was the work of the years following the Norman Conquest.[6] Sometimes, as at Salisbury, York, and Lincoln, it took place about the same time as the adoption of a secular organization at the cathedrals;[7] in other cases, where a secular constitution was introduced more gradually, archdeaconries might be established shortly before the deanery or other cathedral dignities.[8] There seems to have been no question of an archdeacon becoming the head of any of these chapters. Yet, as on the continent, archdeacons were assigned places of honour in the cathedral choir, and, provided they held prebends, might also be admitted as

[1] See above, pp. 8–9. Chrodegang's rule, on which this revival seems to have been based, provided for an archdeacon.

[2] A. Morey, *Bartholomew of Exeter*, p. 114.

[3] C. N. L. Brooke in *Camb. Hist. Jour.*, x, 118 n.; M. Jones, *op. cit.*, p. 48.

[4] See above, pp. 140, 161.

[5] *Ibid.*, pp. 141–2.

[6] See A. H. Thompson, *loc. cit.*, pp. 14–17.

[7] Remigius is said to have instituted seven archdeacons at Lincoln about 1090 when he instituted the other cathedral dignitaries (Henry of Huntingdon, pp. 302–3); an eighth archdeacon of Stow was added in the early to mid-twelfth century. At Salisbury the earliest copies of St. Osmund's institution charter of 1091 do not give the number of archdeacons appointed, but order that two should always be resident at the cathedral (*S.S.*, pp. 26–7). For York see *Hist. Church York*, ii, 108, and C. T. Clay in *Y.A.J.*, xxxvi, 269 *et seq.*

[8] See e.g. J. A. Robinson, *Somerset Hist. Essays*, pp. 73 *et seq.*

members of the chapter. Like the dean, but unlike the other dignitaries and the simple canons, they always continued to take their oath of canonical obedience directly to the bishop, instead of through the dean. Their oath of fidelity to the cathedral church merely bound them to observe and defend the cathedral statutes, in so far as these concerned the archidiaconal dignity; only if they obtained prebends could the dean and chapter exact an additional oath from them to obey the dean, and to keep the chapter's secrets.[1] Friction sometimes developed between archdeacons and chapters on subjects such as their respective powers in the vacancy of the see, or the chapter's exempt jurisdiction.[2] but this rarely seems to have been serious. The position of archdeacons in the English secular chapters seems generally to have been easier than in those continental chapters where the dean and canons had had to assert their independence of the ancient authority of the archdeacon. At English cathedral monasteries the situation was more complicated, because the monks were naturally unwilling to allow any secular clergy to be present at their chapter meetings. Eventually it was agreed at Canterbury about 1160 that the archdeacon's proper place in the chapter of Christ Church should be on the archbishop's footstool; but he had no right to be present unless summoned by the monks for special occasions.[3]

The English secular chapters made it clear in their statutes that the rule, which allowed no dignitary without a prebend to be present at their chapter meetings or elections, or to receive commons, applied with special force to the archdeacons. In the margin of an early copy of the statutes of Salisbury is written, in what is probably a contemporary hand, 'Nota! Contra archidiaconos qui non habent corpora prebendarum.'[4] In a few cases, such as those of the archdeacon of Chester at Lichfield cathedral, or the archdeacons of Wells and Taunton in Wells cathedral, the expedient was adopted of annexing a prebend permanently to

---

[1] Cf. *Salisbury Ceremonies*, p. 111; *R.S.S.P.*, pp. 20, 26–7.

[2] E.g. Swainson, pp. 42–5; *L.S.*, ii, clv–vi.

[3] *Lit. Cant.*, iii, 355–6. At this time Roger the archdeacon, afterwards archbishop of York, had been claiming a seat in the monastic chapter by right of his office. In Archbishop Chichele's pontificate (1414–43) newly appointed archdeacons of Canterbury were still installed in the cathedral choir and assigned their place in chapter (e.g. *Reg. Chichele*, i, 237).

[4] Quoted by Jones, *Fasti Sar.*, p. 126. Cf. *S.S.*, pp. 154–5; *R.S.S.P.*, p. 89; *L.S.*, iii, 314.

their offices.[1] Many archdeacons were collated by their bishop to cathedral prebends for their own lifetime. But there were also cases of archdeacons being without prebends for their whole tenure of office. In 1432, during Bishop Gray's visitation of Lincoln cathedral, only two archdeacons, those of Oxford and Bedford, were prebendaries and residentiaries there; the other six were expressly said to have no prebends.[2] Bradshaw has worked out that between about 1435 and 1445 the archdeacons of Oxford, Buckingham, and Bedford, apparently had no prebends at Lincoln.[3]

On the other hand, if archdeacons held prebends, they were normally granted precedence in chapter over the simple canons both in session and voice,[4] and at certain cathedrals were definitely encouraged to become residentiaries. This was in contrast to their position in cities having monastic cathedrals, where archdeacons had to make their headquarters outside the cathedral close.[5] The statutes of Salisbury and Exeter laid down that if possible two out of their four archdeacons ought always to be resident at the cathedral.[6] Most secular chapters allowed the archdeacons, on account of their exacting duties in the diocese, to have the status of full residentiaries for a much shorter annual period of residence than was obligatory on the simple canons.[7] The chapter of Wells offered to the Archdeacon of Wells the added inducement of double commons, which was usually granted only to the

[1] *L.S.*, i, 138; ii, 23; C. M. Church, 'The Prebendal Stalls in Wells Cathedral,' in *Archaeologia*, lv, 324. About 1151–5 Bishop Robert II of Lincoln granted the church of Langford as a cathedral prebend to be annexed in perpetuity to the archdeaconry of Oxford (*Reg. Antiquissimum*, ii, 38). But Le Neve's later list of the prebendaries of Langford *Ecclesia* (*Fasti*, ii, 163) shows that at any rate from 1330 the archdeacons of Oxford no longer held the prebend.

[2] *Lincoln Visitations*, i, 132–3 n.

[3] *L.S.*, ii, ccxvii n.

[4] E.g. *R.S.S.P.*, p. 20; *L.S.*, iii, 305–6; *Use Sarum*, i, 51.

[5] E.g. at Canterbury Lanfranc gave the archdeacon a dwelling-house near St. Gregory's priory, outside the North Gate of the city, in order that he should not have lodgings within the cathedral precincts. In 1227–8 the archdeacon exchanged this with the monks of Christ Church for the rectory of Hackington in the suburbs and afterwards made his usual residence there (Somner and Battely, *Antiquities Cant.*, i, 150, 156–7; cf. App., i, 65–6). At Norwich in the early fifteenth century the archdeacon's house was in St. Edmund's parish (*Reg. Chichele*, iii, 351).

[6] *S.S.*, pp. 26–7, 56–7, 62; *Ordinale Exon.*, i, 5.

[7] See above, p. 50.

four principal dignitaries because they had to support an especially long period of annual residence.[1]

At all English secular cathedrals the archdeacon's position in the church as distinct from the chapter house was secure and independent of their tenure of prebends. This may have been because in most medieval cathedral churches the archdeacons had come to be regarded as the bishop's official guests, to be treated with the honour due to guests. Special choir stalls were usually reserved for them among or near the four great dignitaries.[2] At Salisbury and Exeter each of the four archdeacons was placed next to a dignitary at the four corners of the choir; at Chichester, where there were only the two archdeacons, one was given the seat next to the dean, the other that next to the precentor. Lincoln, which had eight archdeacons, and York, which had five, adopted rather different arrangements on the same general principle.[3] At St. Paul's the archdeacon of London ranked next to the dean in choir; throughout the middle ages he maintained his right to the north-west terminal stall, which in most English cathedrals belonged to the precentor,[4] while the other three archdeacons of Colchester, Middlesex, and Essex followed the archdeacon of London in dignity, holding the two remaining terminal stalls and the stall next to the dean, and so taking precedence of the treasurer, precentor, and chancellor. A less striking parallel to this was at Wells, where the archdeacons of Wells and Bath took precedence of the chancellor and treasurer in choir, while the archdeacon of Taunton ranked next after the treasurer, above the simple canons.[5] Only at Lichfield and Hereford no special choir stalls were reserved for the archdeacons unless they held prebends; at Lichfield the archdeacon of Chester occupied the seventh stall on the *decani* side of the choir, belonging to his prebend of Bolton.

In England, as in France, it is not always clear whether the medieval archdeacons *ex officio* actually had the right to the title of cathedral dignitaries. The custom seems to have varied at different

[1] *W.S.*, pp. 45, 55; *H.M.C. Wells*, i, 60.
[2] Diagrams of the arrangement of the choir stalls in all the medieval English secular cathedrals are printed in *L.S.*, i, 136–8. Cf. also *Use Sarum*, i, 13; *Ordinale Exon.*, i, 2; *W.S.*, p. 1.
[3] See *L.S.*, i, 136–8.
[4] For the precentor's attempts to wrest this stall from him, see above, p. 161.
[5] In chapter, however, the treasurer and chancellor took precedence of the archdeacon of Bath (*W.S.*, p. 2).

churches. At Salisbury the archdeacons were not usually given the title of dignitaries in the statutes or chapter acts, although if they held prebends, they took precedence of the simple canons in chapter as well as in choir.[1] At St. Paul's, Exeter, and Chichester all archdeacons were normally described as dignitaries.[2] At Wells, in the *Valor Ecclesiasticus* of 1535, the archdeacon of Wells was described as a cathedral dignitary, and the archdeacons of Bath and Taunton as *personae*.[3]

It is interesting to notice that the few functions still remaining to archdeacons in English cathedrals in the later middle ages were mostly connected either with the bishop's duties in the cathedral choir, or with those of the parish clergy of their archdeaconries. The principal archdeacon normally assisted the bishop in the cathedral service on Ash Wednesday; the archdeacon ejected the penitents from the church; then, on Maundy Thursday, he read the lesson, 'Adest tempus' at the church door, and restored the penitents.[4] Three archdeacons were required to be present with the bishop of Salisbury at the making of the chrism in the cathedral church.[5] At Chichester the two archdeacons of Chichester and Lewes preached sermons to the people on Ash Wednesday and Maundy Thursday, and provided the oil for making the chrism and holy oil.[6] The archdeacons were responsible for seeing that the clergy and people of their archdeaconries came to the cathedral church in procession with their offerings in Whitsun week.[7] In those cathedrals where archdeacons had jurisdiction in the city, they had to see that the city clergy were present in the cathedral processions at the statutory times.[8]

---

[1] Cf. Jones, *Fasti Sar.*, p. 126; *Use Sarum*, i, 51.

[2] E.g. *Valor Eccl.*, i, 300, 363; ii, 295–6. Yet in Bishop Grandisson's summary of Exeter customs of about 1337, he gave the title of dignitary only to the four principal *personae* (*Ordinale Exon.*, i, 2, 6).

[3] *Valor Eccl.*, i, 132–3.

[4] *Use Sarum*, i, 138, 143–4; *Salisbury Ceremonies*, pp. 63–4, 68–9.

[5] *Ibid.*, p. 73; *Use Sarum*, i, 202–4.

[6] *Reg. Rede*, i, 103, 116.

[7] E.g. *Reg. Antiquissimum*, i, 257–9.

[8] E.g. *R.S.S.P.*, p. 191.

CHAPTER IV

THE *MINISTRI INFERIORES* AND THE MINOR CORPORATIONS

THE history of the lesser cathedral clergy (the *ministri inferiores*) in the later middle ages has a special interest and importance. The greatest expansion in the numbers of members of the cathedral foundations since the twelfth century had taken place in their ranks. With the increase of non-residence by the canons there might, by the fourteenth century, be only about nine to thirteen canons actually living in Salisbury close. But there would be over fifty vicars choral; about twenty-three chantry priests or cantarists, some of whom would also be vicars choral; at least eight 'altarists' or clerks of the second form; and fourteen choristers. At cathedrals such as St. Paul's which had many more chantry foundations than Salisbury, the numerical preponderance of *ministri inferiores* in relation to residentiary canons was even greater. The story of daily life in the fourteenth-century close is largely the story of the doings of the lesser clergy. They formed in effect the working staff of the cathedral, and the maintenance of the *opus dei* fell mainly on them.

It was in the government of certain groups of these lesser clergy, particularly the vicars and chantry chaplains, that some of the most interesting constitutional experiments were made at the secular cathedrals in the later middle ages. The main lines of the chapters' government had generally been laid down by the late twelfth or early thirteenth centuries; the work of the later thirteenth, fourteenth, and fifteenth centuries added little more than elaboration and definition to the earlier structure. But the vicars only gradually asserted their right to security of tenure, while their demands for some measure of corporate independence only developed fully in the late thirteenth, fourteenth, and fifteenth centuries. A result of the success of these demands, enforced largely through their numerical superiority, was an important modification in the general structure of the cathedral constitutions. In place of the more or less united body of cathedral clergy of earlier times, under the control of the bishop or dean and canons, there now came to be a varying number of minor self-governing corporations of vicars choral or cantarists in addition to the wealthy controlling corporation of the chapter. Interests in the close became more varied and complex. It is especially interesting to find among some of the lesser cathedral clergy a partial revival of the common life, long since abandoned by the canons. Unlike the canons, all lesser *ministri* were bound to continual residence at the cathedral; in the later middle ages the vicars and cantarists frequently came to have common halls of residence; here they usually had separate chambers or houses ranged in a close or round a quadrangle,[1] with a common hall, and in some cases a chapel. Their life in these colleges was in many respects similar to that of university colleges at Oxford and Cambridge or the many independent colleges of chantry priests founded about the same time. The boy choristers were also usually put to live a fairly strict common life in a common hall in the close under the supervision of a master, instead of lodging, as the vicars also had often done in early times, either in the city or with any canon who would take them.

1. THE VICARS CHORAL AND MINOR CANONS

The most important group of *ministri inferiores* at the English secular cathedrals in the middle ages was the vicars choral. They bore 'the heat and burden of the day' at the canonical hours and other cathedral services. Also, they usually had a longer history behind them and belonged more definitely to the cathedral foundation than the chantry priests who formed the second large group of lesser clergy. Therefore those vicars who were priests were normally given precedence of cantarists in the cathedral choir. At Exeter, the whole body of vicars took precedence of the cantarists.[2] At Salisbury and Wells all priests sat together in the upper row of the choir, where the priest vicars had precedence next after the canons.[3] Only at St. Paul's chantry chaplains were said to be superior to vicars choral in dignity, and were given greater honour in habit, rank, station, and processions.[4] But here

---

[1] For the architectural evidence see W. A. Pantin, *Medieval Archaeology*, iii (1959), 247-9.

[2] *Ordinale Exon.*, i, 2.   [3] *Use Sarum*, i, 13; *W.S.*, p. 1.

[4] *R.S.S.P.*, pp. 138-40.

PLATE VI

THE VICARS' CLOSE, CHICHESTER CATHEDRAL, c. 1780-91

PLATE VII

SINGERS, c. 1348–68

the position was exceptional because none of the vicars were priests. The minor canons, who performed the priestly duties allotted to vicars choral in other English secular cathedrals, had undisputed right to rank above the cantarists. In the later middle ages priest vicars frequently held chantries in addition to their vicarages, as a means of augmenting their income; but in England they always preserved their separate identity, and the terms 'vicar' and 'chaplain' or 'cantarist' did not become synonymous, as often happened in Germany.[1]

The practice adopted at nearly all the English secular cathedrals in the course of the twelfth and thirteenth centuries was for each canon to nominate and partly to support his own vicar; thus there came to be the same number of vicars at the cathedral as there were canons. At first each vicar was supposed to be ordained to the order of priest, deacon, or subdeacon required by his canon's prebend. But in the later middle ages this distinction between the orders of vicars was seldom closely observed. A vicar in priest's orders could still minister when necessary in the orders of deacon and subdeacon. At Exeter, where all prebends were priest pre-bends, it was expressly laid down that the vicars should minister in the different holy orders.[2] Elsewhere, most vicars seem to have found it convenient to be ordained priests when they reached the canonical age of thirty, probably largely in order that they might be eligible for collation to a cathedral chantry in addition to their vicarage. Thus at most English cathedrals in the later middle ages there were a number of young vicars between the ages of twenty-two and thirty in deacon's and subdeacon's orders, while the majority of older men were priests. All vicars, however, con-tinued to be attituled to individual canons.

The chief exceptions to these arrangements were at St. Paul's and Hereford. St. Paul's, like other English secular cathedrals, had its body of thirty vicars choral, each nominated by one of the thirty major canons. But, unlike the vicars of other English secular cathedrals, all vicars at St. Paul's were supposed to be deacons or subdeacons, and the functions usually performed by the priest vicars belonged at St. Paul's to a separate body of twelve minor canons, whose status and commons were higher than those of the vicars, and who were in no way dependent on the individual canons. At Hereford, although the cathedral came in time to have

[1] Cf. Hinschius, ii, 78.   [2] Harl. MS. 1027, f. 8b; cf. 10b.

s

about the same number of vicars as canons, most of these vicars, instead of being nominated by the individual canons, were appointed and paid by the dean and chapter jointly from special endowment funds. Furthermore, the six senior vicars, who received higher stipends than the others, were sometimes given the title of 'petty canons'. Apart from its use at Hereford and St. Paul's, this term 'minor' or 'petty' canon seems never to have been used at English secular cathedrals until after the Reformation. Then, in the cathedrals of the New Foundation, set up by Henry VIII in place of the dissolved monastic cathedrals, there were minor or petty canons, whose duties corresponded roughly to those of the vicars choral in the cathedrals of the Old Foundation. Like the minor canons of St. Paul's and Hereford, these new minor canons were subordinate directly to the dean and chapter, and had no separate relations with individual major canons. But their numbers were small and their position markedly inferior to that of the vicars choral of the later middle ages, certainly to that of the medieval minor canons, who in England were superior in rank to the vicars. They did not form a corporation; their common table gave them a certain amount of common life and allowed them a restricted common finance; but any surplus from their common fund was appropriated by the dean and chapter.[1]

The slight evidence available for illustrating the organization of the lesser clergy in medieval cathedrals of northern France suggests that the custom of having vicars choral appointed by individual canons was by no means universal there. There was apparently considerable variety in the titles, methods of appointment, endowments, and size of the various groups of *ministri inferiores*. Small bodies of minor canons, roughly similar to those at Hereford or St. Paul's, are found at Rouen.[2] There were also clerks in the service of individual canons, and large numbers of chantry chaplains, who performed duties fulfilled in England by vicars choral.[3] But at certain of the larger secular chapters in France the group of *ministri* primarily concerned with the main-

---

[1] Cf. Frere, *Visitation Articles*, i, 131–2.

[2] These were the four petty canons 'of fifteen marks' and another four 'of fifteen pounds', founded towards the end of the twelfth century by John, afterwards king of England, and by Richard I of England (Pommeraye, *op. cit.*, p. 293; *Gallia Christiana*, xi, 3).

[3] Cf. *ibid.*; Pommeraye, *op. cit.*, pp. 293–4; Deslandes, *op. cit.*, pp. 268 *et seq.*

tenance of the cathedral services was much smaller than the full chapter of major canons. Chartres cathedral, with a chapter of seventy-seven canons in the fourteenth century, had only twenty-four such *ministri*, described not as vicars, but by the appropriate title of '*heuriers*' and '*matiniers*';[1] their appointment belonged to the dean and chapter jointly. Bayeux, with fifty canons, had in the thirteenth century four or six '*hauts-vicaires*' who were priests, and six '*petits vicaires*', two of whom were deacons, two sub-deacons, and two '*archi-choristes*'.[2] In addition, chaplains and clerks in the service of individual canons were admitted to sing in choir. But it was not until 1377 that a further college of twelve '*heuriers*', charged especially with the maintenance of the song and psalmody, was finally instituted.[3] Appointments to this college were made for a year at a time, but were renewed annually by the general chapter of canons if the *heurier's* service had been satisfactory. All *heuriers* had to be priests; they sat in the second row of the choir stalls and walked in procession with the *petits vicaires*.[4]

The institution of bodies of vicars choral at English cathedrals could therefore have owed little or nothing to particular arrangements in force at Bayeux or Rouen. Indeed, few cathedrals in northern France seem to have had a developed organization of *ministri inferiores* as early as the late eleventh or early twelfth centuries, when the English chapters were being constituted on a secular basis.

There had, naturally, been clerks of all ranks in the early bishops' *familiae*; groups of subdeacons and younger clerks, attached to the *scholae cantorum* of the sixth and seventh centuries, were specially charged with the maintenance of the cathedral song and psalmody;[5] St. Chrodegang's rule mentioned cantors who sang the divine office at the cathedral.[6] But no definite line of descent can be traced from these lesser cathedral clerks of early times to the vicars choral, minor canons, *heuriers*, *matiniers*, and other groups of *ministri inferiores* of medieval secular cathedrals. Hinschius suggests that after the division, in the eleventh or early

---

[1] Amiet, *op. cit.*, pp. 135–7. [2] Deslandes, *op. cit.*, pp. 293–308.
[3] *Ibid.*, pp. 307–17. [4] *Ibid.*
[5] Cf. Leclercq in *Dict. d'archéologie chrétienne et de liturgie*, *s.v.* Chantres, c. 360 *et seq.*; P. Bayart, in *Dict. de droit canonique*, *s.v.* 'Chant,' cc. 501 *et seq.*; 'Chantres,' cc. 511 *et seq.*; Deslandes, *op. cit.*, pp. 254–5.
[6] *Enlarged Rule of Chrodegang*, cc. 48–9.

twelfth centuries, of much of the chapter's income into separate prebends, there were for some time insufficient funds left to maintain an adequate body of lesser clergy.[1] At the same time, in spite of successive attempts to cut down the liturgy and confine it to essentials, both the services and chant were steadily becoming more elaborate. An increasing number of prayers, psalms, masses, and other services were added to the cathedral uses; more saints' days were being observed, and more parts of the liturgy were being sung.[2] Had all the canons been present in person at the cathedrals they would doubtless have been sufficient in numbers to perform the additional services, but they would probably not have had the necessary musical qualifications. No special musical training or ability was required from a secular canon. The need for a body of trained singers would in any case soon have become apparent. As it was, the non-residence of many canons on their prebends, or in the service of king, pope, or bishop, emphasized this need, and many historians have therefore assumed that canonical non-residence was the chief or only cause of the appointment of vicars choral. It is supposed that vicars choral were first provided as deputies by non-resident canons to sing in their places in the cathedral choir.

In England the view that the institution of vicars choral was the direct result of canonical non-residence has rarely been questioned. The title 'vicar' used at English secular cathedrals suggested that its holders were deputies, doing for the canons work which they were unable or unwilling to do for themselves; this impression was strengthened by the fact that throughout the middle ages English vicars were normally nominated by individual canons. Thus the existence of vicars choral has often been looked upon as an abuse. Stephens wrote that the maxim 'qui facit per alium facit per se', which pervaded the feudal world, was applied to ecclesiastical affairs, and so vicars were appointed to do the canons'

[1] Hinschius, ii, 77.
[2] For the general development of the liturgy and chant at this time, see H. Leclercq, in *Dict. d'archéologie chrétienne et de liturgie*, *s.v.* Liturgies Néo Gallicanes, G. Reese, *Music in the Middle Ages*; F. L. Harrison, *Music in Medieval Britain*. A useful outline of their development in English Benedictine monasteries is given by Dom David Knowles, *Monastic Order in England*, pp. 539–59. The celebration of the office in the English Benedictine monasteries and secular cathedrals was in most respects roughly similar.

work at the cathedrals when the canons were absent.[1] He quoted Richard of Devizes, chronicler of the late twelfth century, as saying that, while the monks in cathedral churches praised God with their own lips, the secular canons were absent as often as they pleased, and praised Him only through the mouths of their vicars.[2] He concluded that 'the preponderance of vicars in many cathedrals was so great as to be considered a scandal, even in those days, when men were well accustomed to every form of plurality and of non-residence in civil as well as ecclesiastical departments.[3] E. W. Watson has expressed a similar view, writing that, 'Originally the members [of the chapter] had performed every function, but, when they came to regard their office as a sinecure, inferior officers were introduced, to sing the services and to serve as choir-men, who were not members of the corporation.'[4]

Certain other English historians, including E. A. Freeman, W. H. Frere, and Professor Hamilton Thompson, have accepted this explanation of the institution of vicars choral only with important modifications. They agree that the original need for vicars arose from the absenteeism of the canons, and that vicars were probably first appointed by the non-resident canons. But they do not look upon the presence of vicars in the cathedrals as necessarily a scandal, and draw an important distinction between their position and functions in the early and later middle ages; by the later middle ages the vicars had become an established and necessary group of cathedral clergy, performing regular functions in choir under the direction of a small body of residentiary canons.[5] E. W. Benson and W. W. Capes have gone much further than this. They state that the institution of vicars choral was not an afterthought, resulting from the canons' neglect of their proper work; the vicars were not the canons' deputies, since only a canon could relieve a canon of his duties in choir and chapter; rather they were an integral part of the original cathedral foundation, having

---

[1] *Memorials of the See and Cathedral Church of Chichester*, p. 320.

[2] *Cronicon Richardi Divisensis* (1963), pp. 70–1. Richard of Devizes, himself a monk of Winchester, was attacking the expulsion of the monks from the church of Coventry by Hugh, bishop of Chester, who had put secular canons in their place.

[3] *Memorials Chichester*, p. 322.   [4] *C.M.H.*, vi, 549.

[5] Cf. Freeman, *Hist. Wells Cathedral*, pp. 88, 137–8; 'Cathedral Churches of the Old Foundation', in *Essays on Cathedrals*, pp. 157–8; Frere, *Use Sarum*, i, xvii; A. H. Thompson, *Cathedral Churches*, pp. 183–7.

separate and necessary functions in choir and chapter from the very beginning of every secular cathedral of the Old Foundation.[1]

The weakness of most of these views is that they are usually based on a study of the situation at only a few of the English secular cathedrals in the twelfth century; the evidence from these cathedrals is then used to represent the position at all other cathedrals of the Old Foundation, where vicars were sometimes appointed for different reasons or in different ways. Furthermore, the actual duties which the vicars had to perform are rarely discussed. It is here proposed to examine some of the different ways in which vicars choral came to be instituted at English cathedrals, and to trace briefly the gradual development of their functions and organizations.

The Institution and Functions of Vicars Choral in English Secular Cathedrals

The exceptional arrangements at Hereford cathedral were the result of late development, which in some ways had more similarities with contemporary arrangements in cathedrals of northern France, such as Bayeux, than with the institution of vicars at other English secular cathedrals. According to the mid-thirteenth century customs of the chapter, only the two abbots of Lyre and Cormeilles, who held cathedral prebends, were then bound to appoint four perpetual vicars, and the dean one.[2] There is a suggestion that other canons may have employed temporary vicars for their own convenience, but these had no recognized portion or status in the church.[3] In addition, four perpetual priest vicars were attached to four different altars in the church, and six more, two of them priests, two deacons, and two subdeacons, were vicars, not of individual canons, but of the church.[4] These six had only

---

[1] Benson, *The Cathedral*, p. 36; 'The Relation of the Chapter to the Bishop', in *Essays on Cathedrals*, p. 242; Capes, *The English Church in the Fourteenth and Fifteenth Centuries*, pp. 244, 249–50.

[2] *L.S.*, ii, 60, 62, 72–4. In addition, the precentor appointed a succentor, the treasurer a subtreasurer, and the chancellor a Regent Master in Arts, all of whom had to be present at the canonical hours with the vicars (*ibid.*, pp. 63, 69, 71).

[3] *L.S.*, ii, 81, where 'those who received no certain portion in the church', such as the vicars of individual canons, were said to be punished less severely for their faults than the perpetual vicars.

[4] *Ibid.*, pp. 74–5.

been instituted in 1237. Bishop Maidstone, their founder, secured the appropriation of the tithes of Diddlebury church for their support, and laid down that they should be appointed by the dean and chapter with the bishop's consent.[1] In 1330 a further ten perpetual vicars (eight priests, one deacon, and one subdeacon) were provided through the generosity of Thomas de Chaundos, archdeacon of Hereford, who obtained the appropriation of the tithes of Lugwardine and its dependent chapels for his purpose. After Thomas's death these additional vicars also were to be appointed by the dean and chapter jointly. The object of the foundation was said to be the increase of the number of clerks serving the *opus dei* in the cathedral, particularly the daily mass of the Blessed Virgin Mary, which 'was so meagrely endowed that it was no better celebrated than in a parish church'. The warden of the Lady Chapel, a residentiary canon, was chosen to administer the funds from Lugwardine; he paid the salaries of the ten vicars, and distributed a further hundred shillings annually among the other vicars, priests or clerks attached to the cathedral, whose ancient portions were diminished by having to share their distributions with the ten additional vicars.[2] There were apparently no more foundations. In 1395, when the vicars of Hereford were incorporated as a college, they were said to be twenty-seven,[3] that is, practically the same number as the canons; while in 1411, when Bishop Mascall levelled up the incomes of the seven poorest vicarages and granted additional endowments to all the vicars from the tithes of Westbury, they were twenty-five.[4] The returns made for the *Valor Ecclesiasticus* in 1535 estimated the annual income of the twenty vicars then present at the cathedral as 4 li. 8s. 8¾d. each from their common revenues; fourteen of these vicars held cathedral chantries in addition to their vicarages; the remaining six were described as petty canons, and received an extra 3 li. or 3 li. 10s. a year each from the dean and chapter.[5]

At St. Paul's and Exeter the institution of the full number of minor canons and vicars choral took place earlier than at Hereford. It has even been maintained that they existed from the foundation of the cathedrals as chapters of secular canons. At Exeter the

[1] *Hereford Charters*, pp. 74–5; cf. pp. 123–4.
[2] *Ibid.*, pp. 210–15; *Reg. Thomas de Charlton*, pp. 34–40.
[3] *Hereford Charters*, p. 253.   [4] *Reg. Mascall*, p. 79.
[5] *Valor Eccl.*, iii, 12–15.

authority for this assertion is a statute of 1268 of Bishop Brones-combe and his chapter, who declared that they knew both from ancient tradition and from their own experience that from the foundation of their church there had been and were bound to be twenty-four canons and twenty-four vicars, each vicar being attituled to a canon.[1] At St. Paul's an undated award, probably of the late thirteenth or early fourteenth century, while pointing out that chantry chaplains were an innovation, declared that the original foundation of the church had consisted of thirty major canons, twelve minor canons, and thirty vicars.[2] At neither of these churches is there any other known evidence for the existence of permanent bodies of vicars or minor canons in the late eleventh or early twelfth centuries. The available cathedral records for this period are very meagre, and consist mainly of charters, which, in any case, were rarely witnessed by lesser cathedral clergy; therefore the absence of evidence cannot be taken as proof that such bodies were not present at the cathedrals. But, if taken literally, the statements both at Exeter and St. Paul's would presumably refer to periods when the chapters were following rules for a common life. The foundation of Exeter cathedral was in 1050; the copy of the enlarged rule of Chrodegang which Bishop Leofric then gave to the canons, contained no mention of vicars choral by that name, nor did it specify the number of canons.[3] Possibly it might be said that Bishop Bronescombe was referring, not to the first foundation of the chapter at Exeter, but to the consecration of the new Norman cathedral in 1133. This was about the time when a secular organization was being gradually introduced, and the chapter

[1] Harl. MS. 1027, ff. 8a–b. 'Sicuti antiquorum tradicione accepimus et nos ipsi experimento novimus, a tempore fundacionis ecclesie Exon' certo viz xxiv canonicorum numero ecclesia ipsa floruit. . . . Item a tempore fundacionis predicte fuerunt et esse tenentur in ipsa ecclesia xxiv vicarii singuli singulis canonicis attitulati.'

[2] *R.S.S.P.*, p. 139. 'Primitiva Ecclesie London fundacio consistit in xxx Canonicis Majoribus, xii Canonicis Minoribus, et xxx Vicariis. . . .' The bull of Urban VI of 1378, confirming the privileges of the minor canons, was more cautious. It merely said that for 'a long time past' (*a longis retroactis temporibus*) there had been three grades of persons at the cathedral, namely, major canons, minor canons, and perpetual vicars; but the grant of 1376 of Bishop Sudbury, which it quoted, used the phrase 'a tempore fundacionis ipsius Ecclesie' for the time at which these three grades of clergy had been instituted (*ibid.*, pp. 324–5).

[3] See the edition by A. S. Napier.

then seems to have had about twenty-four canons.[1] It is not until 1159–60 that we have evidence for *ministri inferiores* at the cathedral who may have been fulfilling duties in choir similar to those later assigned to vicars choral. On 1 March 1159–60 thirteen 'clerks of the choir' witnessed a charter of the canons of Exeter granting burial land to the nuns of Polslo.[2] In the time of Bishop Henry Marshall (1194–1206), vicars choral were clearly an established institution. They were then attituled to individual canons, and, in addition to their stipends, shared the revenues of the church of Woodbury granted to them by Bishop Henry.[3]

The situation at St. Paul's in the late eleventh and twelfth centuries is equally puzzling and obscure. It is obvious that the statement quoted could have had no significance for the original foundation of the cathedral in the seventh century. But Miss Gibbs has written that it probably throws light on the customs of Bishop Maurice's episcopate (1086–1107), when the beginnings of a secular organization and of separate prebends for the canons are found. She also suggests that, before possible regulations of Bishop Maurice for various grades of cathedral clergy, the status of the minor canons was junior rather than inferior to that of the major canons.[4] There certainly seems to have been more continuity at St. Paul's than at most English chapters between the Anglo-Saxon customs of the cathedral and those of Norman times. Possibly the minor canons, who were an exceptional body at any rate in English secular cathedrals, may have been in a direct line of descent from junior clerks at the cathedral in the eleventh century; throughout the middle ages they received their prebends from the common revenues of the church, not from special endowment funds, like the vicars of Hereford, or partly in the form of stipends from individual canons, like the vicars of other English cathedrals, including St. Paul's. Yet, in the absence of any evidence for the existence of either minor canons or vicars choral in the eleventh or first half of the twelfth centuries, it is impossible to accept these suggestions as proved. The first known mention of

---

[1] See Mrs. Rose Troup's article, *The Consecration of the Norman Minster at Exeter*, pp. 22–9, in which she has collected evidence for at least twenty-one canons of Exeter in 1133. She suggests that three more canons may recently have died.

[2] *H.M.C. Var. Coll.*, iv, 49.   [3] Harl, MS. 1027, ff. 4b–5a, 8b.

[4] *Early Charters of St. Paul*, pp. xxvi–viii.

minor canons in the records is a reference in 1162 to the 'prebendary clerks of the choir'.[1] The form of the statements made both at
St. Paul's and Exeter, more than two centuries after the events to
which they are supposed to refer, does not suggest that either of
them were based on historical evidence which has since disappeared. Rather it gives the impression that their authors were
speaking in a general way of traditions current in their own times.
Bishop Bronescombe, in stating that there had always been
twenty-four canons and twenty-four vicars at his cathedral, may
only have referred to the period of his own knowledge. At St.
Paul's the thirteenth- or fourteenth-century award was granted in
answer to a petition of the vicars choral who were trying to prove
their antiquity, in order that they might claim precedence of the
chantry chaplains in the cathedral choir; there is no evidence that
the historical information quoted by the vicars was accurate.

But, whatever the situation with regard to vicars and minor
canons at St. Paul's in the twelfth century, it is clear that by the
end of the thirteenth century both groups were fully established,
and their numbers apparently complete. The statutes of Dean
Ralph Baldock (1294–1305), like the earlier statutes of Bishop
Henry Marshall at Exeter show that residentiary as well as non-
resident canons were expected to have their own vicars.[2] Thus at
neither church did the existence of vicars necessarily imply that
their canons were non-resident. The position of the minor canons
of St. Paul's was altogether different. They were not attituled to
individual canons, but were subject directly to the dean and
chapter. From their later statutes, drawn up in 1396, it appears
that they customarily recruited their own members. When a
vacancy occurred in their ranks, they nominated two priests to the
dean, who might choose one for collation to a minor prebend.[3]
Their prebends consisted of weekly distributions of money,
bread, and ale from the cathedral's common fund. These were
supplemented by various pittances, such as oblations from funeral
services, or extra distributions on feast days or at obits, and by the
income from endowments which the minor canons came in time
to hold in common.[4] The three most important minor canons,

[1] *H.M.C. Ninth Rept.*, App., i, 12.
[2] *R.S.S.P.*, pp. 125–33. These statutes also include orders concerning the
minor canons.
[3] *R.S.S.P.*, pp. 330–3; cf. p. 325.   [4] *Ibid.*, pp. 325–6.

elected by their fellows to the offices of senior and junior cardinals of the choir, and of subdean, received double commons.[1] All took an oath of obedience and fidelity to the dean and chapter, and were bound to serve daily at the canonical hours with the vicars choral.[2]

At other English cathedrals there is often considerable doubt as to when vicars choral were first instituted. They are mentioned at Salisbury in St. Osmund's Institution, in the passage describing the dean's office; the dean was said to have authority over both canons and vicars in the rule of souls and correction of behaviour.[3] It has already been suggested that the earliest surviving copies show signs of having been brought up to date at a time later than 1091. Moreover, no indication of the number of vicars is given in the Institution. But the name of the first known vicar choral has been found about 1122, and in the last quarter of the twelfth century Richard le Poore's explanation of the Institution implied that every canon of Salisbury, resident or non-resident, had his vicar;[4] in 1214 it was laid down that vicars at Salisbury should receive commons all the year round, whether their canons were present or absent.[5] Indeed, there is no suggestion at Salisbury that vicars were first appointed only by non-resident canons. On the contrary, an undated letter, written probably in the mid-thirteenth century, from the convent of Salisbury to R., Bishop of Bath, declared, in answer to enquiries from the chapter of Wells, that 'all canons indifferently ought to have a vicar, except those at the schools, or travelling to Rome for the good of the church'.[6] Salisbury chapter, therefore, was apparently willing at this time to exempt certain of its non-resident canons from the necessity of providing a vicar, while it enforced the obligation strictly on its residentiaries.

At Lichfield and Chichester, the first known evidence for vicars choral comes from the last quarter of the twelfth century; here, too, it is clear from cathedral statutes of the late twelfth or early thirteenth centuries that vicars were provided by resident as well

---

[1] *Ibid.*, pp. 75 n., 91, 94–5, 173 n.   [2] *Ibid.*, pp. 325, 334–5; cf. 66–9, 102–3.
[3] *S.S.*, pp. 28–9.
[4] *V.C.H., Wilts*, iii, 158; *Sarum Charters*, pp. 16–17; *S.S.*, p. 57.
[5] *Ibid.*, pp. 48–51.
[6] *H.M.C. Wells*, i, 31. No evidence has been found to suggest that this exemption continued at Salisbury in the later middle ages.

as by non-resident canons.[1] It is possible that vicars at Wells and York may have been appointed in the first instance by non-resident canons only, but the obligation certainly applied to all canons by the end of the thirteenth century. Bishop Jocelin at Wells (1206–42) is said to have ordained vicars choral to all the prebendaries except three;[2] at York in the mid-thirteenth century, both resident and non-resident canons apparently had vicars, and in 1291 the dean and chapter declared that every canon must have a vicar.[3] In fact, Lincoln was the only English medieval cathedral which placed the main burden of providing vicars choral on its non-resident canons. About 1186–1200, and again in 1203–6, the dean and chapter were empowered by the bishop to compel all non-residents to provide vicars.[4] Throughout the later middle ages the chapter continued to observe its early custom of requiring only non-resident canons to maintain vicars choral, while the residentiaries and six canons whose prebends yielded less than six marks a year were exempt from the duty.[5]

It has thus been seen that the full number of vicars choral had been instituted in all English secular cathedrals except Hereford by the end of the thirteenth century. By this time, also, it is clear that the appointment of a vicar did not necessarily imply that a canon was non-resident; normally all canons alike were bound to provide vicars. Yet may not some of these vicars, even when their masters were present in the close, have been acting in a sense as deputies, by performing canonical duties which the canons preferred to neglect? In order to test the truth of this suggestion, it is necessary to examine the vicar's function in more detail.

No vicar choral at any English secular cathedral could represent his master in one important sphere of a canon's duties, his attendance at chapter meetings and share in chapter business. In this, only another canon could act as proctor for an absent canon. The liturgical rules of the cathedrals show, however, that some of the canons' duties in the cathedral services could be performed by their vicars. A vicar could sometimes take his master's place as

---

[1] *L.S.*, ii, 26, 30; cf. *Monasticon*, VI, iii, 1260; *C.S.*, pp. 2, 6–7.

[2] Canon of Wells, 'Historia', in *Anglia Sacra*, i, 564.

[3] *L.S.*, ii, 93, 103, 118–19.   [4] *Reg. Antiquissimum*, i, 259–62.

[5] *L.S.*, ii, 144; iii, 165, 316. As late as the early fifteenth century there were complaints against Dean Macworth, who held a prebend in addition to the deanery, and did not provide a vicar choral when he was absent from the cathedral (*ibid.*, iii, 189; cf. 215).

rector chori, ruling the singing, or as deacon or subdeacon hebdo-madary, ministering at the altar; but the canon was expected to serve in person on important feast days.[1] Naturally, only vicars of residentiary canons could deputize for their masters in these ways, because non-resident canons were not entabled for such duties. No vicar was supposed to celebrate mass at the high altar unless no canon could be present,[2] although exceptions for this could be made, at St. Paul's in favour of the minor canons, at Hereford in favour of the dean's vicar, and at Lichfield for five priest vicars.[3] At York the canons of the neighbouring chapel of the Blessed Virgin and Holy Angels were asked to celebrate at the high altar in the cathedral if no cathedral canon could be present.[4]

It is, however, clear from cathedral ordinals, consuetudinaries, and statutes of the late twelfth century onwards, that in all English secular cathedrals the chief duty of the vicars choral was 'to sing the services for the increase of divine worship'. In this they were subject to the direction, not of their individual masters, but of the chapter of residentiaries in general and to the precentor and his succentor in particular. They all had to undergo an examination in, or to have some knowledge of, singing and music before their first admission;[5] sometimes priests were rejected for not having a musical voice.[6] Then they had to serve for a year on probation, learning by heart the psalter, antiphonary, hymnary, and 'histories',[7] and could only be appointed perpetual vicars after a second examination.[8] They took oath to be present at the daily

[1] E.g. *L.S.*, ii, 73; *S.S.*, p. 68.   [2] *Ibid.*; *L.S.*, i, 293.
[3] *R.S.S.P.*, p. 49; *L.S.*, ii, 73; *Monasticon*, VI, iii, 1260, 1263.
[4] *L.S.*, ii, 102, and below, pp. 297–8.
[5] *S.S.*, pp. 90–1, 210–13; *L.S.*, ii, 29, 111–12, 145; iii, 347; *Monasticon*, VI, iii, 1262–3; Harl. MS. 1027, f. 22b. Senior vicars might sometimes help to examine a new vicar, e.g. *Jones, Fasti Sar.*, p. 272; *W.S.*, p. 81.
[6] *L.S.*, i, 353.
[7] I.e. the responses and verses which followed the lessons, taken on Sundays from the historical books of the Old Testament and on Saints Days from the stories or legends of Saints. Originally the 'histories' were the lessons or legends themselves, but the name had been transferred to the responses at the end.
[8] *S.S.*, pp. 74–7, 212–15; *Salisbury Ceremonies*, pp. 274–5; *W.S.*, pp. 58, 87; *L.S.*, ii, 29, 72, 80, 111–12, 145; iii, 347; *R.S.S.P.*, p. 68. In 1321, when it was decided that the canons of Wells might have their service books and lights by them at matins, this privilege was expressly forbidden to the vicars, lest they should become negligent in learning the office by heart (*H.M.C. Wells*, i, 181–2; *Reg. Drokensford*, p. 218).

and nightly hours, and lost their commons if they were absent for more than a certain number of services a day.[1] Salisbury chapter decreed in 1319 that there must always be at least thirteen vicars on each side of the choir at every service.[2] The chapter of York required twelve on each side.[3] Vicars were also entabled to serve as deacons and subdeacons at the high altar, and to read lessons at the services. In addition, they had important duties connected with the ever-increasing number of prayers, masses, and other services added to the cathedral uses in the course of the eleventh, twelfth, thirteenth, and fourteenth centuries. The celebration and singing of the chapter mass and the mass of the Blessed Virgin Mary usually belonged to them, and, when it became customary to celebrate daily not only the mass but also the hours of the Virgin, this duty fell chiefly on the vicars. With the chantry chaplains, they were responsible for saying the office of the dead and the seven penitential psalms, and for celebrating the many obit and funeral masses and services for benefactors of the cathedral.[4]

Thus, at any rate by the thirteenth century, vicars choral had their separate and necessary functions in the cathedrals, and only occasionally took the place of absent canons. Their essential importance was in singing and in providing staff to celebrate the increasing number of services subsidiary to the main office. Their position was roughly similar to that of the cantors at the cathedrals of the sixth to tenth centuries, who were specially trained in the *scholae cantorum* to be responsible for the maintenance of the cathedral song. Though it cannot be assumed that secular cathedrals had permanent bodies of choir clerks from their foundation, it is clear that such bodies were soon needed. Any delay in instituting them was probably due to financial reasons, while in England the method generally adopted to obtain them seems also to have been dictated by absence of the necessary resources. In the early twelfth century capitular common funds were much smaller

---

[1] *L.S.*, i, 398–9; ii, 29, 72, 80, 109–10, 147–8; *S.S.*, pp. 216–17; *C.S.*, p. 21; *Ordinale Exon.*, i, 6–7; Harl. MS. 1027, ff. 8b, 10a–10b; *W.S.*, pp. 59–60; *H.M.C. Wells*, i, 60; *Monasticon*, VI, iii, 1260.

[2] *S.S.*, pp. 220–1.   [3] *York Fabric Rolls*, p. 252.

[4] Cf. *S.S.*, pp. 250–5; *Salisbury Ceremonies*, p. 158; *Reg. Shrewsbury*, pp. 354–355; *M.R.A.*, p. 114; *Hereford Charters*, pp. 210–15; *Reg. Thomas de Charlton*, pp. 34–40; *L.S.*, i, 294; ii, 148–9; iii, 350. At St. Paul's many of these duties were allotted to the minor canons (*R.S.S.P.*, pp. 48, 66–9, 102–3).

than they became later. Alone they would have been inadequate to pay the salaries of a large permanent body of *ministri inferiores*. Hence the cost of maintaining additional choral staff had to be met, at least in part, from the income of the separate prebends. At most English cathedrals every canon, resident or non-resident, was ordered to appoint and partly to maintain a vicar choral. Sometimes it may have been agreed that only the non-residents need support this burden in the first instance, because they contributed less to the cathedral services than the residentiaries, and had fewer expenses in maintaining a canonical house of residence and in dispensing hospitality. At the large chapter of Lincoln, where, in the fourteenth century, the non-residents and minor residentiaries between them provided a body of from thirty to thirty-five vicars, it was never found necessary to extend the obligation to the greater residentiaries. But at Hereford both the common fund and the prebends were exceptionally poor. Here perpetual vicars were instituted later than in most English cathedrals, and the cost of their salaries was in most cases provided by special endowment funds administered by the dean and chapter. Therefore the vicars of Hereford, like the choir clerks of some cathedrals in northern France, were not attituled to individual canons.

THE RELATIONS OF THE VICARS CHORAL WITH THEIR INDIVIDUAL MASTERS AND WITH THE CHAPTER OF RESIDENTIARY CANONS

Some of the most interesting changes in the position of vicars choral at English medieval cathedrals took place in the sphere of their relations with the individual canons, their masters, and with the chapter of residentiaries. Already from the late twelfth or early thirteenth centuries it is clear that their duties in choir were performed under the direction of the precentor and were for the most part unconnected with any special services to individual canons. Yet at the same time, at most cathedrals, the vicars had ties of a personal nature with the particular canons who paid part of their stipends. These ties gradually became weaker in the later middle ages as the small chapter of residentiaries extended its control, and as the vicars formed themselves into autonomous corporations. It will be interesting to notice here some aspects of the vicars' relations with their different masters.

Both the individual canon and the dean and chapter continued throughout the middle ages to share in the appointment of a vicar. The canon retained his right of presenting whom he pleased as his vicar to the dean and chapter, so long as his presentee was ordained to the holy order required by his prebend. The presentee had to be examined in morals by the dean and in singing and music by the precentor or succentor. If found satisfactory he was solemnly admitted by the chapter to be a vicar of the church for one year on probation, and afterwards in perpetuity. He swore an oath of obedience and fidelity to the dean or dean and chapter and to the cathedral church, promising also to be faithful to the canon, his lord, and to observe those statutes which concerned him and his vicarage.[1] After this no canon might remove his vicar without just cause and the knowledge of the dean and chapter. If a vicarage fell vacant when the canon was abroad, or if the canon for some other reason did not present a new vicar for several months, the dean or president of the chapter was supposed to present in his place; if the dean also failed to present, the duty devolved upon the bishop. Throughout the fourteenth century the statutory number of vicars choral was apparently maintained in most English cathedrals.[2] But in the following century the system seems to have been breaking down. Visitation injunctions complained that the full number of vicars was not present at the cathedrals; the answers were that suitable men could not be found for the work, or that funds were insufficient to support them.[3] At Exeter Bishop Stafford appointed as many as fourteen vicars choral by lapse to his cathedral between 1401 and 1419.[4] In the sixteenth century the breakdown was acknowledged. Lay singing

---

[1] For the rules of the vicars' appointment and their oaths, see *S.S.*, pp. 74–7, 212–15; *Salisbury Ceremonies*, pp. 114–15, 274–5; *L.S.*, i, 398–9; ii, 28–9, 111–12, 145; iii, 347; *R.S.S.P.*, pp. 18–19.

[2] At Exeter cathedral the full number of vicars choral appeared at Bishop Grandisson's visitation in 1337; twenty-one were named at a chapter meeting in 1382, and nineteen were present in 1384 at Archbishop Courtenay's visitation (*Reg. Grandisson*, ii, 857; *Use Exeter*, p. 1; *Reg. Brantyngham*, i, 516). Twenty-eight out of a possible thirty-one vicars were named at Bishop Rede's visitation of Chichester cathedral in 1397 (*Red. Rede*, i, 104–6); fifty-one out of a possible fifty-two or fifty-three were cited to Archbishop Courtenay's visitation of Salisbury cathedral in 1390 (Jones, *Fasti Sar.*, p. 203). Naturally a few vicarages would usually be vacant through death or resignation.

[3] E.g. *Salisbury Ceremonies*, p. 157. Only thirty-one vicars were present at Salisbury in 1468 (*S.S.*, p. 120).

[4] *Reg. Stafford*, p. 169.

men were generally substituted for some of the vicars; the remaining vicars in holy orders were limited to four, six, or seven, one vicar being attituled to seven or eight canons, who shared the cost of his stipend.[1]

In the fourteenth century, however, each canon still normally shared the burden of maintaining his vicar with the chapter only. The chapter provided daily or weekly allowances of money and/or food from its common fund; generally this amounted to about one penny, twopence, or threepence a day, with increased allowances on feast days; while the canon either paid his vicar a fixed termly stipend,[2] or, if he were a residentiary and preferred to do so, he might have his vicar to live in his canonical house and feed him at his table.[3] The canons had to take an oath to pay their vicars' stipends within a definite period after the end of each term, and their prebends might be sequestrated if they neglected to pay.[4] In some churches, such as Lincoln and Exeter, every canon had to allow the same stipend of forty or twenty shillings a year to his vicar, so that all the vicarages were equal in value.[5] But at Salisbury and Wells the stipends were fixed in proportion to the incomes of the prebends;[6] they might vary from twenty to sixty shillings a year, and so the vicars of these churches might compete for promotion to a more lucrative stall.

[1] Cf. Jones, *Fasti Sar.*, pp. 203–4; *V.C.H., Wilts.*, iii, 184; F. Harrison, 'The Bedern College and Chapel', in *Proc. Y.A.A.S.* (1936), pp. 38, 43; W. D. Peckham, 'The Vicars Choral of Chichester Cathedral', in *Sussex Arch. Coll.*, lxxviii, 137–40; *W.S.*, p. clxxvii.

[2] For details of the vicars' commons and stipends at different churches, see *S.S.*, pp. 48–51; *W.S.*, pp. 60, 68, 88–9, 97–9; *Use Exeter*, p. 80; Harl. MS. 1027, f. 8b; *C.S.*, pp. 2, 6–7; Peckham, *loc. cit.*, pp. 128–32; *L.S.*, ii, 30, 108–9, 111, 119, 145–7; iii, 165, 316; *Monasticon*, VI, iii, 1260, 1263; *R.S.S.P.*, p. 186.

[3] E.g. *W.S.*, p. 76; *L.S.*, iii, 166.

[4] *Salisbury Ceremonies*, pp. 111–12; *W.S.*, p. 68; *C.S.*, p. 18; 'Muniments of Lichfield', *Coll. Hist. Staffs.*, II, vi, 62; *Lincoln Visitations*, i, 143.

[5] *L.S.*, ii, 146; iii, 165, 316, 348; *Use Exeter*, p. 80. At Exeter, where the canons' prebends were administered in common, the vicars were paid four quarterly instalments of five shillings direct from the cathedral exchequer, at the same time as the canons received the payments from their prebends. The stipends of the vicars of Lincoln were forty shillings a year payable by the canons.

[6] See the taxation of the vicarages in *W.S.*, pp. 97–9; *Valor Eccl.*, ii, 73–7. At Lichfield each canon had to pay his vicar at least twenty shillings a year, unless the vicar were a priest; in this case the vicar was supposed to have a larger stipend to be arranged between them (*L.S.*, ii, 30).

T

In the twelfth and thirteenth centuries, when more canons kept houses of residence in the close than was customary later, many vicars apparently lived in their masters' houses. At Chichester in 1232 master and vicar were expected to share the daily distribution of bread,[1] and an early statute of York cathedral refers to vicars receiving their late masters' choir habits by ancient custom,[2] which suggests that in some ways the vicars may have acted as the canons' body servants. But later, when common halls of residence were built, probably in the first instance chiefly for the vicars of absent canons, these personal relationships were necessarily weakened. Cathedral statutes laid down that vicars must not expect their masters to give them clothing as a right, nor take possession of their master's personal belongings on his death; they might only accept those possessions which were expressly left to them in the canon's will or offered to them by his executors.[3] Further decrees regulated the entertainment of vicars at the canons' tables. New residentiaries at London, York, and Chichester were supposed to feed their own vicar daily, with the vicars of some non-resident canons; but a full residentiary could use his discretion about inviting vicars of absent canons to his table, provided that he only invited them through his own vicar at matins.[4] If a vicar were in disgrace with the chapter, he might be forbidden by it to eat at any canon's table.[5] Towards the end of the fourteenth century a group of vicars of Exeter cathedral agreed to accept a decision that no vicar of a residentiary canon should expect to be invited to dinner at his master's table by right, but only by grace.[6]

Nevertheless, most residentiary canons at Salisbury seem to have had their vicars living with them in the fourteenth century, and sometimes employed them as personal servants. As late as 1319 Bishop Martival forbade the canons to set their vicars to secular services or bailiff's offices either within or outside their houses, or to order them to do the catering for their households.[7] At the same

---

[1] *C.S.*, pp. 6–7.   [2] *L.S.*, ii, 103.   [3] *L.S.*, ii, 113; *S.S.*, pp. 150–1.

[4] *R.S.S.P.*, p. 129; *S.S.*, pp. 236–7, 242–3; *L.S.*, ii, 103; *C.S.*, p. 17; cf. *Use Exeter*, p. 9. For the hospitality duties of dignitaries and residentiaries, see above, pp. 59 *et seq.* On certain great feasts the dean or other dignitaries would feed the whole choir.

[5] E.g. *S.S.*, pp. 244–7.

[6] *Use Exeter*, p. 13. The dean's vicar accepted this decision publicly in the presence and with the consent of nine other vicars.

[7] *S.S.*, pp. 218–19.

time it was decreed that if a vicar continued to occupy his master's house after his master's death or resignation, he must not make it unsuitable for the next canon by dividing it up into lodgings or little chambers.[1] The obligation of vicars choral to forward to their absent masters any notices or citations attached to their choir stalls, continued throughout the middle ages;[2] it annoyed one vicar at Salisbury so much that, about 1288–97, when he was appointed to the office of subtreasurer, he used his opportunity of access to the chapter muniments to destroy the deed requiring vicars to perform this duty.[3] The spirit of rivalry in personal service to their lords was evidently still lively at Salisbury at the end of the fourteenth century. One Sunday morning in early February, 1394, when William Jakes, vicar, claimed that he was peacefully following his lord, Master Thomas de Southam, to the cathedral church, Thomas Penkyt, another vicar, came up to him and said, 'I am the vicar of Master Thomas de Southam, and it is my office, not yours, to follow him to church. If you follow him again, I will break your head.' The chapter's control over the vicars was however illustrated by the resulting judgement on William Jakes's injuries and Thomas Penkyt's punishment which was given by the dean in chapter, not by Master Thomas de Southam.[4]

Indeed, by the fourteenth century the discipline of the vicars seems to have been almost entirely in the hands of the dean and chapter, except for those domestic matters in which the vicars gradually came to discipline themselves through their own organizations. All the *ministri inferiores* were required to attend the weekly Saturday chapters at which faults or negligence in the cathedral services of the preceding week were corrected by the dean or president.[5] The moral offences of the vicars at York were dealt with by the dean and chapter's auditor in the court of their peculiar jurisdiction.[6] But at Salisbury delinquent vicars were summoned to answer most charges before special sessions of the

---

[1] *Ibid.*, pp. 176–7.

[2] *Ibid.*, pp. 168–71; *R.S.S.P.*, p. 14; *M.R.A.*, p. 274.

[3] *S.S.*, pp. 115, 168–71.

[4] The hearing of the case is recorded in the chapter act book, Reg. Dunham, f. 266.

[5] *R.S.S.P.*, pp. 19–20; Harl. MS. 1027, ff. 29a–29b; cf. *Reg. Grandisson*, ii, 858; *L.S.*, ii, 111, 149–50; iii, 333–4.

[6] Cf. J. S. Purvis, *A Medieval Act Book at York*, pp. 3 *et seq.*

chapter of residentiary canons. The hearing of many such cases is recorded in the Salisbury chapter act books; vicars were found guilty of frequenting taverns and theatricals; playing ball in the close; dining with laymen in the city; wearing a belt of marvellous size, a cape of many colours, or boots of red and green squares, unsuitable to clerks in holy orders; going off to Southampton for the day in a striped costume, carrying arms; defaming members of the chapter; entertaining strangers, especially women in their houses in the close.[1] The dean or president of the chapter, not their individual masters, were the only authorities from whom vicars could obtain permission to be absent for a few days from the cathedral; permission might be given for reasonable causes, such as attending their parents' funerals or for blood-letting, and the cathedral statutes usually laid down that absences should not be longer than from two to fifteen days.[2] But in the later middle ages there were cases of vicars choral being granted licences of absence for much longer periods, to go on pilgrimages or to study at universities.[3] In such cases the chapter usually promised that the vicar should receive back his vicarage on his return, provided that he had obtained no other benefice in the meantime.

Bishops and chapters expended much energy, generally without success, in trying to enforce the rule that vicars choral should not hold other benefices outside the cathedral together with their vicarages.[4] Even an obligation to say mass daily in a neighbouring city church was thought to interfere with their duties in the cathedral. But no ban was placed against their appointment to many cathedral offices, such as clerk of the works, clerk of the common fund, sub-master of the choristers, master or usher of the grammar school, librarian, succentor, sub-treasurer, vice-chancellor;[5]

[1] These cases and others are recorded in *Hemingby's Reg.*, p. 151; Reg. Corffe, ff. 28, 33, 57, 60–1, 114–17, 136; Reg. Coman, ff. 10–11, 64–9; Reg. Dunham, ff. 4, 6, 13–14, 20–1, 35–6, 113–16, 127, 202, 259–62. Cf. *S.S.*, pp. 228–35.

[2] *S.S.*, pp. 220–1; *R.S.S.P.*, p. 133; *Monasticon*, VI, iii, 1257, 1260.

[3] E.g. Reg. Dunham, f. 130; *Reg. Greenfield*, i, 42; *H.M.C. Wells*, i, 208, 293, 298; cf. *Use Exeter*, p. 6.

[4] E.g. Reg. Corffe, ff. 28, 67, 114; Reg. Dunham, f. 262. The certificates of pluralists sent by bishops of the province of Canterbury to the archbishop in 1366 show that a number of vicars choral or minor canons at the cathedrals then held other benefices with cure of souls in the city or diocese (*Reg. Langham*, pp. 5–109; *Reg. Sudbury*, ii, 158–61 *passim*).

[5] See above, Chapter III, *passim*.

most of the priest vicars would be collated also to chantries in the cathedral, while some might be sent on the chapter's business to the court of Rome, to London, or to the chapter's estates within or outside the diocese. In these duties they were naturally responsible directly to the dean and chapter, and had no special relations with their individual masters.

THE FOUNDATION OF THE COLLEGES AND THE VICARS' POWERS OF SELF-GOVERNMENT

By the thirteenth and fourteenth centuries the vicars were taking an increasingly important part in the life, government, and business of the cathedral church. The youngest would be about twenty-two, for they were usually promoted from the ranks of the altarists, poor clerks, or secondaries as soon as they were old enough to be ordained subdeacons.[1] These young vicars may sometimes have appeared to the canons rather as irresponsible undergraduates in need of discipline; they were often in trouble with the chapter for chafing against regulations ordering them to attend the chancellor's grammar school. But many senior vicars were elderly priests, anxious to co-operate in the work of training and disciplining their juniors; in the later middle ages some might hold university degrees. It was impossible for the small chapter of residentiary canons to keep in permanent subjection to themselves the whole body of vicars choral, who by the fourteenth century generally outnumbered them by four or five to one. But, since the canons were loath to surrender their control, a struggle for independence began on the part of the vicars which at most cathedrals lasted throughout the thirteenth and fourteenth centuries. At Salisbury, in particular, feeling on occasion ran high between the chapter and vicars. The fourteenth-century chapter acts reveal a state of frequent defiance and occasional rebellion by the vicars. In 1319 Bishop Martival and the chapter took up an uncompromising attitude. They told the vicars plainly that 'the servant is not greater than his lord', and decreed that, since the vicars had been planning secret conspiracies, and, while eating at their masters' tables, had been saving up the daily pennies which they received

---

[1] Cf. D. H. Robertson, *Sarum Close*, p. 103. Mrs. Robertson has traced the history of choristers at Salisbury who were appointed altarists in the cathedral when their voices broke, and who were later promoted to vicarages.

as commons in order to threaten the canons with law-suits, they had thus constituted themselves open enemies of the canons, and must be shut out utterly from the canons' tables until they desisted and obeyed the chapter's judgement.[1]

Yet, in spite of setbacks, the cause of the vicars steadily advanced. Their first triumph was the establishment of their right to security of tenure. At most English cathedrals this was won at any rate by the middle of the thirteenth century. Bishop Marshall is said to have granted it to the vicars of Exeter in the late twelfth or early thirteenth century.[2] In 1214 the dean and chapter of Salisbury promised that no vicar choral should be dismissed from his vicarage without reasonable and necessary cause proved in chapter.[3] According to customs reduced to writing at Lincoln about 1330 a canon of Lincoln, on coming into residence, still had the right to dismiss his vicar, provided he gave him a term's notice; but such a vicar continued to be a vicar of the church, receiving his daily commons, and was given the next vacant vicarage.[4] At St. Paul's it was established in 1260 that a deceased canon's vicar should not be removed from his stall without cause, even if the new canon wished to present another vicar.[5]

The next stage was generally that of the acquisition and administration of common property by the vicars. At some cathedrals this apparently began as soon as or before the vicars were made perpetual. The vicars of Lincoln received grants of property as early as 1190,[6] and theirs is among the earliest organizations known for managing it. Possibly from as early as 1236, certainly from 1309, the canons of Lincoln paid their vicars' stipends of forty shillings a year direct to the provost of the vicars, who was said to have charge and administration of their common revenues and all things belonging to them, and of all gifts to them.[7] His office was clearly modelled on that of the provost of the canons' common fund. He was elected by the vicars with the assent of the dean and chapter. He paid to each vicar twenty shillings from his

---

[1] *S.S.*, pp. 242–5.   [2] Harl. MS. 1027, f. 8b.
[3] *S.S.*, pp. 48–9.   [4] *L.S.*, iii, 166–7.
[5] *R.S.S.P.*, p. 68.
[6] Cf. *L.S.*, i, 59; Maddison, *Vicars Choral of Lincoln Cathedral*, p. 3.
[7] *L.S.*, ii, 146–7, 149; iii, 316, 348–9. This practice is apparently first mentioned in the copy of the *Statutum Vicariorum* registered in the first chapter act book about 1309. Most other parts of the *Statutum* are known to date from 1236 (cf. *ibid.*, p. 143; i, 57–9).

stipend in two half-yearly instalments, keeping the remaining twenty shillings in their common fund, from which he distributed one penny a day to every vicar present at the cathedral services.[1] A similar system was described at York in 1252, but here the vicar elected to administer the vicars' common fund was to be known, like the keeper of the chapter's common fund, as the chamberlain; he was to receive tenpence a week for his labour in place of the sevenpence earned by the other vicars, and his accounts were to be audited annually by one canon and four vicars.[2] In 1252, when the vicars' status was formally recognized by Archbishop Walter Gray and the dean and chapter, they were definitely granted power to administer their own lands, tenements, rents, and immovable goods. In 1268 this power was confirmed to them by a charter of Henry III, which is regarded by Chancellor Harrison as something very like a first incorporation of their college.[3] Elsewhere there is less information available for the early administration of the vicars' common property. Churches were appropriated to the vicars of Exeter by Bishop Henry Marshall, 1194–1206, and for the support of the vicars of St. Paul's between 1221 and 1228.[4] In 1214 the chapter of Salisbury agreed that the vicars might accept legacies left to them in common,[5] and already in the thirteenth century the vicars apparently had a common seal, bearing the legend, 'Sigillum Commune Vicariorum Ecclesiae Saresbiriensis'.[6] In the same way the vicars choral of Lichfield used

---

[1] *Ibid.*, ii, 146–9; iii, 316, 348–50. A marginal correction in the account of the office of provost of the vicars in the draft *Novum Registrum* of 1440, altered 'provost' to 'two provosts'; these were to receive tenpence a week in place of the sevenpence paid to the other vicars.

[2] *Ibid.*, ii, 109–11. In later records it appears that the vicars' chamberlain was in charge of their real property, while the collection of the vicars' stipends from the canons was made by another official, the bursar, who kept separate rolls of accounts (F. Harrison, *loc. cit.*, p. 42; *Life in a Medieval College*, pp. 52–4).

[3] Cf. *ibid.*, p. 23; *Proc. Y.A.A.S.* (1936), pp. 21. 35. It was not until 1421, when royal charters of incorporation had become fashionable among English bodies of vicars choral, that the vicars of York obtained from Henry V what is generally known as their formal charter of incorporation (see below, p. 284). For their property, see F. Harrison, *loc. cit.*, pp. 21, 33–4, 39–41; *Life in a Medieval College*, pp. 74 *et seq.*

[4] Harl. MS. 1027, f. 8b; *R.S.S.P.*, p. 395–6.

[5] *S.S.*, pp. 50–1. For Robert de Kareville's legacy to them in 1267, see *ibid.*, pp. 320–1; *Sarum Charters*, pp. 342–5.

[6] *S.S.*, p. 320 n. Mr. Malden assigned the seal to the thirteenth century.

a common seal, at any rate from 1340, and administered property granted to them in common at least a century and a half before they obtained recognition of such powers in their royal charter of incorporation as a college.[1]

The establishment of vicars' common halls or colleges of residence in the close gave to the vicars their best opportunity to work together in asserting their independence of the chapter. Everywhere the movement to found these colleges seems to have been encouraged and helped by the bishops and chapters. The Bedern College at York seems to have been the first at an English secular cathedral. The site, near the east end of the cathedral, is said to have been given to the vicars for a common dwelling by William de Laneham, canon of York, about 1248. On it were built separate houses for the vicars with a common hall and refectory and a chapel.[2] The next known evidence for a vicars' common hall is at St. Paul's, where in 1273 the chapter ordered that the vicars must always eat together in their common hall unless specially invited to the canons' houses.[3] Possibly this implies that the hall had been in existence for some time. Then in 1289, since the vicars of St. Paul's, as deacons and subdeacons, had presumably to be kept under strict supervision, two priests, mature men of good and honourable behaviour, were ordered to live in the vicars' houses to watch their comings and goings, and to report any insolence or irregularity to the dean.[4] The vicars took it in turns to ring the rising bell in their houses every morning to wake their fellows, so that no vicar should be absent from matins through not hearing the cathedral bells.[5] The only other common houses for cathedral vicars in thirteenth-century England seem to have been the two houses in the country outside the cities of Lincoln and Lichfield, given for the support and refreshment of sick, old, and broken-down vicars. There was the House of St. Giles without Lincoln, founded and endowed by Bishop Sutton in 1280 for the vicars of Lincoln, and the House at le Stowe for the vicars of Lichfield.[6]

---

[1] 'Catalogue of Muniments of the Lichfield Vicars', in *Coll. Hist. Staffs.*, II, vi, 159 *et seq.*; 'Reg. Norbury', *ibid.*, i, 270, 275, 277–81; *M.R.A.*, pp. 47–8, 318–19, 331–2.

[2] See F. Harrison, *Life in a Medieval College*, pp. 29-42; *Proc. Y.A.A.S.* (1936), p. 21; and J. Solloway in *V.C.H. Yorks.*, iii, 382–3. The college chapel in the Bedern was not consecrated until 1349.

[3] *R.S.S.P.*, p. 68.   [4] *Ibid.*, p. 104.   [5] *Ibid.*, p. 103.

[6] *Reg. Antiquissimum*, iii, 373; *Monasticon*, VI, iii, 1261.

By the fourteenth century the steady increase in the number of non-resident canons, who could not have their vicars to live with them in their canonical houses, was creating a difficult housing problem for most English secular chapters which had not already provided common halls of residence for their vicars choral. In some cases there were not enough houses for the vicars in the close, and they had to lodge in the city, often at a distance from the cathedral. The canons apparently feared that the vicars would get into mischief through living alone without supervision. It was particularly difficult to enforce the vow of chastity on vicars who were scattered in different houses in the city and close; complaints that vicars kept concubines were frequent; the chapter of Wells showed its concern in a series of injunctions ordering that at least two vicars must always lodge together for the sake of honour and good report.[1] In the course of the fourteenth century the movement for the provision of common halls or colleges for the vicars choral spread to all the English secular cathedrals. From the point of view of the chapters of residentiary canons it apparently had two main objects; it helped to alleviate the housing shortage in the close, and, by ensuring that all vicars of absent canons would live together, it allowed the senior and more responsible vicars to help in disciplining their juniors. Between 1300 and 1328, through the generosity of Bishop Sutton, the Vicars' Court at Lincoln was made ready, first for the senior and then for the junior vicars.[2] In 1315 Bishop Walter Langton granted a common house of residence to the vicars choral of Lichfield; 1348 saw the beginning of Bishop Shrewsbury's Vicars' Close at Wells.[3] In 1353 the minor canons of St. Paul's were left a house by a former member of their body to extend and use as a common hall.[4] The vicars of Hereford were already living in their common hall in Castle Street by the cathedral in 1375.[5] The building of a college in the Kalendarhay at

---

[1] E.g. *H.M.C. Wells*, i, 74, 162; *W.S.*, pp. 64–5.
[2] *L.S.*, ii, xlix–li; Maddison, *Vicars Choral of Lincoln Cathedral*, pp. 8–9, cf. p. 43; W. A. Pantin in *Medieval Archaeology*, iii, 247–8.
[3] *Ibid.*, pp. 248–9; *M.R.A.*, pp. 44–5; *W.S.*, p. xxix; Canon of *Wells*, 'Historia', in *Anglia Sacra*, i, 569. For an earlier and apparently unsuccessful project of the dean and chapter to build houses for the vicars at Wells, see *H.M.C. Wells*, i, 181.   [4] *R.S.S.P.*, pp. 321–2.
[5] *Hereford Charters*, pp. 237–8. They agreed to allow an old blind vicar to live with them and share their food until his death, in return for twenty shillings a year, payable to their common fund.

Exeter for the vicars of Exeter was completed by 1388.[1] Another at Chichester, begun in 1394, was ready for the vicars of Chichester by 1403.[2] Lastly, in 1409, there is evidence for the existence of a vicars' common hall in Salisbury close.[3] Here there was no housing shortage, for the close had been planned on a lavish scale by the canons of the early thirteenth century, when they built their new cathedral in the valley below Old Sarum. Throughout the last three-quarters of the thirteenth and during the fourteenth century the vicars of absent canons of Salisbury apparently lived in separate private houses in the close, built and let in accordance with the same regulations as those laid down for the canons' houses.[4] It may have been partly the example of other English cathedrals which caused the canons and vicars of Salisbury finally to institute a vicars' common hall in their close. Also, the canons probably wished to provide a more effective discipline for the vicars, while the vicars may have welcomed the idea of collegiate life as a means of asserting their corporate independence of the chapter.

One of the most important constitutional results of the new system was that the vicars gradually came to govern themselves in many matters of their daily life unconnected with their cathedral duties, and were subject only to general supervision by the dean and chapter. When statutes had to be drawn up for the government of the common halls, the vicars or minor canons usually framed these statutes with the advice and consent of the dean and chapter or bishop.[5] The statutes would then be officially confirmed by the common seals of both dean and chapter and vicars

---

[1] Bishop Brantingham's ordinance for this college is in *Reg. Brantyngham*, ii, 675–6; Harl. MS. 1027, ff. 69a–69b. Cf. *Use Exeter*, pp. 3, 5; E. Lega-Weekes, *Topography of Exeter Close*, pp. 44–8.

[2] *Reg. Rede*, i, 118; cf. Peckham, *loc. cit.*, p. 133. This was replaced by separate houses for the vicars in the late fifteenth century (W. A. Pantin, *loc. cit.*, pp. 248–9).

[3] *S.S.*, p. 55 n.

[4] K. Edwards, 'The Houses of Salisbury Close,' in *British Arch. Jour.* (1939), pp. 81–8.

[5] E.g. *S.S.*, pp. 320–31; *R.S.S.P.*, pp. 329–59; cf. *Dean Cosyn and Wells Cathedral Misc.*, p. 140. At Chichester in 1534 statutes for the vicars' government were made in the bishop's name, with the advice and consent of the dean and chapter and of the principal and commonalty of the vicars, and were sealed with all three seals of bishop, dean and chapter, and of the commonalty of the vicars (*C.S.*, pp. 82–91).

choral; for the future, when a canon presented a new vicar choral, he had to be formally admitted, not only by the dean and chapter, but also by his fellow vicars, taking an additional oath to observe the statutes of the vicars' college.[1]

Four sets of statutes describing the government of the vicars' common halls are available in print: those made for the minor canons of St. Paul's in 1396; for the vicars of Salisbury in 1442; for the vicars of Wells in 1459, and for the vicars of Chichester in 1534;[2] while a fifth manuscript statute book of the vicars choral of York is extant at York.[3] From these statutes, drawn up for the most part some time after the foundation of the common halls, when the rules and way of life were more or less settled, it is possible to form a fairly clear idea of their government and domestic arrangements. In addition, the kitchen book of the York vicars choral, their rolls of accounts, cartulary, and many other records, described in detail by Chancellor Harrison,[4] provide an exceptionally valuable body of material for studying this new form of common life of the vicars at York in the later middle ages and in the sixteenth century.

The head of the college or hall was normally a senior vicar, elected annually by his fellow vicars. Only at Lichfield the succentor was always head of the college *ex officio*;[5] while at York the precentor was apparently usually willing to accept the elected warden of the vicars' college as his *succentor vicariorum*.[6] Elsewhere the warden might be known as the principal or provost of the vicars. The methods of election were sometimes complicated. At Wells it was customary to elect two principals, presumably so that each could act as a check on the other's powers. Every year on the feast of St. Matthew, the two retiring principals, in the presence and with the consent of the other vicars or of the *major et senior pars*, chose five of the more discreet senior vicars, and these, with the principals of the previous year, elected the principals for

---

[1] F. Harrison, *op. cit.*, in *Proc. Y.A.A.S.*, p. 31.

[2] *Dean Cosyn and Wells Cathedral Misc.*, pp. 139–49; *R.S.S.P.*, pp. 329–59; *S.S.*, pp. 321–31; *C.S.*, pp. 82–90.

[3] This has been described by Chancellor Harrison, *op. cit.*, in *Proc. Y.A.A.S.*, pp. 35–8; *Life in a Medieval College*, pp. xii, 48 *et seq.*

[4] *Ibid.*, pp. x–xiii *et passim*; *Proc. Y.A.A.S.* (1936), pp. 32–43.

[5] 'Catalogue of Muniments of Lichfield Vicars', in *Coll. Hist. Staffs.*, II, vi, 161.

[6] F. Harrison, *loc. cit.*, p. 22.

the following year.[1] The minor canons of St. Paul's chose their
warden according to the canonical methods of electing a bishop,
abbot or dean, by scrutiny, compromission or the inspiration of
the Holy Ghost.[2] At Chichester the dean and chapter had the
casting vote if two vicars obtained an equal number of votes from
their fellows; furthermore, if the vicars delayed electing a principal for more than six days after the feast of SS. Cosmas and
Damian, the dean and chapter had the right to appoint.[3]

Everywhere all vicars were bound to swear a special oath of
obedience to the head of their college, while, on his part, the
principal, provost or warden was responsible during his tenure of
office for the spiritual and temporal welfare of all members of the
college. He had power to correct the vicars' moral lapses, to settle
their disputes, and to supervise the administration of their hall and
common property. [4] In addition there were a number of other
elected officials to help him in different parts of his work. At York
the chamberlain and repairer were concerned with the real
property of the college; the bursar paid the vicars' stipends; the
brasiator had charge of the domestic arrangements, including the
provision of drink and meals, while a council of six vicars or 'sex-
men' helped to maintain discipline.[5] The vicars of Chichester
elected a supervisor to help to administer their common property;
the minor canons of St. Paul's chose a pitanciary.[6] At Salisbury the
vicars' college had two dispensers or supervisors of the common
expenses, and, like the chapter, a communar to distribute commons.[7] At Wells there were two receivers and three auditors, in
addition to the inner council of five senior vicars who advised the
principals.[8] Furthermore, every vicar was bound to take his turn as
steward or seneschal for a week, fortnight or month at a time,
when he was responsible for buying the food for the common
table.[9] The vicars had to give due notice to the stewards if they

---

[1] *Dean Cosyn and Wells Cathedral Misc.*, pp. 140–1.

[2] *R.S.S.P.*, pp. 350–1.　　　　　　　　　　　　　[3] *C.S.*, p. 82.

[4] *Dean Cosyn and Wells Cathedral Misc.*, pp. 141–2, 146; *C.S.*, pp. 82–3;
R.S.S.P., pp. 334–5, 350–1.

[5] F. Harrison, *Proc. Y.A.A.S.* (1936), pp. 36–7, 42; *Life in a Medieval College*,
pp. 52–65.

[6] *C.S.*, pp. 84–5, 89; *R.S.S.P.*, pp. 350–3.　　　[7] *S.S.*, pp. 325–9, 410–11 n.

[8] *Dean Cosyn and Wells Cathedral Misc.*, pp. 140–2.

[9] *S.S.*, pp. 326–7; *Dean Cosyn and Wells Cathedral Misc.*, pp. 143, 146–7;
R.S.S.P., pp. 340–3; *C.S.*, p. 86.

were going to be absent from meals, or if they wanted to invite visitors to meals in hall.[1] At Salisbury those vicars whose masters kept houses in the close might be allowed to live with their master when he was in residence, and to come into hall simply for the time when he was absent.[2] Life in college was strictly regulated by the vicars' statutes. Hours of silence were laid down, and the length of time during which the vicars might drink together in hall after supper. There was bible reading at table. Each vicar had his separate house or chamber allotted to him by the head of the college, and was responsible for its upkeep and repair. The hall servants were engaged by the principal; no vicar who was not a hall officer might correct them or give them orders. The duties of servants, such as the cook, butler or gardener, were carefully explained.[3]

The general similarity of all these regulations to those of Oxford and Cambridge colleges, which were being founded at about the same time as the vicars' colleges, is very marked.[4] Even the titles of many of the officials, such as warden, provost, principal, bursar, were often the same. The students and fellows of the Oxford and Cambridge colleges were clerks, who were often bound to celebrate chantry masses daily in their college chapel for the souls of their founders and benefactors; the younger vicars choral were supposed to spend some time in study at the chancellor's school. The government of the vicars' colleges was perhaps more democratic than that of the university colleges, particularly at first. They had grown up under the influence of the older colleges of secular canons, whereas the constitutions of the university colleges seem to have had more in common with those of the independent colleges of chantry priests of the later middle ages. The principal, provost, warden, or dean of a university or chantry college was normally appointed for life, and had considerably more power than the annually elected heads of the vicars' colleges; like the dean of a medieval secular cathedral, the heads of the

[1] *Ibid.*, p. 88; *R.S.S.P.*, pp. 340-3; *S.S.*, 328-31. [2] *Ibid.*
[3] *R.S.S.P.*, pp. 338-45, 354-7; *Dean Cosyn and Wells Cathedral Misc.*, pp. 144-7; *C.S.*, pp. 83-4, 86-7, 90.
[4] For the life and government of the Oxford and Cambridge colleges and halls, see Rashdall, *Universities* (1936), iii, 169-235, 293-464 *passim*; A. B. Emden, *An Oxford Hall in Medieval Times*; H. E. Salter, 'An Oxford Hall in 1424,' in *Essays presented to R. L. Poole*, pp. 421-35; 'The Medieval University of Oxford,' in *History*, xiv (1929-30), 57-61.

colleges of vicars choral were never more than *primus inter pares* among their fellows. Most of the other offices in the vicars' halls were elective and held for short periods only; all the fellows shared in the elections and discussions of common business, and took their turn in the administration. But probably the senior vicars were always given a rather more privileged position than their juniors, and this tendency seems gradually to have become more marked. At Wells the principals could only be chosen from the five senior vicars, who formed a kind of inner council of advice for governing the hall; they might sometimes hold office for longer than a year if the senior vicars thought it advisable.[1] At Salisbury vicars who acted as stewards for their fortnight had to be accompanied by a supervisor, a senior vicar, when they went to the city to pay for food ordered for the common table.[2]

Furthermore, there are indications of a growing exclusiveness among the vicars in the fifteenth century when their numbers were falling, similar to that which had developed earlier among their masters, the residentiary canons. Like the residentiary canons the vicars began to demand an entrance fee of from six shillings and eightpence to twenty-six shillings and eightpence or a feast from a new vicar in return for the privilege of admission to their common hall.[3] In 1432 the vicars of Lincoln were rebuked by Bishop Gray for introducing a kind of greater residence, modelled probably on that of the canons; according to this, a new vicar was to receive nothing from the vicars' common fund for the first seventeen weeks of his residence. As a result new vicars were said to be constrained by famine to demise their vicarages, and other suitable persons, hearing this, were refusing to accept them.[4] As in the case of the residentiary canons, one of the reasons for these rules may have been the increasing poverty of the colleges at the end of the middle ages, which was due to the fall in value of their endowments;[5] at the same time the senior vicars had probably found that their commons were greater when there were fewer

[1] *Dean Cosyn and Wells Cathedral Misc.*, pp. 140-1.
[2] *S.S.*, pp. 326-7.
[3] *Ibid.*, pp. 330-1; *L.S.*, i, 400; *W.S.*, pp. clxxv-vi; *C.S.*, p. 83; *R.S.S.P.*, pp. 334-7.
[4] *Lincoln Visitations*, i, 143.
[5] In the sixteenth century, with the dissolution of the chantries, the vicars' financial position naturally became much worse, since they could no longer supplement their stipends by serving chantries.

vicars to share them. In the sixteenth century at York, when the number of vicars choral fell sharply and lay singing men began to be appointed in their places, the vicars found themselves, like the chapters of residentiary canons in earlier times, in the position of small, exclusive bodies resisting encroachments on their rights and privileges. In 1500 they protested strongly against the insolence of the singing men, who had begun to demand vacant houses in the Bedern as a right, not as a grace.[1] In 1681, when another case of this sort was brought before the dean and chapter, the sub-chanter of the vicars admitted that 'some singing men, well-deserving and of good behaviour, have by grace of the vicars had for their better incouragement some small poore houses allowed them, but never above three at a time.[2]

Many further points of similarity may be noticed between the development and organization of the colleges of vicars choral at the secular cathedrals and those of the chapters of canons, their masters. The form of common life adopted in the early vicars' colleges was never meant to be as strict as that enjoined on his cathedral canons by Bishop Chrodegang of Metz. Yet its purpose was in a sense akin to that of the earlier common life of bishops and cathedral clerks in the Merovingian period in France, when the communal elements in the life were chiefly due to economic motives of convenience, and not enjoined on the clergy universally by the canons. The vicars choral of the thirteenth and fourteenth centuries, attituled to absent masters, and having only small stipends, found economic advantages in a collegiate life, where they could share the expense of housing accommodation and meals. Furthermore, the common life of the vicars, like that of the early 'canonical clerks', had also spiritual and disciplinary purposes; some of their colleges came to have private chapels served by the vicars; rules of life were drawn up and enforced by the vicars. The common life gave to the vicars opportunities of developing a corporate spirit and of asserting their independence of the dean and chapter, as the chapters of the early middle ages had asserted their independence of their absent bishop. The vicars' colleges were granted endowments, and so in time became moderately wealthy and privileged bodies. Then, towards the end of the middle ages and in the sixteenth century, as with the canons, the income from their property seems to have fallen in value;

[1] F. Harrison, *loc. cit.*, in *Proc. Y.A.A.S.*, p. 38.   [2] *Ibid.*, p. 43.

their numbers became fewer, and were gradually limited to only a fraction of the full number at the medieval cathedrals, and the rules for their common life were relaxed.[1] It is also interesting to see how in certain respects the vicars modelled their organization on that of the chapter. The duties of the warden, principal, or provost, who exercised a general authority in both spiritual and temporal matters, corresponded roughly to those of the dean; while the titles of many of the financial officers, such as the vicars' communar at Salisbury, the receiver at Wells, or the chamberlain at York, were often the same as those of the canons who administered the chapter's common fund. Naturally, the vicars' organization was simpler, and more purely concerned with the domestic business of the hall. But the deputies of three of the four great cathedral dignitaries, the precentor, chancellor, and treasurer, were usually senior vicars, who had some authority over the other vicars in their cathedral duties. Sometimes the succentor, the precentor's deputy, was elected as head of the vicars' college.

The final stage in the establishment of the vicars' claims to self-government in the middle ages came when they obtained their formal charter of incorporation under the king's great seal. Bishops or the dean and chapter frequently used their influence to secure these charters for the vicars. The vicars of Wells were apparently the first vicars choral in England to be incorporated; Bishop Shrewsbury obtained the privilege for them as early as 1348, when the building of their college had begun.[2] In the last years of the fourteenth century and in the first half of the fifteenth century the idea became increasingly popular. The minor canons of St. Paul's cathedral were incorporated in 1394; the vicars of Hereford in 1395; the vicars of Exeter in 1405; the vicars of Salisbury in 1409; the vicars of York in 1421; the vicars of Lincoln in 1441, and the vicars of Chichester in 1467.[3] The vicars choral at St. Paul's seem never to have been formally incorporated,[4] possibly because their status as deacons and subdeacons, below

[1] E.g. from the sixteenth century at York it was customary for the vicars to have only one meal a day in their common hall (*ibid.*, pp. 38–9).

[2] *W.S.*, p. xxix.

[3] *R.S.S.P.*, pp. 327–9; *Hereford Charters*, pp. 253–5; E. Lega-Weekes, *Topography of Exeter Close*, pp. 49–50; *S.S.*, p. 320; *C.P.R. 1416–22*, pp. 360–1; Maddison, *Vicars Choral of Lincoln Cathedral*, p. 3; *C.P.R. 1467–77*, p. 35; *C.S.*, pp. 80–1; Peckham, *loc. cit.*, pp. 133–5.

[4] Cf. *V.C.H. London*, i, 428.

that of the minor canons, allowed them less independence and importance than the vicars choral of other English secular cathedrals. Normally, the charters of incorporation constituted the community of vicars as a legal personage with power to elect their own principal; to use a common seal; to acquire and hold in common lands, tenements and rents; to implead and be impleaded, and to prosecute causes. In almost every case the vicars had already exercised all or most of these powers for many years. The royal charters therefore represented little more than a legal confirmation of existing rights.

2. THE CHANTRY CHAPLAINS OR CANTARISTS

The chantry priests were usually the last of the different groups of cathedral clergy to be instituted in the medieval cathedrals; they were the only group which was completely dispensed with in the English cathedrals after the Reformation. For this reason Archbishop Benson has written of them as merely 'a temporary enrichment . . . an accretion which was actually a symptom of decay . . . an aftergrowth having no original place nor true connexion with the cathedral system'.[1] Yet, as Professor Hamilton Thompson has pointed out, the idea of the chantry was at the root of all ecclesiastical establishments in the middle ages.

'The cathedral church, the church of a monastery, the parish church were all institutions whose primary object was to maintain the pious duty of continuous intercession for the living and the departed. It was with this object that those great churches were founded, on whose altars lay, as at Durham, a *Book of Life*, containing long lists of members of the community and others, with those of visitors and benefactors, who had acquired a claim upon the suffrages of the chapter or convent.'[2]

The chantry grew out of the anniversary or obit service. At first, anniversaries or masses commemorating individual persons who had left gifts and bequests to the cathedral with this end in view were probably all celebrated by the cathedral canons in person. But in time the number of obits which had to be celebrated annually increased to such an extent that it became necessary to appoint

[1] *The Cathedral*, p. 37.
[2] 'English Colleges of Chantry Priests', in *Trans. Ecclesiological Soc.*, i (1943), 92.

U

additional clergy to say them. This was often among the reasons which led to the regular appointment of vicars choral or other *ministri inferiores*. From the late twelfth or early thirteenth century priest vicars or minor canons seem usually to have officiated at the celebration of obits in English secular cathedrals, receiving for their labour extra distributions of money or wine from the founders' endowments.[1] At St. Paul's a hundred and eleven obits were celebrated each year in the early fourteenth century, and at Hereford fifty or more.[2]

At the same time, from the late twelfth century onwards, more elaborate foundations known as chantries were becoming increasingly popular as objects for the benefactions of the more wealthy pious founders, such as successful royal clerks, bishops, cathedral canons or lay magnates. Chantries were of various kinds. In the most outstanding instances they consisted of a permanent endowment of land and rent sufficient to maintain one or more priests in perpetuity to say daily masses for the souls of the founder, his kinsmen and friends, but there were also many temporary chantries maintained by bequests of money or other goods for a limited time, usually for a year or a term of years. They might be founded at the altars of cathedral or collegiate churches, in monasteries, in parish churches or chapels. In the later middle ages a special chantry chapel might be built by the founder's tomb, and a college of priests instituted to serve it.

The great increase in the number of chantries founded in the thirteenth and fourteenth centuries has been ascribed to a variety of causes. It has sometimes been said that they took the place of the monasteries as objects for the benefactions of pious founders at a time when the monasteries were on the decline; in the later middle ages pious benefactors, no longer trusting the monks to carry out the obligations attached to their endowments, were

---

[1] See above, p. 266.

[2] W. S. Simpson, 'Dean Colet's Statutes for Chantry Priests', in *Archaeologia*, lii, i, 146; Bannister, *Cathedral Church of Hereford*, p. 156. Obit services could not as a rule be entabled on feasts of nine lessons or greater feasts because of their interference with the main cathedral services (cf. *R.S.S.P.*, pp. 35–6). It is therefore hardly surprising that they could rarely be arranged on the actual anniversary date. Canon Wordsworth concluded from his study of *re* and *ve* rolls at Lincoln that, immediately after the September audit, the cathedral body started on the list of obits and worked through them on vacant days (*L.S.*, ii, 809–10).

thought to have preferred to found a chantry rather than to make gifts to a monastery. Yet the monasteries were at the height of their prestige and influence in the twelfth century when the first records of chantry endowments are found, while both then and later many chantries were established in monastic churches. Probably all sorts of causes occurred. 'Saturation point' had almost been reached in certain districts for monasteries. The cost of founding a religious house was very high, and always demanded the sacrifice of land or at least (for the friars) house property. On the other hand there was an increasing number of men of substance, especially in towns, who had not enough money to found a house, but who could easily afford a chantry. A further reason for the popularity of chantries may have been the natural desire of people to have something private in religion. Before the Conquest, pious founders had built churches on their own estates, appointed a priest, and had, as it were, their own church. Then, gradually, the ecclesiastical authorities insisted on ecclesiastical control over these churches; the priests were instituted by and subject to the bishop, and the church became the parish church of all the parishioners. In the twelfth century the chantry made its appearance to take the place of the private church.[1] More than most pious benefactions, it gave exceptional scope for carrying out the founder's individual wishes. Many founders prescribed in detail the different masses which they wished to have said daily for their souls, drawing up long lists of kinsmen, friends, or patrons whom they wished to share in the spiritual benefits of their chantry; benefactors might ask for two or three thousand masses to be said for their souls as quickly as possible.[2] The foundation of chantries seems also to have been connected with the growing popularity of the mass in the thirteenth century; from about 1250 devotion to the Blessed Sacrament and urban devotion to the mass had somewhat cast into the shade the earlier devotion to the round of liturgical prayer offered by the monks. At the same time chantries reflect the movement towards specialization or departmentalism in church services; in the thirteenth century it was

[1] This suggestion was made by Professor Knowles at a meeting of the Royal Historical Society on 11 November 1944 after the reading of a paper by Miss K. L. Wood-Legh on 'Some Aspects of the History of Chantries in the Later Middle Ages'. He very kindly allows me to quote it here.

[2] E.g. *Reg. Chichele*, ii, xl–i.

becoming usual to have different clergy officiating at different services, more particularly in the cathedrals. It was natural that special priests should be assigned to say the private masses.

One of the chief problems of the founders of chantries was to ensure that the obligations of their endowments would be carried out. Cathedral chapters, like other corporations, such as monasteries, colleges, or town councils, were in a position to give good permanent security for this. Thus it became common for benefactors to grant both the revenues and patronage of their chantries in perpetuity to cathedral chapters, on the understanding that the chapter would administer the revenues, appoint and pay priests to say the masses, and see that they actually said them. Naturally the larger cathedrals in big cities received more of these endowments than churches in more remote parts of the country. St. Paul's in the fourteenth century had as many as seventy-four perpetual chantries, as compared with about the same number at Rouen, the metropolitan see of Normandy, and nineteen at the smaller and more remote English cathedral of Lichfield.[1] At Salisbury nine or ten are known to have been founded in the late twelfth or thirteenth century; fourteen more have been traced in the fourteenth century, and about nine were added in the fifteenth and early sixteenth centuries.[2] Of the fifty-four perpetual chantries known to have existed at York in the middle ages, seventeen were founded in the thirteenth century, twenty-two in the fourteenth century, twelve in the fifteenth century, one in the early sixteenth century, and two at unknown dates.[3] The peak period in the foundation of chantries seems at most cathedrals to have come at about the same time, in the late thirteenth and in the fourteenth centuries.

The most usual names for the new group of clergy which came into existence at the cathedrals to serve the chantries were *cantaristae* or *capellani cantariarum* (cantarists or chantry chaplains);

---

[1] W. S. Simpson, *op. cit.*, in *Archaeologia*, lii, i, 146, 168–70; Pommeraye, *op. cit.*, pp. 293–4; *Gallia Christiana*, xi, 3. A list of nineteen chantries at Lichfield cathedral in 1335 is given in MS. Ashmole 794, ff. 48–9. In 1391 Bishop Braybrooke reduced the number of chantries at St. Paul's by uniting the endowments of many of the poorer chantries (*R.S.S.P.*, pp. 142–8, and below, pp. 292, 300).

[2] *V.C.H., Wilts.*, iii, 168–9, 175, 181; cf. *Salisbury Ceremonies*, pp. 185–6.

[3] See the list of York chantries compiled by Raine, *York Fabric Rolls*, App., pp. 274–306. He did not consider this list to be by any means complete.

custodes altarium or *altaristae*[1] were also commonly used. The description 'stipendiary priests' usually indicated that these were priests holding office for a limited time only, in contrast to the perpetual chaplains appointed for life. The chapter of Exeter almost invariably called all its chantry priests 'annuellars' or 'annivellars', terms usually reserved at other cathedrals for the preists celebrating annuals. One of the most confusing local customs was at York, where the cantarists were normally described in cathedral records as 'parsons' or 'rectors'.[2]

It is difficult to estimate how many additional clergy were actually provided for the cathedral staffs through the chantries, because chantries were frequently given to vicars choral already at the cathedrals in order to supplement their stipends. In Germany, apparently, this was so common that the terms cantarists and vicars choral became synonymous.[3] At Chartres the twenty-four *heuriers* and *matiniers* were regularly collated to the twenty-four canonries of the chantry colleges of St. Piat and St. Nicholas.[4] In England, founders of chantries, fearing perhaps the neglect of their masses by clergy who were supposed to be already fully occupied in the cathedral services, occasionally laid down in their foundation ordinances that vicars choral should not be collated to their chantries.[5] But more often the decision was left to the discretion of the cathedral authorities, whose policy might vary both in different churches and at different periods. At Salisbury in 1319, perhaps because there were few chantries in the cathedral, the granting of them to vicars choral seems to have been discouraged; Bishop Martival's code of statutes laid down that chantries ought to be conferred on priests without any other source of income, so that divine service might be celebrated to the greater glory of God in full numbers.[6] At Lincoln in 1432 Bishop Gray ordered that chantries at the cathedral should be given to those of the

---

[1] At Salisbury and Wells *altaristae* had the special meaning of clerks in minor orders who assisted the chantry priests at their altars (see below, pp. 303 *et seq.*). Elsewhere, both in English and continental cathedrals, the term seems usually to have been an alternative name for chantry priests.

[2] *Personae* or *rectores*, e.g. *L.S.*, ii, 116, 126; *York Fabric Rolls*, pp. 125, 251–2.

[3] Cf. Hinschius, ii, 78.   [4] Amiet, *op. cit.*, pp. 140–3.

[5] E.g. this was the case in the ordinance of the Blunsdon chantry founded in Salisbury cathedral, and in the ordinance of Dean Hussey's chantry at Wells (Reg. Corffe, f. 46; *H.M.C. Wells*, i, 61).

[6] *S.S.*, pp. 258–9.

priest vicars who had not adequate benefices;[1] in 1440 Bishop Alnwick declared that 'those of the church' ought to be preferred to strangers in the collation of chantries, seeing that they had borne the heat and burden of the day.[2]

All vicars choral could not hold chantries, because cantarists were supposed to be priests, while some vicars choral in the cathedrals were usually deacons and subdeacons. Thus nearly always there were a certain number of chantry priests at the English cathedrals in addition to the priest vicars who held chantries. The York chantry certificates of 1546 and 1548 show that, while twenty-one vicars choral then served nineteen chantries in the cathedral, a further twenty-four chantries were served by a separate group of cantarists living in St. William's College.[3] At Lincoln in 1535 the *Valor Ecclesiasticus* records that fifteen vicars then held chantries, but that there were also thirty-three other cantarists in the cathedral attached to twenty more chantries.[4] At the same time fourteen of the twenty-one chantries in Hereford cathedral and nine of the fourteen chantries in Chichester cathedral were served by vicars.[5] An undated list, made possibly about 1339,[6] detailing 'The Form of Collation of Chantries to be conferred annually at Wells on the feast of St. Jerome', shows that at least forty-six of the fifty-four annual appointments were reserved for vicars choral. But there was also another list of anniversary priests or chantry chaplains;[7] from 1401 rooms were available in the College of the Montroy for at least fourteen cantarists who were not entitled to live in the Vicars' Close.[8] An interesting attempt was made by Bishop Grandisson at Exeter in 1358 to fix the number of chantry clergy in relation to the numbers of canons and vicars. He decreed that, seeing there were twenty-four canons and twenty-four vicars in the cathedral, 'so let the annivellars and secondaries [i.e. the clerks in minor orders

---

[1] *Lincoln Visitations*, i, 143.　　　　　　　　　[2] *L.S.*, iii, 360.

[3] *York Chantry Certificates*, ed. W. Page, i, 7–42; ii, 430–49.

[4] *Valor Eccl.*, iv, 22–7.

[5] *Ibid.*, iii, 12; i, 302–3. In 1397 thirteen, and in 1409 ten, vicars of Chichester were said to hold cathedral chantries (*Reg. Rede*, i, 104–5; ii, 367–8).

[6] *W.S.*, pp. 99–100. It may have been drawn up in connexion with the statute of 1339 ordering that all *annalia temporalia* to be celebrated for the souls of the dead were to be conferred annually on the vicars choral of greatest merit (*ibid.*, p. 86).

[7] *Ibid.*, pp. 73–4.　　　　　　　　　　　　　　[8] See below, p. 301.

who assisted the annivellars at their altars] be reduced to the same number, and, from their common revenues and stipends, let it be distributed to each according to the Acts of the Apostles as there is need'.[1] No evidence has been found to suggest that this statute was ever carried out effectively. Nine priests annuellars were cited to Archbishop Courtenay's visitation of Exeter cathedral in 1384;[2] sixteen were serving ten chantries in the cathedral in the deanery of Reginald Pole;[3] in 1535 there were seventeen perpetual chantry priests who were not vicars choral.[4]

The position of such cantarists in secular cathedrals was peculiar. Although primarily concerned with special services subsidiary to the main cathedral services and supported chiefly from separate endowments unconnected with the chapter's common fund, they were regarded as belonging to the cathedral foundation, and were subject to a large measure of control by the dean and chapter. The extent of this control is well illustrated by the methods of their appointment. The right of collation to a chantry was usually laid down in its foundation deed. For the most part collation to chantries in the cathedrals was granted to the dean and chapter jointly. But the founder might sometimes reserve the patronage to himself, his heirs, or his executors during their lifetime; a few cathedral chantries might belong to the bishop's collation, while others were granted to the collation of a particular cathedral dignitary or officer, such as the dean, precentor, succentor, or occasionally to the vicars choral as a body.[5] If these patrons neglected to appoint a chaplain the collation lapsed to the dean and chapter; if they also failed to appoint within a fixed time it devolved on the bishop. But in no case could a chaplain be promoted to a cathedral chantry without the dean and chapter's knowledge and consent. At St. Paul's every cantarist, before admission to the cathedral, was required to undergo an examination by the succentor and one of the cardinals of the choir in singing, to see whether he would be a suitable member of the choir. If

[1] Harl. MS. 1027, f. 57b.

[2] *Reg. Brantyngham*, i, 516. This was a reduction, for twenty-one annuellars had been present at Bishop Grandisson's visitation in 1337 (*Reg. Grandisson*, ii, 857).   [3] *Use Exeter*, p. 84.   [4] *Valor Eccl.*, ii, 297.

[5] In such cases the community of vicars would administer the revenues of the chantry, and usually arranged for its own members to serve it (see e.g. 'Catalogue of Muniments of Lichfield Vicars', in *Coll. Hist. Staffs.* II,, vi, 168–70; *M.R.A.*, pp. 318–19, 331–2; *H.M.C. Wells*, i, 379–80).

found satisfactory and admitted, he had to swear an oath of obedience and fidelity to the dean and chapter, promising both to observe all the cathedral statutes which concerned him and to fulfil all the duties of his chantry.[1] In 1291 the chapter of York strengthened its hold over its 'parsons' by ordering them to be prepared to repeat a similar oath annually before the chapter on the feast of St. Martin, and at the same time to exhibit their letters of appointment to the dean and chapter.[2]

In matters of discipline cantarists were as much subject to the dean and chapter as other *ministri inferiores*. At Salisbury charges against them on the score of incontinence, drunkenness, brawling in the city and the like were heard in the chapter house before the dean or president and a special chapter of residentiary canons; [3] at York similar causes were dealt with in the dean and chapter's peculiar court by their auditor of causes.[4] Like the other cathedral clergy, the cantarists everywhere were bound to attend the weekly Saturday chapters when faults or neglect of duty in the services of the preceding week were investigated. A careful watch was kept upon their performance of the offices for the dead prescribed in the foundation deeds of their chantries. The chapters had power to deprive, suspend, or otherwise punish any cantarists who defrauded the souls of their benefactors of their masses. Furthermore, if the endowments of a chantry failed or decreased in value to such an extent that they were insufficient to support a priest to say the masses, arrangements might be made by the bishop or dean and chapter to combine the revenues of several poorly endowed chantries, so that one priest with a sufficient stipend might perform the obligations to the souls of all the founders. At a number of cathedrals important changes were made in chantry foundations in this way in the late fourteenth and fifteenth centuries, when the value of their endowments fell sharply. In 1391 Bishop Braybrooke at St. Paul's condensed as many as fifty-nine small chantries into twenty-seven groups.[5]

[1] *R.S.S.P.*, pp. 149–50; W. S. Simpson, *op. cit.*, in *Archaeologia*, lii, i, 161–3. For a similar oath taken by cantarists of Lincoln cathedral, see *L.S.*, i, 399.

[2] *Ibid.*, ii, 116.

[3] Records of such causes are entered in the Salisbury chapter act books, e.g. Reg. Dunham, ff. 262–3.

[4] *Medieval Act Book at York*, ed. J. S. Purvis, *passim*.

[5] *R.S.S.P.*, pp. 142–8. Cf. *Lincoln Visitations*, i, 142; H. Jenkins, *op. cit.*, p. 110.

In the thirteenth and fourteenth centuries most cantarists celebrated their chantry masses at altars already existing in the cathedral, which were allotted to them by the dean and chapter, and said their *placebo* and *dirige* in some convenient place.[1] In the later middle ages special chantry chapels, with new altars in them, were sometimes built by the founder's tomb in the cathedral, but naturally this was only done by founders of ample means. The dean and chapter strictly forbade cathedral cantarists to allow any hired or other stipendiary priests, unknown to the chapter, to celebrate other masses at their altars; nor might the cantarists themselves undertake to perform private funeral services or masses for profit without the dean and chapter's express permission.[2] The bread, wine, and incense for the altars seem usually to have been supplied by the cathedral treasurer or his deputy from endowments left by the founder of the chantry.[3] The dean or his *locumtenens* made formal visitations of the altars, inspecting their ornaments, vessels, and other furniture, and requiring the cantarists to exhibit before them their letters of ordination and appointment.[4] Salisbury cathedral had eighteen altars excluding the high altar, which in the early fourteenth century were probably sufficient for its chantry priests.[5] But in cathedrals with more cantarists, such as St. Paul's or York, several chantries had to be attached to one altar, and the chapter arranged the times at which the different masses should be celebrated, ordering the cantarists not to say their masses too loudly, lest they should disturb services at the neighbouring altars.[6] At York in the early sixteenth century there were probably about thirty-two altars for about sixty-four parsons serving at least fifty-four chantries.[7]

Most chantry masses in the cathedrals had to be said by nine in the morning. At Lincoln a special peal of bells (*pella* or 'peal altar') was rung midway between matins and prime, when the cantarists came to celebrate until the ringing for tierce.[8] But the chapters were also careful to arrange that there should always be a

---

[1] For the altars at Salisbury, see Wordsworth, *Salisbury Ceremonies*, pp. 185–213.

[2] *R.S.S.P.*, p. 71; *L.S.*, iii, 359–60.   [3] See above, pp. 221, 224.

[4] *Ibid.*, p. 147 n.

[5] *Salisbury Ceremonies*, pp. 73–9, 187–216.

[6] *R.S.S.P.*, p. 71; *L.S.*, iii, 359–60.

[7] *York Fabric Rolls*, pp. 274–306.   [8] *L.S.*, iii, 361.

mass in the cathedral which workmen, travellers, or other passers-by could attend from dawn until 10 or 11 a.m.[1] Annual tables were drawn up giving the times for these *missae currentes*; if one cantarist did not begin his mass immediately the preceding cantarist had finished, he would be cited before the chapter to answer for neglect of duty.[2] At Lichfield it was always the chaplain of St. Chad's altar who celebrated the daily dawn or morrow mass; he was excused from attending in the cathedral choir at matins on this account, being allowed his commons for matins so long as he celebrated the mass.[3] If oblations were offered at a chantry mass, the cantarist officiating was allowed to retain them.[4]

Just as cantarists serving chantries in parish churches were usually expected to help the parish priest in his church services and in part of the work of his parish, so cathedral cantarists had to take their share in the services and work of the cathedral church. At some continental cathedrals the perpetual cantarists, known as *beneficiati*, were given precedence in the cathedral choir immediately after the canons, and were followed in dignity by other inferior clergy, such as vicars choral, *heuriers*, and poor clerks, who were described as *quasi beneficiati* or *non beneficiati*.[5] But at such churches vicars choral or similar inferior clergy were often less numerous than in English cathedrals, and had not always achieved security of tenure; their appointments were temporary or subject to the will of the chapter. A further reason for the higher status of the cantarists may perhaps have been that at some cathedrals, particularly in Germany, cantarists were very well endowed, and came from more important local families than the vicars choral.[6] In English cathedrals the cantarists do not seem

[1] *S.S.*, pp. 258–61; *L.S.*, iii, 361; *Monasticon*, VI, iii, 1262; Harl. MS. 1027, f. 70b.

[2] *Salisbury Ceremonies*, pp. 224–8; cf. p. 198; *L.S.*, iii, 361; Reg. Corffe, f. 11; Reg. Coman, f. 92; Reg. Dunham, ff. 26, 100, 194; Reg. Holme, f. 32.

[3] *Monasticon*, VI, iii, 1262; cf. *M.R.A.*, p. 352.

[4] *L.S.*, ii, 22–3.

[5] E.g. as at Bayeux (Deslandes, *op. cit.*, pp. 268 *et seq.*).

[6] I owe this suggestion to Miss Kathleen L. Wood-Legh, who points out that the matter could probably only be settled by a careful study of the social background of cantarists serving in various cathedrals. She writes that the wealth and social position of German cantarists varied greatly. At Strasbourg, many were so poorly endowed that they have been justly described as a sort of clerical proletariate. But at Worms they seem to have been drawn largely from patrician families of the town and to have been treated accordingly.

normally to have been wealthier than the vicars,[1] and were usually assigned stalls in choir next to those of the priest vicars, but above those of vicars who were deacons or subdeacons. The chapter of St. Paul's was exceptional in allowing them to rank above all the vicars choral in choir, but this was probably only because the vicars of St. Paul's, unlike those of other English cathedrals, officiated only in the orders of deacon and subdeacon; the cantarists were not superior to the minor canons of St. Paul's, who were priests.[2]

The cantarists' duties, as laid down in English cathedral statutes, were to help the vicars in singing, reading the lessons, and chanting the canonical hours. Their attendances were expected to be laxer than those of the vicars choral,[3] but they were especially enjoined to be present at matins, prime, high mass, and vespers, and in processions on feast days, and to attend all funeral services and offices for the dead. In return they were granted the same commons as vicars for services which they actually attended, were allowed to share the obit distributions and other pittances with the rest of the choir, and were invited in their turns to dine at the residentiaries' tables.[4]

Throughout the greater part of the thirteenth and fourteenth centuries, cantarists usually had to find their own houses or lodgings; only occasionally an especially rich or generous benefactor might provide a house to be reserved in perpetuity for the chaplain of his chantry.[5] In the fourteenth and fifteenth centuries,

---

[1] Their stipends naturally varied according to the wealth or generosity of their founders. In a list of the values of chantries in St. Paul's, made before Bishop Braybrooke's reorganization of their endowments in 1391, the cantarists' annual stipends ranged from ten or twelve marks to as little as eight shillings (W. S. Simpson, *op. cit.*, in *Archaeologia*, lii, i, 148). In 1535 the *Valor Ecclesiasticus* shows that the normal stipend of an English cathedral cantarist was about 4 li to 6 li a year, though some had considerably more.

[2] See above, pp. 252-3.   [3] Cf. *R.S.S.P.*, p. 139.

[4] *S.S.*, pp. 254-7; *R.S.S.P.*, pp. 70, 104, 139-40, 149-51; *Archaeologia*, lii, i, 161-7; *Ordinale Exon.*, i, 6-7; *Use Exeter*, p. 12; Harl. MS. 1027, ff. 13b, 29a, 70a, 71a; *Reg. Grandisson*, ii, 859; *Monasticon*, VI, iii, 1260, 1262, 1265; *L.S.*, ii, 115, 126; iii, 359-60; *York Fabric Rolls*, p. 251.

[5] E.g. in 1365 Roger Clun, archdeacon of Salisbury, bought a small house in Ivy Lane, opening out of the North Highway of Salisbury close, for the chaplain of his chantry; in the early fifteenth century a house in the West Highway of the close was appropriated to the two chaplains of Lord Walter Hungerford's chantry (K. Edwards, 'The Houses of Salisbury Close,' in *British*

however, it was becoming fashionable for benefactors of ample means to found chantries not for one or two priests only, but for a whole college, consisting sometimes of as many as thirteen priests. Examples may be found in the many independent colleges of resident chantry clergy established in parish churches, such as Sibthorpe or Cotterstock in Lincoln diocese.[1] In such cases the founder would usually provide a house or houses for his college, and lay down rules for its members to live a common life under the direction of a provost, warden, or dean. The constitution of these colleges often differed in certain important respects both from those of the older colleges of secular canons, and from the contemporary colleges of vicars choral at the cathedrals. In most cases it was considered necessary for the warden, provost, or dean to have greater power than the head of a college of secular canons, largely in order that he should be able to enforce the obligatory rules of residence on all the members. Professor Hamilton Thompson has pointed out the interest and importance or this new type of collegiate constitution. In the sixteenth century, when Henry VIII reorganized the cathedral bodies in churches which had previously been monastic, the constitutions of these new foundations owed less to the old collegiate chapters of secular canons than to the smaller and more compact bodies of recent times.[2] Like the chantry colleges, the new cathedral chapters had only four to thirteen members in contrast to the fifty or more canons and prebendaries of Salisbury, Lincoln, or Wells. The long growth of ordinance, custom, and precedent on which the cathedrals of the Old Foundation had built up their constitutions formed no possible model for the New Foundations. It was chiefly on the model of the constitutions of the chantry colleges with their precise, ready-made bodies of statutes that the royal commissioners drafted their statutes for the cathedrals of the New Foundation. In these cathedrals the dean was no longer, as in the cathedrals of the Old Foundation, *primus inter pares* among the other canons, but, like the warden of a chantry college, was the parson of the church in whom all authority was vested.

Yet in spite of the widespread influence of these constitutions,

---

Arch. Jour. (1939), pp. 85–6; C. R. Everett, 'Notes on the Prebendal Mansion of Sherborne Monastery', in *W.A.M.*, xlvii, 384).

[1] Cf. A. H. Thompson, 'English Colleges of Chantry Priests', pp. 97–104.

[2] *Ibid.*, p. 107; *The English Clergy and their Organization*, p. 160.

comparatively few traces of their influence can be found in the organization of chantry colleges established in English secular cathedrals. This may have been partly because strict supervision of the cantarists' endowments and discipline by the dean and chapter gave little opportunity for the powers of the heads of these colleges to develop; while, for colleges growing up in the close of a medieval secular cathedral, the natural models would be either the chapter of canons or the college of vicars choral. But there were a few notable exceptions. An unusually early instance was the chapel of St. Mary and the Holy Angels, commonly known as St. Sepulchre's chapel, founded about 1177–81 by Archbishop Roger de Pont l'Evêque at York for a sacrist and twelve canons, 'to the end that divine service may be celebrated for ever to the honour and glory of God, and for the remission of the sins of us and our successors'.[1] This chapel was outside the cathedral, adjoining the gate-house of the archbishop's chapel; the canons were appointed by, and were in most matters subject directly to, the archbishop, not to the dean and chapter. This absence of close supervision by the dean and chapter allowed the powers of the sacrist to be much greater than those of the heads of later chantry colleges in other secular cathedrals. Churches or property appropriated to the college were regarded as appropriated to the sacrist, in whom the *personatus* was legally vested; presentations to vicarages of appropriated churches were made, not by the sacrist and canons as a corporate body, but by the sacrist as an individual; he paid the canons' stipends from a general fund, and was charged with the oversight of the whole establishment.[2] All this is much more similar to the organization of later independent colleges of resident chantry priests than to the older colleges of secular canons. Furthermore, like chantry priests, all clergy of the chapel were supposed to be continually resident.[3] For these reasons,

---

[1] For the constitution and history of this chapel see A. H. Thompson, 'The Chapel of St. Mary and the Holy Angels', in *Y.A.J.*,, xxxvi (1944), 63–77.

[2] A. H. Thompson, *loc. cit.*, p. 66.

[3] It is, however, extremely doubtful if the rule of residence were ever strictly kept, and in time it became little more than a counsel of perfection. Professor Hamilton Thompson's study of the personnel of the canons of the chapel in the thirteenth and fourteenth centuries shows that the type of clerk from which they were chosen did not differ materially from that which furnished members to the cathedral chapter. Many were in the service of archbishop or king, and can seldom have had time to reside (*ibid.*, pp. 72–7).

although they had separate prebends, and were called canons and prebendaries, not cantarists, Professor Hamilton Thompson has described the chapel as a chantry college. The connexion of the canons of the chapel with the cathedral was very close. A communicating doorway led from their chapel into the nave of the cathedral, and a special part in the cathedral services was reserved for them.[1]

Elsewhere in England, later chantry colleges established in secular cathedrals were smaller, having only from about three to seven or eight members; and, as far as we know, their organization was much more closely controlled by the dean and chapter. There are, however, few available records of their government and way of life. At St. Paul's the most considerable was Holmes College, which finally came to have seven members. It was originally founded by Adam of Bury, mayor of London, for three priests, but in 1386 these were increased to seven through the generosity of Roger Holme, Adam's executor, who also provided a common house for their residence. The seven priests each subscribed a fixed sum for their common meals, and every year elected one of their number to preside over the others.[2] Neither this college nor Lancaster College, founded in 1403 for a chantry of priests celebrating in the chapel built by John of Gaunt's executors at his tomb in St. Paul's cathedral, appear ever to have been incorporated.[3] A further chantry college at St. Paul's, known as Thomas More's chantry, did actually obtain a formal charter of incorporation in 1424 which declared its chaplains capable of using a common seal and acquiring land. But their powers were strictly limited, since any such property which they acquired had to be immediately rendered up to the dean and chapter, who held it on

---

[1] A. H. Thompson, *loc. cit.*, pp. 69-70. In 1258 an ordinance of Archbishop Sewall provided that, on the instructions of the precentor of the cathedral, the canons of the chapel should take the places of absent cathedral canons in celebrating the morrow and high masses in York Minster. Normally, none below the rank of cathedral canon was supposed to celebrate at the high altar in English secular cathedrals; but a few other exceptions have been found, such as the minor canons of St. Paul's and certain priest vicars at Lichfield (see above, p. 265).

[2] See the account of this college in *V.C.H. London*, i, 427.

[3] *Ibid.*, In the case of Lancaster College the dean and chapter of the cathedral had power to compel the priests to lodge together in their college and to have meals there in common.

their behalf, paying a yearly rent from it to each of the chantry priests.[1] Lincoln cathedral had three or four chantry colleges of a similar kind: the Cantilupe chantry, founded in 1357 for seven or eight priests;[2] the 'Works Chantry' for three priests supported from the cathedral fabric fund;[3] the Faldingworth chantries;[4] and the Burghersh chantry. This last college was an especially interesting foundation, established by Bishop Burghersh and his brother in the mid-fourteenth century. It consisted of five chaplains, a clerk, and six boys. The boys acted as choristers both at their chantry altar and in the cathedral choir; they wore a livery distinct from that of the cathedral choristers, and had a separate master to instruct them in grammar and song.[5] In 1397 the five chaplains were granted jointly a further 20 li. a year in common income to support another chaplain and a boy to be chosen by themselves.[6] Yet as late as 1535 it was still a canon residentiary of the cathedral, not one of their own number, who acted as supervisor and receiver of the college.[7]

Finally, towards the end of the fourteenth and in the fifteenth centuries, a rather different kind of cantarists' college made its appearance at some cathedrals. A new movement arose to put those cantarists who were not already attached to any other college, and who had no house of residence belonging to their chantries, to live together in a common hall in the close. These halls were generally established rather later than those of the vicars choral. In many cases they were probably suggested by the vicars' colleges, but there were not always the same pressing reasons for founding them. The dean and chapter were not usually so anxious as they had been in the case of the vicars for cantarists to live together for the sake of discipline; all cantarists were supposed to be priests, and might presumably be trusted to live alone or in twos and threes. Nor does the same strength of corporate feeling seem to have developed among the cathedral cantarists as among the vicars choral. The attitude of those cantarists

---

[1] *Ibid.*

[2] *Lincoln Visitations*, i, 142 n. Their house faced eastward on the road from Lincoln cathedral to the Bishop's Palace (A. H. Thompson, *Cathedral Churches*, p. 161).

[3] *L.S.*, iii, 168. These priests were nominated by the *custos* of the fabric to say masses for the souls of benefactors of the fabric.

[4] Their ordinance is printed in *Reg. Antiquissimum*, ii, 105, 107–12.

[5] *Valor Eccl.*, iv, 27.   [6] *C.P.R. 1396–9*, p. 123.   [7] *Valor Eccl.*, iv, 27.

who were not also vicars choral was probably rather more detached from their fellows than that of the vicars; they had their separate duties prescribed for them by their foundation deeds, and, for the most part, seem to have had no special desire to combine in order to obtain privileges from the chapter. The main reason for founding colleges for them seems to have been simply the grow-ing shortage of housing accommodation in the close, and the difficulties encountered by the increasing number of cantarists who had to find lodgings in the city at a distance from the cathe-dral. At cathedrals such as Salisbury, where there were compara-tively few cantarists, and no shortage of houses in the close, it was never found necessary to provide them with a common hall. St. Paul's, however, which had more chantries than any other English secular cathedral, was the first English cathedral chapter to reserve chambers or houses of residence for its cantarists. Before 1318 a piece of land in St. Paul's churchyard was assigned to the cathedral cantarists, and lodgings situated on it, called chambers, might thenceforth be granted to them either by benefactors, or by the dean and chapter.[1] In time a number of chantry priests came to live in the building variously known as the 'Presteshouses' or St. Peter's College; separate chambers were allotted to each, and they were usually bound to keep their own chambers in good repair at their own expense.[2] In 1391, when Bishop Braybrooke united a number of the smaller chantries in the cathedral and re-arranged their revenues, he ordered that in future all chantry priests at St. Paul's, who belonged to no other college, should take their food in common in the Presteshouses, and that the dean and chapter should assign chambers there to as many as possible.[3] Individual chaplains are known to have paid rents to the body of chaplains and the college had statutes which they were bound to observe. In the compilation by Dean Colet they are said to obey their proctor,[4] a statement which suggests that they had some kind of representative official. But their technical position re-mained that of a congregation of individuals. As late as 1424 they had no common seal, and their property was apparently re-garded as being vested for their use in the dean and chapter.[5]

[1] MSS. D. and C., A, Box 74, 1918, 1922, 1938, 1950, quoted by H. Douglas-Irvine, 'Cathedral of St. Paul', in *V.C.H. London*, i, 426.   [2] *Ibid.*
[3] *R.S.S.P.*, p. 149.   [4] W. S. Simpson, *op. cit.*, in *Archaeologia*, lii, i, 167.
[5] *V.C.H. London*, i, 426.

The next evidence for a common hall of residence of this kind at an English secular cathedral is at Wells, where in 1401 Bishop Erghum founded a college for fourteen chantry priests in the quarter north of the cathedral known as the Mountroy.[1] In 1410 Bishop Stafford granted a canonical house in Exeter cathedral close for the common use of the annuellars.[2] In 1415 Bishop Burghill's executors, in accordance with the terms of his will, arranged for the building of a house in Lichfield close in which cantarists serving in the cathedral might live together.[3] Finally, in 1461, the most important of these colleges, St. William's College, was founded at York for twenty-four chantry priests belonging neither to St. Sepulchre's College by the cathedral, nor to the Bedern of the vicars choral.[4] The fellows of St. William's College formed a body corporate, had a common seal, and were able to purchase and hold lands in common. At first, probably with the normal organization of colleges of vicars choral in mind, it was suggested that they should elect annually one of themselves to be supervisor of the college.[5] But the final decision was to have a provost appointed for life, an arrangement more in accordance with that usually adopted at independent chantry colleges. Together with a committee of three, chosen by him from among the fellows, the provost could ordain statutes for the government of the college, punish infringements of them, and, when necessary, expel members from the college.[6]

Of the dissolution of the chantries, Professor Hamilton Thompson has written that it brought about a change in the religious life of England even more widely spread than that effected

[1] Canon of Wells, in *Anglia Sacra*, i, 570.

[2] *Use Exeter*, p. 14. This probably came later to form part of the Annuellars' College (cf. E. Lega-Weekes, *Topography of Exeter Close*, pp. 61 et seq.).

[3] William of Whitlocke in *Anglia Sacra*, i, 452. Bishop Burghill's charter of 1411, granting the land for this building, is printed in *Monasticon*, VI, iii, 1254.

[4] See the account by J. Solloway in *V.C.H. Yorks.*, iii, 385–6. A royal licence to erect the college was first granted to Archbishop Booth, the Earl of Northumberland, and the dean and canons of York in 1455, but was never carried into effect. In 1461 Edward IV made a regrant of the licence with important differences to George Nevill, bishop of Exeter, who became archbishop of York three years later, and to his brother, the earl of Warwick, and their heirs.

[5] This provision was made in the first royal licence of 1455; the final decision was included in the regrant of 1461.

[6] *Ibid.*, p. 386.

by the suppression of the monasteries.[1] It certainly caused changes and left some very definite gaps at the cathedrals, not only in the system of government and in the life of the close, but also in the church services. The cantarists' masses had made an important contribution to the celebration of divine worship at the cathedrals. As the chapter of Lincoln pointed out, the vicars choral were in any case unable to celebrate continuous masses on account of their nightly vigils before the mass of the Blessed Virgin Mary, and, without the cantarists' masses, strangers coming to the church to hear divine service would sometimes have been disappointed.[2] Satirists and moralists of the fourteenth and fifteenth centuries frequently attacked the cathedral cantarists for cupidity and laziness, comparing the few daily offices by which they earned their living with the arduous duties of the conscientious parish priest.[3] Yet the light duties prescribed in the chantry ordinances really give no fair picture of the chaplains' activities. They also gave valuable help to the vicars choral in the celebration of the main cathedral services.[4] Furthermore, they often held administrative offices in the church, such as clerk of the fabric, sub-communar, or master of the choristers; and sometimes did useful work in serving other city churches whose endowments were too small to support a full-time parish priest.[5] The dissolution of the chantries, coming as it did, at a time when the numbers of both residentiary canons and vicars choral were falling, not only put a greater burden of work on the clergy who were left, but caused certain duties and services which had enriched the celebration of the office in the medieval cathedrals to be discontinued altogether. Constitutionally, the disappearance of the various collegiate organizations of the cantarists may have simplified administration within the close. Yet it

---

[1] 'Certificates of Chantry Commissioners for the College of Southwell', in *Trans. Thoroton Soc.*, xv (1911), 65.

[2] *L.S.*, iii, 360–1; cf. *S.S.*, pp. 258–9.

[3] E.g. Chaucer's *Prologue*, ll. 509–14.

[4] When the vicars of St. Paul's complained of the honourable position accorded to the cantarists in their cathedral, saying that chantry clergy did not really belong to the cathedral foundation and that vicars ought to have precedence of them, they were rebuked by the dean and chapter, who reminded them of the valuable help which the cantarists gave both to them and to the minor canons in the daily celebration of the main cathedral services (*R.S.S.P.*, pp. 138–40; cf. p. 150).

[5] E.g. cf. *Reg. Sudbury*, ii, 148–69 passim.

cut short some interesting experiments in self-government and in decentralization, which in many cases had clearly not reached their full development.

3. THE CLERKS OF THE SECOND FORM: ALTARISTS, POOR CLERKS, AND SECONDARIES

At certain English secular cathedrals, as in some continental churches,[1] a further group of 'clerks of the second form' is sometimes mentioned briefly in the cathedral statutes or other records. These were the clerks who sat in the second row of choir stalls below the vicars choral and cantarists, but above the choristers, and whose duties were usually especially connected with the cantarists. At Salisbury and Wells they were called 'altarists', a term which in other churches was more often used as an alternative for cantarists; at Lincoln they were 'poor clerks', and at Exeter 'secondaries' or simply, 'clerks of the second form'. Their number seems rarely to have been more than twelve.[2] None might be priests.[3] In 1277 the chapter of Exeter ordered its secondaries to be divided among the orders of deacon, subdeacon, and acolyte;[4] in 1337 Bishop Grandisson declared that all of them, if possible, ought to be deacons and subdeacons.[5] But at Salisbury the altarists seem frequently to have been in minor orders. Indeed, the chapter of Salisbury declared that it customarily appointed altarists from among the cathedral choristers whose voices had broken and who were not yet old enough to be vicars choral.[6] This was probably the practice at most other English

---

[1] E.g. for the duties and status of the poor clerks or *non-beneficiati* at Bayeux cathedral, see Deslandes, *op. cit.*, pp. 290–1.

[2] At Exeter in 1268 their number was already fixed at twelve (Harl. MS. 1027, ff. 10b–11a, 17b; cf. *Ordinale Exon.*, i, 2). There were eleven poor clerks at Lincoln in 1535 (*Valor Eccl.*, iv, 14). Salisbury cathedral seems to have had about five or six *altaristae intrinseci* and from two to four *altaristae extrinseci* (cf. Jones, *Fasti Sar.*, p. 237). The statutes of Wells cathedral mention only three altarists (*W.S.*, p. 99), but there may have been more.

[3] Thus at Lincoln, if a poor clerk were ordained a priest, his place became *de facto* vacant, and another clerk had to be appointed to it (*L.S.*, i, 350).

[4] Harl. MS. 1027, f. 17b.   [5] *Ordinale Exon.*, i, 2.

[6] This ruling was made in 1388, after the treasurer had unsuccessfully claimed the sole right of appointing altarists at Salisbury (Reg. Dunham, ff. 7–8). No cathedral clerk could be made a vicar choral until he had reached the age of twenty-two, the canonical age for being ordained to the subdiaconate.

cathedrals. There certainly seems to have been no great gap between the choristers and the clerks of the second form. On one occasion in 1530 the secondaries at Exeter were required to take the choristers' places in the cathedral, when the choristers had been ordered to stay away from the church on account of the pesti-lence;[1] while most chapters seem to have felt responsible for the education of their clerks of the second form. At Salisbury and Lincoln, altarists and poor clerks had to attend the chancellor's grammar school in the close as soon as their morning duties in the cathedral were finished.[2] In 1559 this provision was extended by the Injunctions of Queen Elizabeth, which declared that duties in the cathedral interfered too much with the boys' education. In future every chorister, as soon as his voice began to break, was to be given the full stipend of an altarist or secondary and 'meate and drinke provided for two years, so that he might diligently and duly go to the grammar school, being relieved of any obligation to undertake paid duties in the choir'. In the meantime the chapter or treasurer was ordered to find other men to do the altarists' work.[3]

It was naturally easier for the chapter to dispense with the services of the older choristers in 1559 than it would have been before the Dissolution of the chantries, for the Dissolution had ended the altarists' most important duties. In the middle ages each altarist or poor clerk was assigned the custody of a particular cathedral altar, where he served daily in choir habit, at Lincoln from peal altar until tierce, and at Wells from sunrise to high mass, obeying and helping the chantry priests in the celebration of their offices. He was ordered never to allow anyone not wearing the choir habit to take his place. If a cantarist failed to say mass, the altarist was supposed to report him.[4] At Salisbury the six senior

---

[1] *Use Exeter*, pp. 21–2.

[2] Cf. D. H. Robertson, *op. cit.*, in *W.A.M.*, xlviii, 16–17; *Lincoln Visitations*, i, 139; *V.C.H. Lincoln*, ii, 430–1.

[3] *S.S.*, p. 375. For the appointment of lay vicars to do the altarists' work at Salisbury after these injunctions, see *V.C.H., Wilts*, iii, 184–5. Similar injunc-tions were sent to other cathedrals of the Old Foundation, e.g. *Y.S.*, p. 62; *Use Exeter*, p. 51.

[4] *L.S.*, i, 373; iii, 361; *W.S.*, p. 89; *Salisbury Ceremonies*, p. 155; *S.S.*, p. 307 n. No definite evidence has been found for the secondaries at Exeter being assigned to the annuellars' altars, though they are several times mentioned in the cathedral statutes in connexion with the annuellars (e.g. Harl. MS. 1027, f. 57b; *Use Exeter*, p. 12). In 1392 J. Hoper was ordered, on his admission as a secondary

altarists, known as *altaristae intrinseci* or *altaristae antiqui*, seem to have been attached to altars in the inner choir, while the *altaristae extrinseci* were probably attached to those in the outer choir or nave.[1]

Like the cantarists, the clerks of the second form also had duties in choir. They were especially required to be present on feasts of nine lessons and on greater feasts at matins, high mass, and vespers; at these services they might be entabled to serve at the high altar.[2] At Exeter they were also enjoined to attend all choir offices for the dead, the *commendam*, *placebo*, and *dirige*;[3] while at Wells they had the duty of saying the entire psalter daily for the bishop, chapter and benefactors of the church, and for the souls of all the faithful departed.[4] The chapter of Salisbury assigned to its altarists further work in the church under the sacrists' direction. The *altaristae extrinseci* were known as 'the sacrists' boys', and were responsible under the sacrists for cleaning the church and for the bell-ringing.[5] In 1475 it was a disputed point as to how often the sacrists might also call upon the *altaristae intrinseci* to help them with the bell-ringing on feast days.[6] On Maundy Thursday both the *altaristae antiqui* and the *garciones sacristarum* were supposed to help the sacrists to carry round the wine and ale of the bishop's Maundy Loving Cup to the vicars choral and cantarists.[7]

Little evidence is available for the stipends or endowments of these clerks. The statutes of Wells cathedral laid down that the altarists were to receive sufficient stipends from the common goods of the chapter, while a further note added that three altarists received fourpence a week each for guarding the altar and serving in the church.[8] A memorandum of the ordinary termly expenses of Exeter chapter towards the end of the fourteenth century

---

of Exeter cathedral to wait on the vicars who celebrated masses in the choir, and to note their absences (*Use Exeter*, p. 9).

[1] *S.S.*, pp. 379–80; Jones, *Fasti Sar.*, p. 237 n.; cf. *Salisbury Ceremonies*, p. 155.

[2] *S.S.*, pp. 254–7; *Use Exeter*, p. 12; *Ordinale Exon.*, i, 6–7.

[3] Cf. *Reg. Grandisson*, ii, 859.

[4] *W.S.*, pp. 65, 89. This duty was apparently distinct from that of the canons' daily recitation of the psalter (*L.S.*, i, 140–1).

[5] Jones, *Fasti Sar.*, p. 237 n.; cf. *S.S.*, p. 375.

[6] *Salisbury Ceremonies*, pp. 156. The *altaristae intrinseci* maintained that they were only bound to help with the bell-ringing when solemn matins were celebrated after vespers, and at the hour of none on greater and principal feasts.

[7] *Ibid.*, pp. 80–1.　　　　　　　　　　　　[8] *W.S.*, pp. 89, 99.

included a payment of twenty shillings to the secondaries for assisting daily at the mass of the Blessed Virgin Mary.[1] At Salisbury Dean Montacute's Additional Statutes of 1399 mentioned that the salary of an altarist might extend to thirty-six shillings and fourpence a year.[2] In 1475, when Bishop Beauchamp made enquiry into the endowments of altarists at Salisbury, the dean and chapter informed him that the five *altaristae antrinseci* each received a certain portion from the founders' endowments of masses said at their altars; that in addition each of them had one daily refection from the canons residentiary; and that the *altaristae extranseci* were sufficiently provided for by the ordinances of their founders.[3]

The chapter of Lincoln was apparently the only English secular cathedral chapter which acquired a common hall and common endowments for its clerks of the second form. In Bishop Sutton's episcopate, towards the end of the thirteenth century, it decreed that the poor clerks should live together in a house given to them by Master Geoffrey Pollard, canon, on the east side of the close at Lincoln near the priory. However, if a canon particularly wished to have one of the poor clerks living with him in his own house among his *familia*, he might do so by special arrangement with the chapter. In return for their house the poor clerks were to provide a lighted candle in a silver candlestick to burn before the altar on certain days of the year, and to have a solemn mass sung on Master Geoffrey Pollard's obit day.[4] In 1432 Bishop Gray enjoined that repairs should be made to the poor clerks' house, and ordered the chapter to appoint

'one with the office of ruling and governing the poor clerks . . ., to whose commands they may ever listen. . . . Inasmuch as since they are now without a ruler, after they have performed their ministry in the church indifferently or ill, almost every day they spend their time in drinkings and other unseemliness . . . while they might on the same days be giving their attention to learning.' [5]

At the same time he mentioned that disposal ought to be made to

---

[1] *Use Exeter*, p. 80.

[2] *S.S.*, p. 307. This entry is severely calendared in the printed statutes, and the source of the endowment is not clear. It may refer only to one particular altarist.

[3] *Salisbury Ceremonies*, p. 155.   [4] *L.S.*, i, 349; *Reg. Antiquissimum*, ii, 139.

[5] *Lincoln Visitations*, i, 142. The ruler of the poor clerks, like the head of the vicars' court at Lincoln, was called a provost (*L.S.*, i, 75).

the advantage of the poor clerks of forty shillings left to them by John Legburne, canon, 'which the chancellor says he has in his hands with the dean's knowledge and will'.[1] In 1535 the dean and chapter were said to spend a further twenty-nine pounds seven shillings and threepence annually on the maintenance of the poor clerks and their instruction in grammar.[2]

4. THE CHORISTERS

In the course of the late twelfth, thirteenth, and early fourteenth centuries the number of choristers supposed to be admitted to the cathedral had been fixed at Salisbury and Exeter at fourteen; at Lincoln at twelve; at Chichester at ten, later increased to twelve; at Lichfield probably eight, later twelve; at St. Paul's eight, later ten; at York seven, later twelve; at Wells six, and at Hereford five.[3] Nevertheless, the late medieval chapters apparently had difficulty in limiting their boys to the statutory number. In 1337 Bishop Grandisson thought it necessary to include in his visitation articles for Exeter cathedral, 'Are there more than fourteen choristers in the church, and if so, why?'[4] Furthermore, the chapters usually had to allow other boys in addition to the formally admitted choristers to sit on the *prima forma* in the cathedral choir. At Salisbury and Wells boy canons, that is, canons who had not reached the canonical age for ordination to holy orders, were given precedence on this form.[5] Boys attached to the households of individual canons formed a recognized part of the choir at Hereford in the thirteenth century.[6] At Lincoln the six boys of the Burghersh chantry sang in choir with the choristers, while canons and vicars might send young kinsmen or other boys living in their houses to attend the choristers' private grammar school.[7] At Exeter it was laid down in 1268 that boys serving in the church were not to exceed fourteen, unless they were so useful to the

---

[1] *Lincoln Visitations*, i, 144. [2] *Valor Eccl.*, iv, 14.

[3] *C.P.R., 1313–17*, p. 112; *Ordinale Exon.*, i, 7; *L.S.*, i, 410; ii, 76, 83–4; iii, 162; H. Jenkins, *op. cit.*, pp. 113–15; *C.S.*, pp. 7–8; W. D. Peckham, 'The Vicars Choral of Chichester Cathedral,' in *Sussex Arch. Coll.*, lxxviii, 144; *R.S.S.P.*, p. 76; Leach, *Medieval Schools*, p. 216; *York Fabric Rolls*, pp. 124–5; *Y.S.*, p. 144; *W.S.*, p. 99.

[4] *Reg. Grandisson*, ii, 859–60. [5] *Use Sarum*, i, 13; *W.S.*, p. 1.

[6] *L.S.*, ii, 76.

[7] See above, p. 299; *Educational Charters*, ed. Leach, pp. 390–3.

church or of such noble birth that they might be admitted to processions and mass for a time by reason of their progenitors or kinsmen, to be instructed in morals and honourable behaviour.[1] This competition both for choristers' places and for admission to share the choristers' training was evidently due to the value of the education provided.

The custom of admitting children among the communities of clergy serving cathedral churches was very ancient. Boys had an important place in the early episcopal *familiae* in France, where the clergy of the see were recruited mainly from them. By the sixth century there were no secular schools outside Italy; a bishop had to educate his clergy himself, for he was unlikely to get them educated elsewhere. He received them into his household, often at the age of seven, tonsured and blessed them, and admitted them to the minor orders of *ostiarius*, exorcist, and lector. At first he taught them himself; later, in the seventh and eighth centuries, he usually delegated the teaching to one of the priests of his *familia*, who in time came to be called *magister scholarium*, *magister scholarum*, *scholasticus*, or *capischola*.[2] Meanwhile, in the fourth and fifth centuries, important developments in the liturgy and chant had led to the institution in Roman basilicas of a community of clerks specially charged with the song and psalmody. Boys with good voices became especially necessary in these communities. Thus, when Gregory the Great reorganized the papal *schola cantorum* in 595, careful provision was made for training them.[3] The children were maintained by the papal chamber. They lived a common life in common houses, where children of noble families might also be received, to be taught with them by the *primicerius cantorum* or his deputy, the *secundicerius*. All had instruction in the seven liberal arts, as well as in singing. They might be raised from minor orders to the subdiaconate.

With the spread of the Gregorian plain song, the organization of the Roman *schola cantorum* influenced the training of boys in

[1] Harl. MS. 1027, f. 11a.

[2] See above, p. 177. For the training of boys in early episcopal *familiae*, see M. Deanesly, 'The *Familia* at Christ Church, Canterbury, 597–832', in *Essays to Tout*, pp. 1–3; *The Medieval Church*, pp. 32–3; 'Medieval Schools', in *C.M.H.*, v. 767–71.

[3] H. Leclercq in *Dict. d'archéologie chrétienne et de liturgie*, s.v. 'Chantres' cc. 360–2.

many parts of Europe, including England.[1] The school of song at Bishop Chrodegang's cathedral of Metz was one of the most famous in France. Little is known of its organization. But when Bishop Chrodegang drew up his *decretulum* for the common life of his cathedral clergy, he assumed that a number of clerks at the cathedral would be small children and youths in the grades of lector or acolyte. They were ordered to live in a common hall, and to sleep and work together, spending their youth in ecclesiastical discipline under the charge of an elderly and discreet canon; a younger canon might teach them, provided that his teaching were careful and spiritual.[2]

In England similar provisions seem to have been made for children before the Conquest, both at cathedrals which became Benedictine and at the large minsters of clerks. The enlarged rule of Chrodegang which Leofric gave to Exeter included rules for the instruction and discipline of the children,[3] while at Winchester there are references to the feast of the Boy Bishop in the tenth century.[4] The popularity of part-singing at monasteries and other large churches in the tenth and first half of the eleventh centuries gave the boys an important place in the cathedral and conventual choirs.[5] With the adoption of a secular organization at some cathedrals towards the end of the eleventh or in the course of the twelfth centuries, and the resulting abandonment of common buildings, the boys seem generally to have lived in the canons' private houses, receiving food and clothing in return for personal or domestic services. There are few references to them in records surviving from this period, but it is clear from the earliest cathedral statutes that their discipline, instruction, and ordering in choir belonged to the precentor.[6] He taught them singing in his song

---

[1] Cf. *ibid.*, cc. 362–4; 'Chant Romain et Grégorien', cc. 307–8.

[2] 'S. Chrodegangi Regula Canonicorum', in *P.L.*, lxxxix, c. 1073.

[3] *Old English Version of Enlarged Rule of Chrodegang*, c. 46.

[4] E. K. Chambers, *The Medieval Stage*, i, 339.

[5] For the development of part-singing at this time, at first in diaphony, later in polyphony, see M. D. Knowles, *The Monastic Order*, pp. 558–9. He writes that it is uncertain how far polyphony survived the Conquest in monasteries. The twelfth century is one of the darkest periods in the history of music. There are indications that the Normans did not view polyphony in monasteries with favour, and the dwindling number of children in the cloister towards 1050 must have put an obstacle in the way of its execution.

[6] E.g. *S.S.*, p. 58; *Use Sarum*, i, 3; *W.S.*, p. 45; *Ordinale Exon.*, i, 3; *L.S.*, i, 283; ii, 17; *R.S.S.P.*, p. 22.

school, and at Exeter was known throughout the middle ages as
'*Dux Puerorum*'.[1]

Gradually, however, as the number of residentiary canons
became fewer, the support of the boys was regarded as an increasingly heavy burden on those who were left, and the boys
lived on short commons. At Salisbury they are said to have been
'compelled to go round from door to door to crave dole each day,
so as to get enough food to keep the wolf from the door . . . They
had not enough to live upon, and no master to keep them out of
mischief.'[2] It was at this stage, usually in the thirteenth and fourteenth centuries, that the bishop, dean and chapter of most English
cathedrals stepped in, taking the chief direction of the choristers'
lives out of the precentor's hands, and making common provision for their sustenance and education from special endowments.

There was wide variety in the arrangements made at different
cathedrals. The plan adopted by the dean and chapter of St.
Paul's was the most individual and had more in common with the
arrangements in Benedictine monasteries than in other secular
cathedrals. By the late thirteenth century the choristers were living
in the cathedral almonry.[3] Dean Baldock's code of statutes of about
1300 laid down that the almoner was obliged to have living with
him eight boys fit for the service of the church. He had to have
them instructed, either by himself or another master, in subjects
relating to the church services, in grammar, and in good behaviour,
taking no payment.[4] If he chose to send them to the chancellor's
grammar school instead of engaging a separate master to teach
them in the almonry, he had to pay the master of the chancellor's
school five shillings a year.[5] The boys received their food and
clothing from him. They were sometimes invited to dinner at the
canons' houses but were told by the chapter in the early fourteenth
century that on such occasions they must sit on the floor, not at
table with the vicars, lest they should become arrogant, and when
they went back to the almonry despise the food there and blame
their master.[6] It was in the fourteenth century that the great

[1] *Ordinale Exon.*, i, 4.

[2] Quoted by Mrs. Robertson, *Sarum Close*, p. 41, from Bishop Martival's
ordinance of 1322 for the choristers.

[3] For the almonry at St. Paul's, see above, p. 240.

[4] *R.S.S.P.*, p. 76.

[5] Cf. A. F. Leach, 'St. Paul's School before Colet,' in *Archaeologia*, lxii, i, 198.

[6] *R.S.S.P.*, p. 133.

development of this system took place in the English monasteries, where the almoner fed and instructed the choristers in his almonry situated at the gate of the monastery. The monastic almonries might maintain as many as fifty boys, as at St. Mary's Abbey, York, or twenty-four, as at Westminster Abbey. Usually the boys did not exceed thirteen, and were often less. But by the end of the middle ages the almonries provided education for about fifteen hundred boys.[1]

Two English secular chapters, Hereford and Exeter, decided to assign the charge of their boys to the succentor, the precentor's deputy, who in these churches acted also as song schoolmaster. Indeed, at Hereford the succentor seems actually to have chosen the boys. The mid thirteenth-century customs of the cathedral state that he provided from his school to act as choristers in the church five boys, whom he had to train in obedience, reverence, and mature behaviour, seeing that they did not enter the choir without shoes and robes, and that they had a broad and decent tonsure.[2] In 1276 the fourteen choristers of Exeter cathedral were put by the dean and chapter to live with the succentor, who had to board them and instruct them in singing and morals in his school.[3] Few details are known of the chapter of York's arrangements for its choristers, but in 1307 there is evidence that it had arranged for them to live together under the charge of a certain Richard Craven, who agreed to maintain them in board and learning (*in mensa et erudicionibus*) for four shillings and eightpence a week, or eightpence a week each, charged on Brodsworth church; again, in 1346, Stephen, a chaplain, was ordered 'to take care of the choristers and that they should live with him'.[4]

Elsewhere, provisions made by the secular chapters for their choristers usually involved the endowment of a new foundation. In 1264, Richard Gravesend, bishop of Lincoln, drew up his ordinance for the Lincoln Choristers' House,[5] which became the model for several later foundations at other English cathedrals. Already in 1258, when he was dean, he had procured the first separate endowments for the choristers of Lincoln.[6] Now he laid

---

[1] A. F. Leach, *Educational Charters*, pp. xxxi–ii; *Medieval Schools*, pp. 213–34.
[2] *L.S.*, ii, 83–4, 76.   [3] *Reg. Bronescombe*, pp. 77–8.
[4] Agreements quoted by Leach, *Medieval Schools*, pp. 216–17.
[5] Printed in *L.S.*, i, 410; iii, 161–2; *Reg. Antiquissimum*, ii, 137–8.
[6] *Ibid.*, ii, 102–3.

down that for the future their numbers should be limited to twelve, and that they should live together under a master. This master, who administered the revenues assigned for the boys' support, was appointed by the dean and chapter, and rendered annual account to them. He was also supervised by a residentiary canon, known as warden of the choristers. The boys were admitted, by the dean and chapter, after a careful examination in singing, birth, and morals, instead of by the precentor, who, however, seems to have had the right of nominating them to the dean and chapter.[1] Later documents show that the precentor also presented to the chapter one or two other masters to instruct the boys in grammar and song.[2] As Mr. Leach has pointed out,[3] the chapter, which asserted the legal rights of the masters of the chancellor's grammar school and of the precentor's song school to a teaching monopoly in the city, was itself guilty of promoting the most severe form of competition against both masters. The reason for allowing the choristers to have private masters was probably that the boys' ecclesiastical duties and intensive study of singing and music were incompatible with regular attendance at the city schools. But the master of the chancellor's grammar school strongly resented their privilege, especially since the choristers' grammar master was also allowed to teach other commoners who boarded with the choristers, in addition to young kinsmen of the canons and vicars, and members of the canons' households, thus depriving the master of the chancellor's school of their fees. Finally, in 1407, the chapter decreed that the master of the choristers' school might continue to teach all these boys freely, provided that he took them down to the general grammar school in the city for examination once a term.[4]

Between 1314 and 1322 a more ambitious plan was put into force at Salisbury by Bishop Ghent and Bishop Martival. Both these bishops had been at Lincoln, as archdeacons and dean, before their promotion to the episcopate, and may have been influenced by Bishop Gravesend's arrangements for the choristers there. In 1314 Bishop Ghent granted the rents of a cellar in the Fish Shambles in the city of Salisbury and some neighbouring shops for the support of fourteen choristers and a master to teach them

[1] Cf. *L.S.*, iii, 298.
[2] *Ibid.*, pp. 298–9; *V.C.H. Lincoln*, ii, 424–36.
[3] *Ibid.*, p. 424.   [4] *Educational Charters*, pp. 388–93.

grammar.[1] He died early in the next year, but his successor, Roger Martival, obtained the necessary further endowments;[2] arranged for the boys to live together in a house in the north-west corner of the close now known as Hungerford Chantry; and drew up rules for their common life.[3] By this foundation, the bishop declared, all necessity for the choristers' begging should be removed; for the future they were to devote themselves to the cathedral services and the study of letters, under the supervision of a *submagister*, well-grounded in grammar and able to instruct them in letters and morals. One of the residentiary canons was elected warden of the choristers; he administered their revenues and appointed the *submagister*, who might be a senior vicar choral or chantry chaplain. As at Lincoln, the boys were henceforth formally admitted to the church by the dean and chapter, instead of by the precentor; boys born in the diocese were preferred to strangers so long as they were suitable and could sing well.[4] Much more is known of the common life of the choristers at Salisbury than at Lincoln, chiefly through Mrs. Robertson's detailed study of the surviving account rolls of their warden.[5] In 1347 master and boys moved to another house in the close in Bishop's Walk on the site of the present organist's house, where they lived until 1559.[6] Their servants included a cook, barber, and laundress, and arrangements were made to keep the boys in an infirmary when they were ill. In the fifteenth century they had a special singing instructor, who was distinct both from their *submagister* and from the succentor, and who was frequently the cathedral organist.[7] At this time, also, the *submagister* apparently only taught the younger boys, while the older ones attended the chancellor's grammar school in Exeter Street with the altarists

[1] *C.P.R. 1313–17*, p. 112.

[2] The documents relating to Bishop Martival's appropriation of the church of Preshute to the choristers are printed by Mrs. Robertson and Canon Wordsworth, *op. cit.*, *W.A.M.*, xlviii, 201–4.

[3] His ordinance is discussed and largely translated by Mrs. Robertson, *Sarum Close*, pp. 40–3. Cf. *S.S.*, pp. 262–7.

[4] *Ibid.*

[5] *Sarum Close*, pp. 68 *et seq.* Mrs. Robertson has also published extracts from these accounts in *W.A.M.*, xlviii, 6–11.

[6] *Ibid.*, p. 2. Mrs. Robertson has traced all the houses inhabited by the choristers in Salisbury close from 1322 up to the present day, and has published most of the relevant documents (*ibid.*, pp. 1–27).

[7] C. Wordsworth and D. H. Robertson, *op. cit.*, p. 213.

and younger vicars.[1] In 1540 this city grammar school was re-founded in the close for the choristers' benefit.[2]

Other common houses established for English cathedral choristers on a similar plan were those at Wells, founded by Bishop Shrewsbury in 1348, and at Lichfield, founded by Dean Denton with the help of Bishop Geoffrey Blythe in the early sixteenth century.[3] Some interesting details are available of the life of the choristers of Wells in their common hall in the rules published by Bishop Beckington in the mid-fifteenth century.[4] One of the chief differences from the arrangements at Salisbury and Lincoln was that at Wells the precentor kept more of his early responsibility for the boys. The dean and chapter did not insist on their being formally admitted in the chapter house. The precentor appointed the master who lived with the choristers, and himself audited the master's annual accounts with the help of a senior residentiary canon. It was this master who chose and trained the choristers under the precentor's direction. He had to be a priest, and was supposed also to be wise and discreet in judging the capabilities of the boys, moderate in punishing them and trustworthy in managing their temporal goods. He might appoint an under-master to help him to instruct the boys in reading and singing, in matters belonging to the church services, and in behaviour. Special attention was paid to the boys' table manners. Bishop Beckington ordered that they should be trained to drink only when their mouths were empty; to cut or break their bread, not to gnaw it with their teeth or tear it with their nails; not to dirty their tablecloth, or to pick their teeth with their knives. The boys slept three in a bed, the two smaller ones with their heads at the top of the bed, the older one with his head at the foot. A lamp was kept burning in their dormitory at night. Their games were limited to half an hour or an hour at most before supper in winter and after supper in summer.

Many choristers were given permanent employment at the

[1] C. Wordsworth and D. H. Robertson, *op. cit.*, pp. 3, 16–17, 213; *Sarum Close*, pp. 64 *et seq.*

[2] *W.A.M.*, xlviii, 3, 11–22. Leach, *Medieval Schools*, p. 217, had previously maintained in error that there was a medieval grammar school in the close.

[3] Canon of Wells in *Anglia Sacra*, i, 569; William of Whitlocke, *ibid.*, i, 455; cf. *Valor Eccl.*, iii, 135.

[4] They are printed in English in *Dean Cosyn and Wells Cathedral Misc.*, pp. 98–109.

cathedrals after their voices had broken, as clerks of the second form, and later as vicars or chantry chaplains. But Queen Elizabeth's injunctions of 1559, ordering that choristers should be given two or more years' further education at the cathedral grammar school before undertaking such work,[1] introduced little that was new. The clerks of the second form and the younger vicars had always been expected to attend the chancellor's grammar school in their spare time.[2] Moreover, some at least of the medieval chapters had made provision for the higher education of their more promising boys. In 1315 Richard Newport, bishop of London, had granted a house to William de Tolleshunte, almoner of St. Paul's for the support of one or two almonry boys after their voices had broken.[3] In 1329, when William died, he left his grammar books for the use of the boys in the almonry, but his more advanced books on medicine, history, civil and canon law, were to be lent to the boys after they had left the almonry.[4] The dean and chapter of Lincoln in the fifteenth century had the right to nominate one of their choristers to a bible clerkship at Lincoln College, Oxford.[5] At Wells, at any rate from the mid-fifteenth century, all money given to the boys by the canons had to be kept locked up in separate purses by their master. Each boy might see how much he had in his purse; then later, if, with the approval of the precentor and master, he wished to go to an English university, his money was given to him for the purpose.[6]

The chapters usually tried to arrange that the choristers' duties in choir should interfere as little as possible with their general education. On greater feasts all boys had to be present at the hours. But on ordinary days or feasts of three or nine lessons, only the four or five boys entabled to sing or read at the principal hours were required to attend, while the others went to school. During the school vacations, however, the chapter of Exeter decided that all boys indifferently must be present at the whole office.[7]

The boys' chief duty was singing. Groups of them were entabled each week or fortnight to sing the antiphons, responds, versicle, gradual, *Benedicamus*, *O Redemptor* or *Gloria Laus*;[8] the

---

[1] See above, p. 304.   [2] See above, pp. 273, 304.
[3] A. F. Leach, 'St. Paul's School before Colet', in *Archaeologia*, lxii, 199.
[4] *Ibid.*, pp. 198–9.   [5] *Registrum Antiquissimum*, ii, 139–40.
[6] *W.S.*, p. clxxxi.   [7] *Ordinale Exon.*, i, 7.
[8] E.g. *Use Sarum*, i, 304–5, and references there given.

number entabled varied according to the solemnity of the feasts and the uses of different cathedrals; their duties became increasingly important with the development of polyphonic music in the later middle ages.[1] Matins, high mass, and vespers were the most important hours, but a certain number of boys were expected to sing also at prime, compline, the vigils of the dead, and at trigintals and anniversaries.[2] By the late thirteenth and fourteenth centuries, attendance at the daily sung mass of the Blessed Virgin Mary had usually been made compulsory for them. About this time, too, and later, endowments were being granted to enable choristers to sing the matins and vespers of the Blessed Virgin; or, as at Exeter, to sing the antiphons of Our Lady each night at curfew at the north door of the church, before saying vespers in their school.[3]

The boys also helped in reading the lessons and in the ceremonial of the services. Lessons were normally read by the cathedral clergy in ascending order of dignity, from the choristers up to the priests. Therefore a *puer hebdomadarius leccionis* was entabled each week to read the first lesson at matins and to hold the book for the officiating priest, who said the chapter and collect at lauds and vespers. On feast days other lessons might be read by choristers. In addition, the boys were trained to act as cross bearers, censers, taperers, and water bearers; the older boys who were acolytes were entabled as cross bearers and censers, while the younger boys carried the candles and the holy water.[4]

The great day for the choristers was St. Nicholas' or Holy Innocents' Day, when all these duties were reversed. The boys elected their own bishop from among themselves, and conducted the services from matins to vespers, sitting in the dignitaries' and canons' stalls, and entabling priests of the cathedral to act in their places as cross bearers, censers, taperers, and water bearers.[5] The

---

[1] Cf. F. L. Harrison, *Music in Medieval Britain*, pp. 156 *et seq.*

[2] *Use Sarum*, i, 40, 93; *W.S.*, p. 9; *Ordinale Exon.*, i, 7; *L.S.*, ii, 76, 83–4.

[3] E.g. *Use Exeter*, p. 80; *Monasticon*, VI, iii, 1265; D. H. Robertson, *Sarum Close*, p. 61; *Use Exeter*, p. 18; *H.M.C. Wells*, i, 23.

[4] *Use Sarum*, i, 305, and references there given; *L.S.*, ii, 76, 83–4; *R.S.S.P.*, p. 77; *Reg. Antiquissimum*, ii, 120–1, 137–8.

[5] For the origin of and ceremonies connected with the Feast of Boys, see E. K. Chambers, *Medieval Stage*, i, 336–71; A. F. Leach, *Medieval Schools*, pp. 144–5; J. M. J. Fletcher, *The Boy Bishop at Salisbury and Elsewhere*; D. H. Robertson, *Sarum Close*, pp. 78–94. Directions for the services conducted by

boy bishop preached his sermon to the people.[1] This Feast of Boys was much more popular and enduring in England than its riotous rival, the Feast of Fools, conducted by the vicars choral and other lesser clergy on the feast of the Circumcision.[2] The Feast of Fools seems generally to have been stamped out by reformers in England before the end of the fourteenth century, but the Feast of Boys continued to be widely popular until it fell before the austerities of the Reformation in the sixteenth century. Possibly the medieval chapters found that the boys were easier to control on their feast day than the vicars, and so were more reluctant to abolish their privileges. Restrictions were imposed at Salisbury and other southern cathedrals in the later middle ages, when it was said that the feast was made the occasion for mockery, insolence, and physical violence, particularly on the part of the vicars.[3] But at York, in the fourteenth and fifteenth centuries, the boy bishop still had wide powers; he conducted a visitation of neighbouring churches, accompanied by his boy dignitaries and canons; he exacted procurations; and held a quête in the city at intervals between Christmas and Candlemas.[4] The celebrations often lasted for a week or longer. The residentiary canons of St. Paul's prepared feasts for the boys. The boy bishop had the right to visit any canonical house he pleased with his *familia*, while the other boy dignitaries and canons took their *familiae* to the houses of those canons whose places they were filling. After dinner the canons provided them with horses on which to ride round the city and bless the people.[5]

---

the choristers are printed in *Salisbury Ceremonies*, pp. 52–9; *Ordinale Exon.*, i, 74–7, 88–9; cf. *R.S.S.P.*, pp. 91–3. The feast was celebrated in monasteries, colleges, schools, and universities, as well as in secular cathedrals.

[1] William de Tolleshunte, almoner of St. Paul's in 1329, bequeathed to the almonry copies of sermons preached by boy bishops in his time. Probably he was responsible for writing them (cf. Chambers, *op. cit.*, i, 355–6).

[2] Cf. *ibid.*, p. 349. Professor Chambers has written a detailed account of the Feast of Fools, particularly in France (*ibid.*, i, 274–335). The Feast of Boys was sometimes associated with it in the denunciations of reformers.

[3] E.g. *S.S.*, pp. 264–7; *W.A.M.*, xlviii, 211–12; *R.S.S.P.*, pp. 91–3; *Reg. Grandisson*, ii, 723.

[4] Chambers, *op. cit.*, i, 356–8. The office of boy bishop at York was profitable: cf. his computus for 1396, printed *ibid.*, ii, 287–9.

[5] *R.S.S.P.*, pp. 92–3.

Y

CONCLUSION

IN addition to all these groups and colleges of *ministri inferiores*, there were other groups attached to the medieval secular cathedrals, whose members might sometimes be present in the close. These were the clergy and laity, men and women, for the most part benefactors of the cathedrals, who were admitted to confraternity with the chapter; their names were inscribed in the cathedral's 'Book of Life', and they were granted a special share in the benefits of all the prayers and masses said in the cathedral, both in their life and after death.[1] Other fraternities, known as fraternities of the fabric, might be formed from those who had contributed to the particular object of the building and repair of the cathedral fabric;[2] at Lincoln a special 'Works Chantry' was maintained to pray for them.[3] Then there were the more humble members of city gilds, such as the gilds or fraternities of St. Katherine, of St. Anne, of All Souls, or of the Holy Name of Jesus at St. Paul's, and of the Kalendar Fraternity at Exeter, who were allowed by the chapter to hold their services in the cathedral church, and to maintain a chantry priest to celebrate at one of the cathedral altars.[4] These fraternities and gilds had nothing to do with the government of the church and cannot be regarded as part

---

[1] For these fraternities of the secular chapters, see especially C. Wordsworth, *Salisbury Ceremonies*, pp. 145–50; *Canonization of S. Osmund*, pp. 243–5; *L.S.*, i, 408–10; ii, ccxxxv–li. So far little work has been done on them. J. Duhr's article 'La Confrérie dans la vie de l'Église', in *Rev. d'hist. eccl.*, 1939, pp. 437–78, is useful in giving the general background of the movement, but does not deal particularly with the fraternities of the secular chapters. The same is true of W. G. Clark-Maxwell's 'Some Letters of Confraternity', in *Archaeologia*, lxxv, 19–60; lxxix, 179–216, which is concerned chiefly with the fraternities of the monks, friars, hospitals, and gilds.

[2] See e.g. *H.M.C. Wells*, i, 181, 208, 224. Professor Cheney kindly tells me that the earliest text of Richard le Poore's statutes, *c.* 1223, for Salisbury diocese, includes an order to all priests to pray every Sunday for the brethren and sisters, living and dead, of the cathedral fabric. This order is not included in the printed edition of the statutes in *Sarum Charters*, p. 158.

[3] *L.S.*, iii, 168.

[4] *V.C.H. London*, i, 426; *H.M.C. Ninth Rept.*, App., 1, 27; *R.S.S.P.*, pp. lxiv–vii, 435–62; E. Lega-Weekes, *Studies, Exeter Cathedral Close*, pp. 44–5.

of the cathedral constitution. Nevertheless, their existence at the cathedrals, like that of the minor corporations of inferior clergy, helps to illustrate one outstanding characteristic of English secular cathedral government in the later middle ages: the large number of more or less separate organizations which the chapters allowed to grow up in their midst, and the complex and varied interests which were represented in the close.

It is interesting to compare the government of the secular cathedrals of the Old Foundation with those of the medieval cathedral monasteries in England and of the new secular foundations of Henry VIII which took the place of the cathedral monasteries after the Dissolution. The most striking difference is perhaps the much greater centralization of the monasteries under their prior, and later, of the New Foundations under a dean whose powers were far wider than those of the deans of the Old Foundations. The dean of the Old Foundations had never been more than *primus inter pares* among the canons; the chapter had always shared much of his power and responsibility, while the three other principal dignitaries had enjoyed considerable independence of his supervision in their own particular branch of cathedral administration. In the later middle ages the growth of the minor corporations had led to further decentralization of government within the close. In contrast to the clergy of the Old Foundations, those of the New Foundations appear far more as single united bodies in which all ministers alike were subject to the supreme direction of the dean. Even the cathedral monasteries, though they allowed secular chantry chaplains to celebrate at the altars of their church, and though links with members of their fraternities were an essential part of their way of life, formed a much more united whole than the secular cathedrals of the Old Foundation.

How had this complexity of organization developed at the cathedrals of the Old Foundation? The answer seems to be not that it was merely the result of a complete and precise ready-made constitution imported from Normandy in the late eleventh century, but that it grew up gradually in England over a period of several centuries. St. Osmund's Institution of 1091 at Salisbury, the nearest approach which we have to a ready-made constitution being given to any of the English cathedrals, may have come down to us in a form containing additions or modifications made towards the middle of the twelfth century. Even in this form it represents no complete outline of the later medieval constitution of Salisbury chapter, but is merely the basis on which the chapter slowly built up its customs. Furthermore, although the general form of cathedral chapters in northern France in the late eleventh century had a distinct influence on the plans of Osmund, Thomas, and Remigius, it does not seem that at this time any Norman chapter could have provided a precise model for the particular 'four-square' constitution, founded on the four great dignitaries of dean, precentor, chancellor, and treasurer, which later characterized the English cathedrals. Throughout the late eleventh and twelfth centuries, both in Normandy and England, there was much variety and uncertainty with regard to the number, titles, and precedence of the cathedral dignitaries; while, in the thirteenth century and later, the arrangements finally adopted in Normandy were by no means uniform in the different churches. The much greater similarity found among English secular cathedral constitutions from about the middle of the thirteenth century seems to have been due chiefly, not to Norman influence, but to the growing practice of English chapters of borrowing and adopting each others' customs, especially those of Salisbury.

Thus the beginnings of the secular cathedrals' constitutions seem to have been less elaborate than has been sometimes thought. The bishops' plans for their cathedrals in the late eleventh and early twelfth centuries were naturally limited by their resources, and in England these resources may in some cases have been more restricted than in Normandy. Thomas of Bayeux would doubtless have liked to have as fine a chapter at his cathedral of York as Odo had established at Bayeux, but after the Conqueror's harrying of Northumbria his revenues were probably insufficient. Development at the cathedrals could only come with the greatly increased wealth and endowments which all chapters received in the course of the twelfth and thirteenth centuries. It has been seen how, at English cathedrals, the number of prebends and dignities gradually increased during the twelfth and early thirteenth centuries as gifts of land and money were given for the purpose; many dignitaries only received their separate endowments in the middle or last half of the twelfth century, while at Exeter it was as late as 1225 before separate revenues were assigned to the support of a dean and chancellor. The same process has been observed in the institution of the lesser officials and *ministri in-*

feriores. The need for a permanent body of vicars choral was probably felt very early in the history of the English secular cathedrals, but the chapters could not pay salaries until they had the necessary funds. Most chapters probably obtained an adequate number of vicars before the end of the twelfth century, but at others it was not possible until later.

The absence of precision and completeness in the early cathedral constitutions had, however, one great advantage: the chapters were able very easily to use their expanding resources and to adapt their organization in the way best suited both to the changing needs of the times and to local conditions. Compared with the cathedral monasteries they had exceptional freedom to introduce changes and to make statutes, so long as these were conformable to the canon law of the western church. They were not bound by any particular rule, nor had they general chapters or any other central organization of the province which concerned itself with their discipline. They were unhampered by any immediate outside control save that of their bishop, and in time, as they acquired greater wealth and independence, they might sometimes introduce important changes without obtaining even their bishops' consent. Differences can sometimes be distinguished in the approach of the chapters to the task of defining and extending their customs and statutes. Hereford and Exeter, geographically the most isolated, developed what were in some ways the most individual arrangements, and seem to have been least influenced by the customs of other cathedrals. Of the three chapters, Salisbury, Lincoln, and St. Paul's, whose written bodies of customs came to have most influence on the constitutions of other English cathedrals, Salisbury was usually the more ready to introduce changes and to make new statutes; Lincoln, throughout the middle ages, laid exceptional emphasis on the authority of ancient custom. But for the most part, at all the cathedrals changes were regarded as a definition of ancient custom. Since the main constitutional problems were everywhere roughly the same, and since the chapters were frequently in touch with each other, their solutions were naturally similar.

Everywhere two major problems confronted secular cathedral chapters of the twelfth and thirteenth centuries. First was the contemporary need that an increasing proportion of canons and prebendaries should be non-resident in order that they might attend the universities and do necessary work in the administration of the state, of the central church, and of the diocese. At the same time, while fewer canons were thus normally expected to reside, the expansion of the liturgy and chant was requiring larger numbers of cathedral clergy of all grades, trained especially in singing. Directed by general pronouncements of the popes, by the advice of their bishops, and by the example of neighbouring churches, the chapters, in roughly similar ways, gradually readjusted their organization to meet both these needs. The position of the non-resident canons was legalized, while those canons who chose formally to enter residence were assigned very definite duties at the cathedral, with increased revenues from the common fund to enable them to perform their additional tasks. At the same time, each canon, whether resident or non-resident, was required to contribute to the support of a vicar choral at the cathedral, and the chapter devoted a share of its common revenues to the same purpose. In this way the cathedrals obtained a permanent body of inferior clergy, specially trained in singing; under the direction of the precentor and residentiary canons, the vicars choral were able to celebrate the *opus dei* with probably greater skill than the absent canons, who, for the most part, had no special qualifications in singing.

This flexibility of the capitular organizations, which allowed such changes to be introduced gradually, without any drastic upheaval in the life of the church or close, persisted throughout the middle ages. In the later middle ages changed social and economic conditions demanded that the large bodies of vicars choral and chantry chaplains should be allowed greater independence of the chapter, and some measure of corporate life in common halls or colleges. By this time effective government in the close had generally passed into the hands of a fairly small group of residentiary canons. Their outlook was perhaps more conservative and in some ways more limited than that of the larger chapters of the early middle ages. But they could still realize that bold changes were necessary and possible. By allowing the growth of the minor corporations, the chapters again adapted their way of life to contemporary needs. The extension of the vicars' powers of self-government was granted in time to preserve peace and order in the close. Frequently bishops and chapters helped the vicars in the foundation of their colleges.

The history of the secular cathedrals is not a steady decline from an ideal. In most cases there is insufficient evidence to show whether or not the cathedral clergy, when they first became secular, did in fact serve an ideal with any great enthusiasm. The Norman and English bishops, who founded or reconstituted their cathedral chapters on a secular basis, probably hoped that this kind of organization would help their chapters to fulfil the purposes of their cathedrals. But the objects of cathedrals varied at different periods, and the development of the chapters was not always in one fixed direction. Their history is rather one of constant adaptation to meet the changing needs of the church and society. In the late eleventh and twelfth centuries, when the education provided at monasteries was clearly insufficient to satisfy the growing demands of an increasingly urban society, the English secular cathedral schools, like those of northern France, expanded their organization and curriculum to meet these demands. They not only provided teaching in grammar; traces of flourishing cathedral schools in the higher faculties of theology and law have also been found. In the twelfth century, these schools prepared the way for the universities, and in some cases almost developed into universities themselves. Afterwards, when their work was superseded by that of the universities, they retired into the background. Throughout the later middle ages, however, they apparently continued to provide lectures in theology or canon law, probably chiefly for local clergy, such as *ministri inferiores* at the cathedral, or clergy holding benefices in or near the cathedral city. At the same time the cathedral schools of grammar and song remained the diocesan centres for elementary education, usually with a monopoly of teaching in the cathedral city.

Medieval secular cathedrals had three other purposes. In common with monasteries and, indeed, all ecclesiastical institutions of the middle ages, their chief object was always the perpetual celebration of divine worship for the greater glory of God and as intercession for the living and dead by a body of men set apart for the purpose. But, unlike the monks, the secular canons had also work to do in the world. It may at first have been expected that most of this work would consist of helping the bishop in the administration of his diocese and serving the churches which belonged to the canons' prebends or common revenues. But gradually an increasing proportion of the cathedral prebends came to be a recognized means of support not only for clerks doing ecclesiastical work in the service of bishops or archbishops, but for many others studying and teaching at the universities and serving in the royal and papal administrations. The prebends of cathedral or collegiate churches were practically the only kind of ecclesiastical benefice available without a special papal dispensation for clerks employed in this manner; such prebends were legally without cure of souls, and so did not require residence. Much of the work which non-residents did outside the cathedrals was valuable to society. They gave trained service to the state; they enabled universities and learning to flourish, and the central administration of the church to expand and develop. In the later middle ages the popes themselves seem deliberately to have encouraged the extension of the practice of non-residence at cathedrals by providing many royal and papal servants and scholars to cathedral prebends. The result was not a total loss to the cathedrals. The residentiary canons, whose numbers even in the later middle ages seem often to have been larger than has sometimes been thought, might benefit by their contacts, through fellow canons, with contemporary developments in the universal church, in other cathedrals, in royal government, and in learning; such contacts might enable them to form a link between the diocese and the larger organization of the papal curia.

Cathedral churches of the middle ages, however, were generally much more detached from the diocese than they had been either in the early missionary days, when the bishop's cathedral clerks had acted as his council in the work of his diocese and had served with him in its churches, or in the nineteenth century, when the ideal of a cathedral was to become a centre of diocesan activity. The medieval chapters were powerful corporations with individual interests within the close, forming a kind of ecclesiastical republic in the diocese, strongly resentful of episcopal interference with their privileges and jurisdiction. On the other hand, their outside interests and contacts extended far beyond the borders of the diocese to the realms of politics, administration, learning, and the universal church. Nevertheless, throughout its history, the feature which distinguished a cathedral church from all other churches was its special relation to the bishop. It was the church in which the bishop's *cathedra* or throne was set up, and even though, in the later middle ages, bishops rarely stayed for any length of time in their cathedral city for fear of conflicts with their chapters, the cathedral church still remained the mother church of the diocese. The parishes of the diocese still sent their Whitsuntide offerings to the cathedral; the city clergy took part in certain cathedral processions. Some members of the chapter habitually acted as bishop's commissaries in the work of administering the diocese; while, during the bishop's absence from his diocese or during a vacancy of the see, much of the business usually carried on at his manor houses was transferred to the cathedral city.

In sixteenth-century England opinion in state and church apparently considered that the secular cathedral chapters fulfilled this essential function of serving the bishop's church and providing him with a seat of government as well as or better than any other organization. Chiefly for this reason these chapters survived the Reformation when other secular chapters, such as Beverley, which did not serve cathedral churches, were swept away with the monasteries and the chantries. They had to surrender some of their great wealth; they were brought under closer control by bishop and royal government; in addition to the removal of the chantry priests, the numbers of other groups of their clergy were cut down. Yet a gradual process of limiting the numbers of residentiary canons and vicars choral has been traced at the cathedrals as far back as the end of the fourteenth or beginning of the fifteenth century, and seems only to have been accelerated at the Reformation. There was no attempt to reconstitute the chapters on a new basis similar to that of the chapters of the New Foundation, which took the place of the cathedral monasteries, or even drastically to reform or change their medieval constitutions. Indeed, the cathedrals of the Old Foundation were practically untouched by any sweeping measure of reform until the nineteenth century. To-day, in spite of the work of the nineteenth-century reformers, the medieval secular cathedrals still remain, through their constitutions, their services, and their buildings, outstanding instances of continuity in English ecclesiastical life.

APPENDIX I

CANONICAL RESIDENCE AT LINCOLN DURING THE FOURTEENTH CENTURY

THE following lists have been transcribed from the annual accounts of the common fund at Lincoln, extant for fifty-eight years of the fourteenth century in Muniments of the Dean and Chapter of Lincoln, Bj/2/4-10. They give, first, the names of the greater residentiaries, who were present at Lincoln for at least two-thirds of the year; secondly, of the minor residentiaries, who resided for one-third of the year; lastly, of the non-residents. For reasons of space, the lists of 'Nullo modo Residentes' have been included only for the first two years, 1304-5 and 1305-6. They show the amount of the tax of a seventh levied on the income of each canon's prebend as a fine for his non-residence. Furthermore, the marginal sign on the left of the canon's name sometimes indicates the reason for his non-residence. Copies of the signs are given here, so that the reader may judge whether they have been correctly extended:

scʒ	extended to	scribatur
pʒ	,,	,, privilegia
cū epo	,,	,, cum episcopo
dełi	,,	,, deliberetur
nᵗ	,,	,, nichil
īrᵘ	,,	,, in respectu
m⁹	,,	,, mortuus
ī scoł	,,	,, in scolis

The purpose of these signs was apparently to guide the clerk engaged in levying the tax. Thus *privilegia* probably means that the canon had a special privilege or dispensation from the pope, exempting him from paying the tax; *cum episcopo*, that he was exempt by being in the bishop's service; *in scolis*, that he was at a university; *in respectu*, that the hearing of his plea for exemption had been adjourned. The most usual sign, *scribatur*, was probably to remind the clerk that a writ demanding payment must be despatched to the canon.

All the lists have been slightly rearranged, so that the dignitaries on whom residence was obligatory, come first; it can thus be seen at a glance how many dignitaries were performing their statutory duty of residence in any given year. The sum at the end of each annual list represents the amount of the residue of the common fund which was divided up among the greater residentiaries at the close of the financial year. Extensions of christian names or surnames, enclosed in square brackets, have been identified in Le Neve's *Fasti Ecclesiae Anglicanae*. Each canon's name is usually followed by that of his prebend. In cases when the information in the accounts about the holding of prebends contains additions to that given by the Institute of Historical Research's edition of Le Neve 1300-1541, volume i for Lincoln diocese (1962), compiled by Mr. H. P. F. King, the fact is noted the first time it occurs, and the entry is marked with an asterisk★; subsequent entries in which it is repeated are marked with an asterisk only.

1304–05. *Facientes Magnam Residenciam.*

Cancellarius [Ralph Barry] pro [North] Keleseye
Thesaurarius [Gilbert de Eyvill] pro lx s.
H[enricus de Beningworth], subdecanus, pro Welleton' [Westhall].
Archidiaconus Stowe [William de Okham] pro Bedeford maior'.
R[icardus] de Hederyngton' pro Aylesbyr'.
R[icardus] de Rowell' pro Asgerby.
Oliverus [de Sutton] pro Leiton' ecclesia.
W[illemus] de Thornton' pro Longa Stowa.*[1]
R[obertus] de Lascy pro Clifton'.
Thomas de Perrariis pro Dunham.
W[illelmus] de Stocton' pro Lafford.

Facientes Parvam Residenciam.

Archidiaconus Bedeford [Roger de Rowell] pro Welleton' Banastr'.*[2]
Archidiaconus Leycestr' [Roger de Martival] pro Castr'.
Magister Thomas de Birland pro Carleton [Kyme].

Nullo modo Residentes.

	Philippus [Willoughby], Decanus, pro Norton'	xlvs.	viijd.
	Archidiaconus Oxon' [Gilbert de Segrave] pro Milton' Ecclesia	lxxjs.	vd.
scribatur	Archidiaconus Northampton [Thomas de Sutton] pro Thame	cs.	
cum episcopo	Johannes de Nevile pro Welleton' Brinkelhall	xxjs.	vd.
scribatur	W[illelmus] de Astamaco pro Coringham iiij li.	vs.	viijd.
privilegia	Farendon' Romanus [Pandulph de Sabello]	xlijs.	xd.
scribatur	Phillipus de Barton' pro Leyhton' maner'	cxiiijjs.	iijd.
scribatur	J[ohannes] de Wengham pro Hundegat'	xiiijs.	iijd.
privilegia	Carleton' cum Thurleby Romanus*[3]	lviis.	jd.
privilegia	Keten' Romanus [Albert de Lausanne]	cs.	
cum episcopo	Gilbertus de Midelton' pro Bedeford maior' [? *rectius* minor]	xiiijs.	iijd.
scribatur	N[icolaus] de Witherche pro Welleton' Durihall' [4]	lvijs.	jd.

[1] Le Neve–I.H.R., 1300–1541, i, 111, has no information about holders of this stall before William's death as prebendary by 8 June 1313.

[2] This is apparently a variant form for the prebend of Welton Paynshall, which Roger held from 1290–1312 (Le Neve–I.H.R., 1300–1541, i, 124). The list of variants for the Welton prebends given in *L.S.*, iii, 941 (Welton Brinkhall, Welton Brynghall, *olim* Banaster) suggests that it should be Welton Brinkhall, but this is hardly possible, since John de Neville is named in these accounts as prebendary of 'Welleton Brinkelhall' for both 1304–5 and 1305–6, when Roger is said to be holding Welleton Banastr'. The other Welton prebends, Welton Westhall or *Subdecani* (Welleton'), Welton Beckhall (Welleton Bechall) and Welton Ryval (Welleton Durihall) were occupied by Henry de Beningworth, John de Schalby, and Nicholas de Whitchurch respectively.

[3] Le Neve–I.H.R., 1300–1541, i, 45, gives as prebendary of this stall Nicholas de Comite ?–1307, who died as prebendary at the Roman curia by 24 Nov. 1307, or according to a statement of the chapter vacated it by residence at the curia.

[4] I.e. Welton Ryval. Cf. Le Neve–I.H.R., 1300–1541, i, 126, which has no information about holders of this stall before Nicholas's death as prebendary by 19 Sept. 1312.

privilegia	Ecclesia de Langeford Romanus [Francis Gaetani]	ls.	
scribatur	H de Nassington' pro Brampton' ★ [1]	xlijs.	xd.
privilegia	Stokes Romanus [James de Sabello or Bokemar]		
		iiij li. vs.	viijd.
scribatur	I[ohannes] Maunsel pro Leycestr'	lvijs.	jd.
scribatur	Jacobus de Ispania pro cs'. de prepositis★[2]	xs.	viijd.
privilegia	Sutton' [cum Buckingham] Neapoleo [Orsini] cardinal'	lxiiijs.	iiijd.
scribatur	R[obertus] de Keuellyngwrth' pro Lydington'	xlijs.	xd.
deliberetur	J[ohannes] de Langeton' de bursa episcopi[3]	xxjs.	vd.
privilegia	Milton' maner' Romanus [Richard de Anibaldis de Urbe]	lxxjs.	vd.
scribatur	Bannebyr' in sequestro[4]	lxxjs.	vd.
cum episcopo	J[ohannes] de Scalleby pro Welleton' Bechall'	xxjs.	vd.
scribatur	P[etrus] de Ros pro ecclesia sancte crucis★[5]	xxviijs.	vjd.
cum episcopo	H[ugo] de Normanton' pro Crakepoll'	xxviijs.	vjd.
scribatur	W[illelmus] de Brixia pro Bugeden' Decanus[6]	xlijs.	xd.
cum episcopo	G[ocelinus *or* Jocelinus] de Kirmington' pro Empyngham	lxxjs.	vd.
privilegia	Bonifacius de Saluc' pro Gretton' ★[7]	lvijs.	jd.
	Nassington' in sequestro	iiij li. vs.	viijd.
scribatur	Th[omas] de Northflete pro Bikeleswade[8]	xlijs.	xd.
privilegia	P[etrus] de Sabaud' pro Langeford maner'	xlijs.	xd.
scribatur	Cropery Romanus [John de Anibaldis]	cxiiijs.	iijd.
cum episcopo	W[alterus] de Foderyng[eye] pro Merston	xxiijs.	vjd.
deliberetur	Thorngate[9]	xs.	viijd.
scribatur	W[alter] de Wotton' pro Heydor	cs.	
scribatur	R[icardus] de Plumstok' pro Scamlesby	lvijs.	jd.
scribatur	G[ilbertus] de Segrave pro ecclesia sancti Martini	xxjs.	vd.
scribatur	Edwardus de sancto Johanne pro Leyhton' Busard	cxiiijs.	iijd.
scribatur	Thesaurarius Regine pro Luda★[10]	iiij li. vs.	viijd.

[1] Le Neve–I.H.R., 1300–1541, i, 40 has no information before Henry's death as prebendary of this stall by 22 May 1308.

[2] Le Neve–I.H.R., 1300–1541, i, 50, has no information about prebendaries of this stall before March 1330, when John Offord quitted it and James de Hispania succeeded to it by exchange.

[3] I.e. the prebend of Decem Librarum.

[4] There were two claimants to this prebend early in 1304 (*ibid.*, i, 31).

[5] Le Neve–I.H.R., 1300–1541, i, 100, has no information about holders of this stall before the death of Peter de Ross as prebendary of it 22 May 1311.

[6] Jocelin de Kirmington was elected dean in Sept. 1305 on Philip Willoughby's death. He was displaced by Raymond de Got and gave up his claim by 27 Aug. 1309 (*ibid.*, i, 3).

[7] Le Neve–I.H.R., 1300–1541, i, 66, says that Boniface de Saluzzo was admitted to this prebend on the strength of papal provision in 1298, but has no further evidence for its tenure until 1324 when the King granted it to Robert Holden.

[8] Le Neve–I.H.R., 1300–1541, i, 36, has no information before Thomas de Northflete's death as prebendary by 11 Jan. 1318.

[9] Le Neve–I.H.R., 1300–1541, i, 118, says that William Gloucester was collated to Thorngate in 1300 and died in the Roman curia by 7 July 1307.

[10] Le Neve–I.H.R., 1300–1541, i, 86, has no information about holders of this prebend before William de Chessey died in possession of it by 5 Aug. 1309. The

scribatur   Stowa in Lyndesey'   xiiijs. iijd.

clix li. xjs. od. quad'. divided among eleven greater residentiaries: to each, xiiij li.
xs. jd.

1305–06. *Facientes Magnam Residenciam.*

> Cancellarius [Ralph Barry] pro [North] Kelesey
> Thesaurarius [Gilbert de Eyvill] pro Carleton' Kyme
> H[enricus de Beningworth] subdecanus pro Welton' [Westhall]
> Archidiaconus Stowe [William de Okham] pro Bedeford maior
> R[icardus] de Hederington' pro Aylesbyr'
> R[icardus] de Rowell' pro Asgerby
> Oliverus [de Sutton] pro Leyhton' ecclesia
> W[illelmus] de Thornton' pro Long' Stowe★
> R[obertus] de Lascy pro Clifton'
> W[illelmus] de Stocton pro Lafford

> *Facientes Parvam Residenciam*

> Archidiaconus Leycestr' [Roger de Martival] pro Castr'
> Archidiaconus Oxon' [Gilbert de Segrave] pro Milton' ecclesia

> *Nullo modo Residentes.*

nichil	G [Gocelin *or* Jocelin de Kirmington] decanus pro Empingham		lxxjs.	vd.
scribatur	Archidiaconus Northamton [Thomas Sutton] pro Thame		cs.	
deliberetur	Archidiaconus Bedeford [Roger de Rowell] pro Welton Banastr'		xxjs.	vd.
cum episcopo	Johannes de Nevile pro Welton' Brinkelhall'		xxjs.	vd.
scribatur	W[illelmus] de Astamac' pro Coringham	iiij li. vs.	viijd.	
examinetur si habere[t] privilegiam	Farendon' Romanus [Pandulph de Sabello]		xlijs.	xd.
scribatur	P[hillipus] de Barton' pro Leiton maner'		cxiiijs.	iijd.
cum episcopo	W[illelmus] de Foderingeye pro Hundegat'		xiiijs.	iijd.
privilegia	Carleton' cum Thurleby★ Romanus		lvijs.	jd.
privilegia	Ketene' Romanus [Albert de Lausanne]		cs.	
cum episcopo	G[ilbertus] de Middelton' pro Bedeford minor		xiiijs.	iijd.
scribatur	N[icholas] de Wichcherch' pro Welton Durihall'★		lvijs.	jd.

Queen's treasurer between 1300 and 1308 was John of Godley who succeeded
William de Chessey in the office when William went overseas in 1300 (Tout,
Chapters in Administrative History, v, 239). The next annual list of *Nullo modo
Residentes* in the Lincoln Audit Account for 1305–6 again describes the prebendary
of Louth simply as the Queen's treasurer (below, p. 330), but the three following
lists for 1306–7, 1307–8, and 1307–9 give him as William de Chessey without a
descriptive title (Bj/2/4, ff. 29, 39, 49). The first two accounts may mean what
they say, *viz.* that the Queen's treasurer (i.e. John of Godley) held the prebend.
But possibly they mean William de Chessey who had previously been treasurer.
The clerk who made up the accounts at Lincoln may have been out of touch
with the affairs of the non-residents and may until 1306–7 have described William
de Chessey by a title which he no longer held.

privilegia	Ecclesia de Langeford Romanus [Francis Gaetani]		ls.
scribatur	H[enricus] de Nassington' pro Brampton'*		xlijs. xd.
privilegia	Stok' [James de Sabello or Bokemar]	iiij li.	vs. viijd.
scribatur	J[ohannes] Maunsel pro Leycestr'		lvijs. jd.
scribatur	Jacobus de Ispania pro cs. de prepositis*		xs. viijd.
privilegia	Neapoleo [Orsini] Cardinalis pro Sutton' [cum Buckingham]		lxiiijs. iiijd.
scribatur	R[obertus] de Keuellyngwrth pro Lydington'		xlijs. xd.
cum episcopo	H[ugo] de Normanton' pro Norton'		xlvs. viijd.
nichil	R[obertus] de Pykering' pro Bursa Episcopi[1]		xxjs. vd.
in respectu	W[alterus] de Thorp pro sancto Botulpho		xiiijs. iiijd.
privilegia	Milton' maner' Romanus [Richard de Anibaldis de Urbe]		lxxjs. vd.
deliberetur	Bannebyr'		lxxjs. vd.
mortuus	Th[omas] de Perrariis pro Dunham		lvijs. jd.
cum episcopo	J[ohannes] de Scalleby pro Welton' Bechall'		xxjs. vd.
scribatur	P[etrus] de Ros pro ecclesia sancte Crucis*		xxviijs. vjd.
in scolis	P[etrus] de Dalderby pro Crakepol		xxviijs. vjd.
cum episcopo	W[alterus] de Wermyngton' pro lxs.		viijs. vijd.
scribatur	W[illelmus] de Brixia pro Buggeden'		xlijs. xd.
scribatur	Th[omas] de Goldesburg' pro Scarle		xlijs. xd.
privilegia	Bonifacius de Saluc' pro Gretton'*		lvijs. jd.
nichil	Nassington' J[ohannes] de Drokensford	iiij li.	vs. viijd.
scribatur	Th[omas] de Northflet' pro Bykeleswad'*		xlijs. xd.
privilegia	P[etrus] de Sabaud' pro Langeford maner'		xlijs. xd.
cum episcopo	G[ilbertus] de Middelton' pro Cropery		cxiiijs. iijd.
cum episcopo	W[alterus] de Fodering[eye] pro Merston		xxviijs. vjd.
nichil	W[illelmus] de Gloucestria pro Thorngat'		xs. viijd.
scribatur	W[alterus] de Wotton' pro Haydor		cs.
scribatur	R[icardus] de Plumstok' pro Scamlesb' cum Melton		lvijs. jd.
scribatur	G[ilbertus] de Segrave pro ecclesia sancti martini		xxjs. vd.
scribatur	Edwardus de Sancto Johanne pro Leithon Busard		cxiiijs. iijd.
scribatur	Thesaurarius Regine pro Luda*	iiij li.	vs. viijd.
scribatur	Stowa in Lyndeseye		xiiijs. iijd.

cxxxiij li. xvjs. ixd. quad' divided among eleven [*sic*][2] greater residentiaries: to each, xij li. iijs. ivd.

1306–07. *Facientes magnam Residenciam.*

Cancellarius [Ralph Barry] pro [North] Keleseye
G[ilbert de Eyvill] Thesaurarius pro Carleton' Kyme
H[enricus de Beningworth] Subdecanus pro Welton' [Westhall]
Archidiaconus Stowe [William de Okham] pro Bedeford maior'
R[icardus] de Rowell' pro Asgerby
Oliverus [de Sutton] pro Leyhton' ecclesia
W[illelmus] de Thornton pro Long' Stowe*
Thomas Clifford

. [1] I.e. the prebend of Decem Librarum.

[2] Thomas de Perrariis, prebendary of Dunham, who had resided in 1304–5, died this year. Possibly he is counted here as the eleventh residentiary. But his name is entered among the non-residents, with the marginal sign for *mortuus*.

W[illelmus] de Stocton' pro Lafford
R[obertus] de Keuelingworth pro Lydington'

Facientes parvam Residenciam.

Magister Rogerus de Martivallis [Archdeacon of Leicester] pro Castr'
Magister Gilbertus de Segrave [Archdeacon of Oxford] pro Middelton' ecclesia

ccvj li. os. xiijd. divided among ten greater residentiaries: to each, xx li. xijs. jd.

1307–08. *Facientes magnam Residenciam.*

Cancellarius [Ralph Barry] pro [North] Keleseye
H[enricus de Beningworth] Subdecanus pro Welton' [Westhall]
Archidiaconus Stowe [William de Okham] pro Bedeford maior'
R[icardus] de Rowelle pro Asgerby
Oliverus [de Sutton] pro Leyhton' ecclesia
W[illelmus] de Thornton' pro Long' Stowe★
Thomas de Clifford
R[obertus] de Keuellyngworth pro Lydington'
Facientes parvam Residenciam.

Thesaurarius [Robert de Lascy] pro Clifton'
Magister Rogerus de Martivall' [Archdeacon of Leicester] pro Castr'
Magister Gilbertus de Segrave [Archdeacon of Oxford] pro Midelton' ecclesia

cciiij.x li. vijs. iijd. ob' quad' divided among eight greater residentiaries: to each, xxxvj li. vs. xjd.

1308–09. *Facientes magnam Residenciam.*

Cancellarius [Ralph Barry] pro [North] Keleseye
R[obertus] de Lascy Thesaurarius pro Clifton'
H[enricus de Beningworth] subdecanus pro Welton' [Westhall]
R[ogerus de Martival] Archidiaconus Leycestr' pro Castr'
W[illelmus de Okham] Archidiaconus Stowe pro Bedeford maior
R[icardus] de Rowell pro Asgerby
W[illelmus] de Thornton pro Long' Stowe★
Oliverus [de Sutton] pro Leyhton' ecclesia
Thomas de Clifford pro Bedeford minor'
R[obertus] de Keuellyngworth pro Lydington'

ccclij li. xjs. viijd. ob' divided among ten greater residentiaries: to each, xxxv li. vs. ijd.

1309–10. Cancellarius [Ralph Barry] pro [North] Keleseye
R[obertus] de Lascy Thesaurarius pro Clifton'
H[enricus de Beningworth] Subdecanus pro Welton' [Westhall]
W[illelmus de Okham] Archidiaconus Stowe pro Bedeford maior
R[ogerus] de Mortivallis Archidiaconus Leycestr' pro Castr'
R[icardus] de Rowelle pro Asgerby
W[illelmus] de Thornton pro Long' Stowe★
Oliverus [de Sutton] pro Leyhgton' ecclesia
Thomas de Clifford pro Bedeford minor'
R[obertus] de Keuellyngworth pro Lydington'

ccxiiij li. vs. vd. ob' divided among ten greater residentiaries: to each, xxj li. viijs. vjd. ob.

1310–11. R[ogerus de Martival] Decanus pro Castr'
R[adulphus Barry] Cancellarius pro [North] Keleseye
R[obertus] de Lascy Thesaurarius pro Clifton'
H[enricus de Beningworth] subdecanus pro Welton' [Westhall]
W[illelmus de Okham] Archidiaconus Stowe pro Bedeford maior'
R[icardus] de Rowell' pro Asgerby
W[illelmus] de Thornton' pro Long' Stowe★
Oliverus [de Sutton] pro Leyghton' ecclesia
R[obertus] de Keuellyngworth pro Lydington'
J[ohannes] de Scalleby pro Dunham

Facientes parvam Residenciam.
Segrave
G[ilbertus de] Archidiaconus Oxon' pro Middelton' ecclesia
Thomas de Clifford pro Bedeford minor'.

xx
cciiij.xix li. vs. viijd. ob' quad' divided among ten greater residentiaries: to each,
xxix li. xviijs. vjd. ob. quad'.

1311–12. *Facientes magnam Residenciam.*

R[ogerus de Martival] Decanus pro Castr'
R[adulphus Barry] Cancellarius pro [North] Keleseye
R[obertus] de Lascy Thesaurarius pro Clifton'
H[enricus de Beningworth] subdecanus pro Welton' [Westhall]
W[illelmus de Okham] Archidiaconus Stowe pro Bedeford maior'
R[icardus] de Rowell' pro Asgerby
W[illelmus] de Thornton' pro Long' Stowe★
Oliverus [de Sutton] pro Leyghton' ecclesia
R[obertus] de Keuellyngworth pro Lidington'
Thomas de Clifford pro Bedeford minor'
Nicholas de Whitchirch' pro Welton' Durihall'
J[ohannes] de Scalby pro Dunham

ccvij li. xijs. obol' et quadr' divided among twelve greater residentiaries: to each.
xvij li. vjs. od.

1312–13. R[ogerus de Martival] Decanus pro Castr'
R[adulphus Barry] Cancellarius pro [North] Kelleseye
R[obertus] de Lascy Thesaurarius pro Clifton'
H[enricus de Beningworth] Subdecanus pro Welton' [Westhall]
W[illelmus de Okham] Archidiaconus Stowe pro Bedeford maior'
R[icardus] de Rowell' pro Asgerby
W[illelmus] de Thornton' pro Longa Stowa
Johannes de Harington pro ecclesia omnium sanctorum in Hundgat'
Oliverus [de Sutton] pro Leygton' ecclesia
R[obertus] de Keuellingworth pro Lydington'
R[icardus] de Stretton' pro Thorngat'
Johannes de Scalleby pro Dunham

Facientes parvam Residenciam.

Thomas de Clifford pro Bedeford minor
xx
cciiij.iij li. xvjs. xjd. divided among twelve greater residentiaries; to each, xxiij li.
xiijs. od. ob' quad'.

1313-14. *Facientes magnam Residenciam.*

> R[ogerus de Martival] pro Castr'
> R[adulphus Barry] Cancellarius pro [North] Kellesay
> H[enricus de Beningworth] Subdecanus pro Welton' [Westhall]
> W[illelmus de Okham] Archidiaconus Stowe pro Bedeford maiore
> R[icardus] de Rothewell' pro Asgerby
> Johannes de Haryngton pro Hundgat'
> Oliverus [de Sutton] pro Leyghton' ecclesia
> T[homas] de Clifford pro Bedford minore
> R[obertus] de Kyuelingworth' pro Lydington'
> R[icardus] de Stretton' pro Thorngat'
> H[enricus] de Mammesfeld pro ecclesia sancte crucis
> R[adulphus] de Foderyng[eye] pro Langford maner'
> J[ohannes] de Scalleby pro Dunham
> R[obertus] de Lascy pro Clyfton

cxxiv li. os. vjd. divided among fourteen greater residentiaries; to each, viij li. xvijs. ijd.

1314-15.   R[ogerus de Martival] decanus pro Castr'
> R[adulphus Barry] Cancellarius pro [North] Kellesey
> H[enricus de Beningworth] subdecanus pro Welleton [Westhall]
> W[illelmus de Okham] Archidiaconus Stowe pro Bedeford maior'
> R[icardus] de Rowell' pro Asgreby
> Johannes de Harington' pro Hundegate
> Oliverus [de Sutton] pro Leyghton' ecclesia
> T[homas] de Clifford pro Bedeford minor'
> R[obertus] de Kelingworth pro Lidington'
> H[enricus] de Mammesfeld pro ecclesia sancte crucis
> R[obertus] de Lascy pro Norton'
> J[ohannes] de Scalleby pro Donham
> R[icardus] de Stretton pro lxs.

Facientes parvam Residenciam.

> R[adulphus] de Fodering[eye] pro Langford maner'

ⁿⁿ
ciiij.iij li. xviijs. viijd. quad' divided among thirteen greater residentiaries; to each, xiv li. ijs. xjd. ob.

1315-16.[1] *Facientes magnam Residenciam.*

> Henricus [de Mannesfeld] decanus
> R[adulphus Barry] Cancellarius
> H[enricus de Beningworth] Subdecanus
> W[illelmus de Okham] Archidiaconus Stowe
> R[icardus] de Rowell'
> J[ohannes] de Harinton
> Oliverus [de Sutton]
> T[homas] de Clifford
> R[obertus] de Killingworth'
> R[obertus] de Lascy

---

[1] From this year until 1326-7 the canons' prebends are not given in the accounts.

z

J[ohannes] de Scalleby
R[icardus] de Stretton'

ccxxxvj li. viijs. ijd. quad. divided among twelve greater residentiaries; to each, xix li. xivs. od.

1316–17. H[enricus de Mannesfeld] decanus
A[ntonius Bek] Cancellarius
H[enricus de Beningworth] subdecanus
Archidiaconus Stowe [William de Okham]
Johannes de Harinton'
Oliverus de Sutton'
R[obertus] de Kyuelingworth'
T[homas] de Clifford
R[obertus] de Lascy
Johannes de Scalby
R[icardus] de Stretton'

cclviij li. os. xviijd. ob. divided among eleven greater residentiaries; to each, xxiij li. ixs. ijd.

1317–18. H[enricus de Mannesfeld] Decanus
Antonius Bek [Cancellarius]
H[enricus de Beningworth] Subdecanus
Oliverus de Sutton'
T[homas] de Clifford
W[illelmus] de Herpeswell'
W[illelmus] de Ocham
J[ohannes] de Harinton
J[ohannes] de Scalby
Ricardus de Stretton'

ccxiv li. xiijs. ijd. divided among ten greater residentiaries; to each, xxj li. ixs. iijd. ob.

1318–19. Henricus [de Mannesfeld] Decanus
A[ntonius Bek] Cancellarius
W[illelmus] de Ocham
T[homas] de Clifford
Egidius de Redmer
Oliverus de Sutton'
W[illelmus] de Herpeswell'
J[ohannes] de Sutton'
Johannes de Scalby
J[ohannes] de Harington
Ricardus de Stretton'

ccxx li. divided among eleven greater residentiaries; to each, xx li.

1319–20. Henricus [de Mannesfeld] Decanus
Cancellarius [Antony Bek]
Thesaurarius [Jocelin de Kirmington]
Subdecanus [Peter de Medburn].
Thomas de Clifford
Egidius de Redmer
Oliverus de Sutton'

Willelmus de Herpeswelle
Willelmus de Ocham
Johannes de Sutton
Johannes de Scalleby
Johannes de Harington'
Ricardus de Stretton'

clvij li. os. viijd. ob. quad. divided among thirteen greater residentiaries; to each, xij li. os. xixd.

1320–21. Henricus [de Mannesfeld] Decanus
Cancellarius [Antony Bek]
Gocelinus [de Kirmington] Thesaurarius
Subdecanus [Peter de Medburn]
Thomas de Clifford
Egidius de Redmer
Oliverus de Sutton'
Willelmus de Ocham
Johannes de Sutton'
Johannes de Scalleby
Johannes de Harington'
Ricardus de Stretton'

ccxvj li. xviijs. ivd. divided among twelve greater residentiaries; to each, xviij li. os. xviijd.

1321–22. Henricus [de Mannesfeld] Decanus
Antonius [Bek] Cancellarius
Thomas de Luda Thesaurarius
P[etrus de Medburn] Subdecanus
Egidius de Redmer
Oliverus de Sutton'
Willelmus de Ocham
Johannes de Sutton'
Johannes de Harington'
Johannes de Scalleby
Ricardus de Stretton'
Benedictus Feriby

ccxl li. divided among twelve greater residentiaries; to each, xx li.

1322–23. Henricus [de Mannesfeld] Decanus
Antonius [Bek] Cancellarius
Thomas de Luda Thesaurarius
P[etrus de Medburn] Subdecanus
Egidius de Redmer
Thomas de Corbrigge
Oliverus de Sutton'
Willelmus de Ocham
Johannes de Sutton'
Johannes de Scalleby
Johannes de Harington'
Ricardus de Stretton'
Benedictus de Feriby

cccxxiij li. xs. vd. quad. divided among thirteen greater residentiaries; to each, xxiv li. xvijs. viijd.

1323–24. Henricus [de Mannesfeld] Decanus
Antonius [Bek] Cancellarius
Thomas de Luda Thesaurarius
Petrus [de Medburn] Subdecanus
Egidius de Redmer
Thomas de Corbrig'
Thomas Bray
Willelmus de Ocham
Rogerus de Rowell'
Johannes de Scalby
Johannes de Sutton'
Johannes de Harington'
Ricardus de Stretton'
Benedictus de Feryby

cciiij li. ijs. vijd. divided among fourteen greater residentiaries; to each, xx li. os. ijd.

1324–25. Henricus [de Mannesfeld] Decanus
Antonius [Bek] Cancellarius
Thomas de Luda Thesaurarius
Petrus [de Medburn] Subdecanus
Egidius de Redmer
Thomas de Corbrig'
Willelmus de Ocham
Johannes de Scalby
Johannes de Sutton'
Johannes de Haryngton'
Ricardus de Stretton'
Benedictus de Feriby
Stephanus de Scropp'

cccj li. vjs. vjd. divided among thirteen greater residentiaries; to each, xxiij li. iijs. vjd. ob.

1325–26. Henricus [de Mannesfeld] Decanus
Antonius [Bek] Cancellarius
Thomas de Luda Thesaurarius
Petrus [de Medburn] Subdecanus
Egidius de Redmer
Thomas Corbrig'
Willelmus de Dalderby
Willelmus de Ocham
Johannes de Scalby
Johannes de Sutton'
Johannes de Harington'
Ricardus de Stretton'
Benedictus de Feryby
Stephanus de Scropp'

cccxvj li. xivs. ijd. ob quad. divided among fourteen greater residentiaries; to each, xxij li. xijs. vd.

1326–27. Henricus [de Mannesfeld] Decanus pro Asgerby
Antonius [Bek] Cancellarius pro Northekelsey

Thomas de Luda Thesaurarius pro Langford maner'
Petrus [de Medburn] Subdecanus pro Welleton' subdecani
Thomas [?de Northwode] Archidiaconus Stowe★ pro prebenda sancti
    Martini★ [1]
Egidius de Redemer pro ecclesia omnium sanctorum
T[homas] Corbrig' pro Thorngate
W[illelmus] de Ocham pro Bedeford maior'
Johannes de Scalleby pro Donham
Johannes de Sutton' pro Carleton' Kyme
Johannes de Harington' pro sancta Cruce
Ricardus de Stretton' pro sexagint' solid'
Benedictus de Feriby pro Crakpole
Stephanus de Scrop' pro Welleton' Paynshall'

ccccxx li. xs. vd. ob. divided among thirteen greater residentiaries; to each,
xxxij li. vjs. xjd. ob.

1327-28. Henricus [de Mannesfeld] Decanus pro Asgerby
    Antonius [Bek] Cancellarius pro Northkelsey
    Thomas de Luda Thesaurarius pro Langford maner'
    Petrus [de Medburn] Subdecanus quondam pro Welton' subdecani
    T[homas] de Northwod' nunc pro Welton' subdecani
    T[homas] de Corbrig' pro Thorngate
    Egidius de Redmer' pro ecclesia omnium sanctorum in Hundegate
    R[obertus] de Bridlington' pro Welton' Brinkhall'
    Thomas Beek' pro Clifton'
    Walterus Maydenstan pro Norton'
    Willelmus de Ocham pro Bedford maior'
    Johannes de Harington' pro sancta Cruce
    Johannes de Scalby pro Donham
    R[icardus] de Stretton' pro lxs.
    J[ohannes] de Sutton pro Carleton' Kyme

ccclij li. xvs. vijd. ob. quad. divided among fifteen greater residentiaries; to each,
xxiij li. xs. ivd.

1328-29. Antonius [Bek] decanus pro [North] Kelsay
    T[homas] de Northwod Thesaurarius pro Norton
    Walterus de Maydenstan Subdecanus pro Welton' subdecani
    Egidius [de Redmer] pro prebenda omnium sanctorum in Hundegate
    Thomas Beek' pro Clifton'
    Johannes de Harington' pro prebenda sancte crucis
    R[ogerus] de Rowell' pro prebenda de Welton G[? B]ourhall'[2]

---

[1] Le Neve-I.H.R., 1300-1541, i, 18, 89, has gaps in its lists of both the archdeacons of Stow and the prebendaries of St. Martin's at this time. It states (i, 18 n.)
that no trace has been found of Magister Thomas Northwode coll. to the archdeaconry of Stow, 14 April 1328, according to Le Neve-Hardy.

[2] This is most probably the prebend of Welton Ryval (cf. Le Neve-I.H.R.,
1300-1541, i, 126; *Reg. Antiquissimum*, ii, 178-9). Mrs. Varley, archivist to the
bishop of Lincoln, kindly tells me that she has found in a MS. notebook of the
late Canon Foster at Lincoln another reference to the form Welton Bourhall or
Gourhall (Bishop's Register, no. 4, f. 401d); he identified this as Welton Ryval.
Le Neve-I.H.R., 1300-1541, has no evidence for Roger holding this prebend
after 1316.

Johannes de Scalby pro Donham
R[icardus] de Stretton' pro lxs.
J[ohannes] de Sutton' pro Carleton' Kyme

ccccix li. viijs. xd. quad. divided among ten greater residentiaries; to each, xl li.
xviijs. xd. ob.

1329–30. Antonius [Bek] Decanus pro [North] Kelsay
Thomas de Nortwod Thesaurarius pro Norton'
Walterus [de Maydenstan] subdecanus pro Welton' subdecani
Egidius [de Redmer] pro prebenda omnium sanctorum in Hundegat'
Magister J[ohannes] de Harington' pro prebenda Sancte Crucis
Hugo de Walmesford pro prebenda de Bukden'
J[ohannes] de Scalby pro Donham
R[icardus] de Stretton' pro lxs.
Johannes de Sutton' pro Carleton' Kyme

Facientes parvam Residenciam.

Magister T[homas] Beek' pro Clifton

Residentes et nichil oneris facientes in ecclesia

Rogerus de Rothwell' pro Welton' G[? B]ourhall'*
Elias de Wh[e]tle pro Lidington'
Isti erant contenti de communis suis, vinis, et obitis, nichil ultra
recipiendo, quia dictus Rogerus, licet aliquo tempore resedit per
aliquot annos praemodum dum laborare potuit, discontinuauit
residenciam fere per xxiv annos, et rediit in decrepita etate et nichil
fecit. Et predictus Elias nunquam antea resedit, et nunc residere
incipiens semper remansit languide nichil faciendo.

ccccxxxv li. vs. iijd. ob. quad. divided among nine greater residentiaries; to each,
xlviij li. vijs. iijd.

1332–33. *Facientes magnam Residenciam.*

W[alterus] de Stauren' [Thesaurarius] pro Stowe in Lyndesay
W[alterus] de Maydenstan' Subdecanus pro Welleton' subdecani
Thomas de Norwood Archidiaconus Lincoln' pro Norton'
Egidius [de Redmer] pro prebenda omnium sanctorum in Hundegate
Thomas Beek' pro Clifton'
Johannes de Sutton' pro Thorngat'
Johannes de Harington' pro prebenda Sancte Crucis
W[illelmus] Bacheler pro Crakpole
H[ugo] de Walmessforth' pro Bukden'
J[ohannes] de Scalby pro Donham

ccccxxj li. os. vd. ob. divided among ten greater residentiaries; to each, xlij li. ijs.
od. ob.

1335–36. W[alterus] de Stauren' Thesaurarius pro Stowe in Lyndesay
W[alterus] de Maidenstan' subdecanus pro Welton' subdecani
Thomas de Norwood Archidiaconus Lincoln' pro Norton'
Egidius [de Redmer] pro prebenda omnium sanctorum in Hundgate
Johannes de Sutton' pro Thorngate

Galfridus de Edenham pro cs.
Radulphus de Erghum de Bursa Episcopi[1]
Johannes de Harington' pro prebenda sancte crucis
W[illelmus] Bacheler pro Crakpole
Hugo de Walmesford pro Bukden'
Simon de Islep' pro Welton' Bechall
Johannes de Bourn' pro Bedeford maiore

Facientes parvam Residenciam.

Thomas Beek' pro Clifton
Adam Lymbergh' pro Leycestr'

^{xx}
cciiij.x li. vjs. ijd. ob. divided among twelve greater residentiaries; to each, xxiv li. iijs. xd.

1336–37. *Facientes magnam Residenciam.*

Walterus de Stauren' Thesaurarius pro Stowe in Lyndesay
W[alterus] de Maidenstan' subdecanus pro Welton' subdecani
Egidius [de Redmer] pro prebenda omnium sanctorum in Hungate
Johannes de Sutton pro Thorngate
Galfridus de Edenham pro prebenda cs.
Radulphus de Erghum de bursa Episcopi
Thomas Beek' pro Clifton'
Johannes de Harington' pro prebenda sancte Crucis
Willelmus Bacheler pro Crakpole
Hugo de Walmesford pro Bukden'
Simon Islep' pro Welton' Bekhall'
Johannes de Bourne pro Bedford' maior'
Henricus de Edenstowe pro Carleton' Kyme

Facientes parvam Residenciam.

Adam de Lymbergh' pro Leycestr' Ec'
Thomas de Norwod Archidiaconus Linc' pro Norton'

cccxvj li. xivs. viijd. quad. divided among thirteen greater residentiaries; to each, xxiiij li. vjs. iijd. quad.

1337–38. *Facientes magnam Residenciam.*

Walterus de Stauren' Thesaurarius pro Stowe in Lyndesay
Nicholaus de Tarenta Subdecanus pro Welton' Subdecani
Thomas de Norwod Archidiaconus Linc' pro Norton'
Egidius [de Redmer] pro prebenda Omnium Sanctorum in Hungate
Thomas Beek' pro Clifton'
Johannes de Sutton' pro Thorngat'
Adam de Lymbergh' pro Leycestr'
Galfridus de Edenham pro prebenda centum solidorum
Radulphus de Erghum de Bursa Episcopi
Johannes de Harington' pro prebenda Sancte Crucis
Willelmus Bacheler pro Crakpole
Hugo de Walmesford pro Buggeden'
Simon Islep' pro Welton' Bekhall'

---

[1] The prebend of Decem Librarum.

Johannes Bourn' pro Bedeford maior'
Henricus de Edenstowe pro Carleton' Kyme

ccxl li. xijs. ivd. quad. divided among fifteen greater residentiaries; to each, xvj li. os. ixd.

1338–39. Walterus de Stauren' Thesaurarius pro Stowe in Lyndesay
Nicholaus de Tarente [Subdecanus] pro Welleton' Subdecani
Egidius [de Redmer] pro prebenda Omnium Sanctorum in Hundegate
Thomas Beek' pro Clifton
Johannes de Sutton' pro Thorngate
Galfridus de Edenham pro prebenda centum solidorum
Radulphus Erghum pro Bursa Episcopi
Johannes Harington' pro prebenda Sancte Crucis
Willelmus Bacheler pro Crakpole
Hugo Walmesforth pro Bukden'
Simon Islep' pro Welleton Bechall'
Johannes Bourn' pro Bedford maior
Henricus Edenstowe pro Carleton Kyme

Facientes parvam Residenciam.

Thomas Nortwod Archidiaconus Linc' pro Norton'
Adam de Lymbergh' pro Leycestr'

ciiij.xij li. vs. ijd. ob. quad. divided among thirteen greater residentiaries; to each, xiv li. xvs. ixd. quad.

1339–40. *Facientes magnam Residenciam.*

Walterus de Stauren Thesaurarius pro Stowe in L[in]desay
Nicholaus de Tharent' Subdecanus pro Welleton' Subdecani
Thomas de Nortwod Archidiaconus Line' pro Norton
Egidius de Redmer pro prebenda omnium Sanctorum in Hundgat'
Thomas Beek' pro prebenda de Clifton'
Johannes de Sutton' pro prebenda de Thorngate
Galfridus de Edenham pro prebenda centum solidorum
Radulphus de Erghum pro prebenda de bursa Episcopi
Johannes Harington' pro prebenda Sancte Crucis
Willelmus Bacheler pro prebenda de Crakpole
Hugo Walmesford pro prebenda de Bukden'
Simon Islep' pro Welton' Bekhall'
Ricardus de Whitwell' pro Empingham
Johannes Bourn' pro Bedford maior
Henricus Edenstowe pro Carleton' Kyme

ciiij.ij li. xivs. od. ob. divided among fifteen greater residentiaries; to each, xij li. iijs. vijd.

1360–61. Antonius [de Goldesbourgh] precentor pro Merston'
Johannes de Welbourn' [Thesaurarius] pro Asgerby
Hamo Belers [Subdecanus] pro Welton' Subdecani
Galfridus Scropp' pro Haydore
Adam Lymbergth pro xls.[*sic.*]
Thomas Sutton pro x li.
Willelmus Hugat' pro Carleton Kyme

Facientes minorem Residenciam.

Radulphus Erghom pro x li.
Ricardus Wytewell' pro Empingham

cccliij li. xviijs. iijd. divided among seven greater residentiaries; to each, l li. xjs. ijd.

1361–62. *Facientes magnam Residenciam.*

Antonius [de Goldesbourgh] precentor pro Merston'
Johannes Welbourn' [Thesaurarius] pro Asgerby
Hamo Beler [Subdecanus] pro Welton' Subdecani
Galfridus Scrop' pro Haydour
Willelmus Hongat' pro Carlton' Kyme
Adam Lymbergh, pro lxs.
Thomas de Sutton' pro x li.

cclxxij li. xiiijs. ivd. quad. divided among seven greater residentiaries; to each, xxxviij li. xixs. ijd. quad.

1362–63. Antonius [de Goldesbourgh] precentor pro Merston
Johannes de Welbourne [Thesaurarius] pro Asgerby
Hamo Beler [Subdecanus] pro Welton' Subdecani
Galfridus Scrop' pro Haydour
Willelmus Hongat' pro Carleton' Kyme
Thomas Fryskenay pro Dounham
Johannes Selby pro Sancta Cruce
Adam Lymbergh pro lxs.
Thomas de Sutton' pro x li.
J[ohannes] de Carleton' pro Thorngat'

clxvij li. xiijs. ivd. ob. divided among ten greater residentiaries; to each, xvi i. xvs. ivd.

1363–64. Antonius [de Goldesbourgh] precentor pro Merston
Johannes Welbourne [Thesaurarius] pro Asgerby
Hamo Beler [Subdecanus] pro Welton' Subdecani
Galfridus Scropp' pro Haydour
Willelmus Hongat' pro Carleton' Kyme
Thomas Fryskeney pro Donham
Johannes Selby pro Sancta Cruce
Adam Lymbergh pro lxs.
Thomas de Sutton pro x li.
J[ohannes] de Carleton' pro Thorngate
J[ohannes] Haddon' pro Welton' Bekhall'
J[ohannes] Warsopp pro Luda
Johannes Beuer' pro Sancto Bothulpho

iiij.xiij li. xvs. iiijd. ob. quad. divided among thirteen greater residentiaries; to each, vij li. ivs. iijd.

1364–65. Johannes de Stretele [Decanus] pro Bannebury
Antonius [de Goldesbourgh] precentor pro Merston'
Johannes de Welbourne [Thesaurarius] pro Asgerby
Hamo Beler [Subdecanus] pro Welton' Subdecani
Galfridus Scropp' pro Haydor

Thomas Sutton' pro x li.
Johannes de Carleton' pro Thorngate
Johannes Beuer' pro Sancto Bothulpho
Adam Lymbergh pro lxs.
Willelmus Hongat' pro Carleton' Kyme
Thomas Friskeneye pro Donham
Johannes Selby pro Sancta Cruce
Johannes de Warsopp' pro Luda
Johannes Haddon' pro Welton' Bekhall'

cl li. xixs. vd. divided among fourteen greater residentiaries; to each, x li. xvs. viijd.

1365–66. Johannes de Stretle [Decanus] pro Bannebury
Johannes de Welborne [Thesaurarius] pro Asgarby
Hamo Beler [Subdecanus] pro Welton' Subdecani
Galfridus Scropp' pro Haydore
Thomas Sutton' pro x li.
Johannes Carleton' pro Thorngate
Johannes Beuer' pro Sancto Bothulpho
Adam Lymbergh pro lxs.
Willelmus Hugate pro Carleton' Kyme
Johannes Selby pro sancta cruce
Johannes Warsopp' pro Luda
Johannes Haddon' pro Welton' Bekhall'

Facientes minorem Residenciam.

Antonius [de Goldesbourgh] precentor pro Merston'
Thomas Fryskeneye pro Donham

ccli li. iijs. id. ob. quad. divided among twelve greater residentiaries; to each, xx li. xviijs. vijd.

1366–67. Johannes de Stretele [Decanus] pro Bannebury
Johannes de Welborne [Thesaurarius] pro Asgarby
Hamo Belers [Subdecanus] pro Welton' Subdecani
Galfridus Scrop' pro Haydour
Thomas de Sutton pro x li.
Johannes Beuer' pro Sancto Bothulpho
Adam Lymbergh' pro lxs.
Willelmus Hugate pro Carlton' Kyme
Johannes Warsopp pro Luda
Johannes Haddon' pro Welton Bekhall'
Johannes Selby pro Sancta Cruce

Facientes minorem Residenciam

Antonius de Goldesburgh pro Merston [*cancelled*]
Thomas de Fryskeney pro Donham [*cancelled*]
Johannes Carleton pro Thorngate

xx
cciiij.xviij li. ixs. ijd. ob. quad. divided among eleven greater residentiaries; to each, xxvij li. ijs. vijd. ob. quad.

1367–68. *Facientes magnam Residenciam.*

    Johannes de Stretle [Decanus] pro Bannbur'
    Johannes de Welborne [Thesaurarius] pro Asgarby
    Hamo Beler [Subdecanus] pro Welton' Subdecani
    Galfridus Scropp' pro Haydor
    Thomas Sutton pro x li.
    Johannes Beuer' pro Sancto Bothulpho
    Adam Lymbergh' pro lxs.
    Johannes Warsopp' pro Luda
    Johannes Haddon' pro Welton' Bekhall'
    Johannes Selby pro Sancta Cruce

cccxxiv li. ijs. viijd. quad. divided among ten greater residentiaries; to each xxxij li. viijs. iijd.

1378–79. Johannes de Welborne Thesaurarius pro Asgerby
    Johannes de Beluero [Subdecanus] pro Welton' Subdecani
    Thomas de Sutton' pro decem librarum
    Galfridus Scropp' pro Heydore
    Johannes de Rouceby pro Carleton cum Thurleby
    Ricardus de Lyntesford pro Thorngate
    Ricardus de Wynewyk' pro North Kellesay
    Johannes de Warsopp' pro Luda
    Petrus de Dalton' pro Welton' Payneshall'
    Johannes de Stafford pro sexaginta solidorum
    Johannes de Carleton pro Sancto Bothulpho

cccxxxv li. vjs. viijd. divided among eleven greater residentiaries; to each, xxx li. ixs. viijd. quad.

1379–80. Johannes de Welbourne [Thesaurarius] pro Asgerby
    Johannes de Beluero [Subdecanus] pro Welton' Subdecani
    Thomas de Sutton' pro decem librarum
    Galfridus le Scrop' pro Heydore
    Johannes de Rouceby pro Carleton' cum Thurleby
    Ricardus de Lyntesford pro Thorngate
    Johannes de Carleton pro Sancto Bothulpho
    Ricardus de Wynewyk' pro North Kellesay
    Johannes de Warsopp' pro Luda
    Petrus de Dalton' pro Welton' Ryuall'
    Johannes de Stafford pro sexaginta solidorum

    xx
ccciiij.xvij li. xiiis. xid. ob. quad. divided among eleven greater residentiaries; to each, xxxvj li. iijs. id.

1380–81. Johannes de Beluero [Subdecanus] pro Welton' Subdecani
    Thomas de Sutton pro decem librarum
    Galfridus le Scropp' pro Heydore
    Johannes de Rouceby pro Carleton' cum Thurleby
    Johannes de Carleton' pro Sancto Bothulpho
    Ricardus de Beverlay pro Lydyngton'
    Ricardus de Wynewyk' pro North Kellesay
    Johannes de Warsopp' pro Luda
    Petrus de Dalton' pro Welton' Ryuall'

Facientes minorem Residenciam. [*cancelled*]

Johannes de Welborne thesaurarius pro Asgerby [*cancelled*]

Dxxiiij li. xjs. vijd. ob. quad. divided among nine greater residentiaries; to each, lviij li. vs. viijd. quad.

1381–82. *Facientes magnam Residenciam.*

Johannes de Beluere [Subdecanus] pro Welton' Subdecani
Thomas de Sutton' pro decem librarum
Galfridus le Scropp' pro Heydore
Johannes de Rouceby pro Carleton cum Thurleby
Ricardus de Beverlay pro Lydyngton'
Johannes de Carleton' pro Sancto Bothulpho
Ricardus de Wynewyk' pro North Kellesey
Johannes de Warsopp' pro Luda
Petrus de Dalton' pro Welton Ryuall'
Willelmus Welburne pro sexaginta soldidorum

cccciiij. xviij li. xvjs. xid. quad. divided among ten greater residentiaries; to each, xlix li. xvijs. viijd. quad.

1382–83. Johannes de Beluero [Subdecanus] pro Welton' Subdecani
Thomas de Sutton' pro decem librarum
Johannes Rouceby pro Carlton' cum Thurleby
Ricardus de Beverlay pro Lydyngton'
Johannes de Carleton' pro sancto Bothulpho
Thomas de Aston' pro centum solidorum
Ricardus de Wynewyk' pro Northkellesey
Johannes de Warsopp' pro Luda
Petrus de Dalton' pro Dunham
Willelmus de Welburne pro sexaginta solidorum

Facientes minorem Residenciam.

Galfridus Scropp' pro Heydore

cciiij.iiij li. vjs. jd. quad. divided among ten greater residentiaries; to each, xxviij li. viijs. vijd.

1383–84. *Facientes magnam Residenciam.*

Petrus de Dalton' Thesaurarius pro Dunham
Johannes de Beluero [subdecanus] pro Welton Subdecani
Ricardus de Chesterfeld pro Norton'
Johannes Rouceby pro Carleton' cum Thurlby
Ricardus Beuerlay pro Lydyngton'
Johannes de Carleton pro Sancto Botulpho
Thomas de Assheton pro centum solidorum
Ricardus de Wynewyk' pro Northkellesay
Johannes de Warsopp pro Luda
Willelmus de Welburne pro sexaginta solidorum

Facientes minorem Residenciam.

Thomas de Sutton pro Decem librarum

cciiij.xii li. xvs. viijd. quad. divided among ten greater residentiaries; to each, xxix li. vs. vjd. ob. quad.

1384–85. *Facientes magnam Residenciam.*

    Petrus de Dalton' Thesaurarius pro Dunham
    Johannes de Beluero [Subdecanus] pro Welton' Subdecani
    Ricardus de Chesterfeld pro Norton'
    Johannes Rouceby pro Carleton' cum Thurleby
    Ricardus Beuerlay pro Lidyngton'
    Johannes de Carleton pro Sancto Botulpho
    Thomas de Aston' pro centum solidorum
    Ricardus de Wynewik' pro Northkellesey
    Johannes de Warsopp' pro Luda
    Willelmus de Welburn pro sexaginta solidorum

cciiij.vj li. xs. viijd. ob. divided among ten greater residentiaries; to each, xxviij li. xiijs. ob. quad.

1385–86. Johannes Neuport precentor pro Kyldesby
    Petrus de Dalton Thesaurarius pro Dunham
    Johannes de Beluero [Subdecanus] pro Welton' Subdecani
    Thomas Aston' Archidiaconus Stowe pro centum solidorum
    Willelmus de Welbourn Archidiaconus Huntyngdon pro lxs.
    Ricardus Chesterfeld pro Norton'
    Johannes Rouceby pro Carleton' cum Thurleby
    Ricardus de Beuerlay pro Lydyngton'
    Johannes de Carleton' pro Sancto Bothulpho
    Ricardus Wynwyk'pro Northkellesay
    Thomas le Warr pro Lafford'

    Facientes minorem Residenciam.

    Johannes de Warsopp' pro Luda

cxxxiij li. xvijs. iijd. ob. quad. divided among eleven greater residentiaries; to each, xij li. iijs. ivd. ob.

1386–87. *Facientes magnam Residenciam.*

    Johannes Neuport, precentor pro Kildesby
    Petrus de Dalton' Thesaurarius pro Dunham
    Johannes de Beluero [Subdecanus] pro Welton' Subdecani
    Thomas Aston' Archidiaconus Stowe pro cs.
    Willelmus de Welburn' archidiaconus Huntyndon pro lxs.
    Ricardus Chesterfeld pro Norton'
    Johannes de Rouceby pro Carleton' cum Thurleby
    Ricardus de Beuerlay pro Lidyngton'
    Johannes de Carleton' pro Sancto Bothulpho
    Ricardus de Wynewyk' pro Northkellesey
    Thomas la Warr pro Lafford'

ccclxij li. xvs. vijd. divided among eleven greater residentiaries; to each, xxxij li. xixs. vijd.

1389–90. Johannes Shepey Decanus pro Nassyngton'
    Johannes Neuport precentor pro Kildesby

Petrus de Dalton' Thesaurarius pro Dunham'
Johannes de Carleton' [Subdecanus] pro Welton' Subdecani
Thomas Aston' Archidiaconus Stowe pro centum solidorum
Willelmus de Welburn' Archidiaconus Hunt' pro lx solidorum
Johannes de Beluero pro Sancto Bothulpho
Ricardus de Chesterfeld' pro Norton'
Ricardus de Beuerlay pro Lidyngton'
Ricardus de Wynewyk' pro North Kellesey
Thomas la Warr' pro Lafford'

xx
cciiij.j li. xviijs. xjd. divided among eleven greater residentiaries; to each, xxv li
xijs. vijd. ob.

1390–91. Johannes Shepey Decanus pro Nassyngton'
Johannes Neuport precentor pro Kildesby
Petrus de Dalton' Thesaurarius pro Farendon'
Johannes de Carleton' [Subdecanus] pro Welton' Subdecani
Thomas Aston' Archidiaconus Stowe pro Lidyngton'
Willelmus Welburn Archidiaconus Hunt' pro lx solidorum
Johannes de Beluero pro Sancto Botulpho
Ricardus de Chesterfeld' pro Norton'
Ricardus de Wynewyk' pro Northkellesey
Thomas la Warr' pro Lafford'

cccciv li. xs. ixd. ob. divided among ten greater residentiaries; to each, xl li. ixs.
od. ob. quad.

1392–93. Johannes Shepey Decanus pro Nassyngton'
Johannes Neuport precentor pro Kildesby
Johannes Hunteman cancellarius pro Sutton in le mersch'
Petrus de Dalton' Thesaurarius pro Farendon'
Johannes de Carleton' [Subdecanus] pro Welton' Subdecani
Thomas Aston' Archidiaconus Stowe pro Lidyngton'
Willelmus Welburn' Archidiaconus Hunt' pro lx solidorum
Ricardus de Chesterfeld' pro Norton'
Henricus de Brauncewell' pro centum solidorum
Ricardus de Wynewyk' pro Northkellesey
Thomas la Warr' pro Lafford'
Johannes de Kele pro Crakepole

ixxix li. ivs. ijd. divided among twelve greater residentiaries; to each, x li. xvs.
cvd.

1393–94. Johannes Shepey Decanus pro Nassyngton'
Johannes Neuport precentor pro Kildesby
Johannes Hunteman cancellarius pro Sutton' in le mersch'
Petrus de Dalton' thesaurarius pro Farendon'
Johannes de Carleton' [Subdecanus] pro Welton' Subdecani
Thomas Aston' Archidiaconus Stowe pro Lidyngton'
Willelmus de Welburn' pro Empyngham
Ricardus de Chesterfeld' pro Norton'
primus annus Johannes de Southam pro Asgerby
Henricus de Brauncewell' pro centum solidorum
Ricardus de Wynewyk' pro Northkellesey
Thomas la Warre pro Lafford'

primus annus Johannes Waynflete pro Luda
           Johannes de Kele pro Crakepole

iiij.vj. li. ixs. iiijd. divided among fourteen greater residentiaries; to each, vj li.
iijs. vjd. quad.

1394–95. Johannes de Shepey decanus pro Nassyngton'
          Johannes de Neuport precentor pro Kildesby
          Johannes Hunteman cancellarius pro Sutton' in le mersch'
          Petrus de Dalton' thesaurarius pro Farendon'
          Johannes de Carleton' pro Welton' subdecani
          Thomas de Aston' Archidiaconus Stowe pro Lydyngton'
          Ricardus de Chesterfeld' pro Norton'
          Johannes de Southam pro Asgerby
          Ricardus de Wynewyk' pro Northkellesey
          Thomas la Warr' pro Lafford'
          Willelmus de Welburn' pro Empyngham
          Johannes de Waynflete pro Luda
          Johannes de Kele pro Crakepole
          Henricus de Brauncewell' pro Welton' Bekhall'

lx li. xvs. od. quad. divided among fourteen greater residentiaries; to each, iv li.
vjs. ixd. quad.

              anno sequente nullo modo residet
1395–96. Johannes Shepey Decanus pro Nassyngton'
          Johannes de Neuport precentor pro Kildesby
          Johannes Hunteman cancellarius pro Sutton' in le mersch'
          Petrus Dalton' thesaurarius pro Farendon'
          Johannes Carleton' [subdecanus] pro Welton' subdecani
          Thomas de Aston' Archidiaconus Stowe pro Lidyngton'
          Ricardus de Chesterfeld pro Norton'
          Johannes de Southam pro Asgerby
          Johannes de Kele pro Welton' Brynkhall'
          Ricardus de Wynewyk' pro Northkellesey
          Thomas la Warr' pro Lafford'
          Willelmus de Welburn' pro Empyngham
          Johannes de Waynflete pro Luda

li li. xvs. ivd. ob. divided among thirteen greater residentiaries; to each, lxxixs.
vijd. ob.

1396–97. Johannes Neuport precentor pro Kildesby
          Johannes Huntman cancellarius pro Sutton in le mersch
          Petrus Dalton' thesaurarius pro Farendon'
          Johannes Carleton [Subdecanus] pro Welton' Subdecani
          Thomas Aston Archidiaconus Stowe pro Lidyngton'
          Ricardus de Chestrefeld' pro Norton'
          Johannes de Southam pro Asgerby
          Johannes de Kele pro Welton' Brynkhall'
          Ricardus Wynewyk' pro Northkelsey
          Thomas la Warre pro Lafford'
          Willelmus Welburn' pro Empyngham
          Johannes Wayneflete pro Luda

xxxjs. viijd. divided among twelve greater residentiaries; to each, ijs. vijd. ob.

1399–
1400.

Johannes Neuport precentor pro Kildesby
Johannes Huntman cancellarius pro Sutton in le mersche
Petrus Dalton' Thesaurarius pro Farendon'
Johannes Carleton' [Subdecanus] pro Welton' Subdecani
Thomas Aston' Archidiaconus Stowe pro Lidyngton'
Ricardus Chestrefeld' pro Norton'
Johannes Southam pro Asgerby
Johannes Kele pro Welton Brynkhall'
Ricardus Wynewyk' pro Northkelsey
Willelmus Welburn' pro Empyngham
Johannes Waynflete pro Luda

cxxxv li. os. xiijd. ob. quad. divided among eleven greater residentiaries; to each,
xij li. vs. vjd. ob.

1400–01.

Johannes Neuport precentor pro Kildesby
Johannes Huntman cancellarius pro Sutton' in le mersche
Petrus Dalton' thesaurarius pro Farendon'
iste obiit ⎫
hoc anno ⎬ Johannes Carleton' [Subdecanus] pro Welton' Subdecani
7 die ⎪ Thomas Aston' Archidiaconus Stowe pro Lidyngton'
Julii ⎭ Ricardus Chestrefeld' pro Norton'
Johannes Southam pro Asgerby
Johannes Kele pro Welton' Brynkhall'
Ricardus Wynewyk' pro Northkelsey
Willelmus Welburn' pro Empyngham
Johannes Waynflete pro Luda

lxiiij li. ixs. xjd., of which ten greater residentiaries had vj li. iiijs. vjd. quad. each,
and the eleventh had xliiijs. vjd. quad.

CANONS OF SALISBURY PRESENT AT THEIR CATHEDRAL IN 1343, 1347, 1350, 1394, 1398, 1399

THE following tables have been compiled from lists of canons entered in the Salisbury chapter act books as present at chapter meetings, and from payments of commons recorded in the quarterly accounts of the common fund. The six years chosen are those for which most evidence is available; but it is only for one year, 1343, that more than one quarterly account roll has survived. The arrangement is that of the communar's rolls: those canons whose stalls were on the *decani* side of the choir are given first, and are followed by those having stalls on the *cantoris* or precentor's side; a few canons, whose names are not on the roll, but who attended chapter meetings, are added at the end. The four main columns represent the four quarters of the Salisbury financial year. The amount of commons paid to each canon for his attendances at the cathedral services is entered under the relevant quarter, together with the number of chapter meetings at which he is known to have been present. It can thus be seen whether he was present at Salisbury for only one quarter of the year (that is, the time during which he was legally bound by statute to reside), or whether he stayed on for a longer period.

1343

Ex Parte Decani	Jan.–April Commons	C.A.¹	April–July C.A.	July–Oct. Commons	C.A.	Oct.–Jan. C.A.
1. The Bishop (Robert Wyville)	iijs. xd.					
2. Elias of St. Albans, Chancellor	iv li. xvs. ivd.	4	3	cijs. viijd.	5	2
3. John Kirkby, Archdeacon of Dorset	xljs. ivd.	3	1	xljs. vjd.	3	3
4. Robert de Luffenham, Archdeacon of Salisbury	xlviijs. viijd.	2	5	ljs. ivd.	4	
5. Ralph de Querendon, Subdean	xlviijs. viijd.	3	4	ljs. ivd.	3	2
6. Thomas de Luco	xlvjs. xd.	2	1	ijs. viijd. [? *per acquietanciam*]		
7. James de Havant	xviijd.	2		xjs. vjd.	1	2
8. Peter Inkpen	xjs. [?]ijd.			xijd.		
9. Robert Baldock	xxxjs. xd.	1	1	xixs. xd.		1
10. John Pieres	vjs. xijd. received by his vicar					
11. Richard de Thormerton				ijs. xd.		
12. John de Ufford				vjs. viijd. ob. by W. [? Bansity]		

¹ Chapter attendances.

Appendix II

	Jan.–April Commons	C.A.	April–July C.A.	July–Oct. Commons	C.A.	Oct.–Jan. C.A.
13. T. de Hatfeld				vs. viijd. quad. by [? Thomas de Brackle]		
Ex Parte Precentoris						
14. Walter de Wyville, Treasurer	iv li. xvjs. ivd.	2	3	cs. viijd.	1	2
15. Thomas de Bocton	xlviijs. viijd.	3	4	xliijs. viijd.	3	2
16. John de Langebergh	xljs. od.	4	4	ljs. ivd.	3	1
17. John of Salisbury	xlviijs. viijd.	3	3	xlviijs. od.	3	2
18. John de Camera	xljs. xd.	2	2	xls. ivd.	3	1
19. William Salton	xxivs. vjd.	2	2	xxivs. ijd.		1
20. The Abbot of Sherborne	[? d.].			iijs. ijd. received by William Coleshull		
21. John of Abingdon	ivs. vjd.					
22. John Whitchurch, Archdeacon of Wilts				xijs. viijd.	1	1
23. Edmund de Beche				iijs. ijd. quad. [cancelled]		
24. John de Kenewell or Gynewell				ijs. viijd. quad.		
25. John Giffard				xijd. quad.		
26. Richard de Chaddesley		1		ijs. od. quad.		
Not in Communar's Rolls						
27. Thomas of Staunton		1				

The surplus of lvi li. xiijs. ivd., remaining from the Jan.–April account, was distributed among 13 full residentiaries and a half residentiary. Each full residentiary had iv li. ivs. od.

The July–Oct. surplus was distributed among 12 residentiaries, but the details are illegible.

1347

Ex Parte Decani	Jan.–April C.A.	April–July Commons	C.A.	July–Oct. C.A.	Oct.–Jan. C.A.
1. The Bishop (Robert Wyville)		xijd.	2		
2. Elias of St. Albans, Chancellor	1	cvs. ijd.	8	2	1
3. Robert de Luffenham, Archdeacon of Salisbury	1	xljs. ivd.	2	3	2
4. Ralph de Querendon, Subdean	1	lijs. vijd.	8	3	1
5. James de Havant	1	lijs. vijd.	7	3	2
6. Robert Worth	1	xljs. vd.	6	3	1
7. Richard de Thormerton		lijs. vijd.	6		
8. Thomas de Luco	1	lijs. vijd.	6	1	
9. Peter Inkpen	2	xxjs. xd.	2		
10. Robert Baldock		xxjs. od.	1	2	

	Jan.–April C.A.	April–July Commons	C.A.	July–Oct. C.A.	Oct.–Jan. C.A.
Ex Parte Precentoris					
11. John de Camera, precentor		xxixs. ijd.	1	3	1
12. John de Langebergh	1	lijs. vijd.	8	3	1
13. Thomas de Bocton	1	lijs. vijd.	1	2	
14. John of Salisbury	1	lijs. vijd.	8	2	
15. William Salton	1	xxxiijs. xjd.	1	1	
16. Richard de Chaddesley	1	xviijs. od.	1		
17. William de Crouthorne		ixs. xd.	2	1	
18. John Whitchurch		[? vs.] ijd.			
19. Edmund de la Beche		xxijd.	1		

The surplus of xlix li. xvijs. ivd. ob., remaining from the April–July account, was distributed among 14 full residentiaries and a quarter residentiary. Each full residentiary had lixs. xjd.

1350

	Jan.–April C.A.	April–July C.A.	July–Oct. Commons	C.A.	Oct.–Jan. C.A.
Ex Parte Decani					
1. Elias of St. Albans, Chancellor	5	2	cjs. viijd.	3	3
2. Roger Kington, Archdeacon of Salisbury	5	6	x[?vj]s. ijd.	1	2
3. Ralph de Querendon, Subdean	5	3	ljs. ivd.	3	4
4. John Leeche		1	xjs. xd.		
5. Robert Baldock			vs. od.		
Ex Parte Precentoris					
6. John de Camera, precentor	5	5	cijs. viijd.	2	4
7. John Whitchurch			xs. vjd.	1	4
8. Richard of Netheravon	3	6	xxxijs. ivd.	1	2
9. William Salton	1	1	xjs. vjd.		
10. Bartholomew de Bradden	5	6	ls. xd.	3	4
11. John of Salisbury	5	4	xxxs. viijd.	1	
12. John Oliver			xvjs. od.		
13. Walter Waleys		1	iijs. ivd.		
14. John Chardstock			vjs. od.		
Not in Communar's Roll					
15. John Chesterfield	2	1			
16. William Farley		1			
17. John Wolverley		1			

The surplus of xliij li. [? v]s. ivd. ob. quad., remaining from the July to October account, was distributed among 9 full residentiaries. Each full residentiary had iv li. x[   ].

1394

Ex Parte Decani	Jan.–April C.A.	April–July C.A.	July–Oct. C.A.	Oct.-Jan. Commons	C.A.
1. Thomas Montacute, Dean	6	5	1	ijs. od.	
2. John Norton, Chancellor	10	5	1	cijs. viijd.	3
3. John Chitterne	4	2		xxxjs. jd.	1
4. William Loring	6	4		xlixs. xd.	2
5. John Turk	7	1		xlviijs. ivd.	3
6. John of Maidenhead	8	3	1	xliijs. ivd.	1
7. John Cheney			3	ijs. vjd.	
8. Thomas Spert	2			xjs. ijd.	
9. Thomas Worston				xxijd.	

Ex Parte Precentoris

	Jan.–April C.A.	April–July C.A.	July–Oct. C.A.	Oct.-Jan. Commons	C.A.
10. Nicholas Wykeham, Archdeacon of Wilts				xxxjs. ixd.	1
11. Peter Barton	2	4		xxixs. ijd.	
12. Richard Postel	3	4		lijs. xd.	1
13. Thomas Southam	13	5		xlivs. xd.	3
14. John Edington				ivs. ijd.	1
15. Richard Pitts	10	2	1	xlvs. xd.	2
16. Robert Croucheston	10	5	1	xliijs. vjd.	2
17. Thomas Eltisley	7	4	1	liijs. ivd.	2

Not in Communar's Roll

	Jan.–April C.A.	April–July C.A.	July–Oct. C.A.	Oct.-Jan. Commons	C.A.
18. Thomas Bekingham	2				
19. John Chaundler, Treasurer	7	3			
20. Richard Holme		2			
21. George Louthorpe		2			
22. Robert Ragnall	2				
23. Thomas Stow	2				
24. John Upton	4	2			
25. William Waltham		1			
26. Robert de Wicheford	2				
27. H. Winterton	2				

The surplus of lxxix li. xviijs. iijd., remaining from the October to January account, was distributed among 12¼ full residentiaries. Each full residentiary had vj li. xs. ivd.

1398

Ex Parte Decani	Jan.–April C.A.	April–July C.A.	July–Oct. C.A.	Oct.-Jan. Commons	C.A.
1. Thomas Montacute, Dean	5	1	2	cs. vd.	3
2. John Norton, Chancellor	1		2	cvjs. viijd.	3
3. John Chitterne	3			xvs. xjd.	
4. Henry Chichele				xixs. ijd.	

	Jan.–April C.A.	April–July C.A.	July–Oct. C.A.	Oct.–Jan. Commons	C.A.
5. William Loring	3			xljs. xd.	
6. George Louthorpe	4	I	I	lijs. vijd.	4
7. John of Maidenhead	2			xxivs. od.	
8. John Cheney	I			xiijs. od.	I
9. Thomas Worston				xxijd.	
10. William Spaldwick				xxs. ijd.	2
11. Ralph Reppyngton				vjd.	

Ex Parte Precentoris

12. Adam Mottram, Precentor	3	I	2	cvs. viijd.	4
13. John Chaundler, Treasurer	5		2	cvs. vd.	2
14. Nicholas Wykeham				*nichil quia in alio termino*	
15. Peter Barton				xlviijs. ivd.	
16. Richard Postel	3	2	I	liijs. ivd.	I
17. Thomas Southam	5	I	2	xlvijs. viijd.	3
18. Robert Ragnall	5	2	2	liijs. ivd.	4
19. Richard Pitts		I		xlivs. vd.	I
20. Thomas Eltisley	2	I	2	liijs. ivd.	3

Not in Communar's Roll

21. John Scarle — I

The surplus of lxiv li. viijs. ijd., remaining from the October to January account, was distributed among 17 full residentiaries.

1399

	Jan.–April Commons	C.A.[1]	April–July C.A.	July–Oct. C.A.	Oct.–Jan. C.A.
Ex Parte Decani					
1. Thomas Montacute, Dean	iv. li. xiijs. ivd.		8	3	2
2. John Norton, Chancellor	iv li. xixs. ivd.		6	4	
3. John Bere	vs. ijd.				
4. John Chitterne	xxs. vjd.		2	I	
5. William Loring	xxxs. ivd.		2	3	2
6. George Louthorpe	xlixs. viijd.		5	4	2
7. Henry Chichele	vjs. ivd.				
8. John of Maidenhead	xxijs. ivd.		I	3	
9. William Spaldwick	xivs. ijd.		4	2	
Ex Parte Precentoris					
10. Adam Mottram, Precentor	iv li. xviijs. ivd.		7	3	2
11. John Chandler, Treasurer	iv li. xvs. ivd.		8	3	2
12. Peter Barton	xlixs. viijd.		I		
13. Richard Postel	xlixs. viijd.		2	3	I

[1] No Chapter meetings, held in this quarter of the year, are recorded in the Holmes Register.

	Jan.–April Commons		April–July C.A.	July–Oct. C.A.	Oct.–Jan. C.A.
14. Thomas Southam	xlvs.	xd.	8	4	1
15. Robert Ragnall	xlixs.	viijd.	6	5	1
16. Richard Pitts	xlvijs.	viijd.	6	5	2
17. Thomas Eltisley	xlixs.	viijd.	1		

Not in Communar's Roll

18. John Cheney			1	3	
19. Nicholas Wykeham				1	1

The surplus of lxxvij li. xvjs. ivd., remaining from the January to April account, was distributed among 16¾ residentiaries. Each full residentiary had xcijs. ixd.; each half residentiary, xlvijs. ivd. ob.; each quarter residentiary, xxiijs. ijd. quad.

BIBLIOGRAPHY

MANUSCRIPT SOURCES

Muniments of Dean and Chapter of Salisbury.

Registers of Chapter Acts (Press II, Division I):
Hemyngsby Register, 1329–48.
Corffe Register, 1348–58.
Coman Register, 1385–87.
Dunham Register, 1387–95, 1407–8.
Holmes Register, 1395–1402.
Draper Register, 1402–4.
Vyring Register, 1408–13.
Hutchins Register, 1440–1.
Liber Evidentiarum C. Cartulary of the Dean and Chapter, with chapter acts for 1320–6 (Press II, Division 3).
Rolls of Communar's Accounts in two bundles labelled 'Fourteenth Century' and 'Fifteenth Century' (Press II, lower cupboard).
Charters, deeds, and wills in three boxes labelled 'Sarum' in Press I.

Muniments of Dean and Chapter of Lincoln.

Audit Accounts of the Dean and Chapter, bound in volumes called after the clerk of the common fund who wrote them:
Compoti Hervei de Luda, 1304–13, *et Philippi de Gretton,* 1314–17 (Bj/2/4).
Compoti Ricardi de Carleton, 1318–40 (the years 1319–20, 1330–2, and 1333–4 are missing or incomplete) (Bj/2/5).
Compoti Johannis de Braunscepath, 1357–8, 1360–9 (not bound in order) (Bj/2/6).
Compoti Radulphi Bailly de Quadring, 1378–82, 1383–6, *Willelmi de Loft,* 1382–3, *et Simonis de Luffenham,* 1386–7 (Bj/2/7).
Compoti Simonis de Luffenham, 1389–91, 1392–7 (including only part of the year 1395–6) (Bj/2/8).
Compoti Simonis de Luffenham, 1395–6 (Bj/2/9).
Compoti Alani de Humberston, 1399–1408, *et Brianis de le Mak,* 1408–9 (Bj/2/10).
Chapter Acts, *Liber Primus,* 1305–10, 1305–12. Two volumes (A/2/21–22).

British Museum.

Harleian MS. 1027. Statutes of Exeter Cathedral. Twelfth to fifteenth centuries.
Royal MS. 12 D. XI, ff. 69–88. Formulary for Salisbury diocese. Late thirteenth century.

Bodleian Library, Oxford.

Ashmole MS. 794, ff. 1–201. *Acta Capitularia Decani et Canonicorum Ecclesiae Cathedralis Lichefeldensis,* 1321–84.
MS. Wood Empt. 9 (*S.C.* 8597). Statutes of Exeter Cathedral, 1268–1446.
MS. Rawlinson Statutes 38 (*S.C.* 15892). Includes statutes of Exeter Cathedral, c. 1200–1544.
MS. Top. Devon, c. 16 (*S.C.* 22769). Statutes of Exeter Cathedral, 1107–1712.

Digby MS. 96 (*S.C.* 1697). *Meditaciones Godwini, Cantoris Salesberie, ad Rainilvam reclusam.*

Bodley MS. 859 (*S.C.* 2722), ff. 261a–289b. *Lectura Johannis Orum super Apocalipsim in Ecclesia Wellensi.*

New College MS. 264, ff. 262a–265b. Two Hymns, '*De vita et moribus beati Hugonis confessoris episcopi lyncolniensis*'.

Magdalen College, Oxford.

MS. 217, ff. 341r–367r. '*Questiones Roberti de Wynchilse disputate apud Lond' cum ibi legeret.*'

PRINTED ORIGINAL SOURCES

A. RECORDS OF ENGLISH SECULAR CATHEDRALS

Acts of the Dean and Chapter of the Cathedral Church of Chichester, 1472–1544, (*The White Act Book*), ed. W. D. Peckham (Sussex Record Soc., lii for 1951 and 1952).

Ancient Liturgy of the Church of England according to the Uses of Sarum, York, Hereford, and Bangor, and the Roman Liturgy, ed. W. Maskell, 3rd edn., Oxford, 1882.

Breviarium ad Usum Insignis Ecclesiae Eboracensis, ed. S. Lawley (Surtees Soc.), 2 vols., 1880–3.

Breviarium ad Usum Insignis Ecclesiae Sarum, ed. F. Procter and C. Wordsworth, 3 vols., Cambridge, 1879–86.

A Calendar of the Earlier Hereford Cathedral Muniments, ed. B. G. Charles and H. D. Emanuel (National Library of Wales). Typescript reproduced by H.M.C. National Register of Archives, 3 vols., 1955. A typed index to the Calendar by Penelope E. Morgan, 2 vols., 1957–9, is available at H.M.C. National Register of Archives, but has not yet been reproduced.

The Canonization of Saint Osmund, ed. A. R. Malden (Wilts. Record Soc.), 1901.

'Catalogue of Muniments and Manuscript Books of the Dean and Chapter of Lichfield and of the Lichfield Vicars', ed. J. C. Cox in *Coll. Hist. Staffs.*, part II, vol. vi (William Salt Soc.), 1886.

Catalogue of the Records of the Custos and College of Vicars Choral of Exeter Cathedral, ed. Audrey Erskine. Typescript reproduced by H.M.C. National Register of Archives, 1962.

Ceremonies and Processions of the Cathedral Church of Salisbury, ed. C. Wordsworth, Cambridge, 1901.

'Charter and Statutes of the College of Minor Canons in St. Paul's Cathedral, London', ed. W. Sparrow Simpson in *Archaeologia*, xliii (1871), 165–200.

Charters and Documents Illustrating the History of the Cathedral, City, and Diocese of Salisbury in the Twelfth and Thirteenth Centuries, ed. W. R. Jones and W. D. Macray (Rolls Series), 1891.

Charters and Records of Hereford Cathedral, ed. W. W. Capes, Hereford, 1908.

The Chartulary of the High Church of Chichester, ed, W. D. Peckham (Sussex Record Society), 1946.

Dean Cosyn and Wells Cathedral Miscellanea, ed. A. Watkin (Somerset Record Soc., lvi), 1941.

Documents Illustrating the History of St. Paul's Cathedral, ed. W. Sparrow Simpson (Camden Soc.), 1880.

The Domesday of St. Paul's of the Year MCCXXII or Registrum de Visitatione Maneriorum per Robertum Decanum, ed. W. H. Hale (Camden Soc.), 1858.

Bibliography

Early Charters of the Cathedral Church of St. Paul, London, ed. Marion Gibbs (Royal Hist. Soc. Camden 3rd Ser., lviii), 1939.

'Early Statutes of the Cathedral Church of the Holy Trinity, Chichester', ed. M. E. C. Walcott in *Archaeologia*, xlv (1878), 143–234.

Edition of *Liber Albus I* of Wells Cathedral, folios 9 to 61, by Alison E. Cavendish, M.A. thesis, University of London, 1959.

The Fabric Rolls of York Minster, ed. J. Raine (Surtees Soc.), 1859.

The Great Register of Lichfield Cathedral known as Magnum Registrum Album, ed. H. E. Savage (William Salt Soc.), 1926.

Hemingby's Register, ed. Helena M. Chew (Wilts. Arch. and Nat. Hist. Soc., Records Branch, xviii for 1962), 1963.

The Hereford Breviary, ed. W. H. Frere and L. E. G. Brown (Henry Bradshaw Soc.), 3 vols., 1904–15.

History and Constitution of a Cathedral of the Old Foundation Illustrated from Documents in the Registry and Muniment Room of the Cathedral of Chichester, ed. C. A. Swainson, London, 1880.

List of Hereford Cathedral Account Rolls, Court Rolls, Rentals and Surveys, ed. B. G. Charles and H. D. Emanuel, 1955. Typescript available at National Library of Wales and H.M.C., National Register of Archives, with index by Penelope E. Morgan, 2 vols., 1957–9.

Manuale ad usum percelebris ecclesie Sarisburiensis, ed. A. J. Collins (Henry Bradshaw Soc., xci for 1958), 1960.

Monasticon Anglicanum, ed. W. Dugdale, vol. VI, part iii, London, 1846.

Ordinale Exon., ed. J. N. Dalton (Henry Bradshaw Soc.), 3 vols., 1909.

Ordinale Sarum sive Directorium Sacerdotum, ed. W. Cooke and C. Wordsworth (Henry Bradshaw Soc.), 2 vols., 1901–2.

The Registrum Antiquissimum of the Cathedral Church of Lincoln, ed. C. W. Foster and Kathleen Major (Lincoln Record Soc.), 9 vols., 1931–58, in progress.

Registrum Eleemosynariae D. Pauli Londinensis, ed. Maria Hackett, London, 1827.

Registrum Statutorum et Consuetudinum Ecclesiae Cathedralis Sancti Pauli Londinensis, ed. W. Sparrow Simpson, London, 1873.

Reports of the Royal Commission on Historical Manuscripts contain the following reports on muniments of English secular cathedrals, with extracts from or calendars of some of their manuscripts:

'York. The Dean and Chapter', by H. T. Riley in *First Report*, App. (1870), p. 97.

'Manuscripts of the Dean and Chapter of St. Paul's', by H. C. Maxwell-Lyte in *Ninth Report*, part I, App. (1883), pp. 1–72.

'Manuscripts of the Dean and Chapter of Lincoln', and 'The Registry of the Bishop of Lincoln', by J. A. Bennett in *Twelfth Report*, App. IX (1891), pp. 553–79.

'Muniments of the Dean and Chapter of Lichfield', by R. L. Poole in *Fourteenth Report*, App. VIII (1895), pp. 205–36.

'Muniments of the Bishop and Dean and Chapter of Chichester', and 'Muniments of the Dean and Chapter of Salisbury', by R. L. Poole in *Report on Various Collections*, i (1901), pp. 177–204, 338–88.

'Records of the Bishop of Salisbury', 'Records of the Bishop of Exeter', and 'Muniments and Library of the Dean and Chapter of Exeter', by R. L. Poole in *Report on Various Collections*, iv (1907), pp. 1–95.

Calendar of the Manuscripts of the Dean and Chapter of Wells, ed. W. H. B. Bird and W. P. Baildon, 2 vols., 1907, 1914.

Reports of the Royal Commission on the State and Condition of the Cathedral and Collegiate Churches in England and Wales, London, 1854–5, 1884–5.

Statuta et Consuetudines Ecclesiae Cathedralis Beatae Mariae Virginis Sarisberiensis, ed. C. Wordsworth and D. Macleane, London, 1915.

Statuta et Consuetudines Ecclesiae Cathedralis Sarisberiensis, ed. E. A. Dayman and W. H. R. Jones, Bath, 1883.

Statutes and Constitutions of the Cathedral Church of Chichester, ed. F. G. Bennett, R. H. Codrington, and C. Deedes, Chichester, 1904.

Statutes etc. of the Cathedral Church of York, ed. J. Raine, 2nd edn., Leeds, 1900.

Statutes of Lincoln Cathedral, ed. H. Bradshaw and C. Wordswoth, 2 parts in 3 vols., Cambridge, 1892, 1897.

Use of Exeter Cathedral according to John de Grandisson, Bishop of the See, 1327–67. Abstract of Chapter Acts and Other Documents, 1380–1660, ed. H. E. Reynolds, London, 1891.

Use of Sarum, ed. W. H. Frere, 2 vols., Cambridge, 1898–1901.

Vetus Registrum Sarisberiense alias dictum Registrum S. Osmundi Episcopi, ed. W. H. R. Jones (Rolls Series), 2 vols., 1883–4.

Wells Cathedral: Its Foundation, Constitutional History, and Statutes, ed. H. E. Reynolds, Leeds, 1881.

B. ENGLISH BISHOPS' REGISTERS AND *ACTA*

Bath and Wells.

Registers of Walter Giffard, 1265–6, and of Henry Bowett, 1401–7, ed. T. Scott Holmes (Somerset Record Soc.), 1899.

Calendar of the Register of John de Drokensford, 1309–29, ed. E. Hobhouse (Somerset Record Soc.), 1887.

Register of Ralph of Shrewsbury, 1329–63, ed. T. Scott Holmes (Somerset Record Soc.), 2 vols., 1896.

Register of Nicholas Bubwith, 1407–24, ed. T. Scott Holmes (Somerset Record Soc.), 2 vols., 1914.

Register of John Stafford, 1425–43, ed. T. Scott Holmes (Somerset Record Soc.), 2 vols., 1915–16.

Register of Thomas Bekynton, 1443–65, ed. H. C. Maxwell-Lyte and M. C. B. Dawes (Somerset Record Soc.), 2 vols., 1934–5.

Registers of Robert Stillington, 1466–91 and Richard Fox, 1492–4, ed. H. C. Maxwell-Lyte (Somerset Record Soc.), 1937.

Canterbury.

Acta Stephani Langton, 1207–28, ed. Kathleen Major (Canterbury and York Soc.), 1950.

Registrum Epistolarum Johannis Peckham, 1279–92, ed. C. T. Martin (Rolls Series), 3 vols., 1882–6.

Registrum Roberti Winchelsey, 1294–1313, ed. Rose Graham (Canterbury and York Soc.), 2 vols., 1952, 1956.

Registrum Simonis de Langham, 1366–76, ed. A. C. Wood (Canterbury and York Soc.), 1956.

Metropolitan Visitations of William Courteney, 1378–86, ed. J. H. Dahmus (Illinois Studies in Social Sciences, xxii, 2), 1950.

Register of Henry Chichele, 1414–43, ed. E. F. Jacob and H. C. Johnson (Canterbury and York Soc.), 4 vols., 1937–47.

Registrum Thome Bourgchier, 1454–86, ed. F. R. H. Du Boulay Canterbury and York Soc.), 1957.

Bibliography 359

Chichester.

The *Acta of the Bishops of Chichester, 1075–1207*, ed. H. M. R. E. Mayr-Harting (Canterbury and York Soc.), 1965.

Episcopal Register of Robert Rede, 1397–1415, ed. C. Deedes (Sussex Record Soc.), 2 vols., 1908–10.

'Extracts from the Episcopal Register of Richard Praty, S.T.P., 1438–45', ed. C. Deedes, in *Miscellaneous Records*, pp. 83–236 (Sussex Record Soc.), 1905.

Coventry and Lichfield.

'The Register of Roger de Norbury, 1322–58. An Abstract of Contents and Remarks', ed. E. Hobhouse in *Coll. Hist. Staffs.*, i, 241–88 (William Salt Soc.), 1880.

Registers of Robert de Stretton, with the Register of the Guardians of the Spiritualities during the Vacancy of the See, 1358–85, ed. R. A. Wilson (*Coll. Hist. Staffs.*, n.s. viii, x, part i, William Salt Soc.), 2 vols., 1905, 1907.

Exeter.

Registers of Walter Bronescombe, 1257–80, and Peter Quivil, 1280–91, with Some Records of the Episcopate of Bishop Thomas de Bytton, 1292–1307, ed. F. C. Hingeston-Randolph, London and Exeter, 1889.

Register of Walter de Stapeldon, 1307–26, ed. F. C. Hingeston-Randolph, London and Exeter, 1892.

Register of John de Grandisson, 1327–69, with Some Account of the Episcopate of James de Berkeley, 1327, ed. F. C. Hingeston-Randolph, 3 vols., London and Exeter, 1894–9.

Register of Thomas de Brantyngham, 1370–94, ed. F. C. Hingeston-Randolph, 2 vols., London and Exeter, 1901–6.

Register of Edmund Stafford, 1395–1419, ed. F. C. Hingeston-Randolph, London and Exeter, 1886.

Register of Edmund Lacy, 1420–55, with Some Account of the Episcopate of John Catrik, 1419, ed. F. C. Hingeston-Randolph, 2 vols., London and Exeter, 1909–15.

The Register of Edmund Lacy, 1420–55, ed. G. R. Dunstan (Canterbury and York Soc. with Devon and Cornwall Record Soc.), *Registrum Commune*, 2 vols., 1963–6, in progress.

Hereford.

Registrum Thome de Cantilupo, 1275–82, ed. R. G. Griffiths and W. W. Capes (Canterbury and York Soc.), 1907.

Registrum Ricardi de Swinfield, 1283–1317, ed. W. W. Capes (Canterbury and York Soc.), 1909.

Registrum Ade de Orleton, 1317–27, ed. A. T. Bannister (Canterbury and York Soc.), 1908.

Registrum Thome de Charlton, 1327–44, ed. W. W. Capes (Canterbury and York Soc.), 1913.

Registrum Johannis de Trillek, 1344–61, ed. J. H. Parry (Canterbury and York Soc.), 1912.

Registrum Ludowici de Charltone, 1361–70, ed. J. H. Parry (Canterbury and York Soc.), 1914.

Registrum Willelmi de Courtenay, 1370–75, ed. W. W. Capes (Canterbury and York Soc.), 1914.

Registrum Johannis Gilbert, 1375–89, ed. J. H. Parry (Canterbury and York Soc.), 1915.

Registrum Johannis Trefnant, 1389–1404, ed. W. W. Capes (Canterbury and York Soc.), 1916.

Registrum Roberti Mascall, 1404–16, ed. J. H. Parry and C. Johnson (Canterbury and York Soc.), 1917.

Registra Edmundi Lacy, 1417–20, et Thome Poltone, 1420–22, ed. J. H. Parry, A. T. Bannister, and W. W. Capes (Canterbury and York Soc.), 1918.

Registrum Thome Spofford, 1422–48, ed. A. T. Bannister (Canterbury and York Soc.), 1919.

Registra Ricardi Beauchamp, 1449–50, Reginaldi Boulers, 1451–3, et Johannis Stanbury, 1453–74, ed. A. T. Bannister and J. H. Parry (Canterbury and York Soc.), 1919.

Registrum Thome Myllyng, 1471–92, ed. A. T. Bannister (Canterbury and York Soc.), 1920.

Lincoln.

Rotuli Hugonis de Welles, 1209–35, ed. W. P. W. Phillimore and F. N. Davis (Canterbury and York, and Lincoln Record Socs.), 3 vols., 1907–9.

Rotuli Roberti Grosseteste, 1235–53, ed. F. N. Davis (Canterbury and York, and Lincoln Record Socs.), 1913.

Rotuli Ricardi Gravesend, 1258–79, ed. F. N. Davis, C. W. Foster and A. Hamilton Thompson (Canterbury and York, and Lincoln Record Socs.), 1925.

The Rolls and Register of Bishop Oliver Sutton, 1280–99, ed. Rosalind M. T. Hill (Lincoln Record Soc.), vols. 1–5, 1948–64, in progress.

The Register of Bishop Philip Repingdon, 1405–19, ed. Margaret Archer (Lincoln Record Soc.), vols. 1 and 2, 1963, in progress.

Visitations of Religious Houses in the Diocese of Lincoln, 1420–36, vol. i, ed. A. Hamilton Thompson (Canterbury and York, and Lincoln Record Socs.), 1914.

London.

Registrum Radulphi Baldock, Gilberti Segrave, Ricardi Newport, et Stephani Gravesend, 1304–38, ed. R. C. Fowler (Canterbury and York Soc.), 1911.

Registrum Simonis de Sudbiria, 1362–75, ed. R. C. Fowler, C. Jenkins, and S. C. Ratcliff (Canterbury and York Soc.), 2 vols., 1927–38.

Salisbury.

Registrum Simonis de Gandavo, 1297–1315, ed. C. T. Flower and M. C. B. Dawes (Canterbury and York Soc.), 2 vols., 1934.

The Registers of Roger de Martival, 1315–30, ed. Kathleen Edwards, C. R. Elrington and Susan Reynolds (Canterbury and York Soc.), vols. 1–3, 1959–65, in progress.

York.

Historical Letters and Papers from the Northern Registers, ed. J. Raine (Rolls Series), 1873.

Register or Rolls of Walter Gray, 1215–55, ed. J. Raine (Surtees Soc.), 1872.

Register of Walter Giffard, 1266–79, ed. W. Brown (Surtees Soc.), 1904.

Register of William Wickwane, 1279–85, ed. W. Brown (Surtees Soc.), 1907.

Registers of John le Romeyn, 1286–96, and of Henry of Newark, 1296–9, ed. W. Brown (Surtees Soc.), 2 vols., 1913–17.

Register of Thomas of Corbridge, 1300–4, ed. W. Brown and A. Hamilton Thompson (Surtees Soc.), 2 vols., 1925–8.

Register of William Greenfield, 1306–15, ed. W. Brown and A. Hamilton Thompson (Surtees Soc.), 5 vols., 1931–40.

C. OTHER COLLECTIONS OF ECCLESIASTICAL DOCUMENTS

Antiquus Cartularius Ecclesiae Baiocensis (Livre Noir), ed. V. Bourrienne (Soc. Hist. de Normandie), 2 vols., Rouen, 1902–3.

Calendar of Entries in the Papal Registers relating to Great Britain and Ireland. Papal Letters, 1198–1471, ed. W. H. Bliss, C. Johnson, and J. A. Twemlow (H.M.S.O.), 12 vols., 1894–1933; *Petitions to the Pope, 1342–1419*, ed. W. H. Bliss, vol. i (H.M.S.O.), 1897.

Cartulaire de l'Abbaye Cardinale de la Trinité de Vendôme, ed. Ch. Metais (Soc. Archéologique du Vendômais), 4 vols., Paris, 1893.

Cartulaire de l'Abbaye de Saint-Aubin d'Angers, ed. B. de Broussillon, 3 vols., Paris, 1903.

Cartulaire de l'Abbaye de Saint-Père de Chartres, ed. B. Guérard (Collection de Documents Inédits), 2 vols., Paris, 1840.

Cartulaire de l'Abbaye de Saint-Vincent du Mans, ed. R. Charles et M. d'Elbenne, Le Mans, 1886–1913.

Cartulaire des Abbayes de Saint-Pierre de la Couture et de Saint-Pierre de Solesmes, Le Mans, 1881.

Cartulaire de Notre Dame de Chartres, ed. E. de Lépinois et L. Merlet (Soc. Archéologique d'Eure-et-Loir), 3 vols., Chartres, 1862–5.

Cartularium Prioratus de Gyseburne, ed. W. Brown (Surtees Soc.), 2 vols., 1889, 1894.

'The Certificates of the Chantry Commissioners for the College of Southwell in 1546 and 1548, with an Introduction and Notes', ed. A. Hamilton Thompson in *Trans. Thoroton Soc.*, xv. (1911), 63–158.

The Certificates of the Commissioners Appointed to Survey the Chantries, Guilds, Hospitals, etc., in the County of York, ed. W. Page (Surtees Soc.), 2 parts, 1894–5.

Concilia Magnae Britanniae et Hiberniae, ed. D. Wilkins, 4 vols., London, 1737.

Councils and Synods with other Documents relating to the English Church, 1205–1313, ed. F. M. Powicke and C. R. Cheney, 2 parts, Oxford, 1964.

Corpus Iuris Canonici, ed. E. Friedberg, 2 vols., Leipzig, 1879–81.

The Crawford Collection of Early Charters and Documents now in the Bodleian Library, ed. A. S. Napier and W. H. Stevenson, Oxford, 1895.

Le 'De Officiis Ecclesiasticis' de Jean d'Avranches, ed. R. Delamere (*Bibl. Liturgique*, ed. U. Chevalier, vol. 22), Paris, 1923.

The Dignitas Decani of St. Patrick's Cathedral, Dublin, ed. N. B. White and A. Gwynn (Irish MSS. Commission), Dublin S.O., 1957.

Documents Illustrating the Activities of the General and Provincial Chapters of the English Black Monks, 1215–1540, ed. W. A. Pantin (Royal Hist. Soc., Camden 3rd ser.), 3 vols., 1931–7.

Educational Charters and Documents, 598 to 1909, ed. A. F. Leach, Cambridge, 1911.

Episcopal Acts and Cognate Documents relating to Welsh Dioceses, 1066–1272, ed. J. Conway Davies (Hist. Soc. of the Church in Wales), 2 vols., 1946, 1951 (for 1948), in progress.

Fifteenth Century Cartulary of St. Nicholas' Hospital, Salisbury, with other Records, ed. C. Wordsworth, Salisbury, 1902.

Het Rechtsboek van den Dom van Utrecht door Mr. Hugo Wstinc (c. 1345–9), ed. S. Muller (Oude Vaderlandsche Rechtsbronnen), Utrecht, 1895.

'Letters of William Wickwane, Chancellor of York, 1266–1268', ed. C. R. Cheney in *E.H.R.*, xlvii (1932), 626–42.

Literae Cantuarienses. The Letter Books of the Monastery of Christ Church, Canterbury, ed. J. B. Sheppard (Rolls Series), 3 vols., 1887–9.

362 *Bibliography*

Memorials of Beverley Minster: *The Chapter Act Book of the Collegiate Church of St. John of Beverley, 1286–1347*, ed. A. F. Leach (Surtees Soc.), 2 vols., 1898, 1903.

Memorials and Chapter Acts of the Collegiate Church of SS. Peter and Wilfrid, Ripon, ed. J. T. Fowler (Surtees Soc.), 5 vols., 1875–1908.

The Old English Version of the enlarged rule of Chrodegang, together with the Latin Original, ed. A. S. Napier (Early English Text Soc.), 1916.

Ordinaire et Coutumier de l'Église Cathédrale de Bayeux, ed. U. Chevalier (Bibliothèque Liturgique, tom. viiie), Paris, 1902.

Papal Decretals relating to the Diocese of Lincoln in the Twelfth Century, ed. W. Holtzmann and E. W. Kemp (Lincoln Record Soc.), 1954.

Papsturkunden in England, ed. W. Holtzmann, 3 vols., Berlin and Göttingen, 1931–51.

Pouillés de la Province de Rouen, ed. M. A. Longnon (*Receuil des historiens de la France,* publié par l'Académie des Inscriptions et Belles-Lettres, Pouillés, tom. 2), Paris, 1903.

Regestrum Visitationum Archiepiscopi Rothomagensis. Journal des Visites Pastorales d'Eude Rigaud, Archévêque de Rouen, 1248–69, ed. Th. Bonnin, Rouen, 1852.

'The Registers of the Archdeaconry of Richmond, 1361–1477', ed. A. Hamilton Thompson in *Y.A.J.,* xxv (1918–20), 129–268; xxx (1930–1), 1–132; xxxii (1934–6), 111–45.

Roll of the Household Expenses of Richard de Swinfield, Bishop of Hereford during part of the years 1289 and 1290, ed. J. Webb (Camden Soc.), 2 vols., 1854–5.

Sacrorum Conciliorum Nova et Amplissima Collectio, ed. J. D. Mansi, 31 vols., Florence and Venice, 1759–98.

Sancti Benedicti Regula Monasteriorum, ed. C. Butler, Friburgi Brisgoviae, 1927.

'*Sancti Chrodegangi, Episcopi Metensis, Regula Canonicorum*', in *Patrologia Latina,* lxxxix, 1097, *et seq.,* ed. J. P. Migne, Paris, 1863.

Snappe's Formulary and Other Records, ed. H. E. Salter (Oxford Hist. Soc.), 1924.

Studies in Norwich Cathedral History. An Episcopal Visitation of the Priory in 1308, and an Archiepiscopal Adjudication on Priory Rights in 1411, ed. E. H. Carter, Norwich, 1935.

Visitations and Memorials of Southwell Minster, ed. A. F. Leach (Camden Soc.), 1891.

D. OTHER LEGAL MATERIALS

Archives législatives de la ville de Reims. Collections de pièces inédites, tom. i, ed. P. Varin, Paris, 1840.

Bracton, *De Legibus et Consuetudinibus Angliae,* ed. G. E. Woodbine, 4 vols., Yale, 1915–42.

Calendar of Wills proved and enrolled in the Court of Husting, London, 1258–1688, ed. R. R. Sharpe, 2 vols., London, 1889–90.

The Laws of the Kings of England from Edmund to Henry I, ed. A. J. Robertson, Cambridge, 1925.

The Liber Pauperum of Vacarius, ed. F. de Zulueta (Selden Soc.), 1927.

Summa Aurea D. Henrici Cardinalis Hostiensis, ed. N. Superantius, Lyons, 1548.

Wells City Charters, ed. Dorothy O. Shilton and R. Holworthy (Somerset Record Soc.), 1932.

E. PUBLIC RECORDS

Calendar of Chancery Warrants, 1244–1326, vol. i, 1927.
Calendar of Charter Rolls, 1226–1516, 6 vols., 1903–27.

Calendar of Close Rolls, 1272–1509, 47 vols., 1892–1963.
Calendar of Fine Rolls, 1272–1509, 22 vols., 1911–62.
Calendar of Liberate Rolls, 1226–67, 5 vols., 1917–61.
Calendar of Patent Rolls, 1216–1485, 52 vols., 1891–1916.
'Clerical Poll-Taxes in the Diocese of Salisbury, 1377–81, ed. J. L. Kirby in *Collectanea*, ed. N. J. Williams and T. F. T. Plucknett (Wilts. Arch. and Nat. Hist. Soc., Records Branch, 1956), 157–67.
Close Rolls of Henry III, 1227–68, 13 vols., 1902–37.
Regesta Henrici Primi, 1100–1135, ed. C. Johnson and H. A. Cronne (*Regesta Regum Anglo-Normannorum*, vol. ii), Oxford, 1956.
Rotuli Litterarum Clausarum, 1204–27, ed. T. D. Hardy (Record Commission). 2 vols., 1833–44.
The State of the Ex-Religious and Former Chantry Priests in the Diocese of Lincoln, 1547–74, from Returns in the Exchequer, ed. G. A. J. Hodgett (Lincoln Record Soc.), 1959.
Taxatio Ecclesiastica Angliae et Walliae auctoritate P. Nicholai IV circa 1291, ed. S. Ayscough and J. Caley (Record Commission), 1802.
Valor Ecclesiasticus temp. Henrici VIII, auctoritate regia institutus, ed. J. Caley and J. Hunter (Record Commission), 6 vols., 1810–34.

F. CHRONICLES AND ANNALS

'*Actus Pontificum Cenomannis*', in *Vetera Analecta*, ed. J. Mabillon, Paris, 1723, pp. 239–337.
Anglia Sacra, vol. i, ed. H. Wharton, London, 1691, includes:
    Stephani Birchingtoni Historia de Archiepiscopis Cantuariensibus A prima Sedis fundatione ad annum 1369.
    Thomae Chesterfeld Historia de Episcopis Coventrensibus et Lichfeldensibus A prima Sedis fundatione ad annum 1347.
    Gulielmi Whitlocke Additamenta ad Historiam Veteram Lichfeldensem et Ejusdem Auctoris Continuatio Historiae Lichfeldensis, 1359–1559.
    Canonici Wellensis Historia de Episcopis Bathoniensibus et Wellensibus A prima ejus fundatione ad annum 1423.
The Book of John de Schalby, Canon of Lincoln, 1299–1333, concerning the Bishops of Lincoln and their Acts, ed. and trans. J. H. Srawley (Lincoln Minster Pamphlets, no. 2), Lincoln, 1949.
Chronica Magistri Rogeri de Houedene, ed. W. Stubbs (Rolls Series), 4 vols., 1868–71.
Chronicon Abbatiae de Evesham ad Annum 1418, ed. W. D. Macray (Rolls Series), 1863.
Cronicon Richardi Divisensis de Tempore Regis Richardi Primi, ed. and trans. J. T. Appleby (Medieval Texts), London, 1963.
Eadmeri Historia Novorum in Anglia, ed. M. Rule (Rolls Series), 1884.
Giraldi Cambrensis Opera, vols. i, iv, and vii, ed. J. S. Brewer and J. F. Dimock (Rolls Series), 1861, 1877.
'Gregory's Chronicle', in *The Historical Collections of a Citizen of London in the Fifteenth Century*, ed. J. Gairdner (Camden Soc. n.s., xvii), 1876.
Henrici Archidiaconi Huntendunensis Historia Anglorum, ed. T. Arnold (Rolls Series), 1879.
Historians of the Church of York and its Archbishops, ed. J. Raine (Rolls Series), 3 vols., 1879–94.
'*Historiola de Primordiis Episcopatus Somersetensis*', in *Ecclesiastical Documents*, ed. J. Hunter (Camden Soc.), 1840.

Hugh the Chantor, The History of the Church of York, 1066–1127, ed. and trans. C. Johnson (Medieval Texts), London, 1961.

Magna Vita Sancti Hugonis, ed. and trans. Decima L. Douie and H. Farmer (Medieval Texts), 2 vols., London, 1961–2.

Materials for the History of St. Thomas Becket, vol. iii, ed. J. C. Robertson (Rolls Series), 1878.

Matthei Parisiensis Chronica Majora, ed. H. R. Luard (Rolls Series), 7 vols., 1872–84.

Nicholai Triveti Annales sex Regum Angliae, ed. T. Hog (English Hist. Soc.), London, 1845.

Orderici Vitalis Angligenae, Coenobii Uticensis Monachi, Historiae Ecclesiasticae Libri Tredecim, ed. A. le Prévost (Soc. de l'hist. de France), 5 vols., Paris, 1838–55.

Radulphi de Diceto Opera Historica, ed. W. Stubbs (Rolls Series), 2 vols., 1876.

A Scottish Chronicle known as the Chronicle of Holyrood, ed. M. O. and A. O. Anderson (Scottish History Soc.), Edinburgh, 1938.

Venerabilis Bedae Opera Historica, ed. C. Plummer, 2 vols., Oxford, 1896.

Vita Edwardi Secundi Monachi Cujusdam Malmesberiensis, ed. and trans. N. Denholm-Young (Medieval Texts), London, 1957.

William of Newburgh, *Historia Rerum Anglicarum*, ed. R. Howlett in *Chronicles of the Reigns of Stephen, Henry II, and Richard I*, vols. i and ii (Rolls Series), 1884–5.

Willelmi Malmesbiriensis De Gestis Pontificum, ed. N. E. S. A. Hamilton (Rolls Series), 1870.

Willelmi Rishanger Chronica et Annales, 1259–1307, ed. H. T. Riley (Rolls Series), 1865.

G. OTHER LITERARY MATERIALS

Biskupa Sögur gefnar út af *Hinu Islenska Bokmentafèlagi*, 1858.

The Exeter Book of Old English Poetry, ed. R. W. Chambers, M. Förster, and R. Flower, London, 1933.

'Hildeberti Epistolae', in *Patrologia Latina*, vol. clxxi, ed. J. P. Migne, Paris, 1854.

Hungurvaka, Pals Biskups Saga, ok Pattr af Thorvalldi Vidförla, Hafniae, 1778.

The Itinerary of John Leland in or about the years 1535–1543, ed. Lucy Toulmin Smith, 5 vols., London, 1906–10.

'Petri Blesensis Opera Omnia', in *Patrologia Latina*, vol. ccvii, ed. J. P. Migne, Paris, 1904.

Roberti Grosseteste Episcopi quondam Lincolniensis Epistolae, ed. H. R. Luard (Rolls Series), 1861.

Rouleaux des Morts du ixe au xve siècle, ed. L. Delisle (Soc. de l'Hist. de France), Paris, 1866.

'Sancti Aurelii Augustini Hipponensis Confessionum Libri Tredecim', in *Patrologia Latina*, xxxii, 659–867, ed. J. P. Migne, Paris, 1865.

Thómas Saga Erkibyskups. A Life of Archbishop Thomas Becket in Icelandic, ed. E. Magnusson (Rolls Series), 2 vols., 1875, 1883.

The World Map by Richard of Haldingham in Hereford Cathedral, c. 1285, ed. G. R. Crone (Royal Geographical Soc., Reproductions of Early MS. Maps, iii), London, 1954.

SECONDARY SOURCES

A. WORKS OF REFERENCE

Barbosa. A., *Tractatus de Canonicis et Dignitatibus, Aliisque inferioribus Beneficiariis Cathedralium, et Collegiatarum Ecclesiarum, eorumque Officiis, tam in Choro, quam in Capitulo*, Lyons, 1700.

Pastoralis Solicitudinis, sive de Officio et Potestate Episcopi, Paris, 1625.

Birch, W. de G., *Catalogue of Seals in the Department of Manuscripts in the British Museum*, vol. i, London, 1887.

Bouix, D., *Tractatus de Capitulis* and *Tractatus de Episcopo* (*Institutiones Iuris Canonici in Varios Tractatus Divisae*, 10 vols.), 2 vols., Paris, 1852, 1859.

Clay, C. T., *York Minster Fasti, being notes on the Dignitaries, Archdeacons and Prebendaries in the Church of York prior to the year 1307* (Yorks. Arch. Soc., Record Ser., cxxiii, cxxiv for 1957-8), 2 vols., 1958-9.

Davis, G. R. C., *Medieval Cartularies of Great Britain, A Short Catalogue*, London, 1958.

Dictionary of Christian Antiquities, ed. W. Smith and S. Cheetham, 2 vols., London, 1875-80.

Dictionnaire d'Archéologie Chrétienne et de Liturgie, ed. F. Cabrol and H. Leclercq, Paris, 1911, in progress.

Dictionnaire de Droit Canonique, ed. R. Naz and others, Paris, 1935, in progress.

Emden, A. B., *A Biographical Register of the University of Oxford to A.D. 1500*, 3 vols., Oxford, 1957-9.

A Biographical Register of the University of Cambridge to A.D. 1500, Cambridge, 1963.

Fasti Ecclesiae Scoticanae Medii Aevi, ed. D. E. R. Watt, first draft, typescript, St. Andrews, 1959.

Gallia Christiana in provincias ecclesiasticas distributa, ed. D. de Sainte Marthe; editio altera labore et curis P. Piolin recensita et aucta, Paris, 1870, etc.

Harvey, J. and Oswald A., *English Medieval Architects, a Biographical Dictionary down to 1550*, Batsford, 1954.

Hennessy, G., *Novum Repertorium Ecclesiasticum Parochiale Londinense*, London, 1898.

Hinschius, P., *Das Kirchenrecht der Katholiken und Protestanten in Deutschland. System des Katholischen Kirchenrechts*, 6 vols., Berlin, 1869-97.

Jones, W. H., *Fasti Ecclesiae Sarisberiensis*, 2 parts, Salisbury, 1879-81.

Ker, N. R., *Medieval libraries of Great Britain, an Index of Surviving Books* (Royal Hist. Soc. Pubns.), 2nd end., 1964.

Le Neve, J., *Fasti Ecclesiae Anglicanae*, ed. T. Duffus Hardy, 3 vols., Oxford, 1854.

Le Neve, J., *Fasti Ecclesiae Anglicanae*, 3rd edn., *1300-1541*, comp. H. P. F. King, J. M. Horn and B. Jones (Institute of Hist. Research), 11 vols., London, 1962-5, in progress.

Lexikon für Theologie und Kirche, ed. J. Höfer und K. Rahner, 2nd edn., Freiburg, 1957, in progress.

Lunt, W. E., *The Valuation of Norwich*, Oxford, 1926.

Papal Revenues in the Middle Ages, 2 vols., Columbia, 1934.

Major, Kathleen, *A Handlist of the Records of the Bishop of Lincoln and of the Archdeacons of Lincoln and Stow*, Oxford, 1953.

Makower, F., *The Constitutional History and Constitution of the Church of England*, London, 1895.

Newcourt, R., *Repertorium Ecclesiasticum Parochiale Londinense*, 2 vols., London, 1708-10.

Ollard, S. L., *Fasti Wyndesorienses: the Deans and Canons of Windsor*, Windsor, 1950.

Russell, J. C., *Dictionary of Writers of Thirteenth Century England* (*Bulletin of Institute of Historical Research*, Special Supplement, no. 3), 1936.

Survey of Ecclesiastical Archives, 1946 (The Pilgrim Trust), 4 vols., 1951. Stencilled copies available at H.M.C. National Register of Archives, the British Museum, the Bodleian Library, Oxford, the University Library, Cambridge, and other selected libraries.

Thomassin, L., *Dictionnaire de Discipline ecclésiastique*, ed. J. J. Bourassé, in J. P. Migne, *Encyclopédie Théologique*, 3rd ser., vols. 25 and 26, Paris, 1856.
Vetus et Nova Ecclesiae Disciplina, 3 parts in 10 vols., Mainz, 1787.

B. GENERAL WORKS

Amann, E., *L'Époque carolingienne* (*Histoire de l'Église depuis les origines jusqu'à nos jours*, ed. A. Fliche et V. Martin), Paris, 1937.
Amiet, L., *Essai sur l'Organisation du Chapitre Cathédral de Chartres du xie au xviiie siècle*, Chartres, 1922.
Andrieu-Guitrancourt, P., *L'Archévêque Eudes Rigaud et la Vie de l'Église au xiiie siècle, d'après le 'Regestrum Visitationum'*, Paris, 1938.
Bannister, A. T., *The Cathedral Church of Hereford. Its History and Constitution* (S.P.C.K.), London, 1924.
A Descriptive Catalogue of the Manuscripts in the Hereford Cathedral Library, with an introduction by M. R. James, Hereford, 1927.
Barlow, F., *The English Church, 1000–1066. A Constitutional History*, London, 1963.
Barraclough, G., *Papal Provisions*, Oxford, 1935.
Benson, E. W., *The Cathedral: Its Necessary Place in the Life and Work of the Church*, London, 1878.
Berlière, U., *Les Élections abbatiales au Moyen Âge* (Académie Royale de Belgique. Classe des Lettres et des Sciences morales et politiques. Mémoires. Nouv. ser., tom. xx, fasc. 3), Bruxelles, 1927.
Bevan, W. L., and Phillott, H. W., *Medieval Geography: an Essay in Illustration of the Hereford Mappa Mundi*, London, 1873.
Bishop, E., *Liturgica Historica. Papers on the Liturgy and Religious Life of the Western Church*, Oxford, 1918.
Bourrienne, V., *Philippe de Harcourt Évêque de Bayeux*, Paris, 1930.
Brentano, R., *York Metropolitan Jurisdiction and Papal Judges Delegate, 1279–96* (Univ. of California Pubns. in History, xviii), Berkeley and Los Angeles, 1959.
Brooke, C. N. L. and Morey, A., *Gilbert Foliot and his Letters*, Cambridge, 1965.
Callus, D., ed. *Robert Grosseteste, Scholar and Bishop. Essays in Commemoration of the Seventh Centenary of his Death*, Oxford, 1955.
Capes, W. W., *The English Church in the Fourteenth and Fifteenth Centuries*, London, 1900.
Carrière, V., *Introduction aux études d'histoire ecclésiastique locale* (*Bibl. de la Soc. d'Hist. Ecclésiastique de la France*), 3 vols., 1934-40.
Chambers, E. K., *The Medieval Stage*, 2 vols., Oxford, 1903.
Chapman, J., *Saint Benedict and the Sixth Century*, London, 1929.
Cheney, C. R., *Episcopal Visitation of Monasteries in the Thirteenth Century*, Manchester, 1931.
English Bishops' Chanceries, 1100–1250, Manchester, 1950.
From Becket to Langton: English Church Government, 1170–1213, Manchester, 1956.
Church, C. M., *Chapters in the Early History of the Church of Wells, 1136–1333*, London, 1894.
Churchill, Irene J., *Canterbury Administration* (S.P.C.K.), 2 vols., London, 1933.
Clark, J. W., *The Care of Books*, Cambridge, 1909.
Clerval, A., *Les Écoles de Chartres au moyen-âge* (*du ve au xvie siècle*), Paris, 1895.
De Clercq, C., *La législation réligieuse franque de Clovis à Charlemagne*, Louvain et Paris, 1936.

Deanesly, Margaret, *A History of the Medieval Church, 590–1500*, London, 1925.
Sidelights on the Anglo-Saxon Church, London, 1962.

Deslandes, E., *Étude sur l'Église de Bayeux*, Caen, 1917.

Dickinson, J. C., *The Origin of the Austin Canons and their Introduction into England*, London, 1950.

Didier, N., *Les Eglises de Sisteron et de Forcalquier du xie siècle à la Révolution. Le problème de la 'Concathédralité'* (*Essais et Travaux de la Faculté de Droit*, Université de Grenoble, 4), Paris, 1954.

Dix, G., *The Shape of the Liturgy*, Westminster, 1947.

Dixon, W. H., *Fasti Eboracenses. Lives of the Archbishops of York*, ed. J. Raine, London, 1863.

Dodsworth, W., *An Historical Account of the Episcopal See and Cathedral Church of Salisbury*, Salisbury, 1814.

Douglas, D. C., *William the Conqueror. The Norman Impact upon England*, London, 1964.

Douie, Decima L., *Archbishop Pecham*, Oxford, 1946.

Dowden, J., *The Medieval Church in Scotland. Its Constitution, Organization and Law*, Glasgow, 1910.
The Bishops of Scotland, Glasgow, 1912.

Dugdale, W., *History of Saint Paul's Cathedral*, London, 1818.

Duggan, C., *Twelfth Century Decretal Collections and their Importance in English History*, London, 1963.

Emden, A. B., *An Oxford Hall in Medieval Times*, Oxford, 1927.

Fellowes, E. H., *Organists and Masters of the Choristers of St. George's Chapel in Windsor Castle*, London, 1939.

Formeville, H. de, *Histoire de l'ancien Évêché-Comté de Lisieux*, 2 vols., Lisieux, 1873.

Fournier, P., *Les Officialités au moyen-âge. Étude sur l'organisation, la compétence et la procédure des tribunaux ecclésiastiques ordinaires en France de 1180 à 1328*, Paris, 1880.

Fowler, J., *Medieval Sherborne*, Dorchester, 1951. (For the history of the abbot of Sherborne's prebend at Salisbury.)

Freeman, E. A., *History of the Cathedral Church of Wells as illustrating the History of the Cathedral Churches of the Old Foundation*, London, 1870.

Frere, W. H., *Visitation Articles and Injunctions of the Period of the Reformation*, vol. i, *Historical Introduction* (Alcuin Club Collections, xiv), London, 1910.

Fuller, A. R. B., The Minor Corporations of the Secular Cathedrals of the province of Canterbury (excluding the Welsh sees) between the Thirteenth Century and 1536, with special reference to the Minor Canons of St. Paul's Cathedral from their Origin in the Twelfth Century to the Visitation of Bishop Gibson in 1724. M.A. thesis, University of London, 1947.

Gibbs, Marion, and Lang, Jane, *Bishops and Reform, 1215–72*, Oxford, 1934.

Gleason, S. E., *An Ecclesiastical Barony of the Middle Ages. The Bishopric of Bayeux, 1066–1204*, Harvard, 1936.

Greenway, W., The Bishops and Chapter of St. Davids, 1280–1407. M. Litt. thesis, University of Cambridge, 1959.

Gurney, D., *The Record of the House of Gournay*, 3 parts and a supplement, privately printed, 1848–58.

Hallinger, K., *Gorze-Cluny. Studien zu den monastichen Lebensformen und Gegensätzen im Höchmittelalter*, 2 vols. (Studia Anselmiana, fasc. 22–5), Rome, 1950–1.

Harrison, F., *Life in a Medieval College: the Story of the Vicars Choral of York Minster*, London, 1952.

Harrison, F. L., *Music in Medieval Britain*, London, 1958.
Haskins, C. H., *The Renaissance of the Twelfth Century*, Cambridge, Mass., 1927.
  Studies in the History of Medieval Science, Cambridge, Mass., 1927.
Hatcher, H., and Benson, R., *Old and New Sarum or Salisbury* (*The History of Modern Wiltshire*, ed. R. C. Hoare), London, 1843.
Havergal, F. T., *Fasti Herefordenses and other Antiquarian Memorials of Hereford*, Edinburgh, 1869.
Hill, J. W. F., *Medieval Lincoln*, Cambridge, 1948.
Hindley, D. J. B., The Economy and Administration of the Estates of the Dean and Chapter of Exeter in the Fifteenth Century. M.A. thesis (External), London University, 1958.
Hobson, G. D., *English Binding Before 1500*, Cambridge, 1929.
Howell, Margaret, *Regalian Right in Medieval England*, London, 1962.
Imbart de la Tour, P., *Les Élections Épiscopales dans l'Église de France du ixe au xiie siècle*, Paris, 1891.
Jacob, E. F., *Essays in the Conciliar Epoch*, Manchester, 1943.
  The Fifteenth Century, Oxford, 1961.
James, M. R., *The Ancient Libraries of Canterbury and Dover*, Cambridge, 1903.
Jenkins, Hester T., Lichfield Cathedral in the Fourteenth Century. B.Litt. thesis, Oxford University, 1956.
Jones, E. Gwynne and Johnston, J. R. V., *Catalogue of the Bangor Cathedral Library now deposited in the University College of North Wales*, Bangor, 1961.
Jones, Marjorie, The Estates of the Cathedral Church of Hereford, 1066–1317. B.Litt. thesis, Oxford University, 1958.
Judd, A. F., *The Life of Thomas Bekynton, Secretary to King Henry VI and Bishop of Bath and Wells 1443–1465*, Chichester, 1961.
Ker, N. R., *English Manuscripts in the Century after the Norman Conquest*, Oxford, 1960.
Knoop, D., and Jones, G. P., *The Mediaeval Mason*, Manchester, 1933.
Knowles, M. D., *The Monastic Order in England, 943–1216*, 2nd edn., Cambridge, 1963.
  The Religious Orders in England, 3 vols., Cambridge, 1948–59.
  Episcopal Colleagues of Archbishop Thomas Becket, Cambridge, 1951.
La vita comune del clero nei secoli xi e xii (Atti della Settimana di studio, Mendola, 1959), 2 vols., Milan, 1962.
Lawrence, C. H., *St. Edmund of Abingdon. A study in Hagiography and History*, Oxford, 1960.
Leach, A. F., *The Schools of Medieval England*, London, 1915.
Lega-Weekes, Ethel, *Some Studies in the Topography of the Cathedral Close, Exeter*, Exeter, 1915.
Lesne, E., *La Hiérarchie épiscopale*, Lille and Paris, 1905.
  Histoire de la propriété ecclésiastique en France, 6 vols., Lille, 1910–43.
Levison, W., *England and the Continent in the Eighth Century*, Oxford, 1946.
Little, A. G., and Pelster, F., *Oxford Theology and Theologians, c. 1282–1302* (Oxford Hist. Soc.), 1934.
Loyd, Lewis C., The Norman Secular Cathedral Chapters in the Eleventh and Twelfth Centuries (unpublished memorandum).
Lyle, E. K., *Office of an English Bishop in the First Half of the Fourteenth Century*, Pennsylvania, 1903.
McKisack, May, *The Fourteenth Century, 1307–99*, Oxford, 1959.
Maddison, A. R., *A Short Account of the Vicars Choral, Poor Clerks, Organists, and Choristers of Lincoln Cathedral from the Twelfth Century to the Accession of Edward VI*, London, 1878.

Milman, H. H., *Annals of S. Paul's Cathedral*, London, 1868.

Moreau, E. de, *Histoire de l'Eglise en Belgique*, 5 vols. (2nd edn. of vols. 1 and 2), Brussels, 1946–9.

Morey, A., *Bartholomew of Exeter, Bishop and Canonist, A Study in the Twelfth Century*, Cambridge, 1937.

Nicholl, D., *Thurstan, Archbishop of York (1114–1140)*, York, 1964.

Oliver, G., *Lives of the Bishops of Exeter and History of the Cathedral, with an illustrative Appendix*, Exeter, 1861.

Overton, Sylvia E., Ralph Erghum, with special reference to his tenure of the See of Salisbury, 1375–88. B.Litt. thesis, Oxford University, 1960.

Pantin, W. A., *The English Church in the Fourteenth Century*, Cambridge, 1955.

Paré, G., Brunet, A., et Tremblay, P., *La Renaissance du xiie siècle. Les Écoles et l'enseignement*, Paris and Ottawa, 1933.

Pearce, E. H., *Walter de Wenlock, Abbot of Westminster*, London, 1920.

Perroy, E., *L'Angleterre et le Grand Schisme d'Occident. Étude sur la politique réligieuse de l'Angleterre sous Richard II*, Paris, 1933.

Plucknett, T. F. T., *Statutes and their Interpretation in the First Half of the Fourteenth Century*, Cambridge, 1922.

Pommeraye, F., *Histoire de l'Église Cathédrale de Rouen*, Rouen, 1686.

Powicke, F. M., *The Thirteenth Century, 1216–1307*, Oxford, 1953.

Prothero, G. W., *A Memoir of Henry Bradshaw*, London, 1888.

Purvis, J. S., *A Medieval Act Book with some account of Ecclesiastical Jurisdiction at York*, York, 1943.

Rashdall, H., *Universities of Europe in the Middle Ages*, ed. F. M. Powicke and A. B. Emden, 3 vols., Oxford, 1936.

Rathbone, Eleanor, The Influence of Bishops and of Members of Cathedral Bodies in the Intellectual Life of England, 1066–1216. Unpublished London Ph.D. thesis, 1935.

Rawlinson, R., *The History and Antiquities of the City and Cathedral Church of Hereford*, London, 1717.

Reese, G., *Music in the Middle Ages*, London, 1941.

Roberts, A. K. B., *St. George's Chapel, Windsor Castle, 1348–1416. A Study in early Collegiate Administration*, Windsor, 1948.

Robertson, Dora H., *Sarum Close. A History of the Life and Education of the Cathedral Choristers for Seven Hundred Years*, London, 1938.

Robinson, J. Armitage, *Somerset Historical Essays*, London, 1921.

Robson, J. A., *Wyclif and the Oxford Schools*, Cambridge, 1961. (Questions of Thomas Buckingham debated in Exeter cathedral school *c.* 1346–9 are discussed in an appendix.)

Rock, D., *The Church of Our Fathers as seen in St. Osmund's Rite for the Cathedral of Salisbury*, ed. G. W. Hart and W. H. Frere, 4 vols., London, 1903–4.

Salzman, L. F., *Building in England down to 1540*, Oxford, 1952.

Saunders, H. W., *An Introduction to the Obedientiary and Manor Rolls of Norwich Cathedral Priory*, Norwich, 1930.

Shortt, H., ed. *The City of Salisbury*, London, 1957.

Simpson, W. Sparrow, *Chapters in the History of Old St. Paul's*, London, 1881. *Gleanings from Old St. Paul's*, London, 1889.
St. Paul's Cathedral and Old City Life, London, 1894.

Smith, R. A. L., *Canterbury Cathedral Priory. A Study in Monastic Administration*, Cambridge, 1943.

Snape, R. H., *English Monastic Finances in the Later Middle Ages*, Cambridge, 1926.

Somner, W., and Battely, N., *The Antiquities of Canterbury, or A Survey of that Ancient City, with the Suburbs and Cathedral*, 2 parts, London, 1703.

Southern, R. W., *The Making of the Middle Ages*, London, 1953.
Stenton, F. M., *Anglo-Saxon England* (The Oxford History of England), Oxford, 1943.
Stephens, W. R. W., *Memorials of the South Saxon See and Cathedral Church of Chichester*, London, 1876.
Streeter, B. H., *The Chained Library*, London, 1931.
Thompson, A. Hamilton, *The Cathedral Churches of England* (S.P.C.K.), London, 1925.
   The English Clergy and their Organization in the Later Middle Ages, Oxford, 1947.
Thompson, E. M., and Lakin, S. M., *Catalogue of the Library of the Cathedral Church of Salisbury*, London, 1880.
Tout, T. F., *Chapters in the Administrative History of Medieval England*, 6 vols., Manchester, 1920–33.
Troup, Frances B. Rose, *The Consecration of the Norman Minster at Exeter, 1133*, Yeovil, 1932.
   Exeter Vignettes. Clarembald and the Miracles of Exeter; Exeter in Norman Days; the Murder of the Precentor, Manchester, 1942.
Valois, N., *Guillaume d'Auvergne, Évêque de Paris (1228–1249). Sa Vie et ses Ouvrages*, Paris, 1880.
Van Dijk, S. J. P. and Walker, J. Haselden, *The Origins of the Modern Roman Liturgy*, London, 1960.
Veissière, M., *Une communauté canoniale au moyen age. Saint-Quiriace de Provins (xie-xiiie siècles)*, Provins, 1961.
Viollet, P., *Histoire des Institutions politiques et administratives de la France*, 3 vols., Paris, 1890–1903.
Walcott, M. E. C., *Cathedralia: A Constitutional History of Cathedrals of the Western Church*. London, 1865.
   Fasti Cicestrenses (Reprinted from *Journal of British Archaeological Association*), ? London, ? 1866.
Weske, Dorothy Bruce, *Convocation of the Clergy* (S.P.C.K.), London, 1937.
Williams, G., *The Welsh Church from Conquest to Reformation*, Cardiff, 1962.
Wood, A., *Survey of the Antiquities of the City of Oxford*, ed. A. Clark (Oxford Hist. Soc.), 3 vols., 1889–99.
Wood-Legh, Kathleen L., *Perpetual Chantries in Britain*, Cambridge, 1965.
Woolley, R. M., *Catalogue of the Manuscripts of Lincoln Cathedral Library*, Oxford, 1927.
Wormald, F. and Wright, C. E., ed. *The English Library before 1700. Studies in its History*, London, 1958.

C. Articles on Special Subjects

Allen, Hope Emily, 'On the Author of the *Ancren Riwle*', in *P.M.L.A.*, xliv (1929), 635–80.
Archer, Margaret, 'Philip Repingdon, Bishop of Lincoln, and his Cathedral Chapter', in *Univ. Birmingham Hist. Jour.*, iv (1953–4), 81–97.
Bannister, A. T., 'The Origin and Growth of the Cathedral System', in *C.Q.R.* (1927), civ, 86–96.
Barraclough, G., 'The Making of a Bishop in the Middle Ages. The Part of the Pope in Law and Fact', in *Catholic Hist. Rev.*, xix (1933), 275–319.
Barrow, G. W. S., 'The Cathedral Chapter of St. Andrews and the Culdees in the Twelfth and Thirteenth Centuries', in *J.E.H.*, iii (1952), 23–39.
Beaumont, R. M., *The Chapter of Southwell Minster*, Southwell, 1956.
Benson, E. W., 'The Relation of the Chapter to the Bishop', in *Essays on Cathedrals by Various Writers*, ed. J. S. Howson, London, 1872.

Bond, M. F., 'Chapter administration and Archives at Windsor', in *J.E.H.*, viii (1957), 166–81.

Brooke, C. N. L., 'The Composition of St. Paul's Chapter, 1086–1163', in *Camb. Hist. Jour.*, x (1950–2), 111–32.

'English Cathedral Chapters and the Norman Conquest'. An unpublished paper read to the Stubbs Society at Oxford, 1952.

'The Deans of St. Paul's *c.* 1090–1499', in *Bull. Inst. Hist. Research*, xxix (1956), 231–44.

'The Earliest Times to 1485' in *A History of St. Paul's Cathedral and the Men Associated with It*, ed. W. R. Matthews and W. M. Atkins (London, 1957), pp. 1–99.

Continental Influences on English Cathedral Chapters in the XIth and XIIth Centuries', in *Résumés des communications, XIe Congrés International des Sciences Historiques, Stockholm, 1960* (International Committee of Hist. Sciences, Uppsala, 1960), pp. 120–1.

Brooke, Z. N., and C. N. L., 'Hereford Cathedral Dignitaries in the Twelfth Century', in *Cambridge Hist. Jour.*, viii (1944–6), 1–21, 179–85.

Browne, A. L., 'The Medieval Chancellors of Lichfield Cathedral. Biographical Collections.' Reprinted from *Collections for a History of Staffordshire* (William Salt Soc.), 1939.

Browne, G. F., 'On the Constitution of French Chapters', in *Trans. St. Paul's Ecclesiological Soc.* (1895), iii, 225–40.

Callus, D. A., *Introduction of Aristotelian Learning to Oxford*, from *Proc. British Academy*, xxix (1943).

Cheney, C. R., 'Legislation of the Medieval English Church', in *E.H.R.*, l (1935), 193–224, 385–417.

'A Monastic Letter of Fraternity to Eleanor of Aquitaine', *ibid.*, li (1936), 488–93.

'Norwich Cathedral Priory in the Fourteenth Century', in *B.J.R.L.*, xx (1936), 93–120.

'King John's Reaction to the Interdict in England', in *T.R.H.S.*, 4th ser., xxxi (1949), 129–50.

Church, C. M., 'Roger of Salisbury, first Bishop of Bath and Wells, 1244–47', in *Archaeologia*, lii (1890), 89–112.

'The Rise and Growth of the Chapter of Wells from 1242 to 1333', *ibid.*, liv (1894), 1–40.

'The Prebendal Stalls and Misericords in the Cathedral Church of Wells', *ibid.*, lv (1897), 319–42.

'Notes on the Buildings, Books and Benefactors of the Library of the Dean and Chapter of Wells', in *Archaeologia*, lvii, ii (1901), 201–8.

Clark, J. W., 'On Ancient Libraries: Lincoln Cathedral; Westminster Abbey; St. Paul's Cathedral', in *Camb. Antiq. Soc. Proc.*, ix (1894–8), 37–60.

Clark-Maxwell, W. G., 'Some Letters of Confraternity', *ibid.*, lxxv (1925), 19–60.

'Some Further Letters of Confraternity', *ibid.*, lxxix (1929), 179–216.

Clay, C. T., 'Notes on the Chronology of the Early Deans of York', in *Y.A.J.*, xxiv (1939), 361–78.

'The Early Treasurers of York', *ibid.*, xxxv (1940), 7–34.

'The Early Precentors and Chancellors of York', *ibid.*, xxxv (1941), 116–138.

'Notes on the Early Archdeacons in the Church of York', *ibid.*, xxxvi (1946–7), 269–87, 409–34.

Cockerell, D., 'The Development of Book Binding Methods—Coptic Influence', in *Trans. Bibliographical Soc.*, 4th ser., xiii (1932–3), 1–19.

Cole, R. E. G., 'Some Papal Provisions in the Cathedral Church of Lincoln, A.D. 1300–1320', in *Associated Archit. Socs.' Reports*, xxxiv (1918), 219–58.

Colvin, H. M., 'Holme Lacy: an Episcopal Manor and its Tenants in the Twelfth and Thirteenth Centuries', in *Medieval Studies presented to Rose Graham*, ed. V. Ruffer and A. J. Taylor (Oxford, 1950), 15–40.

Darlington, R. R., 'Ecclesiastical Reform in the Late Old English Period', in *E.H.R.*, li (1936), 385–428.

Davis, H. W. C., 'London Lands and Liberties of St. Paul's, 1066–1135', in *Essays in Medieval History Presented to Thomas Frederick Tout*, ed. A. G. Little and F. M. Powicke (Manchester, 1925), pp. 45–59.

De Clercq, C., Review of J. Oswald, *Das alte Passauer Domkapitel. Seine Entwicklung bis zum dreizehnten Jahrhundert und sein Wahlkapitulationswesen*, Munich, 1933, in *Rev. d'hist. eccl.*, xxix, (1933), 1002–04.

Deanesly, Margaret, 'The *Familia* at Christchurch, Canterbury, 597–832', in *Essays in Medieval History Presented to Thomas Frederick Tout*, ed. A. G. Little and F. M. Powicke (Manchester, 1925), pp. 1–13.

'The Archdeacons of Canterbury under Archbishop Ceolnoth (833–70)', in *E.H.R.*, xlii (1927), 1–11.

'Medieval Schools to *c.* 1300', in *C.M.H.*, v (1926), 765–79.

'Early English and Gallic Minsters', in *T.R.H.S.*, 4th ser., xxiii (1941), 25–69.

Deeley, Ann, 'Papal Provision and Royal Rights of Patronage in the Early Fourteenth Century', in *E.H.R.*, xliii (1928), 497 *et seq.*

Dereine, C., 'Vie commune, règle de St. Augustin et chanoines réguliers au xie siècle', in *Rev. d'hist. eccl.*, xli (1946), 365–406.

'Enquête sur la règle de St. Augustin', in *Scriptorium*, II, i (1948), 28–36.

'Chanoines des origines au xiiiie sècle', in *Dict. d'hist. et de géogr. eccl.*, t. xii (Paris, 1951), cc. 353–405.

(These are the more general and relevant for present purposes of a series of articles by Fr. Dereine on the early history of canons, especially of the regular canons, and the rule of St. Augustine. Others are in *Scriptorium*, *Révue Benedictine* and *Studi Gregoriani*.)

Dickens, A. G., 'The "Shire" and Privileges of the Archbishop in Eleventh Century York', in *Y.A.J.*, xxxviii (1953), 131–47.

Dickinson, J. C., 'English Canons and the Continent in the Twelfth Century', in *T.R.H.S.*, 5th ser., i (1951), 71–89.

Didier, N., *Henri de Suse, Evêque de Sisteron (1244–1250)*, Recueil Sirey, 1953.

Douglas, D., 'The Norman Episcopate before the Norman Conquest', in *Camb. Hist. Jour.*, xiii (1957), 101–15.

Douie, Decima, L., *Archbishop Geoffrey Plantagenet and the Chapter of York* (St. Anthony's Hall Pubns., no. 18), York, 1960.

Du Boulay, F. R. H., 'The Quarrel between the Carmelite Friars and the Secular Clergy of London, 1464–68', in *J.E.H.* vi (1955), 156–74.

Duhr, J., 'La Confrérie dans la Vie de l'Église', in *Rev. d'hist. eccl.*, xxxv (1939), 437–78.

Dunlop, Annie, 'Life in a Medieval Cathedral', in *Trans. Soc. Friends of Dunblane Cathedral*, iv, part iv (1945), 70–86.

Dunstan, G. R., 'Some Aspects of the Register of Edmund Lacy, Bishop of Exeter, 1420–55', in *J.E.H.*, vi (1955), 37–47.

Edwards, Kathleen, 'The Houses of Salisbury Close in the Fourteenth Century', in *British Archaeological Jour.*, 3rd ser., iv (1939), 55–115.

'Bishops and Learning in the Reign of Edward II', in *C.Q.R.*, cxxxviii (April–June, 1944), 57–86.

Bibliography

373

'Some Activities of Fellows of De Vaux College at Salisbury and Oxford in the later Middle Ages', in *Oxoniensia*, xix (1954), 61–91.

'The Social Origins and Provenance of the English Bishops during the Reign on Edward II', in *T.R.H.S.*, 5th ser., ix (1959), 51–79.

See also below, *Victoria County History*.

Emanuel, H. D., 'Notaries Public and their Marks recorded in the Archives of the Dean and Chapter of Hereford', in *National Library of Wales Jour.*, viii (1953), 147–63.

Erskine, Audrey M., 'The Medieval Financial Records of the Cathedral Church of Exeter', in *Jour. Soc. Archivists*, ii, 6 (Oct. 1962), 254–66.

Everett, C. R., 'Notes on the Prebendal Mansion of Sherborne Monastery, commonly known as the King's House, in the Close of Sarum, 1220–1850', in *W.A.M.*, xlvii (1936), 379–405.

Fletcher, J. M. J., *The Boy Bishop at Salisbury and Elsewhere*, Salisbury, 1921. *Bishop Giles of Bridport, 1257–62, and De Vaux College which the Bishop founded.* Reprinted from *Wiltshire Gazette* of 22nd and 29th March, 1934.

Freeman, E. A., 'The Cathedral Churches of the Old Foundation', in *Essays on Cathedrals by Various Writers*, ed. J. S. Howson, London, 1872.

Genicot, F., 'Le chapitre de Huy au tournant des xiie et xiiie siècles', in *Rev. d'hist. eccl.*, lix (1964), 5–51.

Godfrey, C. J., 'Pluralists in the Province of Canterbury in 1366', in *J.E.H.*, xi (1960), 23–40.

Graham, Rose, 'Sidelights on the Rectors and Parishioners of Reculver from the Register of Archbishop Winchelsey', in *Archaeologia Cantiana*, lvii (1944), 1–12.

Greenway, W., 'Archbishop Pecham, Thomas Bek and St. Davids', in *J.E.H.*, xi (1960), 152–63.

Hand, G. H., 'Medieval Irish Cathedral Chapters', in *Proc. Irish Catholic Hist. Committee* (1956), 11–14.

'The Medieval Chapter of St. Mary's Cathedral, Limerick', in *Medieval Studies Presented to Aubrey Gwynn*, ed. J. A. Watt, J. B. Morrall and F. X. Martin, Dublin, 1961.

'The Rivalry of the Cathedral Chapters in Medieval Dublin', in *Jour. Royal Soc. Antiquaries Ireland*, xcii (1962), 193–206.

Harrison, F., 'The Early History of York Minster', in *Associated Archit. Socs.' Reports*, xxxvii (1925), 295–307.

'The Sub-Chanter and the Vicars Choral', in *York Minster Historical Tracts, 627–1927*, ed. A. Hamilton Thompson (S.P.C.K.), 1927.

'The Bedern College and Chapel', in *Proc. Y.A.A.S.*, ii, no. 4 (1936), 19–43.

Highfield, J. R. L., 'The English Hierarchy in the Reign of Edward III', in *T.R.H.S.*, 5th ser., vi (1956), 115–38.

Hobson, G. D., 'Further Notes on Romanesque Bindings', in *Trans. Bibliographical Soc.*, 4th ser., xv (1934), 161–211.

Hofmeister, P., 'Die Doppeltitel der Bischöfe' in *Zeitschrift der Savigny-Stiftung für Rechtsgeschichte, Kanonistische Abteilung*, xxxiv (1947), 172–252.

Holtzmann, W., 'Der Katepan Boiannes und die Kirchliche Organization der Capitanata' in *Nachrichtender Akademie der Wissenschaften in Göttingen* (1960), 19–39.

Hunt, R. W., 'English Learning in the Late Twelfth Century', in *T.R.H.S.*, 4th ser., xix (1936), 19–42.

Jacob, E. F., 'Some English Documents of the Conciliar Movement', in *B.J.R.L.*, xv (1931), 358-94.

'Canterbury Administration', in *C.Q.R.*, cxix (1934), 112–24.

'To and From the Court of Rome in the Early Fifteenth Century', in *Studies in French Language and Medieval Literature Presented to Professor Mildred K. Pope*, Manchester, 1939.

'The Medieval Chapter of Salisbury Cathedral', in *W.A.M.*, li (1947), 479–95.

John, E., 'The Division of the *Mensa* in Early English Monasteries', in *J.E.H.*, vi (1955), 143–55.

Jones, J., 'An Account of the Ancient Constitution, Discipline, and Usages of the Cathedral Church of Exeter', in *Archaeologia*, xviii (1817), 385–416.

Judd, A. F., 'The Episcopate of Thomas Bekynton, Bishop of Bath and Wells, 1443–55', in *J.E.H.*, viii (1957), 153–65.

Ker, N. R., 'Salisbury Cathedral Manuscripts and Patrick Young's Catalogue', in *W.A.M.*, liii (1949–50), 153–83.

'Patrick Young's Catalogue of the Manuscripts of Lichfield Cathedral', in *Medieval and Renaissance Studies*, ii (1950), 151–68.

Knecht, R. J., 'The Episcopate and the Wars of the Roses', in *Univ. Birmingham Hist. Jour.*, vi (1957–8), 108 ff.

Knowles, M. D., 'The Early Community at Christ Church, Canterbury', in *J.T.S.*, xxxix (1938), 126–31.

'The English Bishops, 1070–1532', in *Medieval Studies Presented to Aubrey Gwynn*, ed. J. A. Watt, J. B. Morrall, F. X. Martin, Dublin, 1961.

Kuttner, S. and Rathbone, Eleanor, 'Anglo-Norman Canonists of the Twelfth Century', in *Traditio*, vii (1949–51), 279–358.

Le Patourel, J., 'Geoffrey of Montbray, Bishop of Coutances, 1049–93', in *E.H.R.*, lix (1944), 129–61.

Leach, A. F., 'A Clerical Strike at Beverley Minster in the Fourteenth Century', in *Archaeologia*, lv (1896), 1–20.

'St. Paul's School before Colet', *ibid.*, lxii (1910), 191–238.

See also below, *Victoria County History*.

Lesne, E., 'Praebenda, Le sens primitif du terme prébende', in *Mélanges Paul Fournier (Soc. d'hist. de Droit*, Paris, 1929), 443–53.

'Les Origines de la prébende', in *Rev. Hist. de Droit franç. et étranger*, 4th ser., 8 (1929), 242–90.

Lewis, F. R., 'Prelates and Nobles in the Rhineland: a Church Province in the Thirteenth Century', in *History*, xxii (1937), 193–220.

Lincolnshire Archives Committee, 'Muniments of the Dean and Chapter', in *Archivists' Report*, iv (1952–3), 37–69; (1953–4), 58–64.

Little, A. G., 'Theological Schools in Medieval England', in *E.H.R*,. lv (1940), 624–30.

McRoberts, D., 'The Medieval Scottish Liturgy illustrated by surviving Documents', in *Trans. Scottish Ecclesiological Soc.*, xv, i (1957), 24–40.

Major, Kathleen, 'The Office of Chapter Clerk at Lincoln in the Middle Ages', in *Medieval Studies presented to Rose Graham*, ed. V. Ruffer and A. J. Taylor (Oxford 1950), 163–88.

'The Finances of the Dean and Chapter of Lincoln from the Twelfth to the Fourteenth Century', in *J.E.H.*, v (1954), 149–67.

Mayr-Harting, H., *The Bishops of Chichester, 1075–1207. Biographical Notes and Problems* (Chichester Papers, no. 40), Chichester, 1963.

Moor, C., 'Cardinals Beneficed in Sarum Cathedral', in *W.A.M.*, l (1943), 136–48.

Morgan, F. C., *Hereford Cathedral Library*, 2nd edn. revised, Hereford, 1958.

Morris, C., 'The Commissary of the Bishop in the Diocese of Lincoln', in *J.E.H.*, x (1959), 50–65.

Nélis, H., 'La "Congrégation" des Chapitres Cathédraux de la Province Ecclésiastique de Reims à Saint-Quentin (1331–1428)', in *Rev. d hist. eccl.*, xxv (1929), 447–70.

Page, W., 'Some Remarks on the Churches of the Domesday Survey', in *Archaeologia*, 2nd ser., xvi (1915), 61–102.

Pantin, W. A., 'The General and Provincial Chapters of the English Black Monks, 1215–1540', in *T.R.H.S.*, 4th ser., x (1927), 195–263.

'English Monastic Letter Books', in *Hist. Essays in Honour of James Tait*, ed. J. G. Edwards, V. H. Galbraith, and E. F. Jacob (Manchester, 1933), pp. 201–22.

'Chantry Priests' Houses and Other Medieval Lodgings', in *Medieval Archaelogy*, iii (1959), 216–58.

Parker, J. H., 'The Bishop's Palace at Wells', in *Proc. Somersetshire Archaeological Soc.*, xi (1861–2), 143–57.

'The Ecclesiastical Buildings of Wells', *ibid.*, xii, part ii. (1863–4), 24–45.

Peckham, W. D., 'The Vicars Choral of Chichester Cathedral', in *Sussex Archaeological Collections*, lxxviii (1937), 126–59.

Poole, R. L., 'The Early Lives of Robert Pullen and Nicholas Breakspear', in *Essays in Medieval History Presented to Thomas Frederick Tout*, ed. A. G. Little and F. M. Powicke (Manchester, 1925), pp. 61–70.

Post, G., 'Alexander III, the *Licentia Docendi* and the Rise of the Universities', in *Anniversary Essays in Medieval History by Students of Charles Homer Haskins* (Boston and New York, 1929), pp. 255–77.

Purvis, J. S., *The Archives of York Diocesan Registry* (St. Anthony's Hall Pubns., no. 2), London, 1952.

Robertson, Dora H., 'Notes on Some Buildings in the City and Close of Salisbury connected with the Education and Maintenance of the Cathedral Choristers', in *W.A.M.*, xlviii (Dec. 1937), 1–30.

Robertson, Dora H., and Wordsworth, C., 'Salisbury Choristers: Their Endowments, Boy-Bishops, Music Teachers and Headmasters, with the History of the Organ', *ibid.* (June, 1938), 201–31.

Robinson, J. Armitage, 'The Early Community at Christ Church, Canterbury', in *J.T.S.*, xxvii (1926), 225–40.

Round, J. H., 'Bernard, the King's Scribe', in *E.H.R.*, xiv (1899), 417–30.

Salter, H. E., 'An Oxford Hall in 1424', in *Essays in History Presented to Reginald Lane Poole*, ed. H. W. C. Davis, Oxford, 1927, pp. 421–35.

'The Medieval University of Oxford', in *History*, xiv (1929–30), 57–61.

Savage, H. E., *Lichfield Cathedral. The Chapter in the Twelfth Century. An Address given on the Festival of St. Chad, 1917*, Lichfield, 1917.

'*Lichfield Cathedral. A Cathedral Library.' An Address given on the Festival of St. Chad, 1934*, Lichfield, 1934.

Simpson, W. Sparrow, 'On a newly discovered Manscript containing Statutes compiled by Dean Colet for the Government of the Chantry Priests and other Clergy in St. Paul's Cathedral', in *Archaeologia*, lii (1890), 145–74.

'Visitations of certain Churches in the City of London in the patronage of St. Paul's Cathedral Church between the years 1138 and 1250', *ibid.*, lv (1897), 283–300.

Smith, R. A. L., 'The Central Financial System of Christ Church, Canterbury, 1186–1512', in *E.H.R.*, lv (1940), 353–69.

'The *Regimen Scaccarii* in English Monasteries', in *T.R.H.S.*, 4th ser., xxiv (1942), 73–94.

'John of Tours, Bishop of Bath, 1088–1122' and 'The Place of Gundulf in the Anglo-Norman Church', in *Collected Papers*, ed. M. D. Knowles, London, 1947.

Srawley, J. H., *The Origin and Growth of Cathedral Foundations as illustrated by the Cathedral Church of Lincoln* (Lincoln Minster Pamphlets, no. 1), 2nd edn. 1951.

Steer, F. W., *The Vicars' Hall, Chichester, and its Undercroft* (Chichester Papers, no. 12), Chichester, 1958.

Stenton, F. M., *Norman London* (Hist. Association Leaflet), 1934.

Storey, R. L. *Diocesan Administration in the Fifteenth Century* (St. Antony's Hall Pubns. No. 16), York, 1959.

Thompson, A. Hamilton, 'Pluralism in the Medieval Church; with notes on Pluralists in the diocese of Lincoln, 1366', in *Associated Archit. Socs.' Reports*, xxxiii (1915), 35–73; xxxiv (1917), 1–26; xxxv (1919–20), 87–108, 199–242; xxxvi (1921), 1–41.

'Notes on Colleges of Secular Canons in England', in *Archaeological Jour.*, lxxiv (1917), 139–239.

'Cathedral Builders of the Middle Ages', in *History*, x (1925), 139–50.

'The Medieval Archbishops in their Diocese', 'The Medieval Chapter', 'The Fourteenth Century', 'The Fifteenth Century', in *York Minster Historical Tracts 627–1927* (S.P.C.K.), 1927.

Review of *Registrum Simonis de Gandavo*, ed. C. T. Flower and M. C. B. Dawes (Canterbury and York Soc.), 2 vols., 1934, in *E.H.R.*, li (1936), 319–22.

Review of D. Knoop and G. P. Jones, *The Medieval Mason*, Manchester, 1933, *ibid.*, p. 357.

Song Schools in the Middle Ages (Church Music Soc., Occasional Papers, no. 14), S.P.C.K., London, 1942.

'English Colleges of Chantry Priests', in *Trans. Ecclesiological Soc.*, n.s., i (1943), 92–108.

Diocesan Organization in the Middle Ages: Archdeacons and Rural Deans, Raleigh Lecture on History, British Academy, 1943.

'The Chapel of St. Mary and the Holy Angels, otherwise known as St. Sepulchre's Chapel, at York', in *Y.A.J.*, xxxvi (1944), 63–77.

'Master Elias of Dereham and the King's Works', in *Arch. Jour.*, xcviii (1941), 1–35.

See also below, *Victoria County History.*

Thompson, E. Maunde, 'Catalogue of Manuscripts in the Cathedral Library of Salisbury,' in *Catalogue of the Library of the Cathedral Church of Salisbury*, ed. S. M. Lakin, London, 1880.

Thorpe, H. 'Lichfield: A Study of its Growth and Function', in *Coll. Hist. Staffs.* (Staffs. Record Soc., 1954 for 1950–1), 139–211.

Troup, Frances Rose, 'The Establishment of the Office of Dean in Exeter Cathedral', in *Devon and Cornwall Notes and Queries*, xviii (Jan. 1934), 16–20.

Victoria History of the Counties of England, ed. W. Page and R. B. Pugh contains the following relevant articles:

'Lincoln Cathedral', by Phyllis Wragge, in *History of Lincolnshire*, ii (1906), 80–96.

'Schools', by A. F. Leach, *ibid.*, pp. 421–92.

'Cathedral of Chichester', by I. F. Salzman, in *History of Sussex*, ii (1907), 47–51.

'Schools', by A. F. Leach, *ibid.*, pp. 397–409.

'City of Chichester. The Cathedral', by W. H. Godfrey, *ibid.*, iii (1935), 102–69.

'Schools', by A. F. Leach in *History of Yorkshire*, i (1907), 415–30.

'Cathedral Church of St. Peter, York', by A. Hamilton Thompson, *ibid.*, iii (1913), 375–82.

'The Bedern, York', and 'St. William's College, York', by J. Solloway, *ibid.*, pp. 382–3, 385–6.

'Collegiate Church of St. John the Evangelist, Beverley', by A. Hamilton Thompson, *ibid.*, pp. 353–9.

'Collegiate Church of St. Peter and St. Wilfrid, Ripon', by A. Hamilton Thompson, *ibid.*, pp. 367–72.

'The Minster and its Precincts', by P. M. Tillott, in *History of Yorkshire, City of York* (1961), 337–43.

'Worship in the Minster', by L. W. Cowie, *ibid.*, 343–57.

'The Cathedral of St. Paul', by H. Douglas Irvine, in *History of London*, i (1909), 409–33.

'Collegiate Church of Southwell', by J. C. Cox, in *History of Nottinghamshire*, ii (1910), 152–61.

'Cathedral of Wells', by T. Scott Holmes, in *History of Somerset*, ii (1911), 162–9.

'Ecclesiastical History, 1087–1547', by G. Templeman, in *History of Wiltshire*, iii (1956), 1–27.

'The Cathedral of Salisbury, 1075–1950', by Kathleen Edwards, *ibid.*, 156–210.

'The Hospital of St. Nicholas, Salisbury', by Kathleen Edwards, *ibid.*, 343–56.

'The College of De Vaux, Salisbury', by Kathleen Edwards, *ibid.*, 369–85.

'The Borough of Old Salisbury', by J. W. F. Hill in *History of Wiltshire*, vi (1962), 51–67.

'The City of New Salisbury', by Marian K. Dale, *ibid.*, 69–103.

Walcott, M. E. C., 'The Arrangement of Secular Cathedral Closes', in *Associated Archit. Socs.' Reports*, xv (1879), 70–8.

Walker, D., 'The Hereford Cathedral Charters', in *National Library of Wales Journ.*, ix (1955–6), 401–12.

Warichez, J., Review of M. le Grand, *Le Chapitre Cathédral de Langres*, Paris, 1931, in *Rev. d'hist. eccl.*, xxvii (1931), 871–4.

Watson, E. W., 'The Development of Ecclesiastical Organization and its Financial Basis', in *C.M.H.*, vi (Cambridge, 1929), 528–58.

Williams, T. W., 'Wells Cathedral Library', in *Library Assocn. Record*, viii (1906), 372–7.

Williamson, Dorothy M., *The Muniments of the Dean and Chapter of Lincoln* (Lincoln Minster Pamphlets, no. 8), Lincoln, 1956.

'*Sede Vacante* Records of the Diocese of Lincoln', in *Bull. Soc. Local Archivists*, no. 12 (Oct. 1953), 13–20 (duplicated).

Wood-Legh, Kathleen L., 'Some Aspects of the History of the Chantries during the Reign of Edward III', in *Camb. Hist. Jour.*, iv (1932), 26–50.

'Some Aspects of the History of Chantries in the Later Middle Ages', in *T.H.R.S.*, 4th ser., xxviii (1946), 47–60.

Wordsworth, C. (Bishop of Lincoln), 'On English Cathedrals', in *Miscellanies Literary and Religious*, iii (London, 1879), 290–335.

Wordsworth, C. (Chancellor of Salisbury), 'The Use of Salisbury and the Library of the Cathedral Church', in *Notes on the Cathedral Church of Salisbury*, ed. G. H. Bourne and J. M. J. Fletcher, Salisbury, 1924.

INDEX

Cheney, C. R., xiii, xviii, 128, 318 n.
John, c. of Salisbury, vicar
general of bp. of Hereford, 81,
352-4
Chesney, Robt., bp. of Lincoln, 186,
248 n.
Chessey, William de, preby. of Louth,
queen's treasurer, 328-9 n.
Chester (co. Chester): archd. of, 247,
249; bp. of, 10 n.; *see also* Coventry and Lichfield; monks of, 10 n.
Robt. of, 189
Chesterfeld (Chestrefeld), Rd. de,
preby. of Norton, 344-8
Chesterfield, John, c. of Salisbury, 351
Chichele, Henry, c. and chanc. of
Salisbury, abp. of Canterbury,
202 n., 247 n., 352-3. Wm.,
chanc. of Salisbury, 202 n.
Chichester cathedral (co. Sussex):
archd. at, 249-50; act books, 30;
bakehouse, 236; bell-ringers, 225;
bp., 122, 124, 131
canons, 51-2, 57, 61 n., 64, 70, 122,
chanc., 183, 209, 219; chantry
chaplains, 290; chapter, 20, 107,
131, 209; choir stalls, 249; choristers, 307; clerks, 225; common
estates, 148; common fund, 236;
commons, 58, 236, 270; communar, 236; customs, 24; *custos*:
see sub-treasurer
dean, 131, 140-53 *passim*, 249;
dignitaries, 122, 124, 131, 250;
door-keeper, 225; entrance fee,
64; hospitality, 61 n. 64; houses,
124; notary, 208-9; organist, 174;
prebends, 33, 131; precentor
(cantor), 160, 164, 219, 249
residence, 51-2, 57, 61 n., 70, 124,
270; sacrists, 223, 225; secular
cathedral, 11, 20; *servientes*, 225;
statutes, 26, 64, 174, 263, 279;
subdean, 149-51, 153; sub-treasurer (*custos*, sacrist), 223, 225;
succentor, 174; *theologus* and
lectures in theology, 197, 203;
treasurer, 219, 223, 236 n.;
vicars choral, 174, 263-4, 268 n.,
270, 278-80, 284; visitations, 131,
148
Chichester, City of, 131, 153, St.
Peter's, 153 n. See of, 11 n.

Children; see Boys; Choristers
Chitterne, John, c. of Salisbury, 81,
352-3
Choir: altarists in, 304-5; archds. in,
247 n., 249-50; bp. in, 101-4, 164;
canons in, 34-5, 51-9; *cantoris* and
decani, 160-1; chanc. in, 163-4,
175, 214-16; clerks, 165, 175, 267;
dean in, 103, 143, 150-1; discipline
of, 67-8, 175; duties in, 32, 35;
feasts for, 59-67; feeding of, 20;
guarding of, 175; lay singing men
introduced, 283; *ministri inferiores*
in, 252; precentor in, 161, 163-5;
rulers of, 58-9, 164, 265; schoolmaster in, 167, 194-5; services,
56-9, 214-16, 255-7; stalls, 34, 54,
136, 160, 165, 170, 249, 255, 295,
303; sub-treasurer in, 223-4;
succentor in, 167, 169, 173; vicars
of: see Vicars Choral
Choristers, 303, 307-17; admission, 165,
311-14; almoner's responsibilities,
168, 310; in canon's houses, 309-
310; common life and houses,
165-6, 252, 308-14; discipline,
163-6, 309, 314; duties, 299, 315-
316; education and maintenance,
162-3, 165-6, 167-8, 173-4, 194
n., 299, 304, 307-16; endowment
and finance, 168, 310-15; in the
episcopal *familia*, 308; feast of
boys, 316-17; hospitality to, 59,
61; master (warden) of, 67, 135,
272, 302, 311-15; numbers, 307;
precentor's responsibilities, 164-
168, 309-14; promotion, 273 n.,
303, 314-15; succentor's responsibilities, 171, 311
Chrism, 102 n., 103, 250
Christmas, 59, 62, 104-5, 317; plays,
172, 196
Chronicles, 32, 70, 185, 214
Churches, appropriation of, 110; to
chapters, prebendaries or vicars,
147, 235, 238, 275; jurisdiction
over, 125-7; visitations of, 126 n.,
129-32, 147-8, 152-3. Cathedral:
see Cathedrals. City, 1, 7, 272,
302. Collegiate: before Conquest,
9, 309; chanc. in, 206; chantries,
286; dean, 139-40; feast of boys,
317 n.; organist and master of

262; subdean, 127, 149–51, 154;
subtreasurer, 224; succentor, 167,
171, 311; treasurer, 47 n., 127 n.,
141, 161, 219, 221 n.; vicars
choral, 123, 171, 232–3, 241,
252–3, 259–62, 268–70, 274–5,
277–8, 284, 290–1; visitation of,
129, 241 n.
Exeter, City of, 168, 241. See of, 9
Exorcist, 163, 308
Exploratores of faults, 175
Eyvill, Gilbert de, treasurer of Lincoln,
327, 329–30

Fabric of cathedral, 80, 91–2, 123–4,
229–34; craftsmen and workmen,
123 n., 227–34; fund, 63 n., 65,
93, 123, 229–34, 299; keeper of,
47, 67, 123, 229–34; officers, 229–
230, 272, 302; 'works chantry,'
299, 318
Faldingworth chantries, 299
Farendon; *see* Farndon
Fargis, Reymund de, dean of Salisbury,
127, 158 n.
Farley, Wm., c. of Salisbury, 351
Farndon (Farendon) (co. Notts), preb.,
327, 329, 346–8
Fasti, 74, 85
Feast of Boys (Boy Bishop), 309, 317;
of Fools, 317; of the Purification,
222
Feast-days, 57–9, 68, 103–5, 143, 150–1,
164, 172, 227, 265, 295, 305, 315–
316; candles for, 222; treasures
used, 217; distributions on, 42–3,
49, 236 n., 241, 262; hospitality,
270 n., lessons, 215; sermons,
216
Feasts (feasting); *see under* Hospitality
Fécamp (France, dép. Pas de Calais),
abbey, 13
Felix, c. of Lincoln, 150 n., 180
Feriby (Feryby) Benedict de, preby of
Crackpole, 335–7
Feudalism, 6, 139, 256
Finance, officers, 137, 217, 228–9; *see
also*: Accounts; Common fund;
Fabric fund
Fines: of chapters, 100; of non-resident
prebendaries, 39, 48, 50 n., 53, 55,
84, 90–1, 235, 326–30; of residen-
tiaries, 66; *see also* Entrance Fees

Firmicus, Julius, 190
FitzStephen, Wm., 188
Fleming, Rd., bp. of Lincoln, 148
Foderingeye (Foderyngeye, Foderyng-
hay), Ralph de, preby. of Lang-
ford *Manerium*, 333. Walter de,
preby. of Marston, 328, 330.
Wm. de, preby. of Hungate,
329
Foliot, Gilbert, bp. of Hereford, 189–
190
Fordington (co. Dorset), preb., 87
Foreigners, appointed to prebends and
benefices, ix, 83–5
Foresters, 242
Fornesete, Wm. de, S.T.P., 202
Foster, C. W., c. of Lincoln, 337 n.
Fournier, P., 109
France: 139; boys in episcopal *familiae*,
308; cardinals, 84–5, 94
cathedrals in, archd's place, 137, 159,
244–5, 249; archpriest, 137, 139–
140; bp., 109, 114; bp.'s penitentiary, 155 n.; canons, 119–20;
cantor (precentor), 159; cellarer,
238; chamberlain, 238; chanc.,
176–8, 204–5; chapter, 91, 99 n.;
common life, 238, 283; constitutions, 13, 18, 320; dean, 98, 137,
139–40, 159; dignitaries, 16–18,
119, 136; *Ministri inferiores*, 254–5,
258, 267; prebends, 33, 40; provost,
138 n., 139–40, 159, 238; schools,
159 n., 177 n., 178, 181, 185, 204,
308, 323; *magister scholarum* (*scholasticus, capischola*), 177 n., 178,
180–1, 204; sub-dean, 149; succentor, 169–70; treasurer, 218
Fraternities, 69 n., 318–19
Freeman, E. A., 36, 257
Frere, W. H., 128, 257
Fresne, Master Simon de, c. of Hereford, 190
Friars, 287, 318 n.; preacher or
Dominican, 193, 201, 204
Fryskenay (Fryskeney, Fryskeneye)
Thos., preby of Dunholme, 341–2
Fulbert, bp. of Chartres, 177 n., 205.
Chanc. of Rouen, 16 n.
Fuller, A. R. B., xvi
Funeral services, 262, 266, 272, 293,
295
Fyton, John, chanc. of Salisbury, 202 n.

Index

Keuellingworth (Kelingworth, Keuelingworth, Keuellyngworth, Keuellyngwrth, Killingworth, Kyuelingworth, Kyuelingwrth), Robt. de, preby. of Liddington, 328, 330–4
Kilsby (Kildesby, Kyldesby) (co. Northants), preb., 345–8
King: administration, ix, 7, 38, 119, 322, 324; clerks of, ix, 7–8, 20–1, 34, 37–8, 41, 53, 63, 74–5, 82–3, 85–7, 91, 94–5, 189, 256, 324, pluralists among, 86–7; control of chapters, 118–19, 134, 325, influence on appointments, 34, 41, 90, 99, 121, 134, 139, 197 n.; court, 8, 62, 67, 69, 94; custody of temporalities of vacant bprics., 99–100; grants and charters, 6, 27, 33, 99, 118–19, 234, 275 n., 284–5, 301 n.; see also under chancellor, and under name of king
Kington, Roger, archd. of Salisbury, lecturer in theology at Salisbury cathedral, 201, 351
Kirkby, John, archd. of Dorset, 79, 349
Kirmington, Gocelin (Jocelin) de, preby. of Empingham, treasurer and dean of Lincoln, 328–9, 334
Knowles, D., 161 n., 287 n.
Knyght, Wm., chapter clerk at Lichfield, 209 n.

Lacy, Edmd., bp. of Exeter, 199 n.
Lady chapel, 242, 259
Lafford alias Sleaford (co. Lincs), preb., 327, 329, 331, 345–7
Lancaster, Countess of, 201
college, 298
Laneham, Wm, de. c. of York, 276
Lanfranc, abp. of Canterbury, 10–11, 248 n.
Langebergh, John de, c. of Salisbury, 350–1
Langevin, Raoul, c. of Bayeux, 15
Langford Ecclesia (co. Oxford), preb., 248 n., 328, 330; Manor, preb., 328, 330, 333, 337
Langham, Simon, abp. of Canterbury, 86
Langton, John, preby. of Decem Librarum, bp. of Chichester, chanc.,

86 n., 328. Stephen, abp. of Canterbury, 142. Walter, bp. of Coventry and Lichfield, 277
Languedoc (France), cathedrals in, 138 n., 159 n.
Lantony (co. Glos), library of priory, 188
Lascy, Robt. de, preby. of Clifton and Norton and treasurer of Lincoln, 327, 329, 331–4
Lateran Councils, 99, 154, 193–4, 197, 199, 203
Lauds, 56, 316
Laughton (co. Yorks), preb. 87
Laundress, 221, 313
Lausanne, Albert de, 327, 329
Law, books, 79, 187–8. Canon, 1, 34, 37, 87, 89, 119, 130, 321; decretal Postulastis, 109; rulings of, 37, 128, 133, 192; Sext of Boniface VIII, 128, 130. Canon and civil, 88, 142; teaching of, 155, 178, 185–90, 198–9, 203–4. Ius commune of the church, 144. See also under Schools
Lawsuits, 67, 69, 113, 158, 206, 234, 274, 285
Lawyers, ix, 69–70, 88, 94, 109, 113, 188, 203
Laymen at cathedrals, 135, 222; see also under Sacrist; Servientes; Singing men; Vicars
Le Mans (France, dép. Sarthe), cathedral, 18, 182
Le Neve, J., xviii, 180, 183 n., 326 et seq.
Leach, A. F., 111 n., 181, 312
Lechlade, Ralph, dean of Wells, 116
Leclercq, H., 21
Lectors, 162 n., 163, 177, 308; see also Readers
Lectures; see Schools
Leeche, John, c. of Salisbury, 351
Legburne, John, c. of Lincoln, 307
Leicester (Leycester) (co. Leics), archd. of, 49, 85; see also Martival. St. Margaret, preb., 328, 330, 339–40
Leighton Buzzard (Leithon Busard, Leyhton Busard) (co. Beds), preb., 328, 330
ecclesia (Leiton ecclesia, Leygton ecclesia, Leyghton ecclesia, Leyhton

Theologians, 70, 79, 88–9
Theologus, 184 n., 191, 197, 199, 203–4
Theology: books on, 79, 201 n., 211,
213, degrees in, 88, 197, 199–200;
see also under Schools; Theologians; *Theologus*
Thesaurarius; *see* Treasurer
Thetford (co. Norfolk), cathedral of,
10 n.
Thomas, treasurer of Bayeux, abp. of
York, x, 12–14, 17–19, 140, 179,
218, 320
Thomassin, L., 109
Thompson, A. Hamilton, x n., 38, 72,
75, 83, 85, 113, 130, 137 n., 159 n.,
230, 237, 257, 285, 296, 301
Thorlak: *see* St. Thorlak
Thormerton, Rd. de, c. of Salisbury,
349–50
Thorngate, preb.: *see* Lincoln, city
churches
Thornton, Wm. de, preby. of Long
Stow, 327, 329–32
Thorp, Walter de, preby. of St.
Botulph, 330
Thurleby (co. Lincs), preb.: *see*
Carleton cum Thurleby
Tierce, 57, 293, 304
Tingwick, Nicholas, 89
Tolleshunte, Wm. de, 315, 317 n.
Torre, James, 198 n.
Tottenhall (co. Middlesex), preb., 87
Totnes (co. Devon), archd. of, 142
Tours (France, dép. Indre et Loire),
cathedral, 139, 177 n.
Tours, John of, bp. of Bath and Wells,
19
Tout, T. F., 38
Towns, 6–7, 287–8, 323
Treasurer: of Benedictine monastery,
217, 229 n.
of cathedral, 15–17, 84–5, 138 n.,
141, 216–28; duties of, 81 n., 102,
136, 163–4, 212, 216–18, 220–7,
303 n., 304; income and expenses
of 47 n., 221–2; residence of, 50,
222; status of, 13, 135–6, 138 n.,
141, 161, 179, 216–20, 320
of queen, 328, 329 n., 330
Treasures, 136, 216–18, 220–2
Treasury, 28 n., 147 n., 211–12, 217–30
Trefnant, John, bp. of Hereford, 108,
143–4

Tréguier (France, dép. Côtes-du-
Nord), cathedral, 137 n., 160
Turk, John, c. of Salisbury, 80, 352

Ufford, John de, c. of Salisbury, 349
Universities, 8, 185, 191, 195, 204–5,
272, 281, 315, 317 n., 323; chanc.
of, 200, 201 n., 206; degrees at,
197–9, 201, 203–4; libraries of, 79;
masters and students holding prebends, 21, 34, 38, 53, 81, 88–9, 94,
203–4, 263, 322, 324, 326, 330;
rise of, 21, 191–2, 204, 323; *see also*
Cambridge; Oxford; Paris; Salisbury; Schools
Upton, John, c. of Salisbury, 352.
Nicholas, c. of Salisbury, 69 n.
Urban (popes), IV, 111. V, 86. VI, 84,
260 n.
Urbe, *see* Anibaldis
Ursi, Reg. de Filiis, dean of Salisbury,
152
Utrecht cathedral, 1, 5, 40, 106

Vacarius, 187
Varley, Joan, 337 n.
Verdun (France, dép. Meuse), cathedral, 177 n.
Vere, Wm. de, bp. of Hereford, 184 n.
Vergers, 61, 225–6
Vespers, (Evensong), 57–8, 102, 105,
295, 305, 316
Vessels, gold and silver, 217, 221–2,
227, 293
Vestments, 221, 224
Vicaires, hauts et petits, 255
Vicarages, prebendal, 68, 123, 153 n.
Vicars choral, 37, 103 n., 135, 151, 155,
255–6, 317; appointment, 68, 123,
153 n., 165, 253–4, 256–9, 267–8,
303–4 n., 315; chantries allotted
to, 273, 286, 289–90, 299–300;
colleges (common halls), 27, 124,
169–71, 252, 259, 273–85, 296,
322, incorporation, 251–2, 275–6,
284–5; commons, 262–3, 266;
discipline, 67–8, 124, 146, 175,
263, 265–6, 271–2, 276–7, 280–1;
duties of, xiii, 35, 56, 58, 230–2,
241, 256–67, 286, 295, holding
cathedral offices, 228, 230–3,
235–6, 238, 241, 272–3; education,
167, 192, 194 n., 198 n., 265, 268,